Library of Old English Divines,

UNDER THE EDITORIAL SUPERVISION OF

WILLIAM G. T. SHEDD, D.D.,

PROFESSOR IN UNION THEOLOGICAL SEMINARY, NEW YORK.

SERMONS OF ROBERT SOUTH.

VOL. I.

SERMONS

PREACHED UPON

SEVERAL OCCASIONS

BY

ROBERT SOUTH, D.D.,

PREBENDARY OF WESTMINSTER, AND CANON OF CHRIST CHURCH, OXFORD.

IN FIVE VOLUMES.

VOL. I.

NEW YORK:
PUBLISHED BY HURD AND HOUGHTON.
1866.

RIVERSIDE, CAMBRIDGE:
STEREOTYPED AND PRINTED BY
H. O. HOUGHTON AND COMPANY.

PUBLISHERS' PREFACE.

IT is proposed to reprint the works of the most distinguished theologians and preachers of England, previous to the middle of the eighteenth century, under the title of "Library of Old English Divines." The object is, to place within reach of American readers an edition of the principal theological writers of Great Britain during the golden age of both secular and sacred literature, in a style equal to that of the best English editions, and at a much smaller price. The complete writings of such authors as Hooker and Jeremy Taylor, Baxter and Howe, are now inaccessible to many, because of the great expense involved in the importation of foreign books. Only inferior reprints, and imperfect selections, represent these and other great lights of English theology in many of the private libraries of the land; and very many of them are wholly unrepresented. It is believed that the opportunity of obtaining complete editions of these authors, in the best style of the printer's art, and at a cost even less than that which was paid previous to the present enormous rise in all foreign productions, will be welcome to a great number of students and general readers both lay and clerical. For it is, probably more than ever, the conviction amongst thoroughly educated men, that the foundations of a profound and powerful culture in theology must be laid in the study of the Old Divines of England.

It is with this conviction that the publishers venture upon an enterprise that must involve a large outlay, and result in a great number of volumes. They have in contemplation the republication of the writings of ANDREWES, BARROW, BATES, BAXTER, BULL, BUNYAN, BUTLER, CHARNOCK, CHILLINGWORTH, CLARKE, CUDWORTH, DAVENANT, DONNE, FIELD, FLAVEL, HALL, HOOKER, HOPKINS, HOWE, JACKSON, LATIMER, LEIGHTON, MORE, OWEN, PEARSON, SANDERSON, STILLINGFLEET, SIBBS, SMITH, SOUTH, TAYLOR, TILLOTSON,

USHER, and WATERLAND. To these names others may be added, and some of these may, possibly, be dropped; but they are here mentioned as indicative of the general cast and tone of the "Library." The aim will be, to bring into one solid and comprehensive collection the theological wisdom of England in its elder period.

The reprints will be made from the latest and best English editions, and will be accompanied with concise yet full biographical memoirs, and copious indexes. The memoirs, so far as possible, will be selected from existing materials, and preference will in every instance be given to those biographers who from intimate personal acquaintance were in sympathy with the subject of the biography. It is proposed to publish only complete editions of an author. This is the preference of the publishers. But if, owing to very great voluminousness, and the lack of a popular demand, in any particular instance, this rule should be varied from, entire treatises will invariably be given. There will be no compilations, alterations, or mutilations; but each author, even in case he should not appear in all his works, will be represented by entire treatises in the exact form in which he has come down to us.

The prosecution of the enterprise to its completion must, of course, depend upon the public. Should the publishers find that they have presumed too much upon the popular demand, the publication of the first author in the series will disclose the fact, and put a stop to further advance. But should the success of the first be apparent, the second will follow, and the others in their course. Each author will be sold separately as well as collectively, so that all classes of buyers may suit their convenience or preferences.

MEMOIR OF DR. ROBERT SOUTH.

ROBERT SOUTH was born at Hackney, in 1633. His father was an eminent London merchant, and his mother, whose maiden name was Berry, belonged to a good Kentish family. In 1647, after distinguishing himself by his progress in the preliminary studies, he was admitted a king's scholar at Westminster, where he remained for four years under the tuition of the celebrated Dr. Busby. Even so early as 1649 he gave a decided indication of that attachment to an established form of government in Church and State, for which he was conspicuous through life, by praying for Charles I. by name, while reading the Latin prayers in the school on the day of that monarch's execution.

In 1651, he was elected, at the same time with John Locke, a student of Christ Church, Oxford, where he soon attracted attention by his attainments. He took his degree of Bachelor of Arts in 1655, and in the same year published a panegyric in Latin verse, on Oliver Cromwell, on the occasion of his conclusion of the peace with the Dutch,—a circumstance which did not escape the opponents of Dr. South in after years, who ascribed to unsteadiness of principle what perhaps was the mere exercise of scholarship upon a theme imposed by his superiors in the University, and as to which he had himself no choice. It was certainly the last compliment he ever paid to Cromwell. By his adherence to the liturgy and ritual of the Church of England, South appears to have given offense to the members of the dominant political party, who then held the control of the University, and Dr. John Owen, who was Vice-Chancellor at the time, opposed his obtaining the degree of Master of Arts; but fortunately for South, a majority of those with whom the power of conferring the degree lay was in his favor, and he received it in 1657. In 1658 he was admitted to holy orders by a deprived bishop.

The Restoration greatly improved his ecclesiastical position. In August, 1660, he was elected public orator to the University of Oxford, and some time after this he was appointed chaplain to the Chancellor Clarendon, whose attention had been directed to him by an oration delivered in his capacity of public orator, upon the occasion of Clarendon's installation as Chancellor of the University. This opened the door for his advancement, and he was installed Prebendary of Saint Peter's, Westminster, on 30th March, 1663. He obtained his degree of Doctor of Divinity, in the October of that year, after some opposition on the ground of his being a Master of Arts of only six years' standing. This difficulty was overruled, doubtless, from a regard to the high attainments of South. These were universally recognized, and in 1670 he was installed a canon of Christ Church, Oxford.

In 1667 he committed to the press a Latin poem, written in 1655, entitled, "*Musica Inconstans, sive Poema exprimens Musicæ vires, Juvenem in Insaniam adigentis, et Musici inde Periculum.*" This juvenile effusion was highly applauded at the time, says a contemporary biographer, "for the beauty of its language, and the quickness of its turns,"—a species of encomium, which seems to imply that it belonged to the metaphysical school of poetry. The work, which has now become extremely rare, has, no doubt, deservedly passed into oblivion. South himself regretted its publication "as a juvenile and momentary performance."

In June, 1677, South accompanied Mr. Lawrence Hyde, the son of the Earl of Clarendon, and afterwards Lord Rochester, to Poland, on an embassy with which that gentleman was intrusted, to congratulate John Sobieski on his election to the Crown of Poland, and to carry presents to his daughter, the Princess Teresa, afterwards Electress of Bavaria, to whom Charles II. had some time before stood godfather by proxy. Mr. Hyde, whose tutor Dr. South had been, in which capacity he had greatly endeared himself to him, proposed that he should accompany the embassy as chaplain, to which the doctor readily agreed. It is easy to imagine that he should have gladly embraced this opportunity of becoming personally acquainted with a country to which the eyes of all Europe were then earnestly directed, and of seeing Sobieski, who was certainly the most remarkable man of his time. Sobieski had, only two years before, upon the death of the feeble and worthless Michael Wiezsnowiezky, been elected king by the unanimous voice of the Polish diet, and he had, since that period, signalized himself by beating back, with comparatively a handful of men, the overwhelming armies of Mahomet IV., which threatened destruction to the faith and liberties of Europe. The decisive struggle, which was to crush forever the hopes of the Moslem, did not take place for seven years afterwards; but Sobieski's achievements had even then been such, as to be regarded by Europe more as miracles than as ordinary conquests, and to earn him, from the terrors of Turk and Tartar, the title of "The Wizard King."

South has recorded his observations during his visit to Poland in a long and elaborate letter from Dantzic, dated 16th December, 1677, to Dr. Edward Pococke, then Regius Professor of Hebrew at Oxford, and one of the Canons of Christ Church. This letter, which is distinguished by his usual shrewdness of observation, forms a very curious and interesting historical document.

Soon after South's return to England, he was presented by the Dean and Chapter of the Collegiate Church of Westminster, to the Rectory of Islip in Oxfordshire. It is recorded of him, that he applied the whole revenues of the benefice, which amounted to £200 per annum, after setting aside one half to his curate, in educating and apprenticing the poorer children of his parish. He repaired the chancel, which had fallen into disrepair, at his own cost, as appears from a Latin inscription over the entrance. The parsonage house having also fallen into decay, besides being unsuitable to a living of such importance, South purchased a piece of ground, and built a handsome mansion-house upon it, which he settled upon himself and his successors in the cure.

In 1685, Dr. South, who was by this time one of his majesty's chaplains in ordinary, preached his sermon entitled,—"*All contingencies under the direction of God's providence*," in presence of the king. Speaking of the train of mischievous consequences which often spring from trivial beginnings, and the unexpected advancement of persons of the lowest grade to fortune and power, South illustrates his argument by the following passage, which is little creditable to his temper or taste, considering the circumstances in which it was spoken,—"Who," he says,* "that had beheld such a bankrupt, beggarly fellow as Cromwell, first entering the parliament-house with a threadbare torn cloak, and a greasy hat, (and perhaps neither of them paid for,) could have suspected that in the space of a few years, he should, by the murder of one king, and the banishment of another, ascend the throne, be invested in the royal robes, and want nothing of the state of a king, but the changing of his hat into a crown?" On hearing this, the king is said to have burst into a violent fit of laughter, and turning to Lord Rochester, to have exclaimed, "Ods fish, Lory, your chaplain must be a bishop; therefore put me in mind of him at the next death." It was from no sycophantish motive, however, that South indulged in such intemperate and misplaced railing at the protector and his party; for although a bishopric was repeatedly offered to him during the remaining part of Charles's reign, he uniformly declined these offers, saying, that he was amply provided with the means for maintaining the dignities which he

* See Sermon VIII.

already held in the church, and for upholding the charities which he had already settled, or had in contemplation.

Similar offers were made to him during James's reign, and in like manner declined. South was a determined enemy to the Roman Catholic religion, and strongly disapproved of the measures adopted by James for its restoration. He is said to have assisted by his advice in a controversy conducted in presence of the king between Fathers Giffard and Tilden on the one side, and Drs. Jane and Patrick on the other, which ended in the defeat of the advocates of the Romish church, who were dismissed by the king with the remark, "that he could say more in behalf of his religion than they could; and that he never heard a good cause managed so ill, nor a bad one so well." Dr. South had originally been proposed as the party to conduct this controversy on the part of the church of England along with Dr. Jane, but he was objected to by the king, to whom his invectives from the pulpit against the Papists had made him unacceptable.

Notwithstanding his opposition to the king in matters of religion, his loyalty, which was based upon extreme notions of the right divine of kings, remained unshaken. During Monmouth's rebellion, he professed himself ready, if occasion required, to change his black gown for a buff-coat; and when the archbishop of Canterbury, and the bishops who subscribed the invitation to the Prince of Orange to come over, applied to him for his signature, his answer was, that "his religion had taught him to bear all things; and howsoever it should please God that he should suffer, he would, by the divine assistance, continue to abide by his allegiance, and use no other weapons but his prayers and tears for the recovery of his sovereign from the wicked and unadvised counsels wherewith he was entangled."

It was some time before South gave in his adherence to the new government; but after the abdication of James, and the settlement of the crown on the Prince and Princess of Orange, he considered that James's desertion of his kingdom put an end to his claims upon the allegiance of his subjects. He therefore withdrew his opposition, and acknowledged the legality of the Revolution settlement. Offers were made to promote him to one of the episcopal sees vacated by the non-juring bishops, but these he declined, declaring with a noble spirit, "that notwithstanding he himself saw nothing contrary to the laws of God, and the common practice of all nations, to submit to princes in possession of the throne, yet others might have their reasons for a contrary opinion; and he blessed God, that he was neither so ambitious, nor in want of preferment, as, for the sake of it, to build his rise upon the ruins of any one father of the church, who for piety, good morals, and strictness of life, which every one of the deprived bishops was famed for, might be said not to have left their equals."

South, who was extremely jealous of all encroachments upon the power and dignities, as well as upon the ritual, of the Established Church, was by no means friendly to the Act of Toleration. He had used his most vigorous efforts on behalf of the Liturgy and forms of prayer, with the Commissioners appointed by the king in 1689, with the view to an union with dissenting Protestants, anxiously maintaining that they should not part with any of its ceremonies, lest the whole might be endangered. He also preached with the utmost ardor against the admission of dissenters into the revenues of the church, dwelling on their insufficiency and want of all fit knowledge and preparation for the great work of the ministry. In pursuing this theme he leveled against them all the learning and pointed ridicule which he had so readily at command. For example, he thus speaks of them in a sermon preached in the Abbey Church of Westminster, in 1692, upon 1 Cor. xii. 4. "*Now there are diversities of gifts, but the same Spirit.*" "Amongst those of the late reforming age, all learning was utterly cried down; so that with them the best preachers were such as could not read, and the ablest divines such as could hardly spell the letter. To be blind was with them the proper qualification of a spiritual guide; and to be book-learned, as they called it, and to be irreligious, were almost terms convertible. None were thought fit for the ministry but tradesmen and mechanics, because none else were allowed to have the Spirit. Those only were accounted like Saint Paul, who could work with their hands, and, in a literal sense, drive the nail home, and be able to make a pulpit before they preached in it." *

In the year 1693, South became involved in a controversy with Dr. Sherlock, then Dean of Saint Paul's, which originated in a work written by the latter, on the subject of the Socinian heresy, entitled, "A Vindication of the Holy and Ever Blessed Trinity." † The controversy was conducted with great skill and power of argument on both sides, but, like most controversies, it was mingled with more personality and bitterness than befitted the solemnity of the subject. South was generally admitted to have had the best of the discussion. It was only terminated, however, by the interposition of the royal authority, in a direction to the archbishops and bishops, that no

* See Sermon XXXV.

† Sherlock, in prosecuting his argument, however, had himself fallen into the grave heresy of Tritheism. It was to combat this doctrine that South entered the lists.

preacher whatsoever, should, in his sermon or lecture, deliver any other doctrine concerning the Trinity, than what was contained in the Holy Scriptures, and was agreeable to the three creeds, and the thirty-nine articles. The controversy attracted much attention at the time, and the wit and ingenuity in which it was conducted led many to take an interest in it who certainly would not have been induced to do so by the abstract question which was involved in it. But in this strife of wits the interests of religion seem to have been endangered, as they ever must be, when its most sacred mysteries become the familiar themes for the exercise of intellectual ingenuity, and are mingled with passions purely secular.

South was of too ardent a temperament to conduct a controversy with prudence, as well as power. Wherever his sword fell, it carried the whole vigor of his arm, and in this matter he was too much in earnest, and indeed it was at no time his practice, to cast about for holiday terms in speaking of his opponent. "Surely," he says, writing some years after the controversy was closed, "surely it would be thought a very odd way of ridding a man of the plague, by running him through with a sword; or of a lethargy, by casting him into a calenture, — a disease of a contrary nature indeed, but no less fatal to the patient, who equally dies, whether his sickness, or his physic, the malignity of his distemper, or the method of his cure, dispatches him. And in like manner must it fare with a church, which, feeling itself struck with the poison of Socinianism, flies to Tritheism for an antidote."

During the latter years of South's life his health was completely broken. His ailments were of a painful and irritating kind, but he preserved his sprightliness and vivacity in his intercourse with his friends, who were few and well chosen. By many he was charged with moroseness and sullenness of temper, the necessary fate of a man of earnest habits of thought, gifted with keen observation of life, and a natural play of witty expression. So far was he, however, from deserving the character thus attributed to him, says a contemporary biographer, who knew him well, "that whosoever was once in his company, went off with such a relish of his wit and good humor, as to covet the coming into it, though at the expense of bearing a part in the subject of his raillery. So that what was said of Horace, might, on as just grounds, be worked into his character, —

'Ridentem Flaccus amicum
Tangit, et admissus circum præcordia ludit.'"

During the greater part of Queen Anne's reign he was in a state of inactivity, the infirmities of age growing fast upon him, and almost preventing him from performing the duties of his ministerial office. So early as 1709, his infirmities were such, that the eyes of eager expectants were turned to him in hopes of a speedy vacancy in his prebend's stall, and rectory. Swift, in a letter to the Earl of Halifax, dated the 13th January of that year,* in which he presses his suit for preferment, adds in a postscript, "Pray, my Lord, desire Dr. South to die about the fall of the leaf, for he has a prebend of Westminster, which will make me your neighbor, and a sinecure in the country, both in the queen's gift, which my friends have often told me would fit me extremely." Halifax, answering this letter on 6th October, 1709, says, "Dr. South holds out still, but he cannot be immortal." South continued, however, to hold out longer than Swift's patience, and on the 13th of November, in the same year, the latter again wrote Lord Halifax, "If you think this gentle winter will not carry off Dr. South, or that his reversion is not to be compassed, your lordship would please to use your credit that, as my Lord Somers thought of me, last year, for the bishopric of Waterford, so my Lord President may now think of me for that of Cork, if the incumbent dies of the spotted fever he is now under." The infirm old man weathered the "gentle winter," and even outlived by a year the Earl of Halifax himself, who died in 1715.

To the last, South refused to be made a bishop, although the honor was repeatedly pressed upon him, during Queen Anne's reign. When the see of Rochester and deanery of Westminster, vacant by the death of Dr. Sprat, were offered to him, his answer was, "that such a chair would be too uneasy for an old infirm man to sit in, and he held himself much better satisfied with living upon the eaves-droppings of the church, than to fare sumptuously by being placed at the pinnacle of it,"—alluding to his house, which adjoined the Abbey. His zeal for the welfare of his beloved church lost none of its ardor, and we are not surprised to find that among the last acts of his public life was his interesting himself on behalf of the notorious Dr. Sacheverell.

South continued to enjoy his mental faculties to the last amid the increasing infirmities of advanced age, and ended his long and useful life on the 8th of July, 1716, at the age of eighty-three. He was buried in Westminster Abbey, near the grave of his old master, Dr. Busby, where the inscription on his tombstone records he had desired that his remains should be laid. A monument, with his figure in a recumbent posture, marks the spot, and fixes the attention by the peculiar uneasiness of the position in which the sculptor has chosen to place his subject, as if to prevent the natural exclamation of the

* See *Original Letters of Eminent Literary Men*, p. 340. London, 1843. Printed by the Camden Society.

thoughtful passer-by, — "after life's fitful fever he sleeps well!" An elaborate epitaph records the virtues of him that sleeps beneath. It is too long; but it possesses this rarer characteristic of such records, that it is true.

Throughout life South showed himself a man of warm attachments; his friendships were firm and lasting; his dislikes the same. He was conspicuous for his charities, for the simplicity and integrity of his life, and for his energetic devotion to the duties of his high calling. His sincerity cannot be doubted, less because he uniformly declined preferment, than because he feared not to stigmatize vice, and to preach the high duties of Christianity to an unprincipled monarch and a dissolute court, whom his theories of political government led him to look up to with feelings of reverence. He was of a frank, fearless nature, and what he felt strongly, he gave utterance to without reserve.

The same characteristics are conspicuous in his sermons. He speaks from his heart. He has no reserves; his thoughts, feelings, animosities, and predilections animate his words with the warmth of the source that nursed them. In the ardor of his own sentiments he often forgets to make allowance for those of other men, and in matters of political faith or ecclesiastical rule, we find him intolerant and bigoted beyond all measure. He was an enthusiastic advocate of passive obedience and the divine right of kings, and maintained them by arguments, enforced with the hot-headed warmth by which these principles have ever been maintained. He regarded the Church of England royalists as "the best Christians, and the most meritorious subjects in the world." With these views it was to be expected that his fiercest opposition should be directed against the sectarians, with which the country was overrun — the preachers of the tub and the barn, who held all human learning in contempt, and placed at defiance all decency and propriety of language. "Never had man," it has been well said,* "a subject to exert his ingenuity on, more congenial to his temper, and never were poor heretics so assailed with invective and ridicule. He dwelt with delight on their meagre, mortified faces, their droning and snuffling whine, their sanctimonious hypocritical demeanor; but in the midst of his pleasantry, he shot some shafts dipped in the bitterest gall, and pointed by the most inveterate hatred. With a proud consciousness of superior learning, and perhaps a pharisaical conceit of superior integrity; with the keenest sarcasm and the most undisguised contempt, he held up to the detestation of mankind these impudent pretenders to the gifts of the Spirit." "We have thus a picture of a singular

* *Retrospective Review*, vol. ix. page 295.

race of men exhibited in the most striking, but yet the darkest colors, by the hand of a master; for the painter himself was a bigot, and a declared foe to those whom he portrayed. It is, however, useful to have the portrait drawn even by an enemy: we must look elsewhere for the more pleasing lights and colors."

As matters of history, and with reference to our estimate of the man himself, those parts of his sermons which relate to these topics are not devoid of interest. But they form the smallest part of the attraction which these noble monuments of intellect and piety present. South knew mankind well. There is no "pleasant vice," no self-gratulating hypocrisy, no evasion of duty under a complacent admission of its claims, that can escape his searching glance. He strips vice and folly of their frippery, scatters the delusions of pride and passion, and lays down the rules of Christian faith and practice with a precision, which satisfies the intellect, while it leaves the transgressor without an excuse. "Not diffuse, not learned," says Mr. Hallam,* "not formal in argument like Barrow, with a more natural structure of sentences, a more pointed, though by no means a more fair and satisfactory turn of reasoning, with a style clear and English, and free from all pedantry, but abounding with those colloquial novelties of idiom, which, though now vulgar and offensive, the age of Charles II. affected, sparing no personal or temporary sarcasm, but, if he seems for a moment to tread on the verge of buffoonery, recovering himself by some stroke of vigorous sense and language; such was the worthy Dr. South, whom the courtiers delighted to hear. His sermons want all that is called unction, and sometimes even earnestness, which is owing, in a great measure, to a tone of perpetual gibing at rebels and fanatics; but there is a masculine spirit about them, which, combined with their peculiar characteristics, would naturally fill the churches where he might be heard." It is this masculine spirit which gives to the pages of South an interest which never flags, and we never turn from them without feeling that some weakness has been overthrown, some principle placed in a clearer light, and a healthy tone of thought communicated to the mind. His place among divines may not be with the highest, but it is not far beneath them. As a clear and original thinker, and as a master of a manly and forcible style, he is surpassed by none.

"As a judge of men and manners," says the writer in the "Retrospective Review," "and a careful observer of human life, South deserves the highest praise. He seldom attempts the subtleties of metaphysical disquisition, in which he did not excel; his business was with the broad realities of life. To show that the low and con-

* *Literature of Europe*, iv. 177.

temptible things of the earth often govern the great and exalted, to teach man reasonable diffidence and modesty, to discourage unbounded hopes and expectations, to cherish noble and honorable aspirations, and to make his fellow-creatures wiser and better; to do this was the useful and honorable object of this excellent teacher. He thought, no doubt, he had said a witty thing, who called South's discourses not 'Sunday, but week-day sermons;' his meaning was, we presume, if he had any, that they were written too much for worldly every-day affairs; a charge, which a very numerous class of sermon-makers have no cause to fear, who write for no day at all. South's sermons are adapted to all readers and all days; they contain innumerable thoughts and reflections which are true and striking, though not always the most obvious to a common thinker; and this is an unequivocal mark of a good writer. From him we might form a collection of useful maxims, in which sentiments the most profound and just are delivered in language the most expressive and correct.

"His faults, like his virtues, are many and great. His intolerant and persecuting spirit we have before had occasion to notice; words were the only weapons his profession allowed him to use, but he wielded them with a terrible vigor and effect. Doubtless he would have fought with the same spirit that he wrote; for during Monmouth's rebellion, he declared he was ready, if there should be occasion, to change his black gown for a buff-coat. To his detested enemies, the Papists and Puritans, he could show no mercy, and allow no virtue. Milton, with him, is 'the blind adder, who spit venom on the king's person;' Cromwell is 'Baal,' a 'bankrupt beggary fellow, who entered the parliament-house with a threadbare, torn cloak, and greasy hat, and perhaps neither of them paid for;' and Sir Henry Vane, 'that worthy knight, who was executed on Tower Hill.' His crying sin was the contrivance of the covenant; and for this South could triumph over his unjust condemnation.

"Satire, ridicule, and invective, he poured forth in a copious and continuous stream; but he was often carried away by the violence of the torrent, which he could neither direct nor restrain. He would always step aside to have a blow at the schismatics, to slyly insinuate some article of his political creed, something about prerogative, or occasionally relieve himself by a discharge from his inexhaustible fund of wit and humor. This humor often bordered on grossness and indelicacy, and his wit certainly betrayed him into expressions certainly improper, if not profane. What he could not confute by argument, he would overcome by ridicule. He well knew the value of Horace's maxim —

'Ridiculum acri
Fortius et melius magnas plerumque secat res.'

"It may perhaps be objected to some of his sermons that they contain too many divisions and subdivisions, and that order leads to confusion: but all the heads of his discourse are fully examined and discussed; and the infinite variety and fullness of the man's understanding and imagination led him often to crowd into one short sermon what a modern bookmaker would diffuse over a folio.

"His sermons, to be properly appreciated, ought to be carefully studied; and we may venture to say that the labor will not be unprofitable: they bear the unequivocal stamp, which a peculiar turn of mind and a great genius cannot fail to impress. The copious and energetic language of South might serve to invigorate the well-turned and rounded sentences of many a modern scribbler, which fall softly on the ear, but have not strength to penetrate farther. The man of business and active life, who has occasion to state to others what he knows himself, might be supplied from this storehouse with all the necessary stock of words and all the clearness of expression; and, if inclination prompted, or circumstances required, he might from the same magazine arm himself with the weapons of ridicule, sarcasm, invective, and abuse. It is no pedantry to say that we observe considerable resemblance between the style of South and the manner of the great Athenian orator; and it is not surprising that there should be a similarity between two men of ardent temperament, who on all subjects thought clearly and expressed themselves forcibly; both were men of strong common sense, who were deeply interested in the business in which they were engaged; both waged a long and continued warfare with enemies whom they hated, and both had, to support them, the command of a mighty and powerful language."

THE CHIEF HEADS OF THE SERMONS.

VOL. I.

SERMON I.

THE WAYS OF WISDOM ARE WAYS OF PLEASANTNESS.

Prov. iii. 17. — *Her ways are ways of pleasantness.* Page 2.

Some objections against this truth are removed, 3, and the duty of repentance represented under a mixture of sweetness, 7.

The excellencies of the pleasure of wisdom are enumerated:

I. As it is the pleasure of the mind, 9, in reference, 1. To speculation, 10, on the account of the greatness, 10, and newness of the objects, 12. 2. To practice, 12.

II. As it never satiates and wearies, 13. The comparison of other pleasures with it; such as that of an epicure, 13, that of ambition, 15, that of friendship and conversation, 16.

III. As it is in nobody's power, but only in his that has it, 17, which property and perpetuity is not to be found in worldly enjoyments, 17.

A consequence is drawn against the absurd austerities of the Romish profession, 18.

A short description of the religious pleasure, 19.

SERMON II.

OF THE CREATION OF MAN IN THE IMAGE OF GOD.

Genesis i. 27. — *So God created man in his own image, in the image of God created he him.* P. 23.

The several false opinions of the heathen philosophers concerning the original of the world, 23.

The image of God in man considered, 24.

I. Wherein it does not consist, adequately and formally; not in power and dominion, as the Socinians erroneously assert, 24.

II. Wherein it does consist: 1. In the universal rectitude of all the faculties of the soul, 25, viz. of his understanding, 26, both speculative, 26, and practical, 28. Of his will, 30. Concerning the freedom of it, 30. Of his passions, 31; love, 32, hatred, 33, anger, 33, joy, 33, sorrow, 34, hope, 34, fear, 34. 2. In those characters of majesty that God imprinted upon his body, 35.

The consideration of the irreparable loss sustained in the fall of our first parents, 37, and of the excellency of Christian religion, designed by God to repair the breaches of our humanity, 38.

SERMON III.

INTEREST DEPOSED, AND TRUTH RESTORED.

Matthew x. 33. — *But whosoever shall deny me before men, him will I also deny before my Father which is in heaven.* P. 42.

The occasion of those words inquired into, 42, and their explication, by being compared with other parallel scriptures, 44, and some observations deduced from them, 44.

The explication of them, by showing,

I. How many ways Christ and his truths may be denied, 45. 1. By an heretical judgment, 46. 2. By oral expressions, 47. 3. By our actions, 48.

What denial is intended by these words, 49.

II. The causes inducing men to deny Christ in his truths, 50. 1. The seeming absurdity of many truths, 50. 2. Their unprofitableness, 51. 3. Their apparent danger, 53.

III. How far a man may consult his safety in time of persecution, without denying Christ, 54. 1. By withdrawing his person, 54. 2. By concealing his judgment, 55.

When those ways of securing ourselves are not lawful, 55.

IV. What is meant by Christ's denial of us, 57, with reference, 1. To the action itself, 57. 2. To its circumstances, 58.

V. How many uses may be drawn from the words, 59. 1. An exhortation chiefly to persons in authority, to defend Christ in his truth, 59, and in his members, 60. 2. An information, to show us the danger as well as baseness of denying Christ, 61.

SERMON IV.

RELIGION THE BEST REASON OF STATE.

1 Kings xiii. 33, 34. — *After this thing king Jeroboam returned not from his evil way, but made again of the lowest of the people priests of the high places: whosoever would, he consecrated him, and he became one of the priests of the high places. And this thing became sin unto the house of Jeroboam, even to cut it off, and to destroy it from off the face of the earth.* P. 63.

Jeroboam's history and practice, 63. Some observations from it, 66. An explication of the words *high places*, 66, and *consecration*, 67.

The sense of the words drawn into two propositions, 67.

I. The means to strengthen or to ruin the civil power, is either to establish or destroy the right worship of God, 67. Of which proposition the truth is proved by all records of divine and profane history, 68, and the reason is drawn from the judicial proceeding of God; and from the dependence of the principles of government upon religion, 68.

From which may be inferred, 1. The pestilential design of disjoining the civil and ecclesiastical interest, 73. 2. The danger of any thing that may make even the true religion suspected to be false, 75.

II. The way to destroy religion is to embase the dispensers of it, 76, which is done, 1. By divesting them of all temporal privileges and advantages, 76. 2. By admitting unworthy persons to this function, 79. By which means,

1st, ministers are brought under contempt, 82. 2dly, Men of fit parts and abilities are discouraged from undertaking the ministry, 84.

A brief recapitulation of the whole, 86.

SERMON V.

THE DUTIES OF THE EPISCOPAL FUNCTIONS.

Titus ii. 15. — *These things speak, and exhort, and rebuke with all authority. Let no man despise thee.* P. 89.

Titus supposed to be a bishop in all this epistle, 89. The duties of which place are,

I. To teach, 91, either immediately by himself, 93, or mediately by the subordinate ministration of others, 94.

II. To rule, 94, by an exaction of duty from persons under him, 95, by a protection of the persons under the discharge of their duty, 96, and by animadversion upon such as neglect it, 96.

And the means better to execute those duties is, not to be despised, 90, 98, in the handling of which prescription these things may be observed:

1. The ill effects that contempt has upon government, 98. 2. The causes upon which church rulers are frequently despised, 100. And they are

Either groundless; such as their very profession itself, 101, loss of their former grandeur and privilege, 102.

Or just; such as ignorance, 103, viciousness, 103, fearfulness, 104, and a proneness to despise others, 105.

The character of a clergyman, 106.

SERMON VI.

WHY CHRIST'S DOCTRINE WAS REJECTED BY THE JEWS.

John vii. 17. — *If any man will do his will, he shall know of the doctrine, whether it be of God, or whether I speak of myself.* P. 107.

An account of the Jewish and Christian economy, 107.

The gospel must meet with a rightly disposed will, before it can gain the assent of the understanding, 108, which will appear from the following considerations:

I. What Christ's doctrine is, with relation to matters of belief, 109, and to matters of practice, 109.

II. That men's unbelief of that doctrine was from no defect in the arguments, 111, whose strength was sufficient, from the completion of all the predictions, 111, and the authority of miracles, 112. And whose insufficiency (if there could have been any) was not the cause of the unbelief of the Jews, 113, who assented to things less evident, 113, neither evident nor certain, but only probable, 114, neither evident, not certain, nor probable, but false and fallacious, 114.

III. That the Jewish unbelief proceeded from the pravity of the will influencing the understanding to a disbelief of Christianity, 115, the last being prepossessed with other notions, and the first being wholly governed by covetousness and ambition, 115.

IV. That a well-disposed mind, with a readiness to obey the will of God, is the best means to enlighten the understanding to a belief of Christianity, 117, upon the account both of God's goodness, 117, and of a natural efficiency, 119, arising from a right disposition of the will, which will engage the understanding in the search of the truth through diligence, 119, and impartiality, 120.

From which particulars may be learned, 1. The true cause of atheism and skepticism, 122. 2. The most effectual means of becoming good Christians, 124.

SERMON VII.

GOD'S PECULIAR REGARD TO PLACES SET APART FOR DIVINE WORSHIP.

Psalm lxxxvii. 2. — *God hath loved the gates of Sion more than all the dwellings of Jacob.* P. 128.

All comparisons import, in the superior part of them, difference and preëminence, 128, and so from the comparison of this text arise these propositions:

I. That God bears a different respect to consecrated places, from what he bears to all others, 128, which difference he shows, 1. By the interposals of his providence for the erecting and preserving of them, 128. 2. By his punishments upon the violators of them, 131. 3. Not upon the account of any inherent sanctity in the things themselves, but because he has the sole property of them, 136, by appropriating them to his peculiar use, 136, and by deed of gift made by surrender on man's part, 137, and by acceptance on his, 138.

II. That God prefers the worship paid to him in such places above that in all others, 141, because, 1. Such places are naturally apt to excite a greater devotion, 141. 2. In them our worship is a more direct service and homage to him, 143.

From all which we are taught to have these three ingredients in our devotion: desire, reverence, and confidence, 145.

SERMON VIII.

ALL CONTINGENCIES UNDER THE DIRECTION OF GOD'S PROVIDENCE.

Prov. xvi. 33. — *The lot is cast into the lap; but the whole disposing of it is of the Lord.* P. 147.

God's providence has its influence upon all things, even the most fortuitous, such as the casting of lots, 147. Which things, implying in themselves somewhat future and somewhat contingent, are,

I. In reference to men, out of the reach of their knowledge and of their power, 148.

II. In reference to God, comprehended by a certain knowledge, 149, and governed by as certain a providence, 150, and by him directed to both certain, 150, and great ends, 152; in reference,

1. To societies, or united bodies of men, 152. 2. To particular persons, whether public, as princes, 157, or private, touching their lives, 158, health, 159, reputation, 159, friendships, 161, employments, 162.

Therefore we ought to rely on divine Providence; and be neither too confident in prosperity, 164, nor too despondent in adversity, 166; but carry a conscience clear towards God, who is the sole and absolute disposer of all things, 166.

SERMON IX.

THE WISDOM OF THIS WORLD.

1 Cor. iii. 19. — *For the wisdom of this world is foolishness with God.* P. 168.

Worldly wisdom, in scripture, is taken sometimes for philosophy, 168, sometimes, as here, for policy, 168, which,

I. Governs its actions generally by these rules, 169. 1. By a constant dissimulation; not a bare concealment of one's mind; but a man's positive professing what he is not, and resolves not to be, 170. 2. By submitting conscience and religion to one's interest, 172. 3. By making one's self the sole end of all actions, 174. 4. By having no respect to friendship, gratitude, or sense of honor, 175.

Which rules and principles are,

II. Foolish and absurd in reference to God, 177, because in the pursuit of them man pitches, 1. Upon an end, unproportionable, 177, to the measure of his duration, 177, or to the vastness of his desires, 178. 2. Upon means in themselves insufficient for, 180, and frequently contrary to the attaining of such ends, 181, which is proved to happen in the four foregoing rules of the worldly politician, 182.

Therefore we ought to be sincere, 186, and commit our persons and concerns to the wise and good providence of God, 187.

SERMON X.

GOOD INCLINATIONS NO EXCUSE FOR BAD ACTIONS.

2 Cor. viii. 12. — *For if there be first a willing mind, it is accepted according to that a man hath, and not according to that he hath not.* P. 188.

Men are apt to abuse the world and themselves in some general principles of action; and particularly in this, That God accepts the will for the deed, 188. The delusion of which is laid open in these words, 189, expressing, that where there is no power, God accepts the will; but implying, that where there is, he does not. So there is nothing of so fatal an import as the plea of a good intention, and of a good will, 190; for God requires the obedience of the whole man, and never accepts the will but as such, 192. Thence we may understand how far it holds good, that God accepts the will for the deed, 194; a rule whose

I. Ground is founded upon that eternal truth, that God requires of man nothing impossible, 194; and consequently whose

II. Bounds are determined by what power man naturally hath, 194; but whose

III. Misapplication consists in these, 194. 1. That men often mistake for an act of the will what really is not so, 194; as a bare approbation, 194, wishing, 195, mere inclination, 197. 2. That men mistake for impossibilities things which are not truly so, 198; as in duties of very great labor, 198, danger, 199, cost, 203, in conquering an inveterate habit, 207.

Therefore there is not a weightier case of conscience than to know how far God accepts the will, and when men truly will a thing, and have really no power, 209.

SERMON XI.

OF THE ODIOUS SIN OF INGRATITUDE.

Judges viii. 34, 35. — *And the children of Israel remembered not the Lord their God, who had delivered them out of the hands of all their enemies on every side: neither shewed they kindness to the house of Jerubbaal, namely Gideon, according to all the goodness which he had shewed unto Israel.* P. 210.

The history of Gideon, and the Israelites' behavior towards him, 210, are the subject and occasion of these words, which treat of their ingratitude both towards God and man, 212. This vice in this latter sense is described, 212, by showing,

I. What gratitude is, 212; what are its parts, 213; what grounds it hath in the law of nature, 213. Of God's word, 216. Of man, 216.

II. The nature and baseness of ingratitude, 218.

III. That ingratitude proceeds from a proneness to do ill turns with a complacency upon the sight of any mischief befalling another; and from an utter insensibility of all kindnesses, 221.

IV. That it is always attended with many other ill qualities, 222; pride, 222, hard-heartedness, 224, and falsehood, 226. Therefore,

V. What consequences may be drawn from the premises, 226. 1. Never to enter into a league of friendship with an ungrateful person, 226, because, 2. he cannot be altered by any acts of kindness, 227, and, 3. he has no true sense of religion, 228. Exhortation to gratitude as a debt to God, 229.

SERMON XII.

OF THE BASE SINS OF FALSEHOOD AND LYING.

Prov. xii. 22. — *Lying lips are abomination to the Lord.* P. 230.

The universality of lying is described, 230. And this vice is further prosecuted, by showing,

I. The nature of it, 232; wherein it consists, 232; and the unlawfulness of all sorts of lies, whether pernicious, officious, or jocose, 233.

II. The effects of it, 236: all sins that came into the world, 236; all miseries that befall mankind, 237; an utter dissolution of all society, 240; an indisposition to the impressions of religion, 242.

III. The punishments of it: the loss of all credit, 244; the hatred of all whom the liar has or would have deceived, 245; and an eternal separation from God, 248.

All which particulars are briefly summed up, 249.

SERMON XIII.

THE PRACTICE OF RELIGION ENFORCED BY REASON.

Prov. x. 9. — *He that walketh uprightly walketh surely.* P. 254.

The life of man is in scripture expressed by walking; which to do surely, great caution must be taken not to lay down false principles, or mistake in consequences from right ones, 254; but to walk uprightly, under the notion of an infinite mind governing the world, and an expectation of another state hereafter,

255. Which two principles will secure us in all our actions, whether they be considered,

I. As true, 255, the folly of a sinner presuming upon God's mercy, 257, or relying upon a future repentance, 259; or whether supposed,

II. As only probable, 260. No man, in most temporal concerns, acts upon surer grounds than of probability, 261. And self-preservation will oblige a man to undergo a lesser evil to secure himself from the probability of a greater, 262. Probability supposes that a thing may or may not be; both which are examined with relation to a future state, 263.

III. As false, 265. Under this supposition the virtuous walketh more surely than the wicked, with reference to temporal enjoyments: reputation, 265, quietness, 267, health, 268. Answer to an objection, that many sinners enjoy all these, 270.

Thence we may perceive the folly of atheistical persons, 271, and learn to walk uprightly, as the best ground for our present and future happiness, 274.

SERMON XIV.

OF THE LOVE OF CHRIST TO HIS DISCIPLES.

John xv. 15. — *Henceforth I call you not servants; for the servant knoweth not what his lord doeth: but I have called you friends; for all things that I have heard of my Father have I made known unto you.* P. 275.

The superlative love of Christ appears in the several degrees of his kindness to man, before he was created, 275, when created, 276, when fallen, 276; whom even he not only spared, but, from the number of subjects, took into the retinue of his servants, and further advanced to the privilege of a friend, 277. The difference between which two appellations is this:

I. That a servant is, for the most part, 1. unacquainted with his master's designs, 278; 2. restrained with a degenerous awe of mind, 279; 3. endued with a mercenary disposition, 279.

II. That a friend is blessed with many privileges; as, 1. Freedom of access, 280. 2. Favorable construction of all passages, 281. 3. Sympathy in joy and grief, 284. 4. Communication of secrets, 285. 5. Counsel and advice, 287. 6. Constancy and perpetuity, 289.

In every one of which particulars, the excellency of Christ's friendship shining forth, 291, we may learn the high advantage of true piety, 292.

SERMONS XV. XVI.

AGAINST LONG EXTEMPORE PRAYERS.

Eccles. v. 2. — *Be not rash with thy mouth, and let not thine heart be hasty to utter any thing before God: for God is in heaven, and thou upon earth: therefore let thy words be few.* P. 295.

Solomon having been spoken to by God himself, and so the fittest to teach us how to speak to God, here observes to us, that when we are in God's house, we are more especially in his presence; that this ought to create a reverence in our addresses to him, and that this reverence consists in the preparation of our thoughts and the government of our expressions, 295, the two great joint ingredients of prayer, 302. Of which,

The first is premeditation of thought, 296, 302, 303.

The second is, ordering of our words by pertinence and brevity of expression, 296.

Because prayer prevails upon God,

Not, as it does with men, by way of information, 296, persuasion, 296, importunity, 297. An objection to this last is answered, 301.

But as it is the fulfilling of that condition upon which God dispenseth his blessings to mankind, 298. An objection to this is removed, 298.

As it is most properly an act of dependence upon God, 300, a dependence not natural, but moral; for else it would belong indifferently to the wicked as well as to the just, 300.

I. Premeditation ought to respect: 1. The object of our prayers: God and his divine perfections, 303. 2. The matter of our prayers, 305: either things of absolute necessity, as the virtues of a pious life; or of unquestionable charity, as the innocent comforts of it, 305. 3. The order and disposition of our prayers, 306: by excluding every thing which may seem irreverent, incoherent, and impertinent; absurd and irrational, 307; rude, slight, and careless, 307.

Therefore all Christian churches have governed their public worship by a liturgy, or set form of prayer, 308. Which way of praying is truly,

To pray by the Spirit; that is, with the heart, not hypocritically; and according to the rules prescribed by God's holy Spirit, not unwarrantably, or by a pretense to immediate inspiration, 309.

Not to stint, but help and enlarge the spirit of prayer, 311; for the soul being of a limited nature, can not at the same time supply two distinct faculties to the same height of operation; words are the work of the brain; and devotion, properly the business of the heart, indispensably required in prayer, 311.

Whereas, on the contrary,

Extempore prayers stint the spirit, by calling off the faculties of the soul from dealing with the heart both in the minister and in the people, 311, 312. And besides,

They are prone to encourage pride and ostentation, 313, faction and sedition, 314.

II. Brevity of expression, the greatest perfection of speech, 316; authorized by both divine, 317, and human examples, 317; suited best to the modesty, 320, discretion, 320, and respect required in all suppliants, 321; is still further enforced in our addresses to God by these arguments, 321. 1. That all the reasons for prolixity of speech with men cease to be so when we pray to God, 322. 2. That there are but few things necessary to be prayed for, 326. 3. That the person who prays can not keep up the same fervor and attention in a long as in a short prayer, 327. 4. That shortness of speech is the most natural and lively way of expressing the utmost agonies of the soul, 329. 5. That we have examples in scripture, both of brevity and prolixity of speech in prayer, as of brevity in the Lord's Prayer, 330; the practice of it in our Saviour himself, 330; the success of it in several instances; as of the leper, of the blind man, and of the publican, 331. Whereas the heathens and the pharisees, the grand instances of idolatry and hypocrisy, are noted for prolixity, 332.

By these rules we may judge, 1. of our church's excellent liturgy; for its brevity and fullness, for the frequent opportunity of mentioning the name and some great attribute of God; for its alternate responses, which thing properly denominates it a *Book of Common-Prayer*, 334; for appointing even a form of prayer before sermons, 334. 2. Of the dissenters' prayers, always notable for length and tautology, incoherence and confusion, 335;

And, after this comparison, pronounce our liturgy the greatest treasure of rational devotion; and pray God would vouchsafe long to continue to us the use of it, 337.

SERMONS XVII. XVIII.

OF THE HEINOUS GUILT OF TAKING PLEASURE IN OTHER MEN'S SINS.

Romans i. 32. — *Who knowing the judgment of God, that they which commit such things are worthy of death, not only do the same, but have pleasure in them that do them.* Pp. 338, 358.

The sin of taking pleasure in other men's sins is not only distinct from, but also much greater than all those others mentioned in the foregoing catalogue, 338. To arrive at which pitch of sinning there is a considerable difficulty, 342, because every man has naturally a distinguishing sense of good and evil, and an inward satisfaction or dissatisfaction after the doing of either, and can not quickly or easily extinguish this principle, but by another inferior principle gratified with objects contrary to the former, 340. And consequently no man is quickly or easily brought to take pleasure in his own, much less in other men's sins, 341. Of which sin,

I. The causes are: 1. The commission of the same sins in one's own person, 342. 2. The commission of them against the full conviction of conscience, 344. 3. The continuance in them, 346. 4. The inseparable poor-spiritedness of guilt, which is less uneasy in company, 348. 5. A peculiar unaccountable malignity of nature, 349.

II. The reasons why the guilt of that sin is so great, are: 1. That there is naturally no motive to tempt men to it, 352. 2. That the nature of this sin is boundless and unlimited, 355. 3. That this sin includes in it the guilt of many preceding ones, 356.

III. The persons guilty of that sin are generally such as draw others to it, 358; particularly, 1. who teach doctrines, 358, which represent sinful actions either as not sinful, 359, or as less sinful, than they really are, 361. Censure of some modern casuists, 362. 2. Who allure men to sin through formal persuasion or inflaming objects, 363. 3. Who affect the company of vicious persons, 365. 4. Who encourage others in their sins by commendation, 366, or preferment, 367.

Lastly, the effects of this sin are: Upon particular persons; that it quite depraves the natural frame of the heart, 368: it indisposes a man to repent of it, 369; it grows the more as a man lives longer, 370; it will damn more surely, because many are damned who never arrived to this pitch, 372. 2. Upon communities of men; that it propagates the practice of any sin till it becomes national, 372; especially where great sinners make their dependants their proselytes, 373, and the follies of the young carry with them the approbation of the old, 374. This the reason of the late increase of vice, 374.

SERMON XIX.

NATURAL RELIGION WITHOUT REVELATION, SUFFICIENT TO RENDER A SINNER INEXCUSABLE.

Romans i. 20. — *So that they are without excuse.* P. 376.

The apostle in this epistle addresses himself chiefly to the Jews; but in this first chapter he deals with the Greeks and Gentiles, 376, whom he charges with an inexcusable sinfulness, 376. And the charge contains in this, and in the precedent and subsequent verses,

I. The sin; [*that knowing God, they did not glorify him as God,* ver. 21;] idolatry; not that kind of one which worships that for God which is not God; but the other, which worships the true God by the mediation of corporeal resemblances, 377.

II. The persons guilty of this sin; [*such as professed themselves wise,* ver. 22;] not the Gnostics, but the old heathen philosophers, 379.

III. The cause of that sin, [*holding the truth in unrighteousness,* ver. 18;] 381, that the truths which they were accountable for, viz. 1. The being of a God, 381. 2. That he is the maker and governor of the world, 381. 3. That he is to be worshiped, 382. 4. That he is to be worshiped by pious practices, 382. 5. That every deviation from duty is to be repented of, 382. 6. That every guilty person is obnoxious to punishment, 382,

Were by them held in unrighteousness, 1. By not acting up to what they knew, 383. 2. By not improving those known principles into proper consequences, 384. 3. By concealing what they knew, 385.

IV. The judgment passed upon them, [*that they were without excuse,* ver. 20,] 388, that they were unfit not only for a pardon, but even for a plea, 389. Because,

1. The freedom of the will, which they generally asserted, excluded them from the plea of unwillingness, 390. 2. The knowledge of their understanding excluded them from the plea of ignorance, 390.

From all these we may consider,

1. The great mercy of God in the revelation of the gospel, 392.

2. The deplorable condition of obstinate sinners under it, 393.

SERMON XX.

OF SACRAMENTAL PREPARATION.

Matthew xxii. 12.—*And he saith unto him, Friend, how camest thou in hither, not having a wedding-garment?* P. 395.

The design of this parable, under the circumstantial passages of a wedding's royal solemnity, is to set forth the free offer of the gospel to the Jews first, and upon their refusal, to the Gentiles, 396. But it may be more peculiarly applied to the holy eucharist; which not only by analogy, but with propriety of speech, and from the very ceremony of breaking bread, may very well be called a wedding-supper, 397; to the worthy participation whereof there is indispensably required a suitable and sufficient preparation, 398. In which these conditions are required:

I. That the preparation be habitual, 402.

II. That it be also actual, 404; of which the principal ingredients are: 1. Self-examination, 406. 2. Repentance, 408. 3. Prayer, 409. 4. Fasting, 410. 5. Almsgiving, 411. 6. Charitable temper of mind, 412. 7. Reading and meditation, 414.

The reverend author seemed to have designed another discourse upon this text, because in this sermon he only dispatches the first part, viz. the necessity of preparation; but proceeds not to the second, viz. that God is a severe animadverter upon such as partake without such a preparation, 398.

SERMON XXI.

OF THE FATAL IMPOSTURE AND FORCE OF WORDS.

Isaiah v. 20. — *Woe unto them that call evil good, and good evil.* P. 416.

Here a woe is denounced against those, not only in particular, who judicially pronounce the guilty innocent, and the innocent guilty; but in general, who by abusing men's minds with false notions, make evil pass for good, and good for evil, 416. And in the examination of this vile practice it will be necessary,

I. To examine the nature of good and evil, what they are, and upon what they are founded, viz. upon the conformity or unconformity to right reason, 418. Not upon the opinion, 419, or laws of men, 419; because then, 1. The same action under the same circumstances might be both morally good and morally evil, 419. 2. The laws could neither be morally good nor evil, 423. The same action might be in respect of the divine law commanding it, morally good; and of an human, forbidding it, morally evil, 423.

But that the nature of good and evil is founded upon a *jus naturale*, antecedent to all *jus positivum*, may be exemplified in those two moral duties, towards God and towards one's neighbor, 424.

II. To show the way how good and evil operate upon men's minds, viz. by their respective names or appellations, 425.

III. To show the mischief arising from the misapplication of names, 426. For since, 1. the generality of men are absolutely governed by words and names, 426, and 2. chiefly in matters of good and evil, 431, which are commonly taken upon trust, by reason of the frequent affinity between vice and virtue, 431, and of most men's inability to judge exactly of things, 432. Thence may be inferred the comprehensive mischief of this misapplication, by which man is either, 1. deceived, 434, or 2. misrepresented, 435.

SERMON XXII.

PREVENTION OF SIN AN INVALUABLE MERCY.

1 Samuel xxv. 32, 33.—*And David said to Abigail, Blessed be the Lord God of Israel, which sent thee this day to meet me: and blessed be thy advice, and blessed be thou, which hast kept me this day from coming to shed blood, and from avenging myself with my own hand.* P. 438.

This is David's retractation of his revenge resolved upon an insolent wealthy rustic, who had most unthankfully rejected his request with railing at his person and messengers, 438. From which we may,

I. Observe the greatness of sin-preventing mercy, 440. Which appears, 1. From the deplorable condition of the sinner, before that mercy prevents him, 440. 2. From the cause of that mercy, which is God's free grace, 443. 3. From the danger of sin unprevented, which will then be certainly committed; and in such deliberate commission there is a greater probability that it will not, than that it will be pardoned, 445, because every commission hardens the soul in that sin, and disposes the soul to proceed further, and it is not in the sinner's power to repent, 445. 4. From the advantages of the prevention of sin above those of the pardon of it, 447, which are the clearness of a man's condition, 447, and the satisfaction of his mind, 448.

II. Make several useful applications, 449. As, 1. To learn how vastly greater the pleasure is upon the forbearance, than in the commission of sin, 449. 2. To find out the disposition of one's heart by this sure criterion, with what ecstasy he receives a spiritual blessing, 450. 3. To be content, and thankfully to acquiesce in any condition, and under the severest passages of Providence, 452, with relation to health, 452, reputation, 452, and wealth, 453.

SERMONS XXIII. XXIV.

OF THE NATURE AND MEASURE OF CONSCIENCE.

1 John iii. 21. — *Beloved, if our heart condemn us not, we have confidence towards God.* Pp. 456, 479.

It is of great moment and difficulty to be rationally satisfied about the estate of one's soul, 456: in which weighty concern we ought not to rely upon such uncertain rules, 457, as these: 1. The general esteem of the world, 457. 2. The judgment of any casuist, 458. 3. The absolution of any priest, 460. 4. The external profession even of a true religion, 461.

But a man's own heart and conscience, above all other things, is able to give him confidence towards God, 464. In order to which we must know,

I. How the heart or conscience ought to be informed, 464, viz. by right reason and scripture, 464, and endeavoring to employ the utmost of our ability to get the clearest knowledge of our duty; and thus to come to that confidence, which, though it amounts not to an infallible demonstration, yet is a rational, well-grounded hope, 466.

II. By what means we may get our heart thus informed, 467, viz.: 1. By a careful attention to the dictates of reason and natural morality, 467. 2. By a tender regard to every pious motion of God's Spirit, 469. 3. By a study of the revealed word of God, 471. 4. By keeping a frequent and impartial account with our conscience, 473.

With this caution, lest either, on the one side, every doubting may overthrow our confidence, 475, or, on the other, a bare silence of conscience raise it too much, 476.

III. Whence the testimony of conscience is so authentic, 479, viz.: 1. Because it is commissioned to this office by God himself, 481. And there is examined the absurdity and impertinence, 482, the impudence and impiety of false pretenses of conscience, 488; such particularly as those of schismatical dissenters, 484, 489, who oppose the solemn usages of our church; the necessity of which is founded upon sound reason, 486. 2. Because it is quick-sighted, 492, tender and sensible, 493, exactly and severely impartial, 494.

IV. Some particular instances wherein this confidence suggested by conscience exerts itself, 496, viz. 1. In our addresses to God by prayer, 494. 2. At the time of some notable sharp trial, 497, as poverty, 498, calumny and disgrace, 499. 3. Above all others at the time of death, 500.

SERMONS.

SERMON I.

PREACHED BEFORE THE COURT AT CHRIST CHURCH CHAPEL IN OXFORD.

TO THE RIGHT HONORABLE EDWARD EARL OF CLARENDON, LORD HIGH CHANCELLOR OF ENGLAND, AND CHANCELLOR OF THE UNIVERSITY OF OXON, AND ONE OF HIS MAJESTY'S MOST HONORABLE PRIVY COUNCIL.

My Lord,

THOUGH to prefix so great a name to so mean a piece seems like enlarging the entrance of an house that affords no reception; yet since there is nothing can warrant the publication of it, but what can also command it, the work must think of no other patronage than the same that adorns and protects its author. Some indeed vouch great names, because they think they deserve; but I, because I need such: and had I not more occasion than many others to see and converse with your lordship's candor and proneness to pardon, there is none had greater cause to dread your judgment; and thereby in some part I venture to commend my own. For all know, who know your lordship, that in a nobler respect, than either that of government or patronage, you represent and head the best of universities; and have traveled over too many nations and authors to encourage any one that understands himself, to appear an author in your hands, who seldom read any books to inform yourself, but only to countenance and credit them. But, my lord, what is here published pretends no instruction, but only homage; while it teaches many of the world, it only describes your lordship, who have made the ways of labor and virtue, of doing, and doing good, your business and your recreation, your meat and your drink, and, I may add also, your sleep. My lord, the subject here treated of is of that nature, that it would seem but a chimera, and a bold paradox, did it not in the very front carry an instance to exemplify it; and so by the dedication convince the world, that the discourse itself was not impracticable. For such ever was, and is, and will be the temper of the generality of mankind, that, while I send men for pleasure to religion, I can not but expect, that they will look upon me as only having a mind to be pleasant with them myself: nor are men to be worded into new tempers or constitutions: and he that thinks that any one can persuade, but He that made the world, will find that he does not well understand it.

My lord, I have obeyed your command, for such must I account your desire; and thereby design, not so much the publication of my sermon, as of my obedience: for, next to the supreme pleasure described in the ensuing discourse, I enjoy none greater, than in having any opportunity to declare myself,

Your lordship's very humble servant,
and obliged chaplain,
ROBERT SOUTH.

PROV. iii. 17.—*Her ways are ways of pleasantness.*

THE text relating to something going before, must carry our eye back to the thirteenth verse, where we shall find, that the thing, of which these words are affirmed, is wisdom: a name by which the Spirit of God was here pleased to express to us religion, and thereby to tell the world, what before it was not aware of, and perhaps will not yet believe, that those two great things that so engross the desires and designs of both the nobler and ignobler sort of mankind, are to be found in religion; namely, wisdom and pleasure; and that the former is the direct way to the latter, as religion is to both.

That pleasure is man's chiefest good, (because indeed it is the perception of good that is properly pleasure,) is an assertion most certainly true, though under the common acceptance of it, not only false, but odious: for according to this, pleasure and sensuality pass for terms equivalent; and therefore he that takes it in this sense, alters the subject of the discourse. Sensuality is indeed a part, or rather one kind of pleasure, such an one as it is: for pleasure in general is the consequent apprehension of a suitable object, suitably applied to a rightly disposed faculty; and so must be conversant both about the faculties of the body and of the soul respectively; as being the result of the fruitions belonging to both.

Now amongst those many arguments used to press upon men the exercise of religion, I know none that are like to be so successful as those that answer and remove the prejudices that generally possess and bar up the hearts of men against it: amongst which, there is none so prevalent in truth, though so little owned in pretense, as that it is an enemy to men's pleasures, that it bereaves them of all the sweets of converse, dooms them to an absurd and perpetual melancholy, designing to make the world nothing else but a great monastery. With which notion of religion, nature and reason seems to have great cause to be dissatisfied. For since God never created any faculty, either in soul or body, but withal prepared for it a suitable object, and that in order to its gratification; can we think that religion was designed only for a contradiction to nature? and with the greatest and most irrational tyranny in the world to tantalize and tie men up from enjoyment, in the midst of all the opportunities of enjoyment? To place men with the furious affections of hunger and thirst in the very bosom of plenty; and then to tell them, that the envy of providence has sealed up every thing that is suitable under the character of unlawful? For certainly, first to frame appetites fit to receive pleasure, and then to interdict them with a *touch not, taste not*, can be nothing else, than only to give them occasion to devour and prey upon themselves; and so to keep men under the perpetual torment of an unsatisfied desire: a thing hugely contrary to the natural felicity of the creature, and consequently to the wisdom and goodness of the great Creator.

He therefore that would persuade men to religion, both with art and efficacy, must found the persuasion of it upon this, that it interferes not with any rational pleasure, that it bids nobody quit the enjoyment of any one thing that his reason can prove to him ought to be enjoyed. It is confessed, when, through the cross circumstances of a man's temper or condition, the enjoyment of a pleasure would certainly expose him to a greater inconvenience, then religion bids him quit it; that is, it bids him prefer the endurance of a lesser evil before a greater, and nature itself does no less. Religion therefore intrenches upon none of our privileges, invades none of our pleasures; it may indeed sometimes command us to change, but never totally to abjure them.

But it is easily foreseen, that this discourse will in the very beginning of it be encountered by an argument from experience, and therefore not more obvious than strong; namely, that it can not but be the greatest trouble in the world for a man thus (as it were) even to shake off himself, and to defy his nature, by a perpetual thwarting of his innate appetites and desires; which yet is absolutely necessary to a severe and impartial prosecution of a course of piety: nay, and we have this asserted also, by the verdict of Christ himself, who still makes the disciplines of self-denial and the cross, those terrible blows to flesh and blood, the indispensable requisites to the being of his disciples. All which being so, would not he that should be so hardy as to attempt to persuade men to piety from the pleasures of it, be liable to that invective taunt from all mankind, that the Israelites gave to Moses; *Wilt thou put out the eyes of this people?* Wilt thou persuade us out of our first notions? Wilt thou demonstrate, that there is any delight in a cross, any comfort in violent abridgments, and, which is the greatest paradox of all, that the highest pleasure is to abstain from it?

For answer to which, it must be confessed, that all arguments whatsoever against experience are fallacious; and therefore, in order to the clearing of the assertion laid down, I shall premise these two considerations:

1. That pleasure is in the nature of it a relative thing, and so imports a peculiar relation and correspondence to the state and condition of the person to whom it is a pleasure. For as those who discourse of atoms, affirm, that there are atoms of all forms, some round, some triangular, some square, and the like; all which are continually in motion, and never settle till they fall into a fit circumscription or place of the same figure: so there are the like great diversities of minds and objects. Whence it is, that this object striking upon a mind thus or thus disposed, flies off, and rebounds without making any impression; but the same luckily happening upon another, of a disposition as it were framed for it, is presently catched at, and greedily clasped into the nearest unions and embraces.

2. The other thing to be considered is this: that the estate of all men by nature is more or less different from that estate, into which the same persons do or may pass, by the exercise of that which the philosophers called virtue, and into which men are much more effectually and sublimely translated by that which we call grace; that is, by the supernatural, overpowering operation of God's Spirit. The difference of which two estates consists in this: that in the former the sensitive appetites rule and domineer; in the latter, the supreme faculty of the soul, called reason, sways the sceptre, and acts the whole man above the irregular demands of appetite and affection.

That the distinction between these two is not a mere figment, framed only to serve an hypothesis in divinity, and that there is no man but is really under one, before he is under the other, I shall prove, by showing a reason why it is so, or rather indeed why it can not but be so. And it is this: because every man in the beginning of his life, for several years is capable only of exercising his sensitive faculties and desires, the use of reason not showing itself till about the seventh year of his age; and then at length but (as it were) dawning in very imperfect essays and discoveries. Now it being most undeniably evident, that every faculty and power grows stronger and stronger by exercise; is it any wonder at all, when a man for the space of his first six years, and those the years of ductility and impression, has been wholly ruled by the propensions of sense, at that age very eager and impetuous, that then after all, his reason beginning to exert and put forth itself, finds the man prepossessed, and under another power? So that it has much ado, by many little steps and gradual conquests, to recover its prerogative from the usurpations of appetite, and so to subject the whole man to its dictates: the difficulty of which is not conquered by some men all their days. And this is one true ground of the difference between a state of nature and a state of grace, which some are pleased to scoff at in divinity, who think that they confute all that they laugh at, not knowing that it may be solidly evinced by mere reason and philosophy.

These two considerations being premised, namely, that pleasure implies a proportion and agreement to the respective states and conditions of men; and that the state of men by nature is vastly different from the estate into which grace or virtue transplants them; all that objection leveled against the foregoing assertion is very easily resolvable.

For there is no doubt, but a man, while he resigns himself up to the brutish guidance of sense and appetite, has no relish at all for the spiritual, refined delights of a soul clarified by grace and virtue. The pleasures of an angel can never be the pleasures of a hog. But this is the thing that we contend for; that a man having once advanced himself to a state of superiority over the control of his inferior appetites, finds an infinitely more solid and sublime pleasure in the delights proper to his reason, than the same person had ever conveyed to him by the bare ministry of his senses. His taste is absolutely changed, and therefore that which pleased him formerly, becomes flat and insipid to his appetite, now grown more masculine and severe. For as age and maturity passes a real and a marvelous change upon the diet and recreations of the same person; so that no man at the years and vigor of thirty is either fond of sugar-plums or rattles: in like manner, when reason, by the assistance of grace, has prevailed over, and outgrown the encroachments of sense, the delights of sensuality are to such an one but as an hobby-horse would be to a counselor of state, or as tasteless as a bundle of hay to an hungry lion. Every alteration of a man's condition infallibly infers an alteration of his pleasures.

The Athenians laughed the physiognomist to scorn, who, pretending to read men's minds in their foreheads, described Socrates for a crabbed, lustful, proud, ill-natured person; they knowing how directly contrary he was to that dirty character. But Socrates bid them forbear laughing at the man, for that he had given them a most exact account of his nature; but what they saw in him so contrary at the present, was from the conquest that he had got over his natural disposition by philosophy. And now let any one consider, whether that anger, that revenge, that wantonness and ambition, that were the proper pleasures of Socrates, under his natural temper of crabbed, lustful, and proud, could have at all affected or enamored the mind of the same Socrates, made gentle, chaste, and humble by philosophy.

Aristotle says, that were it possible to put a young man's eye into an old man's head, he would see as plainly and clearly as the other: so could we infuse the inclinations and principles of a virtuous person into him that prosecutes his debauches with the greatest keenness of desire and sense of delight, he would loathe and reject them as heartily as he now pursues them. Diogenes, being asked at a feast, why he did not continue eating as the rest did, answered him that asked him with another question, Pray why do you eat? Why, says he, for my pleasure. Why so, says Diogenes, do I abstain for my pleasure. And therefore the vain, the vicious, and luxurious person argues at an high rate of inconsequence, when he makes his particular desires the general measure of other men's delights. But the case is so plain, that I shall not upbraid any man's understanding, by endeavoring to give it any further illustration.

But still, after all, I must not deny, that the change and passage from a state of nature to a state of virtue is laborious, and consequently irksome and unpleasant: and to this it is, that all the forementioned expressions of our Saviour do allude. But surely the baseness of one condition, and the generous excellency of the other, is a sufficient argument to induce any one to a change. For as no man would think it a desirable thing, to preserve the itch upon himself, only for the pleasure of scratching, that attends that loathsome distemper: so neither can any man, that would be faithful to his reason, yield his ear to be bored through by his domineering appetites, and so choose to serve them forever, only for those poor, thin gratifications of sensuality that they are able to reward him with. The ascent up the hill is hard and tedious, but the serenity and fair prospect at the top is sufficient to incite the labor of undertaking it, and to reward it, being undertook. But the difference of these two conditions of men, as the foundation of their different pleasures, being thus made out, to press men with arguments to pass from one to the other, is not directly in the way or design of this discourse.

Yet before I come to declare positively the pleasures that are to be found in the ways of religion, one of the grand duties of which is stated upon repentance, a thing expressed to us by the grim names of mortification, crucifixion, and the like; and that I may not proceed only upon absolute negations, without some concessions; we will see, whether this so harsh, dismal, and affrighting duty of repentance is so entirely gall, as to admit of no mixture, no allay of sweetness, to reconcile it to the apprehensions of reason and nature.

Now repentance consists properly of two things:

1. Sorrow for sin.
2. Change of life.

A word briefly of them both.

1. And first for sorrow for sin: usually, the sting of sorrow is this, that it neither removes nor alters the thing we sorrow for; and so is but a kind of reproach to our reason, which will be sure to accost us with this dilemma. Either the thing we sorrow for is to be remedied, or it is not: if it is, why then do we spend the time in mourning, which should be spent in an active applying of remedies? But if it is not, then is our sorrow vain and superfluous, as tending to no real effect. For no man can weep his father or his friend out of the grave, or mourn himself out of a bankrupt condition. But this spiritual sorrow is effectual to one of the greatest and highest purposes that mankind can be concerned in. It is a means to avert an impendent wrath, to disarm an offended omnipotence, and even to fetch a soul out of the very jaws of hell. So that the end and consequence of this sorrow sweetens the sorrow itself: and as Solomon says, *In the midst of laughter, the heart is sorrowful;* so in the midst of sorrow here, the heart may rejoice: for while it mourns, it reads, that *those that mourn shall be comforted;* and so while the penitent weeps with one eye, he views his deliverance with the other. But then for the external expressions, and vent of sorrow; we know that there is a certain pleasure in weeping; it is the discharge of a big and a swelling grief; of a full and a strangling discontent; and therefore, he that never had such a burden upon his heart, as to give him opportunity thus to ease it, has one pleasure in this world yet to come.

2. As for the other part of repentance, which is change of life, this indeed may be troublesome in the entrance; but it is but the first bold onset, the first resolute violence and invasion upon a vicious habit, that is so sharp and afflicting.

Every impression of the lancet cuts, but it is the first only that smarts. Besides, it is an argument hugely unreasonable, to plead the pain of passing from a vicious estate, unless it were proved, that there was none in the continuance under it: but surely, when we read of the service, the bondage, and the captivity of sinners, we are not entertained only with the air of words and metaphors, and, instead of truth, put off with similitudes. Let him that says it is a trouble to refrain from a debauch, convince us, that it is not a greater to undergo one; and that the confessor did not impose a shrewd penance upon the drunken man, by bidding him go and be drunk again; and that lisping, raging, redness of eyes, and what is not fit to be named in such an audience, is not more toilsome, than to be clean, and quiet, and discreet, and respected for being so. All the trouble that is in it, is the trouble of being sound, being cured, and being recovered. But if there be great arguments for health, then certainly there are the same for the obtaining of it; and so keeping a due proportion between spirituals and temporals, we neither have, nor pretend to greater arguments for repentance.

Having thus now cleared off all, that by way of objection can lie against the truth asserted, by showing the proper qualification of the subject, to whom only the ways of wisdom can be ways of pleasantness; for the further prosecution of the matter in hand, I shall show what are those properties that so peculiarly set off and enhance the excellency of this pleasure.

I. The first is, That it is the proper pleasure of that part of man, which is the largest and most comprehensive of pleasure, and that is his mind: a substance of a boundless comprehension. The mind of man is an image, not only of God's spirituality, but of his infinity. It is not like any of the senses, limited to this or that kind of object: as the sight intermeddles not with that which affects the smell; but with an universal superintendence, it arbitrates upon and takes them in all. It is (as I may so say) an ocean, into which all the little rivulets of sensation, both external and internal, discharge themselves. It is framed by God to receive all, and more than nature can afford it; and so to be its own motive to seek for something above nature. Now this is that part of man to which the pleasures of religion properly belong: and that in a double respect.

1. In reference to speculation, as it sustains the name of understanding.

2. In reference to practice, as it sustains the name of conscience.

1. And first for speculation: the pleasures of which have been sometimes so great, so intense, so engrossing of all the powers of the soul, that there has been no room left for any other pleasure. It has so called together all the spirits to that one work, that there has been no supply to carry on the inferior operations of nature. Contemplation feels no hunger, nor is sensible of any thirst, but of that after knowledge. How frequent and exalted a pleasure did David find from his meditation in the divine law! *All the day long* it was the theme of his thoughts. The affairs of state, the government of his kingdom, might indeed employ, but it was this only that refreshed his mind.

How short of this are the delights of the epicure! How vastly disproportionate are the pleasures of the eating and of the thinking man! Indeed as different as the silence of an Archimedes in the study of a problem, and the stillness of a sow at her wash. Nothing is comparable to the pleasure of an active and a prevailing thought: a thought prevailing over the difficulty and obscurity of the object, and refreshing the soul with new discoveries and images of things; and thereby extending the bounds of apprehension, and (as it were) enlarging the territories of reason.

Now this pleasure of the speculation of divine things is advanced upon a double account:

(1.) The greatness.

(2.) The newness of the object.

(1.) And first for the greatness of it. It is no less than the great God himself, and that both in his nature and his works. For the eye of reason, like that of the eagle, directs itself chiefly to the sun, to a glory that neither admits of a superior nor an equal. Religion carries the soul to the study of every divine attribute.

It poses it with the amazing thoughts of omnipotence; of a power able to fetch up such a glorious fabric, as this of the world, out of the abyss of vanity and nothing, and able to throw it back into the same original nothing again. It drowns us in the speculation of the divine omniscience; that can maintain a steady infallible comprehension of all events in themselves contingent and accidental; and certainly know that, which does not certainly exist. It confounds the greatest subtilties of speculation, with the riddles of God's omnipresence; that can spread a single individual substance through all spaces; and yet without any commensuration of parts to any, or circumscription within any, though totally in every one. And then for his eternity; which nonpluses the strongest and clearest conception, to comprehend how one single act of duration should measure all periods and portions of time, without any of the distinguishing parts of succession. Likewise for his justice; which shall prey upon the sinner forever, satisfying itself by a perpetual miracle, rendering the creature immortal in the midst of the flames; always consuming, but never consumed. With the like wonders we may entertain our speculations from his mercy; his beloved, his triumphant attribute, an attribute, if it were possible, something more than infinite; for even his justice is so, and his mercy transcends that. Lastly, we may contemplate upon his supernatural, astonishing works: particularly in the resurrection, and reparation of the same numerical body, by a reunion of all the scattered parts, to be at length disposed of into an estate of eternal woe or bliss; as also the greatness and strangeness of the beatific vision; how a created eye should be so fortified, as to bear all those glories that stream from the fountain of uncreated light, the meanest expression of which light is, that it is unexpressible. Now what great and high objects are these for a rational contemplation to busy itself upon! Heights that scorn the reach of our prospect; and depths in which the tallest reason will never touch the bottom: yet surely the pleasure arising from thence is great and noble; forasmuch as they afford perpetual matter and employment to the inquisitiveness of human reason, and so are large enough for it to take its full scope and range in: which when it has sucked and drained the utmost of an object, naturally lays it aside, and neglects it as a dry and an empty thing.

(2.) As the things belonging to religion entertain our speculation with great objects, so they entertain it also with new: and novelty, we know, is the great parent of pleasure; upon which account it is that men are so much pleased with variety, and variety is nothing else but a continued novelty. The Athenians, who were the professed and most diligent improvers of their reason, made it their whole business *to hear or to tell some new thing:* for the truth is, newness especially in great matters, was a worthy entertainment for a searching mind; it was (as I may so say) an high taste, fit for the relish of an Athenian reason. And thereupon the mere unheard-of strangeness of Jesus and the resurrection, made them desirous to hear it discoursed of to them again, Acts xvii. 32. But how would it have employed their searching faculties, had the mystery of the Trinity, and the incarnation of the Son of God, and the whole economy of man's redemption been explained to them! For how could it ever enter into the thoughts of reason, that a satisfaction could be paid to an infinite justice? Or, that two natures so unconceivably different as the human and divine, could unite into one person? The knowledge of these things could derive from nothing else but pure revelation, and consequently must be purely new to the highest discourses of mere nature. Now that the newness of an object so exceedingly pleases and strikes the mind, appears from this one consideration; that every thing pleases more in expectation than fruition: and expectation supposes a thing as yet new, the hoped-for discovery of which is the pleasure that entertains the expecting and inquiring mind: whereas actual discovery (as it were) rifles and deflowers the newness and freshness of the object, and so for the most part makes it cheap, familiar, and contemptible.

It is clear therefore, that, if there be any pleasure to the mind from speculation, and if this pleasure of speculation be advanced by the greatness and newness of the things contemplated upon, all this is to be found in the ways of religion.

2. In the next place, religion is a pleasure to the mind, as it respects practice, and so sustains the name of conscience. And conscience undoubtedly is the great repository and magazine of all those pleasures that can afford any solid refresh-

ment to the soul. For when this is calm, and serene, and absolving, then properly a man enjoys all things, and what is more, himself; for that he must do, before he can enjoy any thing else. But it is only a pious life, led exactly by the rules of a severe religion, that can authorize a man's conscience to speak comfortably to him: it is this that must word the sentence, before the conscience can pronounce it, and then it will do it with majesty and authority: it will not whisper, but proclaim a jubilee to the mind; it will not drop, but pour in oil upon the wounded heart. And is there any pleasure comparable to that which springs from hence? The pleasure of conscience is not only greater than all other pleasures, but may also serve instead of them: for they only please and affect the mind *in transitu*, in the pitiful narrow compass of actual fruition; whereas that of conscience entertains and feeds it a long time after with durable, lasting reflections.

And thus much for the first ennobling property of the pleasure belonging to religion; namely, That it is the pleasure of the mind, and that both as it relates to speculation, and is called the understanding, and as it relates to practice, and is called the conscience.

II. The second ennobling property of it is, That it is such a pleasure as never satiates or wearies: for it properly affects the spirit, and a spirit feels no weariness, as being privileged from the causes of it. But can the epicure say so of any of the pleasures that he so much dotes upon? Do they not expire, while they satisfy? And after a few minutes' refreshment, determine in loathing and unquietness? How short is the interval between a pleasure and a burden! How undiscernible the transition from one to the other! Pleasure dwells no longer upon the appetite, than the necessities of nature, which are quickly and easily provided for; and then all that follows is a load and an oppression. Every morsel to a satisfied hunger, is only a new labor to a tired digestion. Every draught to him that has quenched his thirst, is but a further quenching of nature; a provision for rheum and diseases, a drowning of the quickness and activity of the spirits.

He that prolongs his meals, and sacrifices his time, as well as his other conveniences, to his luxury, how quickly does he out-sit his pleasure! And then, how is all the following time bestowed upon ceremony and surfeit! till at length, after a long fatigue of eating, and drinking, and babbling, he concludes the great work of dining genteelly, and so makes a shift to rise from table, that he may lie down upon his bed: where, after he has slept himself into some use of himself, by much ado he staggers to his table again, and there acts over the same brutish scene: so that he passes his whole life in a dozed condition between sleeping and waking, with a kind of drowsiness and confusion upon his senses; which, what pleasure it can be, is hard to conceive; all that is of it, dwells upon the tip of his tongue, and within the compass of his palate: a worthy prize for a man to purchase with the loss of his time, his reason, and himself.

Nor is that man less deceived, that thinks to maintain a constant tenure of pleasure, by a continual pursuit of sports and recreations: for it is most certainly true of all these things, that as they refresh a man when he is weary, so they weary him when he is refreshed; which is an evident demonstration that God never designed the use of them to be continual, by putting such an emptiness in them, as should so quickly fail and lurch expectation.

The most voluptuous and loose person breathing, were he but tied to follow his hawks and his hounds, his dice and his courtships every day, would find it the greatest torment and calamity that could befall him; he would fly to the mines and the galleys for his recreation, and to the spade and the mattock for a diversion from the misery of a continual unintermitted pleasure.

But on the contrary, the providence of God has so ordered the course of things, that there is no action, the usefulness of which has made it the matter of duty, and of a profession, but a man may bear the continual pursuit of it, without loathing or satiety. The same shop and trade that employs a man in his youth, employs him also in his age. Every morning he rises fresh to his hammer and his anvil; he passes the day singing: custom has naturalized his labor to him: his shop is his element, and he can not with any enjoyment of himself live out of it. Whereas no custom can make the painfulness of a debauch easy or pleasing to a man; since nothing can be pleasant that is unnatural. But now, if God has interwoven such a pleasure with the works of our ordinary calling; how much superior and more refined must that be, that arises from the survey of a pious and well-governed life! Surely, as much as Christianity is nobler than a trade.

And then, for the constant freshness of it; it is such a pleasure as can never cloy or overwork the mind: for surely no man was ever weary of thinking, much less of thinking that he had done well or virtuously, that he had conquered such and such a temptation, or offered violence to any of his exorbitant desires. This is a delight that grows and improves under thought and reflection: and while it exercises, does also endear itself to the mind; at the same time employing and inflaming the meditations. All pleasures that affect the body must needs weary, because they transport; and all transportation is a violence; and no violence can be lasting, but determines upon the falling of the spirits, which are not able to keep up that height of motion that the pleasure of the senses raises them to: and therefore how inevitably does an immoderate laughter end in a sigh! which is only nature's recovering itself after a force done to it. But the religious pleasure of a well-disposed mind moves gently, and therefore constantly: it does not affect by rapture and ecstasy; but is like the pleasure of health, which is still and sober, yet greater and stronger than those that call up the senses with grosser and more affecting impressions. God has given no man a body as strong as his appetites; but has corrected the boundlessness of his voluptuous desires, by stinting his strengths, and contracting his capacities.

But to look upon those pleasures also that have an higher object than the body; as those that spring from honor and grandeur of condition; yet we shall find, that even these are not so fresh and constant, but the mind can nauseate them, and quickly feel the thinness of a popular breath. Those that are so fond of applause while they pursue it, how little do they taste it when they have it! Like lightning, it only flashes upon the face, and is gone; and it is well if it does not hurt the man. But for greatness of place, though it is fit and necessary that some persons in the world should be in love with a splendid servitude; yet certainly they must be much beholding to their own fancy, that they can be pleased at it. For he that rises up early, and goes to bed late, only to receive addresses, to read and answer petitions, is really as much tied and abridged in his freedom, as he that waits all that time to present one. And what pleasure can it be to be incumbered with dependences, thronged and surrounded with petitioners? And those perhaps sometimes all suitors for the same thing: whereupon all but one will be sure to depart grumbling, because they miss of what they think their due: and even that one scarce thankful, because he thinks he has no more than his due. In a word, if it is a pleasure to be envied and shot at, to be maligned standing, and to be despised falling, to endeavor that which is impossible, which is to please all, and to suffer for not doing it; then is it a pleasure to be great, and to be able to dispose of men's fortunes and preferments.

But further, to proceed from hence to yet an higher degree of pleasure, indeed the highest on this side that of religion; which is the pleasure of friendship and conversation. Friendship must confessedly be allowed the top, the flower, and crown of all temporal enjoyments. Yet has not this also its flaws and its dark side? For is not my friend a man; and is not friendship subject to the same mortality and change that men are? And in case a man loves, and is not loved again, does he not think that he has cause to hate as heartily, and ten times more eagerly than ever he loved? And then to be an enemy, and once to have been a friend, does it not embitter the rupture, and aggravate the calamity? But admitting that my friend continues so to the end; yet in the mean time, is he all perfection, all virtue and discretion? Has he not humors to be endured, as well as kindnesses to be enjoyed? And am I sure to smell the rose, without sometimes feeling the thorn?

And then lastly for company; though it may reprieve a man from his melancholy, yet it cannot secure him from his conscience, nor from sometimes being alone. And what is all that a man enjoys, from a week's, a month's, or a year's converse, comparable to what he feels for one hour, when his conscience shall take him aside, and rate him by himself?

In short, run over the whole circle of all earthly pleasures, and I dare affirm, that had not God secured a man a solid pleasure from his own actions, after he had rolled from one to another, and enjoyed them all, he would be forced to complain, that either they were not indeed pleasures, or that pleasure was not satisfaction.

III. The third ennobling property of the pleasure that accrues to a man from religion, is, that it is such an one as is in nobody's power, but only in his that has it; so that he that has the property may be also sure of the perpetuity. And tell me so of any outward enjoyment that mortality is capable of. We are generally at the mercy of men's rapine, avarice, and violence, whether we shall be happy or no. For if I build my felicity upon my estate or reputation, I am happy as long as the tyrant or the railer will give me leave to be so. But when my concernment takes up no more room or compass than myself; then so long as I know where to breathe and to exist, I know also where to be happy: for I know I may be so in my own breast, in the court of my own conscience; where, if I can but prevail with myself to be innocent, I need bribe neither judge nor officer to be pronounced so. The pleasure of the religious man is an easy and a portable pleasure, such an one as he carries about in his bosom, without alarming either the eye or envy of the world. A man putting all his pleasures into this one, is like a traveler's putting all his goods into one jewel; the value is the same, and the convenience greater.

There is nothing that can raise a man to that generous absoluteness of condition, as neither to cringe, to fawn, or to depend meanly, but that which gives him that happiness within himself, for which men depend upon others. For surely I need salute no great man's threshold, sneak to none of his friends or servants, to speak a good word for me to my conscience. It is a noble and a sure defiance of a great malice, backed with a great interest; which yet can have no advantage of a man, but from his own expectations of something that is without himself. But if I can make my duty my delight; if I can feast, and please, and caress my mind with the pleasures of worthy speculations or virtuous practices; let greatness and malice vex and abridge me if they can: my pleasures are as free as my will; no more to be controlled than my choice, or the unlimited range of my thoughts and my desires.

Nor is this kind of pleasure only out of the reach of any outward violence, but even those things also that make a much closer impression upon us, which are the irresistible decays of nature, have yet no influence at all upon this. For when age itself, which of all things in the world will not be baffled or defied, shall begin to arrest, seize, and remind us of our mortality, by pains, aches, deadness of limbs, and dullness of senses; yet then the pleasure of the mind shall be in its full youth, vigor, and freshness. A palsy may as well shake an oak, or a fever dry up a fountain, as either of them shake, dry up, or impair the delight of conscience. For it lies within, it centres in the heart, it grows into the very substance of the soul, so that it accompanies a man to his grave; he never outlives it, and that for this cause only, because he can not outlive himself.

And thus I have endeavored to describe the excellency of that pleasure that is to be found in the ways of a religious wisdom, by those excellent properties that do attend it; which, whether they reach the description that has been given them, or no, every man may convince himself, by the best of demonstrations, which is his own trial.

Now from all this discourse, this I am sure is a most natural and direct consequence, that if the ways of religion are ways of pleasantness, then such as are not ways of pleasantness are not truly and properly ways of religion. Upon which ground, it is easy to see what judgment is to be passed upon all those affected, uncommanded, absurd austerities, so much prized and exercised by some of the Romish profession. Pilgrimages, going barefoot, hair shirts, and whips, with other such gospel artillery, are their only helps to devotion: things never enjoined, either by the prophets under the Jewish, or by the apostles under the Christian economy; who yet surely understood the proper and the most efficacious instruments of piety, as well as any confessor or friar of all the order of St. Francis, or any casuist whatsoever.

It seems, that with them a man sometimes can not be a penitent, unless he also turns vagabond, and foots it to Jerusalem; or wanders over this or that part of the world to visit the shrine of such or such a pretended saint; though perhaps, in his life, ten times more ridiculous than themselves: thus, that which was Cain's curse is become their religion. He that thinks to expiate a sin by going barefoot, does the penance of a goose, and only makes one folly the atonement of another. Paul indeed was scourged and beaten by the Jews, but we never read that he beat or scourged himself: and if they think that his *keeping under of his body* imports so much, they must first prove that the body can not be kept under by a virtuous mind, and that the mind can not be made virtuous but by a scourge; and consequently, that thongs and whipcord are means of grace, and things necessary to salvation. The truth is, if men's religion lies no deeper than their skin, it is possible that they may scourge themselves into very great improvements.

But they will find that *bodily exercise* touches not the soul; and that neither pride, nor lust, nor covetousness, nor any other vice, was ever mortified by corporal disciplines: it is not the back, but the heart that must bleed for sin: and consequently, that in this whole course they are like men out of their way; let them lash on never so fast, they are not at all the nearer to their journey's end: and howsoever they deceive themselves and others, they may as well expect to bring a cart as a soul to heaven by such means. What arguments they have to beguile poor, simple, unstable souls with, I know not; but surely the practical, casuistical, that is, the principal, vital part of their religion savors very little of spirituality.

And now upon the result of all, I suppose, that to exhort men to be religious is only in other words to exhort them to take their pleasure. A pleasure, high, rational, and angelical; a pleasure embased with no appendant sting, no consequent loathing, no remorses or bitter farewells: but such an one, as being honey in the mouth, never turns to gall or gravel in the belly. A pleasure made for the soul, and the soul for that; suitable to its spirituality, and equal to all its capacities. Such an one as grows fresher upon enjoyment, and though continually fed upon, yet is never devoured. A pleasure that a man may call as properly his own, as his soul and his conscience; neither liable to accident, nor exposed to injury. It is the foretaste of heaven, and the earnest of eternity. In a word, it is such an one, as being begun in grace, passes into glory, blessedness, and immortality, and those pleasures *that neither eye has seen, nor ear heard, nor has it entered into the heart of man to conceive.*

To which God of his mercy vouchsafe to bring us all: to whom be rendered and ascribed, as is most due, all praise, might, majesty, and dominion, both now and for evermore. Amen.

SERMON II.

PREACHED AT THE CATHEDRAL CHURCH OF ST. PAUL'S, NOVEMBER THE 9TH, 1662.

TO THE RIGHT HONORABLE THE LORD MAYOR AND ALDERMEN OF THE CITY OF LONDON.

RIGHT HONORABLE,

WHEN I consider how impossible it is for a person of my condition to produce, and consequently how imprudent to attempt, any thing in proportion either to the ampleness of the body you represent, or of the places you bear, I should be kept from venturing so poor a piece, designed to live but an hour, in so lasting a publication; did not what your civility calls a request, your greatness render a command. The truth is, in things not unlawful, great persons can not be properly said to request; because, all things considered, they must not be denied. To me it was honor enough to have your audience, enjoyment enough to behold your happy change, and to see the same city, the metropolis of loyalty and of the kingdom, to behold the glory of English churches reformed, that is, delivered from the reformers; and to find at least the service of the church repaired, though not the building; to see St. Paul's delivered from beasts here, as well as St. Paul at Ephesus; and to view the church thronged only with troops of auditors, not of horse. This I could fully have acquiesced in, and received a large personal reward in my particular share of the public joy; but since you are further pleased, I will not say by your judgment to approve, but by your acceptance to encourage the raw endeavors of a young divine, I shall take it for an opportunity, not as others in their sage prudence use to do, to quote three or four texts of scripture, and to tell you how you are to rule the city out of a concordance; no, I bring not instructions, but what much better befits both you and myself, your commendations. For I look upon your city as the great and magnificent stage of business, and by consequence the best place of improvement; for from the school we go to the university, but from the universities to

London. And therefore as in your city meetings you must be esteemed the most considerable body of the nation; so, met in the church, I look upon you as an auditory fit to be waited on, as you are, by both universities. And when I remember how instrumental you have beën to recover this universal settlement, and to retrieve the old spirit of loyalty to kings, (as an ancient testimony of which you bear not the sword in vain;) I seem in a manner deputed from Oxford, not so much a preacher to supply a course, as orator to present her thanks. As for the ensuing discourse, which (lest I chance to be traduced for a plagiary by him who has played the thief) I think fit to tell the world by the way, was one of those that by a worthy hand were stolen from me in the king's chapel, and are still detained; and to which now accidentally published by your honor's order, your patronage must give both value and protection. You will find me in it not to have pitched upon any subject, that men's guilt, and the consequent of guilt, their concernment might render liable to exception; nor to have rubbed up the memory of what some heretofore in the city did, which more and better now detest, and therefore expiate: but my subject is inoffensive, harmless, and innocent as the state of innocence itself, and (I hope) suitable to the present design and genius of this nation; which is, or should be, to return to that innocence, which it lost long since the fall. Briefly, my business is, by describing what man was in his first estate, to upbraid him with what he is in his present: between whom, innocent and fallen, (that in a word I may suit the subject to the place of my discourse,) there is as great an unlikeness, as between St. Paul's a cathedral, and St. Paul's a stable. But I must not forestall myself, nor transcribe the work into the dedication. I shall now only desire you to accept the issue of your own requests; the gratification of which I have here consulted so much before my own reputation; while like the poor widow I endeavor to show my officiousness by an offering, though I betray my poverty by the measure; not so much caring, though I appear neither preacher nor scholar, (which terms we have been taught upon good reason to distinguish,) so I may in this but show myself

Your honors'
very humble servant,
ROBERT SOUTH.

WORCESTER-HOUSE.
Nov. 24, 1662.

Genesis i. 27. — *So God created man in his own image, in the image of God created he him.*

HOW hard it is for natural reason to discover a creation before revealed, or being revealed to believe it, the strange opinions of the old philosophers, and the infidelity of modern atheists, is too sad a demonstration. To run the world back to its first original and infancy, and (as it were) to view nature in its cradle, to trace the outgoings of the Ancient of days in the first instance and specimen of his creative power, is a research too great for any mortal inquiry: and we might continue our scrutiny to the end of the world, before natural reason would be able to find out when it begun.

Epicurus's discourse concerning the original of the world is so fabulous and ridiculously merry, that we may well judge the design of his philosophy to have been pleasure, and not instruction.

Aristotle held, that it streamed by connatural result and emanation from God, the infinite and eternal mind, as the light issues from the sun; so that there was no instant of duration assignable of God's eternal existence, in which the world did not also coexist.

Others held a fortuitous concourse of atoms; but all seem jointly to explode a creation; still beating upon this ground, that to produce something out of nothing is impossible and incomprehensible: incomprehensible indeed I grant, but not therefore impossible. There is not the least transaction of sense and motion in the whole man, but philosophers are at a loss to comprehend, I am sure they are to explain it. Wherefore it is not always rational to measure the truth of an assertion by the standard of our apprehension.

But to bring things even to the bare perceptions of reason, I appeal to any one, who shall impartially reflect upon the ideas and conceptions of his own mind, whether he doth not find it as easy and suitable to his natural notions, to conceive that an infinite almighty power might produce a thing out of nothing, and make that to exist *de novo*, which did not exist before; as to conceive the world to have had no beginning, but to have existed from eternity: which, were it so proper for this place and exercise, I could easily demonstrate to be attended with no small train of absurdities. But then, besides that the acknowledging of a creation is safe, and the denial of it dangerous and irreligious, and yet not more (perhaps much less) demonstrable than the affirmative; so, over and above, it gives me this advantage, that, let it seem never so strange, uncouth, and impossible, the nonplus of my reason will yield a fairer opportunity to my faith.

In this chapter, we have God surveying the works of the creation, and leaving this general impress or character upon them, *that they were exceeding good.* What an omnipotence wrought, we have an omniscience to approve. But as it is reasonable to imagine that there is more of design, and consequently more of perfection, in the last work, we have God here giving his last stroke, and summing up all into man, the whole into a part, the universe into an individual: so that, whereas in other creatures we have but the trace of his footsteps, in man we have the draught of his hand. In him were united all the scattered perfections of the creature; all the graces and ornaments, all the airs and features of being, were abridged into this small, yet full system of nature and divinity: as we might well imagine that the great artificer would be more than ordinarily exact in drawing his own picture.

The work that I shall undertake from these words, shall be to show what this image of God in man is, and wherein it doth consist. Which I shall do these two ways: 1. Negatively, by showing wherein it doth not consist. 2. Positively, by showing wherein it does.

For the first of these, we are to remove the erroneous opinion of the Socinians. They deny that the image of God consisted in any habitual perfections that adorned the soul of Adam: but as to his understanding bring him in void of all notion, a rude unwritten blank; making him to be created as much an infant as others are born; sent into the world only to read and spell out a God in the works of creation, to learn by degrees, till at length his understanding grew up to the stature of his body. Also without any inherent habits of virtue in his will; thus divesting him of all, and stripping him to his bare essence; so that all the perfection they allowed his understanding was aptness and docility; and all that they attributed to his will was a possibility to be virtuous.

But wherein then, according to their opinion, did this image of God consist? Why, in that power and dominion that God gave Adam over the creatures: in that he was vouched his immediate deputy upon earth, the viceroy of the creation, and lord-lieutenant of the world. But that this power and dominion is not adequately and formally the image of God, but only a part of it, is clear from hence; because then he that had most of this, would have most of God's image: and consequently Nimrod had more of it than Noah, Saul than Samuel, the persecutors than the martyrs, and Cæsar than Christ himself, which to assert is a blasphemous paradox. And if the image of God is only grandeur, power, and sovereignty, certainly we have been hitherto much mistaken in our duty: and hereafter are by all means to beware of making ourselves unlike God, by too much self-denial and humility. I am not ignorant that some may distinguish between ἐξουσία and δύναμις, between a lawful authority and an actual power: and affirm, that God's image consists only in the former; which wicked princes, such as Saul and Nimrod, have not, though they possess the latter. But to this I answer,

1. That the scripture neither makes nor owns such a distinction: nor anywhere asserts, that when princes begin to be wicked, they cease of right to be governors. And to this, that when God renewed this charter of man's sovereignty over the creatures to Noah and his family, we find no exception at all, but that Cham stood as fully invested with this right as any of his brethren.

2. But secondly; this savors of something ranker than Socinianism, even the tenents of the fifth monarchy, and of sovereignty founded only upon saintship; and therefore fitter to be answered by the judge, than by the divine; and to receive its confutation at the bar of justice, than from the pulpit.

Having now made our way through this false opinion, we are in the next place to lay down positively what this image of God in man is. It is, in short, that universal rectitude of all the faculties of the soul, by which they stand apt and disposed to their respective offices and operations: which will be more fully set forth, by taking a distinct survey of it, in the several faculties belonging to the soul.

I. In the understanding.

II. In the will.

III. In the passions or affections.

I. And first for its noblest faculty, the understanding: it was then sublime, clear, and aspiring, and, as it were, the soul's upper region, lofty and serene, free from the vapors and disturbances of the inferior affections. It was the leading, controlling faculty; all the passions wore the colors of reason; it did not so much persuade, as command; it was not consul, but dictator. Discourse was then almost as quick as intuition; it was nimble in proposing, firm in concluding; it could sooner determine than now it can dispute. Like the sun, it had both light and agility; it knew no rest, but in motion; no quiet, but in activity. It did not so properly apprehend, as irradiate the object; not so much find, as make things intelligible. It did arbitrate upon the several reports of sense, and all the varieties of imagination; not like a drowsy judge, only hearing, but also directing their verdict. In sum, it was vegete, quick, and lively; open as the day, untainted as the morning, full of the innocence and sprightliness of youth; it gave the soul a bright and a full view into all things; and was not only a window, but itself the prospect. Briefly, there is as much difference between the clear representations of the understanding then, and the obscure discoveries that it makes now, as there is between the prospect of a casement and of a key-hole.

Now as there are two great functions of the soul, contemplation and practice, according to that general division of objects, some of which only entertain our speculation, others also employ our actions; so the understanding with relation to these, not because of any distinction in the faculty itself, is accordingly divided into speculative and practic; in both of which the image of God was then apparent.

1. For the understanding speculative. There are some general maxims and notions in the mind of man, which are

the rules of discourse, and the basis of all philosophy. As, that the same thing cannot at the same time be, and not be; that the whole is bigger than a part; that two proportions equal to a third, must also be equal to one another. Aristotle, indeed, affirms the mind to be at first a mere *rasa tabula;* and that these notions are not ingénite, and imprinted by the finger of nature, but by the latter and more languid impressions of sense; being only the reports of observation, and the result of so many repeated experiments.

But to this I answer two things:

(1.) That these notions are universal; and what is universal must needs proceed from some universal, constant principle, the same in all particulars, which here can be nothing else but human nature.

(2.) These can not be infused by observation, because they are the rules by which men take their first apprehensions and observations of things, and therefore in order of nature must needs precede them: as the being of the rule must be before its application to the thing directed by it. From whence it follows, that these were notions, not descending from us, but born with us; not our offspring, but our brethren: and (as I may so say) such as we were taught without the help of a teacher.

Now it was Adam's happiness in the state of innocence to have these clear and unsullied. He came into the world a philosopher, which sufficiently appeared by his writing the nature of things upon their names; he could view essences in themselves, and read forms without the comment of their respective properties: he could see consequents yet dormant in their principles, and effects yet unborn, and in the womb of their causes: his understanding could almost pierce into future contingents, his conjectures improving even to prophecy, or the certainties of prediction; till his fall, it was ignorant of nothing but of sin; or at least it rested in the notion, without the smart of the experiment. Could any difficulty have been proposed, the resolution would have been as early as the proposal; it could not have had time to settle into doubt. Like a better Archimedes, the issue of all his inquiries was an εὕρηκα, an εὕρηκα, the offspring of his brain without the sweat of his brow. Study was not then a duty, night-watchings were needless; the light of reason wanted not the assistance of a candle. This is the doom of fallen man, to labor in the fire, to seek truth *in profundo*, to exhaust his time and impair his health, and perhaps to spin out his days, and himself, into one pitiful, controverted conclusion. There was then no poring, no struggling with memory, no straining for invention: his faculties were quick and expedite; they answered without knocking, they were ready upon the first summons, there was freedom and firmness in all their operations. I confess, it is difficult for us, who date our ignorance from our first being, and were still bred up with the same infirmities about us with which we were born, to raise our thoughts and imagination to those intellectual perfections that attended our nature in the time of innocence; as it is for a peasant bred up in the obscurities of a cottage, to fancy in his mind the unseen splendors of a court. But by rating positives by their privatives, and other arts of reason, by which discourse supplies the want of the reports of sense, we may collect the excellency of the understanding then, by the glorious remainders of it now, and guess at the stateliness of the building, by the magnificence of its ruins. All those arts, rarities, and inventions, which vulgar minds gaze at, the ingenious pursue, and all admire, are but the relics of an intellect defaced with sin and time. We admire it now, only as antiquaries do a piece of old coin, for the stamp it once bore, and not for those vanishing lineaments and disappearing draughts that remain upon it at present. And certainly that must needs have been very glorious, the decays of which are so admirable. He that is comely, when old and decrepit, surely was very beautiful when he was young. An Aristotle was but the rubbish of an Adam, and Athens but the rudiments of Paradise.

2. The image of God was no less resplendent in that which we call man's practical understanding; namely, that storehouse of the soul, in which are treasured up the rules of action and the seeds of morality. Where, we must observe, that many who deny all connate notions in the speculative intellect, do yet admit them in this. Now of this sort are these maxims; that God is to be worshiped; that parents are to be honored; that a man's word is to be kept, and the

like: which, being of universal influence, as to the regulation of the behavior and converse of mankind, are the ground of all virtue and civility, and the foundation of religion.

It was the privilege of Adam innocent, to have these notions also firm and untainted, to carry his monitor in his bosom, his law in his heart, and to have such a conscience as might be its own casuist: and certainly those actions must needs be regular, where there is an identity between the rule and the faculty. His own mind taught him a due dependence upon God, and chalked out to him the just proportions and measures of behavior to his fellow-creatures. He had no catechism but the creation, needed no study but reflection, read no book, but the volume of the world, and that too, not for rules to work by, but for objects to work upon. Reason was his tutor, and first principles his *magna moralia.* The decalogue of Moses was but a transcript, not an original. All the laws of nations, and wise decrees of states, the statutes of Solon, and the twelve tables, were but a paraphrase upon this standing rectitude of nature, this fruitful principle of justice, that was ready to run out, and enlarge itself into suitable determinations, upon all emergent objects and occasions. Justice then was neither blind to discern, nor lame to execute. It was not subject to be imposed upon by a deluded fancy, nor yet to be bribed by a glozing appetite, for an *utile* or *jucundum* to turn the balance to a false and dishonest sentence. In all its directions of the inferior faculties, it conveyed its suggestions with clearness, and enjoined them with power; it had the passions in perfect subjection; and though its command over them was but suasive and political, yet it had the force of coaction, and despotical. It was not then, as it is now, where the conscience has only power to disapprove, and to protest against the exorbitances of the passions; and rather to wish, than make them otherwise. The voice of conscience now is low and weak, chastising the passions, as old Eli did his lustful, domineering sons; *Not so, my sons, not so;* but the voice of conscience then was not, This should, or This ought to be done; but, This *must,* This *shall be* done. It spoke like a legislator; the thing spoke was a law; and the manner of speaking it a new obligation. In short, there was as great a disparity between the practical dictates of the understanding then and now, as there is between empire and advice, counsel and command, between a companion and a governor.

And thus much for the image of God, as it shone in man's understanding.

II. Let us in the next place take a view of it, as it was stamped upon the will. It is much disputed by divines concerning the power of man's will to good and evil in the state of innocence; and upon very nice and dangerous precipices stand their determinations on either side. Some hold, that God invested him with a power to stand, so that in the strength of that power received, he might, without the auxiliaries of any further influence, have determined his will to a full choice of good. Others hold, that notwithstanding this power, yet it was impossible for him to exert it in any good action, without a superadded assistance of grace, actually determining that power to the certain production of such an act. So that, whereas some distinguish between sufficient and effectual grace; they order the matter so as to acknowledge none sufficient, but what is indeed effectual, and actually productive of a good action. I shall not presume to interpose dogmatically in a controversy, which I look never to see decided. But concerning the latter of these opinions, I shall only give these two remarks :

1. That it seems contrary to the common and natural conceptions of all mankind, who acknowledge themselves able and sufficient to do many things, which actually they never do.

2. That to assert, that God looked upon Adam's fall as a sin, and punished it as such, when, without any antecedent sin of his, he withdrew that actual grace from him, upon the withdrawing of which, it was impossible for him not to fall, seems a thing that highly reproaches the essential equity and goodness of the divine nature.

Wherefore, doubtless the will of man in the state of innocence had an entire freedom, a perfect equipendency and indifference to either part of the contradiction, to stand, or not to stand; to accept, or not accept the temptation. I will grant the will of man now to be as much a slave as any one will have it, and be only free to sin; that is, instead of a liberty, to have only a licentiousness; yet certainly this is not nature, but chance. We were not born crooked; we learnt these windings and turnings of the serpent: and therefore it can not but be a blasphemous piece of ingratitude to ascribe them to God, and to make the plague of our nature the condition of our creation.

The will was then ductile, and pliant to all the motions of right reason; it met the dictates of a clarified understanding half way. And the active informations of the intellect, filling the passive reception of the will, like form closing with matter, grew actuate into a third, and distinct perfection of practice: the understanding and will never disagreed; for the proposals of the one never thwarted the inclinations of the other. Yet neither did the will servilely attend upon the understanding, but as a favorite does upon his prince, where the service is privilege and preferment; or as Solomon's servants waited upon him, it admired its wisdom, and heard its prudent dictates and counsels, both the direction and the reward of its obedience. It is indeed the nature of this faculty to follow a superior guide, to be drawn by the intellect; but then it was drawn as a triumphant chariot, which at the same time both follows and triumphs; while it obeyed this, it commanded the other faculties. It was subordinate, not enslaved to the understanding: not as a servant to a master, but as a queen to her king, who both acknowledges a subjection, and yet retains a majesty.

Pass we now downward from man's intellect and will,

III. To the passions, which have their residence and situation chiefly in the sensitive appetite. For we must know, that inasmuch as man is a compound, and mixture of flesh as well as spirit, the soul, during its abode in the body, does all things by the mediation of these passions and inferior affections. And here the opinion of the Stoics was famous and singular, who looked upon all these as sinful defects and irregularities, as so many deviations from right reason, making passion to be only another word for perturbation. Sorrow, in their esteem, was a sin, scarce to be expiated by another; to pity, was a fault; to rejoice, an extravagance; and the Apostle's advice, to be angry and sin not, was a contradiction in their philosophy. But in this, they were constantly outvoted by other sects of philosophers, neither for fame nor number less than themselves: so that all arguments brought against them from divinity would come in by way of overplus to their confutation. To us let this be sufficient, that our Saviour Christ, who took upon him all our natural infirmities, but none of our sinful, has been seen to weep, to be sorrowful, to pity, and to be angry: which shows that there might be gall in a dove, passion without sin, fire without smoke, and motion without disturbance. For it is not bare agitation, but the sediment at the bottom, that troubles and defiles the water: and when we see it windy and dusty, the wind does not (as we use to say) make, but only raise a dust.

Now, though the schools reduce all the passions to these two heads, the concupiscible, and the irascible appetite; yet I shall not tie myself to an exact prosecution of them under this division; but at this time, leaving both their terms and their method to themselves, consider only the principal and most noted passions, from whence we may take an estimate of the rest.

And first, for the grand leading affection of all, which is love. This is the great instrument and engine of nature, the bond and cement of society, the spring and spirit of the universe. Love is such an affection, as can not so properly be said to be in the soul, as the soul to be in that. It is the whole man wrapt up into one desire; all the powers, vigor, and faculties of the soul abridged into one inclination. And it is of that active, restless nature, that it must of necessity exert itself; and like the fire, to which it is so often compared, it is not a free agent, to choose whether it will heat or no, but it streams forth by natural results and unavoidable emanations. So that it will fasten upon any inferior, unsuitable object, rather than none at all. The soul may sooner leave off to subsist, than to love; and, like the vine, it withers and dies, if it has nothing to embrace. Now this affection in the state of innocence was happily pitched upon its right object; it flamed up in direct fervors of devotion to God, and in collateral emissions of charity to its neighbor. It was not then only another and more cleanly name for lust. It had none of those impure heats, that both represent and deserve hell. It was a vestal, and a virgin fire, and differed as much from that which usually passes by this name nowadays, as the vital heat from the burning of a fever.

Then, for the contrary passion of hatred. This, we know, is the passion of defiance, and there is a kind of aversation and hostility included in its very essence and being. But then, (if there could have been hatred in the world, when there was scarce any thing odious,) it would have acted within the compass of its proper object. Like aloes, bitter indeed, but wholesome. There would have been no rancor, no hatred of our brother: an innocent nature could hate nothing that was innocent. In a word, so great is the commutation, that the soul then hated only that which now only it loves, that is, sin.

And if we may bring anger under this head, as being, according to some, a transient hatred, or at least very like it: this also, as unruly as now it is, yet then it vented itself by the measures of reason. There was no such thing as the transports of malice, or the violences of revenge: no rendering evil for evil, when evil was truly a nonentity, and nowhere to be found. Anger then was like the sword of justice, keen, but innocent and righteous: it did not act like fury, and then call itself zeal. It always espoused God's honor, and never kindled upon any thing but in order to a sacrifice. It sparkled like the coal upon the altar, with the fervors of piety, the heats of devotion, the sallies and vibrations of an harmless activity. In the next place, for the lightsome passion of joy. It was not that, which now often usurps this name; that trivial, vanishing, superficial thing, that only gilds the apprehension, and plays upon the surface of the soul. It was not the mere crackling of thorns, a sudden blaze of the spirits, the exultation of a tickled fancy or a pleased appetite. Joy was then a masculine and a severe thing; the recreation of the judgment, the jubilee of reason. It was the result of a real good, suitably applied. It commenced upon the solidities of truth and the substance of fruition. It did not run out in voice, or undecent eruptions, but filled the soul, as God does the universe, silently and without noise. It was refreshing, but composed; like the pleasantness of youth tempered with the gravity of age; or the mirth of a festival managed with the silence of contemplation.

And, on the other side, for sorrow. Had any loss or disaster made but room for grief, it would have moved according to the severe allowances of prudence, and the proportions of the provocation. It would not have sallied out into complaint or loudness, nor spread itself upon the face, and writ sad stories upon the forehead. No wringing of the hands, knocking the breast, or wishing one's self unborn; all which are but the ceremonies of sorrow, the pomp and ostentation of an effeminate grief: which speak, not so much the greatness of the misery, as the smallness of the mind. Tears may spoil the eyes, but not wash away the affliction. Sighs may exhaust the man, but not eject the burden. Sorrow then would have been as silent as thoughts, as severe as philosophy. It would have rested in inward senses, tacit dislikes; and the whole scene of it been transacted in sad and silent reflections.

Then again for hope. Though indeed the fullness and affluence of man's enjoyments in the state of innocence, might seem to leave no place for hope, in respect of any further addition, but only of the prorogation, and future continuance of what already he possessed: yet doubtless, God, who made no faculty, but also provided it with a proper object, upon which it might exercise and lay out itself, even in its greatest innocence, did then exercise man's hopes with the expectations of a better paradise, or a more intimate admission to himself. For it is not imaginable, that Adam could fix upon such poor, thin enjoyments, as riches, pleasure, and the gayeties of an animal life. Hope indeed was always the anchor of the soul, yet certainly it was not to catch or fasten upon such mud. And if, as the Apostle says, *no man hopes for that which he sees*, much less could Adam then hope for such things as he saw through.

And lastly, for the affection of fear. It was then the instrument of caution, not of anxiety; a guard, and not a torment to the breast that had it. It is now indeed an unhappiness, the disease of the soul: it flies from a shadow, and makes more dangers than it avoids: it weakens the judgment, and betrays the succors of reason: so hard is it to tremble and not to err, and to hit the mark with a shaking hand. Then it fixed upon him who is only to be feared, God: and yet with a filial fear, which at the same time both fears and loves. It was awe without amazement, dread without distraction. There was then a beauty even in this very paleness. It was the color of devotion, giving a lustre to reverence, and a gloss to humility.

Thus did the passions then act without any of their present jars, combats, or repugnances; all moving with the beauty of uniformity, and the stillness of composure. Like a well-governed army, not for fighting, but for rank and order. I confess the scripture does not expressly attribute these several endowments to Adam in his first estate. But all that I have said, and much more, may be drawn out of that short aphorism, *God made man upright,* Eccl. vii. 29. And since the opposite weaknesses now infest the nature of man fallen, if we will be true to the rule of contraries, we must conclude, that those perfections were the lot of man innocent.

Now from this so exact and regular composure of the faculties, all moving in their due place, each striking in its proper time, there arose, by natural consequence, the crowning perfection of all, a good conscience. For, as in the body, when the principal parts, as the heart and liver, do their offices, and all the inferior, smaller vessels act orderly and duly, there arises a sweet enjoyment upon the whole, which we call health: so in the soul, when the supreme faculties of the will and understanding move regularly, the inferior passions and affections following, there arises a serenity and complacency upon the whole soul, infinitely beyond the greatest bodily pleasures, the highest quintessence and elixir of worldly delights. There is in this case a kind of fragrancy, and spiritual perfume upon the conscience; much like what Isaac spoke of his son's garments; *that the scent of them was like the smell of a field which the Lord had blessed.* Such a freshness and flavor is there upon the soul, when daily watered with the actions of a virtuous life. Whatsoever is pure is also pleasant.

Having thus surveyed the image of God in the soul of

man, we are not to omit now those characters of majesty that God imprinted upon the body. He drew some traces of his image upon this also; as much as a spiritual substance could be pictured upon a corporeal. As for the sect of the Anthropomorphites, who from hence ascribe to God the figure of a man, eyes, hands, feet, and the like, they are too ridiculous to deserve a confutation. They would seem to draw this impiety from the letter of the scripture sometimes speaking of God in this manner. Absurdly; as if the mercy of scripture expressions ought to warrant the blasphemy of our opinions. And not rather show us, that God condescends to us, only to draw us to himself; and clothes himself in our likeness, only to win us to his own. The practice of the papists is much of the same nature, in their absurd and impious picturing of God Almighty: but the wonder in them is the less, since the image of a deity may be a proper object for that, which is but the image of a religion. But to the purpose: Adam was then no less glorious in his externals; he had a beautiful body, as well as an immortal soul. The whole compound was like a well-built temple, stately without, and sacred within. The elements were at perfect union and agreement in his body; and their contrary qualities served not for the dissolution of the compound, but the variety of the composure. Galen, who had no more divinity than what his physic taught him, barely upon the consideration of this so exact frame of the body, challenges any one upon an hundred years study, to find how any the least fibre, or most minute particle, might be more commodiously placed, either for the advantage of use or comeliness; his stature erect, and tending upwards to his centre; his countenance majestic and comely, with the lustre of a native beauty, that scorned the poor assistance of art, or the attempts of imitation; his body of so much quickness and agility, that it did not only contain, but also represent the soul: for we might well suppose, that where God did deposit so rich a jewel, he would suitably adorn the case. It was a fit workhouse for sprightly vivid faculties to exercise and exert themselves in. A fit tabernacle for an immortal soul, not only to dwell in, but to contemplate upon: where it might see the world without travel; it being a lesser scheme of the creation, nature contracted, a little cosmography, or map of the universe. Neither was the body then subject to distempers, to die by piecemeal, and languish under coughs, catarrhs, or consumptions. Adam knew no disease, so long as temperance from the forbidden fruit secured him. Nature was his physician; and innocence and abstinence would have kept him healthful to immortality.

Now the use of this point might be various, but at present it shall be only this; to remind us of the irreparable loss that we sustained in our first parents, to show us of how fair a portion Adam disinherited his whole posterity by one single prevarication. Take the picture of a man in the greenness and vivacity of his youth, and in the latter date and declensions of his drooping years, and you will scarce know it to belong to the same person: there would be more art to discern, than at first to draw it. The same and greater is the difference between man innocent and fallen. He is, as it were, a new kind or species; the plague of sin has even altered his nature, and eaten into his very essentials. The image of God is wiped out, the creatures have shook off his yoke, renounced his sovereignty, and revolted from his dominion. Distempers and diseases have shattered the excellent frame of his body; and, by a new dispensation, *immortality is swallowed up of mortality.* The same disaster and decay also has invaded his spirituals: the passions rebel, every faculty would usurp and rule; and there are so many governors, that there can be no government. The light within us is become darkness; and the understanding, that should be eyes to the blind faculty of the will, is blind itself, and so brings all the inconveniences that attend a blind follower under the conduct of a blind guide. He that would have a clear, ocular demonstration of this, let him reflect upon that numerous litter of strange, senseless, absurd opinions, that crawl about the world, to the disgrace of reason, and the unanswerable reproach of a broken intellect.

The two great perfections, that both adorn and exercise man's understanding, are philosophy and religion: for the first of these; take it even amongst the professors of it, where it most flourished, and we shall find the very first notions of common sense debauched by them. For there have been such as have asserted, that there is no such thing in the world as motion; that contradictions may be true. There has not been wanting one, that has denied snow to be white. Such a stupidity or wantonness had seized upon the most raised wits, that it might be doubted, whether the philosophers or the owls of Athens were the quicker sighted. But then for religion; what prodigious, monstrous, misshapen births has the reason of fallen man produced! It is now almost six thousand years, that far the greatest part of the world has had no other religion but idolatry: and idolatry certainly is the first-born of folly, the great and leading paradox; nay, the very abridgment and sum total of all absurdities. For is it not strange, that a rational man should worship an ox, nay, the image of an ox? that he should fawn upon his dog? bow himself before a cat? adore leeks and garlic, and shed penitential tears at the smell of a deified onion? Yet so did the Egyptians, once the famed masters of all arts and learning. And to go a little further; we have yet a stranger instance in Isa. xliv. 14, *A man hews him down a tree in the wood, and part of it he burns,* in ver. 16. and in ver. 17, *with the residue thereof he maketh a god.* With one part he furnishes his chimney, with the other his chapel. A strange thing, that the fire must consume this part, and then burn incense to that. As if there was more divinity in one end of the stick than in the other; or as if it could be graved and painted omnipotent, or the nails and the hammer could give it an apotheosis. Briefly, so great is the change, so deplorable the degradation of our nature, that, whereas before we bore the image of God, we now retain only the image of men.

In the last place, we learn from hence the excellency of Christian religion, in that it is the great and only means that God has sanctified and designed to repair the breaches of humanity, to set fallen man upon his legs again, to clarify his reason, to rectify his will, and to compose and regulate his affections. The whole business of our redemption is, in short, only to rub over the defaced copy of the creation, to reprint God's image upon the soul, and (as it were) to set forth nature in a second and a fairer edition.

The recovery of which lost image, as it is God's pleasure to command, and our duty to endeavor, so it is in his power only to effect.

To whom be rendered and ascribed, as is most due, all praise, might, majesty, and dominion, both now and for evermore. Amen.

SERMON III.

INTEREST DEPOSED, AND TRUTH RESTORED: OR A WORD IN SEASON,

DELIVERED IN TWO SERMONS:

THE FIRST AT ST. MARY'S IN OXFORD, ON THE 24TH OF JULY, 1659, BEING THE TIME OF THE ASSIZES: AS ALSO OF THE FEARS AND GROANS OF THE NATION, IN THE THREATENED AND EXPECTED RUIN OF THE LAWS, MINISTRY, AND UNIVERSITIES. THE OTHER PREACHED BEFORE THE HONORABLE SOCIETY OF LINCOLN'S INN.

TO THE RIGHT WORSHIPFUL EDWARD ATKINS, SERGEANT-AT-LAW, AND FORMERLY ONE OF THE JUSTICES OF THE COMMON PLEAS.

HONORED SIR,

THOUGH at first it was free, and in my choice, whether I should publish these discourses, yet the publication being once resolved, the dedication was not so indifferent; the nature of the subject, no less than the obligations of the author, styling them in a peculiar manner yours: for since their drift is to carry the most endangered and endangering truth, above the safest, when sinful, interest; as a practice upon grounds of reason the most generous, and of Christianity the most religious; to whom rather should this assertion repair as to a patron, than to him whom it has for an instance? Who, in a case of eminent competition, chose duty before interest; and when the judge grew inconsistent with the justice, preferred rather to be constant to sure principles, than to an unconstant government: and to retreat to an innocent and honorable privacy, than to sit and act iniquity by a law; and make your age and conscience (the one venerable, the other sacred) drudges to the tyranny of fanatic, purjured usurpers. The next attempt of this discourse is a defense of the ministry, and that, at such a time, when none owned them upon the bench, (for then you had quitted it;) but when, on the contrary, we lived to hear one in the very face of the university, (as it were in defiance of us and our profession,) openly in his charge to defend the Quakers and fanatics, persons not fit to be named in such courts, but in an indictment. But, sir, in the instructions I here presumed to give to others, concerning what they should do, you may take a narrative of what you have done: what respected their actions as a rule or admonition, applied to yours is only a rehearsal, whose zeal in asserting the ministerial cause is so generally known, so gratefully acknowledged, that I dare affirm, that in what I deliver, you read the words indeed of one, but the thanks of all. Which affectionate concernment of yours for them, seems to argue a spiritual sense, and experimental taste of their works, and that you have reaped as much from their labors, as others have done from their lands: for to me it seemed always strange, and next to impossible, that a man, converted by the word preached, should ever hate and persecute a preacher. And since you have several times in discourse declared yourself for that government in the church, which is founded upon scripture, reason, apostolical practice, and antiquity, and (we are sure) the only one that can consist with the present government of state, I thought the latter discourse also might fitly address itself to you; in the which you may read your judgment, as in the other your practice. And now, since it has pleased Providence at length to turn our captivity, and answer persecuted patience with the unexpected returns of settlement; to remove our rulers, and restore our ruler; and not only to make our *exactors righteousness*, but, what is better, to give us righteousness instead of exaction, and hopes of religion to a church worried with reformation; I believe, upon a due and impartial reflection on what is past, you now find no cause to repent, that you never dipt your hands in the bloody high courts of justice, properly so called only by antiphrasis; nor ever prostituted the scarlet robe to those employments, in which you must have worn the color of your sin in the badge of your office: but, notwithstanding all the enticements of a prosperous villainy, abhorred the purchase, when the price was blood. So that now, being privileged by an happy unconcernment in those legal murders, you may take a sweeter relish of your own innocence, by beholding the misery of others' guilt, who being guilty before God, and infamous before men, obnoxious to both, begin to find the first-fruits of their sin in the universal scorn of all, their apparent danger, and unlikely remedy: which beginnings being at length consummated by the hand of justice, the cry of blood and sacrilege will cease, men's doubts will be satisfied, and Providence absolved.

And thus, sir, having presumed to honor my first essays in divinity, by prefixing to them a name, to which divines are so much obliged; I should here in the close of this address contribute a wish at least to your happiness: but since we desire it not yet in another world, and your enjoyments in this (according to the standard of a Christian desire) are so complete, that they require no addition; I shall turn my wishes into gratulations, and congratulating their fullness, only wish their continuance: praying that you may still possess what you possess, and do what you do; that is, reflect upon a clear, unblotted, acquitting conscience, and feed upon the ineffable comforts of the memorial of a conquered temptation, without the danger of returning to the trial. And this, sir, I account the greatest felicity that you can enjoy, and therefore the greatest that he can desire, who is

Yours in all observance,
ROBERT SOUTH.

Ch. Ch. 25 of
May, 1660.

MATTHEW x. 33. — *But whosoever shall deny me before men, him will I also deny before my Father which is in heaven.*

AS the great comprehensive gospel duty is the denial of self, so the grand gospel sin that confronts it is the denial of Christ. These two are both the commanding and the dividing principles of all our actions: for whosoever acts in opposition to one, does it always in behalf of the other. None ever opposed Christ, but it was to gratify self: none ever renounced the interest of self, but from a prevailing love to the interest of Christ. The subject I have here pitched upon may seem improper in these times, and in this place, where the number of professors and of men is the same; where the cause and interest of Christ has been so cried up; and Christ's personal reign and kingdom so called for and expected. But since it has been still preached up, but acted down; and dealt with, as the eagle in the fable did with the oyster, carrying it up on high, that by letting it fall he might dash it in pieces: I say, since Christ must reign, but his truths be made to serve; I suppose it is but reason to distinguish between profession and pretense, and to conclude, that men's present crying, *Hail king*, and *bending the knee* to Christ, are only in order to his future crucifixion.

For the discovery of the sense of the words, I shall inquire into their occasion. From the very beginning of the chapter we have Christ consulting the propagation of the gospel; and in order to it (being the only way that he knew to effect it) sending forth a ministry; and giving them a commission, together with instructions for the execution of it. He would have them fully acquainted with the nature and extent of their office; and so he joins commission with instruction; by one he conveys power, by the other knowledge. Supposing (I conceive) that upon such an undertaking, the more learned his ministers were, they would prove never the less faithful.* And thus having fitted them, and stript them of all manner of defense, ver. 9, he *sends them forth amongst wolves:* a hard expedition, you will say, to go amongst wolves; but yet much harder to convert them into sheep; and no less hard even to discern some of them, possibly being under sheep's clothing; and so by the advantage of that dress, sooner felt than discovered: probably also such as had both the properties of wolves, that is, they could whine and howl, as well as bite and devour. But that they might not go altogether naked among their enemies, the only armor that Christ allows them is prudence and innocence; *Be ye wise as serpents, but harmless as doves,* ver. 16. Weapons not at all offensive, yet most suitable to their warfare, whose greatest encounters were to be exhortations, and whose only conquest, escape. Innocence is the best caution, and we may unite the expression, to be *wise as a serpent* is to be *harmless as a dove.* Innocence is like polished armor; it adorns, and it defends. In sum, he tells them, that the opposition they should meet with was the greatest imaginable, from ver. 16 to 26. But in the ensuing verses he promises them an equal proportion of assistance; and, as if it were not an argument of force enough to outweigh the forementioned discouragements, he casts into the balance the promise of a reward to such as should execute, and of punishment to such as should neglect their commission: the reward in the former verse, *Whosoever shall confess me before men,* &c. the punishment in this, *But whosoever shall deny,* &c. As if by way of preoccupation he should have said, Well, here you see your commission; this is your duty, these are your discouragements: never seek for shifts and evasions from worldly afflictions; this is your reward, if you perform it; this is your doom, if you decline it.

* In the parliament 1653, it being put to the vote, whether they should support and encourage a *godly* and *learned* ministry, the latter word was rejected, and the vote passed for a *godly* and *faithful* ministry.

As for the explication of the words, they are clear and easy; and their originals in the Greek are of single signification, without any ambiguity; and therefore I shall not trouble you, by proposing how they run in this or that edition; or straining for an interpretation where there is no difficulty, or distinction where there is no difference. The only exposition that I shall give of them, will be to compare them to other parallel scriptures, and peculiarly to that in Mark viii. 38. *Whosoever therefore shall be ashamed of me and of my words in this adulterous and sinful generation; of him also shall the Son of man be ashamed, when he cometh in the glory of his Father, with the holy angels.* These words are a comment upon my text.

1. What is here in the text called a *denying of Christ*, is there termed a *being ashamed of him*, that is, in those words the cause is expressed, and here the effect; for therefore we deny a thing, because we are ashamed of it. First, Peter is ashamed of Christ, then he denies him.

2. What is here termed a denying of Christ, is there called a being ashamed of *Christ and his words:* Christ's truths are his second self. And he that offers a contempt to a king's letters or edicts, virtually affronts the king; it strikes his words, but it rebounds upon his person.

3. What is here said, *before men*, is there phrased, *in this adulterous and sinful generation.* These words import the hinderance of the duty enjoined; which therefore is here purposely enforced with a *non obstante* to all opposition. The term *adulterous*, I conceive, may chiefly relate to the Jews, who being nationally espoused to God by covenant, every sin of theirs was in a peculiar manner spiritual adultery.

4. What is here said, *I will deny him before my Father*, is there expressed, *I will be ashamed of him before my Father and his holy angels;* that is, when he shall come to judgment, when revenging justice shall come in pomp, attended with the glorious retinue of all the host of heaven. In short, the sentence pronounced declares the judgment, the solemnity of it the terror.

From the words we may deduce these observations:

I. We shall find strong motives and temptations from men, to draw us to a denial of Christ.

II. No terrors or solicitations from men, though never so great, can warrant or excuse such a denial.

III. To deny Christ's words, is to deny Christ.

But since these observations are rather implied than expressed in the words, I shall wave them, and instead of deducing a doctrine distinct from the words, prosecute the words themselves under this doctrinal paraphrase:

Whosoever shall deny, disown, or be ashamed of either the person or truths of Jesus Christ, for any fear or favor of man, shall with shame be disowned and eternally rejected by him at the dreadful judgment of the great day.

The discussion of this shall lie in these things:

I. To show, how many ways Christ and his truths may be denied; and what is the denial here chiefly intended.

II. To show, what are the causes that induce men to a denial of Christ and his truths.

III. To show, how far a man may consult his safety in time of persecution, without denying Christ.

IV. To show, what is imported in Christ's denying us before his Father in heaven.

V. To apply all to the present occasion.

But before I enter upon these, I must briefly premise this, that though the text and the doctrine run peremptory and absolute, *Whosoever denies Christ, shall assuredly be denied by him;* yet still there is a tacit condition in the words supposed, unless repentance intervene. For this and many other scriptures, though as to their formal terms they are absolute, yet as to their sense they are conditional. God in mercy has so framed and tempered his word, that we have, for the most part, a reserve of mercy wrapped up in a curse. And the very first judgment that was pronounced upon fallen man, was with the allay of a promise. Wheresoever we find a curse to the guilty expressed, in the same words mercy to the penitent is still understood. This premised, I come now to discuss the first thing, namely, how many ways Christ and his truths may be denied, &c. Here first in general I assert, that we may deny him in all those acts that are capable of being morally good or evil; those are the proper scene in which we act our confessions or denials of him. Accordingly therefore all ways of denying Christ I shall comprise under these three.

1. We may deny him and his truths by an erroneous, heretical judgment. I know it is doubted whether a bare error in judgment can condemn: but since truths absolutely necessary to salvation are so clearly revealed, that we cannot err in them, unless we be notoriously wanting to ourselves; herein the fault of the judgment is resolved into a precedent default in the will; and so the case is put out of doubt. But here it may be replied, Are not truths of absolute and fundamental necessity very disputable; as the deity of Christ, the trinity of persons? If they are not in themselves disputable, why are they so much disputed? Indeed, I believe, if we trace these disputes to their original cause, we shall find, that they never sprung from a reluctancy in reason to embrace them. For this reason itself dictates, as most rational, to assent to any thing, though seemingly contrary to reason, if it is revealed by God, and we are certain of the revelation. These two supposed, these disputes must needs arise only from curiosity and singularity; and these are faults of a diseased will. But some will further demand in behalf of these men, whether such as assent to every word in scripture, (for so will those that deny the natural deity of Christ and the Spirit,) can be yet said in doctrinals to deny Christ? To this I answer, Since words abstracted from their proper sense and signification lose the nature of words, and are only equivocally so called; inasmuch as the persons we speak of, take them thus, and derive the letter from Christ, but the signification from themselves, they can not be said properly to assent so much as to the words of the scripture. And so their case also is clear. But yet more fully to state the matter, how far a denial of Christ in belief and judgment is damnable: we will propose the question, whether those who hold the fundamentals of faith may deny Christ damnably, in respect of those superstructures and consequences that arise from them? I answer in brief, By fundemental truths are understood, (1.) either such, without the belief of which we can not be saved: or, (2.) such, the belief of which is sufficient to save: if the question be proposed of fundamentals in this latter sense, it contains its own answer; for where a man believes those truths, the belief of which is sufficient to save, there the disbelief or denial of their con-

sequences can not damn. But what and how many these fundamentals are, it will then be agreed upon, when all sects, opinions, and persuasions do unite and consent. 2dly, If we speak of fundamentals in the former sense, as they are only truths, without which we can not be saved: it is manifest that we may believe them, and yet be damned for denying their consequences: for that which is only a condition, without which we can not be saved, is not therefore a cause sufficient to save: much more is required to the latter, than to the former. I conclude therefore, that to deny Christ in our judgment, will condemn, and this concerns the learned: Christ demands the homage of your understanding: he will have your reason bend to him; you must put your heads under his feet. And we know, that heretofore, he who had the leprosy in this part was to be pronounced utterly unclean. A poisoned reason, an infected judgment, is Christ's greatest enemy. And an error in the judgment is like an imposthume in the head, which is always noisome, and frequently mortal.

2. We may deny Christ verbally, and by oral expressions. Now our words are the interpreters of our hearts, the transcripts of the judgment, with some further addition of good or evil. He that interprets, usually enlarges. What our judgment whispers in secret, these proclaim upon the housetop. To deny Christ in the former, imports enmity; but in these, open defiance. Christ's passion is renewed in both: he that misjudges of him, condemns him; but he that blasphemes him, spits in his face. Thus the Jews and the Pharisees denied Christ. *We know that this man is a sinner,* John ix. 24, *and a deceiver,* Matt. xxvii. 63. *And he casts out devils by the prince of devils,* Matt. xii. 24. And thus Christ is daily denied, in many blasphemies printed and divulged, and many horrid opinions vented against the truth. The schools dispute whether in morals the external action superadds any thing of good or evil to the internal elicit act of the will: but certainly the enmity of our judgments is wrought up to an high pitch, before it rages in an open denial. And it is a sign that it is grown too big for the heart, when it seeks for vent in our words. Blasphemy uttered, is error heightened with impudence: it is sin

scorning a concealment, not only committed, but defended. He that denies Christ in his judgment, sins; but he that speaks his denial, vouches and owns his sin: and so, by publishing it, does what in him lies to make it universal, and by writing it, to establish it eternal. There is another way of denying Christ with our mouths, which is negative; that is, when we do not acknowledge and confess him: but of this I shall have occasion to treat under the discussion of the third general head.

3. We may deny Christ in our actions and practice; and these speak much louder than our tongues. To have an orthodox belief, and a true profession, concurring with a bad life, is only to deny Christ with a greater solemnity. Belief and profession will speak thee a Christian but very faintly, when thy conversation proclaims thee an infidel. Many, while they have preached Christ in their sermons, have read a lecture of atheism in their practice. We have many here who speak of godliness, mortification, and self-denial; but if these are so, what means the bleating of the sheep, and the lowing of the oxen, the noise of their ordinary sins, and the cry of their great ones? If godly, why do they wallow and steep in all the carnalities of the world, under pretense of Christian liberty? Why do they make religion ridiculous by pretending to prophesy; and when their prophecies prove delusions, why do they blaspheme?* If such are self-deniers, what means the griping, the prejudice, the covetousness, and the pluralities preached against, and retained, and the arbitrary government of many? When such men preach of self-denial and humility, I can not but think of Seneca, who praised poverty, and that very safely, in the midst of his great riches and gardens; and even exhorted the world to throw away their gold, perhaps (as one well conjectures) that he might gather it up: so these desire men to be humble, that they may domineer without opposition. But it is an easy matter to commend patience, when there is no danger

* A noted independent divine, when Oliver Cromwell was sick, of which sickness he died, declared that God had revealed to him that he should recover, and live thirty years longer, for that God had raised him up for a work which could not be done in less time. But Oliver's death being published two days after, the said divine publicly in prayer expostulated with God the defeat of his prophecy, in these words: *Lord, thou hast lied unto us; yea, thou hast lied unto us.*

of any trial, to extol humility in the midst of honors, to begin a fast after dinner.* But, O how Christ will deal with such persons, when he shall draw forth all their actions bare, and stript from this deceiving veil of their heavenly speeches! He will then say, It was not your sad countenance, nor your hypocritical groaning, by which you did either confess or honor me: but your worldliness, your luxury, your sinister partial dealing: these have denied me, these have wounded me, these have gone to my heart; these have caused the weak to stumble, and the profane to blaspheme; these have offended the one, and hardened the other. You have indeed spoke me fair, you have saluted me with your lips, but even then you betrayed me. Depart from me therefore, you professors of holiness, but you workers of iniquity.

And thus having shown the three ways by which Christ may be denied, it may now be demanded, which is the denial here intended in the words.

Answer. (1.) I conceive, if the words are taken as they were particularly and personally directed to the apostles, upon the occasion of their mission to preach the gospel, so the denial of him was the not acknowledgment of the deity or godhead of Christ; and the reason to prove that this was then principally intended is this; because this was the truth in those days chiefly opposed, and most disbelieved; as appears, because Christ and the apostles did most earnestly inculcate the belief of this, and accepted men upon the bare acknowledgment of this, and baptism was administered to such as did but profess this, Act viii. 37, 38. And indeed, as this one aphorism, *Jesus Christ is the Son of God*, is virtually and eminently the whole gospel; so, to confess or deny it, is virtually to embrace or reject the whole round and series of gospel truths. For he that acknowledges Christ to be the Son of God, by the same does consequentially acknowledge, that he is to be believed and obeyed, in whatsoever he does enjoin and deliver to the sons of men: and therefore that we are to repent, and believe, and rest upon him for salvation, and to deny ourselves: and within the compass of this is included whatsoever is called gospel.

* Very credibly reported to have been done in an independent congregation at Oxon.

As for the manner of our denying the deity of Christ here prohibited, I conceive, it was by words and oral expressions verbally to deny and disacknowledge it. This I ground upon these reasons:

1. Because it was such a denial as was *before men*, and therefore consisted in open profession; for a denial in judgment and practice, as such, is not always before men.

2. Because it was such a denial or confession of him as would appear in preaching: but this is managed in words and verbal profession.

But now, (2.) if we take the words as they are a general precept, equally relating to all times and to all persons, though delivered only upon a particular occasion to the apostles, (as I suppose they are to be understood ;) so I think they comprehend all the three ways mentioned of confessing or denying Christ: but principally in respect of practice; and that, 1. Because by this he is most honored or dishonored. 2. Because without this the other two cannot save. 3. Because those who are ready enough to confess him both in judgment and profession, are for the most part very prone to deny him shamefully in their doings.

Pass we now to a second thing, viz. to show,

II. What are the causes inducing men to deny Christ in his truths. I shall propose three:

1. The seeming supposed absurdity of many truths: upon this foundation heresy always builds. The heathens derided the Christians, that still they required and pressed belief; and well they might, say they, since the articles of their religion are so absurd, that upon principles of science they can never win assent. It is easy to draw it forth and demonstrate, how upon this score the chief heresies, that now are said to trouble the church, do oppose and deny the most important truths in divinity. As first, hear the denier of the deity and satisfaction of Christ. What, says he, can the same person be God and man? the creature and the creator? Can we ascribe such attributes to the same thing, whereof one implies a negation and a contradiction of the other? Can he be also finite and infinite, when to be finite is not to be infinite, and to be infinite not to be finite? And when we distinguish between the person and the nature, was not that

distinction an invention of the schools, savoring rather of metaphysics than divinity? If we say, that he must have been God, because he was to mediate between us and God, by the same reason, they will reply, we should need a mediator between us and Christ, who is equally God, equally offended. Then for his satisfaction, they will demand to whom this satisfaction is paid? If to God, then God pays a price to himself: and what is it else to require and need no satisfaction, than for one to satisfy himself? Next comes in the denier of the decrees and free grace of God. What, says he, shall we exhort, admonish, and entreat the saints to beware of falling away finally, and at the same time assert, that it is impossible for them so to fall? What, shall we erect two contradictory wills in God, or place two contradictories in the same will? and make the will of his purpose and intention run counter to the will of his approbation? Hear another concerning the scripture and justification. What, says the Romanist, rely in matters of faith upon a private spirit? How do you know this is the sense of such a scripture? Why, by the Spirit. But how will you try that Spirit to be of God? Why, by the scripture. This he explodes as a circle, and so derides it. Then for justification. How are you justified by an imputed righteousness? Is it yours before it is imputed, or not? If not, as we must say, is this to be justified to have that accounted yours, that is not yours? But again, did you ever hear of any man made rich or wise by imputation? Why then righteous or just? Now these seeming paradoxes, attending gospel truths, cause men of weak, prejudiced intellectuals to deny them, and in them, Christ; being ashamed to own faith so much, as they think, to the disparagement of their reason.

2. The second thing causing men to deny the truths of Christ is their unprofitableness. And no wonder, if here men forsake the truth, and assert interest. To be pious is the way to be poor. Truth still gives its followers its own badge and livery, a despised nakedness. It is hard to maintain the truth, but much harder to be maintained by it. Could it ever yet feed, clothe, or defend its assertors? Did ever any man quench his thirst or satisfy his hunger with a notion? Did ever any one live upon propositions? The

testimony of Brutus concerning virtue is the apprehension of most concerning truth: that it is a name, but lives and estates are things, and therefore not to be thrown away upon words. That we are neither to worship or cringe to any thing under the Deity, is a truth too strict for a Naaman: he can be content to worship the true God, but then it must be in the house of Rimmon: the reason was implied in his condition; he was captain of the host, and therefore he thought it reason good to bow to Rimmon, rather than endanger his place: better bow than break. Indeed sometimes Providence casts things so, that truth and interest lie the same way: and, when it is wrapt up in this covering, men can be content to follow it, to press hard after it, but it is, as we pursue some beasts, only for their skins: take off the covering, and though men obtain the truth, they would lament the loss of that: as Jacob wept and mourned over the torn coat, when Joseph was alive. It is incredible to consider how interest outweighs truth. If a thing in itself be doubtful, let it make for interest, and it shall be raised at least into a probable; and if a truth be certain, and thwart interest, it will quickly fetch it down to but a probability: nay, if it does not carry with it an impregnable evidence, it will go near to debase it to a downright falsity. How much interest casts the balance in cases dubious, I could give sundry instances: let one suffice: and that concerning the unlawfulness of usury. Most of the learned men in the world successively, both heathen and Christian, do assert the taking of use to be utterly unlawful; yet the divines of the reformed church beyond the seas, though most severe and rigid in other things, do generally affirm it to be lawful. That the case is doubtful, and may be disputed with plausible arguments on either side, we may well grant: but what then is the reason, that makes these divines so unanimously concur in this opinion? Indeed I shall not affirm this to be the reason, but it may seem so to many: that they receive their salaries by way of pension, in present ready money, and so have no other way to improve them; so that it may be suspected, that the change of their salary would be the strongest argument to change their opinion. The truth is, interest is the grand wheel and spring that moves the whole universe.

Let Christ and truth say what they will, if interest will have it, gain must be godliness: if enthusiasm is in request, learning must be inconsistent with grace. If pay grows short, the university maintenance must be too great. Rather than Pilate will be counted Cæsar's enemy, he will pronounce Christ innocent one hour, and condemn him the next. How Christ is made to truckle under the world, and how his truths are denied and shuffled with for profit and pelf, the clearest proof would be by induction and example. But as it is the most clear, so here it would be the most unpleasing: wherefore I shall pass this over, since the world is now so peccant upon this account, that I am afraid instances would be mistaken for invectives.

3. The third cause inducing men to deny Christ in his truths is their apparent danger. To confess Christ is the ready way to be cast out of the synagogue. The church is a place of graves, as well as of worship and profession. To be resolute in a good cause is to bring upon ourselves the punishments due to a bad. Truth indeed is a possession of the highest value, and therefore it must needs expose the owner to much danger. Christ is sometimes pleased to make the profession of himself costly, and a man can not buy the truth, but he must pay down his life and his dearest blood for it. Christianity marks a man out for destruction; and Christ sometimes chalks out such a way to salvation as shall verify his own saying, *He that will save his life shall lose it.* The first ages of the church had a more abundant experience of this: what Paul and the rest planted by their preaching, they watered with their blood. We know their usage was such, as Christ foretold; he sent them to wolves, and the common course then was, *Christianos ad leones.* For a man to give his name to Christianity in those days was to list himself a martyr, and to bid farewell, not only to the pleasures, but also to the hopes of this life. Neither was it a single death only that then attended this profession, but the terror and sharpness of it was redoubled in the manner and circumstance. They had persecutors, whose invention was as great as their cruelty. Wit and malice conspired to find out such tortures, such deaths, and those of such incredible anguish, that only the manner of dying was the punishment, death

itself the deliverance. To be a martyr signifies only to witness the truth of Christ, but the witnessing of the truth was then so generally attended with this event, that martyrdom now signifies, not only to witness, but to witness by death: the word, besides its own signification, importing their practice. And since Christians have been freed from heathens, Christians themselves have turned persecutors. Since Rome from heathen was turned Christian, it has improved its persecution into an inquisition. Now, when Christ and truth are upon these terms, that men can not confess him, but upon pain of death, the reason of their apostasy and denial is clear; men will be wise, and leave truth and misery to such as love it; they are resolved to be cunning, let others run the hazard of being sincere. If they must be good at so high a rate, they know they may be safe at a cheaper. *Si negare sufficiat, quis erit nocens?* If to deny Christ will save them, the truth shall never make them guilty. Let Christ and his flock lie open, and exposed to all weather of persecution, foxes will be sure to have holes. And if it comes to this, that they must either renounce their religion, deny and blaspheme Christ, or forfeit their lives to the fire and sword, it is but inverting Job's wife's advice, *Curse God, and live.*

III. We proceed now to the third thing, which is to show, how far a man may consult his safety, &c.

This he may do two ways:

1. By withdrawing his person. Martyrdom is an heroic act of faith: an achievement beyond an ordinary pitch of it; *To you,* says the Spirit, *it is given to suffer,* Phil. i. 29. It is a peculiar additional gift: it is a distinguishing excellency of degree, not an essential consequent of its nature. *Be ye harmless as doves,* says Christ; and it is as natural to them to take flight upon danger, as to be innocent: let every man thoroughly consult the temper of his faith, and weigh his courage with his fears, his weakness and his resolution together, and take the measure of both, and see which preponderates; and if his spirit faints, if his heart misgives and melts at the very thoughts of the fire, let him fly, and secure his own soul, and Christ's honor. *Non negat Christum fugiendo, qui ideo fugit ne neget:* he does not deny Christ by flying, who therefore flies that he may not deny him. Nay, he does

not so much decline, as rather change his martyrdom: he flies from the flame, but repairs to a desert; to poverty and hunger in a wilderness. Whereas, if he would dispense with his conscience, and deny his Lord, or swallow down two or three contradictory oaths, he should neither fear the one, nor be forced to the other.

2. By concealing his judgment. A man sometimes is no more bound to speak, than to destroy himself: and as nature abhors this, so religion does not command that. In the times of the primitive church, when the Christians dwelt amongst heathens, it is reported of a certain maid, how she came from her father's house to one of the tribunals of the gentiles, and declared herself a Christian, spit in the judge's face, and so provoked him to cause her to be executed. But will any say, that this was to confess Christ, to die a martyr? He that, uncalled for, uncompelled, comes and proclaims a persecuted truth, for which he is sure to die, only dies a confessor of his own folly, and a sacrifice to his own rashness. Martyrdom is stamped such only by God's command; and he that ventures upon it without a call, must endure it without a reward: Christ will say, *Who required this at your hands?* His gospel does not dictate imprudence; no evangelical precept justles out that of a lawful self-preservation. He therefore that thus throws himself upon the sword, runs to heaven before he is sent for; where, though perhaps Christ may in mercy receive the man, yet he will be sure to disown the martyr.

And thus much concerning those lawful ways of securing ourselves in time of persecution: not as if these were always lawful: for sometimes a man is bound to confess Christ openly, though he dies for it; and to conceal a truth is to deny it. But now, to show when it is our duty, and when unlawful to take these courses, by some general rule of a perpetual, never-failing truth, none ever would yet presume: for, as Aristotle says, we are not to expect demonstrations in ethics or politics, nor to build certain rules upon the contingency of human actions; so, inasmuch as our flying from persecution, our confessing or concealing persecuted truths, vary and change their very nature, according to different circumstances of time, place, and persons, we can not limit their directions within any one universal precept. You will say then, how shall we know when to confess, when to conceal a truth? when to wait for, when to decline persecution? Indeed, the only way that I think can be prescribed in this case, is to be earnest and importunate with God in prayer for special direction: and it is not to be imagined, that he, who is both faithful and merciful, will leave a sincere soul in the dark upon such an occasion. But this I shall add, that the ministers of God are not to evade, or take refuge in any of these two forementioned ways. They are public persons; and good shepherds must then chiefly stand close to the flock, when the wolf comes. For them to be silent in the cause of Christ, is to renounce it; and to fly, is to desert it. As for that place urged in favor of the contrary, in ver. 23, *When they persecute you in this city, flee into another*, it proves nothing; for the precept was particular, and concerned only the apostles; and that, but for that time in which they were then sent to the Jews, at which time Christ keep them as a reserve for the future: for when after his death they were indifferently sent both to Jews and gentiles, we find not this clause in their commission, but they were to sign the truths they preached with their blood; as we know they actually did. And moreover, when Christ bids them, being persecuted in one city, fly into another, it was not (as Grotius actuely observes) that they might lie hid, or be secure in that city, but that there they might preach the gospel: so that their flight here was not to secure their persons, but to continue their business. I conclude therefore, that faithful ministers are to stand and endure the brunt. A common soldier may fly, when it is the duty of him that holds the standard to die upon the place. And we have abundant encouragement so to do. Christ has seconded and sweetened his command with his promise: yea, the thing itself is not only our duty, but our glory. And he who has done this work, has in the very work partly received his wages. And were it put to my choice, I think I should choose rather with spitting and scorn to be tumbled into the dust in blood, bearing witness to any known truth of our dear Lord, now opposed by the enthusiasts of the present age, than by a denial of those truths through blood and perjury wade to a sceptre, and lord it in a throne. And we need not doubt, but truth, however oppressed, will have some followers, and at length prevail. A Christ, though crucified, will arise: and as it is in Rev. xi. 3, *the witnesses will prophesy, though it be in sackcloth.*

IV. Having thus dispatched the third thing, I proceed to the fourth, which is to show, what it is for Christ to deny us before his Father in heaven. Hitherto we have treated of men's carriage to Christ in this world; now we will describe his carriage to them in the other. These words clearly relate to the last judgment, and they are a summary description of his proceeding with men at that day.

And here we will consider,

1. The action itself, *He will deny them.*

2. The circumstance of the action, *He will deny them before his Father and the holy angels.*

1. Concerning the first: Christ's denying us is otherwise expressed in Luke xiii. 27, *I know you not.* To know, in scripture language, is to approve; and so, not to know, is to reject and condemn. Now who knows how many woes are crowded into this one sentence, *I will deny him?* It is (to say no more) a compendious expression of hell, an eternity of torments comprised in a word: it is condemnation itself, and, what is most of all, it is condemnation from the mouth of a Saviour. O the inexpressible horror that will seize upon a poor sinner, when he stands arraigned at the bar of divine justice! When he shall look about, and see his accuser, his judge, the witnesses, all of them his remorseless adversaries; the law impleading, mercy and the gospel upbraiding him, the devil, his grand accuser, drawing his indictment; numbering his sins with the greatest exactness, and aggravating them with the cruelest bitterness; and conscience, like a thousand witnesses, attesting every article, flying in his face, and rending his very heart: and then after all, Christ, from whom only mercy could be expected, owning the accusation. It will be hell enough to hear the sentence; the very promulgation of the punishment will be part of the punishment, and anticipate the execution. If Peter was so abashed when Christ gave him a look after his denial; if there was so much dread in his looks when he stood as pris-

oner, how much greater will it be when he sits as a judge! If it was so fearful when he looked his denier into repentance, what will it be when he shall look him into destruction! Believe it, when we shall hear an accusation from an advocate, our eternal doom from our intercessor, it will convince us that a denial of Christ is something more than a few transitory words: what trembling, what outcries, what astonishment will there be upon the pronouncing this sentence! Every word will come upon the sinner like an arrow striking through his reins; like thunder, that is heard, and consumes at the same instant. Yea, it will be a denial with scorn, with taunting exprobrations: and to be miserable without commiseration is the height of misery. He that falls below pity, can fall no lower. Could I give you a lively representation of guilt and horror on this hand, and paint out eternal wrath, and decipher eternal vengeance on the other, then might I show you the condition of a sinner hearing himself denied by Christ: and for those whom Christ has denied, it will be in vain to appeal to the Father, unless we can imagine that those whom mercy has condemned, justice will absolve.

2. For the circumstance, *He will deny us before his Father and the holy angels.* As much as God is more glorious than man, so much is it more glorious to be confessed before him, than before men: and so much glory as there is in being confessed, so much dishonor there is in being denied. If there could be any room for comfort after the sentence of damnation, it would be this, to be executed in secret, to perish unobserved: as it is some allay to the infamy of him who died ignominiously, to be buried privately. But when a man's folly must be spread open before the angels, and all his baseness ript up before those pure spirits, this will be a double hell: to be thrust into utter darkness, only to be punished by it, without the benefit of being concealed. When Christ shall compare himself, who was denied, and the thing for which he was denied, together, and parallel his merits with a lust, and lay eternity in the balance with a trifle, then the folly of the sinner's choice shall be the greatest sting of his destruction. For a man shall not have the advantage of his former ignorances and error to approve his sin: things that appear amiable by the light of this world, will appear

of a different odious hue in the clear discoveries of the next: as that which appears to be of this color by a dim candle, will be found to be of another, looked upon in the day. So when Christ shall have cleared up men's apprehensions about the value of things, he will propose that worthy prize for which he was denied; he will hold it up to open view, and call upon men and angels: Behold, look, here 's the thing, here 's that piece of dirt, that windy applause, that poor transitory pleasure, that contemptible danger, for which I was dishonored, my truths disowned, and for which, life, eternity, and God himself was scorned and trampled upon by this sinner: judge, all the world, whether what he so despised in the other life, he deserves to enjoy in this. How will the condemned sinner then crawl forth, and appear in his filth and shame, before that undefiled tribunal, like a toad or a snake in a king's presence-chamber! Nothing so irksome, as to have one's folly displayed before the prudent; one's impurity before the pure. And all this before that company surrounding him, from which he is neither able to look off, nor yet to look upon. A disgrace put upon a man in company is unsupportable: it is heightened according to the greatness, and multiplied according to the number of the persons that hear it. And now as this circumstance [*before his Father*] fully speaks the shame, so likewise it speaks the danger of Christ's then denying us. For when the accusation is heard, and the person stands convict, God is immediately lifting up his hand to inflict the eternal blow; and when Christ denies to exhibit a ransom, to step between the stroke then coming and the sinner, it must inevitably fall upon him, and sink his guilty soul into that deep and bottomless gulph of endless perdition. This therefore is the sum of Christ's denying us before his Father, viz. unsupportable shame, unavoidable destruction.

V. I proceed now to the uses which may be drawn from the truths delivered. And here,

1. (Right honorable) not only the present occasion, but even the words themselves, seem eminently to address an exhortation to your honors. As for others not to deny Christ, is openly to profess him; so for you who are invested with authority, not to deny him, is to defend him. Know there-

fore, that Christ does not only desire, but demand your defense, and that in a double respect.

(1.) In respect of his truth. (2.) Of his members.

(1.) He requires that you should defend and confess him in his truth. Heresy is a tare sometimes not to be pulled up but by the civil magistrate. The word *liberty of conscience* is much abused for the defense of it, because not well understood. Every man may have liberty of conscience to think and judge as he pleases, but not to vent what he pleases. The reason is, because conscience bounding itself within the thoughts is of private concernment, and the cognizance of these belong only to God: but when an opinion is published, it concerns all that hear it; and the public is endamaged, and therefore becomes punishable by the magistrate, to whom the care of the public is intrusted. But there is one truth that concerns both ministry and magistracy, and all; which is opposed by those who affirm, that none ought to govern upon the earth, but Christ in person: absurdly; as if the powers that are destroyed his; as if a deputy were not consistent with a king; as if there were any opposition in subordination. They affirm also, that the wicked have no right to their estates; but only the faithful, that is, themselves, ought to *possess the earth.* And it is not to be questioned, but when they come to explain this principle, by putting it into execution, there will be but few that have estates at present, but will be either found, or made wicked. I shall not be so urgent, to press you to confess Christ, by asserting and owning the truth, contrary to this, since it does not only oppose truth, but property; and here to deny Christ, would be to deny yourselves, in a sense which none is like to do.

(2.) Christ requires you to own and defend him in his members; and amongst these, the chief of them, and such as most fall in your way, the ministers; I say, that despised, abject, oppressed sort of men, the ministers, whom the world would make antichristian, and so deprive them of heaven; and also strip them of that poor remainder of their maintenance, and so allow them no portion upon the earth. You may now spare that distinction of scandalous ministers, when it is even made scandalous to be a minister. And as for their discouragement in the courts of the law, I shall only note this, that for these many years last past, it has been the constant observation of all, that if a minister had a cause depending in the court, it was ten to one but it went against him. I can not believe your law justles out the gospel; but if it be thus used to undermine Christ in his servants, beware that such judgments passed upon them do not fetch down God's judgments upon the land; and that for such abuse of law, Christ does not in anger deprive both you and us of its use. (My lords) I make no doubt but you will meet with many suits in your course, in which the persons we speak of are concerned,* as it is easy to prognosticate from those many worthy petitions preferred against them, for which the well-affected petitioners will one day receive but small thanks from the court of heaven. But however their causes speed in your tribunals, know that Christ himself will recognize them at a greater. And then, what a different face will be put upon things! When the usurping, devouring Nimrods of the world shall be cast with scorn on the left hand; and Christ himself in that great consistory shall deign to step down from his throne, and single out a poor despised minister, and (as it were taking him by the hand) present him to, and openly thus confess him before his Father: Father, here is a poor servant of mine, who, for doing his duty impartially, for keeping a good conscience, and testifying my truths in an hypocritical pretending age, was wronged, trod upon, stripped of all: Father, I will that there be now a distinction made, between such as have owned and confessed me with the loss of the world, and those that have denied, persecuted, and insulted over me. It will be in vain then to come and creep for mercy; and say, Lord, when did we insult over thee? when did we see thee in our courts, and despised or oppressed thee? Christ's reply will be then quick and sharp: Verily, inasmuch as you did it to one of these little, poor despised ones, ye did it unto me.

2. Use is of information, to show us the danger as well as the baseness of a dastardly spirit, in asserting the interest and truth of Christ. Since Christ has made a Christian

* Whensoever any petition was put up to the parliament in the year 1653, for the taking away of tithes, the thanks of the house were still returned to them, and that by the name and elogy of the well-affected petitioners.

course a warfare, of all men living a coward is the most unfit to make a Christian: whose infamy is not so great, but it is sometimes less than his peril. A coward does not always scape with disgrace, but sometimes also he loses his life: wherefore, let all such know, as can enlarge their consciences like hell, and call any sinful compliance submission, and style a cowardly silence in Christ's cause, discretion and prudence; I say, let them know, that Christ will one day scorn them, and spit them, with their policy and prudence, into hell; and then let them consult, how politic they were, for a temporal emolument, to throw away eternity. The things which generally cause men to deny Christ are, either the enjoyments or the miseries of this life: but alas! at the day of judgment all these will expire; and, as one well observes, what are we the better for pleasure, or the worse for sorrow, when it is past? But then sin and guilt will be still fresh, and heaven and hell will be then yet to begin. If ever it was seasonable to preach courage in the despised, abused cause of Christ, it is now, when his truths are reformed into nothing, when the hands and hearts of his faithful ministers are weakened, and even broke, and his worship extirpated in a mockery, that his honor may be advanced. Well, to establish our hearts in duty, let us beforehand propose to ourselves the worst that can happen. Should God in his judgment suffer England to be transformed into a Munster: should the faithful be everywhere massacred: should the places of learning be demolished, and our colleges reduced (not only as one * in his zeal would have it) to three, but to none; yet, assuredly, hell is worse than all this, and is the portion of such as deny Christ: wherefore, let our discouragements be what they will, loss of places, loss of estates, loss of life and relations, yet still this sentence stands ratified in the decrees of Heaven, Cursed be that man, that for any of these shall desert the truth, and deny his Lord.

* A colonel of the army, the perfidious cause of Penruddock's death, and some time after high-sheriff of Oxfordshire, openly and frequently affirmed the uselessness of the universities, and that three colleges were sufficient to answer the occasions of the nation, for the breeding of men up to learning, so far as it was either necessary or useful.

SERMON IV.

ECCLESIASTICAL POLICY THE BEST POLICY: OR RELIGION THE BEST REASON OF STATE:

IN A SERMON PREACHED BEFORE THE HONORABLE SOCIETY OF LINCOLN'S INN.

1 KINGS xiii. 33, 34. — *After this thing Jeroboam returned not from his evil way, but made again of the lowest of the people priests of the high places: whosoever would, he consecrated him, and he became one of the priests of the high places. And this thing became sin unto the house of Jeroboam, even to cut it off, and to destroy it from off the face of the earth.*

JEROBOAM (from the name of a person become the character of impiety) is reported to posterity eminent, or rather infamous, for two things; usurpation of government, and innovation of religion. It is confessed, the former is expressly said to have been from God; but since God may order and dispose what he does not approve, and use the wickedness of men while he forbids it, the design of the first cause does not excuse the malignity of the second: and therefore, the advancement and sceptre of Jeroboam was in that sense only the work of God, in which it is said, Amos iii. 6. *that there is no evil in the city which the Lord hath not done.* But from his attempts upon the civil power, he proceeds to innovate God's worship; and from the subjection of men's bodies and estates, to enslave their consciences, as knowing that true religion is no friend to an unjust title. Such was afterwards the way of Mahomet, to the tyrant to join the impostor, and what he had got by the sword to confirm by the Alcoran; raising his empire upon two pillars, conquest and inspiration. Jeroboam being thus advanced, and thinking policy the best piety, though indeed in nothing ever more befooled, the nature of sin being not only to defile, but to infatuate; in the xiith chapter, and the 27th verse, he thus argues; *If this people go up to do sacrifice in the house of the Lord at Jerusalem, then shall the heart of this people turn again unto their lord, even unto Rehoboam king of Judah, and they shall kill me, and go again unto Rehoboam king of Judah.* As if he should have said: The true worship of God, and the converse of those that use it, dispose men to a considerate lawful subjection. And therefore I must take another course: my practice must not be better than my title; what was won by force, must be continued by delusion. Thus sin is usually seconded with sin; and a man seldom commits one sin to please, but he commits another to defend himself: as it is frequent for the adulterer to commit murder, to conceal the shame of his adultery. But let us see Jeroboam's politic procedure in the next verse. *Whereupon the king took counsel, and made two calves of gold, and said unto them, It is too much for you to go up to Jerusalem: behold thy gods, O Israel.* As if he had made such an edict: I Jeroboam, by the advice of my council, considering the great distance of the temple, and the great charges that poor people are put to in going thither; as also the intolerable burden of paying the first-fruits and tithes to the priest, have considered of a way that may be more easy, and less burdensome to the people, as also more comfortable to the priests themselves; and therefore strictly enjoin, that none henceforth presume to repair to the temple at Jerusalem, especially since God is not tied to any place or form of worship; as also because the devotion of men is apt to be clogged by such ceremonies; therefore, both for the ease of the people, as well as for the advancement of religion, we require and command, that all henceforth forbear going up to Jerusalem. Questionless these and such other reasons the impostor used, to insinuate his devout idolatry. And thus the calves were set up, to which oxen must be sacrificed; the god and the sacrifice out of the same herd. And because Israel was not to return to Egypt, Egypt was brought back to them: that is, the Egyptian way of worship, the Apis, or Serapis, which was nothing but the image of a calf or ox, as is clear from most historians. Thus Jeroboam having procured his people gods, the next thing was to provide priests. Hereupon to the calves he adds a commission for the approving, trying, and admitting the rascality and lowest of the people to minister in that service: such as kept cattle, with a little change of their office, were admitted to make oblations to them. And doubtless, besides the approbation of these, there was a commission also to eject such of the priests and Levites of God, as being too ceremoniously addicted to the temple, would not serve Jeroboam before God, nor worship his calves for their gold, nor approve those two glittering sins for any reason of state whatsoever. Having now perfected divine worship, and prepared both gods and priests; in the next place, that he might the better teach his false priests the way of their new worship, he begins the service himself, and so countenances by his example what he had enjoined by his command, in the 1st verse of this chapter; *and Jeroboam stood by the altar to burn incense.* Burning of incense was then the ministerial office amongst them, as preaching is now amongst us. So that to represent to you the nature of Jeroboam's action; it was as if in a Christian nation the chief governor should authorize and encourage all the scum and refuse of the people to preach, and call them to the ministry by using to preach,* and invade the ministerial function himself. But Jeroboam rested not here, but while he was busy in his work, and a prophet immediately sent by God declares against his idolatry, he endeavors to seize upon and commit him; in ver. 4, *he held forth his hand from the altar, and said, Lay hold of him.* Thus we have him completing his sin, and by a strange imposition of hands persecuting the true prophets, as well as ordaining false. But it was a natural transition, and no ways wonderful to see him, who stood affronting God with false incense in the right hand, persecuting with the left, and abetting the idolatry of one arm with the violence of the other. Now if we lay all these things together, and consider the parts, rise, and degrees of his sin, we shall find, that it was not for nothing that the Spirit of God so frequently and bitterly in scripture stigmatizes this person; for it represents him first encroaching upon the civil government, thence changing that of the church, debasing the office that God had made sacred, introducing a false way of worship, and destroying the true. And in this we have a

* Cromwell (a lively copy of Jeroboam) did so.

full and fair description of a foul thing, that is, of an usurper and an impostor: or, to use one word more comprehensive than both, *of Jeroboam the son of Nebat, who made Israel to sin.*

From the story and practice of Jeroboam, we might gather these observations:

1. That God sometimes punishes a notorious sin, by suffering the sinner to fall into a worse.

Thus God punished the rebellion of the Israelites, by permitting them to fall into idolatry.

2. There is nothing so absurd, but may be obtruded upon the vulgar under pretense of religion.

Certainly, otherwise a golden calf could never have been made either the object or the means of divine worship.

3. Sin, especially that of perverting God's worship, as it leaves a guilt upon the soul, so it perpetuates a blot upon the name.

Hence nothing so frequent, as for the Spirit of God to express wicked, irreligious kings, by comparing them to Ahab or Jeroboam. It being usual to make the first and most eminent in any kind, not only the standard for comparison, but also the rule of expression.

But I shall insist only upon the words of the text, and what shall be drawn from thence. There are two things in the words that may seem to require explication:

1. What is meant by the high places.

2. What by the consecration of the priests.

1. Concerning the high places. The use of these in the divine worship was general and ancient; and as Dionysius Vossius observes in his notes upon Moses Maimonides, the first way that was used, long before temples were either built or thought lawful. The reason of this seems to be, because those places could not be thought to shut up or confine the immensity of God, as they supposed an house did; and withal gave his worshipers a nearer approach to heaven by their height. Hence we read that the Samaritans worshiped upon mount Gerizim, John iv. 20; and Samuel went up to the high place to sacrifice, 1 Sam. ix. 14; and Solomon sacrificed at the high place in Gibeon, 1 Kings iii. 4. Yea, the temple itself was at length built upon a mount or high place, 2 Chron. iii. 1. You will say then, why are these places

condemned? I answer, that the use of them was not condemned, as absolutely and always unlawful in itself, but only after the temple was built, and that God had professed to put his name in that place and no other: therefore, what was lawful in the practice of Samuel and Solomon before the temple was in being, was now detestable in Jeroboam, since that was constituted by God the only place for his worship. To bring this consideration to the times of Christianity. Because the apostles and primitive Christians preached in houses, and had only private meetings, in regard they were under persecution, and had no churches; this can not warrant the practice of those nowadays, nor a toleration of them, that prefer houses before churches, and a conventicle before the congregation.

2. For the second thing, which is the consecration of the priests; it seems to have been correspondent to ordination in the Christian church. Idolaters themselves were not so far gone, as to venture upon the priesthood without consecration and a call. To show all the solemnities of this would be tedious, and here unnecessary: the Hebrew word which we render *to consecrate*, signifies *to fill the hand*, which indeed imports the manner of consecration, which was done by filling the hand: for the priest cut a piece of the sacrifice, and put it into the hands of him that was to be consecrated; by which ceremony he received right to sacrifice, and so became a priest. As our ordination in the Christian church is said to have been heretofore transacted by the bishop's delivering of the Bible into the hands of him that was to be ordained, whereby he received power ministerially to dispense the mysteries contained in it, and so was made a presbyter. Thus much briefly concerning consecration.

There remains nothing else to be explained in the words: I shall therefore now draw forth the sense of them into these two propositions:

I. The surest means to strengthen, or the readiest to ruin the civil power, is either to establish or destroy the worship of God in the right exercise of religion.

II. The next and most effectual way to destroy religion, is to embase the teachers and dispensers of it.

Of both these in their order.

For the prosecution of the former we are to show,

1. The truth of the assertion, that it is so.

2. The reason of the assertion, why and whence it is so.

1. For the truth of it: it is abundantly evinced from all records both of divine and profane history, in which he that runs may read the ruin of the state in the destruction of the church; and that not only portended by it, as its sign, but also inferred from it, as its cause.

2. For the reason of the point; it may be drawn

(1.) From the judicial proceeding of God, the great King of kings, and supreme Ruler of the universe; who for his commands is indeed careful, but for his worship jealous: and therefore in states notoriously irreligious, by a secret and irresistible power, countermands their deepest project, splits their counsels, and smites their most refined policies with frustration and a curse; being resolved that the kingdoms of the world shall fall down before him, either in his adoration, or their own confusion.

(2.) The reason of the doctrine may be drawn from the necessary dependence of the very principles of government upon religion. And this I shall pursue more fully. The great business of government is to procure obedience, and keep off disobedience: the great springs upon which those two move are rewards and punishments, answering the two ruling affections of man's mind, hope and fear. For since there is a natural opposition between the judgment and the appetite, the former respecting what is honest, the latter what is pleasing, which two qualifications seldom concur in the same thing, and since withal man's design in every action is delight; therefore to render things honest also practicable, they must be first represented desirable, which can not be, but by proposing honesty clothed with pleasure; and since it presents no pleasure to the sense, it must be fetched from the apprehension of a future reward: for questionless duty moves not so much upon command as promise. Now therefore, that which proposes the greatest and most suitable rewards to obedience, and the greatest terrors and punishments to disobedience, doubtless is the most likely to enforce one, and prevent the other. But it is religion that does this, which to happiness and misery joins eternity. And these, supposing the immortality of the soul, which philosophy indeed conjectures, but only religion proves, or (which is as good) persuades; I say these two things, eternal happiness and eternal misery, meeting with a persuasion that the soul is immortal, are, without controversy, of all others, the first the most desirable, and the latter the most horrible to human apprehension. Were it not for these, civil government were not able to stand before the prevailing swing of corrupt nature, which would know no honesty but advantage, no duty but in pleasure, nor any law but its own will. Were not these frequently thundered into the understandings of men, the magistrate might enact, order, and proclaim; proclamations might be hung upon walls and posts, and there they might hang, seen and despised, more like malefactors than laws: but when religion binds them upon the conscience, conscience will either persuade or terrify men into their practice. For put the case, a man knew, and that upon sure grounds, that he might do an advantageous murder or robbery, and not be discovered; what human laws could hinder him, which, he knows, can not inflict any penalty, where they can make no discovery? But religion assures him, that no sin, though concealed from human eyes, can either escape God's sight in this world, or his vengeance in the other. Put the case also, that men looked upon death without fear, in which sense it is nothing, or at most very little; ceasing, while it is endured, and probably without pain, for it seizes upon the vitals, and benumbs the senses, and where there is no sense, there can be no pain: I say, if while a man is acting his will towards sin, he should also thus act his reason to despise death, where would be the terror of the magistrate, who can neither threaten nor inflict any more? Hence an old malefactor in his execution at the gallows made no other confession but this; that he had very jocundly passed over his life in such courses; and he that would not for fifty years' pleasure endure half an hour's pain, deserved to die a worse death than himself. Questionless this man was not ignorant before, that there were such things as laws, assizes, and gallows; but had he considered and believed the terrors of another world, he might probably have found a fairer passage out of this. If there was not a minister in every parish, you would quickly find cause to increase the number of constables: and if the churches were not employed to be places to hear God's law, there would be need of them to be prisons for the breakers of the laws of men. Hence it is observable, that the tribe of Levi had not one place or portion together, like the rest of the tribes: but, because it was their office to dispense religion, they were diffused over all the tribes, that they might be continually preaching to the rest their duty to God; which is the most effectual way to dispose them to obedience to man: for he that truly fears God can not despise the magistrate. Yea, so near is the connection between the civil state and religious, that heretofore, if you look upon well-regulated, civilized heathen nations, you will find the government and the priesthood united in the same person; *Anius rex idem hominum, Phœbique sacerdos,* Virg. 3 Æn. if under the true worship of God; *Melchisedech, king of Salem, and priest of the most high God,* Hebrews vii. 1. And afterwards Moses, (whom as we acknowledge a pious, so atheists themselves will confess to have been a wise prince,) he, when he took the kingly government upon himself, by his own choice, seconded by divine institution, vested the priesthood in his brother Aaron, both whose concernments were so coupled, that if nature had not, yet their religious, nay, their civil interests, would have made them brothers. And it was once the design of the emperor of Germany, Maximilian the first, to have joined the popedom and the empire together, and to have got himself chosen pope, and by that means derived the papacy to succeeding emperors. Had he effected it, doubtless there would not have been such scuffles between them and the bishop of Rome; the civil interest of the state would not have been undermined by an adverse interest, managed by the specious and potent pretenses of religion. And to see, even amongst us, how these two are united, how the former is upheld by the latter: the magistrate sometimes can not do his own office dexterously, but by acting the minister: hence it is, that judges of assizes find it necessary in their charges to use pathetical discourses of conscience; and if it were not for the sway of this, they would often lose the best evidence in the world against malefactors, which is confession: for no man would confess and be hanged here, but to avoid being damned hereafter. Thus I have in general shown the utter inability of the magistrate to attain the ends of government, without the aid of religion. But it may be here replied, that many are not at all moved with arguments drawn from hence, or with the happy or miserable state of the soul after death; and therefore this avails little to procure obedience, and consequently to advance government. I answer by concession: that this is true of epicures, atheists, and some pretended philosophers, who have stifled the notions of a Deity and the soul's immortality; but the unprepossessed on the one hand, and the well-disposed on the other, who both together make much the major part of the world, are very apt to be affected with a due fear of these things: and religion, accommodating itself to the generality, though not to every particular temper, sufficiently secures government; inasmuch as that stands or falls according to the behavior of the multitude. And whatsoever conscience makes the generality obey, to that prudence will make the rest conform. Wherefore, having proved the dependence of government upon religion, I shall now demonstrate, that the safety of government depends upon the truth of religion. False religion is, in its nature, the greatest bane and destruction to government in the world. The reason is, because whatsoever is false, is also weak. *Ens* and *verum* in philosophy are the same: and so much as any religion has of falsity, it loses of strength and existence. Falsity gains authority only from ignorance, and therefore is in danger to be known; for from being false, the next immediate step is to be known to be such. And what prejudice this would be to the civil government, is apparent, if men should be awed into obedience, and affrighted from sin by rewards and punishments, proposed to them in such a religion, which afterwards should be detected, and found a mere falsity and cheat; for if one part be but found to be false, it will make the whole suspicious. And men will then not only cast off obedience to the civil magistrate, but they will do it with disdain and rage, that they have been deceived so long, and brought to do that out of conscience, which was imposed upon them out of design: for though men are often willingly deceived, yet still it must be under an opinion of being instructed; though they love the deception, yet they mortally hate it under that appearance: therefore it is no ways safe for a magistrate, who is to build his dominion upon the fears of men, to build those fears upon a false religion. It is not to be doubted, but the absurdity of Jeroboam's calves made many Israelites turn subjects to Rehoboam's government, that they might be proselytes to his religion. Herein the weakness of the Turkish religion appears, that it urges obedience upon the promise of such absurd rewards, as, that after death they should have palaces, gardens, beautiful women, with all the luxury that could be: as if those things, that were the occasions and incentives of sin in this world, could be the rewards of holiness in the other: besides many other inventions, false and absurd, that are like so many chinks and holes to discover the rottenness of the whole fabric, when God shall be pleased to give light to discover and open their reasons to discern them. But you will say, what government more sure and absolute than the Turkish, and yet what religion more false? Therefore, certainly government may stand sure and strong, be the religion professed never so absurd. I answer, that it may do so indeed by accident, through the strange peculiar temper and gross ignorance of a people; as we see it happens in the Turks, the best part of whose policy, supposing the absurdity of their religion, is this, that they prohibit schools of learning; for this hinders knowledge and disputes, which such a religion would not bear. But suppose we, that the learning of these western nations were as great there as here, and the Alcoran as common to them as the Bible to us, that they might have free recourse to search and examine the flaws and follies of it; and withal, that they were of as inquisitive a temper as we: and who knows, but as there are vicissitudes in the government, so there may happen the same also in the temper of a nation? If this should come to pass, where would be their religion? And then let every one judge, whether the *arcana imperii* and *religionis* would not fall together. They have begun to totter already; for Mahomet having promised to come and visit his followers, and translate them to paradise after a thousand years, this being expired, many of the Persians began to doubt and smell the cheat, till the

Mufti or chief priest told them that it was a mistake in the figure, and assured them, that upon more diligent survey of the records, he found it two thousand instead of one. When this is expired, perhaps they will not be able to renew the fallacy. I say therefore, that though his government continues firm in the exercise of a false religion, yet this is by accident, through the present genius of the people, which may change; but this does not prove, but that the nature of such a religion (of which we only now speak) tends to subvert and betray the civil power. Hence Machiavel himself, in his animadversions upon Livy, makes it appear, that the weakness of Italy, which was once so strong, was caused by the corrupt practices of the papacy, in depraving and misusing religion to that purpose, which he, though himself a papist, says, could not have happened, had the Christian religion been kept in its first and native simplicity. Thus much may suffice for the clearing of the first proposition.

The inferences from hence are two:

1. If government depends upon religion, then this shows the pestilential design of those that attempt to disjoin the civil and ecclesiastical interest, setting the latter wholly out of the tuition of the former. But it is clear that the fanatics know no other step to the magistracy, but through the ruin of the ministry. There is a great analogy between the body natural and politic; in which the ecclesiastical or spiritual part justly supplies the part of the soul; and the violent separation of this from the other does as certainly infer death and dissolution, as the disjunction of the body and the soul in the natural; for when this once departs, it leaves the body of the commonwealth a carcass, noisome, and exposed to be devoured by birds of prey. The ministry will be one day found, according to Christ's word, *the salt of the earth*, the only thing that keeps societies of men from stench and corruption. These two interests are of that nature, that it is to be feared they can not be divided, but they will also prove opposite; and not resting in a bare diversity, quickly rise into a contrariety: these two are to the state, what the elements of fire and water to the body, which united compose, separated destroy it. I am not of the papist's opinion, who would make the spiritual above the civil state in power as

well as dignity, but rather subject it to the civil; yet thus much I dare affirm, that the civil, which is superior, is upheld and kept in being by the ecclesiastical and inferior; as it is in a building, where the upper part is supported by the lower; the church resembling the foundation, which indeed is the lowest part, but the most considerable. The magistracy can not so much protect the ministry, but the ministers may do more in serving the magistrate. A taste of which truth you may take from the holy war, to which how fast and eagerly did men go, when the priest persuaded them, that whosoever died in that expedition was a martyr? Those that will not be convinced what a help this is to the magistracy, would find how considerable it is, if they should chance to clash; this would certainly eat out the other. For the magistrate can not urge obedience upon such potent grounds, as the minister, if so disposed, can urge disobedience. As for instance, if my governor should command me to do a thing, or I must die, or forfeit my estate; and the minister steps in, and tells me, that I offend God, and ruin my soul, if I obey that command, it is easy to see a greater force in this persuasion from the advantage of its ground. And if divines once begin to curse Meroz, we shall see that Levi can use the sword as well as Simeon; and although ministers do not handle, yet they can employ it. This shows the imprudence, as well as the danger of the civil magistrate's exasperating those that can fire men's consciences against him, and arm his enemies with religion. For I have read heretofore of some, that, having conceived an irreconcilable hatred of the civil magistrate, prevailed with men so far, that they went to resist him even out of conscience, and a full persuasion and dread upon their spirits, that, not to do it, were to desert God, and consequently to incur damnation.* Now when men's rage is both heightened and sanctified by conscience, the war will be fierce; for what is done out of conscience, is done with the utmost activity. And then Campanella's speech to the king of Spain will be found true, *Religio semper vicit, præsertim armata:* which sentence deserves seriously to be considered by all governors, and timely to be understood, lest it comes to be felt.

* See Serm. on Prov. xii. 22.

2. If the safety of government is founded upon the truth of religion, then this shows the danger of any thing that may make even the true religion suspected to be false. To be false, and to be thought false, is all one in respect of men, who act not according to truth, but apprehension. As on the contrary, a false religion, while apprehended true, has the force and efficacy of truth. Now there is nothing more apt to induce men to a suspicion of any religion, than frequent innovation and change: for since the object of religion, God, the subject of it, the soul of man, and the business of it, truth, is always one and the same; variety and novelty is a just presumption of falsity. It argues sickness and distemper in the mind, as well as in the body, when a man is continually turning and tossing from one side to the other. The wise Romans ever dreaded the least innovation in religion: hence we find the advice of Mæcenas to Augustus Cæsar, in Dion Cassius, in the 52d book, where he counsels him to detest and persecute all innovators of divine worship, not only as contemners of the gods, but as the most pernicious disturbers of the state: for when men venture to make changes in things sacred, it argues great boldness with God, and this naturally imports little belief of him: which if the people once perceive, they will take their creed also, not from the magistrate's laws, but his example. Hence in England, where religion has been still purifying, and hereupon almost always in the fire and the furnace; atheists and irreligious persons have took no small advantage from our changes. For in king Edward the sixth's time, the divine worship was twice altered in two new liturgies. In the first of queen Mary, the protestant religion was persecuted with fire and fagot, by law and public counsel of the same persons, who had so lately established it. Upon the coming in of queen Elizabeth, religion was changed again, and within a few days the public council of the nation made it death for a priest to convert any man to that religion, which before with so much eagerness of zeal had been restored. So that it is observed by an author, that in the space of twelve years there were four changes about religion made in England, and that by the public council and authority of the realm, which were more than were made by any Christian state throughout the world, so soon one after another, in the

space of fifteen hundred years before. Hence it is, that the enemies of God take occasion to blaspheme, and call our religion statism. And now adding to the former, those many changes that have happened since, I am afraid we shall not so easily claw off that name: nor, though we may satisfy our own consciences in what we profess, be able to repel and clear off the objections of the rational world about us, which, not being interested in our changes as we are, will not judge of them as we judge; but debate them by impartial reason, by the nature of the thing, the general practice of the church; against which, new lights, sudden impulses of the Spirit, extraordinary calls, will be but weak arguments to prove any thing but the madness of those that use them, and that the church must needs wither, being blasted with such inspirations. We see therefore how fatal and ridiculous innovations in the church are: and indeed when changes are so frequent, it is not properly religion, but fashion. This, I think, we may build upon as a sure ground, that where there is continual change, there is great show of uncertainty; and uncertainty in religion is a shrewd motive, if not to deny, yet to doubt of its truth.

Thus much for the first doctrine. I proceed now to the second, viz. That the next, and most effectual way to destroy religion, is to embase the teachers and dispensers of it. In the handling of this I shall show,

1. How the dispensers of religion, the ministers of the word, are embased or rendered vile.

2. How the embasing or vilifying them is a means to destroy religion.

1. For the first of these, the ministers and dispensers of the word are rendered base or vile two ways:

(1.) By divesting them of all temporal privileges and advantages, as inconsistent with their calling. It is strange, since the priest's office heretofore was always splendid, and almost regal, that it is now looked upon as a piece of religion, to make it low and sordid. So that the use of the word *minister* is brought down to the literal signification of it, *a servant:* for now *to serve* and *to minister, servile* and *ministerial,* are terms equivalent. But in the Old Testament the same word signifies *a priest,* and *a prince,* or *chief ruler:* hence, though we translate it *priest of On*, (Gen. xli. 45,) and *priest of Midian*, (Exod. iii. 1,) and *as it is with the people so with the priest*, Isa. xxiv. 2, Junius and Tremellius render all these places, not by *sacerdos*, priest, but by *præses*, that is, a prince, or at least a chief counsellor, or minister of state. And it is strange, that the name should be the same, when the nature of the thing is so exceeding different. The like also may be observed in other languages, that the most illustrious titles are derived from things sacred, and belonging to the worship of God. Σεβαστὸς was the title of the Christian Cæsars correspondent to the Latin *Augustus*, and it is derived from the same word that σέβασμα, *cultus*, *res sacra*, or *sacrificium*. And it is usual in our language to make *sacred* an epithet to *majesty;* there was a certain royalty in things sacred. Hence the Apostle, who, I think, was no enemy to the simplicity of the gospel, speaks of a *royal priesthood*, 1 Pet. ii. 9, which shows at least, that there is no contradiction or impiety in those terms. In old time, before the placing this office only in the line of Aaron, the head of the family and the first-born offered sacrifice for the rest; that is, was their priest. And we know, that such rule and dignity belonged at first to the masters of families, that they had *jus vitæ et necis*, jurisdiction and power of life and death in their own family; and from hence was derived the beginning of kingly government: a king being only a civil head, or master of a politic family, the whole people; so that we see the same was the foundation of the royal and sacerdotal dignity. As for the dignity of this office among the Jews, it is so pregnantly set forth in holy writ, that it is unquestionable. Kings and priests are still mentioned together: Lam. ii. 6, *The Lord hath despised in the indignation of his anger the king and the priest.* Hos. v. 1, *Hear, O priests, and give ear, O house of the king.* Deut. xvii. 12, *And the man that doth presumptuously, and will not hearken unto the priest that standeth there to minister before the Lord thy God, or unto the judge, even that man shall die.* Hence Paul, together with a blow, received this reprehension, Acts xxiii. 4, *Revilest thou God's high priest?* And Paul in the next verse does not defend himself, by pleading an extraordinary motion of the Spirit, or that he was sent to reform the church, and might therefore lawfully vilify the priesthood and all sacred orders; but in the 5th verse he makes an excuse, and that from ignorance, the only thing that could take away the fault; namely, *that he knew not that he was the high priest*, and subjoins a reason which further advances the truth here defended: *for it is written, Thou shalt not speak evil of the ruler of thy people.* To holy writ we might add the testimony of Josephus, of next authority to it in things concerning the Jews, who in sundry places of his history sets forth the dignity of the priests; and in his second book against Apion the grammarian has these words πάντων τῶν ἀμφισβητουμένων δικασταὶ οἱ ἱερεῖς ἐτάχθησαν, the priests were constituted judges of all doubtful causes. Hence Justin also in his 36th book has this: *Semper apud Judæos mos fuit, ut eosdem reges et sacerdotes haberent:* though this is false, that they were always so, yet it argues, that they were so frequently, and that the distance between them was not great. To the Jews we may join the Egyptians, the first masters of learning and philosophy. Synesius in his 57th epist. having shown the general practice of antiquity, ὁ πάλαι χρόνος ἤνεγκε τοὺς αὐτοὺς ἱερέας τε καὶ κριτὰς, gives an instance in the Jews and Egyptians, who for many ages ὑπὸ τῶν ἱερέων ἐβασιλεύθησαν, had no other kings but priests. Next, we may take a view of the practice of the Romans: Numa Pompilius, that civilized the fierce Romans, is reported in the first book of Livy sometimes to have performed the priest's office himself. *Tum sacerdotibus creandis animum adjecit, quanquam ipse plurima sacra obibat;* but when he made priests, he gave them a dignity almost the same with himself. And this honor continued together with the valor and prudence of that nation: for the success of the Romans did not extirpate their religion; the college of the priests being in many things exempted even from the jurisdiction of the senate, afterwards the supreme power. Hence Juvenal in his 2d Sat. mentions the priesthood of Mars, as one of the most honorable places in Rome. And Jul. Cæsar, who was chosen priest in his private condition, thought it not below him to continue the same office when he was created absolute governor of Rome, under the name of perpetual dictator. Add to these the practice of the Gauls mentioned by Cæsar in his 6th book *de Bello Gallico*, where he says of the Druids, who were their priests, that they did judge *de omnibus fere controversiis publicis privatisque.* See also Homer in the 1st book of his Iliad representing Chryses priest of Apollo, with his golden sceptre, as well as his golden censer. But why have I produced all these examples of the heathens? Is it to make these a ground of our imitation? No, but to show that the giving honor to the priesthood was a custom universal amongst all civilized nations. And whatsoever is universal is also natural, as not being founded upon compact, or the particular humors of men, but flowing from the native results of reason: and that which is natural neither does nor can oppose religion. But you will say, this concerns not us, who have an express rule and word revealed. Christ was himself poor and despised, and withal has instituted such a ministry. To the first part of this plea I answer, that Christ came to suffer, yet the sufferings and miseries of Christ do not oblige all Christians to undertake the like. For the second, that the ministry of Christ was low and despised by his institution, I utterly deny. It was so, indeed, by the malice and persecution of the heathen princes; but what does this argue or infer for a low, dejected ministry in a flourishing state, which professes to encourage Christianity? But to dash this cavil, read but the practice of Christian emperors and kings all along, down from the time of Constantine, in what respect, what honor and splendor they treated the ministers; and then let our adversaries produce their puny, pitiful arguments for the contrary, against the general, clear, undoubted vogue and current of all antiquity. As for two or three little countries about us, the learned and impartial will not value their practice; in one of which places the minister has been seen, for mere want, to mend shoes on the Saturday, and been heard to preach on the Sunday. In the other place, stating the several orders of the citizens, they place their ministers after their apothecaries; that is, the physician of the soul after the drugster of the body: a fit practice for those, who, if they were to rank things as well as persons, would place their religion after their trade.

And thus much concerning the first way of debasing the ministers and ministry.

(2.) The second way is by admitting ignorant, sordid, illiterate persons to this function. This is to give the royal stamp to a piece of lead. I confess, God has no need of any man's parts or learning; but certainly then, he has much less need of his ignorance and ill behavior. It is a sad thing, when all other employments shall empty themselves into the ministry: when men shall repair to it, not for preferment, but refuge; like malefactors flying to the altar, only to save their lives; or like those of Eli's race, (1 Sam. ii. 36,) that should come crouching, and seek to be put into the priest's office that they might eat a piece of bread. Heretofore there was required splendor of parentage to recommend any one to the priesthood, as Josephus witnesses in a treatise which he wrote of his own life; where he says, to have right to deal in things sacred, was, amongst them, accounted an argument of a noble and illustrious descent. God would not accept the offals of other professions. Doubtless many rejected Christ upon this thought, that he was the carpenter's son, who would have embraced him, had they known him to have been the son of David. The preferring underserving persons to this great service was eminently Jeroboam's sin, and how Jeroboam's practice and offense has been continued amongst us in another guise, is not unknown: for has not learning unqualified men for approbation to the ministry? have not parts and abilities been reputed enemies to grace, and qualities no ways ministerial? while friends, faction, well-meaning, and little understanding have been accomplishments beyond study and the university; and to falsify a story of conversion, beyond pertinent answers and clear resolutions to the hardest and most concerning questions. So that matters have been brought to this pass, that if a man amongst his sons had any blind, or disfigured, he laid him aside for the ministry; and such an one was presently approved, as having a mortified countenance. In short, it was a fiery furnace, which often approved dross, and rejected gold. But thanks be to God, those *spiritual wickednesses* are now discharged from *their high places.* Hence it was, that many rushed into the ministry, as being the only calling that they could profess without serving an apprenticeship. Hence also we had those that could preach sermons, but not defend them. The reason of which is clear, because the works and writings of learned men might be borrowed, but not the abilities. Had indeed the old Levitical hierarchy still continued, in which it was part of the ministerial office to flay the sacrifices, to cleanse the vessels, to scour the flesh-forks, to sweep the temple, and carry the filth and rubbish to the brook Kidron, no persons living had been fitter for the ministry, and to serve in this nature at the altar. But since it is made a labor of the mind; as to inform men's judgments, and move their affections, to resolve difficult places of scripture, to decide and clear off controversies; I can not see how to be a butcher, scavenger, or any other such trade, does at all qualify or prepare men for this work. But as unfit as they were, yet to clear a way for such into the ministry, we have had almost all sermons full of gibes and scoffs at human learning. Away with *vain philosophy, with the disputer of this world, and the enticing words of man's wisdom*, and set up the *foolishness of preaching, the simplicity of the gospel:* thus divinity has been brought in upon the ruins of humanity; by forcing the words of the scripture from the sense, and then haling them to the worst of drudgeries, to set a *jus divinum* upon ignorance and imperfection, and recommend natural weakness for supernatural grace. Hereupon the ignorant have took heart to venture upon this great calling, and instead of cutting their way to it, according to the usual course, through the knowledge of the tongues, the study of philosophy, school divinity, the fathers and councils, they have taken another and a shorter cut; and having read perhaps a treatise or two *upon the Heart, the bruised Reed, the Crumbs of Comfort,* Wollebius in English, and some other little authors, the usual furniture of old women's closets, they have set forth as accomplished divines, and forthwith they present themselves to the service; and there have not been wanting Jeroboams as willing to consecrate and receive them, as they to offer themselves. And this has been one of the most fatal and almost irrecoverable blows that has been given to the ministry.

And this may suffice concerning the second way of embasing God's ministers; namely, by intrusting the ministry with raw, unlearned, ill-bred persons; so that what Solomon speaks of a proverb in the mouth of a fool, the same may be said of the ministry vested in them, that it is like a *pearl in a swine's snout.*

2. I proceed now to the second thing proposed in the discussion of this doctrine, which is, to show how the embasing of the ministers tends to the destruction of religion.

This it does two ways.

(1.) Because it brings them under exceeding scorn and contempt; and then, let none think religion itself secure: for the vulgar have not such logical heads, as to be able to abstract such subtle conceptions as to separate the man from the minister, or to consider the same person under a double capacity, and so honor him as a divine, while they despise him as poor. But suppose they could, yet actions can not distinguish, as conceptions do; and therefore every act of contempt strikes at both, and unavoidably wounds the ministry through the sides of the minister. And we must know, that the least degree of contempt weakens religion, because it is absolutely contrary to the nature of it; religion properly consisting in a reverential esteem of things sacred. Now that which in any measure weakens religion, will at length destroy it: for the weakening of a thing is only a partial destruction of it. Poverty and meanness of condition expose the wisest to scorn, it being natural for men to place their esteem rather upon things great than good; and the poet observes, that this *infelix paupertas* has nothing in it more intolerable than this, that it renders men ridiculous. And then, how easy and natural it is for contempt to pass from the person to the office, from him that speaks, to the thing that he speaks of, experience proves: counsel being seldom valued so much for the truth of the thing, as the credit of him that gives it. Observe an excellent passage to this purpose in Eccles. ix. 14, 15. We have an account of a little city, with few men in it, besieged by a great and potent king, and in the 15th verse, we read, that *there was found in it a poor wise man, and he by his wisdom delivered the city.* A worthy service indeed, and certainly we may expect that some honorable recompense should follow it; a deliverer of his country, and that in such distress, could not but be advanced: but we find a contrary event in the next words of the same verse, *yet none remembered that same poor man.* Why, what should be the reason? Was he not a man of parts and wisdom? and is not wisdom honorable? Yes, but he was poor. But was he not also successful, as well as wise? True; but still he was poor: and once grant this, and you can not keep off that unavoidable sequel in the next verse, *the poor man's wisdom is despised, and his words are not heard.* We may believe it upon Solomon's word, who was rich as well as wise, and therefore knew the force of both: and probably, had it not been for his riches, the queen of Sheba would never have come so far only to have heard his wisdom. Observe her behavior when she came: though upon the hearing of Solomon's wisdom, and the resolution of her hard questions, she expressed a just admiration; yet when Solomon afterwards showed her his palace, his treasures, and the temple which he had built, 1 Kings x. 5, it is said, *there was no more spirit in her.* What was the cause of this? Certainly, the magnificence, the pomp and splendor of such a structure: it struck her into an ecstasy beyond his wise answers. She esteemed this as much above his wisdom, as astonishment is beyond bare admiration: she admired his wisdom, but she adored his magnificence. So apt is the mind, even of wise persons, to be surprised with the superficies, or circumstance of things, and value or undervalue spirituals, according to the manner of their external appearance. When circumstances fail, the substance seldom long survives: clothes are no part of the body; yet take away clothes, and the body will die. Livy observes of Romulus, that being to give laws to his new Romans, he found no better way to procure an esteem and reverence to them, than by first procuring it to himself by splendor of habit and retinue, and other signs of royalty. And the wise Numa, his successor, took the same course to enforce his religious laws, namely, by giving the same pomp to the priest, who was to dispense them. *Sacerdotem creavit, insignique eum veste, et curuli regia sella adornavit.* That is, he adorned him with a rich robe, and a royal chair of state. And in our judicatures, take away the trumpet, the scarlet, the attendance, and the lordship, which would be to make justice naked as well as blind, and the law would lose much of its terror, and consequently of its authority. Let the minister be abject and low, his interest inconsiderable, the word will suffer for his sake: the message will still find reception according to the dignity of the messenger. Imagine an ambassador presenting himself in a poor frieze jerkin and tattered clothes, certainly he would have but small audience, his embassy would speed rather according to the weakness of him that brought, than the majesty of him that sent it. It will fare alike with the ambassadors of Christ, the people will give them audience according to their presence. A notable example of which we have in the behavior of some to Paul himself, 2 Cor. x. 10. Hence in the Jewish church it was cautiously provided in the law, that none that was blind or lame, or had any remarkable defect in his body, was capable of the priestly office; because these things naturally make a person contemned, and this presently reflects upon the function. This therefore is the first way by which the low despised condition of the ministers tends to the destruction of the ministry and religion; namely, because it subjects their persons to scorn, and consequently their calling; and it is not imaginable that men will be brought to obey what they can not esteem.

(2.) The second way by which it tends to the ruin of the ministry is, because it discourages men of fit parts and abilities from undertaking it. And certain it is, that as the calling dignifies the man, so the man much more advances his calling: as a garment, though it warms the body, has a return with an advantage, being much more warmed by it. And how often a good cause may miscarry without a wise manager, and the faith for want of a defender, is, or at least may be known. It is not the truth of an assertion, but the skill of the disputant, that keeps off a baffle; not the justness of a cause, but the valor of the soldiers, that must win the field: when a learned Paul was converted, and undertook the ministry, it stopped the mouths of those that said, None but poor weak fishermen preached Christianity; and so his learning silenced the scandal, as well as strengthened the church. Religion, placed in a soul of exquisite knowledge and abilities, as in a castle, finds not only habitation, but defense. And what a learned foreign divine* said of the English preaching, may be said of all, *Plus est in artifice quam in arte.* So much of moment is there in the professors of any thing, to depress or raise the profession. What

* Gaspar Streso.

is it that kept the church of Rome strong, athletic, and flourishing for so many centuries, but the happy succession of the choicest wits engaged to her service by suitable preferments? And what strength, do we think, would that give to the true religion, that is able thus to establish a false? Religion in a great measure stands or falls according to the abilities of those that assert it. And if, as some observe, men's desires are usually as large as their abilities, what course have we took to allure the former, that we might engage the latter to our assistance? But we have took all ways to affright and discourage scholars from looking towards this sacred calling: for will men lay out their wit and judgment upon that employment, for the undertaking of which both will be questioned? Would men, not long since, have spent toilsome days and watchful nights, in the laborious quest of knowledge preparative to this work, at length to come and dance attendance for approbation upon a junto of petty tyrants, acted by party and prejudice, who denied fitness from learning, and grace from morality? Will a man exhaust his livelihood upon books, and his health, the best part of his life, upon study, to be at length thrust into a poor village, where he shall have his due precariously, and entreat for his own; and when he has it, live poorly and contemptibly upon it; while the same or less labor, bestowed upon any other calling, would bring not only comfort but splendor, not only maintenance but abundance? It is, I confess, the duty of ministers to endure this condition; but neither religion nor reason does oblige either them to approve, or others to choose it. Doubtless, parents will not throw away the towardness of a child, and the expense of education, upon a profession, the labor of which is increased, and the rewards of which are vanished: to condemn promising, lively parts to contempt and penury in a despised calling, what is it else but the casting of a Moses into the mud, or offering a son upon the altar; and instead of a priest, to make him a sacrifice? Neither let any here reply, that it becomes not a ministerial spirit to undertake such a calling for reward; for they must know, that it is one thing to undertake it for a reward, and not to be willing to undertake it without one. It is one thing to perform good works only that we may receive the recompense of them in heaven, and another thing not to be willing to follow Christ and forsake the world, if there were no such recompense. But besides, suppose it were the duty of scholars to choose this calling in the midst of all its discouragements; yet a prudent governor, who knows it to be his wisdom as well as his duty, to take the best course to advance religion, will not consider men's duty, but their practice; not what they ought to do, but what they use to do: and therefore draw over the best qualified to his service, by such ways as are most apt to persuade and induce men. Solomon built his temple with the tallest cedars: and surely, when God refused the defective and the maimed for sacrifice, we can not think that he requires them for the priesthood. When learning, abilities, and what is excellent in the world, forsake the church, we may easily foretell its ruin, without the gift of prophecy. And when ignorance succeeds in the place of learning, weakness in the room of judgment, we may be sure heresy and confusion will quickly come in the room of religion: for undoubtedly there is no way so effectual to betray the truth, as to procure it a weak defender.

Well now, instead of raising any particular uses from the point that has been delivered, let us make a brief recapitulation of the whole. Government, we see, depends upon religion, and religion upon the encouragement of those that are to dispense and assert it. For the further evidence of which truths, we need not travel beyond our own borders; but leave it to every one impartially to judge, whether from the very first day that our religion was unsettled, and church government flung out of doors, the civil government has ever been able to fix upon a sure foundation. We have been changing even to a proverb. The indignation of heaven has been rolling and turning us from one form to another, till at length such a giddiness seized upon government, that it fell into the very dregs of sectaries, who threatened an equal ruin both to minister and magistrate; and how the state has sympathized with the church is apparent. For have not our princes as well as our priests been of the lowest of the people? Have not cobblers, draymen, mechanics, governed, as well as preached? Nay, have not they by preaching come to govern? Was ever that of Solomon more verified, *that servants have rid, while princes and nobles have gone on foot?* But God has been pleased by a miracle of mercy to dissipate this confusion and chaos, and to give us some openings, some dawnings of liberty and settlement. But now, let not those who are to rebuild our Jerusalem think that the temple must be built last: for if there be such a thing as a God, and religion, as whether men believe it or no, they will one day find and feel, assuredly he will stop our liberty, till we restore him his worship. Besides, it is a senseless thing in reason, to think that one of these interests can stand without the other, when in the very order of natural causes, government is preserved by religion. But to return to Jeroboam with whom we first began. He laid the foundation of his government in destroying, though doubtless he colored it with the name of reforming God's worship; but see the issue. Consider him cursed by God, maintaining his usurped title by continual vexatious wars against the kings of Judah: smote in his prosperity, which was made like the dung upon the face of the earth, as low and vile as those priests whom he had employed: consider him branded, and made odious to all after-ages: and now, when his kingdom and glory was at an end, and he and his posterity rotting under ground, and his name stinking above it, judge what a worthy prize he made in getting of a kingdom, by destroying the church. Wherefore the sum of all is this: to advise and desire those whom it may concern, to consider Jeroboam's punishment, and then they will have little heart to Jeroboam's sin.

SERMON V.

A SERMON PREACHED AT LAMBETH CHAPEL ON THE 25TH OF NOVEMBER, 1666.

UPON THE CONSECRATION OF THE RIGHT REVEREND FATHER IN GOD DR. JOHN DOLBEN, LORD BISHOP OF ROCHESTER.

TO THE RIGHT REVEREND FATHER IN GOD JOHN, LORD BISHOP OF ROCHESTER, DEAN OF THE CATHEDRAL CHURCH OF WESTMINSTER, AND CLERK OF THE CLOSET TO HIS MAJESTY.

MY LORD,

THOUGH the interposal of my Lord of Canterbury's command for the publication of this mean discourse may seem so far to determine, as even to take away my choice; yet I must own it to the world, that it is solely and entirely my own inclination, seconded by my obligations to your Lordship, that makes this, that was so lately an humble attendant upon your Lordship's consecration, now ambitious to consecrate itself with your Lordship's name. It was my honor to have lived in the same college with your Lordship, and now to belong to the same cathedral, where at present you credit the church as much by your government, as you did the school formerly by your wit. Your Lordship even then grew up into a constant superiority above others; and all your after-greatness seems but a paraphrase upon those promising beginnings: for whatsoever you are, or shall be, has been but an easy prognostic from what you were. It is your Lordship's unhappiness to be cast upon an age in which the church is in its wane; and if you do not those glorious things that our English prelates did two or three hundred years since, it is not because your Lordship is at all less than they, but because the times are worse. Witness those magnificent buildings in Christ Church in Oxford, begun and carried on by your Lordship; when by your place you governed, and by your wisdom increased the treasure of that college: and, which must eternally set your fame above the reach of envy and detraction, these great structures you attempted at a time when you returned poor and bare, to a college as bare, after a long persecution, and before you had laid so much as one stone in the repairs of your own fortunes: by which incomparably high and generous undertaking, you have shown the world how fit a person you were to build upon Wolsey's foundation: a prelate whose great designs you imitate, and whose mind you equal. Briefly, that Christ Church stands so high above ground, and that the church of Westminster lies not flat upon it, is your Lordship's commendation. And therefore your Lordship is not behindhand with the church, paying it as much credit and support, as you receive from it; for you owe your promotion to your merit, and, I am sure, your merit to yourself. All men court you, not so much because a great person, as a public good. For, as a friend, there is none so hearty, so nobly warm and active to make good all the offices of that endearing relation; as a patron, none more able to oblige and reward your dependents, and, which is the crowning ornament of power, none more willing. And lastly, as a diocesan, you are like even to outdo yourself in all other capacities; and, in a word, to exemplify and realize every word of the following discourse: which is here most humbly and gratefully presented to your Lordship, by

Your Lordship's
most obliged servant,
ROBERT SOUTH.

From St. James's,
Dec. 3, 1666.

TITUS ii. 15. — *These things speak and exhort, and rebuke with all authority. Let no man despise thee.*

IT may possibly be expected, that the very taking of my text out of this epistle to Titus may engage me in a discourse about the nature, original, and divine right of episcopacy; and if it should, it were no more than what some of the greatest and the learnedest persons in the world (when men served truth instead of design) had done before: for I must profess, that I can not look upon Titus as so far unbishoped yet, but that he still exhibits to us all the essentials of that jurisdiction, which to this day is claimed for episcopal. We are told in the fifth verse of the first chapter, *that he was left in Crete to set things in order, and to ordain elders in every city;* which text one would think were sufficiently clear and full, and too big with evidence to be perverted: but when we have seen rebellion commented out of the thirteenth of the Romans; and since there are few things but admit of gloss and probability, and consequently may be expounded as well as disputed on both sides; it is no such wonder, that some would bear the world in hand, that the apostle's design and meaning is for presbytery, though his words are all the time for episcopacy: no wonder, I say, to us at least, who have conversed with too many strange unparalleled actions, occurrences, and events, now to wonder at any thing: wonder is from surprise; and surprise ceases upon experience.

I am not so much a friend to the stale starched formality of preambles, as to detain so great an audience with any previous discourse extrinsic to the subject matter and design of the text; and therefore I shall fall directly upon the words, which run in the form of an exhortation, though in appearance a very strange one; for the matter of an exhortation should be something naturally in the power of him to whom the exhortation is directed. For no man exhorts another to be strong, beautiful, witty, or the like; these are the felicities of some conditions, the object of more wishes, but the effects of no man's choice. Nor seems there any greater reason for the apostle's exhorting Titus, that no man should despise him; for how could another man's action be his duty? Was it in his power that men should not be wicked and injurious; and if such persons would despise him, could any thing pass an obligation upon him not to be despised? No, this can not be the meaning; and therefore it is clear that the exhortation lies not against the action itself, which is only in the despiser's power, but against the just occasion of it, which is in the will and power of him that is despised: it was not in Titus's power that men should not despise him, but it was in his power to bereave them of all just cause of doing so; it was not in his power not to be derided, but it was in his power not to be ridiculous.

In all this epistle it is evident that St. Paul looks upon Titus as advanced to the dignity of a prime ruler of the church, and intrusted with a large diocese, containing many particular churches under the immediate government of their respective elders; and those deriving authority from his ordination, as was specified in the fifth verse of the first chapter. And now looking upon Titus under this qualification, he addresses a long advice and instruction to him, for the discharge of so important a function, all along the first and second chapters; but sums up all in the last verse, which is the subject of the ensuing discourse, and contains in it these two things:

I. An account of the duties of his place or office.

II. Of the means to facilitate and make effectual their execution.

I. The duties of his place were two. 1. To teach. 2. To rule. Both comprised in these words: *These things speak and exhort, and rebuke with all authority.*

And then the means, the only means to make him successful, bright, and victorious in the performance of these great works, was to be above contempt, to shine like the Baptist, with a clear and a triumphant light. In a word, it is every bishop's duty to teach and to govern; and his way to do it is *not to be despised.*

We will discourse of each respectively in their order.

1. And first, for the first branch of the great work incumbent upon a church ruler, which is to teach. A work that none is too great or too high for; it is a work of charity, and charity is the work of heaven, which is always laying itself out upon the needy and the impotent: nay, and it is a work of the highest and the noblest charity; for he that teacheth another, gives an alms to his soul; he clothes the nakedness of his understanding, and relieves the wants of his impoverished reason: he indeed that governs well, leads the blind; but he that teaches, gives him eyes: and it is a glorious thing to have been the repairer of a decayed intellect, and a sub-worker to grace, in freeing it from some of the inconveniences of original sin. It is a benefaction that gives a man a kind of prerogative; for even in the common dialect of the world every teacher is called a master: it is the property of instruction to descend, and upon that very account, it supposes him that instructs, the superior, or at least makes him so.

To say a man is advanced too high to condescend to teach the ignorant, is as much as to say, that the sun is in too high a place to shine upon what is below it. The *sun* is said *to rule the day*, and the *moon to rule the night:* but do they not rule them only by enlightening them? Doctrine is that, that must prepare men for discipline; and men never go on so cheerfully, as when they see where they go.

Nor is the dullness of the scholar to extinguish, but rather to inflame the charity of the teacher: for since it is not in men as vessels, that the smallest capacity is the soonest filled; where the labor is doubled, the value of the work is enhanced; for it is a sowing where a man never expects to reap any thing but the comfort and conscience of having done virtuously. And yet we know moreover, that God sometimes converts even the dull and the slow, turning *very stones* into *sons of Abraham;* where besides that the difficulty of the conquest advances the trophy of the conqueror, it often falls out, that the backward learner makes amends another way, recompensing sure for sudden, expiating his want of docility with a deeper and a more rooted retention: which alone were argument sufficient to enforce the apostle's injunction of being *instant in season and out of season,* even upon the highest and most exalted ruler in the church. He that sits in Moses's chair, sits there to instruct, as well as to rule: and a general's office engages him to lead, as well as to command his army. In the first of Ecclesiastes, Solomon represents himself both as preacher and king of Israel: and every soul that a bishop gains is a new accession to the extent of his power; he preaches his jurisdiction wider, and enlarges his spiritual diocese, as he enlarges men's apprehensions.

The teaching part indeed of a Romish bishop is easy enough, whose grand business is only to teach men to be ignorant, to instruct them how to know nothing, or, which is all one, to know upon trust, to believe implicitly, and in a word, to see with other men's eyes, till they come to be lost in their own souls. But our religion is a religion that dares to be understood; that offers itself to the search of the inquisitive, to the inspection of the severest and the most awakened reason: for being secure of her substantial truth and purity, she knows, that for her to be seen and looked into, is to be embraced and admired: as there needs no greater argument for men to love the light, than to see it. It needs no legends, no service in an unknown tongue, no inquisition against scripture, no purging out the heart and sense of authors, no altering or bribing the voice of antiquity to speak for it; it needs none of all these laborious artifices of ignorance; none of all these cloaks and coverings. The Romish faith indeed must be covered, or it can not be kept warm, and their clergy deal with their religion as with a great crime; if it is discovered, they are undone. But there is no bishop of the church of England, but accounts it his interest, as well as his duty, to comply with this precept of the apostle Paul to Titus, *These things teach and exhort.*

Now this teaching may be effected two ways:

(1.) Immediately by himself.

(2.) Mediately by others.

And first, immediately by himself. Where God gives a talent, the episcopal robe can be no napkin to hide it in. Change of condition changes not the alilities of nature but makes them more illustrious in their exercise; and the episcopal dignity added to a good preaching faculty is like the erecting of a stately fountain upon a spring, which still, for all that, remains as much a spring as it was before, and flows as plentifully, only it flows with the circumstance of greater state and magnificence. Height of place is intended only to stamp the endowments of a private condition with lustre and authority: and, thanks be to God, neither the church's professed enemies, nor her pretended friends, have any cause to asperse her in this respect, she having over her such bishops as are able to silence the factious, no less by their preaching than by their authority.

But then, on the other hand, let me add also, that this is not so absolutely necessary, as to be of the vital constitution of this function. He may teach his diocese, who ceases to be able to preach to it: for he may do it by appointing teachers, and by a vigilant exacting from them the care and the instruction of their respective flocks. He is the spiritual father of his diocese; and a father may see his children taught, though he himself does not turn schoolmaster. It is not the gift of every person nor of every age, to harangue the multitude, to voice it high and loud, *et dominari in concionibus.* And since experience fits for government, and age usually brings experience, perhaps the most governing years are the least preaching years.

(2.) In the second place therefore, there is a teaching mediately, by the subordinate ministration of others; in which, since the action of the instrumental agent is, upon all grounds of reason, to be ascribed to the principal, he, who ordains and furnishes all his churches with able preachers, is an universal teacher; he instructs where he can not be present; he speaks in every mouth of his diocese; and every congregation of it every Sunday feels his influence, though it hears not his voice. That master deprives not his family of their food, who orders a faithful steward to dispense it. Teaching is not a flow of words, nor the draining of an hour-glass, but an effectual procuring, that a man comes to know something which he knew not before, or to know it better. And therefore eloquence and ability of speech is to a church governor, as Tully said it was to a philosopher; *Si afferatur, non repudianda; si absit, non magnopere desideranda:* and to find fault with such an one for not being a popular speaker, is to blame a painter for not being a good musician.

To teach indeed must be confessed his duty, but then there is a teaching by example, by authority, by restraining seducers, and so removing the hinderances of knowledge. And a bishop does his church, his prince and country, more service by ruling other men's tongues, than he can by employing his own. And thus much for the first branch of the great work belonging to a pastor of the church, which was to *teach and to exhort.*

2. The second is to rule, expressed in these words; *rebuke with all authority.* By which I doubt not but the apostle principally intends church censures; and so the words are a metonymy of the part for the whole, giving an instance in ecclesiastical censures, instead of all other ecclesiastical jurisdiction. A jurisdiction, which in the essentials of it is as old as Christianity, and even in those circumstantial additions of secular encouragement, with which the piety and wisdom of Christian princes always thought necessary to support it against the encroachments of the injurious world, much older and more venerable than any constitution that has divested the church of it.

But to speak directly to the thing before us; we see here the great apostle employing the utmost of his authority in commanding Titus to use his: and what he said to him, he says to every Christian bishop after him, *rebuke with all authority*. This authority is a spiritual sword put into the hands of every church ruler; and God put not this sword into his hands, with an intent that he should keep it there for no other purpose, but only for fashion sake, as men used to wear one by their sides. Government is an art above the attainment of an ordinary genius, and requires a wider, a larger, and a more comprehending soul than God has put into every body. The spirit which animates and acts the universe, is a spirit of government; and that ruler that is possessed of it, is the substitute and vicegerent of Providence, whether in church or state: every bishop is God's curate. Now the nature of government contains in it these three parts:

(1.) An exaction of duty from the persons placed under it.

(2.) A protection of them in the performance of their duty.

(3.) Coercion and animadversion upon such as neglect it. All which are, in their proportion, ingredients of that government which we call ecclesiastical.

(1.) And first, it implies exaction of duty from the persons placed under it: for it is both to be confessed and lamented, that men are not so ready to offer it, where it is not exacted: otherwise, what means the service of the church so imperfectly and by halves read over, and that by many who profess a conformity to the rules of the church? What makes them mince and mangle that in their practice, which they could swallow whole in their subscriptions? Why are the public prayers curtailed and left out, prayers composed with sobriety, and enjoined with authority, only to make the more room for a long, crude, impertinent, upstart harangue before the sermon?

Such persons seem to conform (the signification of which word they never make good) only that they may despise the church's injunctions under the church's wing, and contemn authority within the protection of the laws. Duty is but another English word for debt; and God knows, that it is well if men pay their debts when they are called upon. But if governors do not remind men of, and call them to obedience, they will find, that it will never come as a free-will offering, no not from many who even serve at the altar.

(2.) Government imports a protection and encouragement of the persons under it, in the discharge of their duty. It is not for a magistrate to frown upon, and browbeat those who are hearty and exact in the management of their ministry; and with a grave insignificant nod, to call a well-regulated and resolved zeal, want of prudence and moderation. Such discouraging of men in the ways of an active conformity to the church's rules is that, which will crack the sinews of government; for it weakens the hands and damps the spirits of the obedient. And if only scorn and rebuke shall attend men for asserting the church's dignity, and taxing the murder of kings, and the like; many will choose rather to neglect their duty safely and creditably, than to get a broken pate in the church's service, only to be rewarded with that which shall break their hearts too.

(3.) The third thing implied in government is coercion, and animadversion upon such as neglect their duty: without which coercive power all government is but toothless and precarious, and does not so much command as beg obedience. Nothing, I confess, is more becoming a Christian, of what degree soever, than meekness, candor, and condescension; but they are virtues that have their proper sphere and season to act and show themselves in, and consequently not to interfere with others, different indeed in their nature, but altogether as necessary in their use. And when an insolent despiser of discipline, nurtured into impudence and contempt of all order by a long risk of license and rebellion, shall appear before a church governor, severity and resolution are that governor's virtues, and justice itself is his mercy; for by making such an one an example, (as much as in him lies,) he will either cure him, or at least preserve others.

Were indeed the consciences of men as they should be, the censures of the church might be a sufficient coercion upon them; but being, as most of them nowadays are, hell and damnation proof, her bare anathemas fall but like so many *bruta fulmina* upon the obstinate and schismatical; who are like to think themselves shrewdly hurt (forsooth) by being cut off from that body, which they choose not to be of; and so being punished into a quiet enjoyment of their beloved separation. Some will by no means allow the church any further power than only to exhort and to advise; and this but with a proviso too, that it extends not to such as think themselves too wise and too great to be advised; according to the hypothesis of which persons, the authority of the church, and the obliging force of all church sanctions, can bespeak men only thus: These and these things it is your duty to do, and if you will not do them, you may as well let them alone. A strict and efficacious constitution indeed, which invests the church with no power at all, but where men will be so very civil as to obey it, and so at the same time pay it a duty, and do it a courtesy too.

But when in the judgment of some men the spiritual function, as such, must render a churchman, though otherwise never so discreet and qualified, yet merely because he is a churchman, unfit to be intrusted by his prince with a share of that power and jurisdiction, which in many circumstances his prince has judged but too necessary to secure the affairs and dignity of the church; and which every thriving grazier can think himself but ill dealt with, if within his own country he is not mounted to: it is a sign, that such discontented persons intend not that religion shall advise them upon any other terms, than that they may ride and govern their religion.

But surely, all our kings and our parliaments understood well enough what they did, when they thought fit to prop and fortify the spiritual order with some power that was temporal; and such is the present state of the world, in the judgment of any observing eye, that if the bishop has no other defensatives but excommunication, no other power but that of the keys, he may, for any notable effect that he is like to do upon the factious and contumacious, surrender up his pastoral staff, shut up the church, and put those keys under the door.

And thus I have endeavored to show the three things included in the general nature of government; but to prescribe the manner of it in particular is neither in my power nor inclination: only, I suppose, the common theory and speculation of things is free and open to any one whom God has sent into the world with some ability to contemplate, and by continuing him in the world, gives him also opportunity.

In all that has been said, I do not in the least pretend to advise, or chalk out rules to my superiors; for some men can not be fools with so good acceptance as others. But whosoever is called to speak upon a certain occasion, may, I conceive, without offense, take any text suitable to that occasion, and having taken it, may, or at least ought, to speak suitably to that text.

II. I proceed now to the second thing proposed from the words, which is the means assigned for the discharge of the duties mentioned, and exhibited under this one short prescription, *Let no man despise thee:* in the handling of which I shall show,

1. The ill effects and destructive influence that contempt has upon government.

2. The groundless causes upon which church rulers are frequently despised.

3. And lastly, the just causes that would render them, or indeed any other rulers, worthy to be despised. All which being clearly made out, and impartially laid before our eyes, it will be easy and obvious for every one, by avoiding the evil so marked out, to answer and come up to the apostle's exhortation. And,

1. We will discourse of contempt, and the malign hostile influence it has upon government. As for the thing itself, every man's experience will inform him, that there is no action in the behavior of one man towards another, of which human nature is more impatient than of contempt, it being a thing made up of these two ingredients, an undervaluing of a man upon a belief of his utter uselessness and inability, and a spiteful endeavor to engage the rest of the world in the same belief and slight esteem of him. So that the immediate design of contempt is the shame of the person contemned; and shame is a banishment of him from the good opinion of the world, which every man most earnestly desires, both upon a principle of nature and of interest. For it is natural to all men to affect a good name; and he that despises a man, libels him in his thoughts, reviles and traduces him in his judgment. And there is also interest in the case; for a desire to be well thought of, directly resolves itself into that owned and mighty principle of self-preservation: forasmuch

as thoughts are the first wheels and motives of action, and there is no long passage from one to the other. He that thinks a man to the ground, will quickly endeavor to lay him there; for while he despises him, he arraigns and condemns him in his heart; and the after-bitterness and cruelties of his practices are but the executioners of the sentence passed before upon him by his judgment. Centempt, like the planet Saturn, has first an ill aspect, and then a destroying influence.

By all which, I suppose, it is sufficiently proved how noxious it must needs be to every governor: for, can a man respect the person whom he despises? and can there be obedience, where there is not so much as respect? Will the knee bend, while the heart insults? and the actions submit, while the apprehensions rebel? And therefore the most experienced disturbers and underminers of government have always laid their first train in contempt, endeavoring to blow it up in the judgment and esteem of the subject. And was not this method observed in the late most flourishing and successful rebellion? For, how studiously did they lay about them, both from the pulpit and the press, to cast a slur upon the king's person, and to bring his governing abilities under a disrepute? And then after they had sufficiently blasted him in his personal capacity, they found it easy work to dash and overthrow him in his political.

Reputation is power, and consequently to despise is to weaken. For where there is contempt, there can be no awe; and where there is no awe, there will be no subjection; and if there is no subjection, it is impossible, without the help of the former distinction of a politic capacity, to imagine how a prince can be a governor. He that makes his prince despised and undervalued, blows a trumpet against him in men's breasts, beats him out of his subjects' hearts, and fights him out of their affections; and after this, he may easily strip him of his other garrisons, having already dispossessed him of his strongest, by dismantling him of his honor, and seizing his reputation.

Nor is what has been said of princes less true of all other governors, from highest to lowest, from him that heads an army, to him that is master of a family, or of one single servant; the formal reason of a thing equally extending itself to every particular of the same kind. It is a proposition of eternal verity, that none can govern while he is despised. We may as well imagine that there may be a king without majesty, a supreme without sovereignty. It is a paradox, and a direct contradiction in practice; for where contempt takes place, the very causes and capacities of government cease.

Men are so far from being governed by a despised person, that they will not so much as be taught by him. Truth itself shall lose its credit, if delivered by a person that has none. As on the contrary, be but a person in vogue and credit with the multitude, he shall be able to commend and set off whatsoever he says, to authorize any nonsense, and to make popular, rambling, incoherent stuff (seasoned with twang and tautology) pass for high rhetoric and moving preaching; such indeed as a zealous tradesman would even live and die under. And now, I suppose, it is no ill topic of argumentation, to show the prevalence of contempt, by the contrary influences of respect; which thus (as it were) dubs every little, petit, admired person, lord and commander of all his admirers. And certain it is, that the ecclesiastical, as well as the civil governor, has cause to pursue the same methods of securing and confirming himself; the grounds and means of government being founded upon the same bottom of nature in both, though the circumstances and relative considerations of the persons may differ. And I have nothing to say more upon this head, but that if churchmen are called upon to discharge the parts of governors, they may with the highest reason expect those supports and helps that are indispensably requisite thereunto; and that those men are but trepanned, who are called to govern, being invested with authority, but bereaved of power; which, according to a true and plain estimate of things, is nothing else but to mock and betray them into a splendid and magisterial way of being ridiculous. And thus much for the ill effects and destructive influence that contempt has upon government.

2. I pass now to the second thing, which is to show the groundless causes, upon which church rulers are frequently despised.

Concerning which, I shall premise this: that nothing can be a reasonable ground of despising a man, but some fault or other chargeable upon him; and nothing can be a fault that is not naturally in a man's power to prevent; otherwise, it is a man's unhappiness, his mischance, or calamity, but not his fault. Nothing can justly be despised, that can not justly be blamed: and it is a most certain rule in reason and moral philosophy, that where there is no choice, there can be no blame.

This premised, we may take notice of two usual grounds of the contempt men cast upon the clergy, and yet for which no man ought to think himself at all the more worthy to be contemned.

(1.) The first is their very profession itself; concerning which it is a sad, but an experimented truth, that the names derived from it, in the refined language of the present age, are made but the appellatives of scorn. This is not charged universally upon all, but experience will affirm, or rather proclaim it of much the greater part of the world; and men must persuade us that we have lost our hearing and our common sense, before we can believe the contrary. But surely, the bottom and foundation of this behavior towards persons set apart for the service of God, that this very relation should entitle them to such a peculiar scorn, can be nothing else but atheism, the growing rampant sin of the times.

For call a man oppressor, griping, covetous, or overreaching person, and the word indeed, being ill befriended by custom, perhaps sounds not well, but generally, in the apprehension of the hearer, it signifies no more than that such an one is a wise and a thriving, or, in the common phrase, a notable man; which will certainly procure him a respect: and say of another, that he is an epicure, a loose, or a vicious man, and it leaves in men no other opinion of him than that he is a merry, pleasant, and a genteel person, and that he that taxes him is but a pedant, an unexperienced and a morose fellow; one that does not know men, nor understand what it is to eat and drink well: but call a man priest or parson, and you set him, in some men's esteem, ten degrees below his own servant.

But let us not be discouraged or displeased, either with ourselves or our profession, upon this account. Let the virtuosos mock, insult, and despise on: yet after all, they shall never be able to droll away the nature of things; to trample a pearl into a pebble, nor to make sacred things contemptible, any more than themselves, by such speeches, honorable.

(2.) Another groundless cause of some men's despising the governors of our church is their loss of that former grandeur and privilege that they enjoyed. But it is no real disgrace to the church merely to lose her privileges, but to forfeit them by her fault or misdemeanor, of which she is not conscious. Whatsoever she enjoyed in this kind, she readily acknowledges to have streamed from the royal munificence, and the favors of the civil power shining upon the spiritual; which favors the same power may retract and gather back into itself, when it pleases. And we envy not the greatness and lustre of the Romish clergy; neither their scarlet gowns nor their scarlet sins. If our church can not be great; which is better, she can be humble, and content to be reformed into as low a condition as men for their own private advantage would have her; who wisely tell her, that it is best and safest for her to be without any power or temporal advantage; like the good physician, who out of tenderness to his patient, lest he should hurt himself by drinking, was so kind as to rob him of his silver cup. The church of England glories in nothing more, than that she is the truest friend to kings and to kingly government of any other church in the world; that they were the same hands and principles that took the crown from the king's head, and the mitre from the bishops. It is indeed the happiness of some professions and callings, that they can equally square themselves to, and thrive under all revolutions of government: but the clergy of England neither know nor affect that happiness, and are willing to be despised for not doing so. And so far is our church from encroaching upon the civil power, as some, who are back-friends to both, would maliciously insinuate, that, were it stripped of the very remainder of its privileges, and made as like the primitive church for its bareness, as it is already for its purity, it could cheerfully, and, what is more, loyally, want all such privileges; and in the want of them pray heartily that the civil power may flourish as much, and stand as secure from the assaults of fanatic, antimonarchical principles, (grown to such a dreadful height during the church's late confusions,) as it stood while the church enjoyed those privileges. And thus much for the two groundless causes upon which church rulers are frequently despised. I descend now to the

3. And last thing, which is to show those just causes, that would render them, or indeed any other rulers, worthy to be despised. Many might be assigned, but I shall pitch only upon four; in discoursing of which, rather the time than the subject will force me to be very brief.

(1.) And the first is ignorance. We know how great an absurdity our Saviour accounted it, *for the blind to lead the blind;* and to put him that can not so much as see, to discharge the office of a watch. Nothing more exposes to contempt than ignorance. When Samson's eyes were out, of a public magistrate he was made a public sport. And when Eli was blind, we know how well he governed his sons, and how well they governed the church under him. But now the blindness of the understanding is greater and more scandalous; especially in such a seeing age as ours; in which the very knowledge of former times passes but for ignorance in a better dress: an age that flies at all learning, and inquires into every thing, but especially into faults and defects. Ignorance indeed, so far as it may be resolved into natural inability, is, as to men, at least, inculpable; and consequently, not the object of scorn, but pity; but in a governor, it can not be without the conjunction of the highest impudence: for who bid such an one aspire to teach and to govern? A blind man sitting in the chimney-corner is pardonable enough, but sitting at the helm he is intolerable. If men will be ignorant and illiterate, let them be so in private, and to themselves, and not set their defects in an high place, to make them visible and conspicuous. If owls will not be hooted at, let them keep close within the tree, and not perch upon the upper boughs.

(2.) A second thing that makes a governor justly despised, is viciousness and ill morals. Virtue is that which must tip the preacher's tongue and the ruler's sceptre with authority.

And therefore with what a controlling overpowering force did our Saviour tax the sins of the Jews, when he ushered in his rebukes of them with that high assertion of himself, *Who is there amongst you, that convinces me of sin?* Otherwise we may easily guess with what impatience the world would have heard an incestuous Herod discoursing of chastity, a Judas condemning covetousness, or a Pharisee preaching against hypocrisy: every word must have recoiled upon the speaker. Guilt is that which quells the courage of the bold, ties the tongue of the eloquent, and makes greatness itself sneak and lurk, and behave itself poorly. For, let a vicious person be in never so high command, yet still he will be looked upon but as one great vice, empowered to correct and chastise others. A corrupt governor is nothing else but a reigning sin: and a sin in office may command any thing but respect. No man can be credited by his place or power, who by his virtue does not first credit that.

(3.) A third thing that makes a governor justly despised, is fearfulness of, and mean compliances with bold, popular offenders. Some indeed account it the very spirit of policy and prudence, where men refuse to come up to a law, to make the law come down to them. And for their so doing, have this infallible recompense, that they are not at all the more loved, but much the less feared; and, which is a sure consequent of it, accordingly respected. But believe it, it is a resolute, tenacious adherence to well chosen principles that adds glory to greatness, and makes the face of a governor shine in the eyes of those that see and examine his actions. Disobedience, if complied with, is infinitely encroaching, and having gained one degree of liberty upon indulgence, will demand another upon claim. Every vice interprets a connivance and approbation.

Which being so, is it not an enormous indecency, as well as a gross impiety, that any one who owns the name of a divine, hearing a great sinner brave it against Heaven, talk atheistically, and scoff profanely at that religion by which he owns an expectation to be saved, if he cares to be saved at all, should, instead of vindicating the truth to the blasphemer's teeth, think it discretion and moderation (forsooth) with a complying silence, and perhaps a smile to boot, tacitly to approve, and strike in with the scoffer, and so go sharer both in the mirth and guilt of his profane jests?

But let such an one be assured, that even that blasphemer himself would inwardly reverence him, if rebuked by him; as, on the contrary, he in his heart really despises him for his cowardly, base silence. If any one should reply here, that the times and manners of men will not bear such a practice, I confess that it is an answer, from the mouth of a professed time-server, very rational: but as for that man that is not so, let him satisfy himself of the reason, justice, and duty of an action, and leave the event of it to God, who will never fail those who do not think themselves too wise to trust him. For, let the worst come to the worst, a man in so doing would be ruined more honorably than otherwise preferred.

(4.) And lastly. A fourth thing that makes a governor justly despised, is a proneness to despise others. There is a kind of respect due to the meanest person, even from the greatest; for it is the mere favor of Providence, that he, who is actually the greatest, was not the meanest. A man can not cast his respects so low, but they will rebound and return upon him. What Heaven bestows upon the earth in kind influences and benign aspects, is paid it back again in sacrifice, incense, and adoration. And surely, a great person gets more by obliging his inferior, than he can by disdaining him; as a man has a greater advantage by sowing and dressing his ground, than he can have by trampling upon it. It is not to insult and domineer, to look disdainfully, and revile imperiously, that procures an esteem from any one; it will indeed make men keep their distance sufficiently, but it will be distance without reverence.

And thus I have shown four several causes that may justly render any ruler despised; and by the same work, I hope, have made it evident, how little cause men have to despise the rulers of our church.

God is the fountain of honor; and the conduit by which he conveys it to the sons of men, are virtuous and generous practices. But as for us, who have more immediately and nearly devoted both our persons and concerns to his service, it were infinitely vain to expect it upon any other terms. Some indeed may please and promise themselves high matters, from full revenues, stately palaces, court-interests, and great dependences: but that which makes the clergy glorious, is to be knowing in their profession, unspotted in their lives, active and laborious in their charges, bold and resolute in opposing seducers, and daring to look vice in the face, though never so potent and illustrious; and lastly, to be gentle, courteous, and compassionate to all.

These are our robes and our maces, our escutcheons, and highest titles of honor: for by all these things God is honored, who has declared this the eternal rule and standard of all honor derivable upon men, that *those who honor him, shall be honored by him.*

To which God, fearful in praises, and working wonders, be rendered and ascribed as is most due, all praise, might, majesty, and dominion, both now and for evermore. Amen.

SERMON VI.

JOHN vii. 17.—*If any man will do his will, he shall know of the doctrine, whether it be of God, or whether I speak of myself.*

WHEN God was pleased to new-model the world by the introduction of a new religion, and that in the room of one set up by himself, it was requisite that he should recommend it to the reasons of men with the same authority and evidence that enforced the former; and that a religion established by God himself should not be displaced by any thing under a demonstration of that divine power that first introduced it. And the whole Jewish economy, we know, was brought in with miracles; the law was writ and confirmed by the same almighty hand: the whole universe was subservient to its promulgation: the signs of Egypt and the Red Sea; fire and a voice from heaven; the heights of the one, and the depths of the other; so that, as it were, from the top to the bottom of nature there issued forth one universal united testimony of the divinity of the Mosaic law and religion. And this stood in the world for the space of two thousand years; till at length, in the fullness of time, the reason of men ripening to such a pitch as to be above the pedagogy of Moses's rod, and the discipline of types, God thought fit to display the substance without the shadow, and to read the world a lecture of an higher and more sublime religion in Christianity. But the Jewish was yet in possession, and therefore that this might so enter as not to intrude, it was to bring its warrant from the same hand of omnipotence. And for this cause, Christ, that he might not make either a suspected or precarious address to men's understandings, outdoes Moses before he displaces him; shows an ascendant spirit above him, raises the dead, and cures more plagues than he brought upon Egypt, casts out devils, and heals the deaf, speaking such words, as even gave ears to hear them; cures the blind and the lame, and makes the very dumb to speak for the truth of his doctrine. But what was the result of all this? Why, some look upon him as an impostor and a conjurer, as an agent for Beelzebub, and therefore reject his gospel, hold fast their law, and will not let Moses give place to the magician.

Now the cause that Christ's doctrine was rejected must of necessity be one of these two. 1. An insufficiency in the arguments brought by Christ to enforce it. Or, 2. An indisposition in the persons, to whom this doctrine was addressed, to receive it.

And for this, Christ, who had not only an infinite power to work miracles, but also an equal wisdom both to know the just force and measure of every argument or motive to persuade or cause assent; and withal, to look through and through all the dark corners of the soul of man, all the windings and turnings, and various workings of his faculties; and to discern how and by what means they are to be wrought upon; and what prevails upon them, and what does not: he, I say, stakes the whole matter upon this issue; that the arguments by which his doctrine addressed itself to the minds of men, were proper, adequate, and sufficient to compass their respective ends in persuading or convincing the persons to whom they were proposed: and, moreover, that there was no such defect in the natural light of man's understanding, or knowing faculty; but that, considered in itself, it would be apt enough to close with, and yield its assent to, the evidence of those arguments duly offered to and laid before it. And yet, that, after all this, the event proved otherwise; and that, notwithstanding both the weight and fitness of the arguments to persuade, and the light of man's intellect to meet this persuasive evidence with a suitable assent, no assent followed, nor were men thereby actually persuaded; he charges it wholly upon the corruption, the perverseness, and viciosity of man's will, as the only cause that rendered all the arguments, his doctrine came clothed with, unsuccessful. And consequently he affirms here in the text, that men must love the truth before they throughly believe it; and that the gospel has then only a free admission into the assent of the understanding, when it brings a passport from a rightly disposed will, as being the great faculty of dominion, that commands all, that shuts out and lets in what objects it pleases, and, in a word, keeps the keys of the whole soul.

This is the design and purport of the words, which I shall draw forth and handle in the prosecution of these four following heads:

I. I shall show, what the doctrine of Christ was that the world so much stuck at and was so averse from believing.

II. I shall show, that men's unbelief of it was from no defect or insufficiency in the arguments brought by Christ to enforce it.

III. I shall show, what was the true and proper cause into which this unbelief was resolved.

IV. And, lastly, I shall show, that a pious and well disposed mind, attended with a readiness to obey the known will of God, is the surest and best means to enlighten the understanding to a belief of Christianity.

Of these in their order; and,

First, for the doctrine of Christ. We must take it in the known and common division of it, into matters of belief, and matters of practice.

The matters of belief related chiefly to his person and offices. As, That he was the Messias that should come into the world: the eternal son of God, begotten of him before all worlds: that in time he was made man, and born of a pure virgin: that he should die and satisfy for the sins of the world; and that he should rise again from the dead, and ascend into heaven; and there sitting at the right hand of God, hold the government of the whole world, till the great and last day; in which he should judge both the quick and the dead, raised to life again with the very same bodies; and then deliver up all rule and government into the hands of his Father. These were the great articles and *credenda* of Christianity that so much startled the world, and seemed to be such as not only brought in a new religion amongst men, but also required new reason to embrace it.

The other part of his doctrine lay in matters of practice; which we find contained in his several sermons, but principally in that glorious, full, and admirable discourse upon the mount, recorded in the 5th, 6th, and 7th chapters of St. Matthew. All which particulars if we would reduce to one general comprehensive head, they are all wrapt up in the doctrine of self-denial,* prescribing to the world the most inward purity of heart, and a constant conflict with all our sensual appetites and worldly interests, even to the quitting of all that is dear to us, and the sacrificing of life itself, rather than knowingly to omit the least duty, or commit the least sin. And this was that which grated harder upon, and raised greater tumults and boilings in the hearts of men, than the strangeness and seeming unreasonableness of all the former articles, that took up chiefly in speculation and belief.

And that this was so, will appear from a consideration of the state and condition the world was in, as to religion, when Christ promulged his doctrine. Nothing further than the outward action was then looked after, and when that failed, there was an expiation ready in the *opus operatum* of a sacrifice. So that all their virtue and religion lay in their folds and their stalls, and what was wanting in the innocence, the blood of lambs was to supply. The Scribes and Pharisees, who were the great doctors of the Jewish church, expounded the law no further. They accounted no man a murderer, but he that struck a knife into his brother's heart: no man an adulterer, but he that actually defiled his neighbor's bed. They thought it no injustice nor irreligion to prosecute the severest retaliation or revenge; so that at the same time their outward man might be a saint, and their inward man a devil. No care at all was had to curb the unruliness of anger, or the exorbitance of desire. Amongst all their sacrifices, they never sacrificed so much as one lust. Bulls and goats bled apace, but neither the violence of the one, nor the wantonness of the other, ever died a victim at any of their altars. So that no wonder, that a doctrine that arraigned the irregularities of the most inward motions and affections of the soul, and told men that anger and harsh words were murder, and looks and desires, adultery; that a man might stab with his tongue, and assassinate with his mind, pollute himself with a

* See Sermon on Matth. x. 33, *ante*, p. 42.

glance, and forfeit eternity by a cast of his eye: no wonder, I say, that such a doctrine made a strange bustle and disturbance in the world, which then sat warm and easy in a free enjoyment of their lusts; ordering matters so, that they put a trick upon the great rule of virtue, the law, and made a shift to think themselves guiltless, in spite of all their sins; to break the precept, and at the same time to baffle the curse; contriving to themselves such a sort of holiness as should please God and themselves too, justify and save them harmless, but never sanctify nor make them better.

But the severe notions of Christianity turned all this upside down, filling all with surprise and amazement: they came upon the world, like light darting full upon the face of a man asleep, who had a mind to sleep on, and not to be disturbed: they were terrible astonishing alarms to persons grown fat and wealthy by a long and successful imposture; by suppressing the true sense of the law, by putting another veil upon Moses; and, in a word, persuading the world, that men might be honest and religious, happy and blessed, though they never denied nor mortified one of their corrupt appetites.

And thus much for the first thing proposed; which was to give you a brief draught of the doctrine of Christ, that met with so little assent from the world in general, and from the Jews in particular. I come now to the

Second thing proposed: which was to show, That men's unbelief of Christ's doctrine was from no defect or insufficiency in the arguments brought by Christ to enforce it. This I shall make appear two ways:

1. By showing, that the arguments spoken of were in themselves convincing and sufficient.

2. By showing, that upon supposition they were not so, yet their insufficiency was not the cause of their rejection.

And, first, for the first of these: That the arguments brought by Christ for the confirmation of his doctrine were in themselves convincing and sufficient. I shall insist only upon the convincing power of the two principal. One from the prophecies recorded concerning him; the other from the miracles done by him. Of both very briefly. And for the former. There was a full entire harmony and consent of all the divine predictions receiving their completion in Christ. The strength of which argument lies in this, that it evinces the divine mission of Christ's person, and thereby proves him to be the Messias; which by consequence proves and asserts the truth of his doctrine. For he that was so sent by God, could declare nothing but the will of God. And so evidently do all the prophecies agree to Christ, that I dare with great confidence affirm, that if the prophecies recorded of the Messiah are not fulfilled in Jesus of Nazareth, it is impossible to know or distinguish when a prophecy is fulfilled and when not, in any thing or person whatsoever; which would utterly evacuate the use of them. But in Christ they all meet with such an invincible lustre and evidence, as if they were not predictions, but after-relations; and the penmen of them not prophets, but evangelists. And now, can any kind of ratiocination allow Christ all the marks of the Messiah, and yet deny him to be the Messiah? Could he have all the signs, and yet not be the thing signified? Could the shadows that followed him, and were cast from him, belong to any other body? All these things are absurd and unnatural; and therefore the force of this argument was undeniable.

Nor was that other from the miracles done by him at all inferior. The strength and force of which, to prove the things they are alleged for, consists in this, that a miracle being a work exceeding the power of any created agent, and consequently being an effect of the divine omnipotence, when it is done to give credit and authority to any word or doctrine declared to proceed from God, either that doctrine must really proceed from God as it is declared, or God by that work of his almighty power must bear witness to a falsehood, and so bring the creature under the greatest obligation that can possibly engage the assent of a rational nature, to believe and assent to a lie. For surely a greater reason than this can not be produced for the belief of any thing than for a man to stand up and say, This and this I tell you as the mind and word of God; and to prove that it is so, I will do that before your eyes, that you yourselves shall confess can be done by nothing but the almighty power of that God that can neither deceive nor be deceived. Now if this be an irrefragable way to convince, as the reason of all mankind must confess it to be, then Christ's doctrine came attended and enforced with the greatest means of conviction imaginable. Thus much for the argument *in thesi:* and then for the assumption that Christ did such miraculous and supernatural works to confirm what he said, we need only repeat the message sent by him to John the Baptist; *that the dumb spake, the blind saw, the lame walked, and the dead were raised.* Which particulars none of his bitterest enemies ever pretended to deny, they being conveyed to them by an evidence past all exception, even the evidence of sense; nay of the quickest, the surest, and most authentic of all the senses, the sight: which if it be not certain in the reports and representations it makes of things to the mind, there neither is, nor can be naturally, any such thing as certainty or knowledge in the world. And thus much for the first part of the second general thing proposed; namely, That the arguments brought by Christ for the proof of his doctrine were in themselves convincing and sufficient.

I come now to the other part of it, which is to show, That admitting or supposing that they were not sufficient, yet their insufficiency was not the cause of their actual rejection. Which will appear from these following reasons:

(1.) Because those who rejected Christ's doctrine, and the arguments by which he confirmed it, fully believed and assented to other things conveyed to them with less evidence. Such as were even the miracles of Moses himself, upon the credit and authority of which stood the whole economy of the Jewish constitution. For though I grant that they believed his miracles upon the credit of constant unerring tradition, both written and unwritten, and grant also that such tradition was of as great certainty as the reports of sense, yet still I affirm that it was not of the same evidence, which yet is the greatest and most immediate ground of all assent.

The evidence of sense (as I have noted) is the clearest that naturally the mind of man can receive, and is indeed the foundation both of all the evidence and certainty too, that tradition is capable of; which pretends to no other credibility from the testimony and word of some men, but because their word is at length traced up to, and originally terminates in, the sense and experience of some others, which could not be known beyond that compass of time in which it was exercised, but by being told and reported to such as, not living at that time, saw it not, and by them to others, and so down from one age to another. For we therefore believe the report of some men concerning a thing, because it implies that there were some others who actually saw that thing. It is clear therefore, that want of evidence could not be the cause that the Jews rejected and disbelieved the gospel, since they embraced and believed the law, upon the credit of those miracles that were less evident. For those of Christ they knew by sight and sense, those of Moses only by tradition; which, though equally certain, yet were by no means equally evident with the other.

(2.) They believed and assented to things that were neither evident nor certain, but only probable; for they conversed, they traded, they merchandized, and, by so doing, frequently ventured their whole estates and fortunes upon a probable belief or persuasion of the honesty and truth of those whom they dealt and corresponded with. And interest, especially in worldly matters, and yet more especially with a Jew, never proceeds but upon supposal, at least, of a firm and sufficient bottom: from whence it is manifest, that, since they could believe and practically rely upon, and that even in their dearest concerns, bare probabilities, they could not with any color of reason pretend want of evidence for their disbelief of Christ's doctrine, which came enforced with arguments far surpassing all such probabilities.

(3.) They believed and assented to things neither evident nor certain, nor yet so much as probable, but actually false and fallacious. Such as were the absurd doctrines and stories of their rabbins: which, though since Christ's time they have grown much more numerous and fabulous than before, yet even then did so much pester the church, and so grossly abuse and delude the minds of that people, that contradictions themselves asserted by rabbies were equally received and revered by them as the sacred and infallible word of God. And whereas they rejected Christ and his doctrine, though every tittle of it came enforced with miracle, and the best arguments that heaven and earth could back it with, yet Christ then foretold, and after-times confirmed that prediction of his in John v. 43, that they should receive many cheats and deceivers coming to them in their own name:

fellows that set up for Messias's only upon their own heads, without pretending to any thing singular or miraculous, but impudence and imposture.

From all which it follows, that the Jews could not allege so much as a pretense of the want of evidence in the argument brought by Christ to prove the divinity and authority of his doctrine, as a reason of their rejection and disbelief of it; since they embraced and believed many things, for some of which they had no evidence, and for others of which they had no certainty, and for most of which they had not so much as probability. Which being so, from whence then could such an obstinate infidelity, in matters of so great clearness and credibility, take its rise? Why, this will be made out to us in the

Third thing proposed, which was to show, What was the true and proper cause into which this unbelief of the Pharisees was resolved. And that was, in a word, the captivity of their wills and affections to lusts directly opposite to the design and spirit of Christianity. They were extremely ambitious and insatiably covetous, and therefore no impression from argument or miracle could reach them; but they stood proof against all conviction. Now, to show how the pravity of the will could influence the understanding to a disbelief of Christianity, I shall premise these two considerations:

1. That the understanding, in its assent to any religion, is very differently wrought upon in persons bred up in it and in persons at length converted to it. For in the first it finds the mind naked and unprepossessed with any former notions, and so easily and insensibly gains upon the assent, grows up with it, and incorporates into it. But in persons adult, and already possessed with other notions of religion, the understanding can not be brought to quit these, and to change them for new, but by great consideration and examination of the truth and firmness of the one, and comparing them with the flaws and weakness of the other. Which can not be done without some labor and intention of the mind, and the thoughts dwelling a considerable time upon the survey and discussion of each particular.

2. The other thing to be considered is, that in this great

work, the understanding is chiefly at the disposal of the will. For though it is not in the power of the will directly either to cause or hinder the assent of the understanding to a thing proposed and duly set before it, yet it is antecedently in the power of the will to apply the understanding faculty to, or to take it off from the consideration of those objects to which, without such a previous consideration, it can not yield its assent. For all assent presupposes a simple apprehension or knowledge of the terms of the proposition to be assented to. But unless the understanding employ or exercise its cognitive or apprehensive power about these terms, there can be no actual apprehension of them. And the understanding, as to the exercise of this power, is subject to the command of the will, though as to the specific nature of its acts it is determined by the object. As, for instance; my understanding can not assent to this proposition, That Jesus Christ is the Son of God; but it must first consider, and so apprehend, what the terms and parts of it are, and what they signify. And this can not be done, if my will be so slothful, worldly, or voluptuously disposed, as never to suffer me at all to think of them, but perpetually to carry away and apply my mind to other things. Thus far is the understanding at the disposal of the will.

Now these two considerations being premised, namely, that persons grown up in the belief of any religion can not change that for another, without applying their understanding duly to consider and to compare both; and then, that it is in the power of the will, whether it will suffer the understanding thus to dwell upon such objects or no: from these two, I say, we have the true philosophy and reason of the Pharisees' unbelief; for they could not relinquish their Judaism, and embrace Christianity, without considering, weighing, and collating both religions. And this their understanding could not apply to, if it were diverted and took off by their will; and their will would be sure to divert and take it off, being wholly possessed and governed by their covetousness and ambition, which perfectly abhorred the precepts of such a doctrine. And this is the very account that our Saviour himself gives of this matter in John v. 44. *How can ye believe,* says he, *who receive honor one of another?* He looked upon it as a thing morally impossible, for persons infinitely proud and ambitious, to frame their minds to an impartial unbiased consideration of a religion that taught nothing but self-denial and the cross; that humility was honor, and that the higher men climbed, the further they were from heaven. They could not with patience so much as think of it; and therefore, you may be sure, would never assent to it. And again, when Christ discoursed to them of alms, and a pious distribution of the goods and riches of this world, in Luke xvi. it is said in the 14th verse, *that the Pharisees, who were covetous, heard all those things, and derided him.* Charity and liberality is a paradox to the covetous. The doctrine that teaches alms, and the persons that need them, are by such equally sent packing. Tell a miser of bounty to a friend, or mercy to the poor, and point him out his duty with an evidence as bright and piercing as the light, yet he will not understand it, but shuts his eyes as close as he does his hands, and resolves not to be convinced. In both these cases there is an incurable blindness caused by a resolution not to see; and to all intents and purposes, he who will not open his eyes, is for the present as blind as he that can not. And thus I have done with the third thing proposed, and shown what was the true cause of the Pharisees' disbelief of Christ's doctrine: it was the predominance of those two great vices over their will, their covetousness and ambition. Pass we now to the

Fourth and last, which is to show, That a pious and well-disposed mind, attended with a readiness to obey the known will of God, is the surest and best means to enlighten the understanding to a belief of Christianity. That it is so, will appear upon a double account.

First, upon the account of God's goodness, and the method of his dealing with the souls of men; which is, to reward every degree of sincere obedience to his will, with a further discovery of it. *I understand more than the ancients,* says David, Psalm cxix. 100. But how did he attain to such an excellency of understanding? Was it by longer study, or a greater quickness and felicity of parts, than was in those before him? No; he gives the reason in the next words; it was, *because I keep thy statutes.* He got the start of them in point of obedience, and thereby outstript them at length in point of knowledge. And who in old time were the men of extraordinary revelations, but those who were also men of extraordinary piety? Who were made privy to the secrets of Heaven, and the hidden will of the Almighty, but such as performed his revealed will at an higher rate of strictness than the rest of the world? They were the Enochs, the Abrahams, the Elijahs, and the Daniels; such as the scripture remarkably testifies of, *that they walked with God.* And, surely, he that walks with another is in a likelier way to know and understand his mind than he that follows him at a distance. Upon which account, the learned Jews still made this one of the ingredients that went to constitute a prophet, that he should be *perfectus in moralibus*, a person of exact morals, and unblamable in his life: the gift of prophecy being a ray of such a light as never darts itself upon a dunghill. And what I here observe occasionally of extraordinary revelation and prophecy, will by analogy and due proportion extend even to those communications of God's will that are requisite to men's salvation. An honest hearty simplicity and proneness to do all that a man knows of God's will, is the ready, certain, and infallible way to know more of it. For I am sure it may be said of the practical knowledge of religion, *that to him that hath shall be given, and he shall have more abundantly.*

I dare not, I confess, join in that bold assertion of some, that *facienti quod in se est, Deus nec debet, nec potest denegare gratiam*, which indeed is no less than a direct contradiction in the very terms; for if *Deus debet*, then *id quod debetur non est gratia;* there being a perfect inconsistency between that which is of *debt* and that which is of *free gift.* And therefore leaving the *non debet* and the *non potest* to those that can bind and loose the Almighty at their pleasure, so much, I think, we may pronounce safely in this matter, that the goodness and mercy of God is such that he never deserts a sincere person, nor suffers any one that shall live (even according to these measures of sincerity) up to what he knows, to perish for want of any knowledge necessary, and, what is more, sufficient to save him.

If any one should here say, Were there then none living up to these measures of sincerity amongst the heathen? and if there were, did the goodness of God afford such persons knowledge enough to save them? My answer is according to that of St. Paul, *I judge not those that are without the church:* they stand or fall to their own master: I have nothing to say of them. *Secret things belong to God:* it becomes us to be thankful to God, and charitable to men.

2. A pious and well-disposed will is the readiest means to enlighten the understanding to a knowledge of the truth of Christianity, upon the account of a natural efficiency; forasmuch as a will so disposed will be sure to engage the mind in a severe search into the great and concerning truths of religion: nor will it only engage the mind in such a search; but it will also accompany that search with two dispositions, directly tending to, and principally productive of, the discoveries of truth, namely, diligence and impartiality. And,

(1.) For the diligence of the search. Diligence is the great harbinger of truth; which rarely takes up in any mind till that has gone before, and made room for it. It is a steady, constant, and pertinacious study, that naturally leads the soul into the knowledge of that which at first seemed locked up from it. For this keeps the understanding long in converse with an object: and long converse brings acquaintance. Frequent consideration of a thing wears off the strangeness of it, and shows it in its several lights, and various ways of appearance, to the view of the mind.

Truth is a great stronghold, barred and fortified by God and nature; and diligence is properly the understanding's laying siege to it: so that, as in a kind of warfare, it must be perpetually upon the watch; observing all the avenues and passes to it, and accordingly makes its approaches. Sometimes it thinks it gains a point; and presently again it finds itself baffled and beaten off: yet still it renews the onset; attacks the difficulty afresh; plants this reasoning, and that argument, this consequence, and that distinction, like so many intellectual batteries, till at length it forces a way and passage into the obstinate enclosed truth, that so long withstood and defied all its assaults.

The Jesuits have a saying common amongst them, touching the institution of youth, (in which their chief strength and talent lies,) that *vexatio dat intellectum.* As when the mind casts and turns itself restlessly from one thing to another, strains this power of the soul to apprehend, that to judge, another to divide, a fourth to remember; thus tracing out the nice and scarce observable difference of some things, and the real agreement of others, till at length it brings all the ends of a long and various hypothesis together; sees how one part coheres with and depends upon another; and so clears off all the appearing contrarieties and contradictions that seemed to lie cross and uncouth, and to make the whole unintelligible. This is the laborious and vexatious inquest that the soul must make after science. For truth, like a stately dame, will not be seen, nor show herself at the first visit, nor match with the understanding upon an ordinary courtship or address. Long and tedious attendances must be given, and the hardest fatigues endured and digested; nor did ever the most pregnant wit in the world bring forth any thing great, lasting, and considerable, without some pain and travail, some pangs and throes, before the delivery.

Now all this, that I have said, is to show the force of diligence in the investigation of truth, and particularly of the noblest of all truths, which is that of religion. But then, as diligence is the great discoverer of truth, so is the will the great spring of diligence. For no man can heartily search after that which he is not very desirous to find. Diligence is to the understanding as the whetstone to the razor; but the will is the hand that must apply one to the other.

What makes many men so strangely immerse themselves, some in chemical, and some in mathematical inquiries, but because they strangely love the things they labor in? Their intent study gives them skill and proficiency, and their particular affection to these kinds of knowledge puts them upon such study. Accordingly let there be but the same propensity and bent of will to religion, and there will be the same sedulity and indefatigable industry in men's inquiry into it. And then, in the natural course of things, the consequent of a sedulous seeking is finding, and the fruit of inquiry is information.

(2.) A pious and well-disposed will gives not only diligence, but also impartiality to the understanding, in its search into religion, which is as absolutely necessary to give success to our inquiries into truth as the former; it being scarce possible for that man to hit the mark, whose eye is still glancing upon something beside it. Partiality is properly the understanding's judging according to the inclination of the will and affections, and not according to the exact truth of things, or the merits of the cause before it. Affection is still a briber of the judgment; and it is hard for a man to admit a reason against the thing he loves, or to confess the force of an argument against an interest.

In this case he prevaricates with his own understanding, and can not seriously and sincerely set his mind to consider the strength, to poise the weight, and to discern the evidence of the clearest and best argumentations, where they would conclude against the darling of his desires. For still that beloved thing possesses and even engrosses him, and like a colored glass before his eyes casts its own color and tincture upon all the images and ideas of things that pass from the fancy to the understanding; and so absolutely does it sway that, that if a strange irresistible evidence of some unacceptable truth should chance to surprise and force reason to assent to the premises, affection would yet step in at last, and make it quit the conclusion.

Upon which account, Socinus and his followers state the reason of a man's believing or embracing Christianity upon the natural goodness or virtuous disposition of his mind, which they sometimes call *naturalis probitas,* and sometimes *animus in virtutem pronus.* For, say they, the whole doctrine of Christianity teaches nothing but what is perfectly suitable to, and coincident with, the ruling principles that a virtuous and well-inclined man is acted by, and with the main interest that he proposes to himself. So that as soon as ever it is declared to such an one, he presently closes in, accepts, and complies with it: as a prepared soil eagerly takes in and firmly retains such seed or plants as particularly agree with it.

With ordinary minds, such as much the greatest part of the world are, it is the suitableness, not the evidence of a truth, that makes it to be assented to. And it is seldom that any thing practically convinces a man, that does not please him first. If you would be sure of him, you must inform and gratify him too. But now, impartiality strips the mind of prejudice and passion, keeps it right and even from the bias of interest and desire, and so presents it like a *rasa tabula,* equally disposed to the reception of all truth. So that the soul lies prepared, and open to entertain it, and prepossessed with nothing that can oppose or thrust it out. For where diligence opens the door of the understanding, and impartiality keeps it, truth is sure to find both an entrance and a welcome too.

And thus I have done with the fourth and last general thing proposed, and proved by argument, that a pious and well-disposed mind, attended with a readiness to obey the known will of God, is the surest and best means to enlighten the understanding to a belief of Christianity.

Now, from the foregoing particulars, by way of use, we may collect these two things:

1. The true cause of that atheism, that skepticism and caviling at religion, that we see and have cause to lament in too many in these days. It is not from any thing weak or wanting in our religion, to support and enable it to look the strongest arguments and the severest and most controlling reason in the face: but men are atheistical because they are first vicious, and question the truth of Christianity because they hate the practice. And therefore, that they may seem to have some pretense and color to sin on freely, and to surrender up themselves wholly to their sensuality without any imputation upon their judgment, and to quit their morals without any discredit to their intellectuals, they fly to several stale, trite, pitiful objections and cavils, some against religion in general, and some against Christianity in particular, and some against the very first principles of morality, to give them some poor credit and countenance in the pursuit of their brutish courses.

Few practical errors in the world are embraced upon the stock of conviction, but inclination: for though indeed the judgment may err upon the account of weakness, yet where there is one error that enters in at this door, ten are let into it through the will: that, for the most part, being set upon those things, which truth is a direct obstacle to the enjoyment of; and where both can not be had, a man will be sure to buy his enjoyment, though he pays down truth for the purchase. For in this case, the further from truth, the further from trouble: since truth shows such an one what he is unwilling to see, and tells him what he hates to hear. They are the same beams that shine and enlighten, and are apt to scorch too: and it is impossible for a man engaged in any wicked way, to have a clear understanding of it, and a quiet mind in it together.

But these sons of Epicurus, both for voluptuousness and irreligion also, (as it is hard to support the former without the latter,) these, I say, rest not here; but (if you will take them at their word) they must also pass for the only wits of the age: though greater arguments, I am sure, may be produced against this than any they can allege against the most improbable article of Christianity. But heretofore the rate and standard of wit was very different from what it is nowadays. No man was then accounted a wit for speaking such things as deserved to have the tongue cut out that spake them: nor did any man pass for a philosopher, or a man of depth, for talking atheistically: or a man of parts, for employing them against that God that gave them. For then the world was generally better inclined; virtue was in so much reputation as to be pretended to at least. And virtue, whether in a Christian or in an infidel, can have no interest to be served either by atheism or infidelity.

For which cause, could we but prevail with the greatest debauchees amongst us to change their lives, we should find it no very hard matter to change their judgments. For notwithstanding all their talk of reason and philosophy, which (God knows) they are deplorably strangers to; and those unanswerable doubts and difficulties, which, over their cups or their coffee, they pretend to have against Christianity; persuade but the covetous man not to deify his money; the proud man not to adore himself; the lascivious man to throw off his lewd amours; the intemperate man to abandon his revels; and so for any other vice, that is apt to abuse and pervert the mind of man; and I dare undertake, that all their giant-like objections against Christian religion shall presently vanish and quit the field. For he that is a good man, is three quarters of his way towards the being a good Christian, wheresoever he lives, or whatsoever he is called.

2. In the next place, we learn from hence the most effectual way and means of proficiency and growth in the knowledge of the great and profound truths of religion, and how to make us all not only good Christians, but also expert divines. It is a knowledge that men are not so much to study as to live themselves into: a knowledge that passes into the head through the heart. I have heard of some, that in their latter years, through the feebleness of their limbs, have been forced to study upon their knees: and I think it might well become the youngest and the strongest to do so too. Let them daily and incessantly pray to God for his grace; and if God gives grace, they may be sure that knowledge will not stay long behind: since it is the same spirit and principle that purifies the heart, and clarifies the understanding. Let all their inquiries into the deep and mysterious points of theology be begun and carried on with fervent petitions to God; that he would dispose their minds to direct all their skill and knowledge to the promotion of a good life, both in themselves and others; that he would use all their noblest speculations, and most refined notions, only as instruments, to move and set at work the great principles of actions, the will and the affections; that he would convince them of the infinite vanity and uselessness of all that learning that makes not the possessor of it a better man; that he would keep them from those sins that may grieve and provoke his holy Spirit (the fountain of all true light and knowledge) to withdraw from them, and so seal them up under darkness, blindness, and stupidity of mind. For where the heart is bent upon, and held under the power of, any vicious course, though Christ himself should take the contrary virtue for his doctrine, and do a miracle before such an one's eyes, for its application, yet he would not practically gain his assent, but the result of all would end in a *non persuadebis etiamsi persuaseris.* Few consider what a degree of sottishness and confirmed ignorance men may sin themselves into.

This was the case of the Pharisees. And no doubt but this very consideration also gives us the true reason and full explication of that notable and strange passage of scripture, in Luke xvi. and the last verse: *That if men will not hear*

Moses and the prophets, neither will they be persuaded, though one rose from the dead. That is, where a strong inveterate love of sin has made any doctrine or proposition wholly unsuitable to the heart, no argument or demonstration, no nor miracle whatsoever, shall be able to bring the heart cordially to close with and receive it. Whereas, on the contrary, if the heart be piously disposed, the natural goodness of any doctrine is enough to vouch for the truth of it: for the suitableness of it will endear it to the will, and by endearing it to the will, will naturally slide it into the assent also. For in morals, as well as in metaphysics, there is nothing really good but has a truth commensurate to its goodness.

The truths of Christ crucified are the Christian's philosophy, and a good life is the Christian's logic, that great instrumental introductive art that must guide the mind into the former. And where a long course of piety, and close communion with God, has purged the heart, and rectified the will, and made all things ready for the reception of God's Spirit, knowledge will break in upon such a soul, like the sun shining in his full might, with such a victorious light, that nothing shall be able to resist it.

If now at length some should object here, that, from what has been delivered, it will follow, that the most pious men are still the most knowing, which yet seems contrary to common experience and observation, I answer, that, as to all things directly conducing and necessary to salvation, there is no doubt but they are so; as the meanest common soldier, that has fought often in an army, has a truer and better knowledge of war than he that has read and writ whole volumes of it, but never was in any battle.

Practical sciences are not to be learnt but in the way of action. It is experience that must give knowledge in the Christian profession, as well as in all others. And the knowledge drawn from experience is quite of another kind from that which flows from speculation or discourse. It is not the opinion, but the *path of the just*, that, the wisest of men tells us, *shines more and more unto a perfect day*. The obedient, and the men of practice, are those sons of light that shall outgrow all their doubts and ignorances, that shall ride upon these clouds, and triumph over their present imperfections, till persuasion pass into knowledge, and knowledge advance into assurance, and all come at length to be completed in the beatific vision, and a full fruition of those joys which God has in reserve for them whom by his grace he shall prepare for glory.

To which God, infinitely wise, holy, and just, be rendered and ascribed, as is most due, all praise, might, majesty, and dominion, both now and for evermore. Amen.

SERMON VII.

A SERMON PREACHED AT THE CONSECRATION OF A CHAPEL. 1667.

PREFACE.

AFTER the happy expiration of those times which had reformed so many churches to the ground, and in which men used to express their honor to God, and their allegiance to their prince the same way, demolishing the palaces of the one and the temples of the other, it is now our glory and felicity, that God has changed men's tempers with the times, and made a spirit of building succeed a spirit of pulling down, — by a miraculous revolution, reducing many from the head of a triumphant rebellion to their old condition of masons, smiths, and carpenters, that in this capacity they might repair what, as colonels and captains, they had ruined and defaced.

But still it is strange to see any ecclesiastical pile, not by ecclesiastical cost and influence rising above ground; especially in an age in which men's mouths are open against the church, but their hands shut towards it; an age in which, respecting the generality of men, we might as soon expect stones to be made bread, as to be made churches.

But the more epidemical and prevailing this evil is, the more honorable are those who stand and shine as exceptions from the common practice; and may such places, built for the divine worship, derive an honor and a blessing upon the head of the builders, as great and lasting as the curse and infamy that never fails to rest upon the sacrilegious violators of them; and a greater, I am sure I need not, I can not wish.

Now the foundation of what I shall discourse, upon the present subject and occasion, shall be laid in that place in

PSALM lxxxvii. 2. — *God hath loved the gates of Sion, more than all the dwellings of Jacob.*

THE comparison here exhibited between the love God bore to Sion, the great place of his solemn worship, and that which he bore to the other dwellings of Israel, imports, as all other comparisons do in the superior part of them, two things, difference and preëminence: and accordingly I can not more commodiously and naturally contrive the prosecution of these words, than by casting the sense of them into these two propositions:

I. That God bears a different respect to places set apart and consecrated to his worship, from what he bears to all other places designed to the uses of common life.

II. That God prefers the worship paid him in such places, above that which is offered him in any other places whatsoever.

I. As to the former of these, this difference of respect, borne by God to such places, from what he bears to others, may be evinced these three several ways:

1. By those eminent interposals of Providence, for the erecting and preserving of such places.

2. By those notable judgments shown by God upon the violators of them.

3. Lastly, by declaring the ground and reason why God shows such a different respect to those places, from what he manifests to others. Of all which in their order.

1. First of all then, those eminent interposals of the divine Providence for the erecting and preserving such places, will be one pregnant and strong argument to prove the difference of God's respect to them, and to others of common use.

That Providence that universally casts its eye over all the parts of the creation, is yet pleased more particularly to fasten it upon some. God made all the world, that he might be worshiped in some parts of the world; and therefore in the first and most early times of the church, what care did he manifest to have such places erected to his honor! Jacob he admonished by a vision, as by a messenger from heaven, to build him an altar; and then, what awe did Jacob express to it! *How dreadful*, says he, *is this place! for surely it is no other than the house of God.* What particular inspirations were there upon Aholihab to fit him to work about the sanctuary! The Spirit of God was the surveyor, director, and manager of the whole business. But above all, how exact and (as we may say with reverence) how nice was God about the building of the temple! David, though a man of most intimate converse and acquaintance with God, and one who bore a kingly preëminence over others, no less in point of piety than of majesty, after he had made such rich, such vast, and almost incredible provision of materials for the building of the temple; but because he had dipt his hands in blood, though but the blood of God's enemies, had the glory of that work took out of them, and was not permitted to lay a stone in that sacred pile; but the whole work was entirely reserved for Solomon, a prince adorned with those parts of mind, and exalted by such a concurrence of all prosperous events to make him glorious and magnificent, as if God had made it his business to build a Solomon, that Solomon might build him an house. To which, had not God borne a very different respect from what he bore to all other places, why might not David have been permitted to build God a temple, as well as to rear himself a palace? Why might not he, who was so pious as to design, be also so prosperous as to finish it? God must needs have set a more than ordinary esteem upon that which David, the man after his own heart, the darling of Heaven, and the most flaming example of a vigorous love to God that ever was, was not thought fit to have a hand in.

And to proceed, when, after a long tract of time, the sins of Israel had even unconsecrated and profaned that sacred edifice, and thereby robbed it of its only defense, the palladium of God's presence, so that the Assyrians laid it even with the ground; yet after that a long captivity and affliction had made the Jews fit again for so great a privilege as a public place to worship God in, how did God put it into the heart, even of an heathen prince, to promote the building of a second temple! How was the work undertook and carried on amidst all the unlikelihoods and discouraging circumstances imaginable! The builders holding the sword in one hand, to defend the trowel working with the other; yet finished and completed it was, under the conduct and protection of a peculiar providence, that made the instruments of that great design prevalent and victorious, and all those mountains of opposition to become plains before Zorobabel.

And lastly, when Herod the Great, whose magnificence served him instead of piety to prompt him to an action, if not in him religious, yet heroic at least, thought fit to pull down that temple, and to build one much more glorious, and fit for the Saviour of the world to appear and preach in. Josephus, in his 15th book of the Jewish Antiquities, and the 14th chapter, says, that during all the time of its building, there fell not so much as a shower to interrupt the work, but the rain still fell by night, that it might not retard the business of the day. If this were so, I am not of the number of those who can ascribe such great and strange passages to chance, or satisfy my reason in assigning any other cause of this, but the kindness of God himself to the place of his worship; making the common influences of heaven to stop their course, and pay a kind of homage to the rearing of so sacred a structure. Though I must confess, that David's being prohibited, and Herod permitted to build God a temple might seem strange, did not the absoluteness of God's good pleasure satisfy all sober minds of the reasonableness of God's proceedings, though never so strange and unaccountable.

Add to all this, that the extraordinary manifestations of God's presence were still in the sanctuary: the cloud, the Urim and Thummim, and the oracular answers of God, were graces and prerogatives proper and peculiar to the sacredness of this place. These were the dignities that made it, as it were, the presence-chamber of the Almighty, the room of audience, where he declared that he would receive and answer petitions from all places under heaven, and where he displayed his royalty and glory. There was no parlor or dining-room in all the dwellings of Jacob, that he vouchsafed the like privileges to. And moreover, how full are God's expressions to this purpose! *Here have I placed my name, and here will I dwell, for I have a delight therein.*

But to evidence, how different a respect God bears to things consecrated to his own worship, from what he bears to all other things, let that one eminent passage of Corah, Dathan, and Abiram, be proof beyond all exception; in which the censers of those wretches, who, I am sure, could derive no sanctity to them from their own persons, yet upon this account, that they had been consecrated by the offering incense in them, were, by God's special command, sequestered from all common use, and appointed to be beaten into broad plates, and fastened as a covering upon the altar, Numb. xvi. 38. *The censers of these sinners against their own souls, let them make broad plates for a covering of the altar: for they offered them before the Lord, therefore they are hallowed.* It seems this one single use left such an indelible sacredness upon them, that neither the villainy of the persons, nor the impiety of the design, could be a sufficient reason to unhallow and degrade them to the same common use that other vessels may be applied to. And the argument holds equally good for the consecration of places. The apostle would have no reveling, or junketing upon the altar, which had been used, and by that use consecrated to the celebration of a more spiritual and divine repast. *Have ye not houses to eat and to drink in? or despise ye the church of God?* says St. Paul, 1 Cor. xi. 22. It would have been no answer to have told the apostle, What! is not the church stone and wood as well as other buildings? And is there any such peculiar sanctity in this parcel of brick and mortar? And must God, who has declared himself *no respecter of persons,* be now made a respecter of places? No, this is the language of a more spiritualized and refined piety than the apostles and primitive Christians were acquainted with. And thus much for the first argument, brought to prove the different respect that God bears to things and places consecrated and set apart to his own worship, from what he bears to others.

2. The second argument, for the proof of the same assertion, shall be taken from those remarkable judgments shown by God, upon the violators of things consecrated and set apart to holy uses.

A coal, we know, snatched from the altar once fired the nest of the eagle, the royal and commanding bird; and so has sacrilege consumed the families of princes, broke sceptres, and destroyed kingdoms. We read how the victorious Philistines were worsted by the captivated ark, which foraged their country more than a conquering army; they were not able to cohabit with that holy thing; it was like a plague in their bowels, and a curse in the midst of them; so that they were forced to restore their prey, and to turn their triumphs into supplications. Poor Uzzah for but touching the ark, though out of care and zeal for its preservation, was struck dead with a blow from heaven. He had no right to touch it, and therefore his very zeal was a sin, and his care an usurpation; nor could the purpose of his heart excuse the error of his hand. Nay, in the promulgation of the Mosaic law, if so much as a brute beast touched the mountain, the bow of vengeance was ready, and it was to be struck through with a dart, and to die a sacrifice for a fault it could not understand.

But to give some higher and clearer instances of the divine judgments upon sacrilegious persons. In 1 Kings xiv. 26. we find Shishak king of Egypt spoiling and robbing Solomon's temple; and that we may know what became of him, we must take notice that Josephus calls him Susac, and tells us that Herodotus calls him Sesostris; and withal reports, that immediately after his return from this very expedition, such disastrous calamities befell his family, that he burnt two of his children himself; that his brother conspired against him; and lastly, that his son, who succeeded him, was struck blind, yet not so blind (in his understanding at least) but that he saw the cause of all these mischiefs; and therefore, to redeem his father's sacrilege, gave more and richer things to temples than his father had stolen from them: though, by the way, it may seem to be a strange method of repairing an injury done to the true God, by adorning the temples of the false. See the same sad effect of sacrilege in the great Nebuchadnezzar: he plunders the temple of God, and we find the fatal doom that afterwards befell him; he lost his kingdom, and by a new unheard-of judgment was driven from the society and converse of men, to table with the beasts, and to graze with oxen; the impiety and inhumanity of his sin making him a fitter companion for them than for those to whom religion is more natural than reason itself. And since it was his unhappiness to transmit his sin, together with his kingdom, to his son, while Belshazzar was quaffing in the sacred vessels of the temple, which in his pride he sent for to abuse with his impious sensuality, he sees his fatal sentence writ by the finger of God in the very midst of his profane mirth. And he stays not long for the execution of it, that very night losing his kingdom and his life too. And that which makes the story direct for our purpose is, that all this comes upon him for profaning those sacred vessels. God himself tells us so much by the mouth of his prophet in Dan. v. 23, where this only sin is charged upon him, and particularly made the cause of his sudden and utter ruin.

These were violators of the first temple, and those that profaned and abused the second sped no better. And for this, take for instance that first-born of sin and sacrilege, Antiochus; the story of whose profaning God's house you may read in the first book of Maccabees, chap. i. And you may read also at large what success he found after it, in the sixth chapter, where the author tells us, that he never prospered afterwards in any thing, but all his designs were frustrated, his captains slain, his armies defeated; and lastly, himself falls sick, and dies a miserable death. And (which is most considerable as to the present business) when all these evils befell him, his own conscience tells him that it was even for this, that he had most sacrilegiously pillaged and invaded God's house, 1 Maccab. vi. 12, 13. *Now I remember*, says he, *the evils I did at Jerusalem, how I took the vessels of gold and silver: I perceive therefore, that for this cause these evils are come upon me, and, behold, I perish for grief in a strange land.* The sinner's conscience is for the most part the best expositor of the mind of God, under any judgment or affliction.

Take another notable instance in Nicanor, who purposed and threatened to burn the temple, 1 Maccab. vii. 35. And a curse lights upon him presently after: his great army is utterly ruined, he himself slain in it, and his head and right hand cut off, and hung up before Jerusalem. Where two things are remarkable in the text: 1. That he himself was first slain, a thing that does not usually befall a general of an army. 2. That the Jews prayed against him to God, and desired God to destroy Nicanor, for the injury done to his sanctuary only, naming no sin else. And God ratified their prayers by the judgment they brought down upon the head of him whom they prayed against. God stopped his blasphemous mouth, and cut off his sacrilegious hand, and made them teach the world what it was for the most potent sinner under heaven to threaten the almighty God, especially in his own house; for so was the temple.

But now, lest some should puff at these instances, as being such as were under a different economy of religion, in which God was more tender of the shell and ceremonious part of his worship, and consequently not directly pertinent to ours; therefore to show that all profanation, and invasion of things sacred, is an offense against the eternal law of nature, and not against any positive institution after a time to expire, we need not go many nations off, nor many ages back, to see the vengeance of God upon some families, raised upon the ruins of churches, and enriched with the spoils of sacrilege, gilded with the name of reformation. And for the most part, so unhappy have been the purchasers of church lands, that the world is not now to seek for an argument from a long experience to convince it, that though in such purchases men have usually the cheapest pennyworths, yet they have not always the best bargains. For the holy thing has stuck fast to their sides like a fatal shaft, and the stone has cried out of the consecrated walls they have lived within, for a judgment upon the head of the sacrilegious intruder; and Heaven has heard the cry, and made good the curse. So that when the heir of a blasted family has rose up and promised fair, and perhaps flourished for some time upon the stock of excellent parts and great favor, yet at length a cross event has certainly met and stopped him in the career of his fortunes; so that he has ever after withered and declined, and in the end come to nothing, or to that which is worse. So certainly does that, which some call blind superstition, take aim when it shoots a curse at the sacrilegious person. But I shall not engage in the odious task of recounting the families which this sin has blasted with a curse. Only, I shall give one eminent instance in some persons who had sacrilegiously procured the demolishing of some places consecrated to holy uses.

And for this (to show the world that Papists can commit sacrilege as freely as they can object it to Protestants) it shall be in that great cardinal and minister of state, Wolsey, who obtained leave of pope Clement the seventh to demolish forty religious houses; which he did by the service of five men, to whose conduct he committed the effecting of that business; every one of which came to a sad and fatal end. For the pope himself was ever after an unfortunate prince, Rome being twice taken and sacked in his reign, himself taken prisoner, and at length dying a miserable death. Wolsey (as is known) incurred *a premunire*, forfeited his honor, estate, and life, which he ended, some say, by poison, but certainly in great calamity.

And for the five men employed by him, two of them quarreled, one of which was slain, and the other hanged for it; the third drowned himself in a well; the fourth (though rich) came at length to beg his bread; and the fifth was miserably stabbed to death at Dublin in Ireland.

This was the tragical end of a knot of sacrilegious persons from highest to lowest. The consideration of which and the like passages, one would think, should make men keep their fingers off from the church's patrimony, though not out of love to the church, (which few men have,) yet at least out of love to themselves, which, I suppose, few want.

Nor is that instance in one of another religion to be passed over, (so near it is to the former passage of Nicanor,) of a commander in the parliament's rebel army, who, coming to rifle and deface the cathedral at Litchfield, solemnly at the head of his troops begged of God to show some remarkable token of his approbation or dislike of the work they were going about. Immediately after which, looking out at a window, he was shot in the forehead by a deaf and dumb man. And this was on St. Chadd's day, the name of which saint that church bore, being dedicated to God in memory of the same. Where we see, that as he asked of God a sign, so God gave him one, signing him in the forehead, and that with such a mark as he is like to be known by to all posterity.

There is nothing that the united voice of all history proclaims so loud as the certain unfailing curse that has pursued and overtook sacrilege. Make a catalogue of all the prosperous sacrilegious persons that have been from the beginning of the world to this day, and I believe they will come within a very narrow compass, and be repeated much sooner than the alphabet.

Religion claims a great interest in the world, even as great as its object, God, and the souls of men. And since God has resolved not to alter the course of nature, and upon principles of nature, religion will scarce be supported without the encouragement of the ministers of it; Providence, where it loves a nation, concerns itself to own and assert the interest of religion, by blasting the spoilers of religious persons and places. Many have gaped at the church revenues, but, before they could swallow them, have had their mouths stopt in the churchyard.

And thus much for the second argument, to prove the different respect that God bears to things consecrated to holy uses; namely, his signal judgments upon the sacrilegious violators of them.

3. I descend now to the third and last thing proposed for the proof of the first proposition, which is, to assign the ground and reason why God shows such a concern for these things. Touching which we are to observe, (1.) Negatively, that it is no worth or sanctity naturally inherent in the things themselves, that either does or can procure them this esteem from God; for by nature all things have an equally common use. Nature freely and indifferently opens the bosom of the universe to all mankind; and the very *sanctum sanctorum* had originally no more sacredness in it than the valley of the son of Hinnom, or any other place in Judæa. (2.) Positively, therefore, the sole ground and reason of this different esteem vouchsafed by God to consecrated things and places, is this, that he has the sole property of them.

It is a known maxim, that *in Deo sunt jura omnia;* and, consequently, that he is the proprietor of all things, by that grand and transcendent right founded upon creation. Yet notwithstanding he may be said to have a greater, because a sole property in some things, for that he permits not the use of them to men, to whom yet he has granted the free use of all other things. Now this property may be founded upon a double ground.

First, God's own fixing upon, and institution of, a place or thing to his peculiar use. When he shall say to the sons of men, as he spoke to Adam concerning the forbidden fruit, Of all things and places that I have enriched the universe with, you may freely make use for your own occasions; but as for this spot of ground, this person, this thing, I have selected and appropriated, I have enclosed it to myself and my own use; and I will endure no sharer, no rival, or companion in it: he that invades them, usurps, and shall bear the guilt of his usurpation. Now, upon this account, the gates of Sion, and the tribe of Levi, became God's property. He laid his hand upon them, and said, *These are mine.*

Secondly, The other ground of God's sole property in any thing or place, is the gift, or rather the return of it made by man to God; by which act he relinquishes and delivers back to God all his right to the use of that thing, which before had been freely granted him by God. After which donation there is an absolute change and alienation made of the property of the thing given, and that as to the use of it too; which being so alienated, a man has no more to do with it than with a thing bought with another's money, or got with the sweat of another's brow.

And this is the ground of God's sole property in things, persons, and places, now under the gospel. Men by free gift consign over a place to the divine worship, and thereby have no more right to apply it to another use than they have to make use of another man's goods. He that has devoted himself to the service of God in the Christian priesthood, has given himself to God, and so can no more dispose of himself to another employment than he can dispose of a thing that he has sold or freely given away. Now in passing a thing away to another by deed of gift, two things are required:

1. A surrender, on the giver's part, of all the property and right he has in the thing given. And to the making of a thing or place sacred, this surrender of it, by its right owner, is so necessary, that all the rites of consecration used upon a place against the owner's will, and without his giving up his property, make not that place sacred, forasmuch as the property of it is not hereby altered; and therefore says the canonist, *Qui sine voluntate Domini consecrat, revera desecrat.* The like judgment passed that learned Bishop Synesius upon a place so consecrated. Οὐδ' ἱερὸν οὐδὲ μὲν ὅσιον ἡγοῦμαι. *I account it not*, says he, *for any holy thing.*

For we must know, that consecration makes not a place sacred, any more than coronation makes a king, but only solemnly declares it so. It is the gift of the owner of it to God, which makes it to be solely God's, and consequently sacred; after which, every violation of it is as really sacrilege as to conspire against the king is treason before the solemnity of his coronation. And moreover, as consecration makes not a thing sacred without the owner's gift, so the owner's gift of itself alone makes a thing sacred, without the ceremonies of consecration; for we know that tithes and lands given to God are never, and plate, vestments, and other sacred utensils are seldom consecrated: yet certain it is, that after the donation of them to the church, it is as really sacrilege to steal or alienate them from those sacred uses, to which they were dedicated by the donors, as it is to pull down a church, or turn it into a stable.

2. As, in order to the passing away a thing by gift, there is required a surrender of all right to it on his part that gives, so there is required also an acceptation of it on his part to whom it is given. For giving being a relative action, (and so requiring a correlative to answer it), giving on one part transfers no property, unless there be an accepting on the other; for as *volenti non fit injuria*, so in this case *nolenti non fit beneficium.*

And if it be now asked, how God can be said to accept what we give, since we are not able to transact with him in person? To this I answer, 1. That we may and do converse with God in person really, and to all the purposes of giving and receiving, though not visibly: for natural reason will evince that God will receive testimonies of honor from his creatures; amongst which the homage of offerings, and the parting with a right, is a very great one. And where a gift is suitable to the person to whom it is offered, and no refusal of it testified, silence in that case (even amongst those who transact visibly and corporally with one another) is, by the general voice of reason, reputed an acceptance. And therefore much more ought we to conclude that God accepts of a thing suitable for him to receive, and for us to give, where he does not declare his refusal and disallowance of it. But, 2. I add further, that we may transact with God in the person of his and Christ's substitute, the bishop, to whom the deed of gift ought, and uses to be delivered by the owner of the thing given, in a formal instrument signed, sealed, and legally attested by witnesses, wherein he resigns up all his right and property in the thing to be consecrated. And the bishop is as really *vicarius Christi* to receive this from us in Christ's behalf, as the Levitical priest was *vicarius Dei* to the Jews, to manage all transactions between God and them.

These two things therefore concurring, the gift of the owner, and God's acceptance of it, either immediately by himself, which we rationally presume, or mediately by the hands of the bishop, which is visibly done before us, is that which vests the sole property of a thing or place in God. If it be now asked, Of what use then is consecration, if a thing were sacred before it? I answer, Of very much; even as much as coronation to a king, which confers no royal authority upon him, but by so solemn a declaration of it imprints a deeper awe and reverence of it in the people's minds, a thing surely of no small moment. And, 2. The bishop's solemn benediction and prayers to God for a blessing upon those who shall seek him in such sacred places, can not but be supposed a direct and most effectual means to procure a blessing from God upon those persons who shall address themselves to him there, as they ought to do. And surely, this also vouches the great reason of the episcopal consecration. Add to this, in the third place, that all who ever had any awful sense of religion and religious matters (whether Jews or Christians, or even heathens themselves) have ever used solemn dedications and consecrations of things set apart, and designed for divine worship; which surely could never have been so universally practiced, had not right reason dictated the high expediency and great use of such practices.

Eusebius, (the earliest church-historian,) in the tenth book of his "Ecclesiastical History," as also in the "Life of Constantine," speaks of these consecrations of churches as of things generally in use, and withal sets down those actions particularly, of which they consisted, styling them Θεοπρεπεῖς, ἐκκλησίας θεσμοὺς, laws or customs of the church becoming God. What the Greek and Latin churches used to do, may be seen in their pontificals, containing the set forms for these consecrations; though indeed (for these six or seven last centuries) full of many tedious, superfluous, and ridiculous fopperies; setting aside all which, if also our liturgy had a set form for the consecration of places, as it has of persons, perhaps it would be nevertheless perfect. Now from what has been above discoursed of the ground of God's sole property in things set apart for his service, we come at length to see how all things given to the church, whether houses, or lands, or tithes, belong to churchmen. They are but *usufructuarii*, and have only the use of these things, the property and fee remaining wholly in God; and consequently the alienating of them is a robbing of God, Mal. iii. 8, 9. *Ye are cursed with a curse, for ye have robbed me, even this whole nation, in tythes and offerings.* If it was God that was robbed, it was God also that was the owner of what was took away in the robbery: even our own common law speaks as much; for so says our Magna Charta, in the first chapter, *Concessimus Deo—quod ecclesia Anglicana libera erit, &c.* Upon which words, that great lawyer in his "Institutes" comments thus: When any thing is granted *for* God, it is deemed in law to be granted *to* God; and whatsoever is granted to the church for his honor, and the maintenance of his service, is granted *for* and *to* God.

The same also appears from those forms of expression in which the donation of sacred things usually ran. As *Deo omnipotenti hac præsente charta donavimus*, with the like. But most undeniably is this proved by this one argument: That in case a bishop should commit treason or felony, and thereby forfeit his estate with his life, yet the lands of his bishopric become not forfeit, but remain still in the church, and pass entire to his successor; which sufficiently shows that they were none of his.

It being therefore thus proved that God is the sole proprietor of all sacred things or places, I suppose his peculiar property in them is an abundantly pregnant reason of that different respect that he bears to them. For is not the *meum*, and the separate property of a thing, the great cause of its endearment amongst all mankind? Does any one respect a common as much as he does his garden? or the gold that lies in the bowels of a mine as much as that which he has in his purse?

I have now finished the first proposition drawn from the words; namely, that God bears a different respect to places set apart and consecrated to his worship, from what he bears to all other places designed to the uses of common life: and also shown the reason why he does so. I proceed now to the other proposition, which is, That God prefers the worship paid him in such places, above that which is offered him in any other places whatsoever. And that for these reasons:

1. Because such places are naturally apt to excite a greater reverence and devotion in the discharge of divine service, than places of common use. The place properly reminds a man of the business of the place, and strikes a kind of awe into the thoughts, when they reflect upon that great and sacred Majesty they use to treat and converse with there. They find the same holy consternation upon themselves that Jacob did at his consecrated Bethel, which he called *the gate of heaven;* and if such places are so, then surely a daily expectation at the gate is the readiest way to gain admittance into the house.

It has been the advice of some spiritual persons, that such as were able should set apart some certain place in their dwellings for private devotions only, which if they constantly performed there, and nothing else, their very entrance into it would tell them what they were to do in it, and quickly make their chamber-thoughts, their table-thoughts, and their jolly, worldly, but much more their sinful thoughts and purposes, fly out of their hearts.

For is there any man (whose heart has not shook off all sense of what is sacred) who finds himself no otherwise affected, when he enters into a church, than when he enters into his parlor or chamber? If he does, for aught I know, he is fitter to be there always than in a church.

The mind of man, even in spirituals, acts with a corporeal dependence, and so is helped or hindered in its operations, according to the different quality of external objects that incur into the senses. And perhaps sometimes the sight of the altar, and those decent preparations for the work of devotion, may compose and recover the wandering mind much more effectually than a sermon, or a rational discourse. For these things in a manner preach to the eye, when the ear is dull and will not hear, and the eye dictates to the imagination, and that at last moves the affections. And if these little impulses set the great wheels of devotion on work, the largeness and height of that shall not at all be prejudiced by the smallness of its occasion. If the fire burns bright and vigorously, it is no matter by what means it was at first kindled; there is the same force, and the same refreshing virtue in it, kindled by a spark from a flint, as if it were kindled by a beam from the sun.

I am far from thinking that these external things are either parts of our devotion, or by any strength in themselves direct causes of it; but the grace of God is pleased to move us by ways suitable to our nature, and to sanctify these sensible inferior helps to greater and higher purposes. And since God has placed the soul in a body, where it receives all things by the ministry of the outward senses, he would have us secure these cinque ports (as I may so call them) against the invasion of vain thoughts, by suggesting to them such objects as may prepossess them with the contrary. For God knows how hard a lesson devotion is, if the senses prompt one thing when the heart is to utter another. And therefore let no man presume to think that he may present God with as acceptable a prayer in his shop, and much less in an alehouse or a tavern, as he may in a church or in his closet: unless he can rationally promise himself (which is impossible) that he shall find the same devout motions and impresses upon his spirit there that he may here.

What says David, in Psalm lxxvii. 13. *Thy way, O God, is in the sanctuary.* It is no doubt but that holy person continued a strict and most pious communion with God during his wanderings upon the mountains and in the wilderness; but still he found in himself that he had not those kindly, warm meltings upon his heart, those raptures and ravishing transports of affection, that he used to have in the fixed and solemn place of God's worship. See the two first verses of the 63d Psalm, entitled, *A psalm of David, when he was in the wilderness of Judah.* How emphatically and divinely does every word proclaim the truth that I have been speaking of! *O God,* says he, *thou art my God; early will I seek thee: my soul thirsteth for thee, my flesh longeth for thee in a dry and thirsty land, where no water is; to see thy power and thy glory, so as I have seen thee in the sanctuary.* Much different was his wish from that of our nonconforming zealots nowadays, which expresses itself in another kind of dialect; as, When shall I enjoy God as I used to do at a conventicle? When shall I meet with those blessed breathings, those heavenly hummings and hawings, that I used to hear at a private meeting, and at the end of a table?

In all our worshipings of God, we return him but what he first gives us; and therefore he prefers the service offered him in the sanctuary, because there he usually vouchsafes more helps to the piously disposed person, for the discharge of it. As we value the same kind of fruit growing under one climate more than under another; because under one it has a directer and a warmer influence from the sun than under the other, which gives it both a better savor and a greater worth.

And perhaps I should not want a further argument for the confirmation of the truth discoursed of, if I should appeal to the experience of many in this nation, who, having been long bred to the decent way of divine service in the cathedrals of the church of England, were afterwards driven into foreign countries, where, though they brought with them the same sincerity to church, yet perhaps they could not find the same enlargements and flowings out of spirit which they were wont to find here. Especially in some countries, where their very religion smelt of the shop; and their ruder and coarser methods of divine service seemed only adapted to the genius of trade and the designs of parsimony; though one would think that parsimony in God's worship were the worst husbandry in the world, for fear God should proportion his blessings to such devotions.

2. The other reason why God prefers a worship paid him in places solemnly dedicated and set apart for that purpose, is, because in such places it is a more direct service and testification of our homage to him. For surely, if I should have something to ask of a great person, it were greater respect to wait upon him with my petition at his own house, than to desire him to come and receive it at mine.

Set places and set hours for divine worship, as much as the laws of necessity and charity permit us to observe them, are but parts of that due reverence that we owe it: for he that is strict in observing these, declares to the world that he accounts his attendance upon God his greatest and most important business: and surely it is infinitely more reasonable that we should wait upon God than God upon us.

We shall still find, that when God was pleased to vouchsafe his people a meeting, he himself would prescribe the place. When he commanded Abraham to sacrifice his only deand beloved Isaac, the place of the offering was not left untermined, and to the offerer's discretion: but in Gen. xxii. 2. *Get thee into the land of Moriah,* (says God;) *and offer him for a burnt-offering upon one of the mountains that I shall tell thee of.*

It was part of his sacrifice, not only what he should offer, but where. When we serve God in his own house, his service (as I may so say) leads all our other secular affairs in triumph after it. They are all made to stoop and bend the knee to prayer, as that does to the throne of grace.

Thrice a year were the Israelites from all, even the remotest parts of Palestine, to go up to Jerusalem, there to worship and pay their offerings at the temple. The great distance of some places from thence could not excuse the inhabitants from making their appearance there, which the Mosaic law exacted as indispensable.

Whether or no they had coaches, to the temple they must go: nor could it excuse them to plead God's omniscience, that he could equally see and hear them in any place: nor yet their own good will and intentions; as if the readiness of their mind to go, might, forsooth, warrant their bodies to stay at home. Nor, lastly, could the real danger of leaving their dwellings to go up to the temple excuse their journey: for they might very plausibly and very rationally have alleged, that during their absence their enemies round about them might take that advantage to invade their land. And therefore, to obviate this fear and exception, which indeed was built upon so good ground, God makes them a promise, which certainly is as remarkable as any in the whole book of God, Exod. xxxiv. 24. *I will cast out the nations before thee; neither shall any man desire thy land, when thou shalt go up to appear before the Lord thy God thrice in a year.* While they were appearing in God's house, God himself engages to keep and defend theirs, and that by little less than a miracle, putting forth an overpowering work and influence upon the very hearts and wills of men, that when their opportunities should induce, their hearts should not serve them to annoy their neighbors.

For surely, a rich land, guardless and undefended, must needs have been a double incitement, and such an one as might not only admit, but even invite the enemy. It was like a fruitful garden or a fair vineyard without an hedge, that quickens the appetite to enjoy so tempting, and withal so easy a prize. But the great God, by ruling men's hearts, could by consequence hold their hands, and turn the very desires of interest and nature out of their common channel, to comply with the designs of his worship.

But now, had not God set a very peculiar value upon the service paid him in his temple, surely he would not have thus, as it were, made himself his people's convoy, and exerted a supernatural work to secure them in their passage to it. And therefore that eminent hero in religion, Daniel, when in the land of his captivity he used to pay his daily devotions to God, not being able to go to the temple, would at least look towards it, advance to it in wish and desire, and so, in a manner, bring the temple to his prayers, when he could not bring his prayers to that.

And now, what have I to do more, but to wish that all this discourse may have that blessed effect upon us, as to send us both to this and to all other solemn places of divine worship with those three excellent ingredients of devotion, — desire, reverence, and confidence?

1. And first, for desire. We should come hither, as to meet God in a place where he loves to meet us; and where (as Isaac did to his sons) he gives us blessings with embraces. Many frequent the gates of Sion, but is it because they love them; and not rather because their interest forces them, much against their inclination, to endure them?

Do they hasten to their devotions with that ardor and quickness of mind that they would to a lewd play or a masquerade?

Or do they not rather come hither slowly, sit here uneasily, and depart desirously? All which is but too evident a sign that men repair to the house of God, not as to a place of fruition, but of task and trouble, not to enjoy, but to afflict themselves.

2. We should come full of reverence to such sacred places; and where there are affections of reverence, there will be postures of reverence too. Within consecrated walls we are more directly under God's eye, who looks through and through every one that appears before him, and is too jealous a God to be affronted to his face.

3. And lastly; God's peculiar property in such places should give us a confidence in our addresses to him here. Reverence and confidence are so far from being inconsistent, that they are the most direct and proper qualifications of a devout and filial approach to God.

For where should we be so confident of a blessing as in the place and element of blessings; the place where God both promises and delights to dispense larger proportions of his favor, even for this purpose, that he may fix a mark of honor upon his sanctuary; and so recommend and endear it to the sons of men, upon the stock of their own interest as well as his glory; who has declared himself *the high and the lofty One that inhabits eternity, and dwells not in houses made with men's hands, yet is pleased to be present in the assemblies of his saints.*

To whom be rendered and ascribed, as is most due, all praise, might, majesty, and dominion, both now and for evermore. *Amen.*

SERMON VIII.

A SERMON PREACHED AT WESTMINSTER ABBEY,
FEBRUARY 22, 1684–85.

PROV. xvi. 33. — *The lot is cast into the lap; but the whole disposing of it is of the Lord.*

I CANNOT think myself engaged from these words to discourse of lots, as to their nature, use, and allowableness; and that not only in matters of moment and business, but also of recreation; which latter is indeed impugned by some, though better defended by others; but I shall fix only upon the design of the words, which seems to be a declaration of a divine perfection by a signal instance; a proof of the exactness and universality of God's providence from its influence upon a thing, of all others, the most casual and fortuitous, such as is the casting of lots.

A lot is properly a casual event, purposely applied to the determination of some doubtful thing.

Some there are who utterly proscribe the name of *chance*, as a word of impious and profane signification; and indeed, if it be taken by us in that sense in which it was used by the heathen, so as to make any thing casual in respect of God himself, their exception ought justly to be admitted. But to say a thing is a chance, or casualty, as it relates to second causes, is not profaneness, but a great truth; as signifying no more than that there are some events, besides the knowledge, purpose, expectation, and power of second agents. And for this very reason, because they are so, it is the royal prerogative of God himself, to have all these loose, uneven, fickle uncertainties under his disposal.

The subject, therefore, that from hence we are naturally

carried to the consideration of, is, the admirable extent of the divine Providence, in managing the most contingent passages of human affairs; which that we may the better treat of, we will consider the result of a lot:

I. In reference to men.

II. In reference to God.

I. For the first of these, if we consider it as relating to men, who suspend the decision of some dubious case upon it, so we shall find that it naturally implies in it these two things:

1. Something future. 2. Something contingent.

From which two qualifications these two things also follow:

1. That it is absolutely out of the reach of man's knowledge.

2. That it is equally out of his power.

This is most clear; for otherwise, why are men in such cases doubtful, and concerned, what the issue and result should be? for no man doubts of what he sees and knows; nor is solicitous about the event of that which he has in his power to dispose of to what event he pleases.

The light of man's understanding is but a short, diminutive, contracted light, and looks not beyond the present: he knows nothing future, but as it has some kind of presence in the stable, constant manner of operation belonging to its cause; by virtue of which we know, that if the fire continues for twenty years, it will certainly burn so long; and that there will be summer, winter, and harvest, in their respective seasons: but whether God will continue the world till to-morrow or no, we can not know by any certain argument, either from the nature of God or of the world.

But when we look upon such things as relate to their immediate causes with a perfect indifference, so that in respect of them they equally may or may not be, human reason can then, at the best, but conjecture what will be. And in some things, as here in the casting of lots, a man can not, upon any ground of reason, bring the event of them so much as under conjecture.

The choice of man's will is indeed uncertain, because in many things free; but yet there are certain habits and principles in the soul, that have some kind of sway upon it, apt to bias it more one way than another; so that, upon the proposal of an agreeable object, it may rationally be conjectured, that a man's choice will rather incline him to accept than to refuse it. But when lots are shuffled together in a lap, urn, or pitcher, or a man blindfold casts a die, what reason in the world can he have to presume that he shall draw a white stone rather than a black, or throw an ace rather than a size? Now, if these things are thus out of the compass of a man's knowledge, it will unavoidably follow, that they are also out of his power. For no man can govern or command that which he can not possibly know; since to dispose of a thing implies both a knowledge of the thing to be disposed of, and of the end that it is to be disposed of to.

And thus we have seen how a contingent event baffles man's knowledge, and evades his power. Let us now consider the same in respect of God; and so we shall find that it falls under,

1. A certain knowledge. And
2. A determining providence.

1. First of all then, the most casual event of things, as it stands related to God, is comprehended by a certain knowledge. God, by reason of his eternal, infinite, and indivisible nature, is, by one single act of duration, present to all the successive portions of time; and consequently to all things successively existing in them: which eternal, indivisible act of his existence makes all futures actually present to him; and it is the presentiality of the object which founds the unerring certainty of his knowledge. For whatsoever is known, is some way or other present; and that which is present can not but be known by him who is omniscient.

But I shall not insist upon these speculations; which when they are most refined serve only to show how impossible it is for us to have a clear and explicit notion of that which is infinite. Let it suffice us in general to acknowledge and adore the vast compass of God's omniscience. That it is a light shining into every dark corner, ripping up all secrets, and steadfastly grasping the greatest and most slippery uncertainties. As when we see the sun shine upon a river, though the waves of it move and roll this way and that way by the wind; yet for all their unsettledness, the sun strikes them with a direct and a certain beam. Look upon things of the most accidental and mutable nature, accidental in their production, and mutable in their continuance; yet God's prescience of them is as certain in him as the memory of them is or can be in us. He knows which way the lot and the die shall fall, as perfectly as if they were already cast. All futurities are naked before that all-seeing eye, the sight of which is no more hindered by distance of time than the sight of an angel can be determined by distance of place.

2. As all contingencies are comprehended by a certain divine knowledge, so they are governed by as certain and steady a providence.

There is no wandering out of the reach of this, no slipping through the hands of omnipotence. God's hand is as steady as his eye; and certainly thus to reduce contingency to method, instability and chance itself to an unfailing rule and order, argues such a mind as is fit to govern the world; and I am sure nothing less than such an one can.

Now God may be said to bring the greatest casualties under his providence upon a twofold account:

(1.) That he directs them to a certain end.

(2.) Oftentimes to very weighty and great ends.

(1.) And first of all, he directs them to a certain end.

Providence never shoots at rovers. There is an arrow that flies by night as well as by day, and God is the person that shoots it, who can aim then as well as in the day. Things are not left to an *equilibrium*, to hover under an indifference whether they shall come to pass or not come to pass; but the whole train of events is laid beforehand, and all proceed by the rule and limit of an antecedent decree: for otherwise, who could manage the affairs of the world, and govern the dependence of one event upon another, if that event happened at random, and was not cast into a certain method and relation to some foregoing purpose to direct it?

The reason why men are so short and weak in governing is, because most things fall out to them accidentally, and come not into any compliance with their preconceived ends, but they are forced to comply subsequently, and to strike in with things as they fall out, by postliminious after-applications of them to their purposes, or by framing their purposes to them.

But now there is not the least thing that falls within the cognizance of man, but is directed by the counsel of God. *Not an hair can fall from our head, nor a sparrow to the ground, without the will of our heavenly Father.* Such an universal superintendency has the eye and hand of Providence over all, even the most minute and inconsiderable things.

Nay, and sinful actions too are overruled to a certain issue; even that horrid villainy of the crucifixion of our Saviour was not a thing left to the disposal of chance and uncertainty; but in Acts ii. 23. it is said of him, that *he was delivered to the wicked hands of his murderers, by the determinate counsel and foreknowledge of God:* for surely the Son of God could not die by chance, nor the greatest thing that ever came to pass in nature be left to an undeterminate event. Is it imaginable that the great means of the world's redemption should rest only in the number of possibilities, and hang so loose in respect of its futurition as to leave the event in an equal poise, whether ever there should be such a thing or no? Certainly the actions and proceedings of wise men run in a much greater closeness and coherence with one another than thus to derive at a casual issue, brought under no forecast or design. The pilot must intend some port before he steers his course, or he had as good leave his vessel to the direction of the winds and the government of the waves.

Those that suspend the purposes of God, and the resolves of an eternal mind upon the actions of the creature, and make God first wait and expect what the creature will do, (and then frame his decrees and counsels accordingly,) forget that he is the first cause of all things, and discourse most unphilosophically, absurdly, and unsuitably to the nature of an infinite being; whose influence in every motion must set the first wheel agoing. He must still be the first agent, and what he does he must will and intend to do before he does it, and what he wills and intends once, he willed and intended from all eternity; it being grossly contrary to the very first notions we have of the infinite perfection of the divine nature, to state or suppose any new immanent act in God.

The Stoics indeed held a fatality, and a fixed unalterable

course of events; but then they held also, that they fell out by a necessity emergent from and inherent in the things themselves, which God himself could not alter: so that they subjected God to the fatal chain of causes, whereas they should have resolved the necessity of all inferior events into the free determination of God himself; who executes necessarily that which he first purposed freely.

In a word, if we allow God to be the governor of the world, we can not but grant that he orders and disposes of all inferior events; and if we allow him to be a wise and a rational governor, he can not but direct them to a certain end.

(2.) In the next place, he directs all these appearing casualties, not only to certain, but also to very great ends.

He that created something out of nothing, surely can raise great things out of small, and bring all the scattered and disordered passages of affairs into a great, beautiful, and exact frame. Now this overruling, directing power of God may be considered,

First, In reference to societies, or united bodies of men.

Secondly, In reference to particular persons.

First. And first for societies. God and nature do not principally concern themselves in the preservation of particulars, but of kinds and companies. Accordingly, we must allow Providence to be more intent and solicitous about nations and governments than about any private interest whatsoever. Upon which account it must needs have a peculiar influence upon the erection, continuance, and dissolution of every society. Which great effects it is strange to consider, by what small, inconsiderable means they are oftentimes brought about, and those so wholly undesigned by such as are the immediate visible actors in them. Examples of this we have both in holy writ, and also in other stories.

And first for those of the former sort.

Let us reflect upon that strange and unparalleled story of Joseph and his brethren; a story that seems to be made up of nothing else but chances and little contingencies, all directed to mighty ends. For was it not a mere chance that his father Jacob should send him to visit his brethren, just at that time that the Ishmaelites were to pass by that way, and so his unnatural brethren take occasion to sell him to them, and they to carry him into Egypt? and then that he should be cast into prison, and thereby brought at length to the knowledge of Pharaoh in that unlikely manner that he was? Yet by a joint connection of every one of these casual events, Providence served itself in the preservation of a kingdom from famine, and of the church, then circumscribed within the family of Jacob. Likewise by their sojourning in Egypt, he made way for their bondage there, and their bondage for a glorious deliverance through those prodigious manifestations of the divine power, in the several plagues inflicted upon the Egyptians. It was hugely accidental that Joash king of Israel, being commanded by the prophet to *strike upon the ground*, 2 Kings xiii., should strike no oftener than just three times; and yet we find there that the fate of a kingdom depended upon it, and that his victories over Syria were concluded by that number. It was very casual that the Levite and his concubine should linger so long as to be forced to take up their lodging at Gibeah, as we read in Judges xix., and yet we know what a villainy was occasioned by it, and what a civil war that drew after it, almost to the destruction of a whole tribe.

And then for examples out of other histories, to hint a few of them.

Perhaps there is none more remarkable than that passage about Alexander the Great, in his famed expedition against Darius.

When in his march towards him, chancing to bathe himself in the river Cydnus, through the excessive coldness of those waters, he fell sick near unto death for three days; during which short space the Persian army had advanced itself into the strait passages of Cilicia; by which means Alexander with his small army was able to equal them under those disadvantages, and to fight and conquer them. Whereas had not this stop been given him by that accidental sickness, his great courage and promptness of mind would, beyond all doubt, have carried him directly forward to the enemy, till he had met him in the vast open plains of Persia, where his paucity and small numbers would have been contemptible, and the Persian multitudes formidable; and, in all likelihood of reason, victorious. So that this one little accident of that prince's taking a fancy to bathe himself at that time, caused the interruption of his march, and that interruption gave occasion to that great victory that founded the third monarchy of the world. In like manner, how much of casualty was there in the preservation of Romulus, as soon as born exposed by his uncle, and took up and nourished by a shepherd! (for the story of the shewolf is a fable.) And yet in that one accident was laid the foundation of the fourth universal monarchy.

How doubtful a case was it, whether Hannibal, after the battle of Cannæ, should march directly to Rome, or divert into Campania! Certain it is, that there was more reason for the former; and he was a person that had sometimes the command of reason, as well as regiments: yet his reason deserted his conduct at that time; and by not going to Rome he gave occasion to those recruits of the Roman strength that prevailed to the conquest of his country, and at length to the destruction of Carthage itself, one of the most puissant cities in the world.

And to descend to occurrences within our own nation. How many strange accidents concurred in the whole business of King Henry the Eighth's divorce! yet we see Providence directed it and them to an entire change of the affairs and state of the whole kingdom. And surely, there could not be a greater chance than that which brought to light the powder treason, when Providence, as it were, snatched a king and kingdom out of the very jaws of death, only by the mistake of a word in the direction of a letter.

But of all cases in which little casualties produce great and strange effects, the chief is in war; upon the issues of which hangs the fortune of states and kingdoms.

Cæsar, I am sure, whose great sagacity and conduct put his success as much out of the power of chance as human reason could well do, yet upon occasion of a notable experiment that had like to have lost him his whole army at Dyrrachium, tells us the power of it in the third book of his Commentaries, *De Bello Civili:* "Fortuna quæ plurimum potest, cum in aliis rebus, tum præcipue in bello, in parvis momentis magnas rerum mutationes efficit." Nay, and a greater than Cæsar, even the Spirit of God himself, in Eccles. vi. 11., expressly declares, *that the battle is not always to the strong.* So that upon this account every warrior may in some sense be said to be a soldier of fortune; and the best commanders to have a kind of lottery for their work, as, amongst us, they have for their reward. For how often have whole armies been routed by a little mistake, or a sudden fear raised in the soldiers' minds, upon some trivial ground or occasion!

Sometimes the misunderstanding of a word has scattered and destroyed those who have been even in possession of victory, and wholly turned the fortune of the day. A spark of fire or an unexpected gust of wind may ruin a navy. And sometimes a false, senseless report has spread so far, and sunk so deep into the people's minds, as to cause a tumult, and that tumult a rebellion, and that rebellion has ended in the subversion of a government.

And in the late war between the king and some of his rebel subjects, has it not sometimes been at an even cast, whether his army should march this way or that way? Whereas had it took that way, which actually it did not, things afterwards so fell out, that in very high probability of reason, it must have met with such success as would have put an happy issue to that wretched war, and thereby have continued the crown upon that blessed prince's head, and his head upon his shoulders. Upon supposal of which event, most of those sad and strange alterations that have since happened would have been prevented; the ruin of many honest men hindered, the punishment of many great villains hastened, and the preferment of greater spoiled.

Many passages happen in the world, much like that little cloud in 1 Kings xviii., that appeared at first to Elijah's servant, *no bigger than a man's hand,* but presently after grew and spread, and blackened the face of the whole heaven, and then discharged itself in thunder and rain, and a mighty tempest. So these accidents, when they first happen, seem but small and contemptible; but by degrees they branch out, and widen themselves into such a numerous train of mischievous consequences, one drawing after it another, by a continued dependence and multiplication, that the plague becomes victorious and universal, and personal miscarriage determines in a national calamity.

For who that should view the small, despicable beginnings of some things and persons at first, could imagine or prognosticate those vast and stupendous increases of fortune that have afterwards followed them?

Who, that had looked upon Agathocles first handling the clay, and making pots under his father, and afterwards turning robber, could have thought that from such a condition he should come to be king of Sicily?

Who, that had seen Masianello, a poor fisherman, with his red cap and his angle, could have reckoned it possible to see such a pitiful thing, within a week after, shining in his cloth of gold, and with a word or a nod absolutely commanding the whole city of Naples?

And who, that had beheld such a bankrupt, beggarly fellow as Cromwell, first entering the parliament house with a threadbare torn cloak, and a greasy hat, (and perhaps neither of them paid for,) could have suspected that in the space of so few years he should, by the murder of one king and the banishment of another, ascend the throne, be invested in the royal robes, and want nothing of the state of a king but the changing of his hat into a crown?

It is, as it were, the sport of the Almighty thus to baffle and confound the sons of men by such events as both cross the methods of their actings, and surpass the measure of their expectations. For according to both these, men still suppose a gradual natural progress of things; as that from great, things and persons should grow greater, till at length, by many steps and ascents, they come to be at greatest; not considering that when Providence designs strange and mighty changes, it gives men wings instead of legs; and instead of climbing leisurely, makes them at once fly to the top and height of greatness and power. So that the world about them (looking up to those illustrious upstarts) scarce knows who or whence they were, nor they themselves where they are.

It were infinite to insist upon particular instances; histories are full of them, and experience seals to the truth of history.

In the next place, let us consider to what great purposes God directs these little casualties, with reference to particular persons; and those either public or private.

1. And first for public persons, as princes. Was it not a mere accident that Pharaoh's daughter met with Moses? Yet it was a means to bring him up in the Egyptian court, then the school of all arts and policy, and so to fit him for that great and arduous employment that God designed him to. For see upon what little hinges that great affair turned; for had either the child been cast out, or Pharaoh's daughter come down to the river but an hour sooner or later; or had that little vessel not been cast by the parents, or carried by the water, into that very place where it was, in all likelihood the child must have undergone the common lot of the other Hebrew children, and been either starved or drowned; or, however, not advanced to such a peculiar height and happiness of condition. That Octavius Cæsar should shift his tent (which he had never used to do before) just that very night that it happened to be took by the enemy, was a mere casualty; yet such an one as preserved a person who lived to establish a total alteration of government in the imperial city of the world.

But we need not go far for a prince preserved by as strange a series of little contingencies as ever were managed by the art of Providence to so great a purpose.

There was but an hair's breadth between him and certain destruction for the space of many days. For had the rebel forces gone one way rather than another, or come but a little sooner to his hiding-place, or but mistrusted something which they passed over, (all which things might very easily have happened;) we had not seen this face of things at this day; but rebellion had been still enthroned, perjury and cruelty had reigned, majesty had been proscribed, religon extinguished, and both church and state thoroughly reformed and ruined with confusions, massacres, and a total desolation.

On the contrary, when Providence designs judgment or destruction to a prince, nobody knows by what little, unusual, unregarded means the fatal blow shall reach him. If Ahab be designed for death, though a soldier in the enemy's army draws a bow at a venture; yet the sure, unerring directions of Providence shall carry it in a direct course to his heart, and there lodge the revenge of Heaven.

An old woman shall cast down a stone from a wall, and God shall send it to the head of Abimelech, and so sacrifice a king in the very head of his army.

How many warnings had Julius Cæsar of the fatal ides of March! Whereupon sometimes he resolved not to go to the senate, and sometimes again he would go; and when at length he did go, in his very passage thither, one put into his hand a note of the whole conspiracy against him, together with all the names of the conspirators, desiring him to read it forthwith, and to remember the giver of it as long as he lived. But continual salutes and addresses entertaining him all the way, kept him from saving so great a life, but with one glance of his eye upon the paper; till he came to the fatal place where he was stabbed, and died with the very means of preventing death in his hand.

Henry the Second of France, by a splinter, unhappily thrust into his eye at a solemn justing, was dispatched and sent out of the world, by a sad, but very accidental death.

In a word, God has many ways to reap down the grandees of the earth; an arrow, a bullet, a tile, a stone from an house, is enough to do it: and besides all these ways, sometimes, when he intends to bereave the world of a prince or an illustrious person, he may cast him upon a bold, self-opinioned physician, worse than his distemper, who shall dose and bleed, and kill him *secundum artem*, and make a shift to cure him into his grave.

In the last place we will consider this directing influence of God with reference to private persons; and that, as touching things of nearest concernment to them. As,

1. Their lives.
2. Their health.
3. Their reputation.
4. Their friendships. And,
5. Lastly, their employments or preferments.

And first for men's lives. Though these are things for which nature knows no price or ransom, yet I appeal to universal experience whether they have not, in many men, hung oftentimes upon a very slender thread, and the distance between them and death been very nice, and the escape wonderful. There have been some, who upon a slight and perhaps groundless occasion have gone out of a ship, or house, and the ship has sunk, and the house has fell immediately after their departure.

He that, in a great wind, suspecting the strength of his house, betook himself to his orchard, and walking there, was knocked on the head by a tree, falling through the fury of a sudden gust, wanted but the advance of one or two steps to have put him out of the way of that mortal blow.

He that being subject to an apoplexy, used still to carry his remedy about him; but, upon a time, shifting his clothes, and not taking that with him, chanced, upon that very day, to be surprised with a fit, and to die in it, certainly owed his death to a mere accident, to a little inadvertency and failure of memory. But not to recount too many particulars: may not every soldier, that comes alive out of the battle, pass for a living monument of a benign chance, and a happy providence? For was he not in the nearest neighborhood to death? And might not the bullet, that perhaps grazed his cheek, have as easily gone into his head? And the sword that glanced upon his arm, with a little diversion have found the way to his heart? But the workings of Providence are marvelous, and the methods secret and untraceable by which it disposes of the lives of men.

In like manner, for men's health, it is no less wonderful to consider to what strange casualties many sick persons oftentimes owe their recovery. Perhaps an unusual draught or morsel, or some accidental violence of motion, has removed that malady that for many years has baffled the skill of all physicians. So that, in effect, he is the best physician that has the best luck; he prescribes, but it is chance that cures.

That person that (being provoked by excessive pain) thrust his dagger into his body, and thereby, instead of reaching his vitals, opened an imposthume, the unknown cause of all his pain, and so stabbed himself into perfect health and ease, surely had great reason to acknowledge Chance for his chirurgeon, and Providence for the guider of his hand.

And then also for men's reputation; and that either in point of wisdom or of wit. There is hardly any thing which (for the most part) falls under a greater chance. If a man succeeds in any attempt, though undertook with never so much folly and rashness, his success shall vouch him a politician; and good luck shall pass for deep contrivance: for give any one fortune, and he shall be thought a wise man, in spite of his heart; nay, and of his head too. On the contrary, be a design never so artificially laid, and spun in the finest thread of policy, if it chances to be defeated by some cross accident, the man is then run down by an universal vogue; his counsels are derided, his prudence questioned, and his person despised.

Ahithophel was as great an oracle, and gave as good counsel to Absalom, as ever he had given to David; but not having the good luck to be believed, and thereupon losing his former repute, he thought it high time to hang himself. And, on the other side, there have been some, who for several years have been fools with tolerable good reputation, and never discovered themselves to be so, till at length they attempted to be knaves also, but wanted art and dexterity.

And as the repute of wisdom, so that of wit also, is very casual. Sometimes a lucky saying, or a pertinent reply, has procured an esteem of wit, to persons otherwise very shallow, and no ways accustomed to utter such things by any standing ability of mind; so that if such an one should have the ill hap at any time to strike a man dead with a smart saying, it ought, in all reason and conscience, to be judged but a chance-medley: the poor man (God knows) being no way guilty of any design of wit.

Nay, even where there is a real stock of wit, yet the wittiest sayings and sentences will be found in a great measure the issues of chance, and nothing else but so many lucky hits of a roving fancy.

For consult the acutest poets and speakers, and they will confess that their quickest and most admired conceptions were such as darted into their minds like sudden flashes of lightning, they knew not how, nor whence; and not by any certain consequence or dependence of one thought upon another, as it is in matters of ratiocination.

Moreover, sometimes a man's reputation rises or falls as his memory serves him in a performance; and yet there is nothing more fickle, slippery, and less under command than this faculty. So that many, having used their utmost diligence to secure a faithful retention of the things or words committed to it, yet after all can not certainly know where it will trip and fail them. Any sudden diversion of the spirits, or the justling in of a transient thought, is able to deface those little images of things; and so breaking the train that was laid in the mind, to leave a man in the lurch. And for the other part of memory, called reminiscence, which is the retrieving of a thing, at present forgot, or but confusedly remembered, by setting the mind to hunt over all its notions, and to ransack every little cell of the brain. While it is thus busied, how accidentally oftentimes does the thing sought for offer itself to the mind! And by what small, petit hints does the mind catch hold of and recover a vanishing notion!

In short, though wit and learning are certain and habitual perfections of the mind, yet the declaration of them (which alone brings the repute) is subject to a thousand hazards. So that every wit runs something the same risk with the astrologer, who, if his predictions come to pass, is cried up to the stars from whence he pretends to draw them; but if not, the astrologer himself grows more out of date than his almanac.

And then, in the fourth place, for the friendships or enmities that a man contracts in the world; than which surely there is nothing that has a more direct and potent influence upon the whole course of a man's life, whether as to happiness or misery; yet chance has the ruling stroke in them all.

A man by mere peradventure lights into company, possibly is driven into an house by a shower of rain for present shelter, and there begins an acquaintance with a person; which acquaintance and endearment grows and continues, even when relations fail, and perhaps proves the support of his mind and of his fortunes to his dying day.

And the like holds in enmities, which come much more easily than the other. A word unadvisedly spoken on the one side, or misunderstood on the other; any the least surmise of neglect; sometimes a bare gesture; nay, the very unsuitableness of one man's aspect to another man's fancy, has raised such an aversion to him, as in time has produced a perfect hatred of him; and that so strong and so tenacious, that it has never left vexing and troubling him, till perhaps at length it has worried him to his grave; yea, and after death too, has pursued him in his surviving shadow, exercising the same tyranny upon his very name and memory.

It is hard to please men of some tempers, who indeed hardly know what will please themselves; and yet if a man does not please them, which it is ten thousand to one if he does, if they can but have power equal to their malice, (as sometimes, to plague the world, God lets them have,) such an one must expect all the mischief that power and spite, lighting upon a base mind, can possibly do him.

In the last place. As for men's employments and preferments, every man that sets forth into the world, comes into a great lottery, and draws some one certain profession to act, and live by, but knows not the fortune that will attend him in it.

One man perhaps proves miserable in the study of the law, who might have flourished in that of physic or divinity. Another runs his head against the pulpit, who might have been very serviceable to his country at the plow. And a third proves a very dull and heavy philosopher, who possibly would have made a good mechanic, and have done well enough at the useful philosophy of the spade or the anvil.

Now let this man reflect upon the time when all these several callings and professions were equally offered to his choice, and consider how indifferent it was once for him to have fixed upon any one of them, and what little accidents and considerations cast the balance of his choice rather one way than the other; and he will find how easily chance may throw a man upon a profession which all his diligence can not make him fit for.

And then for the preferments of the world, he that would reckon up all the accidents that they depend upon, may as well undertake to count the sands, or to sum up infinity; so that greatness, as well as an estate, may, upon this account, be properly called a man's fortune, forasmuch as no man can state either the acquisition or preservation of it upon any certain rules; every man, as well as the merchant, being here truly an adventurer. For the ways by which it is obtained are various, and frequently contrary: one man, by sneaking and flattering, comes to riches and honor, (where it is in the power of fools to bestow them,) upon observation whereof, another presently thinks to arrive to the same greatness by the very same means; but striving, like the ass, to court his master, just as the spaniel had done before him, instead of being stroked and made much of, he is only rated off and cudgeled for all his courtship.

The source of men's preferments is most commonly the will, humor, and fancy of persons in power; whereupon, when a prince or grandee manifests a liking to such a thing, such an art, or such a pleasure, men generally set about to make themselves considerable for such things, and thereby, through his favor, to advance themselves; and at length, when they have spent their whole time in them, and so are become fit for nothing else, that prince or grandee perhaps dies, and another succeeds him, quite of a different disposition, and inclining him to be pleased with quite different things. Whereupon these men's hopes, studies, and expectations, are wholly at an end. And besides, though the grandee whom they build upon should not die, or quit the stage, yet the same person does not always like the same things. For age may alter his constitution, humor, or appetite; or the circumstances of his affairs may put him upon different courses and counsels; every one of which accidents wholly alters the road to preferment. So that those who travel that road must be (like highwaymen) very dexterous in shifting the way upon every turn; and yet their very doing so sometimes proves the means of their being found out, understood, and abhorred; and for this very cause, that they that are ready to do any thing, are justly thought fit to be preferred to nothing.

Cæsar Borgia (base son to Pope Alexander VI.) used to boast to his friend Machiavel, that he had contrived his affairs and greatness into such a posture of firmness, that, whether his holy father lived or died, they could not but be secure. If he lived, there could be no doubt of them; and if he died, he laid his interest so as to overrule the next election as he pleased. But all this while the politician never thought or considered that he might in the mean time fall dangerously sick, and that sickness necessitate his removal from the court, and during that his absence his father die, and so his interest decay, and his mortal enemy be chosen to the papacy, as indeed it fell out. So that for all his exact plot, down was he cast from all his greatness, and forced to end his days in a mean condition: as it is pity but all such politic opiniators should.

Upon much the like account, we find it once said of an eminent cardinal, by reason of his great and apparent likelihood to step into St. Peter's chair, that in two conclaves he went in pope, and came out again cardinal.

So much has chance the casting voice in the disposal of all the great things of the world. That which men call merit, is a mere nothing. For even when persons of the greatest worth and merit are preferred, it is not their merit, but their fortune that prefers them. And then, for that other so much admired thing called policy, it is but little better. For when men have busied themselves, and beat their brains never so much, the whole result both of their counsels and their fortunes is still at the mercy of an accident. And therefore, whosoever that man was, that said that he had rather have a grain of fortune than a pound of wisdom, as to the things of this life, spoke nothing but the voice of wisdom and great experience.

And now I am far from affirming that I have recounted all, or indeed the hundredth part of those casualties of human life, that may display the full compass of divine Providence; but surely I have reckoned up so many as sufficiently enforce the necessity of our reliance upon it, and that in opposition to two extremes that men are usually apt to fall into.

1. Too much confidence and presumption in a prosperous estate. David, after his deliverances from Saul, and his victories over all his enemies round about him, in Psalm xxx. ver. 7, 8, confesses, that this his prosperity had raised him to such a pitch of confidence, as to make him say, *that he should*

never be moved, God of his favor had made his hill so strong: but presently he adds, almost in the very same breath, *Thou didst hide thy face, and I was troubled.*

The sun shines in his full brightness but the very moment before he passes under a cloud. Who knows what a day, what an hour, nay, what a minute may bring forth! He who builds upon the present, builds upon the narrow compass of a point; and where the foundation is so narrow, the superstructure can not be high and strong too.

Is a man confident of his present health and strength? Why, an unwholesome blast of air, a cold, or a surfeit took by chance, may shake in pieces his hardy fabric, and, in spite of all his youth and vigor, send him, in the very flower of his years, pining and drooping to his long home. Nay, he can not with any assurance so much as step out of his doors, but (unless God commissions his protecting angel to bear him up in his hands) he may dash his foot against a stone, and fall, and in that fall breathe his last.

Or is a man confident of his estate, wealth, and power? Why, let him read of those strange, unexpected dissolutions of the great monarchies and governments of the world. Governments that once made such a noise, and looked so big in the eyes of mankind, as being founded upon the deepest counsels and the strongest force; and yet, by some slight miscarriage or cross accident, (which let in ruin and desolation upon them at first,) are now so utterly extinct, that nothing remains of them but a name, nor are there the least signs or traces of them to be found, but only in story. When, I say, he shall have well reflected upon all this, let him see what security he can promise himself in his own little personal domestic concerns, which at the best have but the protection of the laws to guard and defend them, which, God knows, are far from being able to defend themselves.

No man can rationally account himself secure, unless he could command all the chances of the world: but how should he command them, when he can not so much as number them? Possibilities are as infinite as God's power; and whatsoever may come to pass, no man can certainly conclude shall not come to pass.

People forget how little it is that they know, and how much

less it is that they can do, when they grow confident upon any present state of things.

There is no one enjoyment that a man pleases himself in, but is liable to be lost by ten thousand accidents, wholly out of all mortal power either to foresee or to prevent. Reason allows none to be confident, but Him only who governs the world, who knows all things, and can do all things, and therefore can neither be surprised nor overpowered.

2. The other extreme, which these considerations should arm the heart of man against, is, utter despondency of mind in a time of pressing adversity.

As he who presumes, steps into the throne of God, so he that despairs limits an infinite power to a finite apprehension, and measures Providence by his own little, contracted model. But the contrivances of Heaven are as much above our politics as beyond our arithmetic.

Of those many millions of casualties which we are not aware of, there is hardly one but God can make an instrument of our deliverance. And most men, who are at length delivered from any great distress indeed, find that they are so by ways that they never thought of; ways above or beside their imagination.

And therefore let no man, who owns the belief of a providence, grow desperate or forlorn under any calamity or strait whatsoever; but compose the anguish of his thoughts, and rest his amazed spirits upon this one consideration, that he knows not *which way the lot may fall*, or what may happen to him; he comprehends not those strange unaccountable methods by which Providence may dispose of him.

In a word. To sum up all the foregoing discourse: since the interest of governments and nations, of princes and private persons, and that both as to life and health, reputation and honor, friendships and enmities, employments and preferments, (notwithstanding all the contrivance and power that human nature can exert about them,) remain so wholly contingent as to us; surely all the reason of mankind can not suggest any solid ground of satisfaction, but in making that God our friend who is the sole and absolute disposer of all these things: and in carrying a conscience so clear towards him as may encourage us with confidence to cast ourselves upon him : and in all casualties still to promise ourselves the best events from his providence, to whom nothing is casual : who constantly wills the truest happiness to those that trust in him, and works all things according to the counsel of that blessed will.

To whom be rendered and ascribed, as is most due, all praise, might, majesty, and dominion, both now and for evermore. Amen.

SERMON IX.

A SERMON PREACHED AT WESTMINSTER ABBEY, APRIL 30, 1676.

1 Cor. iii. 19.—*For the wisdom of this world is foolishness with God.*

THE *wisdom of the world,* so called by an Hebraism, frequent in the writings of this apostle, for *worldly wisdom,* is taken in scripture in a double sense.

1. For that sort of wisdom that consists in speculation, called (both by St. Paul and the professors of it) *philosophy;* the great idol of the learned part of the heathen world, and which divided it into so many sects and denominations, as Stoics, Peripatetics, Epicureans, and the like; it was professed and owned by them for the grand rule of life, and certain guide to man's chief happiness. But for its utter insufficiency to make good so high an undertaking, we find it termed by the same apostle, Col. ii. 8, *vain philosophy*; and 1 Tim. vi. 20, *science falsely so called*; and a full account of its uselessness we have in this, 1 Cor. i. 21, where the apostle, speaking of it, says, that *the world by wisdom knew not God.* Such a worthy kind of wisdom is it: only making men accurately and laboriously ignorant of what they were most concerned to know.

2. The *wisdom of this world* is sometimes taken in scripture for such a wisdom as lies in practice, and goes commonly by the name of policy; and consists in a certain dexterity or art of managing business for a man's secular advantage: and so being indeed that ruling engine that governs the world, it both claims and finds as great a preëminence above all other kinds of knowledge, as government is above contemplation,

or the leading of an army above the making of syllogisms, or managing the little issues of a dispute.

And so much is the very name and reputation of it affected and valued by most men, that they can much rather brook their being reputed knaves, than for their honesty be accounted fools; as they easily may: knave, in the mean time, passing for a name of credit, where it is only another word for politician.

Now this is the wisdom here intended in the text; namely, that practical cunning that shows itself in political matters, and has in it really the mystery of a trade, or craft. So that in this latter part of verse 19. God is said *to take the wise in their own craftiness.*

In short, it is a kind of trick or sleight, got not by study, but converse, learned not from books, but men; and those also, for the most part, the very worst of men of all sorts, ways, and professions. So that if it be in truth such a precious jewel as the world takes it for, yet, as precious as it is, we see that they are forced to rake it out of dunghills; and accordingly the apostle gives it a value suitable to its extract, branding it with the most degrading and ignominious imputation of foolishness. Which character running so cross to the general sense and vogue of mankind concerning it, who are still admiring, and even adoring it, as the mistress and queen-regent of all other arts whatsoever, our business, in the following discourse, shall be to inquire into the reason of the apostle's passing so severe a remark upon it: and here, indeed, since we must allow it for an art, and since every art is properly an habitual knowledge of certain rules and maxims, by which a man is governed and directed in his actions, the prosecution of the words will most naturally lie in these two things:

I. To show what are those rules or principles of action, upon which the policy or wisdom here condemned by the apostle does proceed.

II. To show and demonstrate the folly and absurdity of them, in relation to God, in whose account they receive a very different estimate from what they have in the world's.

And first, for the first of these; I shall set down four several rules or principles, which that policy or wisdom, which carries so great a vogue and value in the world, governs its actions by.

1. The first is, That a man must maintain a constant continued course of dissimulation, in the whole tenor of his behavior. Where yet, we must observe, that dissimulation admits of a twofold acception. (1.) It may be taken for a bare concealment of one's mind: in which sense we commonly say, that it is prudence to dissemble injuries, that is, not always to declare our resentments of them; and this must be allowed not only lawful, but, in most of the affairs of human life, absolutely necessary: for certainly it can be no man's duty to write his heart upon his forehead, and to give all the inquisitive and malicious world round about him a survey of those thoughts which it is the prerogative of God only to know, and his own great interest to conceal. Nature gives every one a right to defend himself, and silence surely is a very innocent defence.

(2.) Dissimulation is taken for a man's positive professing himself to be what indeed he is not, and what he resolves not to be; and consequently it employs all the art and industry imaginable, to make good the disguise; and by false appearances to render its designs the less visible, that so they may prove the more effectual: and this is the dissimulation here meant, which is the very groundwork of all worldly policy. The superstructure of which being folly, it is but reason that the foundation of it should be falsity.

In the language of the scripture it is *damnable hypocrisy;* but of those who neither believe scripture nor damnation, it is voted wisdom; nay, the very *primum mobile*, or great wheel, upon which all the various arts of policy move and turn: the soul, or spirit, which, as it were, animates and runs through all the particular designs and contrivances by which the great masters of this mysterious wisdom turn about the world. So that he who hates his neighbor mortally, and wisely too, must profess all the dearness and friendship, all the readiness to serve him, (as the phrase now is,) that words and superficial actions can express.

When he purposes one thing, he must swear and lie, and damn himself with ten thousand protestations, that he designs the clean contrary. If he really intends to ruin and murder his prince, (as Cromwell, an experienced artist in that perfidious and bloody faculty, once did,) he must weep and call upon God, use all the oaths and imprecations, all the sanctified perjuries, to persuade him that he resolves nothing but his safety, honor, and establishment, as the same grand exemplar of hypocrisy did before.

If such persons project the ruin of church and state, they must appeal to God, the searcher of all hearts, that they are ready to sacrifice their dearest blood for the peace of the one and the purity of the other.

And now, if men will be prevailed upon so far as to renounce the sure and impartial judgments of sense and experience, and to believe that black is white, provided there be somebody to swear that it is so; they shall not want arguments of this sort, good store, to convince them: there being knights of the post, and holy cheats enough in the world, to swear the truth of the broadest contradictions, and the highest impossibilities, where interest and pious frauds shall give them an extraordinary call to it.

It is looked upon as a great piece of weakness and unfitness for business, forsooth, for a man to be so clear and open as really to think, not only what he says, but what he swears; and when he makes any promise, to have the least intent of performing it, but when his interest serves instead of veracity, and engages him rather to be true to another than false to himself. He only nowadays speaks like an oracle, who speaks tricks and ambiguities. Nothing is thought beautiful that is not painted: so that, what between French fashions and Italian dissimulations, the old, generous English spirit, which heretofore made this nation so great in the eyes of all the world round about it, seems utterly lost and extinct; and we are degenerated into a mean, sharking, fallacious, undermining way of converse; there being a snare and a trepan almost in every word we hear, and every action we see. Men speak with designs of mischief, and therefore they speak in the dark. In short, this seems to be the true, inward judgment of all our politic sages, that speech was given to the ordinary sort of men, whereby to communicate their mind; but to wise men, whereby to conceal it.

2. The second rule or principle upon which this policy, or

wisdom of the world, does proceed, is, That conscience and religion ought to lay no restraint upon men at all, when it lies opposite to the prosecution of their interest.

The great patron and *coryphæus* of this tribe, Nicolas Machiavel, laid down this for a master rule in his political scheme, That the show of religion was helpful to the politician, but the reality of it hurtful and pernicious. Accordingly, having shown how the former part of his maxim has been followed by these men in that first and fundamental principle of dissimulation already spoken to by us, we come now to show further, that they can not with more art dissemble the appearance of religion than they can with ease lay aside the substance.

The politician, whose very essence lies in this, that he be a person ready to do any thing that he apprehends for his advantage, must first of all be sure to put himself into a state of liberty, as free and large as his principles: and so to provide elbow-room enough for his conscience to lay about, and have its full play in. And for that purpose, he must resolve to shake off all inward awe of religion, and by no means to suffer the liberty of his conscience to be enslaved, and brought under the bondage of observing oaths, or the narrowness of men's opinions, about *turpe et honestum,* which ought to vanish when they stand in competition with any solid, real good; that is, (in their judgment,) such as concerns eating, or drinking, or taking money.

Upon which account, these *children of darkness* seem excellently well to imitate the wisdom of those *children of light*, the great *illuminati* of the late times, who professedly laid down this as the basis of all their proceedings; That whatsoever they said or did for the present, under such a measure of light, should oblige them no longer when a greater measure of light should give them other discoveries.

And this principle, they professed, was of great use to them; as how could it be otherwise, if it fell into skillful hands? For since this light was to rest within them, and the judgment of it to remain wholly in themselves, they might safely and uncontrollably pretend it greater or less, as their occasions should enlighten them.

If a man has a prospect of a fair estate, and sees a way

open to it, but it must be through fraud, violence, and oppression; if he see large preferments tendered him, but conditionally upon his doing base and wicked offices; if he sees he may crush his enemy, but that it must be by slandering, belying, and giving him a secret blow; and conscience shall here, according to its office, interpose, and protest the illegality and injustice of such actions, and the damnation that is expressly threatened to them by the word of God; the thorough-paced politician must presently laugh at the squeamishness of his conscience, and read it another lecture, and tell it, that *just* and *unjust* are but names grounded only upon opinion, and authorized by custom, by which the wise and the knowing part of the world serve themselves upon the ignorant and easy; and that, whatsoever fond priests may talk, there is no devil like an enemy in power, no damnation like being poor, and no hell like an empty purse; and therefore, that those courses, by which a man comes to rid himself of these plagues, are *ipso facto* prudent, and consequently pious: the former being, with such wise men, the only measure of the latter. And the truth is, the late times of confusion, in which the hights and refinements of religion were professed in conjunction with the practice of the most execrable villainies that were ever acted upon the earth; and the weakness of our church discipline since its restoration, whereby it has been scarce able to get any hold on men's consciences, and much less able to keep it; and the great prevalence of that atheistical doctrine of the Leviathan, and the unhappy propagation of Erastianism; these things, I say, with some others, have been the sad and fatal causes that have loosed the bands of conscience, and eaten out the very heart and sense of Christianity amongst us, to that degree, that there is now scarce any religious tie or restraint upon persons, but merely from those faint remainders of natural conscience which God will be sure to keep alive upon the hearts of men, as long as they are men, for the great ends of his own providence, whether they will or no. So that, were it not for this sole obstacle, religion is not now so much in danger of being divided, and torn piecemeal by sects and factions, as of being at once devoured by atheism. Which being so, let none wonder that irreligion is accounted policy, when it is grown even to a fashion; and passes for wit with some, as well as for wisdom with others. For certain it is, that advantage now sits in the room of conscience, and steers all: and no man is esteemed any ways considerable for policy, who wears religion otherwise than as a cloak, that is, as such a garment as may both cover and keep him warm, and yet hang loose upon him too.

3. The third rule or principle upon which this policy, or wisdom of the world, proceeds, is, That a man ought to make himself, and not the public, the chief, if not the sole end of all his actions. He is to be his own centre and circumference too: that is, to draw all things to himself, and to extend nothing beyond himself: he is to make the greater world serve the less; and not only not to love his neighbor as himself, but indeed to account none for his neighbor but himself.

And therefore, to die or suffer for his country, is not only exploded by him as a great paradox in politics, and fitter for poets to sing of than for wise men to practice; but also, to make himself so much as one penny the poorer, or to forbear one base gain to serve his prince, to secure a whole nation, or to credit a church, is judged by him a great want of experience, and a piece of romantic melancholy, unbecoming a politician; who is still to look upon himself as his prince, his country, his church, nay, and his God too.

The general interest of the nation is nothing to him, but only that portion of it that he either does or would possess. It is not the rain that waters the whole earth, but that which falls into his own cistern, that must relieve him: not the common, but the enclosure, that must make him rich.

Let the public sink or swim, so long as he can hold up his head above water: let the ship be cast away, if he may but have the benefit of the wreck: let the government be ruined by his avarice, if by the same avarice he can scrape together so much as to make his peace, and maintain him as well under another: let foreigners invade and spoil the land, so long as he has a good estate in bank elsewhere. Peradventure, for all this, men may curse him as a covetous wretch, a traitor, and a villain: but such words are to be looked upon only as the splendid declaimings of novices, and men of heat, who, while they rail at his person, perhaps envy his fortune:

or possibly of losers and malcontents, whose portion and inheritance is a freedom to speak. But a politician must be above words. Wealth, he knows, answers all, and if it brings a storm upon him, will provide him also a coat to weather it out.

That such thoughts and principles as these lie at the bottom of most men's actions; at the bottom, do I say? nay, sit at the top, and visibly hold the helm in the management of the weightiest affairs of most nations, we need not much history, nor curiosity of observation, to convince us: for though there have not been wanting such heretofore, as have practiced these unworthy arts, (forasmuch as there have been villains in all places and all ages,) yet nowadays they are owned above-board; and whereas men formerly had then in design, amongst us they are openly vouched, argued, and asserted in common discourse.

But this, I confess, being a new, unexemplified kind of policy, scarce comes up to that which the apostle here condemns for the *wisdom of the world*, but must pass rather for the wisdom of this particular age, which, as in most other things it stands alone, scorning the examples of all former ages, so it has a way of policy and wisdom also peculiar to itself.

4. The fourth and last principle that I shall mention, upon which this wisdom of the world proceeds, is this:

That in showing kindness, or doing favors, no respect at all is to be had to friendship, gratitude, or sense of honor; but that such favors are to be done only to the rich or potent, from whom a man may receive a further advantage, or to his enemies, from whom he may otherwise fear a mischief.

I have here mentioned gratitude, and sense of honor, being (as I may so speak) a man's civil conscience, prompting him to many things, upon the accounts of common decency, which religion would otherwise bind him to, upon the score of duty. And it is sometimes found that some, who have little or no reverence for religion, have yet those innate seeds and sparks of generosity as make them scorn to do such things as would render them mean in the opinion of sober and worthy men; and with such persons, shame is instead of piety, to restrain them from many base and degenerous practices.

But now our politician, having baffled his greater conscience, must not be nonplused with inferior obligations; and having leaped over such mountains, at length poorly lie down before a mole-hill: but he must add perfection to perfection; and being past grace, endeavor, if need be, to be past shame too. And accordingly he looks upon friendship, gratitude, and sense of honor, as terms of art to amuse and impose upon weak, undesigning minds. For an enemy's money, he thinks, may be made as good a friend as any; and gratitude looks backward, but policy forward: and for sense of honor, if it impoverisheth a man, it is, in his esteem, neither honor nor sense.

Whence it is, that nowadays only rich men or enemies are accounted the rational objects of benefaction. For to be kind to the former is traffic; and in these times men present, just as they soil their ground, not that they love the dirt, but that they expect a crop: and for the latter, the politician well approves of the Indian's religion; in worshiping the devil, that he may do him no hurt; how much soever he hates him, and is hated by him.

But if a poor, old, decayed friend or relation, whose purse, whose house and heart had been formerly free and open to such an one, shall at length upon change of fortune come to him with hunger and rags, pleading his past services and his present wants, and so crave some relief of one, for the merit and memory of the other; the politician, who imitates the serpent's wisdom, must turn his deaf ear too, to all the insignificant charms of gratitude and honor, in behalf of such a bankrupt, undone friend, who having been already used, and now squeezed dry, is fit only to be cast aside. He must abhor gratitude as a worse kind of witchcraft, which only serves to conjure up the pale, meagre ghosts of dead, forgotten kindnesses, to haunt and trouble him; still respecting what is past; whereas such wise men as himself, in such cases, account all that is past to be also gone; and know that there can be no gain in refunding, nor any profit in paying debts. The sole measure of all his courtesies is, what return they will make him, and what revenue they will bring him in. His expectations govern his charity. And we must not vouch any man for an exact master in the rules of our modern policy, but such an one as hath brought himself so far to hate and despise the absurdity of being kind upon free cost, as (to use a known expression) not so much as to tell a friend what it is a clock for nothing.

And thus I have finished the first general head proposed from the text, and shown some of those rules, principles, and maxims that this wisdom of the world acts by: I say some of them, for I neither pretend nor desire to know them all.

II. I come now to the other general head, which is, to show the folly and absurdity of these principles in relation to God. In order to which we must observe that foolishness, being porperly a man's deviation from right reason in point of practice, must needs consist in one of these two things:

1. In his pitching upon such an end as is unsuitable to his condition; or,

2. In his pitching upon means unsuitable to the compassing of his end.

There is folly enough in either of these; and my business shall be to show, that such as act by the forementioned rules of worldly wisdom are eminently foolish upon both accounts.

1. And first, for that first sort of foolishness imputable to them; namely, that a man, by following such principles, pitches upon that for his end which noways suits his condition.

Certain it is, and indeed self-evident, that the wisdom of this world looks no further than this world. All its designs and efficacy terminate on this side heaven, nor does policy so much as pretend to any more than to be the great art of raising a man to the plenties, glories, and grandeurs of the world. And if it arrives so far as to make a man rich, potent, and honorable, it has its end, and has done its utmost. But now that a man can not rationally make these things his end, will appear from these two considerations:

(1.) That they reach not the measure of his duration or being; the perpetuity of which surviving this mortal state, and shooting forth into the endless eternities of another world, must needs render a man infinitely miserable and forlorn, if he has no other comforts but what he must leave behind him in this. For nothing can make a man happy, but that which shall last as long as he lasts. And all these enjoyments are much too short for an immortal soul to stretch itself upon, which shall persist in being, not only when profit, pleasure, and honor, but when time itself shall cease, and be no more.

No man can transport his large retinue, his sumptuous fare, and his rich furniture into another world. Nothing of all these things can continue with him then, but the memory of them. And surely the bare remembrance that a man was formerly rich or great can not make him at all happier there, where an infinite happiness or an infinite misery shall equally swallow up the sense of these poor felicities. It may indeed contribute to his misery, heighten the anguish, and sharpen the sting of conscience, and so add fury to the everlasting flames, when he shall reflect upon the abuse of all that wealth and greatness that the good providence of God had put as a price into his hand for worthier purposes, than to damn his nobler and better part, only to please and gratify his worse. But the politician has an answer ready for all these melancholy considerations; that he, for his part, believes none of these things; as that there is either a heaven, or a hell, or an immortal soul. No, he is too great a friend to real knowledge, to take such troublesome assertions as these upon trust. Which if it be his belief, as no doubt it is, let him for me continue in it still, and stay for its confutation in another world; which if he can destroy by disbelieving, his infidelity will do him better service than as yet he has any cause to presume that it can. But,

(2.) Admitting that either these enjoyments were eternal, or the soul mortal, and so, that one way or other they were commensurate to its duration, yet still they can not be an end suitable to a rational nature, forasmuch as they fill not the measure of its desires. The foundation of all man's unhappiness here on earth, is the great disproportion between his enjoyments and his appetites; which appears evidently in this, that let a man have never so much, he is still desiring something or other more. Alexander, we know, was much troubled at the scantiness of nature itself, that there were no more worlds for him to disturb: and in this respect, every man living has a soul as great as Alexander, and, put under the same circumstances, would own the very same dissatisfactions.

Now this is most certain, that in spiritual natures, so much as there is of desire, so much there is also of capacity to receive. I do not say there is always a capacity to receive the very thing they desire, for that may be impossible: but for the degree of happiness that they propose to themselves from that thing, this I say they are capable of. And as God is said to have *made man after his own image,* so upon this quality he seems peculiarly to have stampt the resemblance of his infinity. For man seems as boundless in his desires as God is in his being; and therefore nothing but God himself can satisfy him. But the great inequality of all things else to the appetites of a rational soul appears yet further from this; that in all these worldly things, that a man pursues with the greatest eagerness and intention of mind imaginable, he finds not half the pleasure in the actual possession of them, that he proposed to himself in the expectation. Which shows that there is a great cheat or lie which overspreads the world, while all things here below beguile men's expectations, and their expectations cheat their experience.

Let this therefore be the first thing in which the foolishness of this worldly wisdom is manifest. Namely, that by it a man proposes to himself an end wholly unsuitable to his condition; as bearing no proportion to the measure of his duration, or the vastness of his desires.

2. The other thing in which foolishness is seen, is a man's pitching upon means unsuitable to that which he has made his end.

And here we will, for the present, suppose the things of the world to have neither that shortness nor emptiness in them that we have indeed proved them to have. But that they are so adequate to all the concerns of an intelligent nature, that they may be rationally fixed upon by men as the ultimate end of all their designs: yet the folly of this wisdom appears in this, that it suggests those means for the acquisition of these enjoyments, that are noways fit to compass or acquire them, and that upon a double account.

(1.) That they are in themselves unable and insufficient for, and,

(2.) That they are frequently opposite to a successful attainment of them.

(1.) And first for their insufficiency. Let politicians contrive as accurately, project as deeply, and pursue what they have thus contrived and projected, as diligently as it is possible for human wit and industry to do, yet still the success of all depends upon the favor of an overruling hand. For God expressly claims it as a special part of his prerogative, to have the entire disposal of riches, honors, and whatsoever else is apt to command the desires of mankind here below; Deut. viii. 18. *It is the Lord thy God that giveth thee power to get wealth.* And in 1 Sam. ii. 30. God peremptorily declares himself the sole fountain of honor, telling us, that *those that honor him shall be honored, and that those that despise him shall be lightly esteemed.*

And then for dignities and preferments, we have the word of one that could dispose of these things as much as kings could do, Prov. xxix. 26,. where he tells us, that *many seek the ruler's favor :* that is, apply themselves both to his interest and humor, with all the arts of flattery and obsequiousness, the surest and the readiest ways (one would think) to advance a man; and yet, after all, it follows in the next words, that *every man's judgment cometh of the Lord.* And that, whatsoever may be expected here, it is resolved only in the court of heaven, whether the man shall proceed favorite in the courts of princes, and after all his artificial attendance come to sit at the right hand, or be made a footstool. So that upon full trial of all the courses that policy could either devise or practice, the most experienced masters of it have been often forced to sit down with that complaint of the disciples, *We have toiled all night, and have caught nothing.* For do we not sometimes see that traitors can be out of favor, and knaves be beggars, and lose their estates, and be stript of their offices, as well as honester men?

And why all this? Surely not always for want of craft to spy out where their game lay, nor yet for want of irreligion to give them all the scope of ways lawful and unlawful to prosecute their intentions; but because the providence of God strikes not in with them, but dashes, and even dispirits all their endeavors, and makes their designs heartless and ineffectual. So that it is not their seeing this man, their belying another, nor their sneaking to a third, that shall be able to do their business, when the designs of Heaven will be served by their disappointment. And this is the true cause why so many politic conceptions, so elaborately formed and wrought, and grown at length ripe for delivery, do yet in the issue miscarry and prove abortive; for, being come to the birth, the all-disposing providence of God denies them strength to bring forth. And thus the authors of them, having missed of their mighty aims, are fain to retreat with frustration and a baffle; and having played the knaves unsuccessfully, to have the ill luck to pass for fools too.

(2.) The means suggested by policy and worldly wisdom for the attainment of these earthly enjoyments are unfit for that purpose, not only upon the account of their insufficiency for, but also of their frequent opposition and contrariety to, the accomplishment of such ends; nothing being more usual than for these unchristian fishers of men to be fatally caught in their own nets: for does not the text expressly say, that *God taketh the wise in their own craftiness?* And has not our own experience sufficiently commented upon the text, when we have seen some by the very same ways by which they had designed to rise uncontrollably, and to clear off all obstructions before their ambition, to have directly procured their utter downfall, and to have broke their necks from that very ladder by which they had thought to have climbed as high as their father Lucifer; and there from the top of all their greatness to have looked down with scorn upon all below them?

Such persons are the proper and lawful objects of derision, forasmuch as God himself laughs at them.

Haman wanted nothing to complete his greatness but a gallows upon which to hang Mordecai; but it mattered not for whom he provided the gallows, when Providence designed the rope for him.

With what contempt does the apostle here, in the 20th verse of this third chapter of the first epistle to the Corinthians, repeat those words of the psalmist, concerning all the fine artifices of worldly wisdom; *The Lord,* says he, *knoweth the thoughts of the wise that they are vain.* All their contrivances are but thin, slight, despicable things, and, for the most part, destructive of themselves; nothing being more equal in justice, and indeed more natural in the direct consequence and connection of effects and causes, than for men wickedly wise to outwit themselves, and for such as wrestle with Providence, to trip up their own heels.

It is clear, therefore, that the charge of this second sort of foolishness is made good upon worldly wisdom; for that having made men pitch upon an end unfit for their condition, it also makes them pitch upon means unfit to attain that end. And that both by reason of their inability for, and frequent contrariety to, the bringing about such designs.

This, I say, has been made good in the general; but since particulars convince with greater life and evidence, we will resume the forementioned principles of the politician, and show severally in each of them, how little efficacy they have to advance the practicers of them to the things they aspire to by them.

1. And first, for his first principle, That the politician must maintain a constant, habitual dissimulation. Concerning which I shall lay down this as certain; that dissimulation can be no further useful than it is concealed, forasmuch as no man will trust a known cheat: and it is also as certain, that as some men use dissimulation for their interest, so others have an interest as strongly engaging them to use all the art and industry they can to find it out; and to assure themselves of the truth or falsehood of those with whom they deal, which renders it infinitely hard, if not morally impossible, for a man to carry on a constant course of dissimulation without discovery. And being once discovered, it is not only no help, but the greatest impediment of action in the world. For since man is but of a very limited, narrow power in his own person, and consequently can effect no great matter merely by his own personal strength, but as he acts in society and conjunction with others, without first engaging their trust; and moreover, since men will trust no further than they judge a person for his sincerity fit to be trusted, it follows that a discovered dissembler can achieve nothing great or considerable; for not being able to gain men's trust, he can not gain their concurrence, and so is left alone to act singly, and upon his own bottom; and while that is the sphere of his activity, all that he can do must needs be contemptible. We know

how successful the late usurper * was, while his army believed him real in his zeal against kingship. But when they found out the imposture, upon his aspiring to the same himself, he was presently deserted, and opposed by them, and never able to crown his usurped greatness with the addition of that title which he so passionately thirsted after. Add to this the judgment of as great an English author as ever wrote, with great confidence affirming, "that the ablest men that ever were, had all an openness and frankness of dealing; and that, if at any time such did dissemble, their dissimulation took effect merely in the strength of that reputation they had gained by their veracity and clear dealing in the main." From all which it follows, that dissimulation can be of no further use to a man than just to guard him within the compass of his own personal concerns; which yet may be more easily, and not less effectually done, by that silence and reservedness that every man may innocently practice, without the putting on of any contrary disguise.

2. The politician's second principle was, That conscience, or religion, ought never to stand between any man and his temporal advantage. Which indeed is properly atheism; and, so far as it is practiced, tends to the dissolution of society, the bond of which is religion. Forasmuch as a man's happiness or misery in his converse with other men depends chiefly upon their doing or not doing those things which human laws can take no cognizance of: such as are all actions capable of being done in secret, and out of the view of mankind, which yet have the greatest influence upon our neighbor, even in his nearest and dearest concerns. And if there be no inward sense of religion to awe men from the doing unjust actions, provided they can do them without discovery, it is impossible for any man to sit secure or happy in the possession of any thing that he enjoys. And this inconvenience the politician must expect from others, as well as they have felt from him, unless he thinks that he can engross this principle to his own practice, and that others can not be as false and atheistical as himself, especially having had the advantage of his copy to write after.

3. The third principle was, That the politician ought to

* Cromwell.

make himself, and not the public, the chief, if not the sole end of all that he does.

But here we shall quickly find that the private spirit will prove as pernicious in temporals as ever it did in spirituals. For while every particular member of the public provides singly and solely for itself, the several joints of the body politic do thereby separate and disunite, and so become unable to support the whole; and when the public interest once fails, let private interests subsist if they can, and prevent an universal ruin from involving in it particulars. It is not a man's wealth that can be sure to save him, if the enemy be wise enough to refuse part of it tendered as a ransom, when it is as easy for him to destroy the owner, and to take the whole. When the hand finds itself well warmed and covered, let it refuse the trouble of feeding the mouth or guarding the head till the body be starved or killed, and then we shall see how it will fare with the hand. The Athenians, the Romans, and all other nations that grew great out of little or nothing, did so merely by the public-mindedness of particular persons; and the same courses that first raised nations and governments must support them. So that, were there no such thing as religion, prudence were enough to enforce this upon all.

For our own parts, let us reflect upon our glorious and renowned English ancestors, men eminent in church and state, and we shall find that this was the method by which they preserved both.

We have succeeded into their labors, and the fruits of them: and it will both concern and become us to succeed also into their principles. For it is no man's duty to be safe or to be rich, but I am sure, it is the duty of every one to make good his trust. And it is a calamity to a whole nation, that any man should have a place or an employment more large and public than his spirit.

4. The fourth and last principle mentioned was, That the politician must not, in doing kindnesses, consider his friends, but only gratify rich men or enemies. Which principle (as to that branch of it relating to enemies) was certainly first borrowed and fetched up from the very bottom of hell; and uttered, no doubt, by particular and immediate inspiration of the devil. And yet (as much of the devil as it carries in

it) it neither is nor can be more villainous and detestable than it is really silly, senseless, and impolitic.

But to go over the several parts of this principle; and to begin with the supposed policy of gratifying only the rich and opulent. Does our wise man think that the grandee, whom he so courts, does not see through all the little plots of his courtship as well as he himself? And so, at the same time while he accepts the gift, laugh in his sleeve at the design, and despise the giver?

But, for the neglect of friends, as it is the hight of baseness, so it can never be proved rational, till we prove the person using it omnipotent and self-sufficient, and such as can never need any mortal assistance. But if he be a man, that is, a poor, weak creature, subject to change and misery, let him know that it is the friend only that God has made for the day of adversity, as the most suitable and sovereign help that humanity is capable of. And those (though in highest place) who slight and disoblige their friends, shall infallibly come to know the value of them, by having none when they shall most need them.

That prince that maintains the reputation of a true, fast, generous friend, has an army always ready to fight for him, maintained to his hand without pay.

As for the other part of this principle, that concerns the gratifying of enemies; it is (to say no more) an absurdity parallel to the former. For when a man shall have done all he can, given all he has, to oblige an enemy, he shall find that he has armed him indeed, but not at all altered him.

The scripture bids us pray for our enemies, and love our enemies, but nowhere does it bid us trust our enemies; nay, it strictly cautions us against it, Prov. xxvi. 25. *When he speaketh thee fair,* (says the text,) *believe him not; for there are yet seven abominations in his heart*: and, in good earnest, it would be a rarity worth the seeing, could any one show us such a thing as a perfectly reconciled enemy. Men are generally credulous at first, and will not take up this great and safe truth at the cost of other men's experience, till they come to be bitten into a sense of it by their own; but are apt to take fair professions, fawning looks, treats, entertainments, visits, and such like pitiful stuff, for friendship and reconcilement, and so to admit the serpent into their bosom: but let them come once to depend upon this new-made friend, or reconciled enemy, in any great or real concern of life, and they shall find him false as hell, and cruel as the grave. And I know nothing more to be wondered at than that those reconcilements that are so difficult, and even next to impossible in the effect, should yet be so frequent in the attempt; especially since the reason of this difficulty lies as deep as nature itself; which, after it has done an injury, will forever be suspicious; and I would fain see the man that can perfectly love the person whom he suspects.

There is a noted story of Hector and Ajax, who, having combated one another, ended that combat in a reconcilement, and testified that reconcilement by mutual presents: Hector giving Ajax a sword, and Ajax presenting Hector with a belt. The consequence of which was, that Ajax slew himself with the sword given him by Hector, and Hector was dragged about the walls of Troy by the belt given him by Ajax. Such are the gifts, such are the killing kindnesses of reconciled enemies.

Confident men may try what conclusions they please, at their own peril; but let history be consulted, reason heard, and experience called in to speak impartially what it has found, and I believe they will all with one voice declare, that whatsoever the grace of God may do in the miraculous change of men's hearts, yet, according to the common methods of the world, a man may as well expect to make the devil himself his friend, as an enemy that has given him the first blow.

And thus I have gone over the two general heads proposed from the words, and shown both what those principles are upon which this wisdom of the world does proceed; and also wherein the folly and absurdity of them does consist.

And now into what can we more naturally improve the whole foregoing discourse, than into that practical inference of our apostle, in the verse before the text? that *if any man desires the reputation of wisdom, he should become a fool, that he may be wise*; that is, a fool to the world, that he may be wise to God.

Let us not be ashamed of the folly of being sincere, and

without guile; without traps and snares in our converse; of being fearful to build our estates upon the ruin of our consciences; of preferring the public good before our own private emolument; and lastly, of being true to all the offices of friendship, the obligations of which are sacred, and will certainly be exacted of us by the great judge of all our actions. I say, let us not blush to be found guilty of all these follies, (as some account them,) rather than to be expert in that kind of wisdom that God himself, the great fountain of wisdom, has pronounced to be *earthly, sensual, devilish;* and of the wretched absurdity of which all histories, both ecclesiastical and civil, have given us such pregnant and convincing examples.

Reflect upon Ahithophel, Haman, Sejanus, Cæsar Borgia, and other such masters of the arts of policy, who thought they had fixed themselves upon so sure a bottom, that they might even defy and dare Providence to the face; and yet how did God bring an absolute disappointment, like one great blot, over all their fine, artificial contrivances!

Every one of those mighty and profound sages coming to a miserable and disastrous end.

The consideration of which, and the like passages, one would think, should make men grow weary of dodging and showing tricks with God in their own crooked ways: and even force them to acknowledge it for the surest and most unfailing prudence, wholly to commit their persons and concerns to the wise and good providence of God, in the straight and open ways of his own commands.

Who, we may be confident, is more tenderly concerned for the good of those that truly fear and serve him, than it is possible for the most selfish of men to be concerned for themselves: and who, in all the troubles and disturbances, all the cross, difficult, and perplexing passages that can fall out, will be sure to guide all to this happy issue, *that all things shall work together for good to those that love God.*

To which God, infinitely wise, holy, and just, be rendered and ascribed, as is most due, all praise, might, majesty, and dominion, both now and for evermore. *Amen.*

SERMON X.

A SERMON PREACHED AT CHRIST CHURCH, OXON, BEFORE THE UNIVERSITY, MAY 3, 1685.

2 Cor. viii. 12.—*For if there be first a willing mind, it is accepted according to that a man hath, and not according to that he hath not.*

IN dealing with men's consciences, for the taking them off from sin, I know nothing of so direct and efficacious an influence as the right stating of those general rules and principles of action that men are apt to guide their lives and consciences by: for if these be true, and withal rightly applied, men must needs proceed upon firm and safe grounds; but if either false in themselves, or not right in their particular application, the whole course that men are thereby engaged in, being founded in sin and error, must needs lead to, and at length end in, death and confusion: there being (as the wise man tells us) *a way that may seem right in a man's own eyes, when, nevertheless, the end of that way is death.*

Now as amongst these principles or rules of action, the pretenses of the Spirit, and of tenderness of conscience, and the like, have been the late grand artifices, by which crafty and designing hypocrites have so much abused the world; so I shall now instance in another of no less note, by which the generality of men are as apt to abuse themselves; and that is a certain rule or sentence got almost into every man's mouth, that God accepts the will for the deed. A principle (as usually applied) of less malice, I confess; but, considering the easiness, and withal the fatality of the delusion, of more mischief than the other.

And this I shall endeavor to search into, and lay open, in the following discourse.

The words hold forth a general rule or proposition delivered upon a particular occasion: which was the apostle's exhorting the Corinthians to a holy and generous emulation of the charity of the Macedonians, in contributing freely to the relief of the poor saints at Jerusalem: upon this great encouragement, that in all such works of charity, it is the will that gives worth to the oblation, and, as to God's acceptance, sets the poorest giver upon the same level with the richest. Nor is this all; but so perfectly does the value of all charitable acts take its measure and proportion from the will, and from the fullness of the heart, rather than that of the hand, that a lesser supply may be oftentimes a greater charity, and the widow's mite, in the balance of the sanctuary, outweigh the shekels, and perhaps the talents of the most opulent and wealthy: the all and utmost of the one being certainly a nobler alms than the superfluities of the other: and all this upon the account of the great rule here set down in the text: That, in all transactions between God and man, wheresoever there is a full resolution, drift, and purpose of will to please God, there, what a man can do, shall, by virtue thereof, be accepted, and what he can not do, shall not be required. From whence these two propositions, in sense and design much the same, do naturally result.

I. The first of them expressed in the words; to wit, that God accepts the will, where there is no power to perform.

II. The other of them implied; namely, that where there is a power to perform, God does not accept the will.

Of all the spiritual tricks and legerdemain by which men are apt to shift off their duty, and to impose upon their own souls, there is none so common, and of so fatal an import, as these two; the plea of a good intention, and the plea of a good will.

One or both of them being used by men, almost at every turn, to elude the precept, to put God off with something instead of obedience, and so, in effect, to outwit him whom they are called to obey. They are certainly two of the most effectual instruments and engines in the devil's hands to wind and turn the souls of men by, to whatsoever he pleases. For,

1. The plea of a good intention will serve to sanctify and authorize the very worst of actions. The proof of which is

but too full and manifest, from that lewd and scandalous doctrine of the Jesuits concerning the direction of the intention, and likewise from the whole manage of the late accursed rebellion. In which, it was this insolent and impudent pretense, that emboldened the worst of men to wade through the blood of the best of kings, and the loyalest of subjects; namely, that in all that risk of villainy, *their hearts*, forsooth, *were right towards God;* and that all their plunder and rapine was for nothing else, but to place Christ on his throne, and to establish amongst us the power of godliness, and the purity of the gospel; by a further reformation (as the cant goes) of a church which had but too much felt the meaning of that word before.

But such persons consider not, that though an ill intention is certainly sufficient to spoil and corrupt an act in itself materially good, yet no good intention whatsoever can rectify or infuse a moral goodness into an act otherwise evil. To come to church, is no doubt an act in itself materially good; yet he who does it with an ill intention, comes to God's house upon the devil's errand; and the whole act is thereby rendered absolutely evil and detestable before God. But on the other side; if it were possible for a man to intend well, while he does ill; yet no such intention, though never so good, can make that man steal, lie, or murder with a good conscience; or convert a wicked action into a good.

For these things are against the nature of morality; in which nothing is or can be really good, without an universal concurrence of all the principles and ingredients requisite to a moral action; though the failure of any one of them will imprint a malignity upon that act, which, in spite of all the other requisite ingredients, shall stamp it absolutely evil, and corrupt it past the cure of a good intention.

And thus, as I have shown, that the plea of a good intention is used by men to warrant and patronize the most villainous and wicked actions, so, in the next place, the plea of a good will will be found equally efficacious to supersede and take off the necessity of all holy and good actions. For still (as I have observed) the great art of the devil, and the principal deceit of the heart, is to put a trick upon the command, and to keep fair with God himself, while men fall foul upon his laws. For both law and gospel call aloud for active obedience, and such a piety as takes not up either with faint notions, or idle, insignificant inclinations, but such an one as shows itself in the solid instances of practice and performance. For, *Do this and live,* saith the law, Luke x. 28; and, *If ye know these things, happy are ye if ye do them,* says the gospel, John xiii. 17; and, *Not every one that saith, Lord, Lord, shall enter into the kingdom of heaven, but he that doeth the will of my Father which is in heaven,* Matt. vii. 21; and, *Let no man deceive you; he that doth righteousness is righteous,* 1 John iii. 7; with innumerable more such places. All of them terrible and severe injunctions of practice, and equally severe obligations to it.

But then in comes the benign latitude of the doctrine of good will, and cuts asunder all these hard, pinching cords; and tells you, that if this be but piously and well inclined, if the bent of the spirit (as some call it) be towards God and goodness, God accepts of this above, nay, instead of all external works; those being but the shell, or husk, this the kernel, the quintessence, and the very soul of duty. But for all this, these bents and propensities and inclinations will not do the business: the bare bending of the bow will not hit the mark without shooting the arrow; and men are not called to will, but to work out their salvation.

But what then? Is it not as certain from the text, that God sometimes accepts the will, as it is from those forementioned scriptures that God commands the deed? Yes, no doubt: since it is impossible for the Holy Ghost to contradict that in one place of scripture which he had affirmed in another. In all the foregoing places, doing is expressly commanded, and no happiness allowed to any thing short of it; and yet here God is said to accept of the will; and can both these stand together without manifest contradiction? That which enjoins the deed is certainly God's law; and it is also as certain that the scripture that allows of the will is neither the abrogation, nor derogation, nor dispensation, nor relaxation of that law.

In order to the clearing of which, I shall lay down these two assertions:

(1.) That every law of God commands the obedience of the whole man.

(2.) That the will is never accepted by God, but as it is the obedience of the whole man.

So that the allowance or acceptance of the will, mentioned in the text, takes off nothing from the obligation of those laws, in which the deed is so plainly and positively enjoined, but is only an interpretation or declaration of the true sense of those laws, showing the equity of them: which is as really essential to every law, and gives it its obliging force as much as the justice of it; and indeed, is not another, or a distinct thing from the justice of it, any more than a particular case is from an universal rule.

But you will say, how can the obedience of the will ever be proved to be the obedience of the whole man?

For answer to which, we are first to consider every man as a moral, and consequently as a rational agent; and then to consider what is the office and influence of the will in every moral action. Now the morality of an action is founded in the freedom of that principle by virtue of which it is in the agent's power, having all things ready and requisite to the performance of an action, either to perform or not to perform it. And as the will is endued with this freedom, so is it also endued with a power to command all the other faculties, both of soul and body, to execute what it has so willed or decreed, and that without resistance; so that upon the last dictate of the will for the doing of such or such a thing, all the other faculties proceed immediately to act according to their respective offices. By which it is manifest, that in point of action, the will is virtually the whole man; as containing in it all that which by virtue of his other faculties he is able to do: just as the spring of a watch is virtually the whole motion of the watch; forasmuch as it imparts a motion to all the wheels of it.

Thus as to the soul. If the will bids the understanding think, study, and consider, it will accordingly apply itself to thought, study, and consideration. If it bids the affections love, rejoice, or be angry, an act of love, joy, or anger will follow. And then for the body; if the will bids the leg go, it goes; if it bids the hand to do this, it does it. So that a man is a moral agent only as he is endued with, and acts by, a free and commanding principle of will.

And therefore, when God says, *My son, give me thy heart,* (which there signifies the will,) it is as much as if he had commanded the service of the whole man; for whatsoever the will commands, the whole man must do: the empire or dominion of the will over all the faculties of soul and body (as to most of the operations of each of them) being absolutely overruling and despotical. From whence it follows, that when the will has exerted an act of command upon any faculty of the soul, or member of the body, it has, by so doing, done all that the whole man, as a moral agent, can do, for the actual exercise or employment of such a faculty or member. And if so, then what is not done in such a case, is certainly not in a man's power to do; and consequently is no part of the obedience required of him: no man being commanded or obliged to obey beyond his power. And therefore the obedience of the will to God's commands, is the obedience of the whole man, (forasmuch as it includes and infers it,) which was the assertion that we undertook to prove.

But you will say, if the prerogative of the will be such, that where it commands the hand to give an alms, the leg to kneel, or to go to church, or the tongue to utter a prayer, all these things will infallibly be done; suppose we now, a man be bound hand and foot by some outward violence, or be laid up with the gout, or disabled for any of these functions by a palsy; can the will, by its command, make a man in such a condition utter a prayer, or kneel, or go to church? No, it is manifest it can not: but then you are to know also, that neither is vocal prayer, or bodily kneeling, or going to church, in such a case, any part of the obedience required of such a person: but that act of his will hitherto spoken of, that would have put his body upon all these actions, had there been no impediment, is that man's whole obedience; and for that very cause that it is so, and for no other, it stands here accepted by God.

From all which discourse, this must naturally and directly be inferred, as a certain truth, and the chief foundation of all that can be said upon this subject: namely, that whosoever wills the doing of a thing, if the doing of it be in his power, he will certainly do it; and whosoever does not do that thing which he has in his power to do, does not really and properly will it. For though the act of the will commanding, and the act of any other faculty of the soul or body executing that which is so commanded, be physically, and in the precise nature of things, distinct and several; yet morally, as they proceed in subordination, from one entire, free, moral agent, both in divinity and morality they pass but for one and the same action.

Now, that from the foregoing particulars we may come to understand how far this rule of God's accepting the will for the deed holds good in the sense of the apostle, we must consider in it these three things:

1. The original ground and reason of it.
2. The just measure and bounds of it: and,
3. The abuse or misapplication of it.

And first for the original ground and reason of this rule; it is founded upon that great, self-evident, and eternal truth, that the just, the wise, and good God neither does nor can require of man any thing that is impossible, or naturally beyond his power to do: and therefore, in the second place, the measure of this rule, by which the just extent and bounds of it are to be determined, must be that power or ability that man naturally has to do or perform the things willed by him. So that wheresoever such a power is found, there this rule of God's accepting the will has no place; and wheresoever such a power is not found, there this rule presently becomes in force. And accordingly, in the third and last place, the abuse or misapplication of this rule will consist in these two things:

1. That men do very often take that to be an act of the will that really and truly is not so.

2. That they reckon many things impossible that indeed are not impossible.

And first, to begin with men's mistakes about the will, and the acts of it; I shall note these three, by which men are extremely apt to impose upon themselves.

(1.) As first, the bare approbation of the worth and goodness of a thing is not properly the willing of that thing; and yet men do very commonly account it so. But this is properly an act of the understanding or judgment; a faculty wholly distinct from the will; and which makes a principal part of that which in divinity we call natural conscience; and in the strength of which a man may approve of things good and excellent, without ever willing or intending the practice of them. And accordingly the apostle, Rom. ii. 18, gives us an account of some who approved of things excellent, and yet practiced, and consequently willed, things clean contrary; since no man can commit a sin, but he must will it first. Whosoever observes and looks into the workings of his own heart, will find that noted sentence, *Video meliora proboque, deteriora sequor*, too frequently and fatally verified upon himself. The seventh of the Romans (which has been made the unhappy scene of so much controversy about these matters) has several passages to this purpose. In a word, to judge what ought to be done is one thing, and to will the doing of it is quite another.

No doubt virtue is a beautiful and a glorious thing in the eyes of the most vicious person breathing; and all that he does or can hate in it, is the difficulty of its practice; for it is practice alone that divides the world into virtuous and vicious; but otherwise, as to the theory and speculation of virtue and vice, honest and dishonest, the generality of mankind are much the same; for men do not approve of virtue by choice and free election; but it is an homage which nature commands all understandings to pay to it, by necessary determination; and yet, after all, it is but a faint, unactive thing; for in defiance of the judgment, the will may still remain as perverse, and as much a stranger to virtue, as it was before. In fine, there is as much difference between the approbation of the judgment, and the actual volitions of the will, with relation to the same object, as there is between a man's viewing a desirable thing with his eye, and his reaching after it with his hand.

(2.) The wishing of a thing is not properly the willing of it; though too often mistaken by men for such: but it is that which is called by the schools an imperfect velleity, and imports no more than an idle unoperative complacency in, and desire of the end, without any consideration of, nay, for the most part, with a direct abhorrence of the means; of which nature I account that wish of Balaam, in Numbers xxiii. 10, *Let me die the death of the righteous, and let my last end be like his.*

The thing itself appeared desirable to him, and accordingly he could not but like and desire it; but then it was after a very irrational, absurd way, and contrary to all the methods and principles of a rational agent; which never wills a thing really and properly, but it applies to the means by which it is to be acquired. But at that very time that Balaam desired to *die the death of the righteous,* he was actually following the wages of unrighteousness, and so thereby engaged in a course quite contrary to what he desired; and consequently such as could not possibly bring him to such an end. Much like the sot that cried, *Utinam hoc esset laborare,* while he lay lazing and lolling upon his couch.

But every true act of volition imports a respect to the end, by and through the means; and wills a thing only in that way in which it is to be compassed or effected; which is the foundation of that most true aphorism, That he who wills the end, wills also the means. The truth of which is founded in such a necessary connection of the terms, that I look upon the proposition, not only as true, but as convertible; and that, as a man can not truly and properly will the end, but he must also will the means; so neither can he will the means, but he must virtually, and by interpretation at least, will the end. Which is so true, that, in the account of the divine law, a man is reckoned to will even those things that naturally are not the object of desire; such as death itself, Ezek. xviii. 31, only because he wills those ways and courses that naturally tend to and end in it. And even our own common law looks upon a man's raising arms against, or imprisoning his prince, as an imagining or compassing of his death: forasmuch as these actions are the means directly leading to it, and, for the most part, actually concluding in it: and consequently, that the willing of the one is the willing of the other also.

To will a thing therefore is certainly much another thing from what the generality of men, especially in their spiritual concerns, take it to be. I say, in their spiritual concerns; for in their temporal, it is manifest that they think and judge much otherwise; and in the things of this world no man is allowed or believed to will any thing heartily which he does not endeavor after proportionably. A wish is properly a man of desire, sitting or lying still; but an act of the will is a man of business vigorously going about his work: and certainly there is a great deal of difference between a man's stretching out his arms to work, and his stretching them out only to yawn.

(3.) And lastly, a mere inclination to a thing is not properly a willing of that thing; and yet in matters of duty, no doubt, men frequently reckon it for such. For otherwise why should they so often plead and rest in the goodness of their hearts, and the honest and well-inclined disposition of their minds, when they are justly charged with an actual non-performance of what the law requires of them?

But that an inclination to a thing is not a willing of that thing, is irrefragably proved by this one argument, that a man may act virtuously against his inclination, but not against his will. He may be inclined to one thing, and yet will another; and therefore inclination and will are not the same.

For a man may be naturally inclined to pride, lust, anger, and strongly inclined so too, (forasmuch as these inclinations are founded in a peculiar crasis and constitution of the blood and spirits,) and yet by a steady, frequent repetition of the contrary acts of humility, chastity, and meekness, carried thereto by his will, (a principle not to be controlled by the blood or spirits,) he may at length plant in his soul all those contrary habits of virtue: and therefore it is certain that while inclination bends the soul one way, a well-disposed and resolved will may effectually draw it another. A sufficient demonstration, doubtless, that they are two very different things; for where there may be a contrariety, there is certainly a diversity. A good inclination is but the first rude draught of virtue; but the finishing strokes are from the will; which, if well-disposed, will by degrees perfect; if ill-disposed, will, by the superinduction of ill habits, quickly deface it.

God never accepts a good inclination instead of a good action, where that action may be done; nay, so much the contrary, that if a good inclination be not seconded by a good action, the want of that action is thereby made so much the more criminal and inexcusable.

A man may be naturally well and virtuously inclined, and

yet never do one good or virtuous action all his life. A bowl may lie still for all its bias; but it is impossible for a man to will virtue and virtuous actions heartily, but he must in the same degree offer at the practice of them: forasmuch as the dictates of the will are (as we have shown) despotical, and command the whole man. It being a contradiction in morality for the will to go one way, and the man another.

And thus as to the first abuse or misapplication of the great rule mentioned in the text, about God's accepting the will, I have shown three notable mistakes which men are apt to entertain concerning the will; and proved that neither a bare approbation of, nor a mere wishing, or unactive complacency in, nor, lastly, a natural inclination to, things virtuous and good, can pass before God for a man's willing of such things; and consequently, if men upon this account will needs take up and acquiesce in an airy, ungrounded persuasion, that they will those things which really they do not will, they fall thereby into a gross and fatal delusion: a delusion that must and will shut the door of salvation against them. They catch at heaven, but embrace a cloud; they mock God, who will not be mocked; and deceive their own souls, which, God knows, may too easily be both deceived and destroyed too.

2. Come we now in the next place to consider the other way by which men are prone to abuse and pervert this important rule of God's accounting the will for the deed; and that is, by reckoning many things impossible which in truth are not impossible.

And this I shall make appear by showing some of the principal instances of duty, for the performance of which men commonly plead want of power; and thereupon persuade themselves that God and the law rest satisfied with their will.

Now these instances are four.

(1.) In duties of very great and hard labor. Labor is confessedly a great part of the curse; and therefore no wonder if men fly from it: which they do with so great an aversion, that few men know their own strength for want of trying it; and upon that account think themselves really unable to do many things which experience would convince them they have more ability to effect than they have will to attempt.

It is idleness that creates impossibilities; and, where men

care not to do a thing, they shelter themselves under a persuasion that it can not be done. The shortest and the surest way to prove a work possible, is strenuously to set about it; and no wonder if that proves it possible, that, for the most part, makes it so.

Dig, says the unjust steward, *I can not.* But why? Did either his legs or his arms fail him? No; but day-labor was but a hard and a dry kind of livelihood to a man that could get an estate with two or three strokes of his pen; and find so great a treasure as he did, without digging for it.

But such excuses will not pass muster with God, who will allow no man's humor or idleness to be the measure of possible or impossible. And to manifest the wretched hypocrisy of such pretenses, those very things, which upon the bare obligation of duty are declined by men as impossible, presently become not only possible, but readily practicable too, in a case of extreme necessity. As no doubt that forementioned instance of fraud and laziness, the unjust steward, who pleaded that he could neither dig nor beg, would quickly have been brought both to dig and to beg too, rather than starve. And if so, what reason could such an one produce before God, why he could not submit to the same hardships, rather than cheat and lie? The former being but destructive of the body, this latter of the soul: and certainly the highest and dearest concerns of a temporal life are infinitely less valuable than those of an eternal; and consequently ought, without any demur at all, to be sacrificed to them, whensoever they come in competition with them. He who can digest any labor rather than die, must refuse no labor rather than sin.

(2.) The second instance shall be in duties of great and apparent danger. Danger (as the world goes) generally absolves from duty: this being a case in which most men, according to a very ill sense, will needs be a law to themselves. And where it is not safe for them to be religious, their religion shall be to be safe. But Christianity teaches us a very different lesson: for if fear of suffering could take off the necessity of obeying, the doctrine of the cross would certainly be a very idle and a senseless thing; and Christ would never have prayed, *Father, if it be possible, let this cup pass from me,* had the bitterness of the draught made it impossible to be drunk of. If death and danger are things that really can not be endured, no man could ever be obliged to suffer for his conscience, or to die for his religion; it being altogether as absurd to imagine a man obliged to suffer, as to do impossibilities.

But those primitive heroes of the Christian church could not so easily blow off the doctrine of passive obedience, as to make the fear of being passive a discharge from being obedient. No, they found martyrdom not only possible, but in many cases a duty also; a duty dressed up indeed with all that was terrible and afflictive to human nature, yet not at all the less a duty for being so. And such an height of Christianity possessed those noble souls, that every martyr could keep one eye steadily fixed upon his duty, and look death and danger out of countenance with the other: nor did they flinch from duty for fear of martyrdom, when one of the most quickening motives to duty was their desire of it.

But to prove the possibility of a thing, there is no argument like to that which looks backwards; for what has been done or suffered may certainly be done or suffered again. And to prove that men may be martyrs, there needs no other demonstration, than to show that many have been so. Besides that the grace of God has not so far abandoned the Christian world, but that those high primitive instances of passive fortitude in the case of duty and danger rivaling one another have been exemplified, and (as it were) revived, by several glorious copies of them in the succeeding ages of the church.

And (thanks be to God) we need not look very far backward for some of them, even amongst ourselves. For when a violent, victorious faction and rebellion had overrun all, and made loyalty to the king and conformity to the church crimes unpardonable, and of a guilt not to be expiated, but at the price of life or estate; when men were put to swear away all interest in the next world, to secure a very poor one in this; (for they had then oaths to murder souls, as well as sword and pistol for the body; nay,) when the persecution ran so high, that that execrable monster Cromwell made and published that barbarous, heathenish, or rather inhuman edict against the poor suffering episcopal clergy, That they should neither preach nor pray in public, nor baptize, nor marry, nor bury, nor teach school, no, nor so much as live in any gentleman's house, who in mere charity and compassion might be inclined to take them in from perishing in the streets; that is, in other words, that they must starve and die *ex officio*, and being turned out of their churches, take possession only of the church-yard, as so many victims to the remorseless rage of a foul, ill-bred tyrant, professing piety without so much as common humanity: I say, when rage and persecution, cruelty and Cromwellism were at that diabolical pitch, tyrannizing over every thing that looked like loyalty, conscience, and conformity; so that he, who took not their engagement, could not take any thing else, though it were given him; being thereby debarred from the very common benefit of the law, in suing for or recovering of his right in any of their courts of justice; (all of them still following the motion of the high one;) yet even then, and under that black and dismal state of things, there were many thousands who never bowed the knee to Baal-Cromwell, Baal-covenant, or Baal-engagement; but with a steady, fixed, unshaken resolution, and in a glorious imitation of those heroic Christians in the tenth and eleventh chapters of the epistle to the Hebrews, *endured a great fight of afflictions, were made a gazing-stock by reproaches, took joyfully the spoiling of their goods, had trial of cruel mockings; moreover of bonds and imprisonments; sometimes were tempted, sometimes were slain with the sword, wandered about in hunger and nakedness, being destitute, afflicted, tormented.* All which sufferings surely ought to entitle them to that concluding character in the next words, *of whom the world was not worthy.* And I wish I could say of England, that it were worthy of those men now. For I look upon the old church of England royalists (which I take to be only another name for a man who prefers his conscience before his interest) to be the best Christians and the most meritorious subjects in the world; as having passed all those terrible tests and trials, which conquering, domineering malice could put them to, and carried their credit and their conscience clear and triumphant through, and above them all, constantly firm and immovable, by all that they felt either from their professed enemies or their false friends. And what these men did and suffered others might have done and suffered too.

But they, good men, had another and more artificial sort of conscience, and a way to interpret off a command, where they found it dangerous or unprofitable to do it.

"God knows my heart, (says one,) I love the king cordially: and I wish well to the church, (says another,) but you see the state of things is altered; and we can not do what we would do. Our will is good, and the king gracious, and we hope he will accept of this, and dispense with the rest." A goodly present, doubtless, as they meant it; and such as they might freely give, and yet part with nothing; and the king, on the other hand, receive and gain just as much.

But now, had the whole nation mocked God and their king at this shuffling, hypocritical rate, what an odious, infamous people must that rebellion have represented the English to all posterity? Where had been the honor of the reformed religion, that could not afford a man Christian enough to suffer for his God and his prince? But the old royalists did both, and thereby demonstrated to the world that no danger could make duty impossible.

And, upon my conscience, if we may assign any other reason or motive of the late mercies of God to these poor kingdoms, besides his own proneness to show mercy, it was for the sake of the old, suffering cavaliers, and for the sake of none else whatsoever, that God delivered us from the two late accursed conspiracies. For they were the brats and offspring of two contrary factions, both of them equally mortal and inveterate enemies of our church; which they have been, and still are, perpetually pecking and striking at, with the same malice, though with different methods.

In a word: the old, tried church of England royalists were the men, who, in the darkest and foulest day of persecution that ever befell England, never pleaded the will in excuse of the deed, but proved the integrity and loyalty of their wills both by their deeds and their sufferings too.

But, on the contrary, when duty and danger stand confronting one another, and when the law of God says, Obey and assist your king; and the faction says, Do if you dare: for men, in such a case, to think to divide themselves, and to pretend that their will obeys that law, while all besides their will obeys and serves the faction, what is this but a gross fulsome juggling with their duty, and a kind of trimming it between God and the devil?

These things I thought fit to remark to you, not out of any intemperate humor of reflecting upon the late times of confusion, (as the guilt or spite of some may suggest,) but because I am satisfied in my heart and conscience, that it is vastly the concern of his majesty, and of the peace of his government, both in church and state, that the youth of the nation (of which such auditories as this chiefly consist) should be principled and possessed with a full, fixed, and thorough persuasion of the justness and goodness of the blessed old king's cause; and of the excellent piety and Christianity of those principles upon which the loyal part of the nation adhered to him, and that against the most horrid and inexcusable rebellion that was ever set on foot and acted upon the stage of the world: of all which whosoever is not persuaded, is a rebel in his heart, and deserves not the protection which he enjoys.

And the rather do I think such remarks as these necessary of late years, because of the vile arts and restless endeavors used by some sly and venomous factors for the old republican cause, to poison and debauch men from their allegiance; sometimes creeping into houses, and sometimes creeping into studies; but in both equally pimping for the faction, and stealing away as many hearts from the son, as they had formerly employed hands against the father. And this with such success, that it can not but be matter of very sad and melancholy reflection to all sober and loyal minds, to consider, that several who had stood it out, and persevered firm and unalterable royalists in the late storm, have since (I know not by what unhappy fate) turned trimmers in the calm.

(3.) The third instance, in which men use to plead the will instead of the deed, shall be in duties of cost and expense.

Let a business of expensive charity be proposed; and then, as I showed before, that, in matters of labor, the lazy person could find no hands wherewith to work, so neither in this case can the religious miser find any hands wherewith to give.

It is wonderful to consider how a command or call to be liberal, either upon a civil or religious account, all of a sudden impoverishes the rich, breaks the merchant, shuts up every private man's exchequer, and makes those men in a minute have nothing at all to give, who, at the very same instant, want nothing to spend. So that instead of relieving the poor, such a command strangely increases their number, and transforms rich men into beggars presently. For, let the danger of their prince and country knock at their purses, and call upon them to contribute against a public enemy or calamity; then immediately they have nothing, and their riches upon such occasions (as Solomon expresses it) never fail to make themselves wings, and to fly away.

Thus, at the siege of Constantinople, then the wealthiest city in the world, the citizens had nothing to give their emperor for the defense of the place, though he begged a supply of them with tears; but, when by that means the Turks took and sacked it, then those who before had nothing to give, had more than enough to lose. And in like manner, those who would not support the necessities of the old blessed king, against his villainous enemies, found that plunder could take where disloyalty would not give, and rapine open those chests that avarice had shut.

But to descend to matters of daily and common occurrence; what is more usual in conversation, than for men to express their unwillingness to do a thing, by saying they can not do it; and for a covetous man, being asked a little money in charity, to answer that he has none? Which, as it is, if true, a sufficient answer to God and man; so, if false, it is intolerable hypocrisy towards both.

But do men in good earnest think that God will be put off so? or can they imagine that the law of God will be baffled with a lie clothed in a scoff?

For such pretenses are no better, as appears from that notable account given us by the apostle of this windy, insignificant charity of the will, and of the worthlessness of it, not enlivened by deeds, James ii. 15, 16, *If a brother or sister be naked, and destitute of daily food, and one of you say unto them, Depart in peace, be ye warmed and filled; notwithstanding ye give them not those things which are needful to the body; what doth it profit?* Profit, does he say? Why, it profits just as much as fair words command the market, as good wishes buy food and raiment and pass for current payment in the shops. Come to an old, rich, professing vulpony, and tell him that there is a church to be built, beautified, or endowed in such a place, and that he can not lay out his money more to God's honor, the public good, and the comfort of his own conscience, than to bestow it liberally upon such an occasion; and in answer to this, it is ten to one but you shall be told, "how much God is for the inward, spiritual worship of the heart; and that the Almighty neither dwells nor delights in temples made with hands; but hears and accepts the prayers of his people in dens and caves, barns and stables; and in the homeliest and meanest cottages, as well as in the stateliest and most magnificent churches." Thus, I say, you are like to be answered. In reply to which, I would have all such sly, sanctified cheats (who are so often harping upon this string) know, once for all, that that God who accepts the prayers of his people in dens and caves, barns and stables, when by his afflicting providence he has driven them from the appointed places of his solemn worship, so that they can not have the use of them, will not, for all this, endure to be served or prayed to by them in such places, nor accept of their barn-worship, nor their hog-sty-worship; no, nor yet of their parlor or their chamber worship, where he has given them both wealth and power to build him churches. For he that commands us to *worship him in the spirit,* commands us also *to honor him with our substance.* And never pretend that thou hast an heart to pray, while thou hast no heart to give; since he that serves mammon with his estate, can not possibly serve God with his heart. For as in the heathen worship of God, a sacrifice without an heart was accounted ominous, so in the Christian worship of him, an heart without a sacrifice is worthless and impertinent.

And thus much for men's pretenses of the will, when they are called upon to give a religious account; according to which, a man may be well enough said (as the common word is) to be all heart, and yet the arrantest miser in the world.

But come we now to this old rich pretender to godliness,

in another case, and tell him that there is such an one, a man of a good family, good education, and who has lost all his estate for the king, now ready to rot in prison for debt; come, what will you give towards his release? Why, then answers the will instead of the deed, as much the readier speaker of the two, "the truth is, I always had a respect for such men; I love them with all my heart; and it is a thousand pities that any that have served the king so faithfully should be in such want." So say I too, and the more shame is it for the whole nation, that they should be so. But still, what will you give? Why, then answers the man of mouth-charity again, and tells you, that "you could not come in a worse time; that money is nowadays very scarce with him; and that therefore he can give nothing; but he will be sure to pray for the poor gentleman."

Ah thou hypocrite! when thy brother has lost all that ever he had, and lies languishing, and even gasping under the utmost extremities of poverty and distress, dost thou think thus to lick him whole again, only with thy tongue? Just like that old formal hocus, who denied a beggar a farthing, and put him off with his blessing.

Why, what are the prayers of a covetous wretch worth? What will thy blessing go for? What will it buy? Is this the charity that the apostle here, in the text, presses upon the Corinthians? This the case in which God accepts the willingness of the mind, instead of the liberality of the purse? No, assuredly; but the measures that God marks out to thy charity are these: thy superfluities must give place to thy neighbor's great convenience: thy convenience must veil to thy neighbor's necessity: and lastly, thy very necessities must yield to thy neighbor's extremity.

This is the gradual process that must be thy rule; and he that pretends a disability to give short of this, prevaricates with his duty, and evacuates the precept. God sometimes calls upon thee to relieve the needs of thy poor brother, sometimes the necessities of thy country, and sometimes the urgent wants of thy prince: now, before thou fliest to the old, stale, usual pretense, that thou canst do none of all these things, consider with thyself, that there is a God who is not to be flammed off with lies, who knows exactly what thou canst do, and what thou canst not; and consider in the next place that it is not the best husbandry in the world, to be damned to save charges.

(4.) The fourth and last duty that I shall mention, in which men use to plead want of power to do the thing they have a will to, is the conquering of a long, inveterate, ill habit or custom.

And the truth is, there is nothing that leaves a man less power to good than this does. Nevertheless that which weakens the hand does not therefore cut it off. Some power to good, no doubt, a man has left him for all this. And therefore God will not take the drunkard's excuse, that he has so long accustomed himself to intemperate drinking, that now he can not leave it off; nor admit of the passionate man's apology, that he has so long given his unruly passions their head, that he can not now govern or control them. For these things are not so: since no man is guilty of an act of intemperance of any sort, but he might have forborne it; not without some trouble, I confess, from the strugglings of the contrary habit: but still the thing was possible to be done; and he might, after all, have forborne it. And, as he forbore one act, so he might have forborne another, and after that another, and so on, till he had, by degrees, weakened, and at length mortified and extinguished the habit itself. That these things, indeed, are not quickly or easily to be effected, is manifest, and nothing will be more readily granted; and therefore the scripture itself owns so much, by expressing and representing these mortifying courses by acts of the greatest toil and labor; such as are warfare, and taking up the cross: and by acts of the most terrible violence and contrariety to nature; such as are cutting off the right hand, and plucking out the right eye; things infinitely grievous and afflictive, yet still, for all that, feasible in themselves, or else, to be sure, the eternal wisdom of God would never have advised, and much less have commanded them. For, what God has commanded must be done; and what must be done assuredly may be done; and therefore all pleas of impotence, or inability, in such cases, are utterly false and impertinent, and will infallibly be thrown back in the face of such as make them.

But you will say, Does not the scripture itself acknowledge it as a thing impossible for a man, brought under a custom of sin, to forbear sinning? In Jer. xiii. 23, *Can the Ethiopian change his skin, or the leopard his spots? then may ye also do good, that are accustomed to do evil.* Now, if this can be no more done than the former, is it not a demonstration that it can not be done at all?

To this I answer, that the words mentioned are tropical or figurative, and import a hyperbole, which is a way of expressing things beyond what really and naturally they are in themselves; and consequently the design of this scripture, in saying that this can not be done, is no more than to show that it is very hardly and very rarely done; but not, in strict truth, utterly impossible to be done.

In vain therefore do men take sanctuary in such misunderstood expressions as these; and from a false persuasion, that they can not reform their lives, break off their ill customs, and root out their old, vicious habits, never so much as attempt, endeavor, or go about it. For, admit that such a habit, seated in the soul, be, as our Saviour calls it, *a strong man armed, got into possession;* yet still he may be dispossessed, and thrown out by a stronger, Luke xi. 21, 22. Or be it, as St. Paul calls it, *a law in our members,* Rom. vii. 23, yet certainly, ill laws may be broken and disobeyed, as well as good. But, if men will suffer themselves to be enslaved, and carried away by their lusts, without resistance, and wear the devil's yoke quietly, rather than be at the trouble of throwing it off, and thereupon sometimes feel their consciences galled and grieved by wearing it, they must not from these secret stings and remorses, felt by them in the prosecution of their sins, presently conclude that therefore their will is good, and well disposed, and consequently such as God will accept, though their lives remain all the while unchanged, and as much under the dominion of sin as ever.

These reasonings, I know, lie deep in the minds of most men, and relieve and support their hearts, in spite, and in the midst of their sins; but they are all but sophistry and delusion, and false propositions contrived by the devil, to hold men fast in their sins by final impenitence. For though possibly the grace of God may, in some cases, be irresistible, yet it would be an infinite reproach to his providence to affirm that sin either is or can be so. And thus I have given you four principal instances in which men use to plead the will instead of the deed, upon a pretended impotence, or disability for the deed: namely, in duties of great labor; in duties of much danger; in duties of cost and expense; and lastly, in duties requiring a resistance and an extirpation of inveterate, sinful habits.

In the neglect of all which, men relieve their consciences by this one great fallacy running through them all, that they mistake difficulties for impossibilities. A pernicious mistake certainly; and the more pernicious, for that men are seldom convinced of it till their conviction can do them no good. There can not be a weightier or more important case of conscience for men to be resolved in, than to know certainly how far God accepts the will for the deed, and how far he does not: and withal, to be informed truly when men do really will a thing, and when they have really no power to do what they have willed.

For surely it can not but be matter of very dreadful and terrifying consideration to any one sober, and in his wits, to think seriously with himself, what horror and confusion must needs surprise that man, at the last and great day of account, who had led his whole life and governed all his actions by one rule, when God intends to judge him by another.

To which God, the great searcher and judge of hearts, and rewarder of men according to their deeds, be rendered and ascribed, as is most due, all praise, might, majesty, and dominion, both now and for evermore. Amen.

SERMON XI.

A SERMON PREACHED AT CHRIST CHURCH, OXON, BEFORE THE UNIVERSITY, OCTOBER 17, 1675.

JUDGES viii. 34, 35.—*And the children of Israel remembered not the Lord their God, who had delivered them out of the hands of all their enemies on every side: neither shewed they kindness to the house of Jerubbaal, namely, Gideon, according to all the goodness which he had shewed unto Israel.*

THESE words, being a result or judgment given upon matter of fact, naturally direct us to the foregoing story, to inform us of their occasion. The subject of which story was that heroic and victorious judge of Israel, Gideon; who, by the greatness of his achievements, had merited the offer of a crown and kingdom, and, by the greatness of his mind, refused it. The whole narrative is contained and set before us in the 6th, 7th, 8th, and 9th chapters of this book. Where we read, that when the children of Israel, according to their usual method of sinning after mercies and deliverances, and thereupon returning to a fresh enslavement to their enemies, had now passed seven years in cruel subjection to the Midianites, a potent and insulting enemy; and who oppressed them to that degree that they had scarce bread to fill their mouths, or houses to cover their heads: for in the 2d verse of the 6th chapter we find them housing themselves underground, in dens and caves; and in ver. 3, 4, no sooner had they sown their corn, but we have the enemy coming up in armies, and destroying it. In this sad and calamitous condition, I say, in which one would have thought that a deliverance from such an oppressor would have even revived them, and the deliverer eternally obliged them, God raised up the spirit of this great person, and ennobled his courage and conduct with the entire overthrow of this mighty and numerous, or rather innumerable host of the Midianites; and that in such a manner, and with such strange and unparalleled circumstances, that, in the whole action, the mercy and the miracle seemed to strive for the preëminence. And so quick a sense did the Israelites, immediately after it, seem to entertain of the merits of Gideon, and the obligation he had laid upon them, that they all, as one man, tender him the regal and hereditary government of that people, in the 22d verse of this 8th chapter: *Then said the men of Israel to Gideon, Rule thou over us, both thou, and thy son and thy son's son also: for thou hast delivered us from the hand of Midian.* To which he answered as magnanimously, and by that answer redoubled the obligation, in the next verse, *I will not rule over you, neither shall my son rule over you: the Lord shall rule over you.*

Thus far then we see the workings of a just gratitude in the Israelites; and goodness on the one side nobly answered with greatness on the other. And now, after so vast an obligation, owned by so free an acknowledgment, could any thing be expected, but a continual interchange of kindnesses, at least on their part, who had been so infinitely obliged and so gloriously delivered? Yet in the 9th chapter we find these very men turning the sword of Gideon into his own bowels; cutting off the very race and posterity of their deliverer, by the slaughter of three-score and ten of his sons, and setting up the son of his concubine, the blot of his family, and the monument of his shame, to reign over them; and all this without the least provocation or offense given them, either by Gideon himself, or by any of his house. After which horrid fact, I suppose we can no longer wonder at this unlooked-for account given of the Israelites in the text: *That they remembered not the Lord their God, who had delivered them out of the hands of all their enemies on every side: neither shewed they kindness to the house of Gideon, according to all the goodness which he had shewed unto Israel.*

The truth is, they were all along a cross, odd, untoward sort of people, and such as God seems to have chosen, and (as the prophets sometimes phrase it) to have espoused to himself, upon the very same account that Socrates espoused

Xantippe, only for her extreme ill conditions, above all that he could possibly find or pick out of that sex; and so the fittest argument both to exercise and declare his admirable patience to the world.

The words of the text are a charge given in against the Israelites; a charge of that foul and odious sin of ingratitude; and that both towards God and towards man: towards God in the 34th verse, and towards man in the 35th. Such being ever the growing contagion of this ill quality, that if it begins at God, it naturally descends to men; and if it first exerts itself upon men, it infallibly ascends to God. If we consider it as directed against God, it is a breach of religion; if as to men, it is an offense against morality. The passage from one to the other is very easy; breach of duty towards our neighbor still involving in it a breach of duty towards God too; and no man's religion ever survives his morals.

My purpose is, from this remarkable subject and occasion, to treat of ingratitude, and that chiefly in this latter sense; and from the case of the Israelites towards Gideon, to traverse the nature, principles, and properties of this detestable vice; and so drawing before your eyes the several lineaments and parts of it, from the ugly aspect of the picture, to leave it to your own hearts to judge of the original. For the effecting of which I shall do these following things:

I. I shall show what gratitude is, and upon what the obligation to it is grounded.

II. I shall give some account of the nature and baseness of ingratitude.

III. I shall show the principle from which ingratitude proceeds.

IV. I shall show those ill qualities that inseparably attend it, and are never disjoined from it. And,

V. and lastly, I shall draw some useful inferences, by way of application, from the premises.

And first for the first of these: What gratitude is, and upon what the obligation to it is grounded.

"Gratitude is properly a virtue, disposing the mind to an inward sense and an outward acknowledgment of a benefit received, together with a readiness to return the same, or the like, as the occasions of the doer of it shall require, and the abilities of the receiver extend to."

This, to me, seems to contain a full description, or rather definition, of this virtue; from which it appears that gratitude includes in it these three parts:

1. A particular observation, or taking notice of a kindness received, and consequently of the good will and affection of the person who did that kindness. For still, in this case, the mind of the giver is more to be attended to than the matter of the gift; it being this that stamps it properly a favor, and gives it the noble and endearing denomination of a kindness.

2. The second part of gratitude is that which brings it from the heart into the mouth, and makes a man express the sense he has of the benefit done him, by thanks, acknowledgments, and gratulations; and where the heart is full of the one, it will certainly overflow, and run over in the other.

3. The third and last is an endeavor to recompense our benefactor, and to do something that may redound to his advantage, in consideration of what he has done towards ours. I state it upon endeavor, and not upon effect; for this latter may be often impossible. But it is in the power of every one to do as much as he can; to make some essay at least, some offer and attempt this way; so as to show that there is a spring of motion within, and that the heart is not idle or insensible, but that it is full and big, and knows itself to be so, though it wants strength to bring forth. Having thus shown what gratitude is, the next thing is to show the obligation that it brings upon a man, and the ground and reason of that obligation.

As for the obligation, I know no moralists or casuists that treat scholastically of justice, but treat of gratitude under that general head, as a part or species of it. And the nature and office of justice being to dispose the mind to a constant and perpetual readiness to render to every man his due, *suum cuique tribuere*, it is evident, that if gratitude be a part of justice, it must be conversant about something that is due to another. And whatsoever is so, must be so by the force of some law. Now, all law that a man is capable of being obliged by, is reducible to one of these three:

1. The law of nature. 2. The positive law of God revealed in his word. 3. The law of man, enacted by the civil power, for the preservation and good of society.

1. And first for the law of nature, which I take to be nothing else but the mind of God signified to a rational agent, by the bare discourse of his reason, and dictating to him, that he ought to act suitably to the principles of his nature, and to those relations that he stands under. For every thing sustains both an absolute and a relative capacity. An absolute, as it is such a thing endued with such a nature; and a relative, as it is a part of the universe, and so stands in such an order and relation both to the whole and to the rest of the parts.

After which, the next consideration immediately subsequent to the being of a thing, is, what agrees or disagrees with that thing; what is suitable or unsuitable to it; and from this springs the notion of decency or indecency; that which becomes or misbecomes, and is the same with *honestum et turpe.* Which decency, or τὸ πρέπον, (as the Greeks term it,) imports a certain measure or proportion of one thing to another; which to transgress, is to do contrary to the natural order of things; the preservation of which is properly that rule or law by which every thing ought to act; and consequently the violation of it implies a turpitude or indecency. Now those actions that are suitable to a rational nature, and to that πρέπον, that decency or *honestum,* belonging to it, are contained and expressed in certain maxims or propositions, which, upon the repeated exercise of a man's reason about such objects as come before him, do naturally result, and are collected from thence; and so remaining upon his mind, become both a rule to direct and a law to oblige him in the whole course of his actions. Such as are these maxims, That the supreme being, cause, and governor of all things ought to be worshiped and depended upon. That parents are to be honored. That a man should do as he would be done by. From which last alone may sufficiently be deduced all those rules of charity and justice that are to govern the offices of common life; and which alone is enough to found an obligation to gratitude: forasmuch as no man, having done a kindness to another, would acquiesce or think himself justly dealt with in a total neglect and unconcernedness of the person who had received that kindness from him; and consequently neither ought he to be unconcerned in the same case himself.

But I shall, from other and nearer principles, and those the unquestionable documents and dictates of the law of nature, evince the obligation and debt lying upon every man to show gratitude where he has received a benefit. Such as are these propositions:

(1.) That according to the rule of natural justice, one man may merit and deserve of another. (2.) That whosoever deserves of another, makes something due to him from the person of whom he deserves. (3.) That one man's deserving of another is founded upon his conferring on him some good, to which that other had no right or claim. (4.) That no man has any antecedent right or claim to that which comes to him by free gift. (5.) And lastly, that all desert imports an equality between the good conferred and the good deserved, or made due. From whence it follows, that he who confers a good upon another, deserves and consequently has a claim to an equal good from the person upon whom it was conferred. So that from hence, by the law of nature, springs a debt; the acknowledging and repaying of which debt (as a man shall be able) is the proper office and work of gratitude.

As certain therefore as by the law of nature there may be, and often is, such a thing as merit and desert from one man to another; and as desert gives the person deserving a right or claim to some good from the person of whom he deserves; and as a right in one to claim this good infers a debt and obligation in the other to pay it; so certain it is, by a direct gradation of consequences from this principle of merit, that the obligation to gratitude flows from, and is enjoined by, the first dictates of nature. And the truth is, the greatest and most sacred ties of duty that man is capable of, are founded upon gratitude. Such as are the duties of a child to his parent, and of a subject to his sovereign. From the former of which there is required love and honor, in recompense of being; and from the latter, obedience and subjection, in recompense of protection and wellbeing. And, in general, if the conferring of a kindness did not bind the person upon whom it was conferred to the returns of gratitude, why, in the universal dialect of the world, are kindnesses still called obligations?

And thus much for the first ground, enforcing the obligations of gratitude; namely, the law of nature. In the next place,

2. As for the positive law of God revealed in his word, it is evident that gratitude must needs be enjoined and made necessary by all those scriptures that upbraid or forbid ingratitude; as in 2 Tim. iii. 2, the unthankful stand reckoned among the highest and most enormous sinners; which sufficiently evinces the virtue opposite to unthankfulness to bear the same place in the rank of duties that its contrary does in the catalogue of sins. And the like, by consequence, is inferred from all those places in which we are commanded to love our enemies, and to do good to those that hate us: and therefore certainly much more are we by the same commanded to do good to those that have prevented us with good, and actually obliged us. So that it is manifest that by the positive written law of God, no less than by the law of nature, gratitude is a debt.

3. In the third and last place; as for the laws of men, enacted by the civil power, it must be confessed that gratitude is not enforced by them; I say, not enforced, that is, not enjoined by the sanction of penalties, to be inflicted upon the person that shall not be found grateful. I grant indeed that many actions are punished by law that are acts of ingratitude; but this is merely accidental to them, as they are such acts; for if they were punished properly under that notion, and upon that account, the punishment would equally reach all actions of the same kind; but they are punished and provided against by law, as they are gross and dangerous violations of societies, and that common good that it is the business of the civil laws of all nations to protect and to take care of: which good not being violated or endangered by every omission of gratitude between man and man, the laws make no peculiar provision to secure the exercise of this virtue, but leave it as they found it, sufficiently enjoined, and made a duty by the law of God and nature.

Though in the Roman law indeed there is this particular provision against the breach of this duty in case of slaves, that if a lord manumits and makes free his slave, gross ingratitude in the person so made free forfeits his freedom, and reasserts him to his former condition of slavery; though perhaps even this also, upon an accurate consideration, will be found not a provision against ingratitude, properly and formally as such, but as it is the ingratitude of slaves, which, if left unpunished in a commonwealth where it was the custom for men to be served by slaves, as in Rome it was, would quickly have been a public nuisance and disturbance; for such is the peculiar insolence of this sort of men, such the incorrigible vileness of all slavish spirits, that though freedom may rid them of the baseness of their condition, yet it never takes off the baseness of their minds.

And now, having shown both what gratitude is, and the ground and reason of men's obligation to it, we have a full account of the proper and particular nature of this virtue, as consisting adequately in these two things: first, that it is a debt; and, secondly, that it is such a debt as is left to every man's ingenuity, (in respect of any legal coaction,) whether he will pay or no; for there lies no action of debt against him, if he will not. He is in danger of no arrest, bound over to no assize, nor forced to hold up his unworthy hand (the instrument of his ingratitude) at any bar.

And this it is that shows the rare and distinguishing excellency of gratitude, and sets it as a crown upon the head of all other virtues, that it should plant such an overruling generosity in the heart of man, as shall more effectually incline him to what is brave and becoming, than the terror of any penal law whatsoever. So that he shall feel a greater force upon himself from within, and from the control of his own principles, to engage him to do worthily, than all threatenings and punishments, racks and tortures can have upon a low and servile mind, that never acts virtuously but as it is acted; that knows no principle of doing well, but fear; no conscience, but constraint. On the contrary, the grateful person fears no court or judge, no sentence or executioner, but what he carries about him in his own breast: and being still the most severe exactor of himself, not only confesses but proclaims his debts; his ingenuity is his bond, and his conscience a thousand witnesses: so that the debt must needs be sure, yet he scorns to be sued for it; nay, rather, he is always suing, importuning, and even reproaching himself, till he can clear accounts with his benefactor. His heart is, as it were, in continual labor: it even travails with the obligation, and is in pangs till it be delivered: and as David, in the overflowing sense of God's goodness to him, cries out, in the 116th Psalm, ver. 12, *What shall I render unto the Lord for all his benefits towards me?* so the grateful person, pressed down under the apprehension of any great kindness done him, eases his burdened mind a little by such expostulations with himself as these: "What shall I do for such a friend, for such a patron, who has so frankly, so generously, so unconstrainedly relieved me in such a distress; supported me against such an enemy; supplied, cherished, and upheld me when relations would not know me, or at least could not help me; and, in a word, has prevented my desires, and outdone my necessities? I can never do enough for him; my own conscience would spit in my face, should I ever slight or forget such favors." These are the expostulating dialogues and contests that every grateful, every truly noble and magnanimous person has with himself. It was, in part, a brave speech of Luc. Cornelius Sylla, the Roman dictator, who said, "that he found no sweetness in being great or powerful, but only that it enabled him to crush his enemies and to gratify his friends."

I can not warrant or defend the first part of this saying; but surely he that employs his greatness in the latter, be he never so great, it must and will make him still greater.

And thus much for the first general thing proposed, which was to show what gratitude is, and upon what the obligation to it is grounded. I proceed now to the second,

Which is to give some account of the nature and baseness of ingratitude.

There is not any one vice or ill quality incident to the mind of man against which the world has raised such a loud and universal outcry, as against ingratitude: a vice never mentioned by any heathen writer, but with a particular hight of detestation; and of such a malignity, that human nature must be stripped of humanity itself before it can be guilty of it. It is instead of all other vices, and, in the balance of morality, a counterpoise to them all. In the charge of ingratitude, *omnia dixeris*: it is one great blot upon all morality: it is all in a word: it says *Amen* to the black roll of sins: it gives completion and confirmation to them all.

If we would state the nature of it, recourse must be had to what has been already said of its contrary; and so it is properly an insensibility of kindnesses received, without any endeavor either to acknowledge or repay them.

To repay them, indeed, by a return equivalent, is not in every one's power, and consequently can not be his duty; but thanks are a tribute payable by the poorest; the most forlorn widow has her two mites; and there is none so indigent but has an heart to be sensible of, and a tongue to express, its sense of a benefit received.

For, surely, nature gives no man a mouth to be always eating, and never saying grace; nor an hand only to grasp and to receive: but as it is furnished with teeth for the one, so it should have a tongue also for the other; and the hands that are so often reached out to take and to accept, should be sometimes lifted up also to bless. The world is maintained by intercourse; and the whole course of nature is a great exchange, in which one good turn is and ought to be the stated price of another.

If you consider the universe as one body, you shall find society and conversation to supply the office of the blood and spirits; and it is gratitude that makes them circulate. Look over the whole creation, and you shall see that the band or cement that holds together all the parts of this great and glorious fabric is gratitude, or something like it: you may observe it in all the elements; for does not the air feed the flame? and does not the flame at the same time warm and enlighten the air? Is not the sea always sending forth as well as taking in? And does not the earth quit scores with all the elements, in the noble fruits and productions that issue from it? And in all the light and influence that the heavens bestow upon this lower world, though the lower world can not equal their benefaction, yet, with a kind of grateful return, it reflects those rays that it can not recompense: so that there is some return however, though there can be no requital. He who has a soul wholly void of gratitude, should do well to set his soul to learn of his body; for all the parts of that minister to one another. The hands, and all the other limbs, labor to bring in food and provision to the stomach, and the stomach returns what it has received from them in strength and nutriment, diffused into all the parts and members of the body. It would be endless to pursue the like allusions: in short, gratitude is the great spring that sets all the wheels of nature agoing; and the whole universe is supported by giving and returning, by commerce and commutation.

And now, thou ungrateful brute, thou blemish to mankind, and reproach to thy creation, what shall we say of thee, or to what shall we compare thee? For thou art an exception from all the visible world; neither the heavens above, nor the earth beneath, afford any thing like thee: and therefore, if thou wouldest find thy parallel, go to hell, which is both the region and the emblem of ingratitude; for, besides thyself, there is nothing but hell that is always receiving and never restoring.

And thus much for the nature and baseness of ingratitude, as it has been represented in the description given of it. Come we now to the

Third thing proposed, which is to show the principle from which it proceeds. And to give you this in one word, it proceeds from that which we call ill-nature. Which being a word that occurs frequently in discourse, and in the characters given of persons, it will not be amiss to inquire into the proper sense and signification of this expression. In order to which we must observe, that, according to the doctrine of the philosopher, man being a creature designed and framed by nature for society and conversation, such a temper or disposition of mind as inclines him to those actions that promote society and mutual fellowship is properly called good-nature: which actions, though almost innumerable in their particulars, yet seem reducible in general to these two principles of action.

1. A proneness to do good to others.
2. A ready sense of any good done by others.

And where these two meet together, as they are scarce ever found asunder, it is impossible for that person not to be kind, beneficial, and obliging to all whom he converses with. On the contrary, ill-nature is such a disposition as inclines a man to those actions that thwart, and sour, and disturb conversation between man and man; and accordingly consists of two qualities directly contrary to the former.

1. A proneness to do ill turns, attended with a complacency, or secret joy of mind, upon the sight of any mischief that befalls another. And,

2. An utter insensibility of any good or kindness done him by others. I mean not that he is insensible of the good itself; but that, although he finds, feels, and enjoys the good that is done him, yet he is wholly insensible and unconcerned to value, or take notice of the benignity of him that does it.

Now either of these ill qualities, and much more both of them together, denominate a person ill-natured; they being such as make him grievous and uneasy to all whom he deals and associates himself with. For from the former of these proceed envy, an aptness to slander and revile, to cross and hinder a man in his lawful advantages. For these and such like actions feed and gratify that base humor of mind, which gives a man a delight in making, at least in seeing, his neighbor miserable: and from the latter issues that vile thing which we have been hitherto speaking of, to wit, ingratitude: into which all kindnesses and good turns fall, as into a kind of dead sea. It being a quality that confines and, as it were, shuts up a man wholly within himself, leaving him void of that principle which alone should dispose him to communicate and impart those redundancies of good that he is possessed of. No man ever goes sharer with the ungrateful person; be he never so full, he never runs over. But (like Gideon's fleece) though filled and replenished with the dew of heaven himself, yet he leaves all dry and empty about him.

Now this surely, if any thing, is an effect of ill-nature. And what is ill-nature but a pitch beyond original corruption? It is *corruptio pessimi.* A further depravation of that which was stark naught before. But, so certainly does it shoot forth and show itself in this vice, that wheresoever you see ingratitude, you may as infallibly conclude that there is a growing stock of ill-nature in that breast, as you may know that man to have the plague upon whom you see the tokens.

Having thus shown you from whence this ill quality proceeds, pass we now to the

Fourth thing proposed, which is to show those other ill qualities that inseparably attend ingratitude, and are never disjoined from it.

It is a saying common in use, and true in observation, that the disposition and temper of a man may be gathered as well from his companion or associate as from himself. And it holds in qualities as it does in persons: it being seldom or never known, that any great virtue or vice went alone; for greatness in every thing will still be attended on.

How black and base a vice ingratitude is, we have seen by considering it both in its own nature and in the principle from which it springs; and we may see the same yet more fully in those vices which it is always in combination with. Two of which I shall mention, as being of near cognation to it, and constant coherence with it. The first of which is pride. And the second, hard-heartedness, or want of compassion.

1. And first for pride. This is of such intimate, and even essential connection with ingratitude, that the actings of ingratitude seem directly resolvable into pride, as the principal reason and cause of them. The original ground of man's obligation to gratitude was, as I have hinted, from this, that each man has but a limited right to the good things of the world; and that the natural allowed way by which he is to compass the possession of these things, is by his own industrious acquisition of them; and consequently, when any good is dealt forth to him any other way than by his own labor, he is accountable to the person who dealt it to him, as for a thing to which he had no right or claim, by any action of his own entitling him to it.

But now pride shuts a man's eyes against all this, and so fills him with an opinion of his own transcendent worth, that he imagines himself to have a right to all things, as well those that are the effects and fruits of other men's labors, as of his own. So that, if any advantage accrues to him by the liberality and donation of his neighbor, he looks not upon it as matter of free undeserved gift, but rather as a just homage to that worth and merit which he conceives to be in himself, and to which all the world ought to become tributary. Upon which thought, no wonder if he reckons himself wholly unconcerned to acknowledge or repay any good that he receives. For while the courteous person thinks that he is obliging and doing such an one a kindness, the proud person, on the other side, accounts him to be only paying a debt. His pride makes him even worship and idolize himself; and indeed every proud, ungrateful man has this property of an idol, that though he is plied with never so many and so great offerings, yet he takes no notice of the offerer at all.

Now this is the true account of the most inward movings and reasonings of the very heart and soul of an ungrateful person. So that you may rest upon this as a proposition of an eternal, unfailing truth; that there neither is nor ever was any person remarkably ungrateful, who was not also insufferably proud; nor, convertibly, any one proud, who was not equally ungrateful. For, as snakes breed in dunghills not singly, but in knots, so in such base, noisome hearts you shall ever see pride and ingratitude indivisibly wreathed and twisted together. Ingratitude overlooks all kindnesses, but it is because pride makes it carry its head so high.

See the greatest examples of ingratitude equally notorious for their pride and ambition. And to begin with the top and father of them all, the devil himself. That excellent and glorious nature which God had obliged him with could not prevent his ingratitude and apostasy, when his pride bid him aspire to an equality with his maker, and say, *I will ascend, and be like the Most High.* And did not our first parents write exactly after his copy? ingratitude making them to trample upon the command, because pride made them desire to be as gods, and to brave omniscience itself in the knowledge of good and evil. What made that ungrateful wretch, Absalom, kick at all the kindnesses of his indulgent father, but because his ambition would needs be fingering the sceptre, and hoisting him into his father's throne? And in the courts of princes, is there any thing more usual than to see those that have been raised by the favor and interest of some great minister, to trample upon the steps by which they rose, to rival him in his greatness, and at length (if possible) to step into his place?

In a word, ingratitude is too base to return a kindness, and too proud to regard it; much like the tops of mountains, barren indeed, but yet lofty; they produce nothing, they feed nobody, they clothe nobody, yet are high and stately, and look down upon all the world about them.

2. The other concomitant of ingratitude is hard-heartedness, or want of compassion. This, at first, may seem to have no great cognation with ingratitude; but upon a due inspection into the nature of that ill quality, it will be found directly to follow it, if not also to result from it.

For the nature of ingratitude being founded in such a disposition as encloses all a man's concerns within himself, and consequently gives him a perfect unconcernedness in all things not judged by him immediately to relate to his own interest, it is no wonder if the same temper of mind which makes a man unapprehensive of any good done him by others, makes him equally unapprehensive and insensible of any evil or misery suffered by others. No such thought ever strikes his marble, obdurate heart, but it presently flies off and rebounds from it. And the truth is, it is impossible for a man to be perfect and thorough-paced in ingratitude, till he has shook off all fetters of pity and compassion. For all relenting and tenderness of heart makes a man but a puny in this sin; it spoils the growth, and cramps the last and crowning exploits of this vice.

Ingratitude, indeed, put the poniard into Brutus's hand; but it was want of compassion which thrust it into Cæsar's heart. When some fond, easy fathers think fit to strip themselves before they lie down to their long sleep, and to settle their whole estates upon their sons, has it not been too frequently seen, that the father has been requited with want and beggary, scorn and contempt? But now, could bare ingratitude, think we, ever have made any one so unnatural and diabolical, had not cruelty and want of pity come in as a second to its assistance, and cleared the villain's breast of all remainders of humanity? Is it not this which has made so many miserable parents even curse their own bowels, for bringing forth children that seem to have none? Did not this make Agrippina, Nero's mother, cry out to the assassinate sent by her son to murder her, to direct his sword to her belly, as being the only criminal for having brought forth such a monster of ingratitude into the world? And to give you yet a higher instance of the conjunction of these two vices; since nothing could transcend the ingratitude and cruelty of Nero, but the ingratitude and cruelty of an imperious woman; when Tullia, daughter of Servius Tullius, sixth king of Rome, having married Tarquinius Superbus, and put him first upon killing her father, and then invading his throne, came through the street where the body of her father lay newly murdered and wallowing in his blood, she commanded her trembling coachman to drive her chariot and horses over the body of her king and father triumphantly, in the face of all Rome looking upon her with astonishment and detestation. Such was the tenderness, gratitude, filial affection, and good-nature of this weaker vessel.

And then for instances out of sacred story; to go no further than this of Gideon; did not ingratitude first make the Israelites forget the kindness of the father, and then cruelty make them imbrue their hands in the blood of his sons? Could Pharaoh's butler so quickly have forgot Joseph, had not want of gratitude to him as his friend met with an equal want of compassion to him as his fellow-prisoner? A poor, innocent, forlorn stranger languishing in durance, upon the false accusations of a lying, insolent, whorish woman!

I might even weary you with examples of the like nature, both sacred and civil, all of them representing ingratitude, as it were, sitting in its throne, with pride at its right hand and cruelty at its left; worthy supporters of such a stately quality, such a reigning impiety.

And it has been sometimes observed, that persons signally and eminently obliged, yet missing of the utmost of their greedy designs in swallowing both gifts and giver too, instead of thanks for received kindnesses, have betook themselves to barbarous threatenings for defeat of their insatiable expectations.

Upon the whole matter we may firmly conclude, that ingratitude and compassion never cohabit in the same breast. Which remark I do here so much insist upon, to show the superlative malignity of this vice, and the baseness of the mind in which it dwells; for we may with great confidence and equal truth affirm, that since there was such a thing as mankind in the world, there never was any heart truly great and generous, that was not also tender and compassionate. It is this noble quality that makes all men to be of one kind;

for every man would be, as it were, a distinct species to himself, were there no sympathy amongst individuals.

And thus I have done with the fourth thing proposed, and shown the two vices that inseparably attend ingratitude; and now, if falsehood also should chance to strike in as the third, and make up the triumvirate of its attendants, so that ingratitude, pride, cruelty, and falsehood should all meet together, and join forces in the same person; as not only very often, but for the most part they do; in this case, if the devils themselves should take bodies, and come and live amongst us, they could not be greater plagues and grievances to society than such persons.

From what has been said, let no man ever think to meet ingratitude single and alone. It is one of those grapes of gall mentioned by Moses, Deut. xxxii. 32, and therefore expect always to find it one of a cluster. I proceed now to the

Fifth and last thing proposed, which is, to draw some useful consequences, by way of application, from the premises. As, —

1. Never enter into a league of friendship with an ungrateful person. That is, plant not thy friendship upon a dunghill. It is too noble a plant for so base a soil.

Friendship consists properly in mutual offices, and a generous strife in alternate acts of kindness. But he who does a kindness to an ungrateful person, sets his seal to a flint, and sows his seed upon the sand: upon the former he makes no impression, and from the latter he finds no production.

The only voice of ingratitude is, Give, give; but when the gift is once received, then, like the swine at his trough, it is silent and insatiable. In a word, the ungrateful person is a monster which is all throat and belly; a kind of thoroughfare, or common-shore, for the good things of the world to pass into; and of whom, in respect of all kindnesses conferred on him, may be verified that observation of the lion's den; before which appeared the footsteps of many that had gone in thither, but no prints of any that ever came out thence. The ungrateful person is the only thing in nature for which nobody living is the better. He lives to himself, and subsists by the good-nature of others, of which he himself has not the least grain. He is a mere encroachment upon society, and, consequently, ought to be thrust out of the world as a pest, and a prodigy, and a creature of the devil's making, and not of God's.

2. As a man tolerably discreet ought by no means to attempt the making of such an one his friend, so neither is he, in the next place, to presume to think that he shall be able so much as to alter or meliorate the humor of an ungrateful person by any acts of kindness, though never so frequent, never so obliging.

Philosophy will teach the learned, and experience may teach all, that it is a thing hardly feasible. For love such an one, and he shall despise you: commend him, and, as occasion serves, he shall revile you: give to him, and he shall but laugh at your easiness: save his life; but when you have done, look to your own.

The greatest favors to such an one are but like the motion of a ship upon the waves; they leave no trace, no sign behind them; they neither soften nor win upon him; they neither melt nor endear him, but leave him as hard, as rugged, and as unconcerned as ever. All kindnesses descend upon such a temper as showers of rain or rivers of fresh water falling into the main sea: the sea swallows them all, but is not at all changed or sweetened by them. I may truly say of the mind of an ungrateful person, that it is kindness-proof. It is impenetrable, unconquerable; unconquerable by that which conquers all things else, even by love itself. Flints may be melted, (we see it daily,) but an ungrateful heart can not; no, not by the strongest and the noblest flame. After all your attempts, all your experiments, for any thing that man can do, he that is ungrateful will be ungrateful still. And the reason is manifest; for you may remember that I told you that ingratitude sprang from a principle of ill nature; which being a thing founded in such a certain constitution of blood and spirit, as being born with a man into the world, and upon that account called nature, shall prevent all remedies that can be applied by education, and leaves such a bias upon the mind as is beforehand with all instruction.

So that you shall seldom or never meet with an ungrateful person, but if you look backward, and trace him up to his original, you will find that he was born so; and if you could look forward enough, it is a thousand to one but you will find that he also dies so; for you shall never light upon an ill-natured man, who was not also an ill-natured child; and gave several testimonies of his being so, to discerning persons, long before the use of his reason.

The thread that nature spins is seldom broken off by any thing but death. I do not by this limit the operation of God's grace; for that may do wonders: but humanly speaking, and according to the method of the world, and the little correctives supplied by art and discipline, it seldom fails; but an ill principle has its course, and nature makes good its blow. And therefore where ingratitude begins remarkably to show itself, he surely judges most wisely who takes the alarm betimes; and arguing the fountain from the stream, concludes that there is ill-nature at the bottom; and so reducing his judgment into practice, timely withdraws his frustraneous, baffled kindnesses, and sees the folly of endeavoring to stroke a tiger into a lamb, or to court an Ethiopian out of his color.

3. In the third and last place. Wheresoever you see a man notoriously ungrateful, rest assured that there is no true sense of religion in that person. You know the apostle's argument, in 1 John iv. 20. *He who loveth not his brother whom he hath seen, how can he love God whom he hath not seen?* So, by an exact parity of reason, we may argue: If a man has no sense of those kindnesses that pass upon him from one like himself, whom he sees, and knows, and converses with sensibly; how much less shall his heart be affected with the grateful sense of his favors whom he converses with only by imperfect speculations, by the discourses of reason, or the discoveries of faith; neither of which equal the quick and lively impressions of sense? If the apostle's reasoning was good and concluding, I am sure this must be unavoidable.

But the thing is too evident to need any proof. For shall that man pass for a proficient in Christ's school, who would have been exploded in the school of Zeno or Epictetus? Or shall he pretend to religious attainments, who is defective and short in moral? which yet are but the rudiments, the beginnings, and first draught of religion, as religion is the perfection, the refinement, and the sublimation of morality; so that it still presupposes it, it builds upon it, and grace never adds the superstructure, where virtue has not laid the foundation. There may be virtue indeed, and yet no grace; but grace is never without virtue: and therefore, though gratitude does not infer grace, it is certain that ingratitude does exclude it.

Think not to put God off by frequenting prayers, and sermons, and sacraments, while thy brother has an action against thee in the court of heaven; an action of debt, of that clamorous and great debt of gratitude. Rather, as our Saviour commands, *leave thy gift upon the altar*, and first go and clear accounts with thy brother. God scorns a gift from him who has not paid his debts. Every ungrateful person, in the sight of God and man, is a thief, and let him not make the altar his receiver. Where there is no charity, it is certain there can be no religion; and can that man be charitable who is not so much as just?

In every benefaction between man and man, man is only the dispenser, but God the benefactor; and therefore let all ungrateful ones know, that where gratitude is the debt, God himself is the chief creditor: who, though he causes his sun to shine, and his rain to fall upon the evil and unthankful in this world, has another kind of reward for their unthankfulness in the next.

To which God, the great searcher and judge of hearts, and rewarder of men according to their deeds, be rendered and ascribed, as is most due, all praise, might, majesty, and dominion, both now and for evermore. Amen.

SERMON XII.

A SERMON PREACHED AT CHRIST CHURCH, OXON, BEFORE THE UNIVERSITY, OCTOBER 14, 1688.

PROV. xii. 22.—*Lying lips are abomination to the Lord.*

I AM very sensible, that by discoursing of lies and falsehood, which I have pitched upon for my present subject, I must needs fall into a very large commonplace; though yet, not by half so large and common as the practice: nothing in nature being so universally decried, and withal so universally practiced, as falsehood. So that most of those things that have the mightiest and most controlling influence upon the affairs and course of the world, are neither better nor worse than downright lies. For what is common fame, which sounds from all quarters of the world, and resounds back to them again, but generally a loud, rattling, impudent, overbearing lie? What are most of the histories of the world, but lies? lies immortalized, and consigned over as a perpetual abuse and flam upon posterity? What are most of the promises of the world, but lies? of which we need no other proof but our own experience. And what are most of the oaths in the world, but lies? and such as need rather a pardon for being took, than a dispensation from being kept? And lastly, what are all the religions of the world, except Judaism and Christianity, but lies? And even in Christianity itself, are there not those who teach, warrant, and defend lying? and scarce use the Bible for any other purpose but to swear upon it, and to lie against it?

Thus a mighty, governing lie goes round the world, and has almost banished truth out of it; and so reigning triumphantly in its stead, is the true source of most of those confusions and dire calamities that infest and plague the universe. For look over them all, and you shall find that the greatest annoyance and disturbance of mankind has been from one of these two things, force or fraud. Of which, as boisterous and violent a thing as force is, yet it rarely achieves any thing considerable, but under the conduct of fraud. Sleight of hand has done that which force of hand could never do.

But why do we speak of hands? It is the tongue that drives the world before it. The tongue, and the lying lip, which there is no fence against: for when that is the weapon, a man may strike where he can not reach; and a word shall do execution both further and deeper than the mightiest blow. For the hand can hardly lift up itself high enough to strike, but it must be seen; so that it warns while it threatens; but a false, insidious tongue may whisper a lie so close and low, that though you have ears to hear, yet you shall not hear; and indeed we generally come to know it, not by hearing, but by feeling what it says.

A man, perhaps, casts his eye this way and that way, and looks round about him, to spy out his enemy, and to defend himself; but alas! the fatal mischief that would trip up his heels is all the while under them. It works invisibly, and beneath: and the shocks of an earthquake, we know, are much more dreadful than the highest and loudest blusters of a storm. For there may be some shelter against the violence of the one, but no security against the hollowness of the other; which never opens its bosom, but for a killing embrace. The bowels of the earth in such cases, and the mercies of the false in all, being equally without compassion.

Upon the whole matter, it is hard to assign any one thing but lying, which God and man so unanimously join in the hatred of; and it is as hard to tell whether it does a greater dishonor to God, or mischief to man: it is certainly an abomination to both; and I hope to make it appear such in the following discourse. Though I must confess myself very unable to speak to the utmost latitude of this subject; and I thank God that I am so.

Now the words of the text are a plain, entire, categorical proposition; and therefore I shall not go about to darken them by any needless explication, but shall immediately cast the prosecution of them under these three following particulars. As,

I. I shall inquire into the nature of a lie, and the proper essential malignity of all falsehood.

II. I shall show the pernicious effects of it. And,

III. and lastly, I shall lay before you the rewards and punishments that will certainly attend, or at least follow it.

Every one of which, I suppose, and much more all of them together, will afford arguments more than sufficient, to prove, (though it were no part of holy scripture,) that *lying lips are an abomination to the Lord.*

And first, for the first of these.

I. What a lie is, and wherein the nature of it does consist. A lie is properly an outward signification of something contrary to, or, at least, beside the inward sense of the mind; so that when one thing is signified or expressed, and the same thing not meant or intended, that is properly a lie.

And forasmuch as God has endued man with a power or faculty to institute or appoint signs of his thoughts; and that, by virtue hereof, he can appoint, not only words, but also things, actions, and gestures to be signs of the inward thoughts and conceptions of his mind, it is evident that he may as really lie and deceive by actions and gestures, as he can by words; forasmuch as, in the nature of them, they are as capable of being made signs, and consequently of being as much abused and misapplied as the other: though, for distinction sake, a deceiving by words is commonly called a lie, and a deceiving by actions, gestures, or behavior, is called simulation, or hypocrisy.

The nature of a lie, therefore, consists in this, that it is a false signification knowingly and voluntarily used; in which the sign expressing is noways agreeing with the thought or conception of the mind pretended to be thereby expressed. For words signify not immediately and primely things themselves, but the conceptions of the mind concerning things; and therefore, if there be an agreement between our words and our thoughts, we do not speak falsely, though it sometimes so falls out that our words agree not with the things themselves: upon which account, though in so speaking we offend indeed against truth, yet we offend not properly by falsehood, which is a speaking against our thoughts; but by rashness, which is an affirming or denying, before we have sufficiently informed ourselves of the real and true estate of those things whereof we affirm or deny.

And thus having shown what a lie is, and wherein it does consist, the next consideration is, of the lawfulness or unlawfulness of it. And in this we have but too sad and scandalous an instance, both of the corruption and weakness of man's reason, and of the strange bias that it still receives from interest, that such a case as this, both with philosophers and divines, heathens and Christians, should be held disputable.

Plato accounted it lawful for statesmen and governors; and so did Cicero and Plutarch; and the Stoics, as some say, reckoned it amongst the arts and perfections of a wise man, to lie dexterously, in due time and place. And for some of the ancient doctors of the Christian church; such as Origen, Clemens Alexandrinus, Tertullian, Lactantius, and Chrysostom; and generally, all before St. Austin, several passages have fallen from them, that speak but too favorably of this ill thing. So that Paul Layman, a Romish casuist, says, that it is a truth but lately known and received in the world, that a lie is absolutely sinful and unlawful; I suppose he means that part of the world where the scriptures are not read, and where men care not to know what they are not willing to practice.

But then, for the mitigation of what has proceeded from these great men, we must take in that known and celebrated division of a lie into those three several kinds of it. As,

1. The pernicious lie, uttered for the hurt or disadvantage of our neighbor.

2. The officious lie, uttered for our own or our neighbor's advantage: and

3. lastly, The ludicrous and jocose lie, uttered by way of jest, and only for mirth's sake, in common converse. Now for the first of these, which is the pernicious lie; it was and is universally condemned by all; but the other two have found some patronage from the writings of those forementioned authors. The reason of which seems to be, that those

persons did not estimate the lawfulness or unlawfulness of a lie, from the intrinsic nature of the thing itself, but either from those external effects that it produced, or from those ends to which it was directed; which accordingly as they proved either helpful or hurtful, innocent or offensive, so the lie was reputed either lawful or unlawful. And therefore, since a man was helped by an officious lie, and not hurt by a jocose, both of these came to be esteemed lawful, and in some cases laudable.

But the schoolmen and casuists having too much philosophy to go about to clear a lie from that intrinsic inordination and deviation from right reason inherent in the nature of it, and yet withal unwilling to rob the world, and themselves especially, of so sweet a morsel of liberty, held that a lie was indeed absolutely and universally sinful; but then they held also, that only the pernicious lie was a mortal sin, and the other two were only venial. It can be no part of my business here to overthrow this distinction, and to show the nullity of it: which has been solidly and sufficiently done by most of our polemic writers of the protestant church. But at present I shall only take this their concession, that every lie is sinful, and consequently unlawful; and if it be a sin, I shall suppose it already proved to my hands to be, what all sin essentially is and must be, mortal. So that thus far have we gone, and this point have we gained, that it is absolutely and universally unlawful to lie, or to falsify.

Let us now, in the next place, inquire from whence this unlawfulness springs, and upon what it is grounded: to which I answer; that upon the principles of natural reason, the unlawfulness of lying is grounded upon this, that a lie is properly a sort or species of injustice, and a violation of the right of that person to whom the false speech is directed: for all speaking, or signification of one's mind, implies, in the nature of it, an act or address of one man to another: it being evident that no man, though he does speak false, can be said to lie to himself.

Now to show what this right is, we must know, that in the beginnings and first establishments of speech there was an implicit compact amongst men, founded upon common use and consent, that such and such words or voices, actions or gestures, should be means or signs, whereby they would express or convey their thoughts one to another; and that men should be obliged to use them for that purpose; forasmuch as, without such an obligation, those signs could not be effectual for such an end. From which compact there arising an obligation upon every one so to convey his meaning, there accrues also a right to every one, by the same signs to judge of the sense or meaning of the person so obliged to express himself: and consequently, if these signs are applied and used by him so as not to signify his meaning, the right of the person to whom he was obliged so to have done, is hereby violated, and the man, by being deceived and kept ignorant of his neighbor's meaning, where he ought to have known it, is so far deprived of the benefit of any intercourse or converse with him.

From hence therefore we see, that the original reason of the unlawfulness of lying or deceiving is, that it carries with it an act of injustice, and a violation of the right of him to whom we were obliged to signify or impart our minds, if we spoke to him at all.

But then we must observe also, (which I noted at first,) that as it is in man's power to institute, not only words, but also things, actions, or gestures, to be the means whereby he would signify and express his mind, so, on the other side, those voices, actions, or gestures, which men have not by any compact agreed to make the instruments of conveying their thoughts one to another, are not the proper instruments of deceiving, so as to denominate the person using them a liar or deceiver, though the person to whom they are addressed takes occasion from thence to form in his mind a false apprehension or belief of the thoughts of those who use such voices, actions, or gestures towards him. I say, in this case, the person using these things can not be said to deceive; since all deception is a misapplying of those signs which by compact or institution were made the means of men's signifying or conveying their thoughts; but here, a man only does those things from which another takes occasion to deceive himself: which one consideration will solve most of those difficulties that are usually started on this subject.

But yet this I do and must grant, that though it be not

against strict justice or truth for a man to do those things which he might otherwise lawfully do, albeit his neighbor does take occasion from thence to conceive in his mind a false belief, and so to deceive himself, yet Christian charity will in many cases restrain a man here too, and prohibit him to use his own right and liberty, where it may turn considerably to his neighbor's prejudice. For herein is the excellency of charity seen, that the charitable man not only does no evil himself, but that, to the utmost of his power, he also hinders any evil from being done even by another.

And as we have shown and proved that lying and deceiving stand condemned, upon the principles of natural justice, and the eternal law of right reason, so are the same much more condemned, and that with the sanction of the highest penalties, by the law of Christianity, which is eminently and transcendently called the truth, and the word of truth; and in nothing more surpasses all the doctrines and religions in the world, than in this, that it enjoins the clearest, the openest, and the sincerest dealing, both in words and actions; and is the rigidest exacter of truth in all our behavior, of any other doctrine or institution whatsoever.

And thus much for the first general thing proposed, which was to inquire into the nature of a lie, and the proper essential malignity of all falsehood. I proceed now to the

Second, which is to show the pernicious effects of it. Some of the chief and most remarkable of which are these that follow: as,

First of all, it was this that introduced sin into the world. For how came our first parents to sin, and to lose their primitive innocence? Why, they were deceived, and by the subtilty of the devil brought to believe a lie. And, indeed, deceit is of the very essence and nature of sin, there being no sinful action, but there is a lie wrapt up in the bowels of it. For sin prevails upon the soul by representing that as suitable and desirable that really is not so. And no man is ever induced to sin, but by a persuasion that he shall find some good and happiness in it, which he had not before. The wages that sin bargains with the sinner to serve it for, are life, pleasure, and profit; but the wages it pays him with are death, torment, and destruction. He that would understand the falsehood and deceit of sin throughly, must compare its promises and its payments together.

And as the devil first brought sin into the world by a lie, (being equally the base original of both,) so he still propagates and promotes it by the same. The devil reigns over none but those whom he first deceives. Geographers and historians, dividing the habitable world into thirty parts, give us this account of them: that but five of those thirty are Christian; and for the rest, six of them are Jew and Mahometan, and the remaining nineteen perfectly heathen: all which he holds and governs by possessing them with a lie, and bewitching them with a false religion: like the moon and the stars, he rules by night; and his kingdom, even in this world, is perfectly a kingdom of darkness. And therefore our Saviour, who came to dethrone the devil and to destroy sin, did it by being the light of the world, and by bearing witness to the truth. For so far as truth gets ground in the world, so far sin loses it. Christ saves the world, by undeceiving it; and sanctifies the will, by first enlightening the understanding.

2. A second effect of lying and falsehood is all that misery and calamity that befalls mankind. For the proof of which we need go no further than the former consideration: for sorrow being the natural and direct effect of sin, that which first brought sin into the world must by necessary consequence bring in sorrow too. Shame and pain, poverty and sickness, yea, death and hell itself, are all of them but the trophies of those fatal conquests, got by that grand impostor, the devil, over the deluded sons of men. And hardly can any example be produced of a man in extreme misery, who was not one way or other first deceived into it. For have not the greatest slaughters of armies been effected by stratagem? And have not the fairest estates been destroyed by suretyship? In both of which there is a fallacy, and the man is overreached before he is overthrown.

What betrayed and delivered the poor old prophet into the lion's mouth, 1 Kings xiii., but the mouth of a false prophet, much the crueller and more remorseless of the two? How came John Huss and Jerome of Prague to be so cruelly and basely used by the council of Constance, those ecclesiastical commissioners of the court of Rome? Why, they promised those innocent men a safe-conduct, who thereupon took them at their word, and accordingly were burnt alive, for trusting a pack of perfidious wretches, who regarded their own word as little as they did God's.*

And how came so many bonfires to be made in Queen Mary's days? Why, she had abused and deceived her people with lies, promising them the free exercise of their religion before she got into the throne; and when she was once in, she performed her promise to them at the stake. And I know no security we had from seeing the same again in our days, but one or two proclamations forbidding bonfires. Some sort of promises are edged tools, and it is dangerous laying hold on them.

But to pass from hence to fanatic treachery, that is, from one twin to the other; how came such multitudes of our own nation, at the beginning of that monstrous (but still surviving and successful) rebellion, in the year 1641, to be spunged of their plate and money, their rings and jewels, for the carrying on of the schismatical, dissenting, king-killing cause? Why, next to their own love of being cheated, it was the public, or rather prostitute faith of a company of faithless miscreants that drew them in, and deceived them. And how came so many thousands to fight and die in the same rebellion? Why, they were deceived into it by those spiritual trumpeters who followed them with continual alarms of damnation, if they did not venture life, fortune, and all, in that which wickedly and devilishly those impostors called the cause of God. So that I myself have heard one† say, (whose quarters have since hung about that city where he had been first deceived,) that he, with many more, went to that execrable war with such a controlling horror upon their spirits, from those sermons,‡ that they verily believed they should have been accursed by God forever, if they had not acted their part in that dismal tragedy, and heartily done the devil's work, being so effectually called and commanded to it in God's name.

* Of which last, see an instance in the 13th session of this council, in which it decrees, with a *non-obstante* to Christ's express institution of the blessed eucharist in both kinds, that the contrary custom and practice of receiving it only in one kind ought to be accounted and observed as a law; and that, if the priest should administer it otherwise, he was to be excommunicated.

† Colonel Axtell.

‡ He particularly mentioned those of Brooks and Calamy.

Infinite would it be to pursue all instances of this nature: but, consider those grand agents and lieutenants of the devil, by whom he scourges and plagues the world under him, to wit, tyrants; and was there ever any tyrant since the creation, who was not also false and perfidious? Do not the bloody and the deceitful man still go hand in hand together, in the language of the scripture? Psalm lv. 23. Was ever any people more cruel, and withal more false, than the Carthaginians? And had not the hypocritical contrivers of the murder of that blessed martyr king Charles the First, their masks and vizards, as well as his executioners?

No man that designs to rob another of his estate or life, will be so impudent or ignorant, as in plain terms to tell him so. But if it be his estate that he drives at, he will dazzle his eyes, and bait him in with the luscious proposal of some gainful purchase, some rich match, or advantageous project; till the easy man is caught and hampered; and so, partly by lies, and partly by lawsuits together, comes at length to be stripped of all, and brought to a piece of bread, when he can get it. Or if it be a man's life that the malice of his enemy seeks after, he will not presently clap his pistol to his breast, or his knife to his throat; but will rather take Absalom for his pattern, who invited his dear brother to a feast, hugged and embraced, courted and caressed him, till he had well dosed his weak head with wine, and his foolish heart with confidence and credulity; and then, in he brings him an old reckoning, and makes him pay it off with his blood. Or, perhaps, the cut-throat may rather take his copy from the Parisian massacre; one of the horridest instances of barbarous inhumanity that ever the world saw, but ushered in with all the pretenses of amity, and the festival treats of a reconciling marriage,—a new and excellent way, no doubt, of proving matrimony a sacrament. But such butchers know what they have to do. They must soothe and allure before they strike; and the ox must be fed before he is brought to the slaughter; and the same course must be taken with some sort of asses too.

In a word, I verily believe that no sad disaster ever yet befell any person or people, nor any villainy or flagitious action was ever yet committed, but, upon a due inquiry into the causes of it, it will be found that a lie was first or last the principal engine to effect it: and that, whether pride, lust, or cruelty brought it forth, it was falsehood that begot it; this gave it being, whatsoever other vice might give it birth.

3. As we have seen how much lying and falsehood disturbs, so, in the next place, we shall see also how it tends utterly to dissolve society. There is no doubt but all the safety, happiness, and convenience that men enjoy in this life, is from the combination of particular persons into societies or corporations: the cause of which is compact; and the band that knits together and supports all compacts is truth and faithfulness. So that the soul and spirit that animates and keeps up society is mutual trust, and the foundation of trust is truth, either known, or at least supposed in the person so trusted.

But now, where fraud and falsehood, like a plague or canker, comes once to invade society, the band, which held together the parts compounding it, presently breaks; and men are thereby put to a loss where to league and to fasten their dependences; and so are forced to scatter, and shift every one for himself. Upon which account, every notoriously false person ought to be looked upon and detested, as a public enemy, and to be pursued as a wolf or a mad dog, and a disturber of the common peace and welfare of mankind. There being no particular person whatsoever but has his private interest concerned and endangered in the mischief that such a wretch does to the public.

For look into great families, and you shall find some one false, paltry talebearer, who, by carrying stories from one to another, shall inflame the minds and discompose the quiet of the whole family. And from families pass to towns or cities; and two or three pragmatical, intriguing, meddling fellows, (men of business some call them,) by the venom of their false tongues, shall set the whole neighborhood together by the ears. Where men practice falsehood, and show tricks with one another, there will be perpetual suspicions, evil surmisings, doubts, and jealousies, which, by souring the minds of men, are the bane and pest of society. For still society is built upon trust, and trust upon the confidence that men have of one another's integrity.

And this is so evident, that without trusting, there could not only be no happiness, but indeed no living in this world. For in those very things that minister to the daily necessities of common life, how can any one be assured that the very meat and drink that he is to take into his body, and the clothes he is to put on, are not poisoned, and made unwholesome for him, before ever they are brought to him. Nay, in some places, (with horror be it spoke,) how can a man be secure in taking the very sacrament itself? For there have been those who have found something in this spiritual food, that has proved very fatal to their bodies, and more than prepared them for another world. I say, how can any one warrant himself in the use of these things against such suspicions, but in the trust he has in the common honesty and truth of men in general, which ought and uses to keep them from such villainies? Nevertheless, know this certainly beforehand he can not, forasmuch as such things have been done, and consequently may be done again. And therefore, as for any infallible assurance to the contrary, he can have none; but, in the great concerns of life and health, every man must be forced to proceed upon trust, there being no knowing the intention of the cook or baker, any more than of the priest himself. And yet, if a man should forbear his food, or raiment, or most of his business in the world, till he had science and certainty of the safeness of what he was going about, he must starve, and die disputing; for there is neither eating, nor drinking, nor living by demonstration.

Now this shows the high malignity of fraud and falsehood, that, in the direct and natural course of it, tends to the destruction of common life, by destroying that trust and mutual confidence that men should have in one another; by which the common intercourse of the world must be carried on, and without which men must first distrust, and then divide, separate, and stand upon their guard, with their hand against every one, and every one's hand against them.

The felicity of societies and bodies politic consists in this, that all relations in them do regularly discharge their respective duties and offices. Such as are the relation between prince and subject, master and servant, a man and his friend, husband and wife, parent and child, buyer and seller, and the like. But now, where fraud and falsehood take place, there is not one of all these that is not perverted, and that does not, from an help of society, directly become an hinderance. For first, it turns all above us into tyranny and barbarity; and all of the same religion and level with us into discord and confusion. It is this alone that poisons that sovereign and divine thing called friendship; so that when a man thinks that he leans upon a breast as loving and true to him as his own, he finds that he relies upon a broken reed, that not only basely fails, but also cruelly pierces the hand that rests upon it. It is from this that when a man thinks he has a servant or dependent, an instrument of his affairs and a defense of his person, he finds a traitor and a Judas, an enemy that eats his bread and lies under his roof; and perhaps readier to do him a mischief and a shrewd turn than an open and professed adversary. And lastly, from this deceit and falsehood it is, that, when a man thinks himself matched to one who, by the laws of God and nature, should be a comfort to him in all conditions, a consort of his cares, and a companion in all his concerns, instead thereof, he finds in his bosom a beast, a serpent, and a devil.

In a word: he that has to do with a liar, knows not where he is, nor what he does, nor with whom he deals. He walks upon bogs and whirlpools; wheresoever he treads he sinks, and converses with a bottomless pit, where it is impossible for him to fix, or to be at any certainty. In fine, he catches at an apple of Sodom, which, though it may entertain his eye with a florid, jolly white and red, yet upon the touch it shall fill his hand only with stench and foulness; fair in look and rotten at heart; as the gayest and most taking things and persons in the world generally are.

4. And lastly: deceit and falsehood do, of all other ill qualities, most peculiarly indispose the hearts of men to the impressions of religion. For these are sins perfectly spiritual, and so prepossess the proper seat and place of religion, which is the soul or spirit: and, when that is once filled and taken up with a lie, there will hardly be admission or room for truth. Christianity is known in scripture by no name so significantly as by the simplicity of the gospel.

And if so, does it not look like the greatest paradox and

prodigy in nature, for any one to pretend it lawful to equivocate or lie for it? To face God and outface man, with the sacrament and a lie in one's mouth together? Can a good intention, or rather a very wicked one, so miscalled, sanctify and transform perjury and hypocrisy into merit and perfection? Or can there be a greater blot cast upon any church or religion (whatsoever it be) than by such a practice? For will not the world be induced to look upon my religion as a lie, if I allow myself to lie for my religion?

The very life and soul of all religion is sincerity. And therefore the good ground, in which alone the immortal seed of the word sprang up to perfection, is said, in St. Luke viii. 15, to have been those *that received it into an honest heart*, that is, a plain, clear, and well-meaning heart; an heart not doubled, nor cast into the various folds and windings of a dodging, shifting hypocrisy. For the truth is, the more spiritual and refined any sin is, the more hardly is the soul cured of it; because the more difficultly convinced. And in all our spiritual maladies, conviction must still begin the cure.

Such sins indeed as are acted by the body, do quickly show and proclaim themselves; and it is no such hard matter to convince or run down a drunkard, or an unclean person, and to stop their mouths, and to answer any pretenses that they can allege for their sin. But deceit is such a sin as a Pharisee may be guilty of, and yet stand fair for the reputation of zeal and strictness, and a more than ordinary exactness in religion. And though some have been apt to account none sinful, or vicious, but such as wallow in the mire and dirt of gross sensuality, yet no doubt deceit, falsehood, and hypocrisy are more directly contrary to the very essence and design of religion, and carry in them more of the express image and superscription of the devil, than any bodily sins whatsoever. How did that false, fasting, imperious, self-admiring, or rather self-adoring hypocrite, in St. Luke xviii. 11, crow and exult over the poor publican! *God, I thank thee*, says he, *that I am not like other men;* and God forbid, say I, that there should be many others like him, for a glistering outside and a noisome inside, for *tithing mint and cummin, and for devouring widows' houses;* that is, for taking ten parts from his neighbor, and putting God off with one. After all which, had this man of merit and mortification being called to account for his ungodly swallow in gorging down the estates of helpless widows and orphans, it is odds but he would have told you that it was all for charitable uses, and to afford pensions for spies and proselytes. It being no ordinary piece of spiritual good husbandry to be charitable at other men's cost.

But such sons of Abraham, how highly soever they may have the luck to be thought of, are far from being Israelites indeed; for the character that our Saviour gives us of such, in the person of Nathanael, in John i. 47, is, *that they are without guile.* To be so, I confess, is generally reckoned (of late times especially) a poor, mean, sneaking thing, and the contrary, reputed wit and parts, and fitness for business, as the word is: though I doubt not but it will be one day found that only honesty and integrity can fit a man for the main business that he was sent into the world for; and that he certainly is the greatest wit who is wise to salvation.

And thus much for the second general thing proposed, which was to show the pernicious effects of lying and falsehood. Come we now to the

Third and last, which is to lay before you the rewards or punishments that will assuredly attend, or at least follow, this base practice.

I shall mention three: as,

1. An utter loss of all credit and belief with sober and discreet persons; and consequently of all capacity of being useful in the prime and noblest concerns of life. For there can not be imagined in nature a more forlorn, useless, and contemptible tool, or more unfit for any thing, than a discovered cheat. And let men rest assured of this, that there will be always some as able to discover and find out deceitful tricks as others can be to contrive them. For God forbid that all the wit and cunning of the world should still run on the deceiver's side; and when such little shifts and shuffling arts come once to be ripped up and laid open, how poorly and wretchedly must that man needs sneak, who finds himself both guilty and baffled too! a knave without luck is certainly the worst trade in the world. But truth makes the face of that person shine who speaks and owns it: while a lie is like

a vizard, that may cover the face indeed, but can never become it; nor yet does it cover it so but that it leaves it open enough for shame. It brands a man with a lasting, indelible character of ignominy and reproach, and that indeed so foul and odious, that those usurping hectors, who pretend to honor without religion, think the charge of a lie a blot upon them not to be washed out but by the blood of him that gives it.

For what place can that man fill in a commonwealth, whom nobody will either believe or employ? And no man can be considerable in himself, who has not made himself useful to others: nor can any man be so, who is incapable of a trust. He is neither fit for counsel or friendship, for service or command, to be in office or in honor, but, like salt that has lost its savor, fit only to rot and perish upon a dunghill.

For no man can rely upon such an one, either with safety to his affairs or without a slur to his reputation; since he that trusts a knave has no other recompense but to be accounted a fool for his pains. And if he thrusts himself into ruin and beggary, he falls unpitied, a sacrifice to his own folly and credulity; for he that suffers himself to be imposed upon by a known deceiver, goes partner in the cheat, and deceives himself. He is despised and laughed at as a soft and easy person, and as unfit to be relied upon for his weakness, as the other can be for his falseness.

It is really a great misery not to know whom to trust, but a much greater to behave one's self so as not to be trusted. But this is the liar's lot; he is accounted a pest and a nuisance; a person marked out for infamy and scorn, and abandoned by all men of sense and worth, and such as will not abandon themselves.

2. The second reward or punishment that attends the lying and deceitful person, is the hatred of all those whom he either has or would have deceived. I do not say that a Christian can lawfully hate any one; and yet I affirm that some may very worthily deserve to be hated; and of all men living, who may or do, the deceiver certainly deserves it most. To which I shall add this one remark further; that though men's persons ought not to be hated, yet without all peradventure their practices justly may, and particularly that detestable one which we are now speaking of.

For whosoever deceives a man, does not only do all that he can to ruin him, but, which is yet worse, to make him ruin himself; and by causing an error in the great guide of all his actions, his judgment, to cause an error in his choice too; the misguidance of which must naturally engage him in those courses that directly tend to his destruction. Loss of sight is the misery of life, and usually the forerunner of death; when the malefactor comes once to be muffled, and the fatal cloth drawn over his eyes, we know that he is not far from his execution.

And this is so true, that whosoever sees a man who would have beguiled and imposed upon him, by making him believe a lie, he may truly say of that person, That 's the man who would have ruined me, who would have stripped me of the dignity of my nature, and put out the eyes of my reason, to make himself sport with my calamity, my folly, and my dishonor. For so the Philistines used Samson, and every man in this sad case has enough of Samson to be his own executioner. Accordingly, if ever it comes to this, that a man can say of his confidant, he would have deceived me, he has said enough to annihilate and abolish all pretenses of friendship. And it is really an intolerable impudence, for any one to offer at the name of friend, after such an attempt. For can there be any thing of friendship in snares, hooks, and trepans? And therefore, whosoever breaks with his friend upon such terms, has enough to warrant him in so doing, both before God and man; and that without incurring either the guilt of unfaithfulness before the one, or the blemish of inconstancy before the other. For this is not properly to break with a friend, but to discover an enemy, and timely to shake the viver off from one's hand.

What says the most wise author of that excellent book of Ecclesiasticus, Ecclus. xxii. 21, 22? *Though thou drewest a sword at thy friend, yet despair not: for there may be a returning to favor. If thou hast opened thy mouth against thy friend, fear not; for there may be a reconciliation.* That is, an hasty word or an indiscreet action does not presently dissolve the bond, or root out a well-settled habit, but that friendship may be still sound at heart, and so outgrow and wear off these little distempers. But what follows? *Except for up-*

braiding, or disclosing of secrets, or a treacherous wound, (mark that:) *for for these things,* says he, *every friend will depart.* And surely it is high time for him to go, when such a devil drives him away. Passion, anger, and unkindness may give a wound that shall bleed and smart, but it is treachery only that makes it fester.

And the reason of the difference is manifest; for hasty words or blows may be only the effects of a sudden passion, during which a man is not perfectly himself: but no man goes about to deceive, or ensnare, or circumvent another in a passion; to lay trains, and set traps, and give secret blows in a present huff. No; this is always done with forecast and design with a steady aiming; and a long projecting malice, assisted with all the skill and art of an expert and well-managed hypocrisy; and, perhaps, not without the pharisaical feigned guise of something like self-denial and mortification; which are things in which the whole man, and the whole devil too, are employed, and all the powers and faculties of the mind are exerted and made use of.

But for all these masks and vizards, nothing certainly can be thought of or imagined more base, inhuman, or diabolical, than for one to abuse the generous confidence and hearty freedom of his friend, and to undermine and ruin him in those very concerns which nothing but too great a respect to, and too good an opinion of the traitor, made the poor man deposit in his hollow and fallacious breast. Such an one, perhaps, thinks to find some support and shelter in my friendship, and I take that opportunity to betray him to his mortal enemies. He comes to me for counsel, and I show him a trick. He opens his bosom to me, and I stab him to the heart.

These are the practices of the world we live in; especially since the year sixty, the grand epoch of falsehood, as well as debauchery. But God, who is the great guarantee for the peace, order, and good behavior of mankind, where laws can not secure it, may some time or other think it the concern of his justice and providence too, to revenge the affronts put upon them, by such impudent defiers of both, as neither believe a God, nor ought to be believed by man.

In the mean time, let such perfidious wretches know, that

though they believe a devil no more than they do a God, yet in all this scene of refined treachery, they are really doing the devil's journey-work, who was a liar and a murderer from the beginning, and therefore a liar, that he might be a murderer: and the truth is, such an one does all towards his brother's ruin that the devil himself could do. For the devil can but tempt and deceive, and if he can not destroy a man that way, his power is at an end.

But I can not dismiss this head without one further note, as very material in the case now before us. Namely, that since this false, wily, doubling disposition of mind is so intolerably mischievous to society, God is sometimes pleased, in mere pity and compassion to men, to give them warning of it, by setting some odd mark upon such Cains. So that, if a man will be but so true to himself as to observe such persons exactly, he shall generally spy such false lines, and such a sly, treacherous leer upon their face, that he shall be sure to have a cast of their eye to warn him, before they give him a cast of their nature to betray him. And in such cases, a man may see more and better by another's eye than he can by his own.

Let this, therefore, be the second reward of the lying and deceitful person, that he is the object of a just hatred and abhorrence. For as the devil is both a liar himself and the father of liars, so I think that the same cause that has drawn the hatred of God and man upon the father, may justly entail it upon his offspring too; and it is pity that such an entail should ever be cut off. But,

3. And lastly, The last and utmost reward, that shall infallibly reach the fraudulent and deceitful, (as it will all other obstinate and impenitent sinners,) is a final and eternal separation from God, who is truth itself, and with whom no shadow of falsehood can dwell. *He that telleth lies,* says David, in Psalm ci. 7, *shall not tarry in my sight;* and if not in the sight of a poor mortal man, (who could sometimes lie himself,) how much less in the presence of the infinite and all-knowing God! A wise and good prince, or governor, will not vouchsafe a liar the countenance of his eye, and much less the privilege of his ear. The Spirit of God seems to write this upon the very gates of heaven, and to state the

condition of men's entrance into glory chiefly upon their veracity. In Psalm xv. 1, *Who shall ascend into thy holy hill?* says the Psalmist. To which it is answered, in ver. 2, *He that worketh righteousness, and that speaketh the truth from his heart.*

And, on the other side, how emphatically is hell described in the two last chapters of the Revelation; by being the great receptacle and mansion-house of liars, whom we shall find there ranged with the vilest and most detestable of all sinners, appointed to have their portion in that horrid place; Rev. xxi. 8; *The unbelieving, and the abominable, and murderers, and whoremongers, and sorcerers, and idolaters, and all liars, shall have their part in the lake which burneth with fire and brimstone:* and in Rev. xxii. 15, *Without are dogs and sorcerers, &c., and whosoever loveth and maketh a lie.*

Now let those consider this, whose tongue and heart hold no correspondence: who look upon it as a piece of art and wisdom, and the masterpiece of conversation, to overreach and deceive, and make a prey of a credulous and well-meaning honesty. What do such persons think? Are dogs, whoremongers, and sorcerers such desirable company to take up with forever? Will the burning lake be found so tolerable? Or will there be any one to drop refreshment upon the false tongue, when it shall be tormented in those flames? Or do they think that God is a liar like themselves, and that no such things shall ever come to pass, but that all these fiery threatenings shall vanish into smoke, and this dreadful sentence blow off without execution? Few certainly can lie to their own hearts so far as to imagine this: but hell is, and must be granted to be, the deceiver's portion, not only by the judgment of God, but of his own conscience too. And, comparing the malignity of his sin with the nature of the punishment allotted for him, all that can be said of a liar lodged in the very nethermost hell, is this; that if the vengeance of God could prepare any place or condition worse than hell for sinners, hell itself would be too good for him.

And now to sum up all in short; I have shown what a lie is, and wherein the nature of falsehood does consist; that it is a thing absolutely and intrinsically evil; that it is an act of injustice, and a violation of our neighbor's right.

And that the vileness of its nature is equalled by the malignity of its effects. It being this that first brought sin into the world, and is since the cause of all those miseries and calamities that disturb it; and further, that it tends utterly to dissolve and overthrow society, which is the greatest temporal blessing and support of mankind: and, which is yet worst of all, that it has a strange and particular efficacy, above all other sins, to indispose the heart to religion.

And lastly, that it is as dreadful in its punishments as it has been pernicious in its effects. Forasmuch as it deprives a man of all credit and belief, and consequently, of all capacity of being useful in any station or condition of life whatsoever; and next, that it draws upon him the just and universal hatred and abhorrence of all men here; and finally subjects him to the wrath of God and eternal damnation hereafter.

And now, if none of all these considerations can recommend and endear truth to the words and practices of men, and work upon their double hearts so far as to convince and make them sensible of the baseness of the sin and greatness of the guilt that fraud and falsehood leaves upon the soul; let them lie and cheat on, till they receive a fuller and more effectual conviction of all these things, in that place of torment and confusion prepared for the devil and his angels, and all his lying retinue, by the decree and sentence of that God who, in his threatenings as well as in his promises, will be true to his word, and can not lie.

To whom be rendered and ascribed, as is most due, all praise, might, majesty, and dominion, both now and for evermore. Amen.

SERMON XIII.

THE PRACTICE OF RELIGION ENFORCED BY REASON:

IN A SERMON PREACHED AT WESTMINSTER ABBEY, 1667.

TO THE UNIVERSITY OF OXFORD.*

REVEREND AND LEARNED SIRS,

THESE discourses (most of them at least) having by the favor of your patience had the honor of your audience, and being now published in another and more lasting way, do here humbly cast themselves at your feet, imploring the yet greater favor and honor of your patronage, or at least the benevolence of your pardon. Amongst which, the chief design of some of them is, to assert the rights and constitutions of our excellently reformed church, which of late we so often hear reproached (in the modish dialect of the present times) by the name of little things; and that in order to their being laid aside, not only as little, but superfluous. But for my own part, I can account nothing little in any church which has the stamp of undoubted authority, and the practice of primitive antiquity, as well as the reason and decency of the thing itself, to warrant and support it. Though, if the supposed littleness of these matters should be a sufficient reason for the laying them aside, I fear our church will be found to have more little men to spare than little things.

But I have observed all along, that while this innovating spirit has been striking at the constitutions of our church, the same has been giving several bold and scurvy strokes at some of her articles too: an evident demonstration to me, that whensoever her discipline shall be destroyed, her doctrine will not long survive it: and I doubt not but it is for the sake of this, that the former is so much maligned and shot at. Pelagianism and Socinianism, with several other heterodoxies cognate to and dependent upon them, which of late,

* This dedication refers to the twelve sermons next following.

with so much confidence and scandalous countenance, walk about daring the world, are certainly no doctrines of the church of England. And none are abler and fitter to make them appear what they are, and whither they tend, than our excellent and so well stocked universities; and if these will but bestir themselves against all innovators whatsoever, it will quickly be seen, that our church needs none, either to fill her places or to defend her doctrines, but the sons whom she herself has brought forth and bred up. Her charity is indeed great to others, and the greater, for that she is so well provided of all that can contribute either to her strength or ornament without them. The altar receives and protects such as fly to it, but needs them not.

We are not so dull, but we perceive who are the prime designers, as well as the professed actors against our church, and from what quarter the blow chiefly threatens us. We know the spring as well as we observe the motion, and scent the foot which pursues, as well as see the hand which is lifted up against us. The pope is an experienced workman; he knows his tools, and knows them to be but tools, and knows withal how to use them, and that so, that they shall neither know who it is that uses them, or what he uses them for; and we can not in reason presume his skill now in ninety-three, to be at all less than it was in forty-one. But God, who has even to a miracle protected the church of England hitherto, against all the power and spite both of her open and concealed enemies, will, we hope, continue to protect so pure and rational, so innocent and self-denying a constitution still. And next, under God, we must rely upon the old church of England clergy, together with the two universities, both to support and recover her declining state. For so long as the universities are sound and orthodox, the church has both her eyes open; and while she has so, it is to be hoped that she will look about her, and consider again and again what she is to change from, and what she must change to, and where she shall make an end of changing, before she quits her present constitution.

Innovations about religion are certainly the most efficacious, as well as the most plausible way of compassing a total abolition of it. One of the best and strongest arguments we have against popery is, that it is an innovation upon the Christian church; and if so, I can not see why that, which we explode in the popish church, should pass for such a piece of perfection in a reformed one. The papists I am sure (our shrewdest and most designing enemies) desire and push on this to their utmost; and for that very reason one would think that we (if we are not besotted) should oppose it to our utmost too. However, let us but have our liturgy continued to us as it is, till the persons are born who shall be able to mend it, or make a better, and we desire no greater security against either the altering this, or introducing another.

The truth is, such as would new model the church of England ought not only to have a new religion, (which some have been so long driving at,) but a new reason likewise, to proceed by : since experience (which was ever yet accounted one of the surest and best improvements of reason) has been always for acquiescing in things settled with sober and mature advice, (and, in the present case also, with the very blood and martyrdom of the advisers themselves,) without running the risk of new experiments; which, though in philosophy they may be commendable, yet in religion and religious matters are generally fatal and pernicious. The church is a royal society for settling old things, and not for finding out new. In a word, we serve a wise and unchangeable God, and we desire to do it by a religion and in a church (as like him as may be) without changes or alterations.

And now, as in so important a matter I would interest both universities, so I do it with the same honor and deference to both; as abhorring from my heart the pedantic partiality of preferring one before the other: since (if my relation to one should never so much incline me so to do) I must sincerely declare, that I can not see how to place a preference where I can find no preëminence. And therefore, as they are both equal in fame, and learning, and all that is great and excellent, so I hope to see them always one in judgment and design, heart and affection; without any strife, emulation, or contest between them except this one, (which I wish may be perpetual,) viz., which of the two best universities in the world shall be most serviceable to the best church in the world, by their learning, constancy, and integrity.

But to conclude, there remains no more for me to do, but to beg pardon of that august body to which I belong, if I have offended in assuming to myself the honor of mentioning my relation to a society which I could never reflect the least honor upon, nor contribute the least advantage to.

All that I can add is, that as it was my fortune to serve this noble seat of learning for many years, as her public, though unworthy orator, so upon that, and other innumerable accounts, I ought forever to be, and to acknowledge myself,

Her most faithful, obedient,
and devoted servant,
ROBERT SOUTH.

Westminster Abbey,
Nov. 17, 1693.

Prov. x. 9.—*He that walketh uprightly walketh surely.*

AS it were easy to evince, both from reason and experience, that there is a strange, restless activity in the soul of man, continually disposing it to operate, and exert its faculties, so the phrase of scripture still expresses the life of man by walking; that is, it represents an active principle in an active posture. And because the nature of man carries him thus out to action, it is no wonder if the same nature equally renders him solicitous about the issue and event of his actions; for every one, by reflecting upon the way and method of his own workings, will find that he is still determined in them by a respect to the consequence of what he does; always proceeding upon this argumentation: If I do such a thing, such an advantage will follow from it, and therefore I will do it. And if I do this, such a mischief will ensue thereupon, and therefore I will forbear. Every one, I say, is concluded by this practical discourse; and for a man to bring his actions to the event proposed and designed by him, is to walk surely. But since the event of an action usually follows the nature or quality of it, and the quality follows the rule directing it, it concerns a man, by all means, in the framing of his actions, not to be deceived in the rule which he proposes for the measure of them; which, without great and exact caution, he may be these two ways:

1. By laying false and deceitful principles.
2. In case he lays right principles, yet by mistaking in the consequences which he draws from them.

An error in either of which is equally dangerous; for if a man is to draw a line, it is all one whether he does it by a crooked rule, or by a straight one misapplied. He who fixes upon false principles treads upon infirm ground, and so sinks, and he who fails in his deductions from right principles, stumbles upon firm ground, and so falls; the disaster is not of the same kind, but of the same mischief in both.

It must be confessed, that it is sometimes very hard to judge of the truth or goodness of principles, considered barely in themselves, and abstracted from their consequences. But certainly he acts upon the surest and most prudential grounds in the world, who, whether the principles which he acts upon prove true or false, yet secures an happy issue to his actions.

Now he who guides his actions by the rules of piety and religion, lays these two principles as the great ground of all that he does:

1. That there is an infinite, eternal, all-wise mind governing the affairs of the world, and taking such an account of the actions of men as, according to the quality of them, to punish or reward them.

2dly, That there is an estate of happiness or misery after this life, allotted to every man, according to the quality of his actions here. These, I say, are the principles which every religious man proposes to himself; and the deduction which he makes from them is this: That it is his grand interest and concern so to act and behave himself in this world, as to secure himself from an estate of misery in the other. And thus to act, is, in the phrase of scripture, to walk uprightly; and it is my business to prove, that he who acts in the strength of this conclusion, drawn from the two forementioned principles, walks surely, or secures an happy event to his actions, against all contingencies whatsoever.

And to demonstrate this, I shall consider the said principles under a threefold supposition:

1st, As certainly true;

2dly, As probable; and,

3dly, As false.

And if the pious man brings his actions to an happy end, which soever of these suppositions his principles fall under, then certainly there is none who walks so surely, and upon such irrefragable grounds of prudence, as he who is religious.

1. First of all therefore we will take these principles (as we may very well do) under the hypothesis of certainly true: where, though the method of the ratiocination which I have cast the present discourse into, does not naturally engage me to prove them so, but only to show what directly and necessarily follows upon a supposal that they are so; yet to give the greater perspicuity and clearness to the prosecution of the subject in hand, I shall briefly demonstrate them thus.

It is necessary that there should be some first mover; and, if so, a first being; and the first being must infer an infinite, unlimited perfection in the said being: forasmuch as if it were finite or limited, that limitation must have been either from itself or from something else. But not from itself, since it is contrary to reason and nature, that any being should limit its own perfection; nor yet from something else, since then it should not have been the first, as supposing some other thing coevous to it; which is against the present supposition. So that it being clear, that there must be a first being, and that infinitely perfect, it will follow that all other perfection that is, must be derived from it; and so we infer the creation of the world: and then supposing the world created by God, (since it is noways reconcilable to God's wisdom that he should not also govern it,) creation must needs infer providence: and then it being granted that God governs the world, it will follow also that he does it by means suitable to the natures of the things he governs, and to the attainment of the proper ends of government: and moreover, man being by nature a free moral agent, and so capable of deviating from his duty, as well as performing it, it is necessary that he should be governed by laws: and since laws require that they be enforced with the sanction of rewards and punishments, sufficient to sway and work upon the minds of such as are to be governed by them; and lastly, since experience shows that rewards and punishments, terminated only within this life, are not sufficient for that purpose, it fairly and rationally follows that the rewards and punishments, which God governs mankind by, do and must look beyond it.

And thus I have given a brief proof of the certainty of these principles; namely, that there is a supreme governor of the world; and that there is a future estate of happiness or misery for men after this life: which principles, while a man steers his course by, if he acts piously, soberly, and temperately, I suppose there needs no further arguments to evince that he acts prudentially and safely. For he acts as under the eye of his just and severe Judge, who reaches to his creature a command with one hand, and a reward with the other. He spends as a person who knows that he must come to a reckoning. He sees an eternal happiness or misery suspended upon a few days' behavior; and therefore he lives every hour as for eternity. His future condition has such a powerful influence upon his present practice, because he entertains a continual apprehension and a firm persuasion of it. If a man walks over a narrow bridge when he is drunk, it is no wonder that he forgets his caution, while he overlooks his danger. But he who is sober, and views that nice separation between himself and the devouring deep, so that if he should slip, he sees his grave gaping under him, surely must needs take every step with horror, and the utmost caution and solicitude.

But for a man to believe it as the most undoubted certainty in the world, that he shall be judged according to the quality of his actions here, and after judgment receive an eternal recompense, and yet to take his full swing in all the pleasures of sin, is it not a greater frenzy, than for a man to take a purse at Tyburn, while he is actually seeing another hanged for the same fact? It is really to dare and defy the justice of Heaven, to laugh at right-aiming thunderbolts, to puff at damnation, and, in a word, to bid Omnipotence do its worst. He indeed who thus walks, walks surely; but it is because he is sure to be damned.

I confess it is hard to reconcile such a stupid course to the natural way of the soul's acting; according to which, the will moves according to the proposals of good and evil, made by the understanding: and therefore for a man to run headlong into the bottomless pit, while the eye of a seeing conscience assures him that it is bottomless and open, and all return from it desperate and impossible; while his ruin stares him in the face, and the sword of vengeance points directly at his heart, still to press on to the embraces of his sin, is a problem unresolvable upon any other ground, but that sin infatuates before it destroys. For Judas to receive and swallow the sop, when his master gave it him seasoned with those terrible words, *It had been good for that man that he had never been born;* surely this argued a furious appetite and a strong stomach, that could thus catch at a morsel with the fire and brimstone all flaming about it, and, as it were, digest death itself, and make a meal upon perdition.

I could wish that every bold sinner, when he is about to engage in the commission of any known sin, would arrest his confidence, and for a while stop the execution of his purpose, with this short question, Do I believe that it is really true, that God has denounced death to such a practice, or do I not? If he does not, let him renounce his Christianity, and surrender back his baptism, the water of which might better serve him to cool his tongue in hell, than only to consign him over to the capacity of so black an apostasy. But if he does believe it, how will he acquit himself upon the accounts of bare reason? For does he think that if he pursues the means of death, they will not bring him to that fatal end? Or does he think that he can grapple with divine vengeance, and endure the everlasting burnings, or arm himself against the bites of the never-dying worm? No, surely, these are things not to be imagined; and therefore I can not conceive what security the presuming sinner can promise himself, but upon these two following accounts:

1. That God is merciful, and will not be so severe as his word; and that his threatenings of eternal torments are not so decretory and absolute but that there is a very comfortable latitude left in them for men of skill to creep out at. And here it must indeed be confessed that Origen, and some others, not long since, who have been so officious as to furbish up and reprint his old errors, hold that the sufferings of the damned are not to be, in a strict sense, eternal; but that, after a certain revolution and period of time, there shall be a general jail-delivery of the souls in prison, and that not for a further execution, but a final release. And it must be further acknowledged that some of the ancients, like kind-hearted men, have talked much of annual refrigeriums, respites, or intervals of punishment to the damned, as particularly on the great festivals of the resurrection, ascension, pentecost, and the like. In which, as these good men are more to be commended for their kindness and compassion than to be followed in their opinion; (which may be much better argued by wishes than demonstrations;) so, admitting that it were true, yet what a pitiful, slender comfort would this amount to! much like the Jews abating the punishment of malefactors from forty stripes to forty save one. A great indulgence indeed, even as great as the difference between forty and thirty-nine; and yet much less considerable would that indulgence be of a few holidays in the measures of

eternity, of some hours' ease, compared with infinite ages of torment.

Supposing, therefore, that few sinners relieve themselves with such groundless, trifling considerations as these, yet may they not however fasten a rational hope upon the boundless mercy of God, that this may induce him to spare his poor creature, though by sin become obnoxious to his wrath? To this I answer, that the divine mercy is indeed large, and far surpassing all created measures, yet nevertheless it has its proper time; and after this life it is the time of justice; and to hope for the favors of mercy then, is to expect an harvest in the dead of winter. God has cast all his works into a certain, inviolable order; according to which, there is a time to pardon and a time to punish; and the time of one is not the time of the other. When corn has once felt the sickle, it has no more benefit from the sunshine. But,

2dly, If the conscience be too apprehensive (as for the most part it is) to venture the final issue of things upon a fond persuasion that the great Judge of the world will relent, and not execute the sentence pronounced by him; as if he had threatened men with hell rather to fright them from sin than with an intent to punish them for it; I say, if the conscience can not find any satisfaction or support from such reasonings as these, yet may it not, at least, relieve itself with the purposes of a future repentance, notwithstanding its present actual violations of the law? I answer, that this certainly is a confidence of all others the most ungrounded and irrational. For upon what ground can a man promise himself a future repentance, who can not promise himself a futurity? whose life depends upon his breath, and is so restrained to the present that it can not secure to itself the reversion of the very next minute. Have not many died with the guilt of impenitence and the designs of repentance together? If a man dies to-day, by the prevalence of some ill humors, will it avail him that he intended to have bled and purged to-morrow?

But how dares sinful dust and ashes invade the prerogative of Providence, and carve out to himself the seasons and issues of life and death, which the Father keeps wholly within his own power? How does that man, who thinks he sins securely under the shelter of some remote purposes of amendment, know but that the decree above may be already passed against him, and his allowance of mercy spent; so that the bow in the clouds is now drawn, and the arrow levelled at his head: and not many days like to pass, but perhaps an apoplexy, or an imposthume, or some sudden disaster, may stop his breath, and reap him down as a sinner ripe for destruction.

I conclude, therefore, that, upon supposition of the certain truth of the principles of religion, he who walks not uprightly has neither from the presumption of God's mercy reversing the decree of his justice, nor from his own purposes of a future repentance, any sure ground to set his foot upon, but in this whole course acts as directly in contradiction to nature as he does in defiance of grace. In a word, he is besotted, and has lost his reason; and what then can there be for religion to take hold of him by? Come we now to the

2d supposition, under which we show, That the principles of religion laid down by us might be considered, and that is, as only probable. Where we must observe that probability does not properly make any alteration, either in the truth or falsity of things but only imports a different degree of their clearness or appearance to the understanding. So that that is to be accounted probable, which has more and better arguments producible for it than can be brought against it; and surely such a thing at least is religion. For certain it is, that religion is universal, I mean the first rudiments and general notions of religion, called natural religion, and consisting in the acknowledgment of a Deity, and of the common principles of morality, and a future estate of souls after death, (in which also we have all that some reformers and refiners amongst us would reduce Christianity itself to.) This notion of religion, I say, has diffused itself in some degree or other, greater or less, as far as human nature extends. So that there is no nation in the world, though plunged into never such gross and absurd idolatry, but has some awful sense of a Deity, and a persuasion of a state of retribution to men after this life.

But now, if there are really no such things, but all is a

mere lie and a fable, contrived only to chain up the liberty of man's nature from a freer enjoyment of those things, which otherwise it would have as full a right to enjoy as to breathe, I demand whence this persuasion could thus come to be universal? For was it ever known, in any other instance, that the whole world was brought to conspire in the belief of a lie? Nay, and of such a lie as should lay upon men such unpleasing abridgments, tying them up from a full gratification of those lusts and appetites which they so impatiently desire to satisfy, and consequently, by all means, to remove those impediments that might any way obstruct their satisfaction? Since therefore it can not be made out upon any principle of reason, how all the nations in the world, otherwise so distant in situation, manners, interests, and inclinations, should, by design or combination, meet in one persuasion; and withal that men, who so mortally hate to be deceived and imposed upon, should yet suffer themselves to be deceived by such a persuasion as is false; and not only false, but also cross and contrary to their strongest desires; so that if it were false, they would set the utmost force of their reason on work to discover that falsity, and thereby disinthrall themselves; and further, since there is nothing false, but what may be proved to be so; and yet, lastly, since all the power and industry of man's mind has not been hitherto able to prove a falsity in the principles of religion, it irrefragably follows, (and that, I suppose, without gathering any more into the conclusion than has been made good in the premises,) that religion is at least a very high probability.

And this is that which I here contend for, That it is not necessary to the obliging men to believe religion to be true, that this truth be made out to their reason by arguments demonstratively certain; but that it is sufficient to render their unbelief inexcusable, even upon the account of bare reason, if so be the truth of religion carry in it a much greater probability than any of those ratiocinations that pretend the contrary: and this I prove in the strength of these two considerations.

1st, That no man, in matters of this life, requires an assurance either of the good which he designs, or of the evil which he avoids, from arguments demonstratively certain;

but judges himself to have sufficient ground to act upon, from a probable persuasion of the event of things. No man who first traffics into a foreign country has any scientific evidence that there is such a country, but by report, which can produce no more than a moral certainty; that is, a very high probability, and such as there can be no reason to except against. He who has a probable belief that he shall meet with thieves in such a road, thinks himself to have reason enough to decline it, albeit he is sure to sustain some less (though yet considerable) inconvenience by his so doing. But perhaps it may be replied, (and it is all that can be replied,) that a greater assurance and evidence is required of the things and concerns of the other world than of the interests of this. To which I answer, that assurance and evidence (terms, by the way, extremely different; the first, respecting properly the ground of our assenting to a thing; and the other, the clearness of the thing or object assented to) have no place at all here, as being contrary to our present supposition; according to which, we are now treating of the practical principles of religion only as probable, and falling under a probable persuasion. And for this I affirm, that where the case is about the hazarding an eternal or a temporal concern, there a less degree of probability ought to engage our caution against the loss of the former, than is necessary to engage it about preventing the loss of the latter. Forasmuch as where things are least to be put to the venture, as the eternal interests of the other world ought to be, there every, even the least, probability or likelihood of danger, should be provided against; but where the loss can be but temporal, every small probability of it need not put us so anxiously to prevent it, since, though it should happen, the loss might be repaired again; or if not, could not however destroy us, by reaching us in our greatest and highest concern; which no temporal thing whatsoever is or can be. And this directly introduces the

2d consideration or argument, viz. That bare reason, discoursing upon a principle of self-preservation, (which surely is the fundamental principle which nature proceeds by,) will oblige a man voluntarily and by choice to undergo any less evil to secure himself but from the probability of an evil incomparably greater, and that also such an one, as, if that probability passes into a certain event, admits of no reparation by any after-remedy that can be applied to it.

Now that religion, teaching a future estate of souls, is a probability; and that its contrary can not with equal probability be proved, we have already evinced. This therefore being supposed, we will suppose yet further, that for a man to abridge himself in the full satisfaction of his appetites and inclinations, is an evil, because a present pain and trouble: but then it must likewise be granted, that nature must needs abhor a state of eternal pain and misery much more; and that if a man does not undergo the former less evil, it is highly probable that such an eternal estate of misery will be his portion; and if so, I would fain know whether that man takes a rational course to preserve himself, who refuses the endurance of these lesser troubles, to secure himself from a condition infinitely and inconceivably more miserable.

But since probability, in the nature of it, supposes that a thing may or may not be so, for any thing that yet appears, or is certainly determined on either side, we will here consider both sides of this probability: as,

1st, That it is one way possible, that there may be no such thing as a future estate of happiness or misery for those who have lived well or ill here; and then he who, upon the strength of a contrary belief, abridged himself in the gratification of his appetites, sustains only this evil; viz. That he did not please his senses and unbounded desires, so much as otherwise he might and would have done, had he not lived under the captivity and check of such a belief. This is the utmost which he suffers: but whether this be a real evil or no, (whatsoever vulgar minds may commonly think it,) shall be discoursed of afterwards.

2. But then again, on the other side, it is probable that there will be such a future estate; and then how miserably is the voluptuous, sensual unbeliever left in the lurch! For there can be no retreat for him then, no mending of his choice in the other world, no after-game to be played in hell. It fares with men, in reference to their future estate, and the condition upon which they must pass to it, much as it does with a merchant having a vessel richly fraught at sea in a

storm: the storm grows higher and higher, and threatens the utter loss of the ship: but there is one, and but one certain way to save it, which is, by throwing its rich lading overboard; yet still, for all this, the man knows not but possibly the storm may cease, and so all be preserved. However, in the mean time, there is little or no probability that it will do so; and in case it should not, he is then assured that he must lay his life, as well as his rich commodities, in the cruel deep. Now in this case, would this man, think we, act rationally, should he, upon the slender possibility of escaping otherwise, neglect the sure, infallible preservation of his life, by casting away his rich goods? No certainly, it would be so far from it, that should the storm, by a strange hap, cease immediately after he had thus thrown away his riches, yet the throwing them away was infinitely more rational and eligible, than the retaining or keeping them could have been.

For a man, while he lives here in the world, to doubt whether there be any hell or no; and thereupon to live so, as if absolutely there were none; but when he dies, to find himself confuted in the flames; this, surely, must be the height of woe and disappointment, and a bitter conviction of an irrational venture and an absurd choice. In doubtful cases, reason still determines for the safer side; especially if the case be not only doubtful, but also highly concerning, and the venture be of a soul and an eternity.

He who sat at a table, richly and deliciously furnished, but with a sword hanging over his head by one single thread or hair, surely had enough to check his appetite, even against all the ragings of hunger and temptations of sensuality. The only argument that could any way encourage his appetite was, that possibly the sword might not fall; but when his reason should encounter it with another question, What if it should fall? and moreover, that pitiful stay by which it hung should oppose the likelihood that it would, to a mere possibility that it might not; what could the man enjoy or taste of his rich banquet, with all this doubt and horror working in his mind?

Though a man's condition should be really in itself never so safe, yet an apprehension and surmise that it is not safe, is enough to make a quick and a tender reason sufficiently miserable. Let the most acute and learned unbeliever demonstrate that there is no hell: and if he can, he sins so much the more rationally; otherwise, if he can not, the case remains doubtful at least: but he who sins obstinately, does not act as if it were so much as doubtful; for if it were certain and evident to sense, he could do no more; but for a man to found a confident practice upon a disputable principle, is brutishly to outrun his reason, and to build ten times wider than his foundation. In a word, I look upon this one short consideration, were there no more, as a sufficient ground for any rational man to take up his religion upon, and which I defy the subtlest atheist in the world solidly to answer or confute; namely, That it is good to be sure. And so I proceed to the

Third and last supposition, under which the principles of religion may, for argument sake, be considered; and that is, as false; which surely must reach the utmost thoughts of any atheist whatsoever. Nevertheless even upon this account also, I doubt not but to evince that he who walks uprightly walks much more surely than the wicked and profane liver; and that with reference to the most valued temporal enjoyments, such as are reputation, quietness, health, and the like, which are the greatest which this life affords, or is desirable for. And,

1st, For reputation or credit. Is any one had in greater esteem than the just person; who has given the world an assurance, by the constant tenor of his practice, that he makes a conscience of his ways; that he scorns to do an unworthy or a base thing; to lie, to defraud, to undermine another's interest, by any sinister and inferior arts? And is there any thing which reflects a greater lustre upon a man's person, than a severe temperance, and a restraint of himself from vicious and unlawful pleasures? Does any thing shine so bright as virtue, and that even in the eyes of those who are void of it? For hardly shall you find any one so bad, but he desires the credit of being thought what his vice will not let him be; so great a pleasure and convenience is it, to live with honor and a fair acceptance amongst those whom we converse with; and a being without it is not life, but rather the skeleton or *caput mortuum* of life; like time without day, or day itself without the shining of the sun to enliven it.

On the other side, is there any thing that more embitters all the enjoyments of this life than shame and reproach? Yet this is generally the lot and portion of the impious and irreligious; and of some of them more especially.

For how infamous, in the first place, is the false, fraudulent, and unconscionable person! and how quickly is his character known! For hardly ever did any man of no conscience continue a man of any credit long. Likewise, how odious, as well as infamous, is such an one! Especially if he be arrived at that consummate and robust degree of falsehood, as to play in and out, and show tricks with oaths, the sacredest bonds which the conscience of man can be bound with; how is such an one shunned and dreaded, like a walking pest! What volleys of scoffs, curses, and satires, are discharged at him! so that let never so much honor be placed upon him, it cleaves not to him, but forthwith ceases to be honor, by being so placed; no preferment can sweeten him, but the higher he stands, the further and wider he stinks.

In like manner for the drinker and debauched person: is any thing more the object of scorn and contempt than such an one? His company is justly looked upon as a disgrace: and nobody can own a friendship for him without being an enemy to himself. A drunkard is, as it were, outlawed from all worthy and creditable converse. Men abhor, loathe, and despise him, and would even spit at him as they meet him, were it not for fear that a stomach so charged should something more than spit at them.

But not to go over all the several kinds of vice and wickedness, should we set aside the consideration of the glories of a better world, and allow this life for the only place and scene of man's happiness, yet surely Cato will be always more honorable than Clodius, and Cicero than Catiline. Fidelity, justice, and temperance will always draw their own reward after them, or rather carry it with them, in those marks of honor which they fix upon the persons who practice and pursue them. It is said of David in 1 Chron. xxix. 28, *that he died full of days, riches, and honor:* and there was no need of an heaven, to render him in all respects a much happier man than Saul. But in the

2d place, The virtuous and religious person walks upon

surer grounds than the vicious and irreligious, in respect of the ease, peace, and quietness which he enjoys in this world; and which certainly make no small part of human felicity. For anxiety and labor are great ingredients of that curse which sin has entailed upon fallen man. Care and toil came into the world with sin, and remain ever since inseparable from it, both as to its punishment and effect.

The service of sin is perfect slavery; and he who will pay obedience to the commands of it shall find it an unreasonable taskmaster, and an unmeasurable exactor.

And to represent the case in some particulars. The ambitious person must rise early and sit up late, and pursue his design with a constant, indefatigable attendance; he must be infinitely patient and servile, and obnoxious to all the cross humors of those whom he expects to rise by; he must endure and digest all sorts of affronts; adore the foot that kicks him, and kiss the hand that strikes him: while, in the mean time, the humble and contented man is virtuous at a much easier rate: his virtue bids him sleep and take his rest, while the other's restless sin bids him sit up and watch. He pleases himself innocently and easily, while the ambitious man attempts to please others sinfully and difficultly, and perhaps in the issue unsuccessfully too.

The robber, and man of rapine, must run, and ride, and use all the dangerous and even desperate ways of escape; and probably, after all, his sin betrays him to a jail, and from thence advances him to the gibbet: but let him carry off his booty with as much safety and success as he can wish, yet the innocent person, with never so little of his own, envies him not, and, if he has nothing, fears him not.

Likewise the cheat and fraudulent person is put to a thousand shifts to palliate his fraud, and to be thought an honest man: but surely there can be no greater labor than to be always dissembling, and forced to maintain a constant disguise, there being so many ways by which a smothered truth is apt to blaze and break out; the very nature of things making it not more natural for them to be, than to appear as they be. But he who will be really honest, just, and sincere in his dealings, needs take no pains to be thought so; no more than the sun needs take any pains to shine, or, when he is up, to convince the world that it is day.

And here again to bring in the man of luxury and intemperance for his share in the pain and trouble, as well as in the forementioned shame and infamy of his vice. Can any toil or day-labor equal the fatigue or drudgery which such an one undergoes, while he is continually pouring in draught after draught, and cramming in morsel after morsel, and that in spite of appetite and nature, till he becomes a burden to the very earth that bears him; though not so great an one to that, but that (if possible) he is yet a greater to himself? [1]

And now, in the last place, to mention one sinner more, and him a notable, leading sinner indeed, to wit, the rebel. Can any thing have more of trouble, hazard, and anxiety in it, than the course which he takes? For, in the first place, all the evils of war must unavoidably be endured, as the necessary means and instruments to compass and give success to his traitorous designs. In which, if it is his lot to be conquered, he must expect that vengeance that justly attends a conquered, disarmed villain; for when such an one is vanquished, his sins are always upon him. But if, on the contrary, he proves victorious, he will yet find misery enough in the distracting cares of settling an ungrounded, odious, detestable interest, so heartily, and so justly maligned, abhorred, and oftentimes plotted against; so that, in effect, he is still in war, though he has quitted the field. The torment of his suspicion is great, and the courses he must take to quiet his jealous, suspicious mind, infinitely troublesome and vexatious.

But in the mean time, the labor of obedience, loyalty, and subjection is no more, but for a man honestly and discreetly to sit still, and to enjoy what he has, under the protection of the laws. And when such an one is in his lowest condition, he is yet high and happy enough to despise and pity the most prosperous rebel in the world: even those famous ones of forty-one (with all due respect to their flourishing relations be it spoke) not excepted. In the

Third and last place, the religious person walks upon surer grounds than the irreligious, in respect of the very health of his body. Virtue is a friend and an help to nature; but it is

* See above, pp. 14, 15.

vice and luxury that destroys it, and the diseases of intemperance are the natural product of the sins of intemperance. Whereas, on the other side, a temperate, innocent use of the creature, never casts any one into a fever or a surfeit. Chastity makes no work for a chirurgeon, nor ever ends in rottenness of bones. Sin is the fruitful parent of distempers, and ill lives occasion good physicians. Seldom shall one see in cities, courts, and rich families, (where men live plentifully, and eat and drink freely,) that perfect health, that athletic soundness and vigor of constitution, which is commonly seen in the country, in poor houses and cottages, where nature is their cook, and necessity their caterer, and where they have no other doctor but the sun and the fresh air, and that such an one as never sends them to the apothecary. It has been observed in the earlier ages of the church, that none lived such healthful and long lives as monks and hermits, who had sequestered themselves from the pleasures and plenties of the world, to a constant ascetic course, of the severest abstinence and devotion.

Nor is excess the only thing by which sin mauls and breaks men in their health, and the comfortable enjoyment of themselves thereby, but many are also brought to a very ill and languishing habit of body by mere idleness; and idleness is both itself a great sin, and the cause of many more. The husbandman returns from the field, and from manuring his ground, strong and healthy, because innocent and laborious; you will find no diet-drinks, no boxes of pills, nor gallipots, amongst his provisions; no, he neither speaks nor lives French, he is not so much a gentleman, forsooth. His meals are coarse and short, his employment warrantable, his sleep certain and refreshing, neither interrupted with the lashes of a guilty mind, nor the aches of a crazy body. And when old age comes upon him, it comes alone, bringing no other evil with it but itself: but when it comes to wait upon a great and worshipful sinner, (who for many years together has had the reputation of eating well and doing ill,) it comes (as it ought to do, to a person of such quality) attended with a long train and retinue of rheums, coughs, catarrhs, and dropsies, together with many painful girds and achings, which are at least called the gout. How does such an one go about, or is carried rather, with his body bending inward, his head shaking, and his eyes always watering (instead of weeping) for the sins of his ill-spent youth. In a word, old age seizes upon such a person, like fire upon a rotten house; it was rotten before, and must have fallen of itself; so that it is no more but one ruin preventing another.

And thus I have shown the fruits and effects of sin upon men in this world. But peradventure it will be replied, that there are many sinners who escape all these calamities, and neither labor under any shame or disrepute, any unquietness of condition, or more than ordinary distemper of body, but pass their days with as great a portion of honor, ease, and health, as any other men whatsoever. But to this I answer,

First, That those sinners who are in such a temporally happy condition, owe it not to their sins, but wholly to their luck, and a benign chance that they are so. Providence often disposes of things by a method beside and above the discourses of man's reason.

Secondly, That the number of those sinners, who by their sins have been directly plunged into all the forementioned evils, is incomparably greater than the number of those who, by the singular favor of providence, have escaped them. And,

Thirdly and lastly, That notwithstanding all this, sin has yet in itself a natural tendency to bring men under all these evils; and, if persisted in, will infallibly end in them, unless hindered by some unusual accident or other, which no man, acting rationally, can steadily build upon. It is not impossible but a man may practice a sin secretly to his dying day; but it is ten thousand to one, if the practice be constant, but that some time or other it will be discovered; and then the effect of sin discovered, must be shame and confusion to the sinner. It is possible also, that a man may be an old healthful epicure; but I affirm also, that it is next to a miracle, if he be so, and the like is to be said of the several instances of sin, hitherto produced by us. In short, nothing can step between them and misery in this world, but a very great, strange, and unusual chance, which none will presume of who talks surely.

And so, I suppose, that religion can not possibly be enforced (even in the judgment of its best friends and most professed enemies) by any further arguments than what have been produced, (how much better soever the said arguments may be managed by abler hands.) For I have shown and proved, that, whether the principles of it be certain or but probable, nay, though supposed absolutely false, yet a man is sure of that happiness in the practice, which he can not be in the neglect of it; and consequently, that, though he were really a speculative atheist, (which there is great reason to believe that none perfectly are,) yet if he would but proceed rationally, that is, if (according to his own measures of reason) he would but love himself, he could not however be a practical atheist, nor live without God in this world, whether or no he expected to be rewarded by him in another.

And now, to make some application of the foregoing discourse, we may, by an easy but sure deduction, conclude and gather from it these two things:

First, That that profane, atheistical, epicurean rabble, whom the whole nation so rings of, and who have lived so much to the defiance of God, the dishonor of mankind, and the disgrace of the age which they are cast upon, are not indeed (what they are pleased to think and vote themselves) the wisest men in the world; for in matters of choice, no man can be wise in any course or practice in which he is not safe too. But can these high assumers, and pretenders to reason, prove themselves so amidst all those liberties and latitudes of practice which they take? Can they make it out against the common sense and opinion of all mankind, that there is no such thing as a future estate of misery for such as have lived ill here? Or can they persuade themselves, that their own particular reason, denying or doubting of it, ought to be relied upon as a surer argument of truth than the universal, united reason of all the world besides affirming it? Every fool may believe and pronounce confidently; but wise men will, in matters of discourse, conclude firmly, and, in matters of practice, act surely: and if these will do so too in the case now before us, they must prove it, not only probable, (which yet they can never do,) but also certain, and past all doubt, that there is no hell, nor place of torment for the wicked; or at least that they themselves, notwithstanding all their villainous and licentious practices, are not to be reckoned of that number and character, but that, with a *non obstante* to all their revels, their profaneness, and scandalous debaucheries of all sorts, they continue virtuosos still, and are that in truth which the world in favor and fashion (or rather by an antiphrasis) is pleased to call them.

In the meantime, it can not but be matter of just indignation to all knowing and good men, to see a company of lewd, shallow-brained huffs, making atheism and contempt of religion the sole badge and character of wit, gallantry, and true discretion; and then over their pots and pipes, claiming and engrossing all these wholly to themselves; magisterially censuring the wisdom of all antiquity, scoffing at all piety, and, as it were, new modeling the whole world. When yet such as have had opportunity to sound these braggers throughly, by having sometimes endured the penance of their sottish company, have found them in converse so empty and insipid, in discourse so trifling and contemptible, that it is impossible but that they should give a credit and an honor to whatsoever and whomsoever they speak against: they are indeed such as seem wholly incapable of entertaining any design above the present gratification of their palates, and whose very souls and thoughts rise no higher than their throats; but yet withal of such a clamorous and provoking impiety, that they are enough to make the nation like Sodom and Gomorrah in their punishment, as they have already made it too like them in their sins. Certain it is, that blasphemy and irreligion have grown to that daring height here of late years, that had men in any sober civilized heathen nation spoke or done half so much in contempt of their false gods and religion, as some in our days and nation, wearing the name of Christians, have spoke and done against God and Christ, they would have been infallibly burnt at a stake, as monsters and public enemies of society.

The truth is, the persons here reflected upon are of such a peculiar stamp of impiety, that they seem to be a set of fellows got together, and formed into a kind of diabolical society, for the finding out new experiments in vice; and therefore they laugh at the dull, unexperienced, obsolete sinners of former times; and scorning to keep themselves within the common, beaten, broad way to hell, by being vicious only at the low rate of example and imitation, they are for searching out other ways and latitudes, and obliging posterity with unheard of inventions and discoveries in sin; resolving herein to admit of no other measure of good and evil but the judgment of sensuality, as those who prepare matters to their hands allow no other measure of the philosophy and truth of things but the sole judgment of sense. And these, forsooth, are our great sages, and those who must pass for the only shrewd, thinking, and inquisitive men of the age; and such, as by a long, severe, and profound speculation of nature, have redeemed themselves from the pedantry of being conscientious and living virtuously, and from such old-fashioned principles and creeds as tie up the minds of some narrow - spirited, uncomprehensive zealots, who know not the world, nor understand that he only is the truly wise man who, *per fas et nefas*, gets as much as he can.

But for all this, let atheists and sensualists satisfy themselves as they are able. The former of which will find, that as long as reason keeps her ground, religion neither can nor will lose hers. And for the sensual epicure, he also will find, that there is a certain living spark within him, which all the drink he can pour in will never be able to quench or put out; nor will his rotten abused body have it in its power to convey any putrefying, consuming, rotting quality to the soul: no, there is no drinking, or swearing, or ranting, or fluxing a soul out of its immortality. But that must and will survive and abide, in spite of death and the grave; and live forever to convince such wretches to their eternal woe, that the so much repeated ornament and flourish of their former speeches (*God damn 'em*) was commonly the truest word they spoke, though least believed by them while they spoke it.

2dly, The other thing deducible from the foregoing particulars shall be to inform us of the way of attaining to that excellent privilege, so justly valued by those who have it, and so much talked of by those who have it not; which is assurance. Assurance is properly that persuasion or confidence which a man takes up of the pardon of his sins, and his interest in God's favor, upon such grounds and terms as the scripture lays down. But now, since the scripture promises eternal happiness and pardon of sin, upon the sole condition of faith and sincere obedience, it is evident that he only can plead a title to such a pardon, whose conscience impartially tells him that he has performed the required condition. And this is the only rational assurance which a man can with any safety rely or rest himself upon.

He who in this case would believe surely, must first walk surely; and to do so is to walk uprightly. And what that is, we have sufficiently marked out to us in those plain and legible lines of duty, requiring us to demean ourselves to God humbly and devoutly; to our governors obediently; and to our neighbors justly; and to ourselves soberly and temperately. All other pretenses being infinitely vain in themselves and fatal in their consequences.

It was indeed the way of many in the late times, to bolster up their crazy, doting consciences, with (I know not what) odd confidences, founded upon inward whispers of the Spirit, stories of something which they called conversion and marks of predestination: all of them (as they understood them) mere delusions, trifles, and fig-leaves; and such as would be sure to fall off and leave them naked, before that fiery tribunal which knows no other way of judging men but according to their works.

Obedience and upright walking are such substantial, vital parts of religion as, if they be wanting, can never be made up, or commuted for, by any formalities of fantastic looks or language. And the great question, when we come hereafter to be judged, will not be, How demurely have you looked? or, How boldly have you believed? With what length have you prayed? and, With what loudness and vehemence have you preached? But, How holily have you lived? and, How uprightly have you walked? For this, and this only, (with the merits of Christ's righteousness,) will come into account before that great Judge who will pass sentence upon every man according to what he has done here in the flesh, whether it be good, or whether it be evil; and there is no respect of persons with him.

To whom therefore be rendered and ascribed, as is most due, all praise, might, majesty, and dominion, both now and for evermore. Amen.

SERMON XIV.

A SERMON PREACHED BEFORE THE UNIVERSITY, AT CHRIST CHURCH, OXON, 1664.

JOHN xv. 15.—*Henceforth I call you not servants; for the servant knoweth not what his lord doeth: but I have called you friends; for all things that I have heard of my Father I have made known unto you.*

WE have here an account of Christ's friendship to his disciples; that is, we have the best of things represented in the greatest of examples. In other men we see the excellency, but in Christ the divinity of friendship. By our baptism and church-communion we are made one body with Christ; but by this we become one soul.

Love is the greatest of human affections, and friendship is the noblest and most refined improvement of love; a quality of the largest compass. And it is here admirable to observe the ascending gradation of the love which Christ bore to his disciples. The strange and superlative greatness of which will appear from those several degrees of kindness that it has manifested to man in the several periods of his condition. As,

1st, If we consider him antecedently to his creation, while he yet lay in the barren womb of nothing, and only in the number of possibilities: and consequently could have nothing to recommend him to Christ's affection, nor show any thing lovely, but what he should afterwards receive from the stamp of a preventing love. Yet even then did the love of Christ begin to work, and to commence in the first emanations and purposes of goodness towards man; designing to provide matter for itself to work upon, to create its own object, and, like the sun in the production of some animals, first to give a being, and then to shine upon it.

2dly, Let us take the love of Christ as directing itself to man actually created and brought into the world; and so all those glorious endowments of human nature in its original state and innocence, were so many demonstrations of the munificent goodness of him by whom God first made, as well as afterwards redeemed the world. There was a consult of the whole Trinity for the making of man, that so he might shine as a masterpiece, not only of the art, but also of the kindness of his Creator; with a noble and a clear understanding, a rightly disposed will, and a train of affections regular and obsequious, and perfectly conformable to the dictates of that high and divine principle, right reason. So that, upon the whole matter, he stepped forth, not only the work of God's hands, but also the copy of his perfections; a kind of image or representation of the Deity in small. Infinity contracted into flesh and blood; and (as I may so speak) the preludium and first essay towards the incarnation of the divine nature. But,

3dly and lastly, Let us look upon man, not only as created, and brought into the world, with all these great advantages superadded to his being, but also as depraved, and fallen from them, as an outlaw and a rebel, and one that could plead a title to nothing but to the highest severities of a sin-revenging justice. Yet even in this estate also, the boundless love of Christ began to have warm thoughts and actings towards so wretched a creature, at this time not only not amiable, but highly odious.

While indeed man was yet uncreated and unborn, though he had no positive perfection to present and set him off to Christ's view, yet he was at least negatively clear: and, like unwritten paper, though it has no draughts to entertain, yet neither has it any blots to offend the eye; but is white, and innocent, and fair for an after-inscription. But man, once fallen, was nothing but a great blur; nothing but a total universal pollution, and not to be reformed by any thing under a new creation.

Yet, see here the ascent and progress of Christ's love. For first, if we consider man in such a loathsome and provoking condition, was it not love enough that he was spared and permitted to enjoy a being? since, not to put a traitor to death is a singular mercy. But then, not only to continue his being, but to adorn it with privilege, and from the number of subjects to take him into the retinue of servants, this was yet a greater love. For every one that may be fit to be tolerated in a prince's dominions, is not therefore fit to be admitted into his family; nor is any prince's court to be commensurate to his kingdom. But then further, to advance him from a servant to a friend; from only living in his house, to lying in his bosom; this is an instance of favor above the rate of a created goodness, an act for none but the Son of God, who came to do every thing in miracle, to love supernaturally, and to pardon infinitely, and even to lay down the sovereign, while he assumed the savior.

The text speaks the winning behavior and gracious condescension of Christ to his disciples, in owning them for his friends, who were more than sufficiently honored by being his servants. For still these words of his must be understood, not according to the bare rigor of the letter, but according to the arts and allowances of expression: not as if the relation of friends had actually discharged them from that of servants; but that of the two relations, Christ was pleased to overlook the meaner, and without any mention of that, to entitle and denominate them solely from the more honorable.

For the further illustration of which, we must premise this, as a certain and fundamental truth, that, so far as service imports duty and subjection, all created beings, whether men or angels, bear the necessary and essential relation of servants to God, and consequently to Christ, who is *God blessed forever:* and this relation is so necessary, that God himself can not dispense with it, nor discharge a rational creature from it: for although consequentially indeed he may do so, by the annihilation of such a creature, and the taking away his being, yet, supposing the continuance of his being, God can not effect that a creature which has his being from, and his dependence upon, him, should not stand obliged to do him the utmost service that his nature enables him to do. For to suppose the contrary, would be irregular, and opposite to the law of nature, which, consisting in a fixed unalterable relation of one nature to another, is upon that account, even by

God himself, indispensable. Forasmuch as having once made a creature, he can not cause that that creature should not owe a natural relation to his Maker, both of subjection and dependence, (the very essence of a creature importing so much,) to which relation if he behaves himself unsuitably, he goes contrary to his nature, and the laws of it; which God, the author of nature, can not warrant without being contrary to himself. From all which it follows, that even in our highest estate of sanctity and privilege, we yet retain the unavoidable obligation of Christ's servants; though still with an advantage as great as the obligation, where the service is perfect freedom: so that, with reference to such a Lord, to serve, and to be free, are terms not consistent only, but absolutely equivalent.

Nevertheless, since the name of servants has of old been reckoned to imply a certain meanness of mind, as well as lowness of condition, and the ill qualities of many who served have rendered the condition itself not very creditable; especially in those ages and places of the world in which the condition of servants was extremely different from what it is now amongst us; they being generally slaves, and such as were bought and sold for money, and consequently reckoned but amongst the other goods and chattels of their lord or master: it was for this reason that Christ thought fit to waive the appellation of servant here, as, according to the common use of it amongst the Jews, (and at that time most nations besides,) importing these three qualifications, which, being directly contrary to the spirit of Christianity, were by no means to be allowed in any of Christ's disciples.

1st, The first whereof is that here mentioned in the text; viz., an utter unacquaintance with his master's designs, in these words: *The servant knows not what his lord doeth.* For seldom does any man of sense make his servant his counsellor, for fear of making him his governor too. A master for the most part keeps his choicest goods locked up from his servant, but much more his mind. A servant is to know nothing but his master's commands; and in these also, not to know the reason of them.

Neither is he to stand aloof off from his counsels only, but sometimes from his presence also; and so far as decency is duty, it is sometimes his duty to avoid him. But the voice of Christ in his gospel is, *Come to me all ye that are heavy laden.* The condition of a servant staves him off to a distance; but the gospel speaks nothing but allurement, attractives, and invitation. The magisterial law bids the person under it, *Go, and he must go;* but the gospel says to every believer, *Come, and he cometh.* A servant dwells remote from all knowledge of his lord's purposes. He lives as a kind of foreigner under the same roof; a domestic, and yet a stranger too.

2dly, The name of servant imports a slavish and degenerous awe of mind; as it is in Rom. viii. 5, *God has not given us the spirit of bondage again to fear.* He who serves, has still the low and ignoble restraints of dread upon his spirit; which in business, and even in the midst of action, cramps and ties up his activity. He fears his master's anger, but designs not his favor. *Quicken me,* says David, *with thy free spirit.* It is the freedom of the spirit that gives worth and life to the performance. But a servant commonly is less free in mind than in condition; his very will seems to be in bonds and shackles, and desire itself under a kind of durance and captivity. In all that a servant does, he is scarce a voluntary agent, but when he serves himself: all his services otherwise, not flowing naturally from propensity and inclination, but being drawn and forced from him by terror and coaction. In any work he is put to, let the master withdraw his eye, and he will quickly take off his hand.

3dly, The appellation of servant imports a mercenary temper and disposition; and denotes such an one as makes his reward both the sole motive and measure of his obedience. He neither loves the thing commanded, nor the person who commands it, but is wholly and only intent upon his own emolument. All kindnesses done him, and all that is given him, over and above what is strictly just and his due, makes him rather worse than better. And this is an observation that never fails, where any one has so much bounty and so little wit as to make the experiment. For a servant rarely or never ascribes what he receives to the mere liberality and generosity of the donor, but to his own worth and merit, and to the need which he supposes there is of him; which opinion alone will be sure to make any one of a mean servile spirit, insolent and intolerable.

And thus I have shown what the qualities of a servant usually are, (or at least were in that country where our Saviour lived and conversed, when he spake these words,) which, no doubt, were the cause why he would not treat his disciples (whom he designed to be of a quite contrary disposition) with this appellation.

Come we therefore now, in the next place, to show what is included in that great character and privilege which he was pleased to vouchsafe both to them, and to all believers, in calling and accounting them his friends. It includes in it, I conceive, these following things:

1. Freedom of access. House, and heart, and all, are open for the reception of a friend. The entrance is not beset with solemn excuses and lingering delays; but the passage is easy, and free from all obstruction, and not only admits, but even invites the comer. How different, for the most part, is the same man from himself, as he sustains the person of a magistrate, and as he sustains that of a friend! As a magistrate or great officer, he locks himself up from all approaches by the multiplied formalities of attendance, by the distance of ceremony and grandeur; so many hungry officers to be passed through, so many thresholds to be saluted, so many days to be spent in waiting for an opportunity of, perhaps, but half an hour's converse.

But when he is to be entertained, whose friendship, not whose business, demands an entrance, those formalities presently disappear, all impediments vanish, and the rigors of the magistrate submit to the endearments of a friend. He opens and yields himself to the man of business with difficulty and reluctancy, but offers himself to the visits of a friend with facility, and all the meeting readiness of appetite and desire. The reception of one is as different from the admission of the other as when the earth falls open under the incisions of the plow, and when it gapes and greedily opens itself to drink in the dew of heaven, or the refreshments of a shower: or there is as much difference between them as when a man reaches out his arms to take up a burden, and when he reaches them out to embrace.

It is confessed that the vast distance that sin had put between the offending creature and the offended Creator, required the help of some great umpire and intercessor, to open him a new way of access to God; and this Christ did for us as Mediator. But we read of no mediator to bring us to Christ; for though, being God by nature, he dwells in the hight of majesty, and the inaccessible glories of a Deity, yet, to keep off all strangeness between himself and the sons of men, he has condescended to a cognation and consanguinity with us, he has clothed himself with flesh and blood, that so he might subdue his glories to a possibility of human converse. And therefore he that denies himself an immediate access to Christ, affronts him in the great relation of a friend, and as opening himself both to our persons and to our wants, with the greatest tenderness and the freest invitation. There is none who acts a friend by a deputy, or can be familiar by proxy.

2. The second privilege of friendship is a favorable construction of all passages between friends, that are not of so high and so malign a nature as to dissolve the relation. *Love covers a multitude of sins*, says the apostle, 1 Pet. iv. 8. When a scar can not be taken away, the next kind office is to hide it. Love is never so blind as when it is to spy faults. It is like the painter, who, being to draw the picture of a friend having a blemish in one eye, would picture only the other side of his face. It is a noble and a great thing to cover the blemishes and to excuse the failings of a friend; to draw a curtain before his stains, and to display his perfections; to bury his weaknesses in silence, but to proclaim his virtues upon the house-top. It is an imitation of the charities of heaven, which, when the creature lies prostrate in the weakness of sleep and weariness, spreads the covering of night and darkness over it, to conceal it in that condition; but as soon as our spirits are refreshed, and nature returns to its morning vigor, God then bids the sun rise, and the day shine upon us, both to advance and to show that activity.

It is the ennobling office of the understanding to correct the fallacious and mistaken reports of sense, and to assure us that the staff in the water is straight, though our eye would tell us it is crooked. So it is the excellency of friendship to rectify, or at least to qualify, the malignity of those surmises that would misrepresent a friend, and traduce him in our thoughts. Am I told that my friend has done me an injury, or that he has committed any undecent action? Why, the first debt that I both owe to his friendship, and that he may challenge from mine, is rather to question the truth of the report than presently to believe my friend unworthy. Or, if matter of fact breaks out and blazes with too great an evidence to be denied, or so much as doubted of, why still there are other lenitives that friendship will apply, before it will be brought to the decretory rigors of a condemning sentence. A friend will be sure to act the part of an advocate, before he will assume that of a judge. And there are few actions so ill (unless they are of a very deep and black tincture indeed) but will admit of some extenuation at least from those common topics of human frailty; such as are ignorance or inadvertency, passion or surprise, company or solicitation; with many other such things, which may go a great way towards an excusing of the agent, though they can not absolutely justify the action. All which apologies for, and alleviations of, faults, though they are the hights of humanity, yet they are not the favors, but the duties of friendship. Charity itself commands us, where we know no ill, to think well of all. But friendship, that always goes a pitch higher, gives a man a peculiar right and claim to the good opinion of his friend. And if we justly look upon a proneness to find faults, as a very ill and a mean thing, we are to remember that a proneness to believe them is next to it.

We have seen here the demeanor of friendship between man and man: but how is it, think we now, between Christ and the soul that depends upon him? Is he anyways short in these offices of tenderness and mitigation? No, assuredly, but by infinite degrees superior. For where our heart does but relent, his melts; where our eye pities, his bowels yearn. How many frowardnesses of ours does he smother, how many indignities does he pass by, and how many affronts does he put up at our hands, because his love is invincible, and his friendship unchangeable? He rates every action, every sinful infirmity, with the allowances of mercy; and never weighs the sin, but together with it he weighs the force of the inducement; how much of it is to be attributed to choice, how much to the violence of the temptation, to the stratagem of the occasion, and the yielding frailties of weak nature.

Should we try men at that rate that we try Christ, we should quickly find that the largest stock of human friendship would be too little for us to spend long upon. But his compassion follows us with an infinite supply. He is God in his friendship, as well as in his nature, and therefore we sinful creatures are not took upon advantages, nor consumed in our provocations.

See this exemplified in his behavior to his disciples, while he was yet upon earth: how ready was he to excuse and cover their infirmities! At the last and bitterest scene of his life, when he was so full of agony and horror upon the approach of a dismal death, and so had most need of the refreshments of society, and the friendly assistances of his disciples; and when also he desired no more of them but only for a while to sit up and pray with him: yet they, like persons wholly untouched with his agonies, and unmoved with his passionate entreaties, forget both his and their own cares, and securely sleep away all concern for him or themselves either. Now, what a fierce and sarcastic reprehension may we imagine this would have drawn from the friendships of the world, that act but to an human pitch! and yet what a gentle one did it receive from Christ! In Matt. xxvi. 40, no more than, *What, could you not watch with me for one hour?* And when from this admonition they took only occasion to redouble their fault, and to sleep again, so that upon a second and third admonition they had nothing to plead for their unseasonable drowsiness, yet then Christ, who was the only person concerned to have resented and aggravated this their unkindness, finds an extenuation for it, when they themselves could not. *The spirit indeed is willing,* says he, *but the flesh is weak.* As if he had said, I know your hearts, and am satisfied of your affection, and therefore accept your will, and compassionate your weakness. So benign, so gracious is the friendship of Christ, so answerable to our wants, so suitable to our frailties. Happy that man who has a friend to point out to him the perfection of duty; and yet to pardon him in the lapses of his infirmity!

3. The third privilege of friendship is a sympathy in joy and grief. When a man shall have diffused his life, his self, and his whole concernments so far that he can weep his sorrows with another's eyes; when he has another heart besides his own, both to share and to support his griefs; and when, if his joys overflow, he can treasure up the overplus and redundancy of them in another breast; so that he can, as it were, shake off the solitude of a single nature, by dwelling in two bodies at once, and living by another's breath; this surely is the hight, the very spirit and perfection of all human felicities.

It is a true and happy observation of that great philosopher the Lord Verulam, that this is the benefit of communication of our minds to others, that sorrows by being communicated grow less, and joys greater. And indeed sorrow, like a stream, loses itself in many channels; and joy, like a ray of the sun, reflects with a greater ardor and quickness when it rebounds upon a man from the breast of his friend.

Now friendship is the only scene upon which the glorious truth of this great proposition can be fully acted and drawn forth. Which indeed is a summary description of the sweets of friendship: and the whole life of a friend, in the several parts and instances of it, is only a more diffuse comment upon, and a plainer explication of, this divine aphorism. Friendship never restrains a pleasure to a single fruition. But such is the royal nature of this quality, that it still expresses itself in the style of kings, as, *we do* this or that; and, this is *our* happiness; and, such or such a thing belongs *to us;* when the immediate possession of it is vested only in one. Nothing certainly in nature can so peculiarly gratify the noble dispositions of humanity as for one man to see another so much himself as to sigh his griefs, and groan his pains, to sing his joys, and, as it were, to do and feel every thing by sympathy and secret inexpressible communications. Thus it is upon an human account.

Let us now see how Christ sustains and makes good this generous quality of a friend. And this we shall find fully set forth to us in Heb. iv. 15, where he is said to be a *merciful high-priest, touched with the feeling of our infirmities;* and *that in all our afflictions he is afflicted,* Isa. lxiii. 9. And, no doubt, with the same bowels and meltings of affection, with which any tender mother hears and bemoans the groanings of her sick child, does Christ hear and sympathize with the spiritual agonies of a soul under desertion, or the pressures of some stinging affliction. It is enough that he understands the exact measures of our strengths and weaknesses; that *he knows our frame;* as it is in Psalm ciii. 14; and that he does not only know, but emphatically, that *he remembers* also, *that we are but dust.* Observe that signal passage of his loving commiseration; as soon as he had risen from the dead, and met Mary Magdalen, in Mark xvi. 7, he sends this message of his resurrection by her: *Go, tell my disciples, and Peter, that I am risen.* What, was not Peter one of his disciples? Why then is he mentioned particularly and by himself, as if he were exempted out of their number? Why, we know into what a plunge he had newly cast himself by denying his Master: upon occasion of which he was now struggling with all the perplexities and horrors of mind imaginable, lest Christ might in like manner deny and disown him before his Father, and so repay one denial with another. Hereupon Christ particularly applies the comforts of his resurrection to him, as if he had said, Tell all my disciples, but be sure especially to tell poor Peter, that I am risen from the dead; and that, notwithstanding his denial of me, the benefits of my resurrection belong to him, as much as to any of the rest. This is the privilege of the saints, to have a companion and a supporter in all their miseries, in all the doubtful turnings and doleful passages of their lives. In sum, this happiness does Christ vouchsafe to all his, that as a savior he once suffered for them, and that as a friend he always suffers with them.

4. The fourth privilege of friendship is that which is here specified in the text, a communication of secrets. A bosom secret and a bosom friend are usually put together. And this from Christ to the soul is not only kindness, but also honor and advancement; it is for him to vouch it one of his privy council. Nothing under a jewel is taken into the cabinet. A secret is the apple of our eye; it will bear no touch nor approach; we use to cover nothing but what we account a rarity. And therefore to communicate a secret to any one,

is to exalt him to one of the royalties of heaven. For none knows the secrets of a man's mind, but his God, his conscience, and his friend. Neither would any prudent man let such a thing go out of his own heart, had he not another heart besides his own to receive it.

Now it was of old a privilege, with which God was pleased to honor such as served him at the rate of an extraordinary obedience, thus to admit them to a knowledge of many of his great counsels locked up from the rest of the world. When God had designed the destruction of Sodom, the scripture represents him as unable to conceal that great purpose from Abraham, whom he always treated as his friend and acquaintance; that is, not only with love, but also with intimacy and familiarity, in Gen. xviii. 17. *And the Lord said, Shall I hide from Abraham the thing that I go about to do?* He thought it a violation of the rights of friendship to reserve his design wholly to himself. And St. James tells us, in James ii. 23, *that Abraham was called the friend of God;* and therefore had a kind of claim to the knowledge of his secrets, and the participation of his counsels. Also, in Exodus xxxiii. 11, it is said of God, *that he spoke to Moses as a man speaketh to his friend.* And that, not only for the familiarity and facility of address, but also for the peculiar communications of his mind. Moses was with him in the retirements of the mount, received there his dictates and his private instructions, as his deputy and viceroy; and when the multitude and congregation of Israel were thundered away, and kept off from any approach to it, he was honored with an intimate and immediate admission. The priests indeed were taken into a near attendance upon God; but still there was a degree of a nearer converse, and the interest of a friend was above the privileges of the highest servant. In Exod. xix. 24, *Thou shalt come up*, says God, *thou, and Aaron with thee: but let not the priests and the people break through to come up unto the Lord, lest the Lord break forth upon them.* And if we proceed further, we shall still find a continuation of the same privilege; Psalm xxv. 14; *The secret of the Lord is with them that fear him.* Nothing is to be concealed from the other self. To be a friend, and to be conscious, are terms equivalent.

Now if God maintained such intimacies with those whom

he loved under the law, (which was a dispensation of greater distance,) we may be sure that under the gospel, (the very nature of which imports condescension and compliance,) there must needs be the same, with much greater advantage. And therefore when God had manifested himself in the flesh, how sacredly did he preserve this privilege! How freely did Christ unbosom himself to his disciples, in Luke viii. 10. *Unto you,* says he, *it is given to know the mysteries of the kingdom of God: but unto others in parables; that seeing they might not see:* such shall be permitted to cast an eye into the ark, and to look into the very holy of holies. And again, in Matt. xiii. 17, *Many prophets and righteous men have desired to see those things which ye see, and have not seen them; and to hear those things which ye hear and have not heard them.* Neither did he treat them with these peculiarities of favor in the extraordinary discoveries of the gospel only, but also of those incommunicable revelations of the divine love, in reference to their own personal interest in it. In Rev. ii. 17; *To him that overcometh will I give to eat of the hidden manna, and will give him a white stone, and in the stone a new name written, which no man knoweth, saving he that receiveth it.* Assurance is a rarity covered from the inspection of the world. A secret that none can know but God, and the person that is blessed with it. It is writ in a private character, not to be read nor understood but by the conscience, to which the Spirit of God has vouchsafed to decipher it. Every believer lives upon an inward provision of comfort that the world is a stranger to.

5. The fifth advantage of friendship is counsel and advice. A man will sometimes need not only another heart, but also another head besides his own. In solitude there is not only discomfort, but weakness also. And that saying of the wise man, Eccles. iv. 10, *Woe to him that is alone,* is verified upon none so much as upon the friendless person: when a man shall be perplexed with knots and problems of business and contrary affairs, where the determination is dubious, and both parts of the contrariety seem equally weighty, so that, which way soever the choice determines, a man is sure to venture a great concern: how happy then is it to fetch in aid from another person, whose judgment may be greater than my own, and whose concernment is sure not to be less! There are

some passages of a man's affairs that would quite break a single understanding. So many intricacies, so many labyrinths, are there in them, that the succors of reason fail, the very force and spirit of it being lost in an actual intention scattered upon several clashing objects at once; in which case, the interposal of a friend is like the supply of a fresh party to a besieged yielding city.

Now Christ is not failing in this office of a friend also. For in that illustrious prediction of Esay ix. 6, amongst the rest of his great titles, he is called *mighty Counsellor*. And his counsel is not only sure, but also free. It is not under the gospel of Christ, as under some laws of men, where you must be forced to buy your counsel, and oftentimes pay dear for bad advice. No, *he is a light to those that sit in darkness*. And no man fees the sun, no man purchases the light, nor errs, if he walks by it. The only price that Christ sets upon his counsel is, that we follow it, and that we do that which is best for us to do. He is not only light for us to see by, but also light for us to see *with;* He *is understanding to the ignorant*, and *eyes to the blind:* and whosoever has both a faithful and a discreet friend, to guide him in the dark, slippery, and dangerous passages of his life, may carry his eyes in another man's head, and yet see never the worse. In 1 Cor. i. 30, the Apostle tells us, that Christ is made to us not only *sanctification and redemption*, but *wisdom* too: we are his members; and it is but natural that all the members of the body should be guided by the wisdom of the head.

And therefore let every believer comfort himself in this high privilege, that in the great things that concern his eternal peace he is not left to stand or fall by the uncertain directions of his own judgment. No, sad were his condition if he should be so; when he is to encounter an enemy made up of wiles and stratagems, an old serpent, and a long-experienced deceiver, and successful at the trade for some thousands of years.

The inequality of the match between such an one and the subtilest of us, would quickly appear by a fatal circumvention: there must be a wisdom from above, to overreach and master this hellish wisdom from beneath. And this every sanctified person is sure of in his great friend, *in whom all the treasures of wisdom dwell;* treasures that flow out, and are imparted freely, both in direction and assistance, to all that belong to him. He never leaves any of his, perplexed, amazed, or bewildered, where the welfare of their souls requires a better judgment than their own, either to guide them in their duty, or to disentangle them from a temptation. Whosoever has Christ for his friend, shall be sure of counsel; and whosoever is his own friend, will be sure to obey it.

6. The last and crowning privilege, or rather property, of friendship is constancy. He only is a friend whose friendship lives as long as himself, and who ceases to love and to breathe at the same instant. Not that I yet state constancy in such an absurd, senseless, and irrational continuance in friendship, as no injuries or provocations whatsoever can break off. For there are some injuries that extinguish the very relation between friends. In which case, a man ceases to be a friend, not from any inconstancy in his friendship, but from defect of an object for his friendship to exert itself upon. It is one thing for a father to cease to be a father by casting off his son; and another for him to cease to be so, by the death of his son. In this, the relation is at an end for want of a correlate: so in friendship there are some passages of that high and hostile nature, that they really and properly constitute and denominate the person guilty of them, an enemy; and if so, how can the other person possibly continue a friend, since friendship essentially requires that it be between two at least; and there can be no friendship, where there are not two friends?

Nobody is bound to look upon his backbiter or his underminer, his betrayer or his oppressor, as his friend. Nor indeed is it possible that he should do so, unless he could alter the constitution and order of things, and establish a new nature and a new morality in the world. For to remain unsensible of such provocations, is not constancy, but apathy. And therefore they discharge the person so treated from the proper obligations of a friend; though Christianity, I confess, binds him to the duties of a neighbor.

But to give you the true nature and measures of constancy; it is such a stability and firmness of friendship, as overlooks and passes by all those lesser failures of kindness and respect, that, partly through passion, partly through indiscretion, and such other frailties incident to human nature, a man may be sometimes guilty of, and yet still retain the same habitual good-will and prevailing propensity of mind to his friend, that he had before. And whose friendship soever is of that strength and duration as to stand its ground against, and remain unshaken by, such assaults, (which yet are strong enough to shake down and annihilate the friendship of little puny minds,) such an one, I say, has reached all the true measures of constancy: his friendship is of a noble make and a lasting consistency; it resembles marble, and deserves to be wrote upon it.

But how few tempers in the world are of that magnanimous frame as to reach the hights of so great a virtue: many offer at the effects of friendship, but they do not last; they are promising in the beginning, but they fail, and jade, and tire in the prosecution. For most people in the world are acted by levity and humor, by strange and irrational changes. And how often may we meet with those who are one while courteous, civil, and obliging, (at least to their proportion,) but within a small time after are so supercilious, sharp, troublesome, fierce, and exceptious, that they are not only short of the true character of friendship, but become the very sores and burdens of society! Such low, such worthless dispositions, how easily are they discovered, how justly are they despised! But now, that we may pass from one contrary to another, *Christ, who is the same yesterday, to-day, and forever* in his being, is so also in his affection. He is not of the number or nature of those pitiful, mean pretenders to friendship, who perhaps will love and smile upon you one day, and not so much as know you the next: many of which sort there are in the world, who are not so much courted outwardly, but that inwardly they are detested much more.

Friendship is a kind of covenant; and most covenants run upon mutual terms and conditions. And therefore, so long as we are exact in fulfilling the condition on our parts, (I mean, exact according to the measures of sincerity, though not of perfection,) we may be sure that Christ will not fail in the least iota to fulfil every thing on his. The favor of relations, patrons, and princes, is uncertain, ticklish, and variable; and the friendship which they take up, upon the accounts of judgment and merit, they most times lay down out of humor. But the friendship of Christ has none of these weaknesses, no such hollowness or unsoundness in it. *For neither principalities, nor powers, things present, nor things to come*, no, nor all the rage and malice of hell, shall be able to pluck the meanest of Christ's friends out of his bosom: for, *whom he loves, he loves to the end.*

Now, from the particulars hitherto discoursed of, we may infer and learn these two things: 1. The excellency and value of friendship. Christ the Son of the most high God, the second person in the glorious Trinity, took upon him our nature, that he might give a great instance and example of this virtue; and condescended to be a man, only that he might be a friend. Our Creator, our Lord and King, he was before; but he would needs come down from all this, and in a sort become our equal, that he might partake of that noble quality that is properly between equals. Christ took not upon him flesh and blood that he might conquer and rule nations, lead armies, or possess palaces; but that he might have the relenting, the tenderness, and the compassions of human nature, which render it properly capable of friendship; and, in a word, that he might have our heart, and we have his. God himself sets friendship above all considerations of kindred or consanguinity, as the greatest ground and argument of mutual endearment, in Deut. xv. 6: *If thy brother, the son of thy mother, or thy son, or thy daughter, or the wife of thy bosom, or thy friend, which is as thine own soul, entice thee to go and serve other gods, thou shalt not consent unto him.* The emphasis of the expression is very remarkable; it being a gradation or ascent, by several degrees of dearness, to that which is the highest of all. Neither wife nor brother, son nor daughter, though the nearest in cognation, are allowed to stand in competition with a friend; who, if he fully answers the duties of that great relation, is indeed better and more valuable than all of them put together, and may serve instead of them; so that he who has a firm, a worthy, and sincere friend, may want all the rest, without missing them. That which lies in a man's bosom should be dear to him, but that which lies within his heart ought to be much dearer.

2. In the next place, we learn from hence the high advantage of becoming truly pious and religious. When we have said and done all, it is only the true Christian and the religious person who is or can be sure of a friend; sure of obtaining, sure of keeping him. But as for the friendship of the world; when a man shall have done all that he can to make one his friend, employed the utmost of his wit and labor, beaten his brains, and emptied his purse, to create an endearment between him and the person whose friendship he desires, he may, in the end, upon all these endeavors and attempts, be forced to write vanity and frustration: for by them all he may at last be no more able to get into the other's heart than he is to thrust his hand into a pillar of brass. The man's affection, amidst all these kindnesses done him, remaining wholly unconcerned and impregnable; just like a rock, which, being plied continually by the waves, still throws them back again into the bosom of the sea that sent them, but is not at all moved by any of them.

People at first, while they are young and raw, and soft-natured, are apt to think it an easy thing to gain love, and reckon their own friendship a sure price of another man's. But when experience shall have once opened their eyes, and showed them the hardness of most hearts, the hollowness of others, and the baseness and ingratitude of almost all, they will then find that a friend is the gift of God; and that he only, who made hearts, can unite them. For it is he who creates those sympathies and suitableness of nature, that are the foundation of all true friendship, and then by his providence brings persons so affected together.

It is an expression frequent in scripture, but infinitely more significant than at first it is usually observed to be; namely, that God gave such or such a person grace or favor in another's eyes. As for instance, in Gen. xxxix. 21, it is said of Joseph, that *the Lord was with him, and gave him favor in the sight of the keeper of the prison.* Still it is an invisible hand from heaven that ties this knot, and mingles hearts and souls, by strange, secret, and unaccountable conjunctions.

That heart shall surrender itself and its friendship to one man, at first view, which another has in vain been laying siege to for many years, by all the repeated acts of kindness imaginable.

Nay, so far is friendship from being of any human production, that, unless nature be predisposed to it by its own propensity or inclination, no arts of obligation shall be able to abate the secret hatreds and hostilities of some persons towards others. No friendly offices, no addresses, no benefits whatsoever, shall ever alter or allay that diabolical rancor that frets and ferments in some hellish breasts, but that upon all occasions it will foam out at its foul mouth in slander and invective, and sometimes bite too in a shrewd turn or a secret blow. This is true and undeniable upon frequent experience; and happy those who can learn it at the cost of other men's.

But now, on the contrary, he who will give up his name to Christ in faith unfeigned, and a sincere obedience to all his righteous laws, shall be sure to find love for love, and friendship for friendship. The success is certain and infallible; and none ever yet miscarried in the attempt. For Christ freely offers his friendship to all, and sets no other rate upon so vast a purchase, but only that we would suffer him to be our friend. Thou perhaps spendest thy precious time in waiting upon such a great one, and thy estate in presenting him, and probably, after all, hast no other reward but sometimes to be smiled upon, and always to be smiled at; and when thy greatest and most pressing occasions shall call for succor and relief, then to be deserted and cast off, and not known.

Now, I say, turn the stream of thy endeavors another way, and bestow but half that hearty, sedulous attendance upon thy Saviour in the duties of prayer and mortification, and be at half that expense in charitable works, by relieving Christ in his poor members; and, in a word, study as much to please him who died for thee, as thou dost to court and humor thy great patron, who cares not for thee, and thou shalt make him thy friend forever; a friend who shall own thee in thy lowest condition, speak comfort to thee in all thy sorrows, counsel thee in all thy doubts, answer all thy wants, and, in a word, *never leave thee, nor forsake thee.* But when all the hopes that thou hast raised upon the promises or supposed kindnesses of the fastidious and fallacious great ones of the world shall fail, and upbraid thee to thy face, he shall then take thee into his bosom, embrace, cherish, and support thee, and, as the Psalmist expresses it, *he shall guide thee with his counsel here, and afterwards receive thee into glory.*

To which God of his mercy vouchsafe to bring us all; to whom be rendered and ascribed, &c. Amen.

SERMON XV.

A DISCOURSE AGAINST LONG EXTEMPORARY PRAYERS.

ECCLESIASTES v. 2. — *Be not rash with thy mouth, and let not thine heart be hasty to utter any thing before God: for God is in heaven, and thou upon earth: therefore let thy words be few.*

WE have here the wisest of men instructing us how to behave ourselves before God in his own house; and particularly when we address to him in the most important of all duties, which is prayer. Solomon had the honor to be spoken to by God himself, and therefore, in all likelihood, none more fit to teach us how to speak to God. A great privilege certainly for dust and ashes to be admitted to; and therefore it will concern us to manage it so, that in these our approaches to the King of heaven, his goodness may not cause us to forget his greatness, nor (as it is but too usual for subjects to use privilege against prerogative) his honor suffer by his condescension.

In the words we have these three things observable:

1st, That whosoever appears in the house of God, and particularly in the way of prayer, ought to reckon himself, in a more especial manner, placed in the sight and presence of God.

2dly, That the vast and infinite distance between God and him ought to create in him all imaginable awe and reverence in such his addresses to God.

3dly and lastly, That this reverence required of him is to consist in a serious preparation of his thoughts, and a sober government of his expressions: neither is *his mouth to be rash, nor his heart to be hasty, in uttering any thing before God.*

These things are evidently contained in the words, and do

as evidently contain the whole sense of them. But I shall gather them all into this one proposition; namely,

That premeditation of thought, and brevity of expression, are the great ingredients of that reverence that is required to a pious, acceptable, and devout prayer.

For the better handling of which, we will, in the first place, consider how, and by what way it is, that prayer works upon, or prevails with, God, for the obtaining of the things we pray for. Concerning which, I shall lay down this general rule, That the way by which prayer prevails with God is wholly different from that by which it prevails with men. And to give you this more particularly.

1. First of all, it prevails not with God by way of information or notification of the thing to him, which we desire of him. With men indeed this is the common, and with wise men the chief, and should be the only way of obtaining what we ask of them. We represent and lay before them our wants and indigences, and the misery of our condition. Which being made known to them, the quality and condition of the thing asked for, and of the persons who ask it, induces them to give that to us, and to do that for us, which we desire and petition for: but it is not so in our addresses to God; for he knows our wants and our conditions better than we ourselves: he is beforehand with all our prayers; Matt. vi. 8; *Your Father knoweth what things ye have need of before ye ask him;* and in Psalm cxxxix. 2, *Thou understandest my thought afar off.* God knows our thoughts before the very heart that conceives them. And how then can he, who is but of yesterday, suggest any thing new to that eternal mind! how can ignorance inform omniscience!

2dly, Neither does prayer prevail with God by way of persuasion, or working upon the affections, so as thereby to move him to pity or compassion. This indeed is the most usual and most effectual way to prevail with men; who, for the generality, are one part reason, and nine parts affection. So that one of a voluble tongue, and a dexterous insinuation, may do what he will with vulgar minds, and with wise men too, at their weak times. But God, who is as void of passion or affection as he is of quantity or corporeity, is not to be dealt with this way. He values not our rhetoric, nor our pathetical harangues. He who applies to God, applies to an infinite almighty reason, a pure act, all intellect, the first mover, and therefore not to be moved or wrought upon himself. In all passion, the mind suffers, (as the very signification of the word imports,) but absolute, entire perfection can not suffer; it is and must be immovable, and by consequence impassible. And therefore,

In the third and last place, much less is God to be prevailed upon by importunity, and, as it were, wearying him into a concession of what we beg of him. Though with men we know this also is not unusual. A notable instance of which we have in Luke xviii. 4, 5, where the unjust judge being with a restless vehemence sued to for justice, says thus within himself: *Though I fear not God, nor regard man, yet because this widow troubleth me, I will avenge her, lest by her continual coming she weary me.*

In like manner, how often are beggars relieved only for their eager and rude importunity; not that the person who relieves them is thereby informed or satisfied of their real want, nor yet moved to pity them by all their cry and cant, but to rid himself from their vexatious noise and din; so that to purchase his quiet by a little alms he gratifies the beggar, but indeed relieves himself. But now this way is further from prevailing with God than either of the former. For as omniscience is not to be informed, so neither is omnipotence to be wearied. We may much more easily think to clamor the sun and stars out of their courses than to word the great Creator of them out of the steady purposes of his own will by all the vehemence and loudness of our petitions. Men may tire themselves with their own prayers, but God is not to be tired. The rapid motion and whirle of things her below interrupts not the inviolable rest and calmness of the nobler beings above. While the winds roar and bluster here in the first and second regions of the air, there is a perfect serenity in the third. Men's desires can not control God's decrees.

And thus I have shown that the three ways by which men prevail with men in their prayers and applications to them, have no place at all in giving any efficacy to their addresses to God.

But you will ask then, Upon what account is it that prayer

becomes prevalent and efficacious with God, so as to procure us the good things we pray for? I answer, Upon this, that it is the fulfilling of that condition upon which God has freely promised to convey his blessings to men. God of his own absolute, unaccountable good-will and pleasure, has thought fit to appoint and fix upon this as the means by which he will supply and answer the wants of mankind. As for instance, suppose a prince should declare to any one of his subjects, that if he shall appear before him every morning in his bed-chamber, he shall receive of him a thousand talents. We must not here imagine that the subject, by making this appearance, does either move or persuade his prince to give him such a sum of money: no, he only performs the condition of the promise, and thereby acquires a right to the thing promised. He does indeed hereby engage his prince to give him this sum, though he does by no means persuade him: or rather, to speak more strictly and properly, the prince's own justice and veracity is an engagement upon the prince himself, to make good his promise to him who fulfills the conditions of it.

But you will say, that upon this ground it will follow, that when we obtain any thing of God by prayer, we have it upon claim of justice, and not by way of gift, as a free result of his bounty.

I answer, that both these are very well consistent; for though he who makes a promise upon a certain condition is bound in justice upon the fulfilling of that condition to perform his promise, yet it was perfectly grace and goodness, bounty and free mercy, that first induced him to make the promise, and particularly to state the tenor of it upon such a condition. *If we confess our sins,* says the apostle, 1 John i. 9, *God is faithful and just to forgive us our sins.* Can any thing be freer and more the effect of mere grace than the forgiveness of sins? And yet it is certain from this scripture and many more, that it is firmly promised us upon condition of a penitent, hearty confession of them, and consequently as certain it is that God stands obliged here even by his faithfulness and justice, to make good this his promise of forgiveness to those who come up to the terms of it by such a confession.

In like manner, for prayer, in reference to the good things prayed for. He who prays for a thing as God has appointed him, gets thereby a right to the thing prayed for: but it is a right, not springing from any merit or condignity, either in the prayer itself, or the person who makes it, to the blessing which he prays for, but from God's veracity, truth, and justice, who, having appointed prayer as the condition of that blessing, can not but stand to what he himself had appointed; though that he did appoint it was the free result and determination of his own will.

We have a full account of this whole matter from God's own mouth, in Psalm l. *Call upon me*, says God, *in the day of trouble, and I will deliver thee.* These are evidently the terms upon which God answers prayers: in which case there is no doubt but the deliverance is still of more worth than the prayer; and there is as little doubt also, that, without such a previous declaration made on God's part, a person so in trouble or distress might pray his heart out, and yet God not be in the least obliged by all his prayers, either in justice or honor, or indeed so much as in mercy, to deliver him; for mercy is free, and misery can not oblige it. In a word, prayer procures deliverance from trouble, just as Naaman's dipping himself seven times in Jordan procured him a deliverance from his leprosy; not by any virtue in itself adequate to so great an effect, you may be sure; but from this, that it was appointed by God as the condition of his recovery; and so obliged the power of him, who appointed it, to give force and virtue to his own institution, beyond what the nature of the thing itself could otherwise have raised it to.

Let this therefore be fixed upon, as the groundwork of what we are to say upon this subject: that prayer prevails with God for the blessing that we pray for, neither by way of information, nor yet of persuasion, and much less by the importunity of him who prays, and least of all by any worth in the prayer itself, equal to the thing prayed for; but it prevails solely and entirely upon this account, that it is freely appointed by God, as the stated, allowed condition upon which he will dispense his blessings to mankind.

But before I dismiss this consideration, it may be inquired, whence it is that prayer, rather than any other thing, comes to be appointed by God for this condition. In answer to which; Though God's sovereign will be a sufficient reason of its own counsels and determinations, and consequently a more than sufficient answer to all our inquiries, yet, since God in his infinite wisdom still adapts means to ends, and never appoints a thing to any use but what it has a particular and a natural fitness for, I shall therefore presume to assign a reason why prayer, before all other things, should be appointed to this noble use of being the condition and glorious conduit, whereby to derive the bounties of heaven upon the sons of men: and it is this; because prayer, of all other acts of a rational nature, does most peculiarly qualify a man to be a fit object of the divine favor, by being most eminently and properly an act of dependence upon God; since to pray, or beg a thing of another, in the very nature and notion of it, imports these two things: 1. That the person praying stands in need of some good, which he is not able by any power of his own to procure for himself: and, 2. That he acknowledges it in the power and pleasure of the person whom he prays to, to confer it upon him. And this is properly that which men call *to depend.*

But some may reply, There is an universal dependence of all things upon God; forasmuch as he, being the great fountain and source of being, first created, and since supports them by the word of his power; and consequently that this dependence belongs indifferently to the wicked as well as to the just, whose prayer nevertheless is declared an abomination to God.

But to this the answer is obvious, That the dependence here spoken of is meant, not of a natural, but of a moral dependence. The first is necessary, the other voluntary. The first common to all, the other proper to the pious. The first respects God barely as a Creator, the other addresses to him as a Father. Now such a dependence upon God it is, that is properly seen in prayer. And being so, if we should in all humble reverence set ourselves to examine the wisdom of the divine proceeding in this matter, even by the measures of our own reason, what could be more rationally thought of for the properest instrument to bring down God's blessings upon the world, than such a temper of mind as makes a man disown all ability in himself to supply his own wants, and at the same time own a transcendent fullness and sufficiency in God to do it for him? And what can be more agreeable to all principles both of reason and religion than that a creature endued with understanding and will should acknowledge that dependence upon his Maker, by a free act of choice, which other creatures have upon him, only by necessity of nature?

But still, there is one objection more against our foregoing assertion, viz., That prayer obtains the things prayed for, only as a condition, and not by way of importunity or persuasion; for is not prayer said to prevail by frequency, Luke xviii. 7, and by fervency, or earnestness, in James v. 16, and is not this a fair proof that God is importuned and persuaded into a grant of our petitions?

To this I answer two things; 1. That wheresoever God is said to answer prayers, either for their frequency or fervency, it is spoken of him only ἀνθρωποπαθῶς, according to the manner of men; and consequently ought to be understood only of the effect or issue of such prayers, in the success certainly attending them, and not of the manner of their efficiency, that it is by persuading or working upon the passions: as if we should say, frequent, fervent, and importunate prayers are as certainly followed with God's grant of the thing prayed for, as men use to grant that which, being overcome by excessive importunity and persuasion, they can not find in their hearts to deny. 2. I answer further, That frequency and fervency of prayer prove effectual to procure of God the things prayed for, upon no other account but as they are acts of dependence upon God: which dependence we have already proved to be that thing essentially included in prayer, for which God has been pleased to make prayer the condition, upon which he determines to grant men such things as they need and duly apply to him for. So that still there is nothing of persuasion in the case.

And thus having shown (and I hope fully and clearly) how prayer operates towards the obtaining of the divine blessings; namely, as a condition appointed by God for that purpose, and no otherwise: and withal, for what reason it is singled out of all other acts of a rational nature, to be this condition;

namely, because it is the grand instance of such a nature's dependence upon God: we shall now from the same principle infer also, upon what account the highest reverence of God is so indispensably required of us in prayer, and all sort of irreverence so diametrically opposite to, and destructive of, the very nature of it. And it will appear to be upon this, that in what degree any one lays aside his reverence of God, in the same he also quits his dependence upon him: forasmuch as in every irreverent act, a man treats God as if he had indeed no need of him, and behaves himself as if he stood upon his own bottom, absolute and self-sufficient. This is the natural language, the true signification and import of all irreverence.

Now in all addresses, either to God or man, by speech, our reverence to them must consist of, and show itself in these two things:

First, A careful regulation of our thoughts, that are to dictate and to govern our words; which is done by premeditation: and secondly, a due ordering of our words, that are to proceed from and to express our thoughts; which is done by pertinence and brevity of expression.

David, directing his prayer to God, joins these two together as the two great integral parts of it, in Psalm xix. 14. *Let the words of my mouth, and the meditations of my heart, be acceptable in thy sight, O Lord.* So that it seems his prayer adequately and entirely consisted of those two things, meditation and expression, as it were the matter and form of that noble composure. There being no mention at all of distortion of face, sanctified grimace, solemn wink, or foaming at the mouth, and the like; all which are circumstances of prayer of a later date, and brought into request by those fantastic zealots who had a way of praying, as astonishing to the eyes, as to the ears of those that heard them. Well then, the first ingredient of a pious and reverential prayer is a previous regulation of the thoughts, as the text expresses it most emphatically; *Let not thy heart be hasty to utter any thing before God;* that is, in other words, let it not venture to throw out its crude, extemporary, sudden, and misshapen conceptions in the face of infinite perfection. Let not thy heart conceive and bring forth together: this is monstrous and unnatural. All abortion is from infirmity and defect. And time is required to form the issue of the mind, as well as that of the body. The fitness or unfitness of the first thoughts can not be judged of but by reflection of the second: and be the invention never so fruitful, yet in the mind, as in the earth, that which is cast into it must lie hid and covered for a while, before it can be fit to shoot forth. These are the methods of nature, and it is seldom but the acts of religion conform to them.

He who is to pray, would he seriously judge of the work that is before him, has more to consider of than either his heart can hold, or his head well turn itself to. Prayer is one of the greatest and the hardest works that a man has to do in this world; and was ever any thing difficult or glorious achieved by a sudden cast of a thought? a flying stricture of the imagination? Presence of mind is indeed good, but haste is not so. And therefore, let this be concluded upon, that in the business of prayer, to pretend to reverence when there is no premeditation, is both impudence and contradiction.

Now this premeditation ought to respect these three things: 1. The person whom we pray to; 2. The matter of our prayers; and 3. The order and disposition of them.

1. And first, for the person whom we pray to. The same is to employ, who must needs also nonplus and astonish thy meditations, and be made the object of thy thoughts, who infinitely transcends them. For all the knowing and reasoning faculties of the soul are utterly baffled and at a loss when they offer at any idea of the great God. Nevertheless, since it is hard, if not impossible, to imprint an awe upon the affections, without suitable notions first formed in the apprehensions, we must in our prayers endeavor at least to bring these as near to God as we can, by considering such of his divine perfections as have, by their effects, in a great measure, manifested themselves to our senses, and, in a much greater, to the discourses of our reason.

As first; consider with thyself how great and glorious a Being that must needs be, that raised so vast and beautiful a fabric as this of the world out of nothing with the breath of his mouth, and can and will, with the same, reduce it to nothing again; and then consider that this is that high, amazing, incomprehensible Being whom thou addressest thy pitiful self to in prayer.

Consider next, his infinite, all-searching knowledge, which looks through and through the most secret of our thoughts, ransacks every corner of the heart, ponders the most inward designs and ends of the soul in all a man's actions. And then consider, that this is the God whom thou hast to deal with in prayer; the God who observes the postures, the frame and motion of thy mind in all thy approaches to him, and whose piercing eye it is impossible to elude or escape by all the tricks and arts of the subtilest and most refined hypocrisy. And lastly, consider the great, the fiery, and the implacable jealousy that he has for his honor; and that he has no other use of the whole creation, but to serve the ends of it: and, above all, that he will, in a most peculiar manner, *be honored of those who draw near to him;* and will by no means suffer himself to be mocked and affronted, under a pretense of being worshiped; nor endure that a wretched, contemptible, sinful creature, who is but a piece of living dirt at best, should at the same time bend the knee to him, and spit in his face. And now consider, that this is the God whom thou prayest to, and whom thou usest with such intolerable indignity in every unworthy prayer thou puttest up to him; every bold, saucy, and familiar word that (upon confidence of being one of God's elect) thou presumest to debase so great a majesty with: and for an instance of the dreadful curse that attends such a daring irreverence, consider how God used Nadab and Abihu for venturing to offer *strange fire before him;* and then know, that every unhallowed, unfitting prayer is a *strange fire;* a fire that will be sure to destroy the offering, though mercy should spare the offerer. Consider these things seriously, deeply, and severely, till the consideration of them affects thy heart, and humbles thy spirit, with such awful apprehensions of thy Maker, and such abject reflections upon thyself, as may lay thee in the dust before him: and know, that the lower thou fallest, the higher will thy prayer rebound; and that thou art never so fit to pray to God as when a sense of thy own unworthiness makes thee ashamed even to speak to him.

2. The second object of our premeditation is, the matter of our prayers. For, as we are to consider whom we are to pray to, so are we to consider also what we are to pray for; and this requires no ordinary application of thought to distinguish or judge of. Men's prayers are generally dictated by their desires, and their desires are the issues of their affections; and their affections are, for the most part, influenced by their corruptions. The first constituent principle of a well-conceived prayer is, to know what not to pray for: which the scripture assures us that some do not, while they *pray for what they may spend upon their lusts*, James iv. 3, asking such things as it is a contumely to God to hear, and damnation to themselves to receive. No man is to pray for any thing either sinful, or directly tending to sin. No man is to pray for a temptation, and much less to desire God to be his tempter; which he would certainly be, should he, at the instance of any man's prayer, administer fuel to his sinful or absurd appetites. Nor is any one to ask of God things mean and trivial, and beneath the majesty of Heaven to be concerned about, or solemnly addressed to for. Nor, lastly, is any one to admit into his petitions things superfluous or extravagant; such as wealth, greatness, and honor: which we are so far from being warranted to beg of God, that we are to beg his grace to despise and undervalue them: and it were much if the same things should be the proper objects both of our self-denial and of our prayers too; and that we should be allowed to solicit the satisfaction, and enjoined to endeavor the mortification, of the same desires.

The things that we are to pray for are either, 1st, Things of absolute necessity; or, 2dly, Things of unquestionable charity. Of the first sort are all spiritual graces required in us, as the indispensable conditions of our salvation; such as are, repentance, faith, hope, charity, temperance, and all other virtues that are either the parts or principles of a pious life. These are to be the prime subject-matter of our prayers; and we shall find that nothing comes this way so easily from heaven as those things that will assuredly bring us to it. The spirit dictates all such petitions, and God himself is first the author, and then the fulfiller of them; owning and accepting them, both as our duty and his own production. The other sort of things that may allowably be prayed for, are things of manifest, unquestionable charity: such as are a competent measure of the innocent comforts of life, as health, peace, maintenance, and a success of our honest labors: and yet even these but conditionally, and with perfect resignation to the will and wisdom of the sovereign disposer of all that belongs to us; who (if he finds it more for his honor to have us serve him with sick, crazy, languishing bodies; with poverty, and extreme want of all things; and lastly, with our country all in a flame about our ears) ought, in all this, and much more, to overrule our prayers and desires into an absolute acquiescence in his all-wise disposal of things; and to convince us that our prayers are sometimes best answered when our desires are most opposed.

In fine, to state the whole matter of our prayers in one word; Nothing can be fit for us to pray for, but what is fit and honorable for our great mediator and master of requests, Jesus Christ himself, to intercede for. This is to be the unchangeable rule and measure of all our petitions. And then, if Christ is to convey these our petitions to his Father, can any one dare to make him, who was holiness and purity itself, an advocate and solicitor for his lusts? Him, who was nothing but meekness, lowliness, and humility, his providetore for such things as can only feed his pride and flush his ambition? No, certainly; when we come as suppliants to the throne of grace, where Christ sits as intercessor at God's right hand, nothing can be fit to proceed out of our mouth but what is fit to pass through his.

3dly, The third and last thing that calls for a previous meditation to our prayers is, the order and disposition of them; for though God does not command us to set off our prayers with dress and artifice, to flourish it in trope and metaphor, to beg our daily bread in blank verse, or to show any thing of the poet in our devotions but indigence and want; I say, though God is far from requiring such things of us in our prayers, yet he requires that we should manage them with sense and reason. Fineness is not expected, but decency is; and though we can not declaim as orators, yet he will have us speak like men, and tender him the results of that understanding and judgment that essentially constitute a rational nature.

But I shall briefly cast what I have to say upon this particular into these following assertions:

1st, That nothing can express our reverence to God in prayer, that would pass for irreverence towards a great man. Let any subject tender his prince a petition fraught with nonsense and incoherence, confusion and impertinence, and can he expect that majesty should answer it with any thing but a deaf ear, a frowning eye, or, (at best,) vouchsafe it any other reward but, by a gracious oblivion, to forgive the person, and forget the petition?

2dly, Nothing absurd and irrational, and such as a wise man would despise, can be acceptable to God in prayer. Solomon expressly tells us in Ecclesiastes v. 4, that *God has no pleasure in fools;* nor is it possible that an infinite wisdom should. The scripture all along expresses sin and wickedness by the name of folly; and therefore certainly folly is too near of kin to it to find any approbation from God in so great a duty: it is the simplicity of the heart, and not of the head, that is the best inditer of our petitions. That which proceeds from the latter is undoubtedly the sacrifice of fools; and God is never more weary of sacrifice than when a fool is the priest, and folly the oblation.

3dly and lastly, Nothing rude, slight, and careless, or indeed less than the very best that a man can offer, can be acceptable or pleasing to God in prayer. *If ye offer the blind for sacrifice, is it not evil? If ye offer the lame and the sick, is it not evil? Offer it now to thy governor, and see whether he will be pleased with thee, or accept thy person, saith the Lord of hosts.* Malachi i. 8. God rigidly expects a return of his own gifts; and where he has given ability, will be served by acts proportionable to it. And he who has parts to raise and propagate his own honor by, but none to employ in the worship of him that gave them, does (as I may so express it) refuse to wear God's livery in his own service, adds sacrilege to profaneness, strips and starves his devotions, and, in a word, falls directly under the dint of that curse denounced in the last verse of the first of Malachi, *Cursed be the deceiver, that hath in his flock a male, and voweth, and sacrificeth to the Lord a corrupt thing.* The same is here, both the deceiver and the deceived too; for God very well knows what he gives men, and why; and where he has bestowed judgment, learning, and utterance, will not endure that men should be accurate in their discourse, and loose in their devotions; or think that the great *author of every good and perfect gift* will be put off with ramble, and confused talk, babble, and tautology.

And thus much for the order and disposition of our prayers, which certainly requires precedent thought and meditation. God has declared himself the God of order in all things; and will have it observed in what he commands others, as well as in what he does himself. Order is the great rule or art by which God made the world, and by which he still governs it: nay, the world itself is nothing else; and all this glorious system of things is but the chaos put into order: and how then can God, who has so eminently owned himself concerned for this excellent thing, brook such absurdity and confusion as the slovenly and profane negligence of some treats him with in their most solemn addresses to him? All which is the natural unavoidable consequent of unpreparedness and want of premeditation; without which, whosoever presumes to pray can not be so properly said to approach to, as to break in upon God. And surely he who is so hardy as to do so, has no reason in the earth to expect that the success which follows his prayers should be greater than the preparation that goes before them.

Now from what has been hitherto discoursed of, this first and grand qualification of a pious and devout prayer, to wit, premeditation of thought, what can be so naturally and so usefully inferred, as the high expediency, or rather the absolute necessity of a set form of prayer to guide our devotions by? We have lived in an age that has despised, contradicted, and counteracted all the principles and practices of the primitive Christians, in taking the measures of their duty both to God and man, and of their behavior both in matters civil and religious; but in nothing more scandalously than in their vile abuse of the great duty of prayer; concerning which, though it may with the clearest truth be affirmed, that there has been no church yet of any account in the Christian world, but what has governed its public worship of God by a liturgy or set form of prayer; yet these enthusiastic innovators, the bold and blind reformers of all antiquity, and wiser than the whole catholic church besides, introduced into the room of it a saucy, senseless, extemporary way of speaking to God; affirming that this was a praying by the Spirit; and that the use of all set forms was stinting of the Spirit. A pretense, I confess, popular and plausible enough with such idiots as take the sound of words for the sense of them. But for the full confutation of it, (which, I hope, shall be done both easily and briefly too,) I shall advance this one assertion in direct contradiction to that; namely,

That the praying by a set form is not a stinting of the Spirit; and the praying extempore truly and properly is so.

For the proving and making out of which, we will first consider, what it is to pray by the Spirit: a thing much talked of, but not so convenient for the talkers of it, and pretenders to it, to have it rightly stated and understood. In short, it includes in it these two things:

1st, A praying with the heart, which is sometimes called the spirit, or inward man; and so it is properly opposed to hypocritical lip-devotions, in which the heart or spirit does not go along with a man's words.

2dly, It includes in it also a praying according to the rules prescribed by God's holy Spirit, and held forth to us in his revealed word, which word was both dictated and confirmed by this Spirit; and so it is opposed to the praying unlawfully, or unwarrantably; and that either in respect of the matter or manner of our prayers. As, when we desire of God such things, or in such a way, as the Spirit of God, speaking in his holy word, does by no means warrant or approve of. So that to pray by the Spirit, signifies neither more nor less but to pray knowingly, heartily, and affectionately for such things, and in such a manner, as the Holy Ghost in scripture either commands or allows of. As for any other kind of praying by the Spirit, upon the best inquiry that I can make into these matters, I can find none. And if some say (as I know they both impudently and blasphemously do) that, to pray by the Spirit is to have the Spirit immediately inspiring them, and by such inspiration speaking within them, and so dictating their prayers to them, let them either produce plain scripture, or do a miracle to prove this by. But till then, he who shall consider what kind of prayers these pretenders to the Spirit have been notable for, will find that they have as little cause to father their prayers, as their practices, upon the Spirit of God.

These two things are certain, and I do particularly recommend them to your observation. One, That this way of praying by the Spirit, as they call it, was begun and first brought into use here in England in Queen Elizabeth's days, by a Popish priest and Dominican friar, one Faithful Commin by name; who counterfeiting himself a Protestant, and a zealot of the highest form, set up this new spiritual way of praying, with a design to bring the people first to a contempt, and from thence to an utter hatred and disuse of our common prayer; which he still reviled as only a translation of the mass, thereby to distract men's minds, and to divide our church. And this he did with such success, that we have lived to see the effects of his labors in the utter subversion of church and state. Which hellish negotiation, when this malicious hypocrite came to Rome to give the pope an account of, he received of him, (as so notable a service well deserved,) besides a thousand thanks, two thousand ducats for his pains. So that now you see here the original of this extempore way of praying by the Spirit. The other thing that I would observe to you is, that in the neighbor nation of Scotland, one of the greatest * monsters of men that, I believe, ever lived, and actually in league with the devil, was yet, by the confession of all that heard him, the most excellent at this extempore way of praying by the Spirit of any man in his time; none was able to come near him, or to compare with him. But surely now, he who shall venture to ascribe the prayers of such a wretch, made up of adulteries, incest, witchcraft, and other villainies not to be named, to the Spirit of God, may as well strike in with the Pharisees, and ascribe the miracles of Christ to the devil. And thus having shown both what ought to be meant by praying by the Spirit, and what ought not, can not be meant by it, let us now see whether a set form, or this extemporary way, be the greater hinderer and stinter of it: in order to which, I shall lay down these three assertions:

* Major John Weyer. See *Ravaillac Rediviv.*

1st, That the soul or mind of man is but of a limited nature in all its workings, and consequently can not supply two distinct faculties at the same time, to the same hight of operation.

2dly, That the finding words and expressions for prayer is the proper business of the brain and the invention; and that the finding devotion and affection to accompany and go along with those expressions is properly the work and business of the heart.

3dly, That this devotion and affection is indispensably required in prayer, as the principal and most essential part of it, and that in which the spirituality of it does most properly consist.

Now from these three things put together, this must naturally and necessarily follow: that as spiritual prayer, or praying by the Spirit, taken in the right sense of the word, consists properly in that affection and devotion that the heart exercises and employs in the work of prayer, so, whatsoever gives the soul scope and liberty to exercise and employ this affection and devotion, that does most effectually help and enlarge the spirit of prayer; and whatsoever diverts the soul from employing such affection and devotion, that does most directly stint and hinder it. Accordingly, let this now be our rule whereby to judge of the efficacy of a set form, and of the extemporary way in the present business. As for a set form, in which the words are ready prepared to our hands, the soul has nothing to do but to attend to the work of raising the affections and devotions, to go along with those words; so that all the powers of the soul are took up in applying the heart to this great duty; and it is the exercise of the heart (as has been already shown) that is truly and properly a praying by the Spirit. On the contrary, in all extempore prayer, the powers and faculties of the soul are called off from dealing with the heart and the affections; and that both in the speaker and in the hearer; both in him who makes, and in him who is to join in such prayers.

And first, for the minister who makes and utters such extempore prayers. He is wholly employing his invention, both to conceive matter, and to find words and expressions to clothe it in: this is certainly the work which takes up his mind in this exercise; and since the nature of man's mind is such that it can not with the same vigor, at the same time, attend the work of invention and that of raising the affections also, nor measure out the same supply of spirits and intention for the carrying on the operations of the head and those of the heart too, it is certain that, while the head is so much employed, the heart must be idle and very little employed, and perhaps not at all; and consequently, if to pray by the Spirit be to pray with the heart and the affections, it is also as certain that while a man prays extempore, he does not pray by the Spirit; nay, the very truth of it is, that while he is so doing, he is not praying at all, but he is studying; he is beating his brain, while he should be drawing out his affections.

And then for the people that are to hear and join with him in such prayers; it is manifest that they, not knowing beforehand what the minister will say, must, as soon as they do hear him, presently busy and bestir their minds both to apprehend and understand the meaning of what they hear; and withal, to judge whether it be of such a nature as to be fit for them to join and concur with him in. So that the people also are, by this course, put to study, and to employ their apprehending and judging faculties, while they should be exerting their affections and devotions; and consequently, by this means, the spirit of prayer is stinted, as well in the congregation that follows, as in the minister who first conceives a prayer after their extempore way: which is a truth so clear, and indeed self-evident, that it is impossible that it should need any further arguments to demonstrate or make it out.

The sum of all this is: That, since a set form of prayer leaves the soul wholly free to employ its affections and devotions, in which the spirit of prayer does most properly consist, it follows, that the spirit of prayer is thereby, in a singular manner, helped, promoted, and enlarged; and since, on the other hand, the extempore way withdraws and takes off the soul from employing its affections, and engages it chiefly, if not wholly, about the use of its invention, it as plainly follows, that the spirit of prayer is by this means unavoidably cramped and hindered, and (to use their own word) stinted: which was the proposition that I undertook to prove. But there are two things, I confess, that are extremely hindered and stinted by a set form of prayer, and equally furthered and enlarged by the extempore way; which, without all doubt, is the true cause why the former is so much decried, and the latter so much extolled, by the men whom we are now pleading with. The first of which is pride and ostentation; the other, faction and sedition.

1. And first for pride. I do not in the least question, but the chief design of such as use the extempore way is to amuse the unthinking rabble with an admiration of their gifts; their whole devotion proceeding from no other principle but only a love to hear themselves talk. And I believe it would put Lucifer himself hard to it, to outvie the pride of one of those fellows pouring out his extempore stuff amongst his ignorant, whining, factious followers, listening to, and applauding his copious flow and cant with the ridiculous accents of their impertinent groans. And, the truth is, extempore prayer, even when best and most dexterously performed, is nothing else but a business of invention and wit, (such as it is,) and requires no more to it but a teeming imagination, a bold front, and a ready expression; and deserves much the same commendation (were it not in a matter too serious to be sudden upon) which is due to extempore verses: only with this difference, that there is necessary to these latter a competent measure of wit and learning, whereas the former may be done with very little wit, and no learning at all.

And now, can any sober person think it reasonable, that the public devotions of a whole congregation should be under the conduct and at the mercy of a pert, empty, conceited holder-forth, whose chief (if not sole) intent is to vaunt his spiritual clack, and (as I may so speak) to pray prizes; whereas prayer is a duty that recommends itself to the acceptance of Almighty God by no other qualification so much as by the profoundest humility, and the lowest esteem that a man can possibly have of himself?

Certainly the extemporizing faculty is never more out of its element than in the pulpit; though even here it is much more excusable in a sermon than in a prayer; forasmuch as in that, a man addresses himself but to men — men like himself, whom he may therefore make bold with; as no doubt for so doing they will also make bold with him. Besides the peculiar advantage attending all such sudden conceptions, that, as they are quickly born, so they quickly die: it being seldom known, where the speaker has so very fluent an invention, but the hearer also has the gift of as fluent a memory.

2dly, The other thing that has been hitherto so little befriended by a set form of prayer, and so very much by the extempore way, is faction and sedition. It has been always found an excellent way of girding at the government in scripture phrase. And we all know the common dialect in which the great masters of this art used to pray for the king, and which may justly pass for only a cleanlier and more refined kind of libelling him in *the Lord.* As, *that God would turn his heart, and open his eyes:* as if he were a pagan yet to be converted to Christianity; with many other sly, virulent, and malicious insinuations, which we may every day hear of from (those mints of treason and rebellion) their conventicles; and for which, and a great deal less, some princes and governments would make them not only eat their words, but the tongue that spoke them too. In fine, let all their extempore harangues be considered and duly weighed, and you shall find a spirit of pride, faction, and sedition predominant in them all; the only spirit which those impostors do really and indeed pray by.

I have been so much the longer and the earnester against this intoxicating, bewitching cheat of extempore prayer, being fully satisfied in my conscience that it has been all along the devil's masterpiece and prime engine to overthrow our church by. For I look upon this as a most unanswerable truth, that whatsoever renders the public worship of God contemptible amongst us, must, in the same degree, weaken and discredit our whole religion. And I hope I have also proved it to be a truth altogether as clear, that this extempore way naturally brings all the contempt upon the worship of God, that both the folly and faction of men can possibly expose it to: and therefore, as a thing neither subservient to the true purposes of religion, nor grounded upon principles of reason, nor, lastly, suitable to the practice of antiquity, ought by all means to be exploded and cast out of every sober and well-ordered church; or that will be sure to throw the church itself out of doors.

And thus I have at length finished what I had to say of the first ingredient of a pious and reverential prayer, which was premeditation of thought, prescribed to us in these words, *Let not thy mouth be rash, nor thy heart be hasty to utter any thing before God.* Which excellent words and most wise advice of Solomon, whosoever can reconcile to the expediency, decency, or usefulness of extempore prayer, I shall acknowledge him a man of greater ability and parts of mind than Solomon himself.

The other ingredient of a reverential and duly qualified prayer is a pertinent brevity of expression, mentioned and recommended in that part of the text, *Therefore let thy words be few.* But this I can not dispatch now, and therefore shall not enter upon at this time.

Now to God the Father, God the Son, and God the Holy Ghost, three Persons and one God, be rendered and ascribed, as is most due, all praise, might, majesty, and dominion, both now and for evermore. Amen.

SERMON XVI.

A DISCOURSE AGAINST LONG AND EXTEMPORE PRAYERS:

IN BEHALF OF THE LITURGY OF THE CHURCH OF ENGLAND.

UPON THE SAME TEXT.

ECCLESIASTES v. 2.—*Be not rash with thy mouth, and let not thine heart be hasty to utter any thing before God: for God is in heaven, and thou upon earth: therefore let thy words be few.*

I FORMERLY began a discourse upon these words, and observed in them these three things:

1st, That whosoever appears in the house of God, and particularly in the way of prayer, ought to reckon himself, in a more especial manner, placed in the sight and presence of God; and,

2dly, That the vast and infinite distance between God and him ought to create in him all imaginable awe and reverence in such his addresses to God.

3dly and lastly, That this reverence required of him is to consist in a serious preparation of his thoughts, and a sober government of his expressions: neither is his *mouth to be rash, nor his heart to be hasty in uttering any thing before God.*

These three things I show, were evidently contained in the words, and did as evidently contain the whole sense of them. But I gathered them all into this one proposition; namely,

That premeditation of thought and brevity of expression are the great ingredients of that reverence that is required to a pious, acceptable, and devout prayer.

The first of these, which is premeditation of thought, I then fully treated of, and dispatched; and shall now proceed to the other, which is a pertinent brevity of expression; *therefore let thy words be few.*

Concerning which we shall observe, first, in general, that to be able to express our minds briefly, and fully too, is absolutely the greatest perfection and commendation that speech is capable of; such a mutual communication of our thoughts being (as I may so speak) the next approach to intuition, and the nearest imitation of the converse of *blessed spirits made perfect,* that our condition in this world can possibly raise us to. Certainly the greatest and the wisest conceptions that ever issued from the mind of man, have been couched under, and delivered in, a few, close, home, and significant words.

But, to derive the credit of this way of speaking much higher, and from an example infinitely greater than the greatest human wisdom, was it not authorized and ennobled by God himself in his making of the world? Was not the work of all the six days transacted in so many words? There was no circumlocution or amplification in the case; which makes the rhetorician Longinus, in his book of the Loftiness of Speech, so much admire the hight and grandeur of Moses's style in his first chapter of Genesis: Ὁ τῶν Ἰουδαίων θεσμοθέτης, οὐχ ὁ τυχὼν ἀνήρ. "The lawgiver of the Jews," says he, (meaning Moses,) "was no ordinary man," ἐπειδὴ τὴν τοῦ Θεοῦ δύναμιν κατὰ τὴν ἀξίαν ἐγνώρισε κἀξέφηνεν· "because," says he, "he set forth the divine power suitably to the "majesty and greatness of it." But how did he this? Why, εὐθὺς ἐν τῇ εἰσβολῇ γράψας τῶν νόμων, Εἶπεν ὁ Θεὸς, φησὶ, τί; Γενέσθω φῶς, καὶ ἐγένετο· γενέσθω γῆ, καὶ ἐγένετο, &c.; "for that," says he, "in the very entrance of his laws he gives us this short and pleasant account of the whole creation: *God said, Let there be light, and there was light: Let there be an earth, a sea, and a firmament; and there was so.*" So that all this high elogy and encomium, given by this heathen of Moses, sprang only from the majestic brevity of this one expression; an expression so suited to the greatness of a creator, and so expressive of his boundless, creative power, as a power infinitely above all control or possibility of finding the least obstacle or delay in achieving its mightiest and most stupendous works. Heaven and earth, and all the host of both, as it were, dropped from his mouth, and nature itself was but the product of a word; a word not designed to express, but to constitute and give a being; and not so much the representation as the cause of what it signified.

This was God's way of speaking in his first forming of the universe: and was it not so in the next grand instance of his power, his governing of it too? For are not the great instruments of government, his laws, drawn up and digested into a few sentences; the whole body of them containing but ten commandments, and some of those commandments not so many words? Nay, and have we not these also brought into yet a narrower compass by Him who best understood them? *Thou shalt love the Lord thy God with all thy heart, and with all thy soul, and thy neighbor as thyself:* precepts nothing like the tedious, endless, confused trash of human laws; laws so numerous, that they not only exceed men's practice, but also surpass their arithmetic; and so voluminous, that no mortal head, nor shoulders neither, must ever pretend themselves able to bear them. In God's laws, the words are few, the sense vast and infinite. In human laws, you shall be sure to have words enough; but, for the most part, to discern the sense and reason of them, you had need read them with a microscope.

And thus having shown how the Almighty utters himself when he speaks, and that upon the greatest occasions, let us now descend from heaven to earth, from God to man, and show that it is no presumption for us to conform our words, as well as our actions, to the supreme pattern, and, according to our poor measures, to imitate the wisdom that we adore. And for this, has it not been noted by the best observers and the ablest judges both of things and persons, that the wisdom of any people or nation has been most seen in the proverbs and short sayings commonly received amongst them? And what is a proverb but the experience and observation of several ages, gathered and summed up into one expression? The scripture vouches Solomon for the wisest of men: and they are his Proverbs that prove him so. The seven wise men of Greece, so famous for their wisdom all the world over, acquired all that fame each of them by a single sentence, consisting of two or three words: and γνῶθι σεαυτὸν still lives and flourishes in the mouths of all, while many vast volumes are extinct, and sunk into dust and utter oblivion. And then, for books; we shall generally find, that the most excellent, in any art or science, have been still the smallest and most compendious: and this not without ground; for it is an argument that the author was a master of what he wrote, and had a clear notion and a full comprehension of the subject before him. For the reason of things lies in a little compass, if the mind could at any time be so happy as to light upon it. Most of the writings and discourses in the world are but illustration and rhetoric, which signifies as much as nothing to a mind eager in pursuit after the causes and philosophical truth of things. It is the work of fancy to enlarge, but of judgment to shorten and contract; and therefore this must needs be as far above the other, as judgment is a greater and a nobler faculty than fancy or imagination. All philosophy is reduced to a few principles, and those principles comprised in a few propositions. And as the whole structure of speculation rests upon three or four axioms or maxims, so that of practice also bears upon a very small number of rules. And surely there was never yet any rule or maxim that filled a volume, or took up a week's time to be got by heart. No, these are the *apices rerum*, the tops and sums, the very spirit and life of things extracted and abridged; just as all the lines drawn from the vastest circumference do at length meet and unite in the smallest of things, a point: and it is but a very little piece of wood with which a true artist will measure all the timber in the world. The truth is, there could be no such thing as art or science, could not the mind of man gather the general natures of things out of the numberless heap of particulars, and then bind them up into such short aphorisms or propositions; that so they may be made portable to the memory, and thereby become ready and at hand for the judgment to apply and make use of, as there shall be occasion.

In fine, brevity and succinctness of speech is that which in philosophy or speculation we call *maxim*, and first principle: in the counsels and resolves of practical wisdom, and the deep mysteries of religion, *oracle;* and lastly, in matters of wit, and the finenesses of imagination, *epigram*. All of them, severally and in their kinds, the greatest and the noblest things that the mind of man can show the force and dexterity of its faculties in.

And now, if this be the highest excellency and perfection of speech in all other things, can we assign any true, solid reason why it should not be so likewise in prayer? Nay, is there not rather the clearest reason imaginable why it should be much more so; since most of the forementioned things are but addresses to an human understanding, which may need as many words as may fill a volume, to make it understand the truth of one line? whereas prayer is an address to that eternal mind which, as we have shown before, such as rationally invocate pretend not to inform. Nevertheless, since the nature of man is such, that, while we are yet in the body, our reverence and worship of God must of necessity proceed in some analogy to the reverence that we show to the grandees of this world, we will here see what the judgment of all wise men is concerning fewness of words, when we appear as suppliants before our earthly superiors; and we shall find that they generally allow it to import these three things: 1. Modesty; 2. Discretion; and 3dly, Hight of respect to the person addressed to. And first, for modesty. Modesty is a kind of shame or bashfulness, proceeding from the sense a man has of his own defects, compared with the perfections of him whom he comes before. And that which is modesty towards men, is worship and devotion towards God. It is a virtue that makes a man unwilling to be seen, and fearful to be heard; and yet, for that very cause, never fails to make him both seen with favor, and heard with attention. It loves not many words, nor indeed needs them. For modesty, addressing to any one of a generous worth and honor, is sure to have that man's honor for its advocate, and his generosity for its intercessor. And how then is it possible for such a virtue to run out into words? Loquacity storms the ear, but modesty takes the heart; that is troublesome, this gentle but irresistible. Much speaking is always the effect of confidence; and confidence still presupposes, and springs from, the persuasion that a man has of his own worth: both of them certainly very unfit qualifications for a petitioner.

2dly, The second thing that naturally shows itself in paucity of words is, discretion; and particularly that prime and eminent part of it, that consists in a care of offending: which Solomon assures us, that in much speaking it is hardly possible for us to avoid; in Prov. x. 19, *In the multitude of words*, says he, *there wanteth not sin*. It requiring no ordinary skill for a man to make his tongue run by rule, and, at the same time, to give it both its lesson and its liberty too. For seldom or never is there much spoke, but something or other had better been not spoke; there being nothing that the mind of man is so apt to kindle and take distaste at as at words: and therefore, whensoever any one comes to prefer a suit to another, no doubt the fewer of them the better; since, where so very little is said, it is sure to be either candidly accepted, or, which is next, easily excused: but at the same time to petition and to provoke too, is certainly very preposterous.

3dly, The third thing that brevity of speech commends itself by in all petitionary addresses is, a peculiar respect to the person addressed to: for whosoever petitions his superior in such a manner, does, by his very so doing, confess him better able to understand than he himself can be to express his own case. He owns him as a patron of a preventing judgment and goodness, and, upon that account, able, not only to answer, but also to anticipate his requests. For, according to the most natural interpretation of things, this is to ascribe to him a sagacity so quick and piercing, that it were presumption to inform; and a benignity so great, that it were needless to importune him. And can there be a greater and more winning deference to a superior than to treat him under such a character? Or can any thing be imagined so naturally fit and efficacious, both to enforce the petition and to endear the petitioner? A short petition to a great man is not only a suit to him for his favor, but also a panegyric upon his parts.

And thus I have given you the three commendatory qualifications of brevity of speech in our applications to the great ones of the world. Concerning which, as I showed before that it was impossible for us to form our addresses, even to God himself, but with some proportion and resemblance to those that we make to our fellow-mortals in a condition much above us, so it is certain, that whatsoever the general judgment and consent of mankind allows to be expressive and declarative of our honor to those, must (only with due allowance of the difference of the object) as really and properly declare and signify that honor and adoration that is due from us to the great God. And, consequently, what we have said for brevity of speech with respect to the former, ought equally to conclude for it with relation to him too.

But to argue more immediately and directly to the point before us, I shall now produce five arguments, enforcing brevity, and cashiering all prolixity of speech, with peculiar reference to our addresses to God.

1. And the first argument shall be taken from this consideration, That there is no reason allegeable for the use of length or prolixity of speech, that is at all applicable to prayer. For whosoever uses multiplicity of words, or length of discourse, must of necessity do it for one of three purposes: either to inform, or persuade; or, lastly, to weary and overcome the person whom he directs his discourse to. But the very first foundation of what I had to say upon this subject was laid by me in demonstrating that prayer could not possibly prevail with God any of these three ways. Forasmuch as, being omniscient, he could not be informed; and, being void of passion or affections, he could not be persuaded; and, lastly, being omnipotent and infinitely great, he could not, by any importunity, be wearied or overcome. And if so, what use then can there be of rhetoric, harangue, or multitude of words in prayer? For, if they should be designed for information, must it not be infinitely sottish and unreasonable to go about to inform him, who can be ignorant of nothing? Or to persuade him, whose unchangeable nature makes it impossible for him to be moved or wrought upon? Or, lastly, by long and much speaking, to think to weary him out, whose infinite power all the strength of men and angels, and the whole world put together, is not able to encounter or stand before? So that the truth is, by loquacity and prolixity of prayer, a man does really and indeed (whether he thinks so or no) rob God of the honor of those three great attributes, and neither treats him as a person omniscient, or unchangeable, or omnipotent: for, on the other side, all the usefulness of long speech, in human converse, is founded only upon the defects and imperfections of human nature. For he, whose

knowledge is at best but limited, and whose intellect, both in apprehending and judging, proceeds by a small diminutive light, can not but receive an additional light by the conceptions of another man, clearly and plainly expressed, and by such expression conveyed to his apprehension. And he again, whose nature subjects him to want and weakness, and consequently to hopes and fears, can not but be moved this way or that way, according as objects suitable to those passions shall be dexterously represented and set before his imagination, by the arts of speaking; which is that that we call *persuasion*. And lastly, he whose soul and body receive their activity from, and perform all their functions by, the mediation of the spirits, which ebb and flow, consume, and are renewed again, can not but find himself very uneasy upon any tedious, verbose application made to him; and that sometimes to such a degree, that, through mere fatigue, and even against judgment and interest both, a man shall surrender himself, as a conquered person, to the overbearing vehemence of such solicitations: for when they ply him so fast, and pour in upon him so thick, they can not but wear and waste the spirits, as unequal to so pertinacious a charge; and this is properly to weary a man. But now all weariness, we know, presupposes weakness; and consequently, every long, importune, wearisome petition is truly and properly a force upon him that is pursued with it; it is a following blow after blow upon the mind and affections, and may, for the time, pass for a real, though short persecution.

This is the state and condition of human nature; and prolixity or importunity of speech is still the great engine to attack it by, either in its blind or weak side: and I think I may venture to affirm, that it is seldom that any man is prevailed upon by words; but, upon a true and philosophical estimate of the whole matter, he is either deceived or wearied before he is so, and parts with the thing desired of him upon the very same terms that either a child parts with a jewel for an apple, or a man parts with his sword, when it is forcibly wrested or took from him. And that he who obtains what he has been rhetorically or importunately begging for, goes away really a conqueror, and triumphantly carrying off the spoils of his neighbor's understanding, or his will; baffling the former, or wearying the latter, into a grant of his restless petitions.

And now, if this be the case, when any one comes with a tedious, long-winded harangue to God, may not God properly answer him with those words in Psalm l. 21, *Surely thou thinkest I am altogether such an one as thyself?* And perhaps, upon a due and rational examination of all the follies and indecencies that men are apt to be guilty of in prayer, they will be all found resolvable into this one thing, as the true and sole cause of them; namely, That men, when they pray, take God to be such an one as themselves; and so treat him accordingly. The malignity and mischief of which gross mistake may reach further than possibly at first they can well be aware of. For if it be idolatry to pray to God the Father, represented under the shape of a man, can it be at all better to pray to him as represented under the weakness of a man? Nay, if the misrepresentation of the object makes the idolatry; certainly, by how much the worse and more scandalous the misrepresentation is, by so much the grosser and more intolerable must be the idolatry. To confirm which, we may add this consideration, that Christ himself, even now in his glorified estate in heaven, wears the body, and consequently the shape, of a man, though he is far from any of his infirmities or imperfections: and therefore, no doubt, to represent God to ourselves under these latter must needs be more absurd and irreligious than to represent him under the former. But to one particular of the preceding discourse some may reply and object, that, if God's omniscience, by rendering it impossible for him to be informed, be a sufficient reason against prolixity, or length of prayer, it will follow, that it is equally a reason against the using any words at all in prayer, since the proper use of words is to inform the person whom we speak to; and consequently, where information is impossible, words must needs be useless and superfluous.

To which I answer, first by concession, That, if the sole use of words or speech were to inform the person whom we speak to, the consequence would be firm and good, and equally conclude against the use of any words at all in prayer. But therefore, in the second place, I deny information to be the sole and adequate use of words or speech, or indeed any use of them at all, when either the person spoken to needs not to be informed, and withal is known not to need it, as sometimes it falls out with men: or, when he is incapable of being informed, as it is always with God. But the proper use of words, whensoever we speak to God in prayer, is thereby to pay him honor and obedience. God having, by an express precept, enjoined us the use of words in prayer, commanding us in Psalm l. 15, and many other scriptures, *to call upon him:* and in Luke xi. 21, *When we pray, to say, Our Father,* &c. But nowhere has he commanded us to do this with prolixity, or multiplicity of words. And though it must be confessed, that we may sometimes answer this command of calling upon God, and saying, *Our Father,* &c., by mental or inward prayer, yet, since these words, in their first and most proper signification, import a vocal address, there is no doubt but the direct design of the command is to enjoin this also, wheresoever there is ability and power to perform it. So that we see here the necessity of vocal prayer, founded upon the authority of a divine precept; whereas, for long prolix prayer, no such precept can be produced; and consequently, the divine omniscience may be a sufficient reason against multiplicity of words in prayer, and yet conclude nothing simply or absolutely against the bare use of them. Nevertheless, that we may not seem to allege bare command, unseconded by reason, (which yet, in the divine commands, it is impossible to do,) there is this great reason for, and use of, words in prayer, without the least pretense of informing the person whom we pray to; and that is, to acknowledge and own those wants before God that we supplicate for a relief of. It being very proper and rational to own and acknowledge a thing, even to him who knew it before; forasmuch as this is so far from offering to communicate or make known to him the thing so acknowledged, that it rather presupposes in him an antecedent knowledge of it, and comes in only as a subsequent assent and subscription to the reality and truth of such a knowledge. For to acknowledge a thing, in the first sense of the word, does by no means signify a design of notifying that thing to another, but is truly and properly a man's passing sentence upon himself and his own condition: there being no reason in the world for a man to expect that God should relieve and supply those wants that he himself will not own nor take notice of; any more than for a man to hope for a pardon of those sins that he can not find in his heart to confess. And yet, I suppose, no man in his right senses does or can imagine, that God is informed or brought to the knowledge of those sins by any such confession.

And so much for the clearing of this objection; and, in the whole, for the first argument produced by us for brevity, and against prolixity of prayer; namely, That all the reasons that can be assigned for prolixity of speech in our converse with men cease, and become no reasons for it at all, when we are to speak or pray to God.

2dly, The second argument for paucity of words in prayer shall be taken from the paucity of those things that are necessary to be prayed for. And surely, where few things are necessary, few words should be sufficient. For where the matter is not commensurate to the words, all speaking is but tautology; that being truly and really tautology where the same thing is repeated, though under never so much variety of expression; as it is but the same man still, though he appears every day or every hour in a new and different suit of clothes.

The adequate subject of our prayers (I showed at first) comprehended in it things of necessity and things of charity. As to the first of which, I know nothing absolutely necessary but grace here and glory hereafter. And for the other, we know what the Apostle says, 1 Tim. vi. 8; *Having food and raiment, let us be therewith content.* Nature is satisfied with a little, and grace with less. And now, if the matter of our prayers lies within so narrow a compass, why should the dress and outside of them spread and diffuse itself into so wide and disproportioned a largeness? by reason of which our words will be forced to hang loose and light, without any matter to support them; much after the same rate that it is said to be in transubstantiation, where accidents are left in the lurch by their proper subject, that gives them the slip, and so leaves those poor slender beings to uphold and shift for themselves.

In brevity of speech, a man does not so much speak words as things; things in their precise and naked truth, and stripped of their rhetorical mask and their fallacious gloss; and therefore in Athens they circumscribed the pleadings of their orators by a strict law, cutting off prologues and epilogues, and commanding them to an immediate representation of the case, by an impartial and succinct declaration of mere matter of fact. And this was, indeed, to speak things fit for a judge to hear, because it argued the pleader also a judge of what was fit for him to speak.

And now, why should not this be both decency and devotion too, when we come to plead for our poor souls before the great tribunal of heaven? It was the saying of Solomon, *A word to the wise;* and if so, certainly there can be no necessity of many words to Him who is wisdom itself. For can any man think that God delights to hear him make speeches, and to show his parts, (as the word is,) or to jumble a multitude of misapplied scripture-sentences together, interlarded with a frequent, nauseous repetition of "Ah Lord!" which some call *exercising their gifts,* but with a greater exercise of their hearers' patience? Nay, does not he present his Maker, not only with a more decent, but also a more free and liberal oblation, who tenders him much in a little, and brings him his whole heart and soul wrapt up in three or four words, than he who, with full mouth and loud lungs, sends up whole volleys of articulate breath to the throne of grace? For neither in the esteem of God or man ought multitude of words to pass for any more. In the present case, no doubt, God accounts and accepts of the former, as infinitely a more valuable offering than the latter. As that subject pays a prince a much nobler and more acceptable tribute, who tenders him a purse of gold, than he who brings him a whole cart-load of farthings, in which there is weight without worth, and number without account.

3dly, The third argument for brevity, or contractedness of speech in prayer, shall be taken from the very nature and condition of the person who prays; which makes it impossible for him to keep up the same fervor and attention in a long prayer, that he may in a short. For as I first observed, that the mind of man can not with the same force and vigor attend to several objects at the same time, so neither can it with the same force and earnestness exert itself upon one and the same object for any long time: great intention of mind spending the spirits too fast to continue its first freshness and agility long. For while the soul is a retainer to the elements, and a sojourner in the body, it must be content to submit its own quickness and spirituality to the dullness of its vehicle, and to comply with the pace of its inferior companion. Just like a man shut up in a coach, who, while he is so, must be willing to go no faster than the motion of the coach will carry him. He who does all by the help of those subtile, refined parts of matter, called spirits, must not think to persevere at the same pitch of acting while those principles of activity flag. No man begins and ends a long journey with the same pace.

But now, when prayer has lost its due fervor and attention, (which indeed are the very vitals of it,) it is but the carcass of a prayer, and consequently must needs be loathsome and offensive to God: nay, though the greatest part of it should be enlivened and carried on with an actual attention, yet, if that attention fails to enliven any one part of it, the whole is but a joining of the living and the dead together; for which conjunction the dead is not at all the better, but the living very much the worse. It is not length, nor copiousness of language, that is devotion, any more than bulk and bigness is valor, or flesh the measure of the spirit. A short sentence may be oftentimes a large and a mighty prayer. Devotion so managed being like water in a well, where you have fullness in a little compass; which surely is much nobler than the same carried out into many petit, creeping rivulets, with length and shallowness together. Let him who prays bestow all that strength, fervor, and attention upon shortness and significance, that would otherwise run out and lose itself in length and luxuriancy of speech to no purpose. Let not his tongue outstrip his heart, nor presume to carry a message to the throne of grace, while that stays behind. Let him not think to support so hard and weighty a duty with a tired, languishing, and bejaded devotion: to avoid which, let a man contract his expression, where he can not enlarge his affection; still remembering that nothing can be more absurd in itself, nor more unacceptable to God, than for one engaged in the great work of prayer to hold on speaking, after he has left off praying, and to keep the lips at work when the spirit can do no more.

4thly, The fourth argument for shortness or conciseness of speech in prayer shall be drawn from this, That it is the most natural and lively way of expressing the utmost agonies and outcries of the soul to God upon a quick, pungent sense, either of a pressing necessity, or an approaching calamity; which, we know, are generally the chief occasions of prayer, and the most effectual motives to bring men upon their knees in a vigorous application of themselves to this great duty. A person ready to sink under his wants has neither time nor heart to rhetoricate or make flourishes. No man begins a long grace when he is ready to starve: such an one's prayers are like the relief he needs, quick and sudden, short and immediate: he is like a man in torture upon the rack; whose pains are too acute to let his words be many, and whose desires of deliverance too impatient to delay the things he begs for by the manner of his begging it.

It is a common saying, "If a man does not know how to pray, let him go to sea, and that will teach him." And we have a notable instance of what kind of prayers men are taught in that school, even in the disciples themselves, when a storm arose, and the sea raged, and the ship was ready to be cast away, in the eighth of Matthew. In which case we do not find that they fell presently to harangue it about seas and winds, and that dismal face of things that must needs appear all over the devouring element at such a time: all which, and the like, might no doubt have been very plentiful topics of eloquence to a man who should have looked upon these things from the shore, or discoursed of wrecks and tempests safe and warm in his parlor. But these poor wretches, who were now entering, as they thought, into the very jaws of death, struggling with the last efforts of nature upon the sense of a departing life, and consequently could neither speak nor think any thing low or ordinary in such a condition, presently rallied up, and discharged the whole concern of their desponding souls in that short prayer of but three words, though much fuller and more forcible than one of three thousand, in the 25th verse of the forementioned chapter; *Save us, Lord, or we perish.* Death makes short work when it comes, and will teach him who would prevent it to make shorter. For surely no man who thinks himself a-perishing can be at leisure to be eloquent, or judge it either sense or devotion to begin a long prayer, when, in all likelihood, he shall conclude his life before it.

5thly, The fifth and last argument that I shall produce for brevity of speech, or fewness of words in prayer, shall be taken from the examples which we find in scripture, of such as have been remarkable for brevity, and of such as have been noted for prolixity of speech, in the discharge of this duty.

1. And first for brevity. To omit all those notable examples which the Old Testament affords us of it, and to confine ourselves only to the New, in which we are undoubtedly most concerned; was not this way of praying not only warranted but sanctified, and set above all that the wit of man could possibly except against it, by that infinitely exact form of prayer prescribed by the greatest, the holiest, and the wisest man that ever lived, even Christ himself, the Son of God and Saviour of the world? Was it not an instance both of the truest devotion and the fullest and most comprehensive reason that ever proceeded from the mouth of man? and yet, withal, the shortest and most succinct model that ever grasped all the needs and occasions of mankind, both spiritual and temporal, into so small a compass? Doubtless, had our Saviour thought fit to amplify or be prolix, *He, in whom were hid all the treasures of wisdom,* could not want matter; nor he who was himself *the Word,* want variety of the fittest to have expressed his mind by. But he chose rather to contract the whole concern of both worlds into a few lines, and to unite both heaven and earth in his prayer, as he had done before in his person. And indeed one was a kind of copy or representation of the other.

So then we see here brevity in the rule or pattern; let us see it next in the practice; and, after that, in the success of prayer. And first, we have the practice, as well as the pattern of it, in our Saviour himself; and that in the most signal passage of his whole life, even his preparation for his approaching death. In which dolorous scene, when his whole soul was nothing but sorrow, (that great moving spring of invention and elocution,) and when nature was put to its last and utmost stretch, and so had no refuge or relief but in prayer, yet even then all this horror, agony, and distress of spirit delivers itself but in two very short sentences, in Matt. xxvi. 39; *O my Father, if it be possible, let this cup pass from me; nevertheless, not as I will, but as thou wilt.* And again, the second time, with the like brevity and the like words: *O my Father, if this cup may not pass from me, except I drink it, thy will be done.* And lastly, the third time also, he used the same short form again; and yet in all this he was (as we may say without a metaphor) even praying for life, so far as the great business he was then about, to wit, the redemption of the world, would suffer him to pray for it. All which prayers of our Saviour, and others of like brevity, are properly such as we call ejaculations; an elegant similitude from a dart or arrow, shot or thrown out; and such an one (we know) of a yard long, will fly further, and strike deeper, than one of twenty.

And then, in the last place, for the success of such brief prayers, I shall give you but three instances of this; but they shall be of persons praying under the pressure of as great miseries as human nature could well be afflicted with. And the first shall be of the leper, Matt. viii. 2, or, as St. Luke describes him, *a man full of leprosy, who came to our Saviour, and worshipped him;* and, as St. Luke again has it more particularly, *fell on his face before him,* (which is the lowest and most devout of all postures of worship,) saying, *Lord, if thou wilt, thou canst make me clean.* This was all his prayer: and the answer to it was, that he was immediately cleansed. The next instance shall be of the poor blind man, in Luke xviii. 38, following our Saviour with this earnest prayer: *Jesus, thou son of David, have mercy upon me.* His whole prayer was no more: for it is said in the next verse, that he went on repeating it again and again: *Jesus, thou son of David, have mercy upon me.* And the answer he received was, that his eyes were opened and his sight restored.

The third and last instance shall be of the publican, in the same chapter of St. Luke, praying under a lively sense of as great a leprosy and blindness of soul as the other two could have of body: in the 13th verse, *he smote upon his breast, saying, God be merciful to me a sinner.* He spoke no more; though it is said in the 10th verse, that he went solemnly and purposely up to the temple to pray: the issue and success of which prayer was, that he went home justified, before one of those whom all the Jewish church revered as absolutely the highest and most heroic examples of piety, and most beloved fovorites of Heaven, in the whole world. And now, if the force and virtue of these short prayers could rise so high as to cleanse a leper, to give sight to the blind, and to justify a publican; and if the worth of a prayer may at all be measured by the success of it, I suppose no prayers whatsoever can do more; and I never yet heard or read of any long prayer that did so much. Which brings on the other part of this our fifth and last argument, which was to be drawn from the examples of such as have been noted in scripture for prolixity or length of prayer. And of this there are only two mentioned, the heathens and the Pharisees. The first, the grand instance of idolatry; the other, of hypocrisy: but Christ forbids us the imitation of both; *When ye pray,* says our Saviour in the 6th of Matthew, *be ye not like the heathens:* but in what? Why in this, *That they think they shall be heard for their much speaking;* in the 7th verse. It is not the multitude that prevails in armies, and much less in words. And then for the Pharisees, whom our Saviour represents as the very vilest of men, and the greatest of cheats. We have them amusing the world with pretenses of a more refined devotion, while their heart was all that time in their neighbor's coffers. For does not our Saviour expressly tell us in Luke xx. and the two last verses, that the great tools, the hooks or engines, by which they compassed their worst, their wickedest, and most rapacious designs, were long prayers? prayers made only for a show or color; and that to the basest and most degenerous sort of villainy, even the robbing the spittal, and devouring the houses of poor, helpless, forlorn widows. Their devotion served all along but as an instrument to their avarice, as a factor or under-agent to their extortion. A practice which, duly seen into, and stripped of its hypocritical blinds, could not but look very odiously and ill-favoredly; and therefore in come their long robes, and their long prayers together, and cover all. And the truth is, neither the length of one nor of the other is ever found so useful as when there is something more than ordinary that would not be seen. This was the gainful godliness of the Pharisees; and, I believe, upon good observation, you will hardly find any like the Pharisees for their long prayers, who are not also extremely like them for something else. And thus having given you five arguments for brevity, and against prolixity of prayer, let us now make this our other great rule whereby to judge of the prayers of our church, and the prayers of those who dissent and divide from it. And,

First, for that excellent body of prayers contained in our liturgy, and both compiled and enjoined by public authority. Have we not here a great instance of brevity and fullness together, cast into several short significant collects, each containing a distinct, entire, and well-managed petition? the whole set of them being like a string of pearls, exceeding rich in conjunction; and therefore of no small price or value, even single and by themselves. Nothing could have been composed with greater judgment; every prayer being so short, that it is impossible it should weary; and withal so pertinent, that it is impossible it should cloy the devotion. And indeed so admirably fitted are they all to the common concerns of a Christian society, that when the rubric enjoins but the use of some of them, our worship is not imperfect; and when we use them all, there is none of them superfluous.

And the reason assigned by some learned men for the preference of many short prayers before a continued long one is unanswerable; namely, that by the former there is a more frequently repeated mention made of the name, and some great attribute of God, as the encouraging ground of our praying to him; and withal, of the merits and mediation of Christ, as the only thing that can promise us success in what we pray for: every distinct petition beginning with the former and ending with the latter: by thus annexing of which to each particular thing that we ask for, we do manifestly confess and declare that we can not expect to obtain any one thing at the hands of God, but with a particular renewed respect to the merits of a Mediator; and withal, remind the congregation of the same, by making it their part to renew a distinct *Amen* to every distinct petition.

Add to this the excellent contrivance of a great part of our liturgy, into alternate responses; by which means the people are put to bear a considerable share in the whole service: which makes it almost impossible for them to be only idle hearers, or, which is worse, mere lookers-on: as they are very often, and may be always, (if they can but keep their eyes open,) at the long tedious prayers of the nonconformists. And this indeed is that which makes and denominates our liturgy truly and properly a book of common prayer. For I think I may truly avouch, (how strange soever it may seem at first,) that there is no such thing as common or joint prayer anywhere amongst the principal dissenters from the church of England: for in the Romish communion, the priest says over the appointed prayers only to himself; and the rest of the people, not hearing a word of what he says, repeat also their own particular prayers to themselves, and when they have done, go their way: not all at once, as neither do they come at once, but scatteringly, one after another, according as they have finished their devotions. And then, for the nonconformists, their prayers being all extempore, it is, as we have shown before, hardly possible for any, and utterly impossible for all, to join in them: for surely people can not join in a prayer before they understand it; nor can it be imagined that all capacities should presently and immediately understand what they hear, when, possibly, Holder-forth himself understands not what he says. From all which we may venture to conclude, that that excellent thing, common prayer, which is the joint address of an whole congregation with united voice, as well as heart, sending up their devotions to Almighty God, is nowhere to be found in these kingdoms, but in that best and nearest copy of primitive Christian worship, the divine service, as it is performed according to the orders of our church.

As for those long prayers so frequently used by some before their sermons; the constitution and canons of our church are not at all responsible for them, having provided us better things, and with great wisdom appointed a form of prayer to be used by all before their sermons. But as for this way of praying, now generally in use, as it was first took up upon an humor of novelty and popularity, and by the same carried on till it had passed into a custom, and so put the rule of the church first out of use, and then out of countenance also, so, if it be rightly considered, it will, in the very nature of the thing itself, be found a very senseless and absurd practice. For can there be any sense or propriety in beginning a new, tedious prayer in the pulpit, just after the church has, for near an hour together, with great variety of offices, suitable to all the needs of the congregation, been praying for all that can possibly be fit for Christians to pray for? Nothing certainly can be more irrational. For which cause, amongst many more, that old sober form of bidding prayer, which, both against law and reason, has been justled out of the church by this upstart, puritanical encroachment, ought, with great reason, to be restored by authority; and both the use and users of it, by a strict and solemn reinforcement of the canon upon all, without exception, be rescued from that unjust scorn of the factious and ignorant, which the tyranny of the contrary usurping custom will otherwise expose them to. For surely it can neither be decency nor order for our clergy to conform to the fanatics, as many in their prayers before sermon nowadays do.

And thus having accounted for the prayers of our church, according to the great rule prescribed in the text, *Let thy words be few*, let us now, according to the same, consider also the way of praying, so much used and applauded by such as have renounced the communion and liturgy of our church; and it is but reason that they should bring us something better, in the room of what they have so disdainfully cast off. But, on the contrary, are not all their prayers exactly after the heathenish and pharisaical copy? always notable for those two things, length and tautology? Two whole hours for one prayer, at a fast, used to be reckoned but a moderate dose; and that, for the most part, fraught with such irreverent, blasphemous expressions, that to repeat them would profane the place I am speaking in; and indeed they seldom "carried on the work of such a day," (as their phrase was,) but they left the church in need of a new consecration. Add to this the incoherence and confusion, the endless repetitions, and the insufferable nonsense that never failed to hold out, even with their utmost prolixity; so that in all their long fasts, from first to last, from seven in the morning to seven in the evening, (which was their measure,) the pulpit was always the emptiest thing in the church: and I never knew such a fast kept by them, but their hearers had cause to begin a thanksgiving as soon as they had done. And the truth is, when I consider the matter of their prayers, so full of ramble and inconsequence, and in every respect so very like the language of a dream; and compare it with their carriage of themselves in prayer, with their eyes for the most part shut, and their arms stretched out in yawning posture, a man that should hear any of them pray, might, by a very pardonable error, be induced to think that he was all the time hearing one talking in his sleep: besides the strange virtue which their prayers had to procure sleep in others too. So that he who should be present at all their long cant, would show a greater ability in watching, than ever they could pretend to in praying, if he could forbear sleeping, having so strong a provocation to it, and so fair an excuse for it. In a word, such were their prayers, both for matter and expression, that, could any one truly and exactly write them out, it would be the shrewdest and most effectual way of writing against them that could possibly be thought of.

I should not have thus troubled either you or myself, by raking into the dirt and dunghill of these men's devotions, upon the account of any thing either done or said by them in the late times of confusion; for as they have the king's, so I wish them God's pardon also, whom, I am sure, they have offended much more than they have both kings put together. But that which has provoked me thus to rip up and expose to you their nauseous and ridiculous way of addressing to God, even upon the most solemn occasions, is, that intolerably rude and unprovoked insolence and scurrility with which they are every day reproaching and scoffing at our liturgy, and the users of it, and thereby alienating the minds of the people from it, to such a degree, that many thousands are drawn by them into a fatal schism; a schism that, unrepented of, and continued in, will as infallibly ruin their souls, as theft, whoredom, murder, or any other of the most crying, damning sins whatsoever. But leaving this to the justice of the government, to which it belongs to protect us in our spiritual as well as in our temporal concerns, I shall only say this, that nothing can be more for the honor of our liturgy than to find it despised only by those who have made themselves remarkable to the world for despising the Lord's prayer as much.

In the mean time, for ourselves of the church of England, who, without pretending to any new lights, think it equally a duty and commendation to be wise, and to be devout only to sobriety, and who judge it no dishonor to God himself to be worshiped according to law and rule. If the directions of Solomon, the precept and example of our Saviour, and lastly, the piety and experience of those excellent men and martyrs, who first composed, and afterwards owned our liturgy with their dearest blood, may be looked upon as safe and sufficient guides to us in our public worship of God; then, upon the joint authority of all these, we may pronounce our liturgy the greatest treasure of rational devotion in the Christian world. And I know no prayer necessary, that is not in the liturgy, but one, which is this; That God would vouchsafe to continue the liturgy itself in use, honor, and veneration in this church forever. And I doubt not but all wise, sober, and good Christians will with equal judgment and affection give it their *Amen.*

Now to God the Father, God the Son, and God the Holy Ghost, three Persons and one God, be rendered and ascribed, as is most due, all praise, might, majesty, and dominion, both now and for evermore. Amen.

SERMON XVII.

THE FIRST SERMON PREACHED UPON ROMANS I. 32.

Who knowing the judgment of God, that they which commit such things are worthy of death, not only do the same, but have pleasure in them that do them.

FROM the beginning of the 18th verse to the end of the 31st, (the verse immediately going before the text,) we have a catalogue of the blackest sins that human nature, in its highest depravation, is capable of committing; and this so perfect, that there seems to be no sin imaginable but what may be reduced to, and comprised under, some of the sins here specified. In a word, we have an abridgment of the lives and practices of the whole heathen world; that is, of all the baseness and villainy that both the corruption of nature and the instigation of the devil could for so many ages, by all the arts and opportunities, all the motives and incentives of sinning, bring the sons of men to. And yet, as full and comprehensive as this catalogue of sin seems to be, it is but of sin under a limitation; and universality of sin under a certain kind, that is, of all sins of direct and personal commission. And you will say, is not this a sufficient comprehension of all? For is not a man's person the compass of his actions? Or, can he operate further than he does exist? Why yes, in some sense he may; he may not only commit such and such sins himself, but also take pleasure in others that do commit them; which expression implies these two things: first, That thus to take pleasure in other men's sins, is a distinct sin from all the former; and, secondly, That it is much greater than the former. Forasmuch as these terms, *not only do the same, but also take pleasure*, &c., import aggravation as well as distinction, and are properly an advance *a minore ad majus*, a progress to a further degree. And this indeed is the furthest that human pravity can reach, the highest point of villainy that the debauched powers of man's mind can ascend unto. For surely that sin that exceeds idolatry, monstrous unnatural lusts, covetousness, maliciousness, envy, murder, deceit, backbiting, hatred of God, spitefulness, pride, disobedience to parents, covenant-breaking, want of natural affection, implacableness, unmercifulness, and the like: I say, that sin, that is a pitch beyond all these, must needs be such an one as must nonplus the devil himself to proceed further: it is the very extremity, the fullness, and the concluding period of sin, the last line and finishing stroke of the devil's image drawn upon the soul of man.

Now the sense of the words may be fully and naturally cast into this one proposition, which shall be the subject of the following discourse; viz.,

That the guilt arising from a man's delighting or taking pleasure in other men's sins, or (which is all one) in other men for their sins, is greater than he can possibly contract by a commission of the same sins in his own person.

For the handling of which, I can not but think it superfluous to offer at any explication of what it is, to take pleasure in other men's sins; it being impossible for any man to be so far unacquainted with the motions and operations of his own mind as not to know how it is affected and disposed, when any thing pleases or delights him. And therefore I shall state the prosecution of the proposition upon these following things:

1. I shall show what it is that brings a man to such a disposition of mind as to take pleasure in other men's sins.

II. I shall show the reasons why a man's being disposed to do so, comes to be attended with such an extraordinary guilt; and,

III. and lastly, I shall declare what kind of persons are to be reckoned under this character. Of each of which in their order.

And first, for the first of these, What it is that brings a man, &c.

In order to which, I shall premise these four considerations:

1. That every man naturally has a distinguishing sense of *turpe et honestum;* of what is honest and what is dishonest; of what is fit, and what is not fit to be done. There are those practical principles and rules of action, treasured up in that part of man's mind, called by the schools συντήρησις, that, like the candle of the Lord, set up by God himself in the heart of every man, discovers to him both what he is to do, and what to avoid: they are *a light, lighting every man that cometh into the world.*

And in respect of which principally it is, that God is said not to have *left himself without witness* in the world; there being something fixed in the nature of man that will be sure to testify and declare for him.

2. The second thing to be considered is, That there is consequently upon this distinguishing principle an inward satisfaction or dissatisfaction arising in the heart of every man, after he has done a good or an evil action; an action agreeable to, or deviating from, this great rule. And this, no doubt, proceeds not only from the real unsuitableness that every thing sinful or dishonest bears to the nature of man, but also from a secret, inward, foreboding fear, that some evil or other will follow the doing of that which a man's own conscience disallows him in. For no man naturally is or can be cheerful immediately upon the doing of a wicked action: there being something within him that presently gives sentence against him for it: which, no question, is the voice of God himself, speaking in the hearts of men, whether they understand it or no; and by secret intimations giving the sinner a foretaste of that direful cup which he is like to drink more deeply of hereafter.

3. The third thing to be considered is, That this distinguishing sense of good and evil, and this satisfaction or dissatisfaction of mind consequent upon a man's acting suitably or unsuitably to it, is a principle neither presently nor easily to be worn out or extinguished. For besides that it is founded in nature, (which kind of things are always most durable and lasting,) the great important end that God designs it for, (which is no less than the government of the noblest part of the world, mankind,) sufficiently shows the necessity of its being rooted deep in the heart, and put be-

yond the danger of being torn up by any ordinary violence done to it.

4. The fourth and last thing to be considered is, That that which weakens, and directly tends to extinguish this principle, (so far as it is capable of being extinguished,) is an inferior, sensitive principle, which receives its gratifications from objects clean contrary to the former; and which affect a man in the state of this present life much more warmly and vividly than those which affect only his nobler part, his mind. So that there being a contrariety between those things that conscience inclines to and those that entertain the senses, and since the more quick and affecting pleasure still arises from these latter, it follows that the gratifications of these are more powerful to command the principles of action than the other, and consequently are, for the most part, too hard for, and victorious over, the dictates of right reason.

Now from these four considerations, thus premised, we naturally infer these two things:

First, That no man is quickly or easily brought to take a full pleasure and delight in his own sins. For though sin offers itself in never so pleasing and alluring a dress at first, yet the remorse, and inward regrets of the soul, upon the commission of it, infinitely overbalance those faint and transient gratifications it affords the senses. So that, upon the whole matter, the sinner, even at his highest pitch of enjoyment, is not pleased with it so much, but he is afflicted more. And, as long as these inward rejolts and recoilings of the mind continue, (which they will certainly do for a considerable part of a man's life,) the sinner will find his accounts of pleasure very poor and short, being so mixed and indeed overdone with the contrary impressions of trouble upon his mind, that it is but a bitter-sweet at best; and the fine colors of the serpent do by no means make amends for the smart and poison of his sting.

Secondly, The other thing to be inferred is, that, as no man is quickly or easily brought to take a full pleasure or delight in his own sins, so much less easily can he be brought to take pleasure in those of other men. The reason is, because the chief motive, as we have observed, that induces a man to sin, which is the gratification of his sensitive part, by a sinful act, can not be had from the sins of another man; since naturally, and directly, they affect only the agent that commits them. For certainly another man's intemperance can not affect my sensuality, any more than the meat and drink that I take into my mouth can please his palate: but of this more fully in some of the following particulars.

In the mean time, it is evident from reason, that there is a considerable difficulty in a man's arriving to such a disposition of mind as shall make him take pleasure in other men's sins; and yet it is also as evident from the text, and from experience too, that some men are brought to do so. And therefore, since there is no effect, of what kind soever, but is resolvable into some cause, we will inquire into the cause of this vile and preternatural temper of mind, that should make a man please himself with that which can noways reach or affect those faculties and principles which nature has made the proper seat and subject of pleasure. Now the causes (or at least some of the causes) that debauch and corrupt the mind of man to such a degree as to take pleasure in other men's sins, are these five:

1. A commission of the same sins in a man's own person. This is imported in the very words of the text; where it is said of such persons, that *they not only do the same things;* which must therefore imply that they do them. It is conversation and acquaintance, that must give delight in things and actions, as well as in persons: and it is trial that must begin the acquaintance. It being hardly imaginable, that one should be delighted with a sin at second hand, till he has known it at the first. Delight is the natural result of practice and experiment; and when it flows from any thing else, so far it recedes from nature. None look with so much pleasure upon the works of art as those who are artists themselves. They are therefore their delight, because they were heretofore their employment; and they love to see such things, because they once loved to do them. In like manner, a man must sin himself into a love of other men's sins; for a bare notion or speculation of this black art will not carry him so far. No sober, temperate person in the world, (whatsoever other sins he may be inclinable to, and guilty of,) can look with any complacency upon the drunkenness and sottishness of his

neighbor; nor can any chaste person (be his other failings what they will) reflect with any pleasure or delight upon the filthy, unclean conversation of another, though never so much in fashion, and vouched, not by common use only, but applause. No, he must be first an exercised, thorough-paced practitioner of these vices himself, and they must have endeared themselves to him by those personal gratifications he had received from them, before he can come to like them so far as to be pleased and enamored with them wheresoever he sees them. It is possible indeed, that a sober or a chaste person, upon the stock of ill-will, envy, or spiritual pride, (which is all the religion that some have,) may be glad to see the intemperance and debauchery of some about them; but it is impossible that such persons should take any delight in the men themselves for being so. The truth is, in such a case, they do not properly delight in the vice itself, though they inwardly rejoice (and after a godly sort, no doubt) to see another guilty of it; but they delight in the mischief and disaster which they know it will assuredly bring upon him whom they hate and wish ill to: they rejoice not in it, as in a delightful object, but as in a cause and means of their neighbor's ruin. So grateful, nay, so delicious, are even the horridest villainies committed by others to the pharisaical piety of some; who in the mean time can be wholly unconcerned for the reproach brought thereby upon the name of God and the honor of religion, so long as by the same their sanctified spleen is gratified in their brother's infamy and destruction.

This therefore we may reckon upon, that scarce any man passes to a liking of sin in others, but by first practicing it himself; and consequently may take it for a shrewd indication and sign, whereby to judge of the manners of those who have sinned with too much art and caution to suffer the eye of the world to charge some sins directly upon their conversation. For though such kind of men have lived never so much upon the reserve, as to their personal behavior, yet, if they be observed to have a particular delight in, and fondness for, persons noted for any sort of sin, it is ten to one but there was a communication in the sin, before there was so in affection. The man has, by this, directed us to a copy of himself; and though we can not always come to a sight of the original, yet by a true copy we may know all that is in it.

2dly, A second cause that brings a man to take pleasure in other men's sins is, not only a commission of those sins in his own person, but also a commission of them against the full light and conviction of his conscience. For this also is expressed in the text; where the persons charged with this wretched disposition of mind are said to have been such as *knew the judgment of God, that they who committed such things were worthy of death.* They knew that there was a righteous and a searching law, directly forbidding such practices; and they knew that it carried with it the divine stamp, that it was the law of God; they knew also, that the sanction of it was under the greatest and dreadfullest of all penalties, death. And this surely, one would think, was knowledge enough to have opened both a man's eyes, and his heart too; his eyes to see, and his heart to consider, the intolerable mischief that the commission of the sin set before him must infallibly plunge him into. Nevertheless, the persons here mentioned were resolved to venture, and to commit the sin, even while conscience stood protesting against it. They were such as broke through all mounds of law, such as laughed at the sword of vengeance, which divine justice brandished in their faces. For we must know that God has set *a flaming sword,* not only before paradise, but before hell itself also, to keep men out of this, as well as out of the other. And conscience is the angel into whose hand this sword is put. But if now the sinner shall not only wrestle with this angel, but throw him too, and win so complete a victory over his conscience that all these considerations shall be able to strike no terror into his mind, lay no restraint upon his lusts, no control upon his appetites, he is certainly too strong for the means of grace, and his heart lies open, like a broad and high road, for all the sin and villainy in the world freely to pass through.

The truth is, if we impartially consider the nature of these sins against conscience, we shall find them such strange paradoxes, that a man must balk all common principles, and act contrary to the natural way and motive of all human actions, in the commission of them. For that which naturally moves a man to do any thing, must be the apprehension and expectation of some good from the thing which he is about to do; and that which naturally keeps a man from doing of a thing must be the apprehension and fear of some mischief likely to ensue from that thing or action that he is ready to engage in. But now, for a man to do a thing, while his conscience, the best light that he has to judge by, assures him that he shall be infinitely, unsupportably miserable if he does it, this is certainly unnatural, and, one would imagine, impossible.

And therefore, so far as one may judge, while a man acts against his conscience, he acts by a principle of direct infidelity, and does not really believe that those things that God has thus threatened shall ever come to pass. For, though he may yield a general faint assent to the truth of those propositions, as they stand recorded in scripture, yet, for a thorough, practical belief, that those general propositions shall be particularly made good upon his person, no doubt, for the time that he is sinning against conscience, such a belief has no place in his mind. Which being so, it is easy to conceive how ready and disposed this must needs leave the soul to admit of any, even the most horrid, unnatural proposals that the devil himself can suggest: for conscience being once extinct, and the Spirit of God withdrawn, (which never stays with a man, when conscience has once left him,) the soul, like the first matter to all forms, has an universal propensity to all lewdness. For every violation of conscience proportionably wears off something of its native tenderness; which tenderness being the cause of that anguish and remorse that it feels upon the commission of sin, it follows that, when by degrees it comes to have worn off all this tenderness, the sinner will find no trouble of mind upon his doing the very wickedest and worst of actions; and consequently, that this is the most direct and effectual introduction to all sorts and degrees of sin.

For which reason it was that I alleged sinning against conscience for one of the causes of this vile temper and habit of mind, which we are now discoursing of: not that it has any special productive efficiency of this particular sort of sinning, more than of any other, but that it is a general cause of this, as of all other great vices; and that it is impossible but a man must have first passed this notable stage, and got his conscience throughly debauched and hardened, before he can arrive to the hight of sin; which I account the delighting in other men's sins to be.

3dly, A third cause of this villainous disposition of mind, besides a man's personal commission of such and such sins, and his commission of them against conscience, must be also his continuance in them. For God forbid that every single commission of a sin, though great for its kind, and withal acted against conscience for its aggravation, should so far deprave the soul, and bring it to such a reprobate sense and condition, as to *take pleasure in other men's sins.* For we know what a foul sin David committed, and what a crime St. Peter himself fell into; both of them, no doubt, fully and clearly against the dictates of their conscience; yet we do not find that either of them was thereby brought to such an impious frame of heart as to delight in their own sins, and much less in other men's. And therefore it is not every sinful violation of conscience that can *quench the Spirit* to such a degree as we have been speaking of; but it must be a long inveterate course and custom of sinning after this manner, that at length produces and ends in such a cursed effect. For this is so great a masterpiece in sin, that no man begins with it: he must have passed his *tyrocinium,* or novitiate, in sinning, before he can come to this, be he never so quick a proficient. No man can mount so fast as to set his foot upon the highest step of the ladder at first. Before a man can come to be pleased with a sin, because he sees his neighbor commit it, he must have had such a long acquaintance with it himself as to create a kind of intimacy or friendship between him and that; and then, we know, a man is naturally glad to see his old friend not only at his own house, but wheresoever he meets him. It is generally the property of an old sinner to find a delight in reviewing his own villainies in the practice of other men; to see his sin and himself, as it were, in reversion; and to find a greater satisfaction in beholding him who succeeds him in his vice, than him who is to succeed him in his estate. In the matter of sin, age makes a greater change upon the soul than it does or can upon the body. And as in this, if we compare the picture of a man, drawn at the years of seventeen or eighteen, with a picture of the same person at threescore and ten, hardly the least trace or similitude of one face can be found in the other. So for the soul, the difference of the dispositions and qualities of the inner man will be found much greater. Compare the harmlessness, the credulity, the tenderness, the modesty, and the ingenuous pliableness to virtuous counsels, which is in youth, as it comes fresh and untainted out of the hands of nature, with the mischievousness, the slyness, the craft, the impudence, the falsehood, and the confirmed obstinacy in most sorts of sin, that is to be found in an aged, long-practiced sinner, and you will confess the complexion and hue of his soul to be altered more than that of his face. Age has given him another body, and custom another mind. All those seeds of virtue and good morality, that were the natural endowments of our first years, are lost, and dead forever. And in respect of the native innocence of childhood, no man, through old age, becomes twice a child. The vices of old age have in them the stiffness of it too. And as it is the unfittest time to learn in, so the unfitness of it to unlearn will be found much greater.

Which considerations, joined with that of its imbecility, make it the proper season for a superannuated sinner to enjoy the delights of sin in the rebound; and to supply the impotence of practice by the airy, fantastic pleasure of memory and reflection. For all that can be allowed him now, is to refresh his decrepit, effete sensuality with the transcript and history of his former life, recognized, and read over by him, in the vicious rants of the vigorous youthful debauchees of the present time, whom (with an odd kind of passion, mixed of pleasure and envy too) he sees flourishing in all the bravery and prime of their age and vice. An old wrestler loves to look on, and to be near the lists, though feebleness will not let him offer at the prize. An old huntsman finds a music in the noise of hounds, though he can not follow the chase. An old drunkard loves a tavern, though he can not go to it, but as he is supported, and led by another, just as some are observed to come from thence. And an old wanton will be doting upon women, when he can scarce see them without spectacles. And to show the true love and faithful allegiance that the old servants and subjects of vice ever after bear to it, nothing is more usual and frequent than to hear that such as have been strumpets in their youth, turn procurers in their age. Their great concern is, that the vice may still go on.

4thly, A fourth cause of men's taking pleasure in the sins of others, is from that meanness and poor-spiritedness that naturally and inseparably accompanies all guilt. Whosoever is conscious to himself of sin, feels in himself (whether he will own it or no) a proportionable shame, and a secret depression of spirit thereupon. And this is so irksome, and uneasy to man's mind, that he is restless to relieve and rid himself from it: for which he finds no way so effectual as to get company in the same sin. For company, in any action, gives both credit to that, and countenance to the agent; and so much as the sinner gets of this, so much he casts off of shame. Singularity in sin puts it out of fashion; since to be alone in any practice seems to make the judgment of the world against it; but the concurrence of others is a tacit approbation of that in which they concur. Solitude is a kind of nakedness, and the result of that, we know, is shame. It is company only that can bear a man out in an ill thing; and he who is to encounter and fight the law, will be sure to need a second. No wonder therefore if some take delight in the immoralities and baseness of others; for nothing can support their minds drooping, and sneaking, and inwardly reproaching them, from a sense of their own guilt, but to see others as bad as themselves.

To be vicious amongst the virtuous, is a double disgrace and misery; but where the whole company is vicious and debauched, they presently like, or at least easily pardon one another. And as it is observed by some that there is none so homely but loves a looking-glass, so it is certain that there is no man so vicious, but delights to see the image of his vice reflected upon him, from one who exceeds, or at least equals him in the same.

Sin in itself is not only shameful, but also weak; and it seeks a remedy for both in society: for it is this that must give it both color and support. But on the contrary, how great and (as I may so speak) how self-sufficient a thing is virtue! It needs no credit from abroad, no countenance from the multitude. Were there but one virtuous man in the world, he would hold up his head with confidence and honor; he would shame the world, and not the world him. For, according to that excellent and great saying, Prov. xiv. 14, *A good man shall be satisfied from himself.* He needs look no further. But if he desires to see the same virtue propagated and diffused to those about him, it is for their sakes, not his own. It is his charity that wishes, and not his necessity that requires it. For solitude and singularity can neither daunt nor disgrace him; unless we could suppose it a disgrace for a man to be singularly good.

But a vicious person, like the basest sort of beasts, never enjoys himself but in the herd. Company, he thinks, lessens the shame of vice, by sharing it; and abates the torrent of a common odium, by driving it into many channels; and therefore, if he can not wholly avoid the eye of the observer, he hopes to distract it at least by a multiplicity of the object. These, I confess, are poor shifts, and miserable shelters, for a sick and a self-upbraiding conscience to fly to; and yet they are some of the best that the debauchee has to cheer up his spirits with in this world. For if, after all, he must needs be seen and took notice of, with all his filth and noisomeness about him, he promises himself however, that it will be some allay to his reproach to be but one of many, to march in a troop, and by a preposterous kind of ambition to be seen in bad company.

5. The fifth and last cause, (that I shall mention,) inducing men to take pleasure in the sins of others, is a certain, peculiar, unaccountable malignity that is in some natures and dispositions. I know no other name or word to express it by. But the thing itself is frequently seen in the temporal concerns of this world. For are there not some who find an inward, secret rejoicing in themselves, when they see or hear of the loss or calamity of their neighbor, though no imaginable interest or advantage of their own is or can be served thereby? But it seems there is a base, wolfish principle within, that is fed and gratified with another's misery; and no other account or reason in the world can be given of its being so, but that it is the nature of the beast to delight in such things.

And as this occurs frequently in temporals, so there is no doubt but that with some few persons it acts the same way also in spirituals. I say, with some few persons; for, thanks be to God, the common, known corruption of human nature, upon the bare stock of its original depravation, does not usually proceed so far. Such an one, for instance, was that wretch who made a poor captive renounce his religion, in order to the saving of his life; and when he had so done, presently run him through, glorying that he had thereby destroyed his enemy, both body and soul. But more remarkably such was that monster of diabolical baseness here in England, who, some years since, in the reign of King Charles the First, suffered death for crimes scarce ever heard of before; having frequently boasted, that as several men had their several pleasures and recreations, so his peculiar pleasure and recreation was to destroy souls, and accordingly to put men upon such practices as he knew would assuredly do it. But above all, the late saying of some of the dissenting brotherhood ought to be proclaimed and celebrated to their eternal honor; who, while there was another new oath preparing, which they both supposed and hoped most of the clergy would not take, in a most insulting manner gave out thereupon, that they were resolved either to have our livings, or to damn our souls. An expression, so fraught with all the spite and poison which the devil himself could infuse into words, that it ought to remain as a monument of the humanity, charity, and Christianity of this sort of men forever.

Now such a temper or principle as these and the like passages do import, I call a peculiar malignity of nature; since it is evident, that neither the inveterate love of vice, nor yet the long practice of it, and that even against the reluctancies and light of conscience, can of itself have this devilish effect upon the mind, but as it falls in with such a villainous preternatural disposition as I have mentioned. For to instance in the particular case of parents and children, let a father be never so vicious, yet, generally speaking, he would not have his child so. Nay, it is certain that some, who have been as corrupt in their morals as vice could make them, have yet been infinitely solicitous to have their children soberly, virtuously, and piously brought up: so that, although they have *begot sons after their own likeness*, yet they are not willing to breed them so too.

Which, by the way, is the most pregnant demonstration in the world, of that self-condemning sentence, that is perpetually sounding in every great sinner's breast; and of that inward, grating dislike of the very thing he practices, that he should abhor to see the same in any one whose good he nearly tenders, and whose person he wishes well to. But if now, on the other side, we should chance to find a father corrupting his son, or a mother debauching her daughter, (as God knows such monsters have been seen within the four seas,) we must not charge this barely upon an high predominance of vice in these persons, but much more upon a peculiar anomaly and baseness of nature: if the name of nature may be allowed to that which seems to be an utter cashiering of it; a deviation from, and a contradiction to, the common principles of humanity. For this is such a disposition as strips the father of the man; as makes him sacrifice his children to Moloch; and as much outdo the cruelty of a cannibal or a Saturn, as it is more barbarous and inhuman to damn a child than to devour him. We sometimes read and hear of monstrous births, but we may often see a greater monstrosity in educations: thus when a father has begot a man, he trains him up into a beast, making even his own house a stews, a bordel, and a school of lewdness, to instill the rudiments of vice into the unwary, flexible years of his poor children, poisoning their tender minds with the irresistible, authentic venom of his base example; so that all the instruction they find within their father's walls shall be only to be disciplined to an earlier practice of sin, to be catechized into all the mysteries of iniquity, and, at length, confirmed into a mature, grown-up, incorrigible state of debauchery. And this some parents call a-teaching their children to know the world, and to study men: thus leading them, as it were, by the hand, through all the forms and classes, all the varieties and modes of villainy, till at length they make them ten times more the children of the devil than of themselves. Now, I say, if the unparalleled wickedness of the age should at any time cast us upon such blemishes of mankind as these, who, while they thus treat their children, should abuse and usurp the name of parents, by assuming it to themselves; let us not call them by the low, diminutive term or title of sinful, wicked, or ungodly men, but let us look upon them as so many prodigious exceptions from our common nature, as so many portentous animals, like the strange unnatural productions of Africa, and fit to be publicly shown, were they not unfit to be seen: for certainly where a child finds his own parents his perverters, he can not be so properly said to be born, as to be damned into the world; and better were it for him by far to have been unborn, and unbegot, than to come to ask blessing of those whose conversation breathes nothing but contagion and a curse. So impossible, and so much a paradox is it, for any parent to impart to his child his blessing and his vice too.

And thus I have dispatched the first general thing proposed for the handling of the words, and shown in five several particulars, what it is that brings a man to such a disposition of mind as to take pleasure in other men's sins. I proceed now to the

Second, which is, To show the reasons why a man's being disposed to do so, comes to be attended with such an extraordinary guilt. And the first shall be taken from this, that naturally there is no motive to induce or tempt a man to this way of sinning. And this is a most certain truth, that the lesser the temptation is, the greater is the sin. For in every sin, by how much the more free the will is in its choice, by so much is the act the more sinful. And where there is nothing to importune, urge, or provoke it to any act, there is so much an higher and perfecter degree of freedom about that act. For albeit the will is not capable of being compelled to any of its actings, yet it is capable of being made to act with more or less difficulty, according to the different impressions it receives from motives or objects. If the object be extremely pleasing, and apt to gratify it, there, though the will has still a power of refusing it, yet it is not without some difficulty: upon which account it is that men are so strongly carried out to, and so hardly took off from, the practice of vice; namely, because the sensual pleasure arising from it is still importuning and drawing them to it.

But now, from whence springs this pleasure? Is it not

from the gratification of some desire founded in nature? An irregular gratification it is indeed very often; yet still the foundation of it is, and must be, something natural: so that the sum of all is this, that the naturalness of a desire is the cause that the satisfaction of it is pleasure, and pleasure importunes the will; and that which importunes the will, puts a difficulty in the will's refusing or forbearing it. Thus drunkenness is an irregular satisfaction of the appetite of thirst; uncleanness an unlawful gratification of the appetite of procreation; and covetousness a boundless, unreasonable pursuit of the principle of self-preservation. So that all these are founded in some natural desire, and are therefore pleasurable, and upon that account tempt, solicit, and entice the will. In a word, there is hardly any one vice or sin of direct and personal commission, but what is the irregularity and abuse of one of those two grand natural principles; namely, either that which inclines a man to preserve himself, or that which inclines him to please himself.

But now, what principle, faculty, or desire, by which nature projects either its own pleasure or preservation, is or can be gratified by another man's personal pursuit of his own vice? It is evident that all the pleasure that naturally can be received from a vicious action can immediately and personally affect none but him who does it; for it is an application of the pleasing object only to his own sense; and no man feels by another man's senses. And therefore the delight that a man takes from another's sin can be nothing else but a fantastical, preternatural complacency arising from that which he has really no sense or feeling of. It is properly a love of vice, as such; a delighting in sin for its own sake; and is a direct imitation, or rather an exemplification of the malice of the devil; who delights in seeing those sins committed which the very condition of his nature renders him incapable of committing himself. For the devil can neither drink, nor whore, nor play the epicure, though he enjoys the pleasures of all these at a second hand, and by malicious approbation. If a man plays the thief, says Solomon, *and steals to satisfy his hunger*, Prov. vi. 30, though it can not wholly excuse the fact, yet it sometimes extenuates the guilt. And we know there are some corrupt affections in the soul of man, that urge and push him on to their satisfaction with such an impetuous fury, that when we see a man overborne and run down by them, considering the frailty of human nature, we can not but pity the person, while we abhor the crime. It being like one ready to drink poison, rather than to die with thirst.

But when a man shall, with a sober, sedate, diabolical rancor, look upon and enjoy himself in the sight of his neighbor's sin and shame, and secretly hug himself upon the ruins of his brother's virtue, and the dishonors of his reason, can he plead the instigation of any appetite in nature inclining him to this; and that would otherwise render him uneasy to himself, should he not thus triumph in another's folly and confusion? No, certainly; this can not be so much as pretended. For he may as well carry his eyes in another man's head, and run races with another man's feet, as directly and naturally taste the pleasures that spring from the gratification of another man's appetites.

Nor can that person, whosoever he is, who accounts it his recreation and diversion to see one man wallowing in his filthy revels, and another made infamous and noisome by his sensuality, be so impudent as to allege for a reason of his so doing, that either all the enormous draughts of the one do or can leave the least relish upon the tip of his tongue, or that all the fornications and whoredoms of the other do or can quench or cool the boilings of his own lust. No, this is impossible. And if so, what can we then assign for the cause of this monstrous disposition? Why, all that can be said in this case is, that nature proceeds by quite another method; having given men such and such appetites, and allotted to each of them their respective pleasures; the appetite and the pleasure still cohabiting in the same subject: but the devil and long custom of sinning have superinduced upon the soul new, unnatural, and absurd desires; desires that have no real object; desires that relish things not at all desirable; but, like the sickness and distemper of the soul, feeding only upon filth and corruption, fire and brimstone, and giving a man the devil's nature and the devil's delight; who has no other joy or happiness but to dishonor his Maker, and to destroy his fellow-creature; to corrupt him here, and to torment him hereafter. In fine, there is as much difference between the pleasure a man takes in his own sins, and that which he takes in other men's, as there is between the wickedness of a man and the wickedness of a devil.

2. A second reason why a man's taking pleasure in the sins of others comes to be attended with such an extraordinary guilt, is, from the boundless, unlimited nature of this way of sinning. For by this a man contracts a kind of an universal guilt, and, as it were, sins over the sins of all other men; so that while the act is theirs, the guilt of it is equally his. Consider any man as to his personal powers and opportunities of sinning, and comparatively they are not great; for at greatest they must still be limited by the measure of a man's acting, and the term of his duration. And a man's active powers are but weak, and his continuance in the world but short. So that nature is not sufficient to keep pace with his corruptions, by answering desire with proportionable practice.

For to instance in those two grand extravagances of lust and drunkenness: surely no man is of so general and diffusive a lust as to prosecute his amours all the world over; and let it burn never so outrageously for the present, yet age will in time chill those heats; and the impure flame will either die of itself, or consume the body that harbors it. And so for intemperance in drinking; no man can be so much a swine as to be always pouring in, but in the compass of some years he will drown his health and his strength in his own belly; and after all his drunken trophies, at length drink down himself too; and that certainly will and must put an end to the debauch.

But now, for the way of sinning which we have been speaking of, it is neither confined by place, nor weakened by age; but the bed-rid, the gouty, and the lethargic may, upon this account, equal the activity of the strongest and the most vegete sinner. Such an one may take his brother by the throat, and act the murderer, even while he can neither stir a hand nor a foot; and he may invade his neighbor's bed, while weakness has tied him down to his own. He may sin over all the adulteries and debauches, all the frauds and oppressions of the whole neighborhood, and, as I may so speak, he may break every command of God's law by proxy, and it were well for him if he could be damned by proxy too. A man, by delight and fancy, may grasp in the sins of all countries and ages, and by an inward liking of them communicate in their guilt. He may take a range all the world over, and draw in all that wide circumference of sin and vice, and centre it in his own breast. For whatsoever sin a man extremely loves, and would commit if he had opportunity, and, in the mean time, pleases himself with the speculation of the same, whether ever he commits it or no, it leaves a stain and a guilt upon his conscience; and, according to the spiritual and severe accounts of the law, is made, in a great respect, his own. So that by this means there is a kind of transmigration of sins, much like that which Pythagoras held of souls. Such an one to be sure it is, as makes a man not only (according to the apostle's phrase) a *partaker of other men's sins*, but also a deriver of the whole entire guilt of them to himself; and yet so as to leave the committer of them as full of guilt as he was before.

From whence we see the infinitely fruitful and productive power of this way of sinning; how it can increase and multiply beyond all bounds and measures of actual commission, and how vastly it swells the sinner's account in an instant. So that a man shall, out of all the various and even numberless kinds of villainy, acted by all the people and nations round about him, as it were, extract one mighty, comprehensive guilt, and adopt it to himself; and so become chargeable with, and accountable for, a world of sin without a figure.

3. The third and last reason that I shall assign of the extraordinary guilt attending a man's being disposed to take pleasure in other men's sins, shall be taken from the soul's preparation and passage to such a disposition. For that it presupposes and includes in it the guilt of many preceding sins. For, as it has been shown, a man must have passed many periods of sin before he can arrive to it, and have served a long apprenticeship to the devil before he can come to such a perfection and maturity in vice as this imports. It is a collection of the guilt of a long and numerous train of villainies, the compendium and sum total of several particular impieties, all united and cast up into one. It is, as it were, the very quintessence and sublimation of vice, by which, as

in the spirit of liquors, the malignity of many actions is contracted into a little compass, but with a greater advantage of strength and force, by such a contraction.

In a word, it is the wickedness of a whole life discharging all its filth and foulness into this one quality, as into a great sink or common shore. So that nothing is or can be so properly and significantly called the *very sinfulness of sin*, as this. And therefore no wonder if, containing so many years' guilt in the bowels of it, it stands here stigmatized by the apostle as a temper of mind rendering men so detestably bad, that the great enemy of mankind, the devil himself, neither can nor desires to make them worse. I can not, I need not say any more of it. It is indeed a condition not to be thought of (by persons serious enough to think and consider) without the utmost horror. But such as truly fear God shall both be kept from it and from those sins that lead to it.

To which God, infinitely wise, holy, and just, be rendered and ascribed, as is most due, all praise, might, majesty, and dominion, both now and for evermore. Amen.

SERMON XVIII.

THE SECOND SERMON PREACHED UPON ROMANS I. 32.

Who knowing the judgment of God, that they which commit such things are worthy of death, not only do the same, but have pleasure in them that do them.

THE sense of these words I show, in the preceding discourse, fell naturally into this one proposition: viz.

That the guilt arising from a man's delighting or taking pleasure in other men's sins, or (which is all one) in other men for their sins, is greater than he can possibly contract by a commission of the same sins in his own person.

The prosecution of which I stated upon these three things:

First, To show what it is that brings a man to such a disposition of mind as to take pleasure in other men's sins.

Secondly, To show the reasons why a man's being disposed to do so comes to be attended with such an extraordinary guilt.

Thirdly and lastly, To declare what kind of persons are to be reckoned under this character.

The two first of which being dispatched already, I proceed now to the third and last. Concerning which I shall lay down this general assertion; That whosoever draws others to sin ought to be looked upon as one delighting in those sins that he draws them to. Forasmuch as no man is brought to do any thing, especially if it be ill or wicked, but in order to the pleasing of himself by it: it being absurd and incredible that any one should venture to damn himself hereafter for that which does not some way or other gratify and please him here. But to draw forth this general into particulars.

1. First of all: Those are to be accounted to take pleasure in other men's sins who teach doctrines directly tending to

engage such as believe them in a sinful course. For there is none so compendious and efficacious a way to prepare a man for all sin as this: this being properly to put out the eyes of that which is to be his guide, by perverting his judgment; and when that is once done, you may carry him whither you will. Chance must be his rule, and present appetite his director. A man's judgment or conscience is the great spring of all his actions; and consequently to corrupt or pervert this is to derive a contagion upon all that he does. And therefore we see how high a guilt our Saviour charges upon this in Matt. v. 19; *Whosoever shall break one of these least commandments, and shall teach men so, shall be called the least in the kingdom of heaven:* that is, in truth shall never come thither. And we find the great sin of the Pharisees was, that they promoted and abetted the sins of other men, taught the devil's doctrine out of Moses's chair, and by false descants upon the divine precepts cut asunder the binding force of them: so that, according to their wretched comments, men might break the law, and yet never sin against it. For in Matt. xv. 5, 6, they had taught men how *to dishonor their parents,* without any violation of the fifth commandment. Thus they preached: and what design can any one imagine the authors of such doctrines could have, but the depravation of men's manners! For, if some men teach wicked things, it must be that others should practice them. And if one man sets another a copy, it is no doubt with a purpose that he should write after it.

Now these doctrines are of two sorts:

1. Such as represent actions that are in themselves really wicked and sinful, as not so.

2. Such as represent them much less sinful as to their kind or degrees than indeed they are.

For the first of which; to instance in one very gross one, instead of many, take the doctrine of those commonly called Antinomians, who assert positively that believers, or persons regenerate, and within the covenant of grace, can not sin. Upon which account, no wonder if some very liberally assume to themselves the condition and character of believers; for then they know that other mighty privilege belongs to them of course. But what? may not these believers cheat and lie, commit adultery, steal, murder, and rebel? Why, yes; they may, and nothing is more common than to see such believers do such things. But how then can they escape the charge of all that guilt that naturally follows from such enormities? Why, thus; you must in this case with great care and accuracy distinguish between the act of lying and the sin of lying, the act of stealing and the sin of stealing, and the act of rebellion and the sin of rebellion. Now, though all these acts are frequent and usual with such persons, yet they are sure (as they order the matter) never to be guilty of the sin. And the reason is, because it is not the quality of the action that derives a qualification upon the person, so as to render him such or such, good or bad; but it is the antecedent quality or condition of the person that denominates his actions, and stamps them good or evil. So that they are those only who are first wicked, that do wicked actions. But believers, and the godly, though they do the very same things, yet they so much outwit the devil in the doing of them, that they never commit the same sins. But you will say, how came they by such a great and strange privilege? Why, they will tell you, it is because they are not under the obliging power of the law. And if you ask further, how they come to get from under that common obligation that lies so hard and heavy upon all the rest of the world; they will tell you, it is from this, that believers, instead of the law, have the Spirit actually dwelling in them, and by an admirable kind of invisible clock-work moving them, just as a spring does a watch; and that immediately by himself alone, without the meditation of any written law or rule to guide, or direct, and much less to command or oblige them. So that the Spirit, we see, is to be their sole director, without, and very often contrary to, the written law. An excellent contrivance, doubtless, to authorize and sanctify the blackest and most flagitious actions that can proceed from man. For since the motions of the Spirit (which they so confidently suppose themselves to have) can not so much as in things good and lawful, by any certain diagnostic, be distinguished from the motions of a man's own heart, they very easily make a step further, and even in things unlawful conclude the motions of their own hearts to be the impulse of the Spirit; and this presently alters the whole complexion of an action that would otherwise look but very scurvily; and makes it absolutely pure and unblamable, or rather perfect and meritorious. So that let a man have but impudence and wickedness enough to libel his Maker, and to entitle the Spirit of God to all that he does or desires, surnaming his own inclinations and appetites (though never so irregular and impure) the Holy Ghost; and you may, upon very sure grounds, turn him loose, and bid him sin if he can. And thus much for the first sort of doctrines, which once believed, like the floodgates of hell pulled up, lets in a deluge and inundation of all sin and vice upon the lives of men. And if this be the natural effect of the doctrines themselves, we can not in all reason but infer, that the interest of the teachers of them must needs be agreeable.

2. The other sort of doctrines tending to engage such as believe them in a sinful course, are such as represent many sins much less, as to their kind or degree, than indeed they are. Of which number is that doctrine, that asserts all sins committed by believers, or persons in a state of grace, to be but infirmities. That there are such things as sins of infirmity, in contradistinction to those of presumption, is a truth not to be questioned; but *in hypothesi*, to state exactly which are sins of infirmity, and which are not, is not so easy a work. This is certain, that there is a vast difference between them; indeed, as vast as between inadvertency and deliberation, between surprise and set purpose: and that persons truly regenerate have sinned this latter way, and consequently may sin so again, is as evident as the story (already referred to by us) of David's murder and adultery: sins acted not only with deliberation, but with artifice, study, and deep contrivance. And can sins, that carry such dismal marks and black symptoms upon them, pass for infirmities? for sins of daily incursion, and such as human frailty, and the very condition of our nature in this world, is so unavoidably liable to, (for so are sins of infirmity,) that *a righteous man may fall into them seven times in a day*; and yet, according to the merciful tenor of the covenant of grace, stand accepted before God as a righteous man still? No, certainly, if such are infirmities, it will be hard to assign what are presumptions. And what a

sin-encouraging doctrine that is, that avouches them for such, is sufficiently manifest from hence; that although every sin of infirmity, in its own nature and according to the strict rigor of the law, merits eternal death, yet it is certain from the gospel, that no man shall actually suffer eternal death barely for sins of infirmity: which being so, persuade but a man that a regenerate person may cheat and lie, steal, murder, and rebel, by way of infirmity, and at the same time you persuade him also that he may do all this without any danger of damnation. And then, since these are oftentimes such desirable privileges to flesh and blood; and since withal, every man by nature is so very prone to think the best of himself and of his own condition; it is odds but he will find a shrewd temptation to believe himself regenerate, rather than forbear a pleasurable or profitable sin, by thinking that he shall go to hell for committing it. Now this being such a direct manuduction to all kind of sin, by abusing the conscience with undervaluing persuasions concerning the malignity and guilt even of the foulest, it is evident that such as teach and promote the belief of such doctrines are to be looked upon as the devil's prophets and apostles; and there is no doubt but the guilt of every sin, that either from pulpit or from press they influence men to the commission of, does as certainly rest upon them, and will one day be as severely exacted of them, as if they had actually and personally committed it themselves.

And thus I have instanced in two notable doctrines, that may justly be looked upon as the general inlets, or two great gates, through which all vice and villainy rush in upon the manners of men professing religion. But the particulars into which these generals diffuse themselves, you may look for and find in those well-furnished magazines and storehouses of all immorality and baseness, the books and writings of some modern casuists; who, like the devil's amanuenses, and secretaries to the prince of darkness, have published to the world such notions and intrigues of sin out of his cabinet, as neither the wit or wickedness of man, upon the bare natural stock either of invention or corruption, could ever have found out.

The writings both of the Old and New Testament make it

very difficult for a man to be saved; but the writings of these men make it more difficult, if not impossible, for any one to be damned: for where there is no sin, there can be no damnation. And as these men have obscured and confounded the natures and properties of things by their false principles and wretched sophistry, though an act be never so sinful, they will be sure to strip it of its guilt; and to make the very law and rule of action so pliable and bending, that it shall be impossible to be broke. So that he who goes to hell must pass through a narrower gate than that which the gospel says leads to heaven. For that, we are told, is only strait, but this is absolutely shut; and so shut that sin can not pass it, and therefore it is much if a sinner should.

So insufferably have these impostors poisoned the fountains of morality, perverted and embased the very standard and distinguishing rule of good and evil. So that all their books and writings are but debauchery upon record, and impiety registered and consigned over to posterity.

In every volume there is a nursery and plantation of vice, where it is sure to thrive, and from thence to be transplanted into men's practice. For here it is manured with art and argument, sheltered with fallacy and distinction, and thereby enabled both to annoy others and to defend itself.

And to show how far the malignity of this way of sinning reaches, he who has vented a pernicious doctrine, or published an ill book, must know that his guilt and his life determine not together: no, such an one, as the apostle says, *being dead, yet speaketh;* he sins in his very grave, corrupts others while he is rotting himself, and has a growing account in the other world after he has paid nature's last debt in this; and, in a word, quits this life like a man carried off by the plague, who, though he dies himself, yet does execution upon others by a surviving infection.

2. Such also are to be reckoned to take pleasure in other men's sins, as endeavor by all means to allure men to sin; and that either by formal persuasion, importunity, or desire, as we find the harlot described, enticing the young man, in Prov. vii. from ver. 13 to 22; or else by administering objects and occasions fit to inflame and draw forth a man's corrupt affections; such as are the drinking of a choleric or revenge-

ful person into a fit of rage and violence against the person of his neighbor; thus heating one man's blood, in order to the shedding of another's. Such also as the provoking of a lustful, incontinent person, by filthy discourse, wanton books and pictures, and, that which equals and exceeds them all, the incentives of the stage; till a man's vice and folly works over all bounds, and grows at length too mad and outrageous to be either governed or concealed.

Now, with great variety of such kind of traders for hell as these has the nation of late years abounded. Wretches who live upon the shark, and other men's sins, the common poisoners of youth, equally desperate in their fortunes and their manners, and getting their very bread by the damnation of souls. So that if any inexperienced young novice happens into the fatal neighborhood of such pests, presently they are upon him, plying his full purse and his empty pate with addresses suitable to his vanity; telling him, what pity it is that one so accomplished for parts and person should smother himself in the country, where he can learn nothing of gallantry or behavior; as, how to make his court, to hector a drawer, to cog the die, or storm a whorehouse; but must of necessity live and die ignorant of what it is to trepan or be trepanned, to sup or rather dine at midnight in a tavern, with the noise of oaths, blasphemies, and fiddlers about his ears, and to fight every watch and constable at his return from thence, and to be beaten by them: but must at length, poor man! die dully of old age at home; when here he might so fashionably and genteelly, long before that time, have been duelled or fluxed into another world.

If this be not the guise and practice of the times, especially as to the principal cities of the kingdom, let any one judge; and whether for such a poor deluded wretch, instead of growing rusty in the country, (as some call it,) to be thus brought by a company of indigent, debauched, soul-and-body-destroying harpies, to lose his estate, family, and virtue, amongst them in the city, be not a much greater violation of the public weal and justice of any government, than most of those crimes that bring the committers of them to the gallows, we may at present easily see, and one day perhaps sadly feel.

Nor is this trade of corrupting the gentry and nobility, and seasoning them with the vices of the great town, as soon as they set foot into it, carried on secretly, and in a corner, but openly, and in the face of the sun; by persons who have formed themselves into companies, or rather corporations. So that a man may as easily know where to find one to teach him to debauch, whore, game, and blaspheme, as to teach him to write or cast accompt: it is their support and business; nay, their very profession and livelihood; getting their living by those practices, for which they deserve to forfeit their lives.

Now these are another sort of men, who are justly charged with the guilt and character of delighting in other men's sins: men, who are the devil's setters; who contrive, study, and beat their brains how to draw in some poor, innocent, unguarded heir into their hellish net, learning his humor, prying into his circumstances, and observing his weak side; and all this to plant the snare and apply the temptation effectually and successfully; and when by such insinuations they have once got within him, and are able to drill him on from one lewdness to another, by the same arts corrupting and squeezing him as they please; no wonder if they rejoice to see him guilty of all sorts of villainy, and take pleasure in those sins in which they find their profit too.

3. Such as affect the company of infamous and vicious persons are also to be reckoned in the number of those who take pleasure in such men's vices. For otherwise, what is there in such men which they can pretend to be pleased with? For generally such sots have neither parts nor wit, ingenuity of discourse, nor fineness of conversation, to entertain or delight any one, that, coming into their company, brings but his reason along with him. But, on the contrary, their rude, impertinent loudness, their quarrels, their nastiness, their dull, obscene talk and ribaldry, (which from them you must take for wit, or go without it,) can not but be very nauseous and offensive to any one who does not balk his own reason, out of love to their vice, and, for the sake of the sin itself, pardon the ugliness of its circumstances: as a father will hug and embrace his beloved son, for all the dirt and foulness of his clothes; the dearness of the person easily apologizing for the disagreeableness of the habit.

One would think it should be no easy matter to bring any man of sense to love an alehouse; indeed of so much sense, as seeing and smelling amounts to; there being such strong encounters of both as would quickly send him packing, did not the love of good fellowship reconcile him to these nuisances, and the deity he adored compound for the homeliness of its shrine.

It is clear therefore, that where a man can like and love the conversation of lewd, debauched persons, amidst all the natural grounds and motives of loathing and dislike, it can proceed from nothing but the inward affection he bears to their lewd, debauched humor. It is this that he enjoys, and, for the sake of this, the rest he endures.

4thly and lastly, Such as encourage, countenance, and support men in their sins, are to be reckoned in the number of those who take pleasure in other men's sins. Now this may be done two ways:

First, By commendation. Concerning which, we may take this for granted; that no man commends another any further than he likes him: for indeed to commend any one, is to vouch him to the world, to undertake for his worth, and, in a word, to own the thing which he is chiefly remarkable for. He who writes an *encomium Neronis*, if he does it heartily, is himself but a transcript of Nero in his mind; and would no doubt gladly enough see such pranks as he was famous for, acted again, though he dares not be the actor of them himself.

From whence we see the reason of some men's giving such honorable names and appellations to the worst of men and actions, and base, reproachful titles to the best: such as are calling faction, and a spitting in their prince's face, *petitioning;* fanaticism and schism, *true Protestantism;* sacrilege and rapine, *thorough reformation*, and the like. As, on the contrary, branding conformity to the rules and rites of the best church in the world with the false and odious name of *formality;* and traducing all religious, conscientious observers of them, as *mongrel Protestants*, and *Papists in masquerade.* And indeed many are and have been called Papists of late years, whom those very persons who call them so know to be far from being so. But what then do they mean by fixing such false characters upon men, even against their own consciences? Why, they mean and design this: they would set such a mark upon those whom they hate, as may cause their throats to be cut, and their estates to be seized upon, when the rabble shall be let loose upon the government once again; which such beggarly, malicious fellows impatiently hope and long for.

Though I doubt not (how much soever knaves may abuse fools with words for a time) but there will come a day, in which the most active Papists will be found under the Puritan mask; in which it will appear, that the conventicle has been the Jesuits' safest kennel, and the Papists themselves, as well as the fanatics, have been managers of all those monstrous outcries against Popery, to the ruin of those Protestants whom they most hate, and whom alone they fear. It being no unheard-of trick for a thief, when he is closely pursued, to cry out, Stop the thief, and thereby diverting the suspicion from himself, to get clear away. It is also worth our while to consider with what terms of respect and commendation knaves and sots will speak of their own fraternity. As, What an honest, what a worthy man is such an one! And, What a good-natured person is another! According to which terms, such as are factious, by *worthy men* mean only such as are of the same faction, and united in the same designs against the government with themselves. And such as are brothers of the pot, by a *good-natured person* mean only a true, trusty debauchee, who never stands out at a merry-meeting, so long as he is able to stand at all; nor ever refuses an health, while he has enough of his own to pledge it with; and, in a word, is as honest as drunkenness and debauchery, want of sense and reason, virtue and sobriety, can possibly make him.

2dly, The other way by which some men encourage others in their sins is, by preferment. As, when men shall be advanced to places of trust and honor for those qualities that render them unworthy of so much as sober and civil company. When a lord or master shall cast his favors and rewards upon such beasts and blemishes of society, as live only to the dishonor of Him who made them, and the reproach of him who maintains them. None certainly can love to see vice in power but such as love to see it also in practice. Place and honor do of all things most misbecome it; and a goat or a swine in a chair of state can not be more odious than ridiculous.

It is reported of Cæsar, that, passing through a certain town, and seeing all the women of it standing at their doors with monkeys in their arms, he asked, whether the women of that country used to have any children or no? thereby wittily and sarcastically reproaching them for misplacing that affection upon brutes, which could only become a mother to her child. So, when we come into a great family or government, and see this place of honor allotted to a murderer, another filled with an atheist or blasphemer, and a third with a filthy parasite, may we not as appositely and properly ask the question, whether there be any such thing as virtue, sobriety, or religion amongst such a people, with whom vice wears those rewards, honors, and privileges, which in other nations the common judgment of reason awards only to the virtuous, the sober, and religious? And certainly it is too flagrant a demonstration, how much vice is the darling of any people, when many amongst them are preferred for those practices for which, in other places, they can scarce be pardoned.

And thus I have finished the third and last general thing proposed, for the handling of the words, which was, to show the several sorts or kinds of men which fall under the charge and character of taking pleasure in other men's sins.

Now the inferences from the foregoing particulars shall be twofold:

1. Such as concern particular persons; and,
2. Such as concern communities, or bodies of men.

And first for the malignity of such a disposition of mind as induces a man to delight in other men's sins, with reference to the effects of it upon particular persons. As,

1. It quite alters and depraves the natural frame of a man's heart: for there is that naturally in the heart of man, which abhors sin, as sin; and consequently would make him detest it, both in himself and in others too. The first and most genuine principles of reason are certainly averse to it, and find a secret grief and remorse from every invasion that sin makes upon a man's innocence; and that must needs render the first entrance and admission of sin uneasy, because dis-

agreeable. Yet time, we see, and custom of sinning, can bring a man to such a pass, that it shall be more difficult and grievous to him to part with his sin, than ever it was to him to admit it. It shall get so far into, and lodge itself so deep within, his heart, that it shall be his business and his recreation, his companion and his other self; and the very dividing between his flesh and his bones, or rather, between his body and his soul, shall be less terrible and afflictive to him than to be took off from his vice.

Nevertheless, as unnatural as this effect of sin is, there is one yet more so: for, that innate principle of self-love, that very easily and often blinds a man, as to any impartial reflection upon himself, yet, for the most part, leaves his eyes open enough to judge truly of the same thing in his neighbor, and to hate that in others which he allows and cherishes in himself. And therefore, when it shall come to this, that he also approves, embraces, and delights in sin, as he observes it even in the person and practice of other men, this shows that the man is wholly transformed from the creature that God first made him; nay, that he has consumed those poor remainders of good that the sin of Adam left him; that he has worn off the very remote dispositions and possibilities to virtue; and, in a word, turned grace first, and afterwards nature itself, out of doors. No man knows, at his first entrance upon any sin, how far it may carry him and where it will stop; the commission of sin being generally like the pouring out of water, which, when once poured out, knows no other bounds but to run as far as it can.

2dly, A second effect of this disposition of mind is, that it peculiarly indisposes a man to repent, and recover himself from it. For the first step to repentance is a man's dislike of his sin: and how can we expect that a man should conceive any thorough dislike of that which has took such an absolute possession of his heart and affections, that he likes and loves it, not only in his own practice, but also in other men's? nay, that he is pleased with it, though he is past the practice of it. Such a temper of mind is a downright contradiction to repentance; as being founded in the destruction of those qualities which are the only dispositions and preparatives to it. For that natural tenderness of conscience, which must first create in the soul a sense of sin, and from thence produce a sorrow for it, and at length cause a relinquishment of it; that, I say, (we have already shown,) is took away by a customary, repeated course of sinning against conscience: so that the very first foundation of virtue, which is the natural power of distinguishing between the moral good and evil of any action, is, in effect, plucked up and destroyed; and the Spirit of God finds nothing in the heart of such an one to apply the means of grace to; all taste, relish, and discernment of the suitableness of virtue, and the unsuitableness of vice, being utterly gone from it.

And as this is a direct bar to that part of repentance which looks back with sorrow and indignation upon what is past, so is it equally such to that greater part of repentance which is to look forward, and to prevent sin for the future. For this properly delivers a man up to sin; forasmuch as it leaves his heart destitute of all those principles which should resist it. So that such an one must be as bad as the devil will have him, and can be no better than the devil will let him. In both he must submit to his measures. And what is this but a kind of entrance into, or rather an anticipation of hell? What is it but judgment and damnation already begun? For a man in such a case is as sure of it as if he were actually in the flames.

3dly, A third effect of this disposition of mind (which also naturally follows from the former) is, that the longer a man lives the wickeder he grows, and his last days are certainly his worst. It has been observed, that to delight in other men's sins was most properly the vice of old age; and we shall also find that it may be as truly and properly called the old age of vice. For, as first, old age necessarily implies a man's having lived so many years before it comes upon him; and withal, this sort of viciousness supposes the precedent commission of many sins, by which a man arrives to it; so it has this further property of old age: that, as when a man comes once to be old, he never retreats, but still goes on, and grows every day older and older; so when a man comes once to such a degree of wickedness as to delight in the wickedness of other men, it is more than ten thousand to one odds, if he ever returns to a better mind, but grows every day worse and worse. For he has nothing else to take up his thoughts, and nothing to entertain his desires with; which, by a long estrangement from better things, come at length perfectly to loathe and fly off from them.

A notable instance of which we have in Tiberius Cæsar, who was bad enough in his youth, but superlatively and monstrously so in his old age: and the reason of this was, because he took a particular pleasure in seeing other men do vile and odious things. So that all his diversion at his beloved Capreæ, was to be a spectator of the devil's actors, representing the worst of vices upon that infamous stage.

And therefore let not men flatter themselves, (as no doubt some do,) that though they find it difficult at present to combat and stand out against an ill practice, and upon that account give way to a continuance in it, yet that old age shall do that for them which they in their youth could never find in their heart to do for themselves; I say, let not such persons mock and abuse themselves with such false and absurd presumptions. For they must know that a habit may continue when it is no longer able to act; or rather the elicit, internal acts of it may be quick and vigorous, when the external, imperate acts of the same habit utterly cease: and let men but reflect upon their own observation, and consider impartially with themselves, how few in the world they have known made better by age. Generally they will see, that such leave not their vice, but their vice leaves them; or rather retreats from their practices, and retires into their fancy; and that, we know, is boundless and infinite: and when vice has once settled itself there, it finds a vaster and a wider compass to act in than ever it had before. I scarce know any thing that calls for a more serious consideration from us than this: for still men are apt to persuade themselves that they shall find it an easy matter to grow virtuous as they grow old. But it is a way of arguing highly irrational and fallacious. For this is a maxim of eternal truth; that nothing grows weak with age but that which will at length die with age, which sin never does. The longer a blot continues, the deeper it sinks. And it will be found a work of no small difficulty to dispossess and throw out a vice from that heart where long possession begins to plead prescription. It is naturally impossible for an old man to grow young again; and it is next to impossible for a decrepit aged sinner to become a new creature, and *be born again.*

4thly and lastly, We need no other argument of the malign effects of this disposition of mind, than this one consideration, that many perish eternally who never arrived to such a pitch of wickedness as to take any pleasure in, or indeed to be at all concerned about, the sins of other men. But they perish in the pursuit of their own lusts, and the obedience they personally yield to their own sinful appetites: and that, questionless, very often not without a considerable mixture of inward dislike of themselves for what they do: yet for all that, their sin, we see, proving too hard for them, the overpowering stream carries them away, and down they sink into the bottomless pit, though under the weight of a guilt by vast degrees inferior to that which we have been discoursing of. For doubtless many men are finally lost, who yet have no men's sins to answer for but their own: who never enticed nor perverted others to sin, and much less applauded or encouraged them in their sin: but only being slaves to their own corrupt affections, have lived and died under the killing power of them, and so passed to a sad eternity.

But that other devilish way of sinning, hitherto spoken of, is so far beyond this, that this is a kind of innocence, or rather a kind of charity, compared to it. For this is a solitary, single, that a complicated, multiplied guilt. And indeed, if we consider at what a rate some men sin nowadays, that man sins charitably who damns nobody but himself. But the other sort of sinners, who may properly enough be said to people hell, and, in a very ill sense, to bear the sins of many; as they have a guilt made up of many guilts, so what can they reasonably expect but a damnation equivalent to many damnations?

And thus much for the first general inference from the foregoing discourse, showing the malignity of such a disposition of mind as induces a man to delight in other men's sins with reference to particular persons.

2dly, The other inference shall be with reference to communities, or bodies of men; and so such a disposition has a most direct and efficacious influence to propagate, multiply, and spread the practice of any sin, till it becomes general and national. For this is most certain, that some men's taking pleasure in other men's sins, will cause many men to sin, to do them a pleasure; and this will appear upon these three accounts. 1. That it is seldom or never that any man comes to such a degree of impiety as to take pleasure in other men's sins, but he also shows the world by his actions and behavior that he does so. 2. That there are few men in the world so inconsiderable, but there are some or other who have an interest to serve by them. And, 3. That the natural course that one man takes to serve his interest by another is, by applying himself to him in such a way as may most gratify and delight him.

Now from these three things put together, it is not only easy, but necessary to infer, that since the generality of men are wholly acted by their present interest, if they find those who can best serve them in this their interest, most likely also to be gained over so to do by the sinful and vile practices of those who address to them; no doubt such practices shall be pursued by such persons, in order to the compassing their desired ends. Where greatness takes no delight in goodness, we may be sure there shall be but little goodness seen in the lives of those who have an interest to serve by such an one's greatness. For take any illustrious, potent sinner, whose power is wholly employed to serve his pleasure, and whose chief pleasure is to see others as bad and wicked as himself; and there is no question but in a little time he will also make them so; and his dependents shall quickly become his proselytes. They shall sacrifice their virtue to his humor, spend their credit and good name, nay, and their very souls too, to serve him; and that by the worst and basest of services, which is, by making themselves like him. It is but too notorious how long vice has reigned, or rather raged amongst us; and with what a bare face and a brazen forehead it walks about the nation, as it were, *elato capite,* and looking down with scorn upon virtue as a contemptible and a mean thing. Vice could not come to this pitch by chance. But we have sinned apace, and at an higher strain of villainy than the fops our ancestors (as some are pleased to call them) could ever arrive to. So that we daily see maturity and age in vice joined with youth and greenness of years; a manifest argument, no doubt, of the great docility and pregnancy of parts, that is, in the present age, above all the former.

For, in respect of vice, nothing is more usual nowadays than for boys *illico nasci senes.* They see their betters delight in ill things; they observe reputation and countenance to attend the practice of them; and this carries them on furiously to that which, of themselves, they are but too much inclined to; and which laws were purposely made by wise men to keep them from. They are glad, you may be sure, to please and prefer themselves at once, and to serve their interest and their sensuality together.

And as they are come to this heght and rampancy of vice, in a great measure, from the countenance of their betters and superiors, so they have took some steps higher in the same from this, That the follies and extravagances of the young too frequently carry with them the suffrage and approbation of the old. For age, which naturally and unavoidably is but one remove from death, and consequently should have nothing about it but what looks like a decent preparation for it, scarce ever appears of late days but in the high mode, the flaunting garb, and utmost gaudery of youth; with clothes as ridiculously, and as much in the fashion, as the person that wears them is usually grown out of it. The eldest equal the youngest in the vanity of their dress, and no other reason can be given of it, but that they equal, if not surpass them in the vanity of their desires. So that those who by the majesty and, as I may so say, the prerogative of their age, should even frown youth into sobriety and better manners, are now striving all they can to imitate and strike in with them, and to be really vicious, that they may be thought to be young.

The sad and apparent truth of which makes it very superfluous to inquire after any further cause of that monstrous increase of vice, that like a torrent, or rather a breaking in of the sea upon us, has of late years overflowed and victoriously carried all before it. Both the honorable and the aged have contributed all they could to the promotion of it; and, so far as they are able, to give the best color to the worst of things. This they have endeavored, and thus much they have effected, that men now see that vice makes them acceptable to those who are able to make them considerable. It is the key that lets them into their very heart, and enables them to command all that is there. And if this be the price of favor, and the market of honor, no doubt where the trade is so quick, and withal so certain, multitudes will be sure to follow it.

This is too manifestly our present case. All men see it; and wise and good men lament it: and where vice, pushed on with such mighty advantages, will stop its progress, it is hard to judge: it is certainly above all human remedies to control the prevailing course of it; unless the great Governor of the world, who quells the rage and swelling of the sea, and sets bars and doors to it, beyond which the proudest of its waves can not pass, shall, in his infinite compassion to us, do the same to that ocean of vice which now swells, and roars, and lifts up itself above all banks and bounds of human laws; and so, by his omnipotent word, reducing its power, and abasing its pride, shall at length say to it, *Hitherto shalt thou come, and no further.* Which God in his good time effect.

To whom be rendered and ascribed, as is most due, all praise, might, majesty, and dominion, both now and for evermore. Amen.

SERMON XIX.

NATURAL RELIGION, WITHOUT REVELATION, SHOWN ONLY SUFFICIENT TO RENDER A SINNER INEXCUSABLE:

IN A SERMON PREACHED BEFORE THE UNIVERSITY, AT CHRIST CHURCH, OXON, NOVEMBER 2, 1690.

ROMANS i. 20. . . . . *So that they are without excuse.*

THIS excellent epistle, though in the front of it it bears a particular inscription, yet, in the drift and purpose of it, is universal; as designing to convince all mankind (whom it supposes in pursuit of true happiness) of the necessity of seeking for it in the Gospel, and the impossibility of finding it elsewhere. All without the church, at that time, were comprehended under the division of Jews and Gentiles, called here by the apostle, Greeks; the nobler and more noted part being used for the whole. Accordingly, from the second chapter, down along, he addresses himself to the Jews, showing the insufficiency of their law to justify, or make them happy, how much soever they doated upon it. But here, in this first chapter, he deals with the Greeks, or Gentiles, who sought for and promised themselves the same happiness from the dictates of right reason, which the Jews did from the Mosaic law. Where, after he had took an account of what their bare reason had taught them in the things of God, and compared the superstructure with the foundation, their practice with their knowledge, he finds them so far from arriving at the happiness which they aspire to by this means, that upon a full survey of the whole matter, the result of all comes to this sad and deplorable issue, that they were sinful and miserable, and that without excuse. In the words, taken with the coherence of the precedent and subsequent verses, we have these four things considerable:

I. The sin here followed upon a certain sort of men, with this so severe a judgment; namely, that *knowing God, they did not glorify him as God*, ver. 21.

II. The persons guilty of this sin; they were *such as professed themselves wise*, ver. 22.

III. The cause or reason of their falling into this sin; which was their *holding the truth in unrighteousness*, ver. 18. And,

IV. and lastly, The judgment, or rather the state and condition, penally consequent upon these sinners; namely, that *they were without excuse*, ver. 20.

Of each of which in their order: and first, for the first of them.

The sin here followed with so severe a judgment, and so highly aggravated and condemned by the apostle, is, by the united testimony of most divines upon this place, the sin of idolatry; which the apostle affirms to consist in this: *That the Gentiles glorified not God, as God.* Which general charge he also draws forth into particulars; as, that they *changed his glory into the similitude and images of men, and beasts, and birds;* where, by glory, he means God's worship, to wit, that by which men glorify him, and not the essential glory of his nature; it being such a glory as was in men's power to change and to debase; and therefore must needs consist, either in those actions, or those means, which they performed the divine worship by. I know no place from which we may more clearly gather what the scripture accounts idolatry, than from this chapter. From whence, that I may represent to you what idolatry is, and wherein one sort of it, at least, does consist, you may observe, that the persons who are here charged with it are positively affirmed to have known and acknowledged the true God. For it is said of them, that they knew his *eternal power and godhead*, in this twentieth verse; nay, and they worshiped him too. From whence this undeniably and invincibly follows, that they did not look upon those images which they addressed to, as gods, nor as things in which the divine nature did or could enclose itself; nor, consequently, to which they gave, or ultimately designed their religious worship. This conclusion therefore I infer, and assert, that idolatry is not only an accounting or worshiping that for God which is not God, but it is also a worshiping the true God in a way wholly unsuitable to his nature; and particularly by the mediation of images and corporeal resemblances of him. This is idolatry: for the persons here spoken of pretended to glorify the true God, but *they did not glorify him as God,* and upon that account stand arraigned for idolaters. Common sense and experience will and must evince the truth of this. For can any one imagine that men of reason, who had their senses quick, and their wits and discourse entire, could take that image or statue, which they fell down before, to be a god? Could they think that to be infinite and immense, the ubiquity of which they could thrust into a corner of their closet? Or, could they conceive that to be eternal, which a few days before they had seen a log, or a rude trunk, and perhaps the other piece of it a joint-stool in the workman's shop?

The ground and reason of all worship is, an opinion of power and will in the person worshiped to answer and supply our desires; which he can not possibly do, unless he first apprehend them. But can any man, who is master of sense himself, believe the rational heathens so void of it, as to think that those images could fulfill the petitions which they could not hear, pity the wants they could not see, do all things when they could not stir an hand or a foot? It is impossible they should; but it is also certain that they were idolaters.

And therefore it is clear that their idolatry consisted in something else, and the history of it would demonstrate so much, were it proper to turn a sermon into a history. So that we see here, that the sin condemned in the text was the worshiping of the true God by images. For the defense of which there is no doubt but they might have pleaded, and did plead for those images, that they used them not as objects, but only as means and instruments of divine worship, not as what they worshiped, but as that by which they directed their worship to God. Though still, methinks it is something hard to conceive, that none of the worship should fall upon the image by the way, or that the water can be conveyed into the sea, without so much as wetting the channel through which it passes. But however, you see it requires a very distinguishing head, and an even hand, and no small skill in directing the intention, to carry a prayer quite through to its journey's end: though, after all, the mischief of it is, that the distinction, which looks so fine in the theory, generally miscarries in the practice; especially where the ignorant vulgar are the practicers, who are the worst in the world at distinguishing, but yet make far the greatest part of mankind, and are as much concerned and obliged to pray as the wisest and the best; but withal, infinitely unhappy, if they can not perform a necessary duty without school-distinctions, nor beg their daily bread without metaphysics. And thus much for the first thing proposed; namely, the sin here spoken against by the apostle in the text; which was idolatry.

2. The second is the persons charged with this sin. And they were not the Gnostics, as some whimsically imagine, who can never meet with the words γινώσκοντες, γινώσκειν, γνῶσις, or γνωστὸν, but presently the Gnostics must be drawn in by the head and shoulders; but the persons here meant were plainly and manifestly the old heathen philosophers; such as not only in the apostle's, but also in their own phrase, *professed themselves to be wise.* Their great title was σοφοὶ, and the word of applause still given to their lectures was σοφῶς. And Pythagoras was the first who abated of the invidiousness of the name, and from σοφὸς brought it down to φιλόσοφος, from a master to a lover of wisdom, from a professor to a candidate.

These were the men here intended by St. Paul; men famous in their respective ages; the great favorites of nature, and the top and masterpiece of art; men whose aspiring intellectuals had raised them above the common level, and made them higher by the head than the world round about them. Men of a polite reason, and a notion refined and enlarged by meditation. Such, as with all these advantages of parts and study, had been toiling and plodding many years, to outwit and deceive themselves; sat up many nights, and spent many days to impose a fallacy upon their reason; and, in a word, ran the round of all the arts and sciences to arrive, at length, at a glorious and elaborate folly; even these, I say, these grandees and giants in knowledge, who thus looked down, as it were, upon the rest of mankind, and laughed at all besides themselves, as barbarous and insignificant, (as quick and sagacious as they were to look into the little intrigues of matter and motion, which a man might *salva scientia*, or at least, *salva anima ignorare*,) yet blundered and stumbled about their grand and principal concern, the knowledge of their duty to God, sinking into the meanest and most ridiculous instances of idolatry; even so far as to worship the great God under the form of *beasts and creeping things;* to adore eternity and immensity in a brute or a plant, or some viler thing; bowing down, in their adoration, to such things as they would scarce otherwise have bowed down to take up. Nay, and to rear temples, and make altars to *fear*, *lust*, and *revenge*; there being scarce a corrupt passion of the mind, or a distemper of the body, but what they worshiped. So that it could not be expected that they should ever repent of those sins which they thought fit to deify, nor mortify those corrupt affections to which they ascribed a kind of divinity and immortality. By all which they fell into a greater absurdity in matter of practice, than ever any one of them did in point of opinion; (which yet certainly was very hard;) namely, that having confessed a God, and allowed him the perfections of a God, to wit, an infinite power and an eternal godhead, they yet denied him the worship of God: thus reversing the great truths they had subscribed to in speculation, by a brutish, senseless devotion, managed with a greater prostration of reason than of body.

Had the poor vulgar rout only, who were held under the prejudices and prepossessions of education, been abused into such idolatrous superstitions as to adore a marble or a golden deity, it might have been detested indeed, or pitied, but not so much to be wondered at: but for the stoa, the academy, or the peripaton to own such a paradox; for an Aristotle or a Plato to think their Νοῦς ἀΐδιος, their eternal mind or universal spirit, to be found in, or served by, the images of four-footed beasts; for the Stagirite to recognize his gods in his own book *de Animalibus*; this, as the apostle says, *was without excuse*: and how will these men answer for their sins, who stand thus condemned for their devotions? And thus, from the persons here charged by the apostle with the sin of idolatry, pass we now to the

3d thing proposed; namely, the cause or reason of their falling into this sin; and that was their holding of the truth in unrighteousness. For the making out of which, we must inquire into these two things:

1. What was the truth here spoken of.
2. How they held it in unrighteousness.

For the first of them; there were these six great truths, the knowledge of which the Gentile philosophers stood accountable for: as,

1. That there was a God; a being distinct from this visible, material world; infinitely perfect, omniscient, omnipotent, eternal, transcendently good and holy. For all this is included in the very notion of a God. And this was a truth wrote with a sunbeam, clear and legible to all mankind, and received by universal consent.

2. That this God was the maker and governor of this visible world. The first of which was evident from the very order of causes; the great argument by which natural reason evinces a God. It being necessary, in such an order or chain of causes, to ascend to, and terminate in, some first: which should be the original of motion, and the cause of all other things, but itself be caused by none. And then, that God also governed the world, this followed from the other; for that a creature should not depend upon its Creator in all respects in which it is capable of depending upon him, (amongst which, to be governed by him, is certainly one,) is contrary to the common order and nature of things, and those essential relations which (by virtue thereof) they bear to one another; and consequently absurd and impossible. So that upon a bare principle of reason, creation must needs infer providence; and God's making the world, irrefragably prove that he governs it too; or that a Being of a dependent nature remains nevertheless independent upon him in that respect. Besides all which, it is also certain that the heathens did actually acknowledge the world governed by a supreme mind; which knowledge, whether they had it from tradition or the discourses of reason, they stood however equally accountable for upon either account.

3dly, That this God, or supreme Being, was to be worshiped. For this was founded upon his omnipotence and his providence. Since he, who would preserve or destroy as he pleased, and withal governed the world, ought surely to be depended upon by those who were thus obnoxious to his power and subject to his government; which dependence could not manifest itself but by acts of worship, homage, and address to the person thus depended upon.

4thly, That this God was to be worshiped, or addressed to, by virtuous and pious practices. For so much his essential holiness required, and those innate notions of *turpe et honestum*, wrote in the consciences of all men, and joined with the apprehensions they had of the infinite purity of the divine nature, could not but suggest.

5thly, That upon any deviation from virtue and piety, it was the duty of every rational creature so deviating, to condemn, renounce, and be sorry for every such deviation: that is, in other words, to repent of it. What indeed the issue or effect of such a repentance might be, bare reason could not of itself discover, but that a peccant creature should disapprove, and repent of every violation of, and declination from, the rules of just and honest, this, right reason, discoursing upon the stock of its own principles, could not but infer. And the conscience of every man, before it is debauched and hardened by habitual sin, will recoil after the doing of an evil action, and acquit him after a good.

6thly and lastly, That every such deviation from duty rendered the person so deviating liable and obnoxious to punishment. I do not say that it made punishment necessary, but that it made the person so transgressing worthy of it; so that it might justly be inflicted on him, and consequently ought rationally to be feared and expected by him. And upon this notion, universally fixed in the minds of men, were grounded all their sacrifices, and rites of expiation, and lustration; the use of which has been so general, both as to times and places, that there is no age or nation of the world in which they have not been used as principal parts of religious worship.

Now these six grand truths were the talent intrusted and deposited by God in the hands of the Gentiles for them to traffic with, to his honor and their own happiness. But what little improvement they made of this noble talent, shall now be shown in the next particular; namely, their holding of it in unrighteousness: which they did several ways. As,

1. By not acting up to what they knew. As in many things their knowledge was short of the truth, so, almost in all things, their practice fell short of their knowledge. The principles by which they walked were as much below those by which they judged as their feet were below their head. By the one they looked upwards, while they placed the other in the dirt. Their writings sufficiently show what raised and sublime notions they had of the divine nature, while they employed their reason about that glorious object, and what excellent discourses of virtue and morality the same reason enabled them to furnish the world with. But when they came to transcribe these theories into practice, one seemed to be of no other use to them at all, but only to reproach them for the other. For they neither depended upon this God as if he were almighty, nor worshiped him as if they believed him holy; but in both prevaricated with their own principles to that degree, that their practice was a direct contradiction to their speculations. For the proof of which, go over all the heathen temples, and take a survey of the absurdities and impieties of their worship, their monstrous sacrifices, their ridiculous rites and ceremonies. In all which, common sense and reason could not but tell them, that the good and gracious God could not be pleased, nor consequently worshiped, with any thing barbarous or cruel; nor the most holy God with any thing filthy and unclean; nor a God infinitely wise with any thing sottish or ridiculous; and yet these were the worthy qualifications of the heathen worship, even amongst their greatest and most reputed philosophers.

And then, for the duties of morality; surely they never wanted so much knowledge as to inform and convince them of the unlawfulness of a man's being a murderer, a hater of God, a covenant-breaker, without natural affection, implacable, unmerciful. These were enormities branded and condemned by the first and most natural verdict of common humanity; and so very gross and foul, that no man could pretend ignorance that they ought to be avoided by him: and yet the apostle tells us, in the last verse of this chapter, that they practiced so much short of their knowledge, even as to these particulars, *That though they knew the judgment of God, that those who committed such things were worthy of death, yet not only did the same themselves, but also had pleasure in those that did them.* Which certainly is the greatest demonstration of a mind wholly possessed and even besotted with the love of vice, that can possibly be imagined. So notoriously did these wretches balk the judgment of their consciences, even in the plainest and most undeniable duties relating to God, their neighbor, and themselves, as if they had owned neither God nor neighbor, but themselves.

2dly, These men held the truth in unrighteousness, by not improving those known principles into the proper consequences deducible from them. For surely had they discoursed rightly but upon this one principle, that God was a being infinitely perfect, they could never have been brought to assert or own a multiplicity of gods. For can one god include in him all perfection, and another god include in him all perfection too? Can there be any more than all? and if this all be in one, can it be also in another? Or, if they allot and parcel out several perfections to several deities, do they not, by this, assert contradictions, making a deity only to such a measure perfect; whereas a deity, as such, implies perfection beyond all measure or limitation? Nor could they, in the next place, have slid into those brutish immoralities of life, had they duly manured those first practical notions and dictates of right reason, which the nature of man is originally furnished with; there being not any one of them but what is naturally productive of many more. But they quickly stifled and overlaid those infant principles, those seeds of piety and virtue sown by God and nature in their own hearts; so that they brought a voluntary darkness and stupidity upon their minds; and, by not *exercising their senses to discern between good and evil,* came at length to lose all sense and discernment of either: whereupon, as the apostle says of them in the 21st verse of this chapter to the Romans, *their foolish heart was darkened:* and that, not only by the just judgment of God, but also by the very course of nature; nothing being more evident from experience than that the not using or employing any faculty or power, either of body or soul, does insensibly weaken and impair that faculty; as a sword by long lying still will contract a rust, which shall not only deface its brightness, but by degrees also consume its very substance. Doing nothing, naturally ends in being nothing.

It holds in all operative principles whatsoever, but especially in such as relate to morality; in which, not to proceed is certainly to go backward; there being no third estate between not advancing and retreating in a virtuous course. Growth is of the very essence and nature of some things. To be and to thrive is all one with them; and they know no middle season between their spring and their fall.

And therefore, as it is said in Matt. xiii. 12, that *from him who hath not, shall be taken away even that which he hath:* so he, who neglects the practice, shall in the end also lose the very power and faculty of doing well. That which stops a man's actual breathing very long, will, in the issue, take away his very power of breathing too. To hide one's talent in the ground is to bury it; and the burial of a thing either finds it dead, or will quickly make it so.

3dly, These men held the truth in unrighteousness by concealing what they knew. For how rightly soever they might conceive of God and of virtue, yet the illiterate multitude, who, in such things, must see with better eyes than their own, or see not at all, were never the wiser for it. Whatsoever the inward sentiments of those sophisters were, they kept them wholly to themselves; hiding all those important truths, all those useful notions from the people, and teaching the world much otherwise from what they judged themselves. Though I think a greater truth than this can not well be uttered; That never any thing or person was really good, which was good only to itself. But from hence it was that, even in a literal sense, sin came to be established by a law. For amongst the Gentiles the laws themselves were the greatest offenders. They made little or no provision for virtue, but very much for vice: for the early and universal practice of sin had turned it into a custom, and custom, especially in sin, quickly passed into common law.

Socrates was the only martyr for the testimony of any truth

that we read of amongst the heathens, who chose rather to be condemned, and to die, than either to renounce or conceal his judgment touching the unity of the Godhead. But as for the rest of them, even Zeno and Chrysippus, Plato and Aristotle, and generally all those heroes in philosophy, they swam with the stream, (as foul as it ran,) leaving the poor vulgar as ignorant and sottish, as vicious and idolatrous, as they first found them.

But it has been always the practice of the governing cheats of all religions, to keep the people in as gross ignorance as possibly they could; for, we see, the heathen impostors used it before the Christian impostors took it up and improved it. *Si populus decipi vult, decipiatur*, was ever a gold and silver rule amongst them all; though the pope's legate first turned it into a benediction: and a very strange one it was, and enough, one would think, to have made all that heard it look about them, and begin to bless themselves. For as Demetrius, a great master in such arts, told his fellow-artists, Acts xix. 25, *it was by this craft that they got their wealth:* so long experience has found it true of the unthinking *mobile ;* that the closer they shut their eyes, the wider they open their hands. But this base trade the church of England always abhorred; and for that cause, as to its temporal advantages, has fared accordingly; and, by this time, may be thought fit for another reformation.

And thus I have shown three notable ways by which the philosophers and learned men amongst the Gentiles held the truth in unrighteousness: as first, That they did not practice up to it; 2dly, That they did not improve it; and 3dly and lastly, That they concealed and dissembled it. And this was that which prepared and disposed them to greater enormities: for, *changing the truth of God into a lie*, they became like those who, by often repeating a lie to others, came at length to believe it themselves. They owned the idolatrous worship of God so long, till, by degrees, even in spite of reason and nature, they thought that he ought so to be worshiped. But this stopped not here: for as one wickedness is naturally a step and introduction to another, so, from absurd and senseless devotions, they passed into vile affections, practicing vices against nature, and that in such strange and abominable instances of sin, that nothing could equal the corruption of their manners but the delusion of their judgments; both of them the true and proper causes of one another.

The consideration of which, one would think, should make men cautious and fearful how they suppress or debauch that spark of natural light which God has set up in their souls. When nature is in the dark, it will venture to do any thing. And God knows how far the spirit of infatuation may prevail upon the heart, when it comes once to court and love a delusion. Some men hug an error, because it gratifies them in a freer enjoyment of their sensuality: and for that reason, God in judgment suffers them to be plunged into fouler and grosser errors, such as even unman and strip them of the very principles of reason and sober discourse. For surely it could be no ordinary declension of nature that could bring some men, after an ingenuous education in arts and philosophy, to place their *summum bonum* upon their trenchers, and their utmost felicity in wine and women, and those lusts and pleasures which a swine or a goat has as full and quick a sense of as the greatest statesmen or the best philosopher in the world.

Yet this was the custom, this the known voice of most of the Gentiles; *Dum vivimus vivamus; Let us eat and drink to-day, for to-morrow we must die.* That soul which God had given them, comprehensive of both worlds, and capable of looking into the great mysteries of nature, of diving into the depths beneath, and of understanding the motions and influences of the stars above; even this glorious, active thing did they confine within the pitiful compass of the present fruition, forbidding it to take a prospect so far as into the morrow; as if to think, to contemplate, or be serious, had been high treason against the empire and prerogative of sense, usurping the throne of their baffled and deposed reason.

And how comes it to pass that even nowadays there is often seen such a vast difference between the former and the latter part of some men's lives? that those who first stepped forth into the world with high and promising abilities, vigorous intellectuals, and clear morals, come at length to grow sots and epicures, mean in their discourses, and dirty in their practices; but that, as by degrees, they remitted of their industry, loathed their business, and gave way to their pleasures, they let fall those generous principles which in their youthful days had borne them upon the wing, and raised them to worthy and great thoughts; which thoughts and principles not being kept up and cherished, but smothered in sensual delights, God, for that cause, suffered them to flag and sink into low and inglorious satisfactions, and to enjoy themselves more in a revel or a merry-meeting, a strumpet or a tavern, than in being useful to a church or a nation, in being a public good to society, and a benefit to mankind. The parts that God gave them they held in unrighteousness, sloth, and sensuality; and this made God to desert and abandon them to themselves; so that they have had a doting and a decrepit reason long before age had given them such a body.

And therefore I could heartily wish that such young persons as hear we now would lodge this one observation deep in their minds; viz., that God and nature have joined wisdom and virtue by such a near cognation, or rather such an inseparable connection, that a wise, a prudent, and an honorable old age is seldom or never found but as the reward and effect of a sober, a virtuous, and a well-spent youth.

4. I descend now to the fourth and last thing proposed; namely, The judgment, or rather the state and condition penally consequent upon the persons here charged by the apostle with idolatry; which is, *That they were without excuse.*

After the commission of sin, it is natural for the sinner to apprehend himself in danger, and, upon such apprehension, to provide for his safety and defense; and that must be one of these two ways: viz., either by pleading his innocence, or by using his power. But since it would be infinitely in vain for a finite power to contend with an infinite, innocence, if any thing, must be his plea; and that must be either by an absolute denial, or, at least, by an extenuation or diminution of his sin. Though indeed this course will be found altogether as absurd as the other could be; it being every whit as irrational for a sinner to plead his innocence before omniscience, as it would be to oppose his power to omnipotence. However, the last refuge of a guilty person is to take shelter under an excuse; and so to mitigate, if he can not divert, the blow. It was the method of the great pattern and parent of all sinners, Adam, first to hide, and then to excuse himself; to wrap the apple in the leaves, and to give his case a gloss at least, though not a defense. But now, when the sinner shall be stripped of this also, have all his excuses blown away, be stabbed with his own arguments, and, as it were, sacrificed upon that very altar which he fled to for succor, this surely is the hight and crisis of a forlorn condition. Yet this was the case of the malefactors who stand here arraigned in the text; this was the consummation of their doom, that they were persons, not only unfit for a pardon, but even for a plea.

Now an excuse, in the nature of it, imports these two things:

1. The supposition of a sin.
2. The extenuation of its guilt.

As for the sin itself, we have already heard what that was, and we will now see how able they are to acquit themselves in point of its extenuation. In which, according to the two grand principles of human actions which determine their morality, the understanding and the will, the excuse must derive either from ignorance or unwillingness.

As for unwillingness, (to speak of this last first,) the heathen philosophers generally asserted the freedom of the will, and its inviolable dominion over its own actions; so that no force or coaction from without could intrench upon the absolute empire of this faculty.

It must be confessed indeed, that it hath been something lamed in this its freedom by original sin; of which defect the heathens themselves were not wholly ignorant, though they were of its cause. So that hereupon, the will is not able to carry a man out to a choice so perfectly, and in all respects good, but that still there is some adherent circumstance of imperfection, which, in strictness of morality, renders every action of it evil; according to that known and most true rule, *Malum ex quolibet defectu.*

Nevertheless, the will has still so much freedom left as to enable it to choose any act in its kind good, whether it be an act of temperance, justice, or the like; as also to refuse any act in its kind evil, whether of intemperance, injustice, or the like; though yet it neither chooses one, nor refuses the other, with such a perfect concurrence of all due ingredients of action, but that still, in the sight of God, judging according to the rigid measures of the law, every such choice or refusal is indeed sinful and imperfect. This is most certain, whatsoever Pelagius and his brethren assert to the contrary.

But however, that measure of freedom which the will still retains, of being able to choose any act materially, and in its kind good, and to refuse the contrary, was enough to cut off all excuse from the heathen, who never duly improved the utmost of such a power, but gave themselves up to all the filthiness and licentiousness of life imaginable. In all which it is certain that they acted willingly and without compulsion, or rather indeed greedily, and without control.

The only persons amongst the heathens who sophisticated nature and philosophy in this particular, were the Stoics; who affirmed a fatal, unchangeable concatenation of causes, reaching even to the elicit acts of man's will. So that according to them there was no act of volition exerted by it, but, all circumstances considered, it was impossible for the will not to exert that volition. But these were but one sect of philosophers; that is, but a handful in comparison of the rest of the Gentiles: ridiculous enough for what they held and taught, and consequently not to be laid in the balance with the united judgment of all other learned men in the world unanimously exploding this opinion. Questionless therefore, a thing so deeply engraven upon the first and most inward notions of man's mind, as a persuasion of the will's freedom, would never permit the heathens (who are here charged by the apostle) to patronize and excuse their sins upon this score, that they committed them against their will, and that they had no power to do otherwise. In which, every hour's experience, and reflection upon the method of their own actings, could not but give them the lie to their face.

The only remaining plea therefore, which these men can take sanctuary in, must be that of ignorance; since there could be no pretense for unwillingness. But the apostle divests them even of this also: for he says expressly, in verse 19, *that what might be known of God*, that famous and so much disputed of τὸ γνωστὸν τοῦ Θεοῦ, was manifested in them; and in verse 21, their inexcusableness is stated upon the supposition of this very thing, *that they knew God*, but, for all that, *did not glorify him as God.* This was the sum of their charge; and how it has been made good against them we have already shown, in what we have spoken about their idolatry, very briefly, I confess, but enough to show its absurdity, though not to account for its variety, when Vossius's very abridgment of it makes a thick volume in folio.

The plea of ignorance therefore is also taken out of their hands; forasmuch as they knew that there was a God; and that this God made and governed the world; and upon that account was to be worshiped and addressed to; and that with such a worship as should be agreeable to his nature, both in respect of the piety and virtue of the worshiper, and also of the means of the worship itself. So that he was neither to be worshiped with impious and immoral practices, nor with corporeal resemblances. For how could an image help men in directing their thoughts to a Being which bore no similitude or cognation to that image at all? And what resemblance could wood or stone bear to a spirit void of all sensible qualities and bodily dimensions? How could they put men in mind of infinite power, wisdom, and holiness, and such other attributes, of which they had not the least mark or character?

But now, if these things could not possibly resemble any perfection of the Deity, what use could they be of to men in their addresses to God? For can a man's devotions be helped by that which brings an error upon his thoughts? And certain it is, that it is natural for a man, by directing his prayers to an image, to suppose the Being he prays to represented by that image. Which how injurious, how contumelious it must needs be to the glorious, incomprehensible nature of God, by begetting such false and low apprehensions of him in the minds of his creature, let common sense, not perverted by interest and design, be judge. From all which it follows, that the idolatrous heathens, and especially the most learned of them, not being able to charge their idolatry either upon ignorance or unwillingness, were wholly *without excuse.* So that it is to be feared that Averroes had not the right way of blessing himself, when, in defiance of Christianity, he wished, *Sit anima mea cum philosophis.*

And now, after all, I can not but take notice, that all that

I have said of the heathen idolatry is so exactly applicable to the idolatry of another sort of men in the world, that one would think this first chapter of the Epistle to the Romans were not so much an address to the ancient Romans, as a description of the modern.

But to draw towards a close. The use and improvement of the foregoing discourse shall be briefly to inform us of these two things:

1st, The signally great and peculiar mercy of God to those to whom he has revealed the gospel, since there was nothing that could have obliged him to it upon the account of his justice: for if there had, the heathens, to whom he revealed it not, could not have been thus *without excuse*, but might very rationally have expostulated the case with their great Judge, and demurred to the equity of the sentence, had they been condemned by him. But it appears from hence, that what was sufficient to render men inexcusable, was not therefore sufficient to save them.

It is not said by the apostle, nor can it be proved by any one else, that God vouchsafed to the heathens the means of salvation, if so be the gospel be the only means of it. And yet I will not, I dare not affirm, that God will save none of those to whom the sound of the gospel never reached: though this is evident, that if he does save any of them, it must not be by that ordinary, stated, appointed method, which the scripture has revealed to us, and which they were wholly ignorant of. For grant that the heathens knew that there was a God, who both made and governed the world, and who, upon that account, was to be worshiped, and that with such a worship as should be suitable to such a Being; yet what principle of mere reason could assure them, that *this God would be a rewarder of such as diligently sought and served him?* For certain it is that there is nothing in the nature of God to oblige him to reward any service of his creature; forasmuch as all that the creature can do is but duty; and even now, at this time, God has no other obligation upon him but his own free promise to reward the piety and obedience of his servants; which promise reason of itself could never have found out, till God made it known by revelation. And moreover, what principle of reason could assure a man that God would pardon sinners upon any terms whatsoever? Possibly it might know that God could do so; but this was no sufficient ground for men to depend upon. And then, last of all, as for the way of his pardoning sinners, that he should do it upon a satisfaction paid to his justice by such a Saviour as should be both God and man; this was utterly impossible for all the reason of mankind to find out.

For that these things could be read in the book of nature, or the common works of God's providence, or be learned by the sun and moon's preaching the gospel, as some have fondly (not to say profanely) enough asserted, it is infinitely sottish to imagine, and can indeed be nothing else but the turning the grace of God into wanton and unreasonable propositions.

It is clear therefore, that the heathens had no knowledge of that way by which alone we expect salvation. So that all the hope which we can have for them is, that the gospel may not be the utmost limit of the divine mercy; but that the merits of Christ may overflow, and run over the pale of the church, so as to reach even many of those who lived and died invincibly ignorant of him.

But whether this shall be so, or no, God alone knows, who only is privy to the great counsels of his own will. It is a secret hid from us; and therefore, though we may hope compassionately, yet I am sure we can pronounce nothing certainly: it is enough for us that God has asserted his justice, even in his dealing with those whom he treats not upon terms of evangelical mercy. So that such persons can neither excuse themselves, nor yet accuse him; who, in the severest sentence that he can pronounce upon the sinner, will (as the Psalmist tells us) *be justified when he speaks, and clear when he is judged.*

2dly, In the next place, we gather hence the unspeakably wretched and deplorable condition of obstinate sinners under the gospel. The sun of mercy has shined too long and too bright upon such, to leave them any shadow of excuse. For, let them argue over all the topics of divine goodness and human weakness, and whatsoever other pretenses poor sinking sinners are apt to catch at, to support and save themselves by, yet how trifling must be their plea! how impertinent their defense!

For admit an impenitent heathen to plead, that, albeit his conscience told him that he had sinned, yet it could not tell him that there was any provision of mercy for him upon his repentance. He knew not whether amendment of life would be accepted, after the law was once broke; or that there was any other righteousness to atone or merit for him, but his own.

But no Christian, who has been taken into the arms of a better covenant, and grown up in the knowledge of a Saviour, and the doctrine of faith and repentance from dead works, can speak so much as one plausible word for his impenitence. And therefore it was said of him who came to the *marriage-feast without a wedding-garment*, that, being charged, and apprehended for it, ἐφιμώθη, *he was speechless*, struck with shame and silence, the proper effects of an overpowering guilt, too manifest to be denied, and too gross to be defended. His reason deserted, and his voice failed him, finding himself arraigned, convicted, and condemned in the court of his own conscience.

So that if, after all this, his great Judge had freely asked him what he could allege or say for himself, why he should not have judgment to die eternally, and sentence to be awarded according to the utmost rigors of the law, he could not, in this forlorn case, have made use of the very last plea of a cast criminal: nor so much as have cried, *Mercy, Lord, mercy*. For still his conscience would have replied upon him, that mercy had been offered and abused; and that the time of mercy was now past. And so, under this overwhelming conviction, every gospel-sinner must pass to his eternal execution, taking the whole load of his own damnation solely and entirely upon himself, and acquitting the most just God, *who is righteous in all his works, and holy in all his ways.*

To whom, therefore, be rendered and ascribed, as is most due, all praise, might, majesty, and dominion, both now and for evermore. Amen.

SERMON XX.

SACRAMENTAL PREPARATION:

SET FORTH IN A SERMON PREACHED AT WESTMINSTER ABBEY,

APRIL 8, 1688; BEING PALM SUNDAY.

MATTHEW xxii. 12. — *And he saith unto him, Friend, how camest thou in hither, not having a wedding-garment?*

THE whole scheme of these words is figurative, as being a parabolical description of God's vouchsafing to the world the invaluable blessing of the gospel, by the similitude of a king, with great magnificence, solemnizing his son's marriage, and with equal bounty bidding and inviting all about him to that royal solemnity; together with his severe animadversion, both upon those who would not come, and upon one who did come in a very unbeseeming manner.

For the better understanding of which words, we must observe, that in all parables two things are to be considered:

First, The scope and design of the parable; and,

Secondly, The circumstantial passages, serving only to complete and make up the narration.

Accordingly, in our application of any parable to the thing designed and set forth by it, we must not look for an absolute and exact correspondence of all the circumstantial or subservient passages of the metaphorical part of it, with just so many of the same or the like passages in the thing intended by it; but it is sufficient that there be a certain analogy or agreement between them, as to the principal scope and design of both.

As for the design of this parable, it is, no doubt, to set

forth the free offer of the gospel, with all its rich privileges, to the Jewish church and nation, in the first place; and upon their refusal of it, and God's rejection of them for that refusal, to declare the calling of the Gentiles in their room, by a free, unlimited tender of the gospel to all nations whatsoever; adding withal a very dreadful and severe sentence upon those who, being so freely invited and so generously admitted to such high and undeserved privileges, should nevertheless abuse and despise them by an unworthy, wicked, and ungrateful deportment under them.

For men must not think that the gospel is all made up of privilege and promise, but that there is something of duty to be performed, as well as of privilege to be enjoyed. No welcome to a wedding-supper without a wedding-garment; and no coming by a wedding-garment for nothing. In all the transactions between God and the souls of men, something is expected on both sides; there being a fixed, indissoluble, and (in the language of the parable) a kind of marriage-tie between duty and privilege, which renders them inseparable.

Now, though I question not but that this parable of the wedding-supper comprehends in it the whole complex of all the blessings and privileges exhibited by the gospel, yet I conceive that there is one principal privilege amongst all the rest, that it seems more peculiarly to aim at, or at least may more appositely and emphatically be applied to, than to any other whatsoever: and that is the blessed sacrament of the eucharist, by which all the benefits of the gospel are in a higher, fuller, and more divine manner conveyed to the faithful, than by any other duty or privilege belonging to our excellent religion. And for this I shall offer these three following reasons:

1. Because the foundation of all parables is, as we have shown, some analogy or similitude between the tropical or allusive part of the parable, and the thing couched under it and intended by it. But now, of all the benefits, privileges, or ordinances of the gospel, which of them is there that carries so natural a resemblance to a wedding-supper as that which every one of a very ordinary, discerning faculty may observe in the sacrament of the eucharist? For, surely, nei-

ther the preaching of the word, nor yet the sacrament of baptism, bears any such resemblance or affinity to it. But, on the other side, this sacrament of the eucharist so lively resembles, and so happily falls in with it, that it is indeed itself a supper, and is called a supper, and that by a genuine, proper, as well as a common and received appellation.

2. This sacrament is not only with great propriety of speech called a supper, but moreover, as it is the grand and prime means of the nearest and most intimate union and conjunction of the soul with Christ, it may, with a peculiar significancy, be called also a *wedding-supper*. And as Christ frequently in scripture owns himself related to the church as a husband to a spouse, so, if these nuptial endearments, by which Christ gives himself to the soul, and the soul mutually gives itself to Christ, pass between Christ and believers in any ordinance of the gospel, doubtless it is most eminently and effectually in this: which is another pregnant instance of the notable resemblance between this divine sacrament and the wedding-supper in the parable, and consequently a further argument of the elegant and expressive signification of one by the other.

3dly and lastly, The very manner of celebrating this sacrament, which is by the breaking of bread, was the way and manner of transacting marriages in some of the eastern countries. Thus Q. Curtius reports, that when Alexander the Great married the Persian Roxana, the ceremony they used was no other but this; *panem gladio divisum uterque libabat;* he divided a piece of bread with his sword, of which each of them took a part, and so thereby the nuptial rites were performed. Besides, that this ceremony of feasting belongs most properly both to marriage and to the eucharist, as both of them have the nature of a covenant. And all covenants were, in old times, solemnized and accompanied with festival eating and drinking; the persons newly confederate always thereupon feasting together in token of their full and perfect accord, both as to interest and affection.

And now these three considerations together, so exactly suiting the parable of the wedding-supper to this spiritual, divine banquet of the gospel, if it does not primarily, and in its first design, intend it, yet certainly it may with greater advantage of resemblance be applied to it than to any other duty or privilege belonging to Christianity.

Upon the warrant of which so very particular and extraordinary a cognation between them, I shall at present treat of the words wholly with reference to this sacred and divine solemnity, observing and gathering from them, as they lie in coherence with the foregoing and following parts of the parable, these two propositions:

1. That to a worthy participation of the holy mysteries and great privileges of the gospel, and particularly that of the Lord's supper, there is indispensably required a suitable preparation.

2. That God is a strict observer of, and a severe animadverter upon, such as presume to partake of those mysteries without such a preparation.

And first, for the first of these; viz. That to a worthy participation of the holy mysteries, &c.

Now this proposition imports in it two things:

1. That to a right discharge of this duty a preparation is necessary.

2. That every preparation is not sufficient. And first, for the

First of these: That a preparation is necessary. And this, I confess, is a subject which I am heartily sorry that any preacher should find it needful to speak so much as one word upon. For would any man in his wits venture to die without preparation? And if not, let me tell you that nothing less than that which will fit a man for death, can fit him for the sacrament. The truth is, there is nothing great or considerable in the world, which ought to be done, or ventured upon, without preparation; but, above all, how dangerous, sottish, and irrational is it, to engage in any thing or action extempore, where the concern is eternity!

None but the careless and the confident (and few are confident but what are first careless) would rush rudely into the presence of a great man: and shall we, in our applications to the great God, take that to be religion which the common reason of mankind will not allow to be manners? The very rules of worldly civility might instruct men how to order their addresses to God. For who, that is to appear before his prince or patron, would not view and review himself over and over, with all imaginable care and solicitude, that there be nothing justly offensive in his habit, language, or behavior? But especially, if he be vouchsafed the honor of his table, it would be infinitely more absurd and shameful to appear foul and sordid there, and in the dress of the kitchen receive the entertainments of the parlor.

What previous cleansings and consecrations, and what peculiar vestments were the priests, under the law, enjoined to use, when they were to appear before God in the sanctuary! And all this upon no less a penalty than death. This and this they were to do, lest they died, lest God should strike them dead upon the spot; as we read in Levit. viii. 35, and in many other places in the books of Moses. And so exact were the Jews in their preparations for the solemn times of God's worship, that every σάββατον had its προσάββατον or παρασκευὴ, that is, a part of the sixth day, from the hour of six in the evening, to fit them for the duties of the seventh day: nor was this all; but they had also a προπαρασκευὴ, beginning about three in the afternoon, to prepare them for that: and indeed the whole day was, in a manner, but preparative to the next; several works being disallowed and forborne amongst them on that day, which were not so upon any of the foregoing five: so careful, even to scrupulosity, were they to keep their sabbath with due reverence and devotion, that they must not only have a time to prepare them for that, but a further time also to prepare them for their very preparations.

Nay, and the heathens, (many of them at least,) when they were to sacrifice to their greatest and most revered deities, used, on the evening before, to have a certain preparative rite or ceremony, called by them *cœna pura;* that is, a supper, consisting of some peculiar meats, in which they imagined a kind of holiness; and by eating of which they thought themselves sanctified, and fitted to officiate about the mysteries of the ensuing festival. And what were all their lustrations but so many solemn purifyings, to render both themselves and their sacrifices acceptable to their gods?

So that we see here a concurrence both of the Jews and heathens in this practice, before Christianity ever appeared: which to me is a kind of demonstration that the necessity of men's preparing themselves for the sacred offices of religion was a lesson which the mere light and dictates of common reason, without the help of revelation, taught all the knowing and intelligent part of the world.

I will wash my hands in innocency, says David, *and so will I compass thine altar,* Psalm xxvi. 6. And as the apostle told the Hebrews, Heb. xiii. 10, *We also,* we Christians, *have an altar* as well as they; an altar as sacred, an altar to be approached with as much awe and reverence; and though there be no fire, upon it, yet there is a dreadful one that follows it; a fire, that does not indeed consume the offering, but such an one as will be sure to seize and prey upon the unworthy offerer. *I will be sanctified,* says God, *in them that come nigh me,* Levit. x. 3. And God then accounts himself sanctified in such persons, when they sanctify themselves. Nadab and Abihu were a dreadful exposition of this text.

And for what concerns ourselves; he that shall thoroughly consider what the heart of man is, what sin and the world is, and what it is to approve one's self to an all-searching eye, in so sublime a duty as the sacrament, must acknowledge that a man may as well go about it without a soul, as without preparation.

For the holiest man living, by conversing with the world, insensibly draws something of soil and taint from it: the very air and mien, the way and business of the world, still, as it were, rubbing something upon the soul, which must be fetched off again, before it can be able heartily to converse with God. Many secret indispositions, coldnesses, and aversions to duty will undiscernibly steal upon it; and it will require both time and close application of mind to recover it to such a frame as shall dispose and fit it for the spiritualities of religion.

And such as have made trial find it neither so easy nor so ready a passage from the noise, the din, and hurry of business to the retirements of devotion, from the exchange to the closet, and from the freedoms of conversation to the recollections and disciplines of the spirit.

The Jews, as soon as they came from markets, or any other such promiscuous resorts, would be sure to use accurate and more than ordinary washings. And had their washings soaked through the body into the soul, and had not their inside reproached their outside, I see nothing in this custom but what was allowable enough, and (in a people which needed washing so much) very commendable. Nevertheless, whatsoever it might have in it peculiar to the genius of that nation, the spiritual use and improvement of it, I am sure, may very well reach the best of us. So that if the Jews thought this practice requisite before they sat down to their own tables, let us Christians think it absolutely necessary, when we come to God's table, not to eat till we have washed. And when I have said so, I suppose I need not add, that our washing is to be like our eating, both of them spiritual; that we are to carry it from the hand to the heart, to improve a ceremonial nicety into a substantial duty, and the modes of civility into the realities of religion.

And thus much for the first thing, that a preparation in general is necessary. But then, 2dly, the other thing imported in the proposition is, That every preparation is not sufficient. It must be a suitable preparation; none but a wedding-garment will serve the turn; a garment as much fitted to the solemnity as to the body itself that wears it.

Now all fitness lies in a particular commensuration, or proportion of one thing to another; and that such an one as is founded in the very nature of things themselves, and not in the opinions of men concerning them. And for this cause it is that the soul, no less than the body, must have its several distinct postures and dispositions, fitting it for several distinct offices and performances. And as no man comes with folded arms to fight or wrestle, nor prepares himself for the battle as he would compose himself to sleep, so, upon a true estimate of things, it will be found every whit as absurd and irrational for a man to discharge the most extraordinary duty of his religion at the rate of an ordinary devotion. For this is really a paradox in practice, and men may sometimes do, as well as speak, contradictions.

There is a great festival now drawing on; a festival designed chiefly for the acts of a joyful piety, but generally made only an occasion of bravery. I shall say no more of it at present, but this; that God expects from men something more than ordinary at such times, and that it were much to be wished, for the credit of their religion, as well as the satisfaction of their consciences, that their Easter devotions would, in some measure come up to their Easter dress.

Now that our preparation may answer the important work and duty which we are to engage in, these two conditions, or qualifications, are required in it.

1. That it be habitual.
2. That it be also actual.

For it is certain that there may both be acts which proceed not from any preëxisting habits; and, on the other side, habits which lie for a time dormant, and do not at all exert themselves in action. But in the case now before us, there must be a conjunction of both; and one without the other can never be effectual for that purpose for which both together are but sufficient. And,

First, For habitual preparation. This consists in a standing, permanent habit, or principle of holiness, wrought chiefly by God's Spirit, and instrumentally by his word, in the heart or soul of man: such a principle as is called, both by our Saviour and his apostles, the *new birth*, the *new man*, the *immortal seed*, and the like; and by which a man is so universally changed and transformed in the whole frame and temper of his soul, as to have a new judgment and sense of things, new desires, new appetites and inclinations.

And this is first produced in him by that mighty spiritual change which we call conversion: which, being so rarely and seldom found in the hearts of men, (even where it is most pretended to,) is but too full and sad a demonstration of the truth of that terrible saying, *That few are chosen*, and consequently, *but few saved*. For who almost is there, of whom we can with any rational assurance, or perhaps so much as likelihood, affirm, Here is a man, whose nature is renewed, whose heart is changed, and the stream of whose appetites is so turned, that he does with as high and quick a relish taste the ways of duty, holiness, and strict living, as others, or as he himself before this, grasped at the most enamoring proposals of sin; who almost, I say, is there, who can reach and verify the hight of this character? and yet, without which, the scripture absolutely affirms, *that a man cannot see the kingdom of God*, John iii. 3. For, let preachers say and suggest what they will, men will do as they use to do; and custom generally is too hard for conscience, in spite of all its convictions. Possibly sometimes in hearing or reading the word, the conscience may be alarmed, the affections warmed, good desires begin to kindle, and to form themselves into some degrees of resolution; but the heart remaining all the time unchanged, as soon as men slide into the common course and converse of the world, all those resolutions and convictions quickly cool and languish, and after a few days are dismissed as troublesome companions. But assuredly no man was ever made a true convert, or a new creature, at so easy a rate; sin was never dispossessed, nor holiness introduced, by such feeble, vanishing impressions. Nothing under a total, thorough change will suffice; neither tears, nor trouble of mind, neither good desires nor intentions, nor yet the relinquishment of some sins, nor the performance of some good works will avail any thing, *but a new creature:* a word that comprehends more in it than words can well express; and perhaps, after all that can be said of it, never thoroughly to be understood by what a man hears from others, but by what he must feel within himself.

And now, that this is required as the groundwork of all our preparations for the sacrament, is evident from hence: because this sacrament is not first designed to make us holy, but rather supposes us to be so; it is not a converting, but a confirming ordinance: it is properly our spiritual food. And, as all food presupposes a principle of life in him who receives it, which life is, by this means, to be continued and supported, so the sacrament of the Lord's supper is originally intended to preserve and maintain that spiritual life which we do or should receive in baptism, or at least by a thorough conversion after it. Upon which account, according to the true nature and intent of this sacrament, men should not expect life, but growth from it: and see that there be something to be fed, before they seek out for provision. For the truth is, for any one who is not passed from death to life, and has not in him that new living principle which we have been hitherto speaking of, to come to this spiritual repast, is upon the matter as absurd and preposterous as if he who makes a feast should send to the graves and the churchyards for guests, or entertain and treat a corpse at a banquet.

Let men therefore consider, before they come hither, whether they havè any thing besides the name they received in baptism to prove their Christianity by. Let them consider whether, as by their baptism they formerly washed away their original guilt, so they have not since, by their actual sins, washed away their baptism. And, if so, whether the converting grace of God has set them upon their legs again, by forming in them a new nature. And that such an one as exerts and shows itself by the sure, infallible effects of a good life: such an one, as enables them to reject and trample upon all the alluring offers of the world, the flesh, and the devil, so as not to be conquered or enslaved by them; and to choose the hard and rugged paths of duty, rather than the easy and voluptuous ways of sin: which every Christian, by the very nature of his religion, as well as by his baptismal vow, is strictly obliged to do: and if, upon an impartial survey of themselves, men find that no such change has passed upon them, either let them prove that they may be Christians upon easier terms, or have a care how they intrude upon so great and holy an ordinance, in which God is so seldom mocked but it is to the mocker's confusion. And thus much for habitual preparation. But,

2dly, Over and above this, there is required also an actual preparation; which is, as it were, the furbishing or rubbing up of the former habitual principle.

We have both of them excellently described in Matt. xxv. in the parable of the ten virgins; of which the *five wise* are said to have had *oil in their lamps;* yet, notwithstanding that, midnight and weariness was too hard for them, and they all slumbered and slept, and their lamps cast but a dim and a feeble light till the bridegroom's approach; but then, upon the first alarm of that, they quickly *rose, and trimmed their lamps,* and without either trimming or painting themselves, (being as much too wise as some should be too old for such follies,) they presently put themselves into a readiness to receive their surprising guest. Where, by their *having oil in their lamps,* no doubt, must be understood a principle of grace infused into their hearts, or the new nature formed within them; and, by their *trimming their lamps,* must be meant their actual exercise and improvement of that standing principle, in the particular instances of duty suitable and appropriate to the grand solemnity of the bridegroom's reception. In like manner, when a man comes to this sacrament, it is not enough that he has an habitual stock of grace, that he has the immortal seed of a living faith sown in his heart. This indeed is necessary, but not sufficient; his faith must be, not only living, but lively too; it must be brightened and stirred up, and, as it were, put into a posture by a particular exercise of those several virtues that are specifically requisite to a due performance of this duty: habitual grace is the life, and actual grace the beauty and ornament of the soul; and therefore, let people in this high and great concern be but so just to their souls as, in one much less, they never fail to be to their bodies; in which the greatest advantages of natural beauty make none think the further advantage of a decent dress superfluous.

Nor is it at all strange, if we look into the reason of things, that a man habitually good and pious should, at some certain turns and times of his life, be at a loss how to exert the highest acts of that habitual principle. For no creature is perfect and pure in act; especially a creature so compounded of soul and body, that body seems much the stronger part in the composition.

Common experience shows that the wisest of men are not always fit and disposed to act wisely, nor the most admired speakers to speak eloquently and exactly. They have indeed an acquired, standing ability of wisdom and eloquence within them, which gives them an habitual sufficiency for such performances. But, for all that, if the deepest statesman should presume to go to council immediately from his cups, or the ablest preacher think himself fitted to preach, only by stepping up to the pulpit, notwithstanding the policy of the one, and the eloquence of the other, they may chance to get the just character of bold fools for venturing, whatsoever good fortune may bring them off.

And therefore the most active powers and faculties of the mind require something besides themselves, to raise them to the full hight of their natural activity; something to excite and quicken, and draw them forth into immediate action. And this holds proportionably in all things, animate or inanimate, in the world. The bare nature and essential form of fire will enable it to burn; but there must be an enlivening breath of air besides, to make it flame. A man has the same strength, sleeping and waking; but while he sleeps, it fits him no more for business than if he had none. Nor is it the having of wheels and springs, though never so curiously wrought and artificially set, but the winding of them up, that must give motion to the watch. And it would be endless to illustrate this subject by all the various instances that art and nature could supply us with.

But the case is much the same in spirituals: for grace in the soul, while the soul is in the body, will always have the ill neighborhood of some remainders of corruption; which, though they do not conquer and extinguish, yet will be sure to slacken and allay the vigor and briskness of the renewed principle; so that when this principle is to engage in any great duty, it will need the actual intention, the particular stress and application of the whole soul, to disencumber and set it free, to scour off its rust, and remove those hinderances which would otherwise clog and check the freedom of its operations.

And thus having shown, that to fit us for a due access to the holy sacrament, we must add actual preparation to habitual, I shall now endeavor to show the several parts or ingredients of which this actual preparation must consist.

And here I shall not pretend to give an account of every particular duty that may be useful for this purpose, but shall only mention some of the principal, and such as may most peculiarly contribute towards it: as,

First, Let a man apply himself to the great and difficult work of self-examination by a strict scrutiny into, and survey of, the whole estate of his soul, according to that known and excellent rule of the apostle, in the very case now before us, 1 Cor. xi. 28, *Let a man examine himself, and so let him eat of that bread*, &c. If a man would have such a wedding-garment as may fit him exactly, let self-examination take the measure, a duty of so mighty an influence upon all that concerns the soul, that it is indeed the very root and groundwork of all true repentance, and the necessary antecedent, if not also the direct cause, of a sinner's return to God.

For, as there are some sins which require a particular and distinct repentance by themselves, and can not be accounted for in the general heap of sins known and unknown, so, how is it possible for a man to repent rightly of such sins, unless, by a thorough search into the nature, number, and distinguishing circumstances of them, he comes to see how, and in what degree, they are to be repented of?

But the sovereign excellency and necessity of this duty needs no other nor greater proof of it, than this one consideration, That nothing in nature can be more grievous and offensive to a sinner than to look into himself; and generally what grace requires, nature is most averse to. It is indeed as offensive as to rake into a dunghill; as grievous, as for one to read over his debts, when he is not able to pay them; or for a bankrupt to examine and look into his accounts, which at the same time that they acquaint, must needs also upbraid him with his condition.

But as irksome as the work is, it is absolutely necessary. Nothing can well be imagined more painful than to pròbe and search a purulent old sore to the bottom; but for all that the pain must be endured, or no cure expected. And men certainly have sunk their reason to the very gross, low, and absurd conceptions of God, when in the matter of sin they can make such false and short reckonings with him and their own hearts; for can they imagine that God has therefore forgot their sins, because they are not willing to remember them? or will they measure his pardon by their own oblivion? What pitiful fig-leaves, what senseless and ridiculous shifts are these, not able to silence, and much less satisfy, an accusing conscience!

But now for the better management of this examination of our past lives, we must thoroughly canvass them with these and the like questions.

As for instance; let a man inquire what sins he has committed, and what breaches he has made upon those two great standing rules of duty, the decalogue, and our Saviour's divine sermon upon the mount. Let him inquire also what particular aggravations lie upon his sins; as, whether they have not been committed against strong reluctancy and light of conscience? after many winning calls of mercy to reclaim, and many terrible warnings of judgment to affright him? Whether resolutions, vows, and protestations have not been made against them? Whether they have not been repeated frequently, and persisted in obstinately? And lastly, whether the same appetites to sin have not remained as active and unmortified after sacraments, as ever they had been before?

How important these considerations and heads of inquiry are, all who understand any thing will easily perceive. For this we must know, that the very same sin, as to the nature of it, stamped with any one of these aggravations, is, in effect, not the same. And he who has sinned the same great sin, after several times receiving the sacrament, must not think that God will accept him under ten times greater repentance and contrition for it than he brought with him to that duty formerly. Whether God, by his grace, will enable him to rise up to such a pitch, or no, is uncertain; but most certain, that both his work is harder, and his danger greater, than it was or could be at the first.

Secondly, When a man has, by such a close and rigorous examination of himself, found out the *accursed thing*, and discovered his sin, the next thing in order must be, to work up his heart to the utmost hatred of it, and the bitterest sorrow and remorse for it. For self-examination having first presented it to the thoughts, these naturally transmit and hand it over to the passions. And this introduces the next ingredient of our sacramental preparations, to wit, repentance. Which arduous work I will suppose not now to begin, but to be renewed; and that with special reference to sins not repented of before; and yet more especially to those new scores which we still run ourselves upon since the last preceding sacrament. Which method, faithfully and constantly observed, must needs have an admirable and mighty effect upon the conscience, and keep a man from breaking, or running behindhand in his spiritual estate, which, without frequent accountings, he will hardly be able to prevent.

But, because this is a duty of such high consequence, I would by all means warn men of one very common, and yet very dangerous mistake about it; and that is, the taking of mere sorrow for sin for repentance. It is indeed a good introduction to it; but the porch, though never so fair and spacious, is not the house itself. Nothing passes in the accounts of God for repentance, but change of life: ceasing to do evil, and doing good, are the two great integral parts that complete this duty. For not to do evil is much better than the sharpest sorrow for having done it; and to do good is better and more valuable than both.

When a man has found out sin in his actions, let him resolutely arrest it there; but let him also pursue it home to his inclinations, and dislodge it thence; otherwise it will be all to little purpose; for the root being still left behind, it is odds but in time it will shoot out again.

Men befool themselves infinitely, when, by venting a few sighs or groans, putting the finger in the eye, and whimpering out a few melancholy words; and lastly, concluding all with, "I wish I had never done so, and I am resolved never to do so more;" they will needs persuade themselves that they have repented; though perhaps in this very thing their heart all the while deceives them, and they neither really wish the one nor resolve the other.

But whether they do or no, all true penitential sorrow will and must proceed much further. It must force and make its way into the very inmost corners and recesses of the soul; it must shake all the powers of sin, producing in the heart strong and lasting aversions to evil, and equal dispositions to good, which, I must confess, are great things; but if the sorrow which we have been speaking of carry us not so far, let it express itself never so loudly and passionately, and discharge itself in never so many showers of tears and volleys of sighs, yet by all this it will no more purge a man's heart than the washing of his hands can cleanse the rottenness of his bones. But,

Thirdly, When self-examination has both shown us our sin, and repentance has disowned and cast it out, the next thing naturally consequent upon this is, with the highest importunity to supplicate God's pardon for the guilt, and his grace against the power of it. And this brings in prayer as the third preparative for the sacrament: a duty, upon which all the blessings of both worlds are entailed; a duty, appointed by God himself as the great conduit and noble instrument of commerce between heaven and earth; a duty, founded on man's essential dependence upon God ; and so, in the ground and reason of it, perpetual, and consequently in the practice of it indispensable.

But I shall speak of it now only with reference to the sacrament. And so, whatsoever other graces may furnish us with a wedding-garment, it is certain that prayer must put it on. Prayer is that by which a man engages all the auxiliaries of omnipotence itself against his sin ; and is so utterly contrary to and inconsistent with it, that the same heart can not long hold them both, but one must soon quit possession of it to the other ; and either praying make a man leave off sinning, or sinning force him to give over praying.

Every real act of hatred of sin is, in the very nature of the thing, a partial mortification of it ; and it is hardly possible for a man to pray heartily against his sin, but he must at the same time hate it too. I know a man may think that he hates his sin when indeed he does not ; but then it is also as true that he does not sincerely pray against it, whatsoever he may imagine.

Besides, since the very life and spirit of prayer consists in an ardent, vehement desire of the thing prayed for, and since the nature of the soul is such that it strangely symbolizes with the thing it mightily desires, it is evident, that if a man would have a devout, humble, sin-abhorring, self-denying frame of spirit, he can not take a more efficacious course to attain it than by praying himself into it. And so close a connection has this duty with the sacrament, that whatsoever we receive in the sacrament is properly in answer to our prayers. And consequently we may with great assurance conclude, that he who is not frequently upon his knees before he comes to that holy table, kneels to very little purpose when he is there. But then,

Fourthly, Because prayer is not only one of the highest and hardest duties in itself, but ought to be more than ordinarily fervent and vigorous before the sacrament, let the body be also called in as an assistant to the soul, and abstinence and fasting added to promote and highten her devotions. Prayer is a kind of wrestling with God ; and he who would win the prize at that exercise, must be severely dieted for that purpose.

The truth is, fasting was ever acknowledged by the church, in all ages, as a singular instrument of religion, and a particular preparative to the sacrament. And hardly was there ever any thing great or heroic either done or attempted in religion without it. Thus, when Moses received the law from God, it was with fasting, Deut. ix. 9. When Christ entered upon the great office of his mediatorship, it was with fasting, Matt. iv. 2. And when Paul and Barnabas were separated to that high and difficult charge of preaching to the Gentiles, Acts xiii. 2, still it was managed with fasting. And we know the rubric of our own church always, almost, enjoins a fast to prepare us for a festival.

Bodily abstinence is certainly a great help to the spirit; and the experience of all wise and good men has ever found it so. The ways of nature and the methods of grace are vastly different. Good men themselves are never so surprised as in the midst of their jollities; nor so fatally overtaken and caught as when their *table is made the snare.* Even our first parents ate themselves out of paradise; and Job's children junketed and feasted together often, but the reckoning cost them dear at last. *The heart of the wise,* says Solomon, *is in the house of mourning;* and the house of fasting adjoins to it.

In a word, fasting is the diet of angels, the food and refection of souls, and the richest and highest aliment of grace. And he who fasts for the sake of religion, *hungers and thirsts after righteousness,* without a metaphor.

Fifthly, Since every devout prayer is designed to ascend and fly up to heaven; as fasting (according to St. Austin's allusion) has given it one wing, so let almsgiving to the poor supply it with another. And both these together will not only carry it up triumphant to heaven, but, if need require, bring heaven itself down to the devout person who sends it thither; as, while Cornelius was fasting and praying, (to which he still joined giving alms,) an angel from heaven was dispatched to him with this happy message, Acts x. 4, *Thy prayers and thine alms are come up for a memorial before God.* And nothing certainly can give a greater efficacy to prayer, and a more peculiar fitness for the sacrament, than a hearty and conscientious practice of this duty; without which all that has been mentioned hitherto is nothing but wind and air, pageantry and hypocrisy: for if there be any truer measure of a man than by what he does, it must be by what he gives. He who is truly pious will account it a wedding-supper to feed the hungry, and a wedding-garment to clothe the naked. And God and man will find it a very unfit garment for such a purpose, which has not in it a purse or pocket for the poor.

But so far are some from considering the poor before the sacrament, that they have been observed to give nothing to the poor, even at the sacrament: and those such, that if rich clothes might pass for a wedding-garment, none could appear better fitted for such a solemnity than themselves; yet some such, I say, I myself have seen at a communion, drop nothing into the poor's basin.

But, good God! what is the heart of such worldlings made of, and what a mind do they bring with them to so holy an ordinance! an ordinance in which none can be qualified to receive, whose heart does not serve them also to give.

From such indeed as have nothing, God expects nothing; but where God has given, as I may say, with both hands, and men return with none, such must know that the poor have an action of debt against them, and that God himself will undertake and prosecute their suit for them: and if he does, since they could not find in their hearts to proportion their charity to their estates, nothing can be more just than for God to proportion their estates to their charity; and by so doing, he can not well give them a shrewder and a shorter cut.

In the mean time, let such know further, that whosoever dares, upon so sacred and solemn an occasion, approach the altar with bowels so shut up as to leave nothing behind him there for the poor, shall be sure to carry something away with him from thence which will do him but little good.

Sixthly, Since the charity of the hand signifies but little, unless it springs from the heart and flows through the mouth, let the pious communicant, both in heart and tongue, thoughts and speech, put on a charitable, friendly, Christian temper of mind and carriage towards all. Wrath and envy, malice and backbiting, and the like, are direct contradictions to the very spirit of Christianity, and fit a man for the sacrament just as much as a stomach overflowed with gall would help him to digest his meat. St. Paul often rebukes and schools such disturbers of the world very sharply, correcting a base humor by a very generous rule, Phil. ii. 3; *Let each,* says he, *esteem others better than themselves.* No man, doubtless, shall ever be condemned of God for not judging his brother: for, be thy brother or neighbor never so wicked and ungodly, satisfy thyself with this, that another's wickedness shall never damn thee; but thy own bitterness and rancor may, and, continued in, certainly will: rather let his want of grace give thee occasion to exercise thine, if thou hast any, in thinking and speaking better of him than he deserves: and if thy charity proves mistaken, assure thyself that God will accept the charity, and overlook the mistake. But if in judging him whom thou hast nothing to do with, thou chancest to judge one way, and God and truth to judge another, take heed of that dreadful tribunal, where it will not be enough to say that "I thought this," or "I heard that;" and where no man's mistake will be able to warrant an unjust surmise, and much less justify a false censure. Such would find it much better for them to retreat inwards, and view themselves in the law of God and their own consciences; and that will tell them their own impartially, that will fetch off all their paint, and show them a foul face in a true glass. Let them read over their catechism, and lay aside spite and virulence, gossiping and meddling, calumny and detraction; and let not all about them be villains and reprobates, because they themselves are envious and forlorn, idle and malicious: such vermin are to be looked upon by all sober Christians as the very cankers of society, and the shame of any religion; and so far from being fit to come to the sacrament, that really they are not fit to come to church; and would much better become the house of correction than the house of prayer.

Nevertheless, as custom in sin makes people blind, and blindness makes them bold, none come more confidently to the sacrament than such wretches. But when I consider the pure and blessed body of our Saviour, passing through the open sepulchres of such throats, into the noisome receptacles of their boiling, fermenting breasts, it seems to me a lively but sad representation of Christ's being first buried, and then descending into hell. Let this diabolical leaven therefore be purged out; and while such pretend to be so busy in cleansing their hearts, let them not forget to wash their mouths too.

Seventhly and lastly; As it is to be supposed that the pious communicant has all along carried on, so let him likewise in the issue close his preparatory work with reading and meditation. Of which, since the time will not serve me to speak more now, I shall only remark this, that they are duties of so near an import to the wellbeing of the soul, that the proper office of reading is to take in its spiritual food, and of meditation to digest it.

And now, I hope, that whosoever shall in the sincerity of his heart acquit himself as to all the foregoing duties, and thereby prepare and adorn himself to meet and converse with his Saviour at this divine feast, shall never be accosted with the thunder of that dreadful increpation from him, *Friend, how camest thou in hither, not having a wedding-garment?*

But because I am very sensible that all the particular instances of duty, which may one way or other contribute to the fitting of men for this great one, can hardly be assigned, and much less equally and universally applied, where the conditions of men are so very different, I shall gather them all into this one plain, full, and comprehensive rule; namely, That all those duties which common Christianity always obliges a Christian to, ought most eminently, and with a higher and more exalted pitch of devotion, to be performed by him before the sacrament; and convertibly, whatsoever duties divines prescribe to be observed by him with a peculiar fervor and application of mind upon this occasion, ought, in their proportion, to be practiced by him through the whole course of his Christian conversation.

And this is a solid and sure rule; a rule that will never deceive or lurch the sincere communicant; a rule, that by adding discretion to devotion, will both keep him from being humorsome, singular, and fantastic in his preparations before the sacrament, and (which is worse, and must fatally unravel all again) from being, as most are, loose and remiss after it; and thinking that, as soon as the sacrament is over, their great business is done, whereas indeed it is but begun.

And now I fear, that as I have been too long upon the whole, so I have been but too brief upon so many, and those such weighty particulars. But I hope you will supply this defect, by enlarging upon them in your practice, and make up the omissions of the pulpit by the meditations of the closet. And God direct and assist us all in so concerning a work.

To whom be rendered and ascribed, as is most due, all praise, might, majesty, and dominion, both now and for evermore. Amen.

SERMON XXI.

THE FATAL IMPOSTURE AND FORCE OF WORDS:

SET FORTH IN A SERMON PREACHED ON ISAIAH V. 20.

MAY 9, 1686.

ISAIAH V. 20. — *Woe unto them that call evil good, and good evil, &c.*

THESE words contain in them two things:

1. A woe denounced; and,

2. The sin for which it is denounced; to wit, *the calling evil good, and good evil:* which expression may be taken two ways:

First, In a judicial and more restrained sense; as it signifies the pronouncing of a guilty person innocent, and an innocent, guilty, in the course of judgment. But this I take to be too particular to reach the design of the words here.

Secondly, It may be taken in a general and more enlarged sense; as it imports a misrepresentation of the qualities of things and actions to the common apprehensions of men, abusing their minds with false notions, and so by this artifice making evil pass for good, and good for evil, in all the great concerns of life. Where, by *good,* I question not, but *good* morally so called, *bonum honestum,* ought, chiefly at least, to be understood; and that the good of profit, or pleasure, the *bonum utile,* or *jucundum,* hardly come into any account here, as things extremely below the principal design of the Spirit of God in this place.

It is wonderful to consider, that, since *good* is the natural and proper object which all human choice is carried out to; and *evil,* that which with all its might it shuns and flies from; and since withal there is that controlling worth and beauty in goodness, that, as such, the will can not but like and desire it; and, on the other side, that odious deformity in vice, that it never so much as offers itself to the affections or practice of mankind, but under the disguise and colors of the other; and since all this is easily discernible by the ordinary discourses of the understanding; and lastly, since nothing passes into the choice of the will, but as it comes conveyed and warranted by the understanding, as worthy of its choice; I say, it is wonderful to consider, that, notwithstanding all this, the lives and practices of the generality of men (in which men certainly should be most in earnest) are almost wholly took up in a passionate pursuit of what is evil, and in an equal neglect, if not also an abhorrence, of what is good. This is certainly so; and experience, which is neither to be confuted nor denied, does every minute prove the sad truth of this assertion.

But now, what should be the cause of all this? For so great, so constant, and so general a practice must needs have not only a cause, but also a great, a constant, and a general cause; a cause every way commensurate to such an effect: and this cause must of necessity be from one of those two commanding powers of the soul, the understanding or the will. As for the will, though its liberty be such, that, a suitable or proper good being proposed to it, it has a power to refuse, or not to choose it, yet it has no power to choose evil, considered absolutely as evil, this being directly against the nature and natural method of its workings.

Nevertheless it is but too manifest that things evil, extremely evil, are both readily chosen, and eagerly pursued and practiced by it. And therefore this must needs be from that other governing faculty of the soul, the understanding, which represents to the will things really evil under the notion and character of good. And this, this is the true source and original of this great mischief. The will chooses, follows, and embraces things evil and destructive; but it is because the understanding first tells it that they are good and wholesome, and fit to be chosen by it. One man gives another a cup of poison, a thing as terrible as death; but at the same time he tells him that it is a cordial; and so he drinks it off, and dies.

From the beginning of the world to this day, there was never any great villainy acted by men, but it was in the strength of some great fallacy put upon their minds by a false representation of evil for good, or good for evil. *In the day that thou eatest thereof thou shalt surely die*, says God to Adam; and so long as Adam believed this, he did not eat. But, says the devil, in the day that thou eatest thereof thou shalt be so far from *surely dying*, that thou shalt be immortal, and from a man grow into an angel; and upon this different account of the thing, he presently took the fruit, and ate mortality, misery, and destruction to himself and his whole posterity.

And now, can there be a woe or curse in all the stores and magazines of vengeance, equal to the malignity of such a practice; of which one single instance could involve all mankind, past, present, and to come, in one universal and irreparable confusion? God commanded and told man what was good, but the devil surnamed it evil, and thereby baffled the command, turned the world topsy-turvy, and brought a new chaos upon the whole creation.

But that I may give you a more full discussion of the sense and design of the words, I shall do it under these following particulars: as,

First, I shall give you some general account of the nature of good and evil, and the reason upon which they are founded.

Secondly, I shall show that the way by which good and evil commonly operate upon the mind of man, is by those respective names or appellations by which they are notified and conveyed to the mind. And,

Thirdly and lastly, I shall show the mischief, directly, naturally, and unavoidably following from the misapplication and confusion of those names.

And, I hope, by going over all these particulars, you may receive some tolerable satisfaction about this great subject which we have now before us.

1. And first for the nature of good and evil, what they are, and upon what they are founded. The knowledge of this I look upon as the foundation and groundwork of all those rules that either moral philosophy or divinity can give for

the direction of the lives and practices of men; and consequently ought to be reckoned as a first principle; and that such an one, that, for aught I see, the thorough speculation of good will be found much more difficult than the practice. But when we shall have once given some account of the nature of *good*, that of *evil* will be known by consequence; as being only a privation, or absence of good, in a subject capable of it, and proper for it.

Now *good*, in the general nature and notion of it, over and above the bare being of a thing, connotes also a certain suitableness or agreeableness of it to some other thing: according to which general notion of good, applied to the particular nature of moral goodness, (upon which only we now insist,) a thing or action is said to be morally good or evil, as it is agreeable or disagreeable to right reason, or to a rational nature; and as right reason is nothing else but the understanding or mind of man, discoursing and judging of things truly and as they are in themselves; and as all truth is unchangeably the same; (that proposition which is true at any time being so forever;) so it must follow that the moral goodness or evil of men's actions, which consist in their conformity or unconformity to right reason, must be also eternal, necessary, and unchangeable. So that, as that which is right reason at any time, or in any case, is always right reason with relation to the same time and case; in like manner, that which is morally good or evil at any time, or in any case, (since it takes its whole measure from right reason,) must be also eternally and unchangeably a moral good or evil, with relation to that time and to that case. For propositions concerning the goodness, as well as concerning the truth of things, are necessary and perpetual.

But you will say, may not the same action, as for instance, the killing of a man, be sometimes morally good, and sometimes morally evil? to wit, *good*, when it is the execution of justice upon a malefactor, and *evil*, when it is the taking away the life of an innocent person?

To this I answer, that this indeed is true of actions considered in their general nature or kind, but not considered in their particular individual instances. For, generally speaking, to take away the life of a man is neither morally good nor morally evil, but capable of being either, as the circumstances of things shall determine it; but every particular act of killing is of necessity accompanied with, and determined by, several circumstances, which actually and unavoidably constitute and denominate it either good or evil. And that which, being performed under such and such circumstances, is morally good, can not possibly, under the same circumstances, ever be morally evil. And so on the contrary.

From whence we infer the villainous falsehood of two assertions, held and maintained by some persons, and too much countenanced by some others in the world. As,

First, That good and evil, honest and dishonest, are not qualities existing or inherent in things themselves; but only founded in the opinions of men concerning things. So that any thing or action that has gained the general approbation of any people, or society of men, ought, in respect of those persons, to be esteemed morally good, or honest; and whatsoever falls under their general disapprobation, ought, upon the same account, to be reckoned morally evil, or dishonest; which also they would seem to prove from the very signification of the word *honestus*; which, originally and strictly, signifies no more than creditable, and is but a derivative from *honor*, which signifies *credit* or *honor*; and according to the opinion of some, we know that is lodged only in the esteem and thoughts of those who pay it, and not in the thing or person whom it is paid to. Thus for example; thieving or robbing was accounted amongst the Spartans a gallant, worthy, and a creditable thing; and consequently, according to the principle which we have mentioned, thievery, amongst the Spartans, was a practice morally good and honest. Thus also, both with the Grecians and the Romans, it was held a magnanimous and highly laudable act for a man, under any great or insuperable misery or distress, to put an end to his own life; and accordingly, with those who had such thoughts of it, that which we call self-murder was properly a good, an honest, and a virtuous action. And persons of the highest and most acknowledged probity and virtue amongst them, such as Marcus Cato, and Pomponius Atticus, actually did it, and stand celebrated both by their orators and historians for so doing. And I could also instance in other actions of a fouler and more unnatural hue, which yet, from the approbation and credit they have found in some countries and places, have passed for good morality in those places: but, out of respect to common humanity, as well as divinity, I shall pass them over. And thus much for the first assertion or opinion.

Secondly, The second opinion, or position, is, that good and evil, honest and dishonest, are originally founded in the laws and constitutions of the sovereign civil power, enjoining some things or actions, and prohibiting others. So that when any thing is found conducing to the welfare of the public, and thereupon comes to be enacted by governors into a law, it is forthwith thereby rendered morally good and honest; and, on the contrary, evil and dishonest, when, upon its contrariety to the public welfare, it stands prohibited and condemned by the same public authority.

This was the opinion heretofore of Epicurus, as it is represented by Gassendus; who understood his notions too well to misrepresent them. And lately of one amongst ourselves, a less philosopher, though the greater heathen of the two, the infamous author of the Leviathan. And the like lewd, scandalous, and immoral doctrine, or worse, if possible, may be found in some writers, of another kind of note and character; whom, one would have thought, not only religion, but shame of the world, might have taught better things.

Such as, for instance, Bellarmine himself; who, in his 4th book and 5th chapter *De Pontifice Romano*, has this monstrous passage: "That if the pope should through error or mistake command vices, and prohibit virtues, the church would be bound in conscience to believe vice to be good, and virtue evil." I shall give you the whole passage in his own words to a tittle: "Fides catholica docet omnem virtutem esse bonam, omne vitium esse malum. Si autem erraret papa, præcipiendo vitia vel prohibendo virtutes, teneretur ecclesia credere vitia esse bona et virtutes malas, nisi vellet contra conscientiam peccare." Good God! that any thing that wears the name of a Christian, or but of a man, should venture to own such a villainous, impudent, and blasphemous assertion in the face of the world, as this! What! must murder, adultery, theft, fraud, extortion, perjury, drunkenness, rebellion, and the like, pass for good and commendable actions, and fit to be practiced? And mercy, chastity, justice, truth, temperance, loyalty, and sincere dealing, be accounted things utterly evil, immoral, and not to be followed by men, in case the pope, who is generally weak, and almost always a wicked man, should, by his mistake and infallible ignorance, command the former, and forbid the latter? Did Christ himself ever assume such a power as to alter the morality of actions, and to transform vice into virtue, and virtue into vice, by his bare word? Certainly never did a grosser paradox, or a wickeder sentence, drop from the mouth or pen of any mortal man, since reason or religion had any being in the world.

And, I must confess, I have often with great amazement wondered how it could possibly come from a person of so great a reputation, both for learning and virtue too, as the world allows Bellarmine to have been. But when men give themselves over to the defense of wicked interests and false propositions, it is just with God to smite the greatest abilities with the greatest infatuations.

But as for these two positions or assertions; That the moral good or evil, the honesty or dishonesty of human actions, should depend either upon the opinions or upon the laws of men; they are certainly false in themselves, because they are infinitely absurd in their consequences. Some of which are such as these. As,

First, If the moral goodness or evil of men's actions were originally founded in, and so proceeded wholly from, the opinions or laws of men, then it would follow that they must change and vary according to the change and difference of the opinions and laws of men: and consequently, that the same action, under exactly the same circumstances, may be morally good one day, and morally evil another; and morally good in one place, and morally evil in another: forasmuch as the same sovereign authority may enact or make a law, commanding such or such an action to-day, and a quite contrary law forbidding the same action to-morrow; and the very same action, under the same circumstances, may be commanded by law in one country, and prohibited by law in another. Which being so, the consequence is manifest, and the absurdity of the consequent intolerable.

Secondly, If the moral goodness or evil of men's actions depended originally upon human laws, then those laws themselves could neither be morally good nor evil: the consequence is evident; because those laws are not commanded or prohibited by any antecedent human laws; and consequently, if the moral goodness or evil of any act were to be derived only from a precedent human law, laws themselves, not supposing a dependence upon other precedent human laws, could have no moral goodness or evil in them. Which to assert of any human act (such as all human laws essentially are and must be) is certainly a very gross absurdity.

Thirdly, If the moral goodness or evil of men's actions were sufficiently derived from human laws or constitutions, then, upon supposal that a divine law should (as it often does) command what is prohibited by human laws, and prohibit what is commanded by them, it would follow, that either such commands and prohibitions of the divine law do not at all affect the actions of men in point of their morality, so as to render them either good or evil; or that the same action, at the same time, may, in respect of the divine law commanding it, be morally good; and, in respect of a human law forbidding it, be morally evil: than which consequence, nothing can be more clear, nor withal more absurd.

And many more of the like nature I could easily draw forth, and lay before you. Every false principle or proposition being sure to be attended with a numerous train of absurdities.

But, as to the subject-matter now in hand; so far is the morality of human actions, as to the goodness or evil of them, from being founded in any human law, that in very many, and those the principal instances of human action, it is not originally founded in, or derived from, so much as any positive divine law. There being a *jus naturale* certainly antecedent to all *jus positivum*, either human or divine; and that such as results from the very nature and being of things, as they stand in such a certain habitude or relation to one another: to which relation whatsoever is done agreeably is morally and essentially good; and whatsoever is done otherwise is, at the same rate, morally evil.

And this I shall exemplify in those two grand, comprehensive, moral duties, which man is forever obliged to, his duty towards God, and his duty towards his neighbor.

And first, for his duty towards God; which is, *to love and obey him with all his heart and all his soul.* It is certain that for a rational, intelligent creature to conform himself to the will of God in all things, carries in it a moral rectitude, or goodness; and to disobey or oppose his will in any thing, imports a moral obliquity, before God ever deals forth any particular law or command to such a creature; there being a general obligation upon man to obey all God's laws, whensoever they shall be declared, before any particular instanee of law comes actually to be declared. But now whence is this? Why, from that essential suitableness which obedience has to the relation which is between a rational creature and his Creator. Nothing in nature being more irrational and irregular, and consequently more immoral, than for an intelligent being to oppose or disobey that sovereign, supreme will, which gave him that being, and has withal the sole and absolute disposal of him in all his concerns. So that there needs no positive law or sanction of God to stamp an obliquity upon such a disobedience; since it cleaves to it essentially, and by way of natural result from it, upon the account of that utter unsuitableness which disobedience has to the relation which man naturally and necessarily stands in towards his Maker.

And then, in the next place, for his duty to his neighbor. The whole of which is comprised in that great rule, *of doing as a man would be done by.* We may truly affirm, that the morality of this rule does not originally derive itself from those words of our Saviour, Matt. vii. 12; *Whatsoever ye would that men should do unto you, do ye even so unto them:* no, nor yet from Moses or the prophets; but it is as old as Adam, and bears date with human nature itself; as springing from that primitive relation of equality which all men, as fellow-creatures, and fellow-subjects to the same supreme Lord, bear to one another, in respect of that common right which every man has equally to his life, and to the proper comforts of life, and consequently to all things naturally necessary to the support of both.

Now, whatsoever one man has a right to keep or possess, no other man can have a right to take from him. So that no man has a right to expect that from or to do that to another, which that other has not an equal right to expect from and to do to him. Which parity of right, as to all things purely natural, being undoubtedly the result of nature itself, can any thing be inferred from thence more conformable to reason, and consequently of a greater moral rectitude, than that such an equality of right should also cause an equality of behavior, between man and man, as to all those mutual offices and intercourses in which life and the happiness of life are concerned? Nothing certainly can shine out and show itself by the mere light of reason, as a higher and more unquestionable piece of morality than this, nor as a more confessed deviation from morality than the contrary practice.

From all which discourse I think we may without presumption conclude, that the *rationes boni et mali*, the nature of good and evil, as to the principal instances of both, spring from that essential habitude, or relation, which the nature of one thing bears to another by virtue of that order which they stand placed in, here in the world, by the very law and condition of their creation; and for that reason do and must precede all positive laws, sanctions, or institutions whatsoever. Good and evil are in morality as the east and west are in the frame of the world; founded in and divided by that fixed and unalterable situation which they have respectively in the whole body of the universe; or, as the right hand is discriminated from the left, by a natural, necessary, and never to be confounded distinction.

And thus I have done with the first thing proposed, and given you such an account of the nature of good and evil, as the measure of the present exercise and occasion would allow. Pass we now to the

2d, which is to show, That the way by which good and evil generally operate upon the mind of man, is by those words or names by which they are notified and conveyed to the mind. Words are the signs and symbols of things; and as in accompts, ciphers and figures pass for real sums, so in the course of human affairs, words and names pass for things themselves. For things, or objects, can not enter into the mind, as they subsist in themselves, and by their own natural bulk pass into the apprehension; but they are taken in by their ideas, their notions or resemblances; which imprinting themselves after a spiritual immaterial manner in the imagination, and from thence, under a further refinement, passing into the intellect, are by that expressed by certain words or names, found out and invented by the mind, for the communication of its conceptions, or thoughts, to others. So that as conceptions are the images or resemblances of things to the mind within itself, in like manner are words, or names, the marks, tokens, or resemblances of those conceptions to the minds of them whom we converse with: τὰ ἐν τῇ φωνῇ τῶν ἐν τῇ ψυχῇ παθημάτων σύμβολα, being the known maxim laid down by the philosopher as the first and most fundamental rule of all discourse.

This therefore is certain, that in human life, or conversation, words stand for things; the common business of the world not being capable of being managed otherwise. For by these, men come to know one another's minds. By these they covenant and confederate. By these they buy and sell, they deal and traffic. In short, words are the great instruments both of practice and design; which, for the most part, move wholly in the strength of them: forasmuch as it is the nature of man both to will and to do according to the persuasion he has of the good and evil of those things that come before him, and to take up his persuasions according to the representations made to him of those qualities by their respective names or appellations.

This is the true and natural account of this matter; and it is all that I shall remark upon this second head. I proceed now to the

3d. Which is, to show the mischief which directly, naturally, and unavoidably follows from the misapplication and confusion of those names. And in order to this, I shall premise these two considerations:

1. That the generality of mankind is wholly and absolutely governed by words or names; without, nay, for the most part, even against the knowledge men have of things. The multitude, or common rout, like a drove of sheep, or a herd of oxen, may be managed by any noise or cry which their drivers shall accustom them to.

And he who will set up for a skillful manager of the rabble, so long as they have but ears to hear, needs never inquire whether they have any understanding whereby to judge; but with two or three popular empty words, such as *popery and superstition, right of the subject, liberty of conscience, Lord Jesus Christ*, well tuned and humored, may whistle them backwards and forwards, upwards and downwards, till he is weary; and get up upon their backs when he is so.

As for the meaning of the word itself, that may shift for itself: and as for the sense and reason of it, that has little or nothing to do here; only let it sound full and round, and chime right to the humor, which is at present agog, (just as a big, long, rattling name is said to command even adoration from a Spaniard,) and no doubt, with this powerful senseless engine, the rabble-driver shall be able to carry all before him, or to draw all after him, as he pleases. For a plausible, insignificant word, in the mouth of an expert demagogue, is a dangerous and a dreadful weapon.

You know, when Cæsar's army mutinied, and grew troublesome, no argument from interest or reason could satisfy or appease them: but as soon as he gave them the appellation of Quirites, the tumult was immediately hushed; and all were quiet and content, and took that one word in good payment for all. Such is the trivial slightness and levity of most minds. And indeed, take any passion of the soul of man, while it is predominant and afloat, and, just in the critical hight of it, nick it with some lucky or unlucky word, and you may as certainly overrule it to your own purpose, as a spark of fire, falling upon gunpowder, will infallibly blow it up.

The truth is, he who shall duly consider these matters, will find that there is a certain bewitchery, or fascination in words, which makes them operate with a force beyond what we can naturally give an account of. For would not a man think ill deeds and shrewd turns should reach further and strike deeper than ill words? And yet many instances might be given in which men have much more easily pardoned ill things *done*, than ill things *said* against them: such a peculiar rancor and venom do they leave behind them in men's minds, and so much more poisonously and incurably does the serpent bite with his tongue than with his teeth.

Nor are men prevailed upon at this odd unaccountable rate,

by bare words, only through a defect of knowledge; but sometimes also do they suffer themselves to be carried away with these puffs of wind, even contrary to knowledge and experience itself. For otherwise, how could men be brought to surrender up their reason, their interest, and their credit to flattery? gross, fulsome, abusive flattery; indeed more abusive and reproachful, upon a true estimate of things and persons, than the rudest scoffs and the sharpest invectives. Yet so it is, that though men know themselves utterly void of those qualities and perfections which the impudent sycophant, at the same time, both ascribes to them, and in his sleeve laughs at them for believing; nay, though they know that the flatterer himself knows the falsehood of his own flatteries; yet they swallow the fallacious morsel, love the impostor, and with both arms hug the abuse; and that to such a degree, that no offices of friendship, no real services, shall be able to lie in the balance against those luscious falsehoods which flattery shall feed the mind of a fool in power with: the sweetness of the one infinitely overcomes the substance of the other.

And therefore you shall seldom see, that such an one cares to have men of worth, honesty, and veracity about him; for such persons can not fall down and worship stocks and stones, though they are placed never so high above them; but their *yea* is *yea*, and their *nay, nay;* and they can not admire a fox for his sincerity, a wolf for his generosity, nor an ass for his wit and ingenuity; and therefore can never be acceptable to those whose whole credit, interest, and advantage lies in their not appearing to the world what they are really in themselves. None are or can be welcome to such, but those who speak paint and wash; for that is the thing they love; and no wonder, since it is the thing they need.

There is hardly any rank, order, or degree of men, but, more or less, have been captivated and enslaved by words. It is a weakness, or rather a fate, which attends both high and low; the statesman who holds the helm, as well as the peasant who holds the plough. So that, if ever you find an ignoramus in place and power, and can have so little conscience, and so much confidence, as to tell him to his face that he has a wit and an understanding above all the world besides; and "that what his own reason can not suggest to him, neither can the united reason of all mankind put together;"* I dare undertake, that, as fulsome a dose as you give him, he shall readily take it down, and admit the commendation, though he can not believe the thing: *Blanditiæ, etiam cum excluduntur, placent,* says Seneca. Tell him, that no history or antiquity can match his policies and his conduct; and presently the sot (because he knows neither history nor antiquity) shall begin to *measure himself by himself,* (which is the only sure way for him not to fall short,) and so immediately, amongst his outward admirers and his inward despisers, vouched also by a *teste meipso,* he steps forth an exact politician, and, by a wonderful and new way of arguing, proves himself no fool, because, forsooth, the sycophant who tells him so is an egregious knave.

But to give you yet a grosser instance of the force of words, and of the extreme vanity of man's nature in being influenced by them, hardly shall you meet with any person, man or woman, so aged or ill-favored, but, if you will venture to commend them for their comeliness, nay, and for their youth too, though "time out of mind" is wrote upon every line of their face; yet they shall take it very well at your hands, and begin to think with themselves that certainly they have some perfections which the generality of the world are not so happy as to be aware of.

But now, are not these, think we, strange self-delusions, and yet attested by common experience almost every day? But whence, in the mean time, can all this proceed, but from that besotting intoxication which this verbal magic, as I may so call it, brings upon the mind of man? For can any thing in nature have a more certain, deep, and undeniable effect, than folly has upon man's mind, and age upon his body? And yet we see, that in both these, words are able to persuade men out of what they find and feel, to reverse the very impressions of sense, and to amuse men with fancies and paradoxes, even in spite of nature and experience. But since it would be endless to pursue all the particulars in which this humor shows itself, whosoever would have one full, lively, and complete view of an empty, shallow, self-opinioned gran-

* The words of a great self-opiniator, and a bitter reviler of the clergy.

dee, surrounded by his flatterers, (like a choice dish of meat by a company of fellows commending and devouring it at the same time,) let him cast his eye upon Ahab in the midst of his false prophets, 1 Kings xxii., where we have them all with one voice for giving him a cast of their court-prophecy, and sending him, in a compliment, to be knocked on the head at Ramoth Gilead. But, says Jehoshaphat, (who smelt the parasite through the prophet,) in the seventh verse, *Is there not a prophet of the Lord besides, that we may inquire of him? Why, yes,* says Ahab, *there is yet one man by whom we may inquire of the Lord; but I hate him, for he doth not prophesy good concerning me, but evil.* Ay! that was his crime; the poor man was so good a subject, and so bad a courtier, as to venture to serve and save his prince, whether he would or no; for, it seems, to give Ahab such warning as might infallibly have prevented his destruction, was esteemed by him evil; and to push him on headlong into it, because he was fond of it, was accounted good. These were his new measures of good and evil. And therefore those who knew how to *make their court* better, (as the word is,) tell him a bold lie in God's name, and therewith send him packing to his certain doom; thus calling evil good at the cost of their prince's crown and his life too. But what cared they? they knew that it would please, and that was enough for them; there being always a sort of men in the world (whom others have an interest to serve by) who had rather a great deal be pleased than be safe. Strike them under the fifth rib, provided at the same time you kiss them too, as Joab served Abner, and you may both destroy and oblige them with the same blow.

Accordingly, in the thirtieth of Isaiah, we find some arrived to that pitch of sottishness, and so much in love with their own ruin, as to own plainly and roundly what they would be at; in the tenth verse, *Prophesy not unto us,* say they, *right things, but prophesy to us smooth things.* As if they had said, "Do but oil the razor for us, and let us alone to cut our own throats." Such an enchantment is there in words; and so fine a thing does it seem to some to be ruined plausibly, and to be ushered to their destruction with panegyric and acclamation: a shameful, though irrefragable argument, of the absurd empire and usurpation of words over things; and that the greatest affairs and most important interests of the world are carried on by things, not as they are, but as they are called.

And thus much for the first thing which I thought necessary to premise to the prosecution of our third particular.

2. The other thing to be premised is this; That as the generality of men are wholly governed by names and words, so there is nothing in which they are so remarkably and powerfully governed by them, as in matters of good and evil, so far as these qualities relate to, and affect the actions of, men: a thing certainly of a most fatal and pernicious import. For though, in matters of mere speculation, it is not much the concern of society whether or no men proceed wholly upon trust, and take the bare word of others for what they assent to; since it is not much material to the welfare either of government or of themselves whether they opine right or wrong, and whether they be philosophers or no. But it is vastly the concern both of government and of themselves too, whether they be morally good or bad, honest or dishonest. And surely it is hardly possible for men to make it their business to be virtuous or honest, while vices are called and pointed out to them by the names of virtues; and they all the while suppose the nature of things to be truly and faithfully signified by their names, and thereupon believe as they hear, and practice as they believe. And that this is the course of much the greatest part of the world, thus to take up their persuasions concerning good and evil by an implicit faith, and a full acquiescence in the word of those who shall represent things to them under these characters, I shall prove by two reasons; and those such as, I fear, will not only be found reasons to evince that men actually do so, but also sad demonstrations to conclude that they are never like to do otherwise.

First, The first of which shall be taken from that similitude, neighborhood, and affinity, which is between vice and virtue, good and evil, in several notable instances of each. For though the general natures and definitions of these qualities are sufficiently distant from one another, and so in no danger of a promiscuous confusion; yet when they come to subsist in particulars, and to be clothed and attended with several accidents and circumstances, the case is hereby much altered; for then the discernment is neither so easy, nor yet so certain. Thus it is not always so obvious to distinguish between an act of liberality and an act of prodigality; between an act of courage and an act of rashness; an act of pusillanimity, and an act of great modesty or humility: nay, and some have had the good luck to have their very dullness dignified with the name of *gravity*, and to be no small gainers by the mistake. And many more such actions of dubious quality might be instanced in, too numerous to be here recounted or insisted on. In all which, and the like, it requiring too great a sagacity for vulgar minds to draw the line nicely and exactly between vice and virtue, and to adjust the due limits of each; it is no wonder if most men attempt not a laborious scrutiny into things themselves, but only take names and words as they first come, and so without any more ado rest in them; it being so much easier, in all disquisitions of truth, to suppose than to prove, and to believe than to distinguish.

Secondly, The other reason of the same shall be taken from the great and natural inability of most men to judge exactly of things; which makes it very difficult for them to discern the real good and evil of what comes before them; to consider and weigh circumstances, to scatter and look through the mists of error, and so separate appearances from realities. For the greater part of mankind is but slow and dull of apprehension, and therefore, in many cases, under a necessity of seeing with other men's eyes, and judging with other men's understandings; nature having manifestly contrived things so, that the vulgar and the many are fit only to be led or driven, but by no means fit to guide or direct themselves.

To which their want of judging or discerning abilities, we may add also their want of leisure and opportunity to apply their minds to such a serious and attent consideration as may let them into a full discovery of the true goodness and evil of things, which are qualities which seldom display themselves to the first view: for in most things good and evil lie shuffled and thrust up together in a confused heap; and it is study and intention of thought which must draw them forth, and range them under their distinct heads. But there can be no study without time; and the mind must abide and dwell upon things, or be always a stranger to the inside of them. *Through desire,* says Solomon, *a man having separated himself, seeketh and intermeddleth with all wisdom,* Prov. xviii. 1. There must be leisure and a retirement, solitude, and a sequestration of a man's self from the noise and toil of the world: for truth scorns to be seen by eyes too much fixed upon inferior objects. It lies too deep to be fetched up with the plow, and too close to be beaten out with the hammer. It dwells not in shops or workhouses; nor till the late age was it ever known that any one served seven years to a smith or a tailor, that he might at the end thereof proceed master of any other arts but such as those trades taught him; and much less that he should commence doctor or divine from the shop-board or the anvil; or from whistling to a team, come to preach to a congregation.

These were the peculiar, extraordinary privileges of the late blessed times of light and inspiration: otherwise nature will still hold on in its old course, never doing any thing which is considerable, without the assistance of its two great helps, art and industry. But above all, the knowledge of what is good and what is evil, what ought and what ought not to be done, in the several offices and relations of life, is a thing too large to be compassed, and too hard to be mastered, without brains and study, parts and contemplation; which providence never thought fit to make much the greatest part of mankind possessors of. And consequently those who are not so, must, for the knowledge of most things, depend upon those who are, and receive their information concerning good and evil from such verbal or nominal representations of each as shall be imparted to them by those whose ability and integrity they have cause to rely upon for a faithful account of these matters.

And thus from these two great considerations premised; 1st, That the generality of the world are wholly governed by words and names; and 2dly, That the chief instance in which they are so, is in such words and names as import the good or evil of things; (which both the difficulty of things themselves, and the very condition of human nature, constrains much the greatest part of mankind to take wholly upon trust;) I say, from these two considerations must needs be inferred, what a fatal, devilish, and destructive effect the misapplication and confusion of those great governing names of *good* and *evil* must inevitably have upon the societies of men; the comprehensive mischief of which will appear from this, that it takes in both those ways by which the greatest evils and calamities which are incident to man do directly break in upon him.

The first of which is by his being deceived, and the second by his being misrepresented. And first, for the first of these. I do not in the least doubt, but if a true and just computation could be made of all the miseries and misfortunes that befall men in this world, two thirds of them, at least, would be found resolvable into their being deceived by false appearances of good; first deluding their apprehensions, and then by natural consequence perverting their actions, from which are the great issues of life and death; since, according to the eternal sanction of God and nature, such as a man's actions are for good or evil, such ought also his condition to be for happiness or misery.

Now all deception in the course of life is indeed nothing else but a lie reduced to practice, and falsehood passing from words into things.

For is a man impoverished and undone by the purchase of an estate? Why, it is because he bought an imposture, paid down his money for a lie, and by the help of the best and ablest counsel, forsooth, that could be had, took a bad title for a good.

Is a man unfortunate in marriage? Still it is because he was deceived; and put his neck into the snare before he put it into the yoke, and so took that for virtue and affection which was nothing but vice in a disguise, and a devilish humor under a demure look.

Is he again unhappy and calamitous in his friendships? Why, in this also it is because he built upon the air, and trod upon a quicksand, and took that for kindness and sincerity which was only malice and design, seeking an opportunity to ruin him effectually, and to overturn him in all his interests by the sure but fatal handle of his own good nature and credulity.

And lastly, is a man betrayed, lost, and blown by such agents and instruments as he employs in his greatest and nearest concerns? Why, still the cause of it is from this, that he misplaced his confidence, took hypocrisy for fidelity, and so relied upon the services of a pack of villains, who designed nothing but their own game, and to stake him, while they played for themselves.

But not to mention any more particulars, there is no estate, office, or condition of life whatsoever, but groans and labors under the killing truth of what we have asserted.

For it is this which supplants not only private persons, but kingdoms and governments, by keeping them ignorant of their own strengths and weaknesses; and it is evident that governments may be equally destroyed by an ignorance of either. For the weak, by thinking themselves strong, are induced to venture and proclaim war against that which ruins them: and the strong, by conceiting themselves weak, are thereby rendered as unactive, and consequently as useless, as if they really were so. In Luke xiv. 31, when *a king with ten thousand is to meet a king coming against him with twenty thousand*, our Saviour advises him, before he ventures the issue of a battle, *to sit down and consider*. But now a false glozing parasite would give him quite another kind of counsel, and bid him only reckon his ten thousand forty, call his fool-hardiness valor, and then he may go on boldly, because blindly, and by mistaking himself for a lion, come to perish like an ass.

In short, it is this great plague of the world, deception, which takes wrong measures, and makes false musters almost in every thing; which sounds a retreat instead of a charge, and a charge instead of a retreat; which overthrows whole armies; and sometimes by one lying word treacherously cast out, turns the fate and fortune of states and empires, and lays the most flourishing monarchies in the dust. A blind guide is certainly a great mischief; but a guide that blinds those whom he should lead is undoubtedly a much greater.

Secondly, The other great and undoing mischief which befalls men upon the forementioned account is, by their being misrepresented. Now as by calling evil good, a man is misrepresented to himself in the way of flattery, so by calling good evil he is misrepresented to others in the way of slander and detraction. I say detraction, that killing, poisoned arrow drawn out of the devil's quiver, which is always flying abroad, and doing execution in the dark; against which no virtue is a defense, no innocence a security. For as by flattery a man is usually brought to open his bosom to his mortal enemy, so by detraction, and a slanderous misreport of persons, he is often brought to shut the same even to his best and truest friends. In both cases he receives a fatal blow, since that which lays a man open to an enemy, and that which strips him of a friend, equally attacks him in all those interests that are capable of being weakened by the one and supported by the other.

The most direct and efficacious way to ruin any man, is to misrepresent him; and it often so falls out that it wounds on both sides, and not only mauls the person misrepresented, but him also to whom he is misrepresented: for if he be great and powerful, (as spies and pickthanks seldom apply to any others,) it generally provokes him through mistake to persecute and tyrannize over, nay, and sometimes even to dip his hands in the blood of the innocent and the just, and thereby involve himself in such a guilt as shall arm heaven and earth against him, the vengeance of God, and the indignation of men; who will both espouse the quarrel of a bleeding innocence, and heartily join forces against an insulting baseness, especially when backed with greatness, and set on by misinformation. Histories are full of such examples.

Besides that, it is rarely found that men hold their greatness for term of life; though their baseness, for the most part, they do; and then, according to the common vicissitude and wheel of things, the proud and the insolent must take their turn too; and after long trampling upon others, come at length, *plaudente et gaudente mundo*, to be trampled upon themselves. For, as Tully has it in his oration for Milo, *non semper viator a latrone, nonnunquam etiam latro a viatore occiditur.*

But to pass from particulars to communities, nothing can be imagined more destructive to society than this villainous practice. For it robs the public of all that benefit and advantage that it may justly claim and ought to receive from the worth and virtue of particular persons, by rendering their virtue utterly insignificant. For good itself can do no good while it passes for evil; and an honest man is, in effect, useless, while he is accounted a knave. Both things and persons subsist by their reputation.

An unjust sentence from a tribunal may condemn an innocent person, but misrepresentation condemns innocence itself. For it is this which revives and imitates that inhuman barbarity of the old heathen persecutors, wrapping up Christians in the skins of wild beasts, that so they might be worried and torn in pieces by dogs. Do but paint an angel black, and that is enough to make him pass for a devil. "Let us blacken him, let us blacken him what we can," said that miscreant Harrison * of the blessed king, upon the wording and drawing up his charge against his approaching trial. And when any man is to be run down, and sacrificed to the lust of his enemies, as that royal martyr was, even his *good* (according to the apostle's phrase) *shall be evil spoken of.* He must first be undermined, and then undone. The practice is usual, and the method natural. But, to give you the whole malice of it in one word, it is a weapon forged in hell, and formed by the prime artificer and engineer of all mischief, the devil; and none but that God who knows all things, and can do all things, can protect the best of men against it.

To which God, the fountain of all good, and the hater of all evil, be rendered and ascribed, as is most due, all praise, might, majesty, and dominion, both now and for evermore. Amen.

* A preaching colonel of the parliament-army, and a chief actor in the murder of King Charles the First; notable before for having killed several after quarter given them by others, and using these words in the doing it; *Cursed be he who does the work of the Lord negligently.* He was by extraction a butcher's son; and accordingly, in his practices all along, more a butcher than his father.

SERMON XXII.

PREVENTION OF SIN AN INVALUABLE MERCY:

OR A SERMON PREACHED UPON THAT SUBJECT ON 1 SAMUEL, XXV. 32, 33,

AT CHRIST CHURCH, OXON, NOVEMBER 10, 1678.

1 Samuel xxv. 32, 33.—*And David said to Abigail, Blessed be the Lord God of Israel, which sent thee this day to meet me.*
And blessed be thy advice, and blessed be thou, which hast kept me this day from coming to shed blood, and from avenging myself with mine own hand.

THESE words are David's retractation, or laying down of a bloody and revengeful resolution; which, for a while, his heart had swelled with, and carried him on with the highest transport of rage to prosecute. A resolution took up from the sense of a gross indignity and affront passed upon him, in recompense of a signal favor and kindness received from him. For during his exile and flight before Saul, in which he was frequently put to all the hardships which usually befall the weak flying before the strong; there happening a great and solemn festivity, such as the sheep-shearings used to be in those eastern countries, he condescends, by an honorable and kind message, to beg of a rich and great man some small repast and supply for himself and his poor harassed companions, at that notable time of joy and feasting: a time that might make any thing that looked like want or hunger no less an absurdity than a misery to all that were round about him. And, as if the greatness of the asker, and the smallness of the thing asked, had not been sufficient to enforce his request, he adds a commemoration of his own generous and noble usage of the person whom he thus addressed to; showing how that he had been a wall and a bulwark to all that belonged to him, a safeguard to his estate, and a keeper of his flocks; and that both from the violence of robbers, and the license of his own soldiers; who could much more easily have carved themselves their own provisions than so great a spirit stoop so low as to ask them.

But in answer to this, (as nothing is so rude and insolent as a wealthy rustic,) all this his kindness is overlooked, his request rejected, and his person most unworthily railed at. Such being the nature of some base minds, that they can never do ill turns but they must double them with ill words too. And thus David's messengers are sent back to him like so many sharks and runagates, only for endeavoring to compliment an ill nature out of itself, and seeking that by petition which they might have commanded by their sword.

And now, who would not but think that such ungrateful usage, hightened with such reproachful language, might warrant the justice of the sharpest revenge; even of such a revenge as now began to boil and burn in the breast of this great warrior? For surely, if any thing may justly call up the utmost of a man's rage, it should be bitter and contumelious words from an unprovoked inferior; and if any thing can legalize revenge, it should be injuries from an extremely obliged person. But for all this, revenge, we see, is so much the prerogative of the Almighty, so absolutely the peculiar of Heaven, that no consideration whatsoever can empower even the best men to assume the execution of it in their own case. And therefore David, by an happy and seasonable pacification, being took off from acting that bloody tragedy which he was just now entering upon, and so turning his eyes from the baseness of him who had stirred up his revenge, to the goodness of that God who had prevented it; he breaks forth into these triumphant praises and doxologies expressed in the text: *Blessed be the Lord God of Israel, who has kept me this day from shedding blood, and from avenging myself with my own hand.*

Which words, together with those going before in the same verse, naturally afford us this doctrinal proposition, which shall be the subject of the following discourse: namely, That prevention of sin is one of the greatest mercies that God can vouchsafe a man in this world.

The prosecution of which shall lie in these two things: first, to prove the proposition; secondly, to apply it.

And first, for the proof of it: the transcendent greatness of this sin-preventing mercy is demonstrable from these four following considerations:

1. Of the condition which the sinner is in when this mercy is vouchsafed him.

2. Of the principle or fountain from whence this prevention of sin does proceed.

3. Of the hazard a man runs, if the commission of sin be not prevented, whether ever it will come to be pardoned: and,

4thly and lastly, Of the advantages accruing to the soul from the prevention of sin, above what can be had from the bare pardon of it, in case it comes to be pardoned.

Of these in their order: and first, we are to take an estimate of the greatness of this mercy, from the condition it finds the sinner in when God is pleased to vouchsafe it to him. It finds him in the direct way to death and destruction; and, which is worse, wholly unable to help himself. For he is actually under the power of a temptation and the sway of an impetuous lust; both hurrying him on to satisfy the cravings of it by some wicked action. He is possessed and acted by a passion which, for the present, absolutely overrules him; and so can no more recover himself than a bowl rolling down a hill stop itself in the midst of its career. It is a maxim in the philosophy of some, that whatsoever is once in actual motion, will move forever, if it be not hindered.

So a man, being under the drift of any passion, will still follow the impulse of it, till something interpose and by a stronger impulse turn him another way: but in this case we can find no principle within him strong enough to counteract that principle, and to relieve him. For if it be any, it must be either, first, the judgment of his reason, or, secondly, the free choice of his will.

But from the first of these there can be no help for him in his present condition. For while a man is engaged in any sinful purpose, through the prevalence of any passion, during the continuance of that passion he fully approves of whatsoever he is carried on to do in the strength of it; and judges it, under his present circumstances, the best and most rational course that he can take. Thus we see when Jonas was under the passion of anger, and God asked him, *Whether he did well to be angry?* he answered, *I do well to be angry, even unto death,* Jonas iv. 9. And when Saul was under his persecuting fit, what he did appeared to him good and necessary, Acts xxvi. 9; *I verily thought with myself that I ought to do many things contrary to the name of Jesus.* But to go no further than the text; do we not think that while David's heart was full of his revengeful design, it had blinded and perverted his reason so far that it struck in wholly with his passion, and told him that the bloody purpose he was going to execute was just, magnanimous, and most becoming such a person, and so dealt with, as he was? This being so, how is it possible for a man under a passion to receive any succor from his judgment or reason, which is made a party in the whole action, and influenced to a present approbation of all the ill things which his passion can suggest? This is most certain; and every man may find it by experience, (if he will but impartially reflect upon the method of his own actings, and the motions of his own mind,) that while he is under any passion, he thinks and judges quite otherwise of the proper objects of that passion, from what he does when he is out of it. Take a man under the transports of a vehement rage or revenge, and he passes a very different judgment upon murder and bloodshed from what he does when his revenge is over and the flame of his fury spent. Take a man possessed with a strong and immoderate desire of any thing, and you shall find that the worth and excellency of that thing appears much greater and more dazzling to the eye of his mind than it does when that desire, either by satisfaction or otherwise, is quite extinguished. So that while passion is upon the wing, and the man fully engaged in the prosecution of some unlawful object, no remedy or control is to be expected from his reason, which is wholly gained over to judge in favor of it. The fumes of his passion do as really intoxicate and confound his judging and discerning faculty, as the fumes of drink discompose and stupefy the brain of a man overcharged with it. When his drink indeed is over, he sees the folly and the absurdity, the madness and the vileness of those things which before he acted with full complacency and approbation. Passion is the drunkenness of the mind; and therefore, in its present workings, not controllable by reason; forasmuch as the proper effect of it is, for the time, to supersede the workings of reason. This principle therefore being able to do nothing to the stopping of a man in the eager pursuit of his sin, there remains no other that can be supposed able to do any thing upon the soul, but that second mentioned, to wit, the choice of his will. But this also is as much disabled from recovering a man fully intent upon the prosecution of any of his lusts, as the former. For all the time that a man is so, he absolutely wills, and is fully pleased with what he is designing or going about. And whatsoever perfectly pleases the will, overpowers it; for it fixes and determines the inclination of it to that one thing which is before it; and so fills up all its possibilities of indifference, that there is actually no room for choice. He who is under the power of melancholy, is pleased with his being so. He who is angry, delights in nothing so much as in the venting of his rage. And he who is lustful, places his greatest satisfaction in a slavish following of the dictates of his lust. And so long as the will and the affections are pleased, and exceedingly gratified in any course of acting, it is impossible for a man, so far as he is at his own disposal, not to continue in it; or, by any principle within him, to be diverted or took off from it.

From all which we see, that when a man has took up a full purpose of sinning, he is hurried on to it in the strength of all those principles which nature has given him to act by: for sin having depraved his judgment, and got possession of his will, there is no other principle left him naturally by which he can make head against it. Nor is this all; but to these internal dispositions to sin, add the external opportunities and occasions concurring with them, and removing all lets and rubs out of the way, and, as it were, making the path of destruction plain before the sinner's face; so that he may run his course freely and without interruption. Nay, when opportunities shall lie so fair as not only to permit, but even to invite, and further a progress in sin; so that the sinner shall set forth like a ship launched into the wide sea, not only well built and rigged, but also carried on with full wind and tide, to the port or place it is bound for: surely, in this case, nothing under heaven can be imagined able to stop or countermand a sinner, amidst all these circumstances promoting and pushing on his sinful design. For all that can give force and fury to motion, both from within and from without, jointly meet to bear him forward in his present attempt. He presses on like a horse rushing into the battle, and all that should withstand him giving way before him.

Now under this deplorable necessity of ruin and destruction does God's preventing grace find every sinner, when it *snatches him like a brand out of the fire,* and steps in between the purpose and the commission of his sin. It finds him going on resolutely in the high and broad way to perdition; which yet his perverted reason tells him is right, and his will, pleasant. And therefore he has no power of himself to leave or turn out of it; but he is ruined jocundly and pleasantly, and damned according to his heart's desire. And can there be a more wretched and woful spectacle of misery, than a man in such a condition? a man pleasing and destroying himself together? a man, as it were, doing violence to damnation, and taking hell by force? So that when the preventing goodness of God reaches out its arm, and pulls him out of this fatal path, it does by main force even wrest him from himself, and save him, as it were, against his will.

But neither is this his total inability to recover or relieve himself the worst of his condition; but, which is yet much worse, it puts him into a state of actual hostility against, and defiance of, that almighty God from whom alone, in this helpless and forlorn condition, he is capable of receiving help. For surely, while a man is going on in a full purpose of sin, he is trampling upon all law, spitting in the face of Heaven, and provoking his Maker in the highest manner; so that none is or can be so much concerned as God himself, to destroy and cut off such an one, and to vindicate the honor of his great name, by striking him dead in his rebellion. And this brings us to the

Second thing proposed; which was to show, What is the fountain or impulsive cause of this prevention of sin. It is perfectly free grace. A man at best, upon all principles of divinity and sound philosophy, is incapable of meriting any thing from God. But surely, while he is under the dominion of sin, and engaged in full design and purpose to commit it, it is not imaginable what can be found in him to oblige the divine grace in his behalf. For he is in high and actual rebellion against the only giver of such grace. And therefore it must needs flow from a redundant, unaccountable fullness of compassion; showing mercy because it will show mercy; from a compassion which is and must be its own reason, and can have no argument for its exercise but itself. No man in the strength of the first grace can merit the second, (as some fondly speak, for reason they do not,) unless a beggar, by receiving one alms, can be said to merit another. It is not from what a man is, or what he has done; from any virtue or excellency, any preceding worth or desert in him, that God is induced thus to interpose between him and ruin, and so stop him in his full career to damnation. No, says God, in Ezek. xvi. 6, *When I passed by, and saw thee polluted in thine own blood, I said unto thee, Live; yea, I said unto thee, when thou wast in thy blood, Live.* The Spirit of God speaks this great truth to the hearts of men with emphasis and repetition, knowing what an aptness there is in them to oppose it. God sees a man wallowing in his native filth and impurity, delivered over as an absolute captive to sin, polluted with its guilt, and enslaved by its power; and in this most loathsome condition fixes upon him as an object of his distinguishing mercy. And to show yet further that the actings of this mercy in the work of prevention are entirely free, do we not sometimes see, in persons of equal guilt and demerit, and of equal progress and advance in the ways of sin, some of them maturely diverted and took off, and others permitted to go on without check or control, till they finish a sinful course in final perdition? So true is it, that if things were cast upon this issue, that God should never prevent sin till something in man deserved it, the best of men would fall into sin, continue in sin, and sin on forever.

And thus much for the second thing proposed; which was to show, What was the principle, or fountain, from whence this prevention of sin does proceed. Come we now to the

Third demonstration or proof of the greatness of this preventing mercy, taken from the hazard a man runs, if the commission of sin be not prevented, whether ever it will come to be pardoned.

In order to the clearing of which, I shall lay down these two considerations:

1. That if sin be not thus prevented, it will certainly be committed; and the reason is, because on the sinner's part there will be always a strong inclination to sin. So that, if other things concur, and Providence cuts not off the opportunity, the act of sin must needs follow. For an active principle, seconded with the opportunities of action, will infallibly exert itself.

2dly, The other consideration is, That in every sin deliberately committed, there are (generally speaking) many more degrees of probability that that sin will never come to be pardoned, than that it will.

And this shall be made to appear upon these three following accounts:

1. Because every commission of sin introduces into the soul a certain degree of hardness, and an aptness to continue in that sin. It is a known maxim, that it is much more difficult to throw out, than not to let in. Every degree of entrance is a degree of possession. Sin taken into the soul is like a liquor poured into a vessel; so much of it as it fills, it also seasons. The touch and tincture go together. So that although the body of the liquor should be poured out again, yet still it leaves that tang behind it which makes the vessel fitter for that than for any other. In like manner, every act of sin strangely transforms and works over the soul to its own likeness: sin in this being to the soul like fire to combustible matter; it assimilates before it destroys it.

2dly, A second reason is, because every commission of sin imprints upon the soul a further disposition and proneness to sin. As the second, third, and fourth degrees of heat are more easily introduced than the first. Every one is both a preparative and a step to the next. Drinking both quenches the present thirst and provokes it for the future. When the soul is beaten from its first station, and the mounds and outworks of virtue are once broken down, it becomes quite another thing from what it was before. In one single eating of the forbidden fruit, when the act is over, yet the relish remains; and the remembrance of the first repast is an easy allurement to the second. One visit is enough to begin an acquaintance; and this point is gained by it, that when the visitant comes again he is no more a stranger.

3dly, The third and grand reason is, because the only thing that can entitle the sinner to pardon, which is repentance, is not in the sinner's power: and he who goes about the work will find it so. It is the gift of God: and though God has certainly promised forgiveness of sin to every one who repents, yet he has not promised to any one to give him grace to repent. This is the sinner's hard lot, that the same thing which makes him need repentance, makes him also in danger of not obtaining it. For it provokes and offends that holy Spirit which alone can bestow this grace: as the same treason which puts a traitor in need of his prince's mercy, is a great and a just provocation to his prince to deny it him.

Now, let these three things be put together: First, That every commission of sin, in some degree, hardens the soul in that sin. Secondly, That every commission of sin disposes the soul to proceed further in sin. And, thirdly, That to repent and turn from sin, (without which all pardon is impossible,) is not in the sinner's power; and then, I suppose, there can not but appear a greater likelihood, that a sin once committed will in the issue not be pardoned, than that it will. To all which, add the confirmation of general experience, and the real event of things, that where one man ever comes to repent, an hundred, I might say a thousand at least, end their days in final impenitence.

All which considered, surely there can not need a more pregnant argument of the greatness of this preventing mercy, if it did no more for a man than this; that his grand, immortal concern, more valuable to him than ten thousand worlds, is not thrown upon a critical point; that he is not brought to his last stake; that he is rescued from the first descents into hell and the high probabilities of damnation.

For whatsoever the issue proves, it is certainly a miserable thing to be forced to cast lots for one's life; yet in every sin, a man does the same for eternity. And therefore let the boldest sinner take this one consideration along with him, when he is going to sin, that, whether the sin he is about to act ever comes to be pardoned or no, yet, as soon as it is acted, it quite turns the balance, puts his salvation upon the venture, leaves him but one cast for all; and, which is yet much more dreadful, makes it ten to one odds against him.

But let us now alter the state of the matter, so as to leave no doubt in the case; but suppose that the sin, which, upon non-prevention, comes to be committed, comes also to be repented of, and consequently to be pardoned. Yet, in the

Fourth and last place, The greatness of this preventing mercy is eminently proved from those advantages accruing to the soul from the prevention of sin, above what can be had from the bare pardon of it: and that, in these two great respects:

1. Of the clearness of a man's condition.
2. Of the satisfaction of his mind. And,

First, For the clearness of his condition. If innocence be preferable to repentance, and to be clean be more desirable than to be cleansed, then surely prevention of sin ought to have the precedence of its pardon. For so much of prevention, so much of innocence. There are indeed various degrees of it; and God, in his infinite wisdom, does not deal forth the same measure of his preventing grace to all. Sometimes he may suffer the soul but just to begin the sinful production, in reflecting upon a sin, suggested by the imagination, with some complacency and delight; which, in the apostle's phrase, is to *conceive sin*; and then, in these early, imperfect beginnings, God perhaps may presently dash and extinguish it. Or possibly he may permit the sinful conception to receive life and form, by passing into a purpose of committing it; and then he may make it prove abortive, by stifling it before ever it comes to the birth. Or perhaps God may think fit to let it come even *to the birth,* by some strong endeavors to commit it, and yet then deny it *strength to bring forth*; so that it never comes into actual commission. Or, lastly, God may suffer it to be born, and see the world, by permitting the endeavor of sin to pass into the commission of it. And this is the last fatal step but one; which is, by frequent repetition of the sinful act, to continue and persist in it, till at length it settles into a fixed, confirmed habit of sin; which, being properly that which the apostle calls the *finishing of sin*, ends certainly in *death*, — death, not only as to merit, but also as to actual infliction.

Now peradventure in this whole progress, preventing grace may sometimes come in to the poor sinner's help, but *at the last hour of the day;* and having suffered him to run all the former risk and maze of sin, and to descend so many steps downwards to the black regions of death: as first, from the bare thought and imagination of sin, to look upon it with some beginnings of appetite and delight; from thence, to purpose and intend it; and from intending, to endeavor it; and from endeavoring, actually to commit it; and, having committed it, perhaps for some time to continue in it: and then, I say, after all this, God may turn the fatal stream, and by a mighty grace interrupt its course, and keep it from passing into a settled habit, and so hinder the absolute completion of sin in final obduracy.

Certain it is, that wheresoever it pleases God to stop the sinner on this side hell, how far soever he has been advanced in his way towards it, is a vast, ineffable mercy; a mercy as great as life from the dead, and salvation to a man tottering with horror upon the very edge and brink of destruction. But if, more than all this, God shall be pleased by an early grace to prevent sin so soon as to keep the soul in the virginity of its first innocence, not tainted with the desires, and much less defloured with the formed purpose of any thing vile and sinful, what an infinite goodness is this! It is not a converting, but a crowning grace; such an one as irradiates, and puts a circle of glory about the head of him upon whom it descends; it is the Holy Ghost coming down upon him *in the form of a dove*, and setting him triumphant above the necessity of tears and sorrow, mourning and repentance, the sad after-games of a lost innocence. And this brings in the consideration of that other great advantage accruing to the soul from the prevention of sin, above what can be had from the bare pardon of it; namely,

2. The satisfaction of a man's mind. There is that true joy, that solid and substantial comfort, conveyed to the heart by preventing grace, which pardoning grace, at the best, very

seldom, and, for the most part, never gives. For since all joy passes into the heart through the understanding, the object of it must be known by one before it can affect the other. Now, when grace keeps a man so within his bounds that sin is prevented, he certainly knows it to be so; and so rejoices upon the firm, infallible ground of sense and assurance. But, on the other side, though grace may have reversed the condemning sentence, and sealed the sinner's pardon before God, yet it may have left no transcript of that pardon in the sinner's breast. The handwriting against him may be cancelled in the court of heaven, and yet the indictment run on in the court of conscience. So that a man may be safe as to his condition, but in the mean time dark and doubtful as to his apprehensions; secure in his pardon, but miserable in the ignorance of it; and so, passing all his days in the disconsolate, uneasy vicissitudes of hopes and fears, at length go out of the world, not knowing whither he goes. And what is this, but a black cloud drawn over all a man's comforts? a cloud which, though it can not hinder the supporting influence of heaven, yet will be sure to intercept the refreshing light of it. The pardoned person must not think to stand upon the same vantage-ground with the innocent. It is enough that they are both equally safe; but it can not be thought that, without a rare privilege, both can be equally cheerful. And thus much for the advantageous effects of preventing, above those of pardoning grace; which was the fourth and last argument brought for the proof of the proposition. Pass we now to the next general thing proposed for the prosecution of it; namely,

2. Its application. Which, from the foregoing discourse, may afford us several useful deductions; but chiefly by way of information, in these three following particulars. As,

First, This may inform and convince us how vastly greater a pleasure is consequent upon the forbearance of sin than can possibly accompany the commission of it; and how much higher a satisfaction is to be found from a conquered, than from a conquering passion. For the proof of which, we need look no further than the great example here before us. Revenge is certainly the most luscious morsel that the devil can put into the sinner's mouth. But do we think that

David could have found half that pleasure in the execution of his revenge that he expresses here upon the disappointment of it? Possibly it might have pleased him in the present heat and hurry of his rage, but must have displeased him infinitely more in the cool, sedate reflections of his mind. For sin can please no longer than for that pitiful space of time while it is committing; and surely the present pleasure of a sinful act is a poor countervail for the bitterness of the review, which begins where the action ends, and lasts forever. There is no ill thing which a man does in his passion, but his memory will be revenged on him for it afterwards.

All pleasure springing from a gratified passion (as most of the pleasure of sin does) must needs determine with that passion. It is short, violent, and fallacious; and as soon as the imagination is disabused, will certainly be at an end. And therefore Des Cartes prescribes excellently well for the regulation of the passions; viz. That a man should fix and forearm his mind with this settled persuasion, that, during that commotion of his blood and spirits, in which passion properly consists, whatsoever is offered to his imagination in favor of it, tends only to deceive his reason. It is indeed a real trepan upon it; feeding it with colors and appearances, instead of arguments; and driving the very same bargain which Jacob did with Esau, a mess of pottage for a birthright, a present repast for a perpetuity.

Secondly, We have here a sure, unfailing criterion, by which every man may discover and find out the gracious or ungracious disposition of his own heart. The temper of every man is to be judged of from the thing he most esteems; and the object of his esteem may be measured by the prime object of his thanks. What is it that opens thy mouth in praises, that fills thy heart, and lifts up thy hands in grateful acknowledgments to thy great Creator and Preserver? Is it that thy bags and thy barns are full, that thou hast escaped this sickness or that danger? Alas, God may have done all this for thee in anger! All this fair sunshine may have been only to harden thee in thy sins. He may have given thee riches and honor, health and power with a curse; and if so, it will be found but a poor comfort to have had never so great a share of God's bounty without his blessing.

But has he at any time kept thee from thy sin? stopped thee in the prosecution of thy lust? defeated the malicious arts and stratagems of thy mortal enemy the tempter? And does not the sense of this move and affect thy heart more than all the former instances of temporal prosperity, which are but, as it were, the promiscuous scatterings of his common providence, while these are the distinguishing kindnesses of his special grace?

A truly pious mind has certainly another kind of relish and taste of these things; and if it receives a temporal blessing with gratitude, it receives a spiritual one with ecstasy and transport. David, an heroic instance of such a temper, overlooks the rich and seasonable present of Abigail, though pressed with hunger and travel; but her advice, which disarmed his rage, and calmed his revenge, draws forth those high and affectionate gratulations from him: *Blessed be thy advice, and blessed be thou, who hast kept me this day from shedding blood, and avenging myself with mine own hand.* These were his joyful and glorious trophies; not that he triumphed over his enemy, but that he insulted over his revenge; that he escaped from himself, and was delivered from his own fury. And whosoever has any thing of David's piety, will be perpetually plying the throne of grace with such like acknowledgments; as, "Blessed be that Providence which delivered me from such a lewd company, and such a vicious acquaintance, which was the bane of such and such a person. And, Blessed be that God who cast rubs, and stops, and hinderances in my way, when I was attempting the commission of such or such a sin; who took me out of such a course of life, such a place, or such an employment, which was a continual snare and temptation to me. And, Blessed be such a preacher, and such a friend, whom God made use of to speak a word in season to my wicked heart, and so turned me out of the paths of death and destruction, and saved me in spite of the world, the devil, and myself."

These are such things as a man shall remember with joy upon his deathbed; such as shall cheer and warm his heart even in that last and bitter agony, when many, from the very bottom of their souls, shall wish that they had never been rich, or great, or powerful; and reflect with anguish and remorse upon those splendid occasions of sin, which served them for little but to highten their guilt, and at best to inflame their accounts at that great tribunal which they are going to appear before.

In the third and last place. We learn from hence the great reasonableness of, not only a contented, but also a thankful acquiescence in any condition, and under the crossest and severest passages of Providence which can possibly befall us: since there is none of all these but may be the instrument of preventing grace in the hands of a merciful God, to keep us from those courses which would otherwise assuredly end in our confusion. This is most certain, that there is no enjoyment which the nature of man is either desirous or capable of, but may be to him a direct inducement to sin, and consequently is big with mischief, and carries death in the bowels of it. But to make the assertion more particular, and thereby more convincing, let us take an account of it with reference to the three greatest and deservedly most valued enjoyments of this life.

1. Health; 2dly, Reputation; and 3dly, Wealth.

First, And first for health. Has God made a breach upon that? Perhaps he is building up thy soul upon the ruins of thy body. Has he bereaved thee of the use and vigor of thy limbs? Possibly he saw that otherwise they would have been the instruments of thy lusts, and the active ministers of thy debaucheries. Perhaps thy languishing upon thy bed has kept thee from rotting in a jail, or in a worse place. God saw it necessary by such mortifications to quench the boilings of a furious, overflowing appetite, and the boundless rage of an insatiable intemperance; to make the weakness of the flesh the physic and restaurative of the spirit; and, in a word, rather to save thee diseased, sickly, and deformed, than to let strength, health, and beauty drive thee headlong (as they have done many thousands) into eternal destruction.

Secondly, Has God in his providence thought fit to drop a blot upon thy name, and to blast thy reputation? He saw perhaps that the breath of popular air was grown infectious, and would have derived a contagion upon thy better part. Pride and vainglory had mounted thee too high, and therefore it was necessary for mercy to take thee down, to prevent a greater fall. *A good name is*, indeed, *better than life;* but a sound mind is better than both. Praise and applause had swelled thee to a proportion ready to burst; it had vitiated all thy spiritual appetites, and brought thee to feed upon the air, and to surfeit upon the wind, and, in a word, to starve thy soul, only to pamper thy imagination.

And now if God makes use of some poignant disgrace to prick this enormous bladder, and to let out the poisonous vapor, is not the mercy greater than the severity of the cure? *Cover them with shame*, says the psalmist, *that they may seek thy name.* Fame and glory transports a man out of himself; and, like a violent wind, though it may bear him up for a while, yet it will be sure to let him fall at last. It makes the mind loose and garish, scatters the spirits, and leaves a kind of dissolution upon all the faculties. Whereas shame, on the contrary, as all grief does, naturally contracts and unites, and thereby fortifies the spirits, fixes the ramblings of fancy, and so reduces and gathers the man into himself. This is the sovereign effect of a bitter potion, administered by a wise and merciful hand: and what hurt can there be in all the slanders, obloquies, and disgraces of this world, if they are but the arts and methods of Providence to shame us into the glories of the next. But then,

Thirdly and lastly, Has God thought fit to cast thy lot amongst the poor of this world, and that either by denying thee any share of the plenties of this life, which is something grievous; or by taking them away, which is much more so? Yet still all this may be but the effect of preventing mercy. For so much mischief as riches have done and may do to the souls of men, so much mercy may there be in taking them away. For does not the wisest of men, next our Saviour, tell us of *riches kept to the hurt of the owners of them?* Eccles. v. 13. And does not our Saviour himself speak of the intolerable difficulty which they cause in men's passage to heaven? Do they not make the *narrow way* much narrower, and contract *the gate which leads to life* to the straitness of a *needle's eye?*

And now, if God will fit thee for this passage by taking off thy load, and emptying thy bags, and so suit the narrowness of thy fortune to the narrowness of the way thou art to pass, is there any thing but mercy in all this? Nay, are not the riches of his mercy conspicuous in the poverty of thy condition?

Thou who repinest at the plenty and splendor of thy neighbor, at the greatness of his incomes, and the magnificence of his retinue, consider what are frequently the dismal, wretched consequences of all this, and thou wilt have little cause to envy this gaudy great one, or to wish thyself in his room.

For do we not often hear of this or that young heir newly come to his father's vast estate? An happy man, no doubt! But does not the town presently ring of his debaucheries, his blasphemies, and his murders? Are not his riches and his lewdnesses talked of together? and the odiousness of one hightened and set off by the greatness of the other? Are not his oaths, his riots, and other villainies reckoned by as many thousands as his estate?

Now consider, had this grand debauchee, this glistering monster, been born to thy poverty and mean circumstances, he could not have contracted such a clamorous guilt, he could not have been so bad: nor, perhaps, had thy birth instated thee in the same wealth and greatness, wouldest thou have been at all better.

This God foresaw and knew, in the ordering both of his and thy condition: and which of the two now, can we think, is the greater debtor to his preventing mercy? Lordly sins require lordly estates to support them: and where Providence denies the latter, it cuts off all temptation to the former.

And thus have I shown by particular instances, what cause men have to acquiesce in and submit to the harshest dispensations that Providence can measure out to them in this life; and with what satisfaction, or rather gratitude, that ought to be endured by which the greatest of mischiefs is prevented. The great physician of souls sometimes can not cure without cutting us. Sin has festered inwardly, and he must lance the imposthume, to let out death with the suppuration. He who ties a madman's hands, or takes away his sword, loves his person, while he disarms his frenzy. And whether by health or sickness, honor or disgrace, wealth or poverty, life or death, mercy is still contriving, acting, and carrying on the spiritual good of all those who love God, and are loved by him.

To whom, therefore, be rendered and ascribed, as is most due, all praise, might, majesty, and dominion, both now and for evermore. Amen.

SERMON XXIII.

AN ACCOUNT OF THE NATURE AND MEASURES OF CONSCIENCE:

IN TWO SERMONS ON 1 JOHN III. 21, PREACHED BEFORE THE UNIVERSITY, AT CHRIST CHURCH, OXON.

THE FIRST PREACHED ON THE 1ST OF NOVEMBER, 1691.

1 JOHN iii. 21.—*Beloved, if our heart condemn us not, we have confidence toward God.*

AS nothing can be of more moment, so few things, doubtless, are of more difficulty, than for men to be rationally satisfied about the estate of their souls, with reference to God and the great concerns of eternity. In their judgment about which, if they err finally, it is like a man's missing his cast when he throws dice for his life; his being, his happiness, and all that he does or can enjoy in the world, is involved in the error of one throw. And therefore it may very well deserve our best skill and care, to inquire into those rules by which we may guide our judgment in so weighty an affair, both with safety and success. And this, I think, can not be better done than by separating the false and fallacious from the true and certain. For if the rule we judge by be uncertain, it is odds but we shall judge wrong; and if we should judge right, yet it is not properly skill, but chance; not a true judgment, but a lucky hit: which, certainly, the eternal interests of an immortal soul are of much too high a value to be left at the mercy of.

First of all then: he who would pass such a judgment upon his condition as shall be ratified in heaven and confirmed at that great tribunal from which there lies no appeal, will find himself wofully deceived, if he judges of his spiritual estate by any of these four following measures: as,

1. The general esteem of the world concerning him. He who owes his piety to fame and hearsay, and the evidences of his salvation to popular voice and opinion, builds his house not only upon the sand, but, which is worse, upon the wind; and writes the deeds, by which he holds his estate, upon the face of a river. He makes a bodily eye the judge of things impossible to be seen; and humor and ignorance (which the generality of men both think and speak by) the great proofs of his justification. But surely no man has the estate of his soul drawn upon his face, nor the decree of his election wrote upon his forehead. He who would know a man thoroughly, must follow him into the closet of his heart, the door of which is kept shut to all the world besides, and the inspection of which is only the prerogative of omniscience.

The favorable opinion and good word of men, (to some persons especially,) comes oftentimes at a very easy rate; and by a few demure looks and affected whines, set off with some odd, devotional postures and grimaces, and such other little arts of dissimulation, cunning men will do wonders, and commence presently heroes for sanctity, self-denial, and sincerity, while within perhaps they are as proud as Lucifer, as covetous as Demas, as false as Judas; and, in the whole course of their conversation, act and are acted, not by devotion, but design.

So that, for aught I see, though the Mosaical part of Judaism be abolished amongst Christians, the Pharisaical part of it never will. A grave, stanch, skillfully managed face, set upon a grasping, aspiring mind, having got many a sly formalist the reputation of a primitive and severe piety, forsooth, and made many such mountebanks pass admired, even for saints upon earth, (as the word is,) who are like to be so nowhere else.

But a man who had never seen the stately outside of a tomb, or painted sepulchre, before, may very well be excused if he takes it rather for the repository of some rich treasure, than of a noisome corpse; but should he but once open and rake into it, though he could not see, he would quickly smell out his mistake. The greatest part of the world is nothing but appearance, nothing but show and surface; and many make it their business, their study, and concern, that it should be so; who, having for many years together deceived all about them, are at last willing to deceive themselves too; and by a long, immemorial practice, and, as it were, prescription of an aged, thoroughpaced hypocrisy, come at length to believe that for a reality which, at the first practice of it, they themselves knew to be a cheat. But if men love to be deceived and fooled about so great an interest as that of their spiritual estate, it must be confessed that they can not take a surer and more effectual course to be so, than by taking their neighbor's word for that which can be known to them only from their own hearts. For certainly it is not more absurd to undertake to tell the name of an unknown person by his looks, than to vouch a man's saintship from the vogue of the world, founded upon his external behavior.

2. The judgment of any casuist, or learned divine, concerning the estate of a man's soul, is not sufficient to give him confidence towards God. And the reason is, because no learning whatsoever can give a man the knowledge of another's heart. Besides, that it is more than possible that the most profound and experienced casuist in the world may mistake in his judgment of a man's spiritual condition; and if he does judge right, yet the man can not be sure that he will declare that judgment sincerely and impartially, (the greatest clerks being not always the honestest, any more than the wisest men,) but may purposely soothe a man up for hope or fear, or the service of some sinister interest; and so show him the face of a foul soul in a flattering glass: considering how much the raising in some men a false hope of another world may, with others, serve a real interest in this.

There is a generation of men who have framed their casuistical divinity to a perfect compliance with all the corrupt affections of a man's nature; and by that new-invented engine of the doctrine of probability, will undertake to warrant and quiet the sinner's conscience in the commission of any sin whatsoever, provided there be but the opinion of one learned man to vouch it. For this, they say, is a sufficient ground for the conscience of any unlearned person to rely and to act upon. So that if but one doctor asserts that I may lawfully kill a man to prevent a box on the ear, or a calumny, by which he would otherwise asperse my good name, I may with a good conscience do it; nay, I may safely rest upon this one casuist's judgment, though thousands, as learned as himself, yea, and the express law of God besides, affirm the quite contrary. But these spiritual engineers know well enough how to deal with any commandment, either by taking or expounding it away, at their pleasure.

Such an ascendant have these Romish casuists over scripture, reason, and morality; much like what is said of the stupid, modern Jews, that they have subdued their sense and reason to such a sottish servitude to their rabbies, as to hold, that in case two rabbies should happen to contradict one another, they were yet bound to believe the contradictory assertions of both to be equally certain, and equally the word of God: such an iron-digesting faith have they, and such pity it is that there should be no such thing in Judaism as transubstantiation to employ it upon.

But as for these casuists whom I have been speaking of; if the judgment of one doctor may authorize the practice of any action, I believe it will be hard to find any sort or degree of villainy which the corruption of man's nature is capable of committing, which shall not meet with a defense. And of this I could give such an instance from something wrote by a certain prelate of theirs, cardinal and archbishop of Beneventum, as were enough, not only to astonish all pious ears, but almost to unconsecrate the very church I speak in.

But the truth is, the way by which these Romish casuists speak peace to the consciences of men, is either by teaching them that many actions are not sins, which yet really are so, or by suggesting something to them which shall satisfy their minds, notwithstanding a known, actual, avowed continuance in their sins: such as are their pardons and indulgences, and giving men a share in the saints' merits, out of the common bank and treasury of the church, which the pope has the sole custody and disposal of, and is never kept shut to such as come with an open hand. So that according to these new evangelists, well may we pronounce, Blessed are the rich, for theirs is the kingdom of heaven. But God deliver the world from such guides, or rather such hucksters of souls, the very shame of religion, and the shameless subverters of morality. And it is really matter both of wonder and indignation, that such impostors should at all concern themselves about rules or directions of conscience, who seem to have no consciences to apply them to.

3. The absolution pronounced by a priest, whether Papist or Protestant, is not a certain, infallible ground, to give the person so absolved confidence towards God; and the reason is, because, if absolution, as such, could of itself secure a man, as to the estate of his soul, then it would follow that every person so absolved should, by virtue thereof, be *ipso facto* put into such a condition of safety which is not imaginable.

For the absolution pronounced must be either conditional, as running upon the conditions of faith and repentance; and then, if those conditions are not found in the person so absolved, it is but a seal to a blank, and so a mere nullity to him. Or, the absolution must be pronounced in terms absolute and unconditional: and if so, then the said absolution becomes valid and effectual, either by virtue of the state of the person to whom it was pronounced, as being a true penitent, or by virtue of the *opus operatum*, or bare action itself of the priest absolving him. If it receives its validity from the former, then it is clear, that although it runs in forms absolute, yet it is indeed conditional, as depending upon the qualification of the person to whom it is pronounced; who therefore owes the remission of his sins, not properly to the priest's absolution, but to his own repentance, which made that absolution effectual, and would undoubtedly have saved him, though the priest had never absolved him.

But if it be asserted that the very action of the priest absolving him has of itself this virtue, then we must grant also, that it is in the priest's power to save a man who never repented, nor did one good work in all his life; forasmuch as it is in his power to perform this action upon him in full form, and with full intention to absolve him. But the horrible absurdity, blasphemy, and impiety of this assertion sufficiently proclaims its falsity without any further confutation.

In a word, if a man be a penitent, his repentance stamps

his absolution effectual. If not, let the priest repeat the same absolution to him ten thousand times, yet for all his being absolved in this world, God will condemn him in the other. And consequently, he who places his salvation upon this ground, will find himself like an imprisoned and condemned malefactor, who in the night dreams that he is released, but in the morning finds himself led to the gallows.

4thly and lastly, No advantages from external church-membership, or profession of the true religion, can themselves give a man confidence towards God. And yet perhaps there is hardly any one thing in the world, which men, in all ages, have generally more cheated themselves with. The Jews were an eminent instance of this: who, because they were the sons of Abraham, as it is readily acknowledged by our Saviour, John viii. 37, *and because they were entrusted with the oracles of God*, Rom. iii. 2, *together with the covenants, and the promises*, Rom. ix. 4, that is, in other words, because they were the true church, and professors of the true religion, (while all the world about them lay wallowing in ignorance, heathenism, and idolatry,) they concluded from hence, that God was so fond of them, that, notwithstanding all their villainies and immoralities, they were still the darlings of heaven, and the only heirs apparent of salvation. They thought, it seems, God and themselves linked together in so fast, but withal so strange a covenant, that, although they never performed their part of it, God was yet bound to make good every tittle of his.

And this made John the Baptist set himself with so much acrimony and indignation to baffle this senseless, arrogant conceit of theirs, which made them huff at the doctrine of repentance, as a thing below them, and not at all belonging to them, in Matt. iii. 9. *Think not*, says he, *to say within yourselves, We have Abraham to our father.* This, he knew, lay deep in their hearts, and was still in their mouths, and kept them insolent and impenitent under sins of the highest and most clamorous guilt; though our Saviour himself also, not long after this, assured them, that they were of a very different stock and parentage from that which they boasted of; and that whosoever was their father upon the natural account, the devil was certainly so upon a moral.

In like manner, how vainly do the Romanists pride and value themselves upon the name of *Catholics*, of the *catholic religion*, and of the *catholic church!* though a title no more applicable to the church of Rome, than a man's finger, when it is swelled and putrefied, can be called his whole body: a church which allows salvation to none without it, nor awards damnation to almost any within it. And therefore, as the former empty plea served the sottish Jews, so, no wonder if this equally serves these, to put them into a fool's paradise, by feeding their hopes without changing their lives; and, as an excellent expedient, first to assure them of heaven, and then to bring them easily to it; and so, in a word, to save both their souls and their sins too.

And to show how the same cheat runs through all professions, though not in the same dress; none are more powerfully and grossly under it than another sort of men, who, on the contrary, place their whole acceptance with God, and indeed their whole religion, upon a mighty zeal, or rather outcry, against popery and superstition; verbally, indeed, uttered against the church of Rome, but really against the church of England. To which sort of persons I shall say no more but this, and that in the spirit of truth and meekness; namely, that zeal and noise against popery, and real services for it, are no such inconsistent things as some may imagine; indeed no more than invectives against Papists, and solemn addresses of thanks to them for that very thing by which they would have brought in popery upon us. And if those of the separation do not yet know so much, thanks to them for it, we of the church of England do; and so may they themselves too, in due time. I speak not this by way of sarcasm, to reproach them, (I leave that to their own consciences, which will do it more effectually,) but by way of charity, to warn them: for let them be assured that this whole scene and practice of theirs is as really superstition, and as false a bottom to rest their souls upon, as either the Jews alleging Abraham for their father, while the devil claimed them for his children; or the Papists relying upon their indulgences, their saints' merits and supererogations, and such other fopperies, as can never settle, nor indeed so much as reach, the conscience; and much less recommend it to that Judge who is not to be flammed off with words, and phrases, and names, though taken out of the scripture itself.

Nay, and I shall proceed yet further. It is not a man's being of the church of England itself, (though undoubtedly the purest and best reformed church in the world; indeed so well reformed, that it will be found a much easier work to alter than to better its constitution;) I say, it is not a man's being even of this excellent church, which can of itself clear accounts between God and his conscience. Since bare communion with a good church can never alone make a good man: for if it could, I am sure we should have no bad ones in ours; and much less such as would betray it.

So that we see here that it is but too manifest that men of all churches and persuasions are strangely apt to flatter and deceive themselves with what they believe and what they profess; and if we throughly consider the matter, we shall find the fallacy to lie in this: that those religious institutions, which God designed only for means, helps, and advantages, to promote and further men in the practice of holiness, they look upon rather as a privilege to serve them instead of it, and really to commute for it. This is the very case, and a fatal self-imposture it is certainly, and such an one as defeats the design and destroys the force of all religion.

And thus I have shown four several uncertain and deceitful rules, which men are prone to judge of their spiritual estate by.

But now, have we any better or more certain, to substitute and recommend in the room of them? Why, yes; if we believe the apostle, a man's own heart or conscience is that which, above all other things, is able to give him confidence towards God. And the reason is, because the heart knows that by itself, which nothing in the world besides can give it any knowledge of, and without the knowledge of which it can have no foundation to build any true confidence upon. Conscience, under God, is the only competent judge of what the soul has done, and what it has not done; what guilt it has contracted, and what it has not; as it is in 1 Cor. ii. 11, *What man knoweth the things of a man, save the spirit of man which is in him?* Conscience is its own counsellor, the sole master of its own secrets: and it is the privilege of our nature, that every man should keep the key of his own breast.

Now for the further prosecution of the words, I shall do these four things:

1. I shall show how the heart or conscience ought to be informed, in order to its founding in us a rational confidence towards God.

2. I shall show how and by what means we may get it thus informed, and afterwards preserve and keep it so.

3. I shall show whence it is that the testimony of conscience thus informed, comes to be so authentic, and so much to be relied upon; and,

4thly and lastly, I shall assign some particular cases or instances, in which the confidence suggested by it does most eminently show and exert itself.

1. And first for the first of these, how the heart or conscience, &c. It is certain, that no man can have any such confidence towards God, only because his heart tells him a lie; and that it may do so is altogether as certain. For there is the erroneous, as well as the rightly informed conscience; and if the conscience happens to be deluded, and thereupon to give false directions to the will, so that by virtue of those directions it is betrayed into a course of sin: sin does not therefore cease to be sin, because a man committed it conscientiously. If conscience comes to be perverted so far as to bring a man under a persuasion that it is either lawful or his duty to resist the magistrate, to seize upon his neighbor's just rights or estate, to worship stocks and stones, or to lie, equivocate, and the like, this will not absolve him before God; since error, which is in itself evil, can never make another thing good. He who does an unwarrantable action through a false information, which information he ought not to have believed, can not in reason make the guilt of one sin the excuse of another.

Conscience therefore must be rightly informed, before the testimony of it can be authentic in what it pronounces concerning the estate of the soul. It must proceed by the two grand rules of right reason and scripture; these are the compass which it must steer by. For conscience comes formally to oblige, only as it is the messenger of the mind of God to the soul of man; which he has revealed to him, partly by the impression of certain notions and maxims upon the practical understanding, and partly by the declared oracles of his word. So far therefore as conscience reports any thing agreeable to, or deducible from these, it is to be hearkened to as the great conveyer of truth to the soul; but when it reports any thing dissonant to these, it obliges no more than the falsehood reported by it.

But since there is none who follows an erroneous conscience, but does so because he thinks it true; and moreover thinks it true, because he is persuaded that it proceeds according to the two forementioned rules of scripture and right reason; how shall a man be able to satisfy himself, when his conscience is rightly informed, and when possessed with an error? For to affirm that the sentence passed by a rightly informed conscience gives a man a rational confidence towards God; but, in the mean time, not to assign any means possible by which he may know when his conscience is thus rightly informed, and when not, it must equally bereave him of such a confidence, as placing the condition upon which it depends wholly out of his knowledge.

Here therefore is the knot, here the difficulty, how to state some rule of certainty, by which infallibly to distinguish when the conscience is right, and to be relied upon; when erroneous, and to be distrusted, in the testimony it gives about the sincerity and safety of a man's spiritual condition.

For the resolution of which, I answer, that it is not necessary for a man to be assured of the rightness of his conscience, by such an infallible certainty of persuasion as amounts to the clearness of a demonstration; but it is sufficient, if he knows it upon grounds of such a convincing probability as shall exclude all rational grounds of doubting of it. For I can not think that the confidence here spoken of rises so high as to assurance. And the reason is, because it is manifestly such a confidence as is common to all sincere Christians; which yet assurance, we all know, is not.

The truth is, the word in the original, which is παῤῥησία, signifies properly *freedom* or *boldness of speech*; though the Latin translation renders it by *fiducia*, and so corresponds with the English, which renders it *confidence*. But whether *fiducia* or *confidence* reaches the full sense of *παῤῥησία*, may very well be disputed. However, it is certain that neither the word in the original, nor yet in the translation, imports *assurance*. For *freedom* or *boldness of speech*, I am sure, does not; and *fiducia*, or *confidence*, signifies only a man's being actually persuaded of a thing, upon better arguments for it than any that he can see against it; which he may very well be, and yet not be assured of it.

From all which I conclude, that the confidence here mentioned in the text amounts to no more than a rational well-grounded hope. Such an one as the apostle tells us, in Rom. v. 5, *maketh not ashamed*.

And upon these terms, I affirm, that such a conscience as has employed the utmost of its ability to give itself the best information and clearest knowledge of its duty that it can, is a rational ground for a man to build such an hope upon; and, consequently, for him to confide in.

There is an innate light in every man, discovering to him the first lines of duty, in the common notions of good and evil, which, by cultivation and improvement, may be advanced to higher and brighter discoveries. And from hence it is that the schoolmen and moralists admit not of any *ignorantia juris*, speaking of natural moral right, to give excuse to sin. Since all such ignorance is voluntary, and therefore culpable, forasmuch as it was in every man's power to have prevented it, by a due improvement of the light of nature, and the seeds of moral honesty sown in his heart.

If it be here demanded, whether a man may not remain ignorant of his duty, after he has used the utmost means to inform himself of it, I answer, that so much of duty as is absolutely necessary to save him, he shall upon the use of such a course come to know; and that which he continues ignorant of, having done the utmost lying in his power that he might not be ignorant of it, shall never damn him. Which assertion is proved thus: The gospel damns nobody for being ignorant of that which he is not obliged to know; but that which upon the improvement of a man's utmost power he can not know, he is not obliged to know; for that otherwise he would be obliged to an impossibility; since that which is out of the compass of any man's power, is to that man impossible.

He therefore who exerts all the powers and faculties of his soul, and plies all means and opportunities in the search of truth, which God has vouchsafed him, may rest upon the judgment of his conscience so informed, as a warrantable guide of those actions which he must account to God for. And if by following such a guide he falls into the ditch, the ditch shall never drown him, or if it should, the man perishes not by his sin, but by his misfortune. In a word, he who endeavors to know the utmost of his duty that he can, and practices the utmost that he knows, has the equity and goodness of the great God to stand as a mighty wall or rampart between him and damnation, for any errors or infirmities which the frailty of his condition has invincibly, and therefore inculpably, exposed him to.

And if a conscience thus qualified and informed, be not the measure by which a man may take a true estimate of his absolution before the tribunal of God, all the understanding of human nature can not find out any ground for the sinner to pitch the sole of his foot upon, or rest his conscience with any assurance, but is left in the plunge of infinite doubts and uncertainties, suspicions and misgivings, both as to the measures of his present duty, and the final issues of his future reward.

Let this conclusion therefore stand as the firm result of the foregoing discourse, and the foundation of what is to follow; that such a conscience as has not been wanting to itself, in endeavoring to get the utmost and clearest information about the will of God, that its power, advantages, and opportunities could afford it, is that internal judge whose absolution is a rational and sure ground of confidence towards God: and so I pass to the second thing proposed. Which is to show, How, and by what means, we may get our heart or conscience thus informed, and afterwards preserve and keep it so.

In order to which, amongst many things that might be alleged as highly useful, and conducing to this great work, I shall insist upon these four: as,

1. Let a man carefully attend to the voice of his reason, and all the dictates of natural morality, so as by no means to

do any thing contrary to them. For though reason is not to be relied upon as a guide universally sufficient to direct us what to do, yet it is generally to be relied upon and obeyed, where it tells us what we are not to do. It is indeed but a weak and diminutive light, compared to revelation; but it ought to be no disparagement to a star, that it is not a sun. Nevertheless, as weak and as small as it is, it is a light always at hand, and though enclosed, as it were, in a dark lantern, may yet be of singular use to prevent many a foul step, and to keep us from many a dangerous fall. And every man brings such a degree of this light into the world with him, that though it can not bring him to heaven, yet, if he be true to it, it will carry him a great way; indeed so far, that if he follows it faithfully, I doubt not but he shall meet with another light, which shall carry him quite through.

How far it may be improved is evident from that high and refined morality which shined forth both in the lives and writings of some of the ancient heathens, who yet had no other light but this, both to live and to write by. For how great a man in virtue was Cato, of whom the historian gives this glorious character: *Esse quam videri bonus malebat!* And of what an impregnable integrity was Fabricius, of whom it was said, that a man might as well attempt to turn the sun out of his course, as to bring Fabricius to do a base or a dishonest action! And then for their writings; what admirable things occur in the remains of Pythagoras, and the books of Plato, and of several other philosophers! short, I confess, of the rules of Christianity, but generally above the lives of Christians.

Which being so, ought not the light of reason to be looked upon by us as a rich and a noble talent, and such an one as we must account to God for? for it is certainly from him. It is a ray of divinity darted into the soul. *It is the candle of the Lord,* as Solomon calls it, and God never lights us up a candle either to put out or to sleep by. If it be made conscious to a work of darkness, it will not fail to discover and reprove it; and therefore the checks of it are to be revered, as the echo of a voice from heaven; for, whatsoever conscience binds here on earth, will be certainly bound there too; and it were a great vanity to hope or imagine, that either law or gospel will absolve what natural conscience condemns. No man ever yet offended his own conscience, but first or last it was revenged upon him for it. So that it will concern a man to treat this great principle awfully and warily, by still observing what it commands, but especially what it forbids: and if he would have it always a faithful and sincere monitor to him, let him be sure never to turn a deaf ear to it; for not to hear it is the way to silence it. Let him strictly observe the first stirrings and intimations; the first hints and whispers of good and evil, that pass in his heart; and this will keep conscience so quick and vigilant, and ready to give a man true alarms upon the least approach of his spiritual enemy, that he shall be hardly capable of a great surprise.

On the contrary, if a man accustoms himself to slight or pass over these first motions to good, or shrinkings of his conscience from evil, which originally are as natural to the heart of man as the appetites of hunger and thirst are to the stomach, conscience will by degrees grow dull and unconcerned, and, from not spying out motes, come at length to overlook beams; from carelessness it shall fall into a slumber, and from a slumber it shall settle into a deep and long sleep; till at last perhaps it sleeps itself into a lethargy, and that such an one that nothing but hell and judgment shall be able to awaken it. For long disuse of any thing made for action will in time take away the very use of it. As I have read of one, who, having for a disguise kept one of his eyes a long time covered, when he took off the covering found his eye indeed where it was, but his sight was gone. He who would keep his conscience awake, must be careful to keep it stirring.

2. Let a man be very tender and regardful of every pious motion and suggestion made by the Spirit of God to his heart. I do not hereby go about to establish enthusiasm, or such fantastic pretenses of intercourse with God, as Papists and fanatics (who in most things copy from one another, as well as rail at one another) do usually boast of. But certainly, if the evil spirit may and often does suggest wicked and vile thoughts to the minds of men, as all do and must grant, and is sufficiently proved from the *devil's putting it into the heart of Judas to betray Christ*, John xiii. 2, and his *filling the heart of*

Ananias to lie to the Holy Ghost, Acts v. 3, it can not after this, with any color of reason, be doubted, but that the holy Spirit of God, whose power and influence to good is much greater than that of the wicked spirit to evil, does frequently inject into and imprint upon the soul many blessed motions and impulses to duty, and many powerful avocations from sin. So that a man shall not only, as the prophet says, *hear a voice behind him*, but also a voice within him, telling him which way he ought to go.

For doubtless there is something more in those expressions of *being led by the Spirit*, and *being taught by the Spirit*, and the like, than mere tropes and metaphors; and nothing less is or can be imported by them, than that God sometimes speaks to, and converses with, the hearts of men, immediately by himself; and happy those who by thus hearing him speak in a *still voice*, shall prevent his speaking to them in thunder.

But you will here ask, perhaps, how we shall distinguish in such motions, which of them proceed immediately from the Spirit of God, and which from the conscience? In answer to which, I must confess that I know no certain mark of discrimination to distinguish them by, save only in general, that such as proceed immediately from God use to strike the mind suddenly and very powerfully. But then I add also, that, as the knowledge of this, in point of speculation, is so nice and difficult, so, thanks be to God, in point of practice it is not necessary. But let a man universally observe and obey every good motion rising in his heart, knowing that every such motion proceeds from God, either mediately or immediately; and that whether God speaks immediately by himself to the conscience, or mediately by the conscience to the soul, the authority is the same in both, and the contempt of either is rebellion.

Now the thing which I drive at, under this head of discourse, is to show, that as God is sometimes pleased to address himself in this manner to the hearts of men, so, if the heart will receive and answer such motions, by a ready and obsequious compliance with them, there is no doubt but they will both return more frequently, and still more and more powerfully, till at length they produce such a degree of light in the conscience, as shall give a man both a clear sight of his duty and a certain judgment of his condition.

On the contrary, as all resistance whatsoever of the dictates of conscience, even in the way of natural efficiency, brings a kind of hardness and stupefaction upon it, so the resistance of these peculiar suggestions of the Spirit will cause in it also a judicial hardness, which is yet worse than the other. So that God shall withdraw from such a heart, and the Spirit being grieved shall depart, and these blessed motions shall cease, and affect and visit it no more. The consequence of which is very terrible, as rendering a man past feeling: and then the less he feels in this world, the more he shall be sure to feel in the next. But,

3. Because the light of natural conscience is in many things defective and dim, and the internal voice of God's Spirit not always distinguishable, above all, let a man attend to the mind of God, uttered in his revealed word. I say, his revealed word. By which I do not mean that mysterious, extraordinary (and of late so much studied) book called the Revelation, and which perhaps the more it is studied the less it is understood, as generally either finding a man cracked, or making him so: but I mean those other writings of the prophets and apostles, which exhibit to us a plain, sure, perfect, and intelligible rule; a rule that will neither fail nor distract such as make use of it. A rule to judge of the two former rules by: for nothing that contradicts the revealed word of God is either the voice of right reason or of the Spirit of God: nor is it possible that it should be so, without God's contradicting himself.

And therefore we see what high elogies are given to the written word by the inspired penmen of both Testaments. *It giveth understanding to the simple,* says David, in Psalm cxix. 130. And that, you will say, is no such easy matter to do.

It is able to *make the man of God perfect,* says St. Paul, 2 Tim. iii. 17. *It is quick and powerful, and sharper than any two-edged sword, piercing even to the dividing asunder of soul and spirit; and is a discerner of the thoughts and intents of the heart,* Heb. iv. 12. Now what a force and fullness, what a vigor and emphasis is there in all these expressions! Enough, one would think, to recommend and endear the scriptures even to the Papists themselves. For if, as the text says, *they give understanding to the simple,* I know none more concerned to read and study them than their popes.

Wherefore since the light and energy of the written word is so mighty, let a man bring and hold his conscience to this steady rule; the unalterable rectitude of which will infallibly discover the rectitude or obliquity of whatsoever it is applied to. We shall find it a rule, both to instruct us what to do, and to assure us in what we have done. For though natural conscience ought to be listened to, yet it is revelation alone that is to be relied upon: as we may observe in the works of art, a judicious artist will indeed use his eye, but he will trust only to his rule.

There is not any one action whatsoever which a man ought to do or to forbear, but the scripture will give him a clear precept or prohibition for it.

So that if a man will commit such rules to his memory, and stock his mind with portions of scripture answerable to all the heads of duty and practice, his conscience can never be at a loss, either for a direction of his actions, or an answer to a temptation: it was the very course which our Saviour himself took, when the devil plied him with temptation upon temptation. Still he had a suitable scripture ready to repel and baffle them all, one after another: every pertinent text urged home being a direct stab to a temptation.

Let a man therefore consider and recount with himself the several duties and virtues of a Christian. Such as temperance, meekness, charity, purity of heart, pardoning of enemies, patience. (I had almost said passive obedience too, but that such old-fashioned Christianity seems as much out of date with some as Christ's divinity and satisfaction.) I say, let a man consider these and the like virtues, together with the contrary sins and vices that do oppose them, and then, as out of a full armory or magazine, let him furnish his conscience with texts of scripture, particularly enjoining the one, and forbidding or threatening the other. And yet I do not say that he should stuff his mind like the margent of some authors, with chapter and verse heaped together, at all adventures; but only that he should fortify it with some few texts which are home and apposite to his case. And a conscience thus supplied will be like a man armed at all points; and always ready either to receive or to attack his enemy. Otherwise it is not a man's having arms in his house; no, nor yet his having courage and skill to use them; but it is his having them still about him, which must both secure him from being set upon, and defend him when he is.

Accordingly, men must know that without taking the forementioned course, all that they do in this matter is but lost labor; and that they read the scriptures to as little purpose as some use to quote them; much reading being like much eating, wholly useless without digestion; and it is impossible for a man to digest his meat, without also retaining it.

Till men get what they read into their minds, and fix it in their memories, they keep their religion as they used to do their Bibles, only in their closet, or carry it in their pocket; and that, you may imagine, must improve and affect the soul just as much as a man's having plenty of provision only in his stores, will nourish and support his body. When men forget the word heard or read by them, the devil is said *to steal it out of their hearts*, Luke viii. 12. And for this cause we do with as much reason as propriety of speech call the committing of a thing to memory, the getting it by heart. For it is the memory that must transmit it to the heart; and it is in vain to expect that the heart should keep its hold of any truth when the memory has let it go.

4. The fourth and last way that I shall mention for the getting of the conscience rightly informed, and afterwards keeping it so, is frequently and impartially to account with it. It is with a man and his conscience as with one man and another; amongst whom we use to say that *even reckoning makes lasting friends;* and the way to make reckonings even, I am sure, is to make them often. Delays in accounts are always suspicious; and bad enough in themselves, but commonly much worse in their cause. For to defer an account is the ready way to perplex it; and when it comes to be perplexed and intricate, no man, either as to his temporal or spiritual estate, can know of himself what he is, or what he has, or upon what bottom he stands. But the amazing difficulty and greatness of his account will rather terrify than in-

form him; and keep him from setting heartily about such a task as he despairs ever to go through with. For no man willingly begins what he has no hope to finish.

But let a man apply to this work by frequent returns and short intervals, while the heap is small, and the particulars few, and he will find it easy and conquerable; and his conscience, like a faithful steward, shall give him in a plain, open, and entire account of himself, and hide nothing from him. Whereas we know, if a steward or cashier be suffered to run on from year to year without bringing him to a reckoning, it is odds but such a sottish forbearance will in time teach him to shuffle, and strongly tempt him to be a cheat, if not also to make him so; for as the account runs on, generally the accountant goes backward.

And for this cause some judge it advisable for a man to account with his heart every day; and this, no doubt, is the best and surest course; for still the oftener the better. And some prescribe accounting once a week; longer than which it is by no means safe to delay it: for a man shall find his heart deceitful, and his memory weak, and nature extremely averse from seeking narrowly after that which it is unwilling to find; and being found, will assuredly disturb it.

So that upon the whole matter it is infinitely absurd to think, that conscience can be kept in order without frequent examination. If a man would have his conscience deal clearly with him, he must deal severely with that. Often scouring and cleansing it will make it bright; and when it is so, he may see himself in it: and if he sees any thing amiss, let this satisfy him, that no man is or can be the worse for knowing the very worst of himself.

On the contrary, if conscience, by a long neglect of and disacquaintance with itself, comes to contract an inveterate rust or soil, a man may as well expect to see his face in a mud-wall, as that such a conscience should give him a true report of his condition; no, it leaves him wholly in the dark as to the greatest concern he has in both worlds. He can neither tell whether God be his friend or his enemy, or rather he has shrewd cause to suspect him his enemy, and can not possibly know him to be his friend. And this being his case, he must live in ignorance and die in ignorance;

and it will be hard for a man to die in it, without dying for it too.

And now, what a wretched condition must that man needs be in, whose heart is in such a confusion, such darkness, and such a settled blindness, that it shall not be able to tell him so much as one true word of himself! Flatter him it may, I confess, (as those are generally good at flattering who are good for nothing else,) but in the mean time the poor man is left under the fatal necessity of a remediless delusion: for in judging of a man's self, if conscience either can not or will not inform him, there is a certain thing called *self-love* that will be sure to deceive him. And thus I have shown, in four several particulars, what is to be done, both for the getting and keeping of the conscience so informed as that it may be able to give us a rational confidence towards God. As,

1. That the voice of reason, in all the dictates of natural morality, ought carefully to be attended to by a strict observance of what it commands, but especially of what it forbids.

2. That every pious motion from the Spirit of God ought tenderly to be cherished, and by no means checked or quenched either by resistance or neglect.

3. That conscience is to be kept close to the rule of the written word.

4thly and lastly, That it is frequently to be examined, and severely accounted with.

And I doubt not but a conscience thus disciplined shall give a man such a faithful account of himself as shall never shame nor lurch the confidence which he shall take up from it.

Nevertheless, to prevent all mistakes in so critical a case and so high a concern, I shall close up the foregoing particulars with this twofold caution.

First, Let no man think that every doubting or misgiving about the safety of his spiritual estate overthrows the confidence hitherto spoken of. For, as I showed before, the confidence mentioned in the text is not properly assurance, but only a rational, well-grounded hope; and therefore may very well consist with some returns of doubting. For we know, in that pious and excellent confession and prayer made by the poor man to our Saviour, in Mark ix. 24, how in the very same breath in which he says, *Lord, I believe,* he says also, *Lord, help my unbelief.* So that we see here, that the sincerity of our faith or confidence will not secure us against all vicissitudes of wavering or distrust; indeed no more than a strong athletic constitution of body will secure a man always against heats, and colds, and rheums, and such like indispositions.

And one great reason of this is, because such a faith or confidence as we have been treating of resides in the soul or conscience as a habit. And habits, we know, are by no means either inconsistent with, or destroyed by, every contrary act. But especially in the case now before us, where the truth and strength of our confidence towards God does not consist so much in the present act, by which it exerts itself, no, nor yet in the habit producing this act, as it does in the ground or reason which this confidence is built upon; which being the standing sincerity of a man's heart, though the present act be interrupted, (as, no doubt, through infirmity or temptation it may be very often,) yet, so long as that sincerity, upon which this confidence was first founded, does continue, as soon as the temptation is removed and gone, the forementioned faith, or affiance, will, by renewed, vigorous, and fresh acts, recover and exert itself, and with great comfort and satisfaction of mind give a man confidence towards God. Which, though it be indeed a lower and a lesser thing than assurance, yet, as to all the purposes of a pious life, may, for aught I see, prove much more useful; as both affording a man due comfort, and yet leaving room for due caution too; which are two of the principal uses that religion serves for in this world.

2. The other caution, with reference to the foregoing discourse, is this: Let no man, from what has been said, reckon a bare silence of conscience in not accusing or disturbing him, a sufficient argument for confidence towards God. For such a silence is so far from being always so, that it is usually worse than the fiercest and loudest accusations; since it may, and for the most part does, proceed from a kind of numbness or stupidity of conscience, and an absolute dominion obtained

by sin over the soul; so that it shall not so much as dare to complain or make a stir. For, as our Saviour says, Luke xi. 21, *While the strong man armed keepeth his palace, his goods are in peace.* So, while sin rules and governs with a strong hand, and has wholly subdued the conscience to a slavish subjection to its tyrannical yoke, the soul shall be at peace, such a false peace as it is; but for that very cause worse a great deal, and more destructive, than when, by continual alarms and assaults, it gives a man neither peace nor truce, quiet nor intermission. And therefore it is very remarkable that the text expresses the sound estate of the heart or the conscience here spoken of, not barely by its not accusing, but by its not condemning us, which word imports properly an acquitment or discharge of a man upon some precedent accusation, and a full trial and cognizance of his cause had thereupon. For as *condemnation*, being a law term, and so relating to the judicial proceedings of law courts, must still presuppose a hearing of the cause, before any sentence can pass, so likewise in the court of conscience there must be a strict and impartial inquiry into all a man's actions, and a thorough hearing of all that can be pleaded for and against him, before conscience can rationally either condemn or discharge him: and if indeed upon such a fair and full trial he can come off, he is then *rectus in curia*, clear and innocent, and consequently may reap all that satisfaction from himself which it is natural for innocence to afford the person who has it. I do not here speak of a legal innocence, (none but sots and Quakers dream of such things,) for, as St. Paul says, Galat. ii. 16, *by the works of the law shall no flesh living be justified;* but I speak of an evangelical innocence; such an one as the economy of the gospel accepts, whatsoever the law enjoins; and though mingled with several infirmities and defects, yet amounts to such a pitch of righteousness as we call *sincerity*. And whosoever has this shall never be damned for want of the other.

And now, how vastly does it concern all those who shall think it worth their while to be in earnest with their immortal souls, not to abuse and delude themselves with a false confidence? a thing so easily taken up, and so hardly laid down. Let no man conclude, because his conscience says nothing to him, that therefore it has nothing to say. Possibly some never so much as doubted of the safety of their spiritual estate in all their lives; and if so, let them not flatter themselves, but rest assured that they have so much the more reason a great deal to doubt of it now. For the causes of such a profound stillness are generally gross ignorance, or long custom of sinning, or both; and these are very dreadful symptoms indeed to such as are not hell and damnation proof. When a man's wounds cease to smart, only because he has lost his feeling, they are nevertheless mortal for his not seeing his need of a chirurgeon. It is not mere, actual, present ease, but ease after pain, which brings the most durable and solid comfort. Acquitment before trial can be no security. Great and strong calms usually portend and go before the most violent storms. And therefore, since storms and calms (especially with reference to the state of the soul) do always follow one another, certainly of the two it is much more eligible to have the storm first and the calm afterwards: since a calm before a storm is commonly a peace of a man's own making; but a calm after a storm, a peace of God's.

To which God, who only can speak such peace to us as neither the world nor the devil shall be able to take from us, be rendered and ascribed, as is most due, all praise, might, majesty, and dominion, both now and for evermore. Amen.

SERMON XXIV.

A FURTHER ACCOUNT OF THE NATURE AND MEASURES OF CONSCIENCE:

IN A SERMON ON 1 JOHN III. 21, PREACHED BEFORE THE UNIVERSITY, AT CHRIST CHURCH, OXON.

OCTOBER 30, 1692

1 JOHN iii. 21.—*Beloved, if our heart condemn us not, we have confidence toward God.*

I HAVE discoursed once already upon these words in this place. In which discourse, after I had set down four several false grounds upon which men, in judging of the safety of their spiritual estate, were apt to found a wrong confidence towards God, and shown the falsity of them all; and that there was nothing but a man's own heart or conscience which, in this great concern, he could with any safety rely upon; I did, in the next place, cast the further prosecution of the words under these four following particulars:

1. To show, How the heart or conscience ought to be informed, in order to its founding in us a rational confidence, towards God.

2. To show, How and by what means we may get our conscience thus informed, and afterwards preserve and keep it so.

3. To show, Whence it is that the testimony of conscience, thus informed, comes to be so authentic, and so much to be relied upon. And,

4thly and lastly, To assign some particular cases or instances in which the confidence suggested by it does most eminently show and exert itself.

Upon the first of which heads, to wit, How the heart or conscience ought to be informed, in order to its founding in us a rational confidence towards God, after I had premised something about an erroneous conscience, and shown both what influence that ought to have upon us, and what regard we ought to have to that in this matter, I gathered the result of all into this one conclusion; namely, That such a conscience as has not been wanting to itself, in endeavoring the utmost knowledge of its duty, and the clearest information about the will of God, that its power, advantages, and opportunities could afford it, is that great internal judge whose absolution is a rational and sure ground of confidence towards God. This I then insisted upon at large, and from thence proceeded to the

Second particular, which was to show, How and by what means we might get our conscience thus informed, and afterwards preserve and keep it so.

Where, amongst those many ways and methods which might, no doubt, have been assigned as highly conducing to this purpose, I singled out and insisted upon only these four. As,

1st, That the voice of reason, in all the dictates of natural morality, was still carefully to be attended to by a strict observance of what it commanded, but especially of what it forbade.

2dly, That every pious motion from the Spirit of God was tenderly to be cherished, and by no means quenched or checked, either by resistance or neglect.

3dly, That conscience was still to be kept close to the rule of God's written word; and,

4thly and lastly, That it was frequently to be examined, and severely accounted with.

These things also I then more fully enlarged upon; and so closed up all with a double caution, and that of no small importance as to the case then before us: as,

First, That no man should reckon every doubting or misgiving of his heart, about the safety of his spiritual estate, inconsistent with that confidence towards God which is here spoken of in the text; and, secondly, That no man should account a bare silence of conscience, in not accusing or disturbing him, a sufficient ground for such a confidence. Of both which I then showed the fatal consequence. And so, not to trouble you with any more repetitions than these, which were just and necessary to lay before you the coherence of one thing with another, I shall now proceed to the third of those four particulars first proposed; which was to show, Whence it is that the testimony of conscience (concerning a man's spiritual estate) comes to be so authentic, and so much to be relied upon.

Now the force and credit of its testimony stands upon this double ground.

1st, The high office which it holds immediately from God himself, in the soul of man ; and,

2dly, Those properties or qualities which peculiarly fit it for the discharge of this high office, in all things relating to the soul.

1. And first, for its office. It is no less than God's vicegerent or deputy, doing all things by immediate commission from him. It commands and dictates every thing in God's name, and stamps every word with an almighty authority. So that it is, as it were, a kind of copy or transcript of the divine sentence, and an interpreter of the sense of Heaven. And from hence it is, that sins against conscience (as all sins against light and conviction are, by way of eminence, so called) are of so peculiar and transcendent a guilt. For that every such sin is a daring and direct defiance of the divine authority, as it is signified and reported to a man by his conscience, and thereby ultimately terminates in God himself.

Nay, and this vicegerent of God has one prerogative above all God's other earthly vicegerents; to wit, that it can never be deposed. Such a strange, sacred, and inviolable majesty has God imprinted upon this faculty; not indeed as upon an absolute, independent sovereign, but yet with so great a communication of something next to sovereignty, that while it keeps within its proper compass, it is controllable by no mortal power upon earth. For not the greatest monarch in the world can countermand conscience so far as to make it condemn where it would otherwise acquit, or acquit where it would otherwise condemn; no, neither sword nor sceptre can come at it; but it is above and beyond the reach of both.

And if it were not for this awful and majestic character which it bears, whence could it be that the stoutest and bravest hearts droop and sneak when conscience frowns: and the most abject and afflicted wretch feels an unspeakable and even triumphant joy when the judge within absolves and applauds him. When a man has done any villainous act, though under countenance of the highest place and power, and under covert of the closest secrecy, his conscience, for all that, strikes him like a clap of thunder, and depresses him to a perpetual trepidation, horror, and poorness of spirit; so that, like Nero, though surrounded with his Roman legions and Pretorian bands, he yet skulks, and hides himself, and is ready to fly *to* every thing for refuge, though he sees nothing to fly *from*. And all this, because he has heard a condemning sentence from within, which the secret forebodings of his mind tell him will be ratified by a sad and certain execution from above: on the other side, what makes a man so cheerful, so bright and confident in his comforts, but because he finds himself acquitted by God's high commissioner and deputy? Which is as much as a pardon under God's own hand, under the broad seal of Heaven, (as I may so express it.) For a king never condemns any whom his judges have absolved, nor absolves whom his judges have condemned, whatsoever the people and republicans may.

Now from this principle, that the authority of conscience stands founded upon its vicegerency and deputation under God, several very important inferences may, or rather indeed unavoidably must, ensue. Two of which I shall single out and speak of; as,

First, We collect from hence the absurdity and impertinence; and,

Secondly, The impudence and impiety of most of those pretenses of conscience which have borne such a mighty sway all the world over, and in these poor nations especially.

1. And first, for the absurdity and impertinence of them. What a rattle and a noise has this word *conscience* made! How many battles has it fought! How many churches has it robbed, ruined, and *reformed* to ashes! How many laws has

it trampled upon, dispensed with, and addressed against! And, in a word, how many governments has it overturned! Such is the mischievous force of a plausible word applied to a detestable thing.

The allegation or plea of conscience ought never to be admitted barely for itself: for when a thing obliges only by a borrowed authority, it is ridiculous to allege it for its own. Take a lieutenant, a commissioner, or ambassador of any prince; and, so far as he represents his prince, all that he does or declares under that capacity has the same force and validity as if actually done or declared by the prince himself in person. But then how far does this reach? Why, just so far as he keeps close to his instructions: but when he once balks them, though what he does may be indeed a public crime or a national mischief, yet it is but a private act; and the doer of it may chance to pay his head for the presumption. For still, as great as the authority of such kind of persons is, it is not founded upon their own will, nor upon their own judgment, but upon their commission.

In like manner, every dictate of this vicegerent of God, where it has a divine word or precept to back it, carries a divine authority with it. But if no such word can be produced, it may indeed be a strong opinion or persuasion, but it is not conscience: and no one thing in the world has done more mischief, and caused more delusions amongst men, than their not distinguishing between conscience and mere opinion or persuasion.

Conscience is a Latin word, (though with an English termination,) and, according to the very notation of it, imports *a double* or *joint knowledge*; to wit, one of a divine law or rule, and the other of a man's own action: and so is properly the application of a general law to a particular instance of practice. The law of God, for example, says, *Thou shalt not steal;* and the mind of man tells him that the taking of such or such a thing from a person lawfully possessed of it is stealing. Whereupon the conscience, joining the knowledge of both these together, pronounces in the name of God, that such a particular action ought not to be done. And this is the true procedure of conscience, always supposing a law from God before it pretends to lay any obligation upon man: for still

I aver that conscience neither is nor ought to be its own rule.

I question not, I confess, but mere opinion or persuasion may be every whit as strong, and have as forcible an influence upon a man's actions as conscience itself. But then, we know, strength or force is one thing, and authority quite another. As a rogue upon the highway may have as strong an arm, and take off a man's head as cleverly as the executioner. But then there is a vast disparity in the two actions, when one of them is *murder*, and the other *justice*: nay, and our Saviour himself told his disciples, *that men should both kill them, and think that in so doing they did God's service.* So that here, we see, was a full opinion and persuasion, and a very zealous one too, of the high meritoriousness of what they did; but still there was no law, no word or command of God to ground it upon, and consequently it was not conscience.

Now the notion of conscience thus stated, if firmly kept to and thoroughly driven home, would effectually baffle and confound all those senseless, though clamorous pretenses of the schismatical opposers of the constitutions of our church. In defense of which I shall not speak so much as one syllable against the indulgence and toleration granted to these men. No; since they have it, let them, in God's name, enjoy it, and the government make the best of it. But since I can not find that the law which tolerates them in their way of worship (and it does no more) does at all forbid us to defend ours, it were earnestly to be wished that all hearty lovers of the church of England would assert its excellent constitution more vigorously now than ever: and especially in such congregations as this; in which there are so many young persons, upon the well or ill principling of whom, next under God, depends the happiness or misery of this church and state. For if such should be generally prevailed upon by hopes or fears, by base examples, by trimming and time-serving, (which are but two words for the same thing,) to abandon and betray the church of England, by nauseating her pious, prudent, and wholesome orders, (of which I have seen some scurvy instances,) we may rest assured that this will certainly produce confusion, and that confusion will as certainly end in popery.

And therefore, since the Liturgy, rites, and ceremonies of our church have been and still are so much caviled and struck at, and all upon a plea of conscience, it will concern us, as becomes men of sense, seriously to examine the force of this plea, which our adversaries are still setting up against us as the grand pillar and buttress of the *good old cause* of nonconformity. For come to any dissenting brother, and ask him, Why can not you communicate with the church of England? "Oh," says he, "it is against my conscience; my conscience will not suffer me to pray by a set form, to kneel at the sacrament, to hear divine service read by one in a surplice, or to use the cross in baptism," or the like.

Very well; and is this the case then, that it is all pure conscience that keeps you from complying with the rule and order of the church in these matters? If so, then produce me some word or law of God forbidding these things. For conscience never commands or forbids any thing authentically, but there is some law of God which commands or forbids it first. Conscience (as might be easily shown) being no distinct power or faculty from the mind of man, but the mind of man itself applying the general rule of God's law to particular cases and actions. This is truly and properly conscience. And therefore show me such a law; and that, either as a necessary dictate of right reason, or a positive injunction in God's revealed word: (for these two are all the ways by which God speaks to men nowadays:) I say, show me something from hence which countermands or condemns all or any of the forementioned ceremonies of our church, and then I will yield the cause. But if no such reason, no such scripture can be brought to appear in their behalf against us, but that with screwed face and doleful whine they only ply you with senseless harangues of conscience against *carnal ordinances*, *the dead letter*, and *human inventions* on the one hand, and loud outcries for a *further reformation* on the other; then rest you assured that they have a design upon your pocket, and that the word *conscience* is used only as an instrument to pick it; and more particularly as it calls it a *further reformation*, signifies no more, with reference to the church, than as if one man should come to another and say, "Sir, I have already taken away your cloak, and do fully intend, if I can, to take away your coat also." This is the true meaning of this word *further reformation*; and so long as you understand it in this sense, you can not be imposed upon by it.

Well, but if these mighty men at chapter and verse can produce you no scripture to overthrow our church ceremonies, I will undertake to produce scripture enough to warrant them; even all those places which absolutely enjoin obedience and submission to lawful governors in all not unlawful things: particularly that in 1 Pet. ii. 13, and that in Heb. xiii. 17, (of which two places more again presently,) together with the other in 1 Cor. xiv., last verse, enjoining order and decency in God's worship, and in all things relating to it. And consequently, till these men can prove the forementioned things, ordered by our church, to be either intrinsically unlawful or indecent, I do here affirm by the authority of the foregoing scriptures, that the use of them, as they stand established amongst us, is necessary; and that all pretenses or pleas of conscience to the contrary are nothing but cant and cheat, flam and delusion. In a word, the ceremonies of the church of England are as necessary as the injunctions of an undoubtedly lawful authority, the practice of the primitive church, and the general rules of decency, determined to particulars of the greatest decency, can make them necessary. And I would not for all the world be arraigned at the last and great day for disturbing the church, and disobeying government, and have no better plea for so doing than what those of the separation were ever yet able to defend themselves by.

But some will here say perhaps, If this be all that you require of us, we both can and do bring you scripture against your church ceremonies; even that which condemns all *will worship*, Col. ii. 23, and such other like places. To which I answer, first, that the *will worship*, forbidden in that scripture, is so termed, not from the circumstance, but from the object of religious worship; and we readily own that it is by no means in the church's power to appoint or choose whom or what it will worship. But that does not infer that it is not therefore in the church's power to appoint how and in what manner it will worship the true object of religious worship; provided that in so doing it observes such rules of decency as are proper and conducing to that purpose. So that this scripture is wholly irrelative to the case before us, and as impertinently applied to it as any poor text in the Revelation was ever applied to the grave and profound whimseys of some modern interpreters. But secondly, to this objection about *will worship*, I answer yet further, that the forementioned ceremonies of the church of England are no worship, nor part of God's worship at all, nor were ever pretended so to be; and, if they are not so much as *worship*, I am sure they can not be *will worship*. But we own them only for circumstances, modes, and solemn usages, by which God's worship is orderly and decently performed: I say, we pretend them not to be parts of divine worship, but, for all that, to be such things as the divine worship, in some instance or other, can not be without: for that which neither does nor can give vital heat, may yet be necessary to preserve it: and he who should strip himself of all that is no part of himself would quickly find, or rather feel, the inconvenience of such a practice, and have cause to wish for a body as void of sense as such an argument.

Now the consequence in both these cases is perfectly parallel: and if so, you may rest satisfied that what is *nonsense* upon a principle of reason, will never be *sense* upon a principle of religion. But as touching the necessity of the aforesaid usages in the church of England, I shall lay down these four propositions:

1. That circumstantials in the worship of God (as well as in all other human actions) are so necessary to it, that it can not possibly be performed without them.

2. That decency in the circumstantials of God's worship is absolutely necessary.

3. That the general rule and precept of decency is not capable of being reduced to practice, but as it is exemplified in, and determined to, particular instances. And,

4thly and lastly, That there is more of the general nature of decency in those particular usages and ceremonies which the church of England has pitched upon, than is or can be shown in any other whatsoever.

These things I affirm; and when you have put them all together, let any one give me a solid and sufficient reason for the giving up those few ceremonies of our church, if he can. All the reason that I could ever yet hear alleged by the chief factors for a general intromission of all sorts, sects, and persuasions into our communion is, that those who separate from us are stiff and obstinate, and will not submit to the rules and orders of our church, and that therefore they ought to be taken away. Which is a goodly reason indeed, and every way worthy of the wisdom and integrity of those who allege it. And to show that it is so, let it be but transferred from the ecclesiastical to the civil government, from church to state; and let all laws be abrogated which any great or sturdy multitude of men have no mind to submit to. That is, in other words, let laws be made to obey, and not to be obeyed; and upon these terms I doubt not but you will find that kingdom (or rather that commonwealth) finely governed in a short time.

And thus I have shown the absurdity, folly, and impertinence of alleging the obligation of conscience, where there is no law or command of God mediate or immediate to found that obligation upon. And yet, as bad as this is, it were well if the bare absurdity of these pretenses were the worst thing which we had to charge them with. But it is not so. For our second and next inference from the foregoing principle of the vicegerency of conscience under God, will show us also the daring impudence and downright impiety of many of those fulsome pleas of conscience which the world has been too often and too scandalously abused by. For a man to sin against his conscience, is doubtless a great wickedness. But to make God himself a party in the sin, is a much greater. For this is to plead God's authority against God's very law; which doubles the sin, and adds blasphemy to rebellion. And yet such things we have seen done amongst us. An horrid, unnatural civil war raised and carried on; the purest and most primitively reformed church in the world laid in the dust; and one of the best and most innocent princes that ever sat upon a throne, by a barbarous, unheard-of violence, hurried to his grave in a bloody sheet, and not so much as suffered to rest there to this day; and all this by men acting under the most solemn pretenses of conscience, that hypocrisy perhaps ever yet presumed to outface the world with.

And are not the principles of those wretches still owned, and their persons sainted by a race of men of the same stamp, risen up in their stead, the sworn mortal enemies of our church? And yet, for whose sake some projectors amongst us have been turning every stone to transform, mangle, and degrade its noble constitution to the homely, mechanic model of those republican, imperfect churches abroad; which, instead of being any rule or pattern to us, ought in all reason to receive one from us. Nay, and so short-sighted are some in their politics as not to discern all this while, that it is not the service but the revenue of our church which is struck at; and not any passages of our Liturgy, but the property of our lands, which these reformers would have altered.

For I am sure no other alteration will satisfy dissenting consciences; no, nor this neither very long, without an utter abolition of all that looks like order or government in the church. And this we may be sure of, if we do but consider both the inveterate malice of the Romish party, which sets these silly, unthinking tools a-work, and withal that monstrous principle or maxim which those who divide from us (at least most of them) roundly profess, avow, and govern their consciences by; namely, That in all matters that concern religion or the church, though a thing or action be never so indifferent or lawful in itself, yet if it be commanded or enjoined by the government, either civil or ecclesiastical, it becomes *ipso facto*, by being so commanded, utterly unlawful, and such as they can by no means with good conscience comply with.

Which one detestable tenet or proposition, carrying in it the very quintessence and vital spirit of all nonconformity, absolutely cashiers and cuts off all church government at one stroke, and is withal such an insolent, audacious defiance of Almighty God, under the mask of conscience, as perhaps none in former ages, who so much as wore the name of Christians, ever arrived to or made profession of.

For to resume the scriptures afore quoted by us; and particularly that in 1 Pet. ii. 13. *Submit yourselves to every ordinance of man,* says the Spirit of God, speaking by that apostle. But say these men, If the ordinance of man enjoins you the practice of any thing with reference to religion or the church, though never so lawful in itself, you can not with a good conscience submit to the ordinance of man in that case: that is, in other words, God says they must submit, and they say they must not.

Again, in the forementioned Heb. xiii. 17. The apostle bids them (and in them all Christians whatsoever) *to obey those who have the rule over them*; speaking there of church rulers; for he tells them, *that they were such as watched for their souls*. But, says the Separatist, If those who have the rule over you should command you any thing about church affairs, you can not, you ought not in conscience to obey them; forasmuch as, according to that grand principle of theirs, newly specified by us, every such command makes obedience to a thing otherwise lawful, to become unlawful; and consequently, upon the same principle, rulers must not, can not be obeyed: unless we could imagine that there may be such a thing as obedience on the one side, when there must be no such thing as a command on the other; which would make pleasant sense of it indeed, and fit for none but a dissenting reason, as well as conscience, to assert. For though these men have given the world too many terrible proofs of their own example that there may be commands and no obedience, yet, I believe, it will put their little logic hard to it to prove that there can be any obedience where there is no command. And therefore it unanswerably follows, that the abettors of the forementioned principles plead conscience in a direct and barefaced contradiction to God's express command.

And now, I beseech you, consider with yourselves; (for it is no slight matter that I am treating of;) I say, consider what you ought to judge of those insolent, unaccountable boasts of conscience, which, like so many fireballs or mouth-granadoes, as I may so term them, are every day thrown at our church. The apostle bids us *prove all things*. And will you then take conscience at every turn upon its own word? upon the forlorn credit of every bold impostor who pleads it? Will you sell your reason, your church, and your religion, and both of them the best in the world, for a name? and that a wrested, abused, misapplied name? Knaves, when they design some more than ordinary villainy, never fail to make use of this plea; and it is because they always find fools ready to believe it.

But you will say then, What course must be taken to fence against this imposture? Why truly, the best that I know of, I have told you before; namely, that whensoever you hear any of these sly, sanctified sycophants, with turned-up eye and shrug of shoulder, pleading conscience for or against any thing or practice, you would forthwith ask them what word of God they have to bottom that judgment of their conscience upon? Forasmuch as conscience, being God's vicegerent, was never commissioned by him to govern us in its own name; but must still have some divine word or law to support and warrant it. And therefore call for such a word; and that, either from scripture or from manifest universal reason, and insist upon it, so as not to be put off without it. And if they can produce you no such thing from either of them, (as they never can,) then rest assured that they are errant cheats and hypocrites; and that, for all their big words, the conscience of such men is so far from being able to give them any true confidence towards God, that it can not so much as give them confidence towards a wise and good man, no, nor yet towards themselves, who are far from being either.

And thus I have shown you the first ground upon which the testimony of conscience (concerning a man's spiritual estate) comes to be so authentic and so much to be relied upon; to wit, the high office which it holds as the vicegerent of God himself in the soul of man: together with the two grand inferences drawn from thence. The first of them showing the absurdity, folly, and impertinence of pretending conscience against any thing, when there is no law of God mediate or immediate against it: and the other, setting forth the intolerable blasphemy and impiety of pretending conscience for any thing which the known law of God is directly against and stands in open defiance of.

Proceed we now to the second ground from which conscience derives the credit of its testimony in judging of our spiritual estate; and that consists in those properties and qualities which so peculiarly fit it for the discharge of its forementioned office in all things relating to the soul. And these are three:

First, The quickness of its sight.

Secondly, The tenderness of its sense; and,

Thirdly and lastly, Its rigorous and impartial way of giving sentence.

Of each of which in their order. And first for the extraordinary quickness and sagacity of its sight, in spying out every thing which can any way concern the estate of the soul. As the voice of it, I showed, was as loud as thunder, so the sight of it is as piercing and quick as lightning. It presently sees the guilt, and looks through all the flaws and blemishes of a sinful action; and on the other side, observes the candidness of a man's very principles, the sincerity of his intentions, and the whole carriage of every circumstance in a virtuous performance. So strict and accurate is this spiritual inquisition.

Upon which account it is that there is no such thing as perfect secrecy, to encourage a rational mind to the perpetration of any base action. For a man must first extinguish and put out the great light within him, his conscience, he must get away from himself, and shake off the thousand witnesses which he always carries about him, before he can be alone. And where there is no solitude, I am sure there can be no secrecy.

It is confessed indeed that a long and a bold course of sinning may (as we have shown elsewhere) very much dim and darken the discerning faculty of conscience. For so the apostle assures us it did with those in Rom. i. 21, and the same, no doubt, it does every day; but still so as to leave such persons, both then and now, many notable lucid intervals; sufficient to convince them of their deviations from reason and natural religion; and thereby to render them inexcusable; and so, in a word, to stop their mouths, though not save their souls. In short, their conscience was not stark dead, but under a kind of spiritual apoplexy or deliquium. The operation was hindered, but the faculty not destroyed. And now, if conscience be naturally thus apprehensive and sagacious, certainly this ought to be another great ground, over and above its bare authority, why we should trust and rely upon the reports of it. For knowledge is still the ground and reason of trust: and so much as any one has of discernment, so far he is secured from error and deception, and for that cause fit to be confided in. No witness so much to be credited as an eye-witness. And conscience is like the great eye of the world, the sun, always open, always making discoveries. Justly therefore may we by the light of it take a view of our condition.

2dly, Another property or quality of conscience, enabling it to judge so truly of our spiritual estate, is the tenderness of its sense. For as, by the quickness of its sight, it directs us what to do, or not to do, so, by this tenderness of its sense, it excuses or accuses us, as we have done or not done according to those directions. And it is altogether as nice, delicate, and tender in feeling as it can be perspicacious and quick in seeing. For conscience, you know, is still called and accounted the eye of the soul: and how troublesome is the least mote or dust falling into the eye! and how quickly does it weep and water, upon the least grievance that afflicts it!

And no less exact is the sense which conscience, preserved in its native purity, has of the least sin. For as great sins waste, so small ones are enough to wound it; and every wound, you know, is painful, till it festers beyond recovery. As soon as ever sin gives the blow, conscience is the first thing that feels the smart. No sooner does the poisoned arrow enter, but that begins to bleed inwardly; sin and sorrow, the venom of one and the anguish of the other, being things inseparable.

Conscience, if truly tender, never complains without a cause; though, I confess, there is a new-fashioned sort of tenderness of conscience which always does so: but that is like the tenderness of a bog or quagmire; and it is very dangerous coming near it, for fear of being swallowed up by it. For when conscience has once acquired this artificial tenderness, it will strangely enlarge or contract its swallow, as it pleases; so that sometimes a camel shall slide down with ease, where at other times even a gnat may chance to stick by the way. It is indeed such a kind of tenderness as makes the person who has it generally very tender of obeying the laws, but never so of breaking them. And therefore, since it is commonly at such variance with the law, I think the law is the fittest thing to deal with it.

In the mean time, let no man deceive himself, or think

that true tenderness of conscience is any thing else but an awful and exact sense of the rule which should direct, and of the law which should govern it. And while it steers by this compass, and is sensible of every declination from it, so long it is truly and properly tender, and fit to be relied upon, whether it checks or approves a man for what he does. For from hence alone springs its excusing or accusing power: all accusation, in the very nature of the thing, still supposing, and being founded upon, some law: for where there is no law there can be no transgression: and where there can be no transgression, I am sure there ought to be no accusation.

And here, when I speak of law, I mean both the law of God and of man too. For where the matter of a law is a thing not evil, every law of man is virtually, and at a second hand, the law of God also: forasmuch as it binds in the strength of the divine law, commanding obedience to *every ordinance of man*, as we have already shown. And therefore all tenderness of conscience against such laws is hypocrisy, and patronized by none but men of design, who look upon it as the fittest engine to get into power by; which, by the way, when they are once possessed of, they generally manage with as little tenderness as they do with conscience: of which we have had but too much experience already, and it would be but ill venturing upon more.

In a word, conscience, not acting by and under a law, is a boundless, daring, and presumptuous thing: and for any one by virtue thereof to challenge to himself a privilege of doing what he will, and of being unaccountable for what he does, is in all reason too much either for man or angel to pretend to.

3dly, The third and last property of conscience which I shall mention, and which makes the verdict of it so authentic, is its great and rigorous impartiality. For as its wonderful apprehensiveness made that it could not easily be deceived, so this makes that it will by no means deceive. A judge, you know, may be skillful in understanding a cause, and yet partial in giving sentence. But it is much otherwise with conscience; no artifice can induce it to accuse the innocent, or to absolve the guilty. No; we may as well bribe the light and the day to represent white things black, or black white.

What pitiful things are power, rhetoric, or riches, when

they would terrify, dissuade, or buy off conscience from pronouncing sentence according to the merit of a man's actions! For still, as we have shown, conscience is a copy of the divine law; and though judges may be bribed or frightened, yet laws cannot. The law is impartial and inflexible; it has no passions or affections, and consequently never accepts persons, nor dispenses with itself.

For let the most potent sinner upon earth speak out, and tell us whether he can command down the clamors and reviling of a guilty conscience, and impose silence upon that bold reprover. He may perhaps for a while put on a high and a big look; but can he, for all that, look conscience out of countenance? And he may also dissemble a little forced jollity; that is, he may court his mistress, and quaff his cups, and perhaps sprinkle them now and then with a few *Dammees;* but who, in the mean time, besides his own wretched, miserable self, knows of those secret, bitter infusions which that terrible thing, called *conscience*, makes into all his draughts? Believe it, most of the appearing mirth in the world is not mirth, but art. The *wounded spirit* is not seen, but walks under a disguise; and still the less you see of it, the better it looks.

On the contrary, if we consider the virtuous person, let him declare freely whether ever his conscience checked him for his innocence, or upbraided him for an action of duty; did it ever bestow any of its hidden lashes or concealed bites on a mind severely pure, chaste, and religious?

But when conscience shall complain, cry out, and recoil, let a man descend into himself with too just a suspicion that all is not right within. For surely that hue and cry was not raised upon him for nothing. The spoils of a rifled innocence are borne away, and the man has stolen something from his own soul, for which he ought to be pursued, and will at last certainly be overtook.

Let every one therefore attend the sentence of his conscience: for he may be sure it will not daub nor flatter. It is as severe as law, as impartial as truth. It will neither conceal nor pervert what it knows.

And thus I have done with the third of those four particulars at first proposed, and shown whence, and upon what account it is, that the testimony of conscience, concerning our spiritual estate, comes to be so authentic, and so much to be relied upon: namely, for that it is fully empowered and commissioned to this great office by God himself; and withal, that it is extremely quicksighted to apprehend and discern; and moreover very tender and sensible of every thing that concerns the soul. And lastly, that it is most exactly and severely impartial in judging of whatsoever comes before it. Every one of which qualifications justly contributes to the credit and authority of the sentence which shall be passed by it. And so we are at length arrived at the fourth and last thing proposed from the words; which was to assign some particular cases or instances, in which this confidence towards God, suggested by a rightly informed conscience, does most eminently show and exert itself.

I shall mention three.

1. In our addresses to God by prayer. When a man shall presume to come and place himself in the presence of the great Searcher of hearts, and to ask something of him, while his conscience is all the while smiting him on the face, and telling him what a rebel and a traitor he is to the majesty which he supplicates, surely such an one should think with himself, that the God whom he prays to is greater than his conscience, and pierces into all the filth and baseness of his heart with a much clearer and more severe inspection. And if so, will he not likewise resent the provocation more deeply, and revenge it upon him more terribly, if repentance does not divert the blow? Every such prayer is big with impiety and contradiction, and makes as odious a noise in the ears of God as the harangues of one of those rebel fasts, or humiliations in the year forty-one; invoking the blessings of Heaven upon such actions and designs as nothing but hell could reward.

One of the most peculiar qualifications of a heart rightly disposed for prayer is, a well-grounded confidence of a man's fitness for that duty. In Heb. x. 22, *Let us draw near with a true heart, in full assurance of faith,* says the apostle. But whence must this assurance spring? Why, we are told in the very next words of the same verse: *having our hearts sprinkled from an evil conscience:* otherwise the voice of an impure conscience will cry much louder than our prayers, and speak more effectually against us than these can intercede for us.

And now, if prayer be the great conduit of mercy, by which the blessings of heaven are derived upon the creature, and the noble instrument of converse between God and the soul, then surely that which renders it ineffectual and loathsome to God, must needs be of the most mischievous and destructive consequence to mankind imaginable; and consequently to be removed with all that earnestness and concern with which a man would rid himself of a plague or a mortal infection. For it taints and pollutes every prayer; it turns an oblation into an affront; and the odors of a sacrifice into the exhalations of a carcass. And, in a word, makes the heavens over us brass, denying all passage either to descending mercies or ascending petitions.

But on the other side, when a man's breast is clear, and the same heart which indites does also encourage his prayer, when his innocence pushes on the attempt, and vouches the success; such an one goes boldly to the throne of grace, and his boldness is not greater than his welcome. God recognizes the voice of his own Spirit interceding within him, and his prayers are not only followed, but even prevented with an answer.

2dly, A second instance, in which this confidence towards God does so remarkably show itself, is at the time of some notable trial or sharp affliction. When a man's friends shall desert him, his relations disown him, and all dependencies fail him, and, in a word, the whole world frown upon him, certainly it will then be of some moment to have a friend in the court of conscience, which shall, as it were, buoy up his sinking spirits, and speak greater things for him than all these together can declaim against him.

For as it is most certain that no hight of honor, nor affluence of fortune, can keep a man from being miserable, nor indeed contemptible, when an enraged conscience shall fly at him, and take him by the throat, so it is also as certain that no temporal adversities can cut off those inward, secret, invincible supplies of comfort, which conscience shall pour in upon distressed innocence, in spite and in defiance of all worldly calamities.

Naturalists observe, that when the frost seizes upon wine, they are only the slighter and more waterish parts of it that are subject to be congealed; but still there is a mighty spirit which can retreat into itself, and there within its own compass lie secure from the freezing impression of the element round about it. And just so it is with the spirit of a man, while a good conscience makes it firm and impenetrable. An outward affliction can no more benumb or quell it, than a blast of wind can freeze up the blood in a man's veins, or a little shower of rain soak into his heart, and there quench the principle of life itself.

Take the two greatest instances of misery, which, I think, are incident to human nature; to wit, poverty and shame, and I dare oppose conscience to them both.

And first for poverty. Suppose a man stripped of all, driven out of house and home, and perhaps out of his country too, (which having, within our memory, happened to so many, may too easily, God knows, be supposed again,) yet if his conscience shall tell him that it was not for any failure in his own duty, but from the success of another's villainy, that all this befell him, why then his banishment becomes his preferment, his rags his trophies, his nakedness his ornament; and so long as his innocence is his repast, he feasts and banquets upon bread and water. He has disarmed his afflictions, unstung his miseries; and though he has not the proper happiness of the world, yet he has the greatest that is to be enjoyed in it.

And for this we might appeal to the experience of those great and good men who, in the late times of rebellion and confusion, were forced into foreign countries, for their unshaken firmness and fidelity to the oppressed cause of majesty and religion, whether their conscience did not, like a *fidus Achates*, still bear them company, stick close to them, and suggest comfort, even when the causes of comfort were invisible; and, in a word, verify that great saying of the apostle in their mouths: *We have nothing, and yet we possess all things.*

For it is not barely a man's abridgment in his external accommodations which makes him miserable, but when his conscience shall hit him in the teeth, and tell him that it was his sin and his folly which brought him under these abridgments. That his present scanty meals are but the natural effects of his former over-full ones. That it was his tailor, and his cook, his fine fashions, and his French ragouts, which sequestered him; and, in a word, that he came by his poverty as sinfully as some usually do by their riches; and consequently, that Providence treats him with all these severities, not by way of trial, but by way of punishment and revenge. The mind surely, of itself, can feel none of the burnings of a fever; but if my fever be occasioned by a surfeit, and that surfeit caused by my sin, it is that which adds fuel to the fiery disease, and rage to the distemper.

2dly, Let us consider also the case of calumny and disgrace; doubtless, the sting of every reproachful speech is the truth of it; and to be conscious, is that which gives an edge and keenness to the invective. Otherwise, when conscience shall plead not guilty to the charge, a man entertains it not as an indictment, but as a libel. He hears all such calumnies with a generous unconcernment; and receiving them at one ear, gives them a free and easy passage through the other: they fall upon him like rain or hail upon an oiled garment; they may make a noise indeed, but can find no entrance. The very whispers of an acquitting conscience will drown the voice of the loudest slander.

What a long charge of hypocrisy, and many other base things, did Job's friends draw up against him! but he regarded it no more than the dunghill which he sat upon, while his conscience enabled him to appeal even to God himself; and, in spite of calumny, to assert and hold fast his integrity.

And did not Joseph lie under as black an infamy as the charge of the highest ingratitude and the lewdest villainy could fasten upon him? Yet his conscience raised him so much above it, that he scorned so much as to clear himself, or to recriminate the strumpet by a true narrative of the matter. For we read nothing of that in the whole story: such confidence, such greatness of spirit, does a clear conscience give a man; always making him more solicitous to preserve his innocence than concerned to prove it. And so we come now to the

Third, and last instance, in which, above all others, this confidence towards God does most eminently show and exert itself; and that is at the time of death. Which surely gives the grand opportunity of trying both the strength and worth of every principle. When a man shall be just about to quit the stage of this world, to put off his mortality, and to deliver up his last accounts to God; at which sad time his memory shall serve him for little else but to terrify him with a sprightful review of his past life, and his former extravagances stripped of all their pleasure, but retaining their guilt. What is it then that can promise him a fair passage into the other world, or a comfortable appearance before his dreadful Judge, when he is there? Not all the friends and interests, all the riches and honors under heaven, can speak so much as a word for him, or one word of comfort to him in that condition; they may possibly reproach, but they can not relieve him.

No, at this disconsolate time, when the busy tempter shall be more than usually apt to vex and trouble him, and the pains of a dying body to hinder and discompose him, and the settlement of worldly affairs to disturb and confound him; and, in a word, all things conspire to make his sick-bed grievous and uneasy: nothing can then stand up against all these ruins, and speak life in the midst of death, but a clear conscience.

And the testimony of that shall make the comforts of heaven descend upon his weary head, like a refreshing dew or shower upon a parched ground. It shall give him some lively earnests and secret anticipations of his approaching joy. It shall bid his soul go out of the body undauntedly, and lift up its head with confidence before saints and angels. Surely the comfort which it conveys at this season is something bigger than the capacities of mortality; mighty and unspeakable, and not to be understood till it comes to be felt.

And now, who would not quit all the pleasures, and trash, and trifles, which are apt to captivate the heart of man, and pursue the greatest rigors of piety and austerities of a good life, to purchase to himself such a conscience as, at the hour of death, when all the friendships of the world shall bid him adieu, and the whole creation turn its back upon him, shall dismiss his soul, and close his eyes with that blessed sentence, *Well done, thou good and faithful servant, enter thou into the joy of thy Lord!*

For he whose conscience enables him to look God in the face with confidence here, shall be sure to see his face also with comfort hereafter.

Which God of his mercy grant to us all ; to whom be rendered and ascribed, as is most due, all praise, might, majesty, and dominion, both now and for evermore. Amen.

END OF VOL. I.

www.ingramcontent.com/pod-product-compliance
Lightning Source LLC
LaVergne TN
LVHW021305110826
845150LV00003B/482

* 9 7 8 1 4 2 5 5 5 9 9 0 8 *